Edition

JUSTICE ADMINISTRATION
Police, Courts, and Corrections Management

KENNETH J. PEAK
University of Nevada, Reno

Prentice Hall

Upper Saddle River, New Jersey 07458

Library of Congress Cataloging-in-Publication Data

Peak, Kenneth J. (date)
    Justice administration: police, courts, and corrections management / Kenneth J. Peak—
3rd ed.
        p. cm.
    Includes bibliographical references and index.
    ISBN 0-13-020539-7
    1. Criminal justice, Administration of—United States. 2. Law enforcement—United
States. 3. Prison administration—United States. I. Title.

HV9950 .P43 2001
364.973—dc21   00-036329

Publisher: Dave Garza
Senior Acquisitions Editor: Kim Davies
Assistant Editor: Marion Gottlieb
Managing Editor: Mary Carnis
Production Editor: Linda B. Pawelchak
Production Liaison: Adele M. Kupchik
Director of Manufacturing and Production: Bruce Johnson
Manufacturing Buyer: Ed O'Dougherty
Creative Director: Marianne Frasco
Cover Design Coordinator: Miguel Ortiz
Cover Design: Joseph Sengotta
Typesetting: Lithokraft II
Editorial Assistant: Lisa Schwartz
Marketing Manager: Chris Ruel
Marketing Assistant: Adam Kloza
Printer/Binder: R. R. Donnelley & Sons Company
Cover Illustration: Alan Leiner, SIS/Images.com
Cover Printer: Phoenix Color Corp.

Prentice-Hall International (UK) Limited, *London*
Prentice-Hall of Australia Pty. Limited, *Sydney*
Prentice-Hall Canada Inc., *Toronto*
Prentice-Hall Hispanoamericana, S.A., *Mexico*
Prentice-Hall of India Private Limited, *New Delhi*
Prentice-Hall of Japan, Inc., *Tokyo*
Pearson Education Asia Pte. Ltd., *Singapore*
Editora Prentice-Hall do Brasil, Ltda., *Rio de Janeiro*

10 9 8 7 6 5

ISBN 0-13-020539-7

To the memory of Betty Jean Peak

CONTENTS

Chapter 2

Organization and Administration: Principles and Practices 20

PART II

THE POLICE

Chapter 3

Police Organization and Operation 54

Chapter 4

Police Personnel Roles and Functions   88

Chapter 5

Police Issues and Practices   **124**

PART III

THE COURTS

Chapter 6

Court Organization and Operation   158

Chapter 7

Court Personnel Roles and Functions   175

Chapter 10

Corrections Personnel Roles and Functions   244

Chapter 11

Community Corrections: Probation and Parole   270

Chapter 12

Corrections Issues and Practices   293

Chapter 15

Financial Administration   387

Chapter 16

Technology Review   414

Chapter 17

Peeking Over the Rim: What Lies Ahead?   **440**

Appendix I

Appendix II

PREFACE

This third edition of *Justice Administration: Police, Courts, and Corrections Management* continues to be the sole book of its kind: a single author's examination of all facets of the criminal justice system as well as several related matters of interest to prospective and actual administrators. This edition represents a general updating of materials, with a new chapter concerning special administrative challenges: personnel discipline, liability, and labor relations. Several real-world vignettes have been included as well, taken from such sources as *Law Enforcement News* and courts- and corrections-related newsletters. In addition, new chapter sections have been incorporated on sexual harassment, ethics and values, workload allocation and deployment, and truth in sentencing. New community policing case studies are included as well. Several chapter sections have been expanded, including those on communication, stress, technology, community oriented policing and problem solving, and alternative dispute resolution. A new appendix lists related Web sites.

The author brings both a scholarly and practical administrative background to this effort. As a result, the chapters contain a "real-world" flavor not found in most administration textbooks.

The purpose and organization of this book are discussed in Chapter 1. I would like to add some prefatory comments as well, however. First, it is still my belief that while the criminal justice system is currently much maligned in many quarters in our society and may well continue to be criticized for many years in the new millennium, it is still the best system in the world. During my 30 years in "the business" as a police and corrections practitioner and administrator, planner, and educator, I have met hundreds of dedicated practitioners, both administrative and rank and file. I can say unequivocally that this discipline continues to be a special calling, containing countless dedicated people of exceedingly high ability and moral character.

Criminal justice is a people business. This book reflects that fact as it looks at human foibles and some of the problems of personnel and policy in justice administration. Thanks to many innovators in the field, however, a number of exciting innovations and positive activities are occurring. The general goal of the book is to inform the reader of the primary *people, practices,* and *terms* that are utilized in justice administration.

There may well be activities, policies, actions, and my own views with which the reader will disagree. This is not at all bad, because in the management of people and agencies there are no absolutes, only ideas and attempts to make the system better. The case studies appearing at the end of each major part of the book are intended to allow the reader to experience some of the kinds of problems confronted daily by justice administrators. With a fundamental knowledge of the system, and a reading of the chapters in the respective book part, readers should be able to arrive at several feasible solutions to each problem that is presented.

From its beginning through the final chapter, the text provides the reader with a comprehensive and penetrating view of what is certainly one of the most difficult and challenging positions that one can occupy in America: administrator of a criminal justice agency.

I kindly solicit your input concerning any facet of this textbook. Feel free to contact me if you have ideas for improving it.

Acknowledgments

This edition, like its two predecessors, is the result of the professional assistance of several people. First, I continue to benefit from the guidance of the staff at Prentice Hall. This effort again involved Neil Marquardt, former acquisitions editor, and Kim Davies and Marian Gottlieb, my new editors. I was again (for the sixth occasion) quite fortunate in being able to work with my friend and production editor, Linda Pawelchak. Copy editing was masterfully accomplished by Nancy Menges.

The author also wishes to acknowledge the invaluable assistance of John O. Ballard, Rochester Institute of Technology, and Michael T. Hanna, Missouri Western State College, whose reviews resulted in many beneficial changes in this third edition.

Furthermore, case study materials were contributed by the following administrators and practitioners, all of whom I am proud to consider friends and thorough professionals (their titles and affiliations are listed in the text, following their respective case study): Ron Angelone, Linda Dits, Ron Glensor, Ted Heim, Richard Kirkland, Matt Leone, Catherine Lowe, Dennis Metrick, Burt Scott, and Glen Whorton.

Ken Peak
peak_k@unr.edu

ABOUT THE AUTHOR

Ken Peak is a full professor and former chairman of the Department of Criminal Justice, University of Nevada, Reno, where he was named "Teacher of the Year" by the university's Honor Society, 1984–85. He served as chairman of the Police Section of the Academy of Criminal Justice Sciences from 1997 to 1999 and recently served as president of the Western and Pacific Association of Criminal Justice Educators. He entered municipal policing in Kansas in 1970 and subsequently held positions as a nine-county criminal justice planner for southeast Kansas, director of a four-state Technical Assistance Institute for LEAA, director of university police at Pittsburg State University, and assistant professor of criminal justice at Wichita State University. He has also served as acting director of public safety at the University of Nevada, Reno.

His earlier Prentice Hall books include *Policing America: Methods, Issues, Challenges* (3d ed., 2000) and *Community Policing and Problem Solving: Strategies and Practices* (2d ed., 1999, with Ronald W. Glensor). Other books include *Police Supervision* (with Ronald W. Glensor and Larry K. Gaines, 1999) and *Kansas Bootleggers* (with Patrick G. O'Brien, Sunflower University Press, Kansas State University, 1991). Two additional books, *Kansas Temperance: Much Ado About Booze, 1870–1920* (Sunflower University Press) and *Policing Communities: Understanding Crime and Solving Problems* (an anthology, co-edited with R. Glensor and M. Correia, Roxbury Press), are in press. He also has published more than 50 journal articles and book chapters. His teaching interests include policing, administration, and comparative justice systems. While residing in Kansas he received two gubernatorial appointments to statewide criminal justice committees. He has a doctorate from the University of Kansas.

JUSTICE ADMINISTRATION: AN INTRODUCTION

PART

I

This part, consisting of two chapters, sets the stage for our later analysis of criminal justice agencies and their successes and challenges in Parts II through V. In Chapter 1, we examine why we study justice administration and its scope. In Chapter 2, we discuss organization and administration in general, looking at both how organizations are managed and how people are motivated. The introductory section of each chapter provides specific chapter content.

THE STUDY AND SCOPE OF JUSTICE ADMINISTRATION

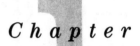

> *[T]he ordinary administration of criminal and civil justice ...*
> *contributes, more than any other circumstance, to impressing upon*
> *the minds of the people affection, esteem, and reverence towards the*
> *government.*
>
> —Alexander Hamilton,
> *The Federalist* No. 17

> *If men were angels, no government would be necessary.*
>
> —James Madison,
> *The Federalist* No. 51

Why Study Justice Administration?

This book is grounded on the assumption that the reader is an undergraduate or possibly even a graduate student, or an in-service practitioner, with a fundamental knowledge of the history and operations of the police, courts, and corrections subsystems. It is further assumed that whether or not you now possess, or seek to possess, the mantle of leadership, you will one day have thrust upon you greater administrative responsibilities within your organization. To coin a phrase, you may one day be "wearing the gold badge."

All of us may find it difficult at an early stage in life to imagine ourselves assuming a leadership role. As one person quipped, we may even have difficulty envisioning ourselves serving as captain of our neighborhood block watch program. The fact is, however, that organizations increasingly seek people with a high level of education and experience as prospective administrators. The college experience, in addition to the transmission of important and sought-after knowledge, is believed to make a person more tolerant, more secure, and less susceptible to debilitating stress and anxiety than those who do not have this experience. We also assume that administration is a science that can be taught; it is not a talent that one must be born with. Unfortunately, administration is an endeavor that is often left to on-the-job training. Many of us who have suffered a boss with inadequate administrative skills can attest to that fact.

Purpose of the Book and Key Terms

This book alone, as with any other on the subject of administration, cannot instantly transform the reader into a bona fide expert in organizational behavior and administrative techniques. It alone cannot prepare anyone to accept the reins of administration, supervision, or leadership; formal education, training, and experience are also necessary for those undertakings.

Many good, basic books about administration exist. They discuss general aspects of leadership, the use of power and authority, and a number of esoteric subjects that are beyond the reach of this book. Rather, here we simply consider some of the major theories, aspects, and issues of administration, laying the foundation for the reader's future study and experience.

Many textbooks have been written about *police* administration; a few have addressed administering courts and corrections agencies. Even fewer have analyzed justice administration from a *systems* perspective, considering all of the components of the justice system, their administration, issues, and practices. This book contributes to the demand for that perspective. Further, most existing books on administration are immersed in "pure" administrative theory and concepts. In doing so, the *practical* criminal justice perspective is often lost on many college and university students. Conversely, many books dwell on minute concepts, thereby obscuring the administrative principles involved. This book, which necessarily delves into some theory and esoteric subject matter, is intended to focus on the practical aspects of justice administration.

Neither is *Justice Administration* written as a guidebook for major, sweeping reform of the U.S. justice system. Rather, its primary intent is to familiarize the reader with the methods and challenges of criminal justice administrators. It also challenges readers to consider what reforms are desirable or even necessary and to be open-minded and visualize where changes might be implemented.

Although the terms *administration, management,* and *supervision* are often used synonymously, it should be noted that each is a unique concept that relates to the others.

Administration encompasses both management and supervision; it is a process by which a group of people is organized and directed toward achieving the group's objective. The exact nature of the organization will vary among the different types and sizes of agencies, but the general principles and the form of administration are similar. Administration focuses on the overall organization, its mission, and its relationship with other organizations and groups external to it.

Management, which is a part of administration, is most closely associated with the day-to-day operation of the various elements within the organization. *Supervision* involves the one-to-one direction of staff members in their day-to-day activities. Confusion may arise because a chief administrator may act in all three capacities. Perhaps the most useful and clearest description is to define top-level personnel as administrators, mid-level personnel as managers, and those who oversee the work as it is being done as supervisors.[1]

The terms *police* and *law enforcement* are generally used interchangeably. Many people in the police field believe, however, that the police do more than merely enforce laws; they prefer to use the term *police.* Although we tend to think of the chief executive of a police division as the administrator, the bureau chiefs or commanders as the managers, and the sergeants as supervisors, it is important to note that often all three of these tasks are required of one administrator.

Organization of the Book

To understand the challenges that administrators of justice organizations face, we first need to place justice administration within the "big picture." Thus, in Part I, "Justice Administration: An Introduction," we discuss the organization and administration of the U.S. justice system; the state of our country with respect to crime and government control; and the evolution of justice administration in its three components: police, courts, and corrections.

Parts II, III, and IV, which discuss contemporary police, courts, and corrections administration, respectively, follow the same organization: The first chapter of each part deals with the *organization and operation* of the component, followed in the second chapter by an examination of the component's *personnel roles and functions,* and in the third chapter, a discussion of *issues and practices.* Parts II, III, and IV conclude with several case studies. As indicated in the Preface, these case studies allow the reader to encounter some of the problems justice administrators confront daily. Several discussion questions follow each case study. With a fundamental knowledge of the system and a reading of the chapters in the respective book part, readers should be able to engage in some critical analysis— even, it is hoped, some spirited discussions—and arrive at several feasible solutions to the problems presented.

Part V examines administrative problems and factors that span and influence the entire justice system, including the rights of criminal justice employees, financial administration, technology, and the future.

This first chapter sets the stage for later discussions of the criminal justice system and its administration. We first consider whether the justice system comprises a "process," a "network," a "nonsystem," or a true "system." Discussion then ensues about the legal and historical bases for justice and administration, followed by an examination of what some great thinkers have said about governance in general. The differences between public- and private-sector administration are reviewed next, and the chapter concludes with a discussion of policymaking in justice administration. After completing this chapter, the reader will have a better grasp of the structure, purpose, and foundation of our criminal justice system.

A True *System* of Justice?

What do justice administrators—police, courts, and corrections administrators— actually *administer*? Do they provide leadership over a system that has succeeded in accomplishing its mission? Do individuals within the system work amiably and communicate well with one another? Do they all share the same goals? Do their efforts effectively result in crime reduction? In short, do they compose a *system*? We now turn to these questions, still taking a fundamental yet expansive view of justice administration.

Succinctly, the U.S. criminal justice system attempts to decrease criminal behavior through a wide variety of uncoordinated and sometimes uncomplementary efforts. Each system component—police, courts, and corrections—has varying degrees of responsibility and discretion for dealing with crime. Each system component fails, however, to engage in any coordinated planning effort; hence, relations among and between these components are often characterized by friction, conflict, and deficient communication. Role conflicts also serve to ensure that planning and communication are stifled.

For example, one role of the police is to arrest suspected offenders. Police typically are not judged publicly on the quality of their arrests, but on the number of them. A common complaint prosecutors voice is the poor quality of police case reports. Prosecutors, on the other hand, are partially judged by their success in obtaining convictions; public defenders or defense attorneys are judged by their success in getting suspected offenders' charges dropped. The courts are more independent in their operation, largely sentencing offenders as they see fit. Corrections agencies are torn between the philosophies of punishment and rehabilitation and, in the view of many, wind up performing neither function with any large degree of success. These agencies are further burdened with overcrowded conditions, high caseloads, and antiquated facilities.[2] Unfortunately, this situation has existed for several decades.

This criticism of the criminal justice system or process—that it is fragmented and rife with role conflicts and other problems—is a common refrain. The following points of view describe the criminal justice system as it currently operates: process, network, and nonsystem. Following our discussion of these three viewpoints, we consider whether or not criminal justice truly represents a system.

A Criminal Justice Process?

What is readily seen in the foregoing discussion is that our criminal justice system may not be a system at all. Given its current operation and fragmentation, it might be better described as a *process.* As a process, it involves the decisions and actions taken by an institution, offender, victim, or society that influence the offender's movement into, through, or out of the justice system.[3] In its purest form, the criminal justice process occurs as shown in Figure 1.1. Note that the horizontal effects are a result of such factors as the amount of crime, the number of prosecutions, and the type of court disposition affecting the population in correctional facilities and rehabilitative programs. Vertical effects are exemplified by the primary system steps or procedures.[4]

At one end of this process are the police, who understandably may view their primary role as getting lawbreakers off the street. At the other end of the process are the corrections officials, who may see their role as being primarily rehabilitative in nature. Somewhere between are the courts, which try to ensure a fair application of the law to each case coming to the bar.

As a process, we assume that the justice system cannot reduce crime by itself, nor can any of the component parts afford to be insensitive to the needs and problems of the other parts. In criminal justice planning jargon, "You can't rock one end of the boat." In other words, every action has a reaction, especially in the justice process. If, for example, a bond issue for funds that provide 10 percent more police officers on the streets is passed in a community, the additional arrests made by those added police personnel will have a decided impact on the courts and corrections components. Obviously, although each component operates largely in a vacuum, the actions and reactions of each with respect to crime sends ripples throughout the process.

Much of the failure to deal effectively with crime may be attributed to organizational and administrative fragmentation of the justice process. Fragmentation exists among the components of the process, within the individual components, among political jurisdictions, and among persons.

A Criminal Justice Network?

Still other observers contend that U.S. justice systems constitute a *network.*[5] In the view of Steven Cox and John Wade, the justice system functions much like a television or radio network whose stations share many programs, but each station also may present programs that the network does not air on other stations. The network appears as a three-dimensional model in which the public, legislators, police, prosecutors, judges, and correctional officials interact with one another and with others who are outside the traditionally conceived criminal justice system.[6]

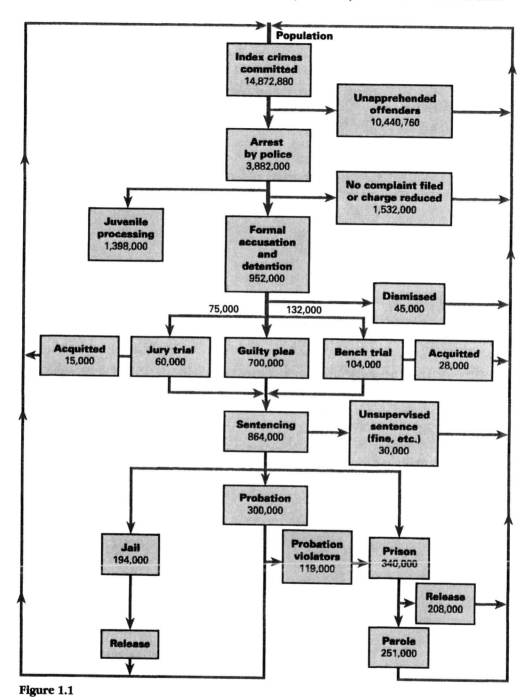

Figure 1.1

Criminal justice model. (*Source:* Adapted from the President's Commission on Law Enforcement and Administration of Justice, *The Challenge of Crime in a Free Society.* Washington, D.C.: U.S. Government Printing Office, 1967, pp. 262–263.)

Furthermore, the justice system is said to be based on several key yet erroneous assumptions, including the following:

1. The components of the network cooperate and share similar goals.
2. The network operates according to a set of formal procedural rules to ensure uniform treatment of all persons, the outcome of which constitutes "justice."
3. Each person accused of a crime receives due process and is presumed innocent until proven guilty.
4. Each person receives a speedy public trial before an impartial jury of his or her peers, and is represented by competent legal counsel.[7]

Cox and Wade assert that these key assumptions are erroneous because

1. The three components have incompatible goals and are continually competing with one another for budgetary dollars.
2. Evidence indicates that blacks and whites, males and females, and middle- and lower-class citizens receive differential treatment in the criminal justice network.
3. Some persons are prosecuted, some are not; some are involved in plea bargaining, others are not; some are convicted and sent to prison, whereas others convicted of the same type of offense are not. A great deal of the plea negotiation remains largely invisible, such as that of "unofficial probation" with juveniles (described later). Also, they argue, there is considerable evidence pointing to the fact that criminal justice employees do not presume their clients or arrestees to be innocent.
4. Finally, these proponents for a "network" view of the justice process argue that the current tremendous backlog of cases ensures that a speedy trial is more fluff than substance, especially when a vast majority (at least 90 percent) of all arrestees plead guilty prior to trial.[8]

Considering these facts, the adherents to this position are compelled to believe that justice appears to be in the eyes of the beholder and that ours is probably not a just network in the eyes of the poor, the minority group, or the individual victim. Citizens, they also assert, may not know what to expect from the network. Some may believe that the network does not work at all and is not worth their support.[9]

A Criminal Justice Nonsystem?

Many observers argue that the three components of the justice system actually compose a *nonsystem*. They maintain that the three segments of the system used in the United States to deal with criminal behavior do not always function in harmony and that the system is neither efficient enough to create a credible fear of punishment nor fair enough to command respect for its values.

Indeed, these theorists are given considerable weight by the President's Commission on Law Enforcement and the Administration of Justice (commonly known as the *Crime Commission*), which made the following comment:

> The system of criminal justice used in America to deal with those crimes it cannot prevent and those criminals it cannot deter is not a monolithic, or even a consistent, system. It was not designed or built in one piece at one time. Its philosophic core is that a person may be punished by the Government, if, and only if, it has been proven by an impartial and deliberate process that he has violated a specific law. Around that core, layer upon layer of institutions and procedures, some carefully constructed and some improvised, some inspired by principle and some by expediency, have accumulated. Parts of the system—magistrates, courts, trial by jury, bail—are of great antiquity. Other parts—juvenile courts, probation and parole, professional policemen—are relatively new. Every village, town, county, city and State has its own criminal justice system, and there is a Federal one as well. All of them operate somewhat alike, no two of them operate precisely alike.[10]

Alfred Cohn and Roy Udolf stated that criminal justice "is not a system, and it has little to do with justice as that term is ordinarily understood."[11] Also in this school of thought are Burton Wright and Vernon Fox, who asserted that "the criminal justice system ... is frequently criticized because it is not a coordinated structure—not really a system. In many ways this is true."[12]

These writers would probably agree that little has changed since 1971, when *Newsweek* stated in a special report entitled "Justice on Trial" that

> America's system of criminal justice is too swamped to deliver more than the roughest justice—and too ragged really to be called a system. "What we have," says one former government hand, "is a non-system in which the police don't catch criminals, the courts don't try them, and the prisons don't reform them. The system, in a word, is in trouble. The trouble has been neglect. The paralysis of the civil courts, where it takes five years to get a judgment in a damage suit ... the courts—badly managed, woefully undermanned and so inundated with cases that they have to run fast just to stand still.[13]

Unfortunately, as we will demonstrate time and again throughout this book, those words still ring true. Clearly, the onus on modern-day justice administrators is not to be innovators or reformers, but rather to simply "make do." As one law professor stated, "Oliver Wendell Holmes could not survive in our criminal court. How can you be an eminent jurist when you have to deal with this mess?"[14]

Those who hold that the justice system is in reality no system at all can also point to the fact that many practitioners in the field (the police, judges, prosecutors, correctional workers, private attorneys) and academicians concede that the entire justice system is in crisis, even rapidly approaching a major breakdown. They can cite overcrowding everywhere—police calls for service, court dockets, prison populations—as well as riots (on the streets as well as within institutions).

In short, they contend that the system is in a state of dysfunction, largely as a result of its fragmentation and lack of cohesion.[15]

System fragmentation is largely believed to affect directly the amount and type of crime that exists. The parts of the system are disunified. Contributing to this fragmentation are the wide discretionary powers possessed by actors in the justice system. For example, police officers (primarily those having the least experience, education, and training) have great discretion over whom they arrest and are effectively able to dictate policy as they go about performing their duties. Here again, the Crime Commission was moved to comment, realizing that how the police officer moves around his or her territory depends largely on this discretion:

> Crime does not look the same on the street as it does in a legislative chamber. How much noise or profanity makes conduct "disorderly" within the meaning of the law? When must a quarrel be treated as a criminal assault: at the first threat, or at the first shove, or at the first blow, or after blood is drawn, or when a serious injury is inflicted? How suspicious must conduct be before there is "probable cause," the constitutional basis for an arrest? Every [officer], however sketchy or incomplete his education, is an interpreter of the law.[16]

Judicial officers also possess great discretionary latitude. The state statutes require judges to provide deterrence, retribution, rehabilitation, and incapacitation—all in the same sentence. Well-publicized studies of the sentencing tendencies of judges—in which participant judges were given identical facts in cases and were to impose sentences based on offenders' violations of the law—have demonstrated considerable discretion and unevenness in their sentences. The nonsystem advocates believe this to be further evidence that a basic inequality exists—an inequality in justice that is communicated to the offender.[17]

Finally, in corrections—the part of the criminal justice process that the U.S. public sees the least of and knows the least about—fragmentation also occurs, according to some people. Indeed, as the Crime Commission noted, the federal government, all 50 states, the District of Columbia, and most of the country's 3,047 counties now engage in correctional activities in some form or another. Each level of government acts independently of the others, and responsibility for the administration of corrections is divided within given jurisdictions as well.[18]

With this fragmentation comes polarity in identifying and establishing the primary goals of the system. The police, enforcing the laws, emphasize community protection; the courts weigh both sides of the issue—individual rights and community needs; and correctional facilities work with the individual. Each of these groups has varied perceptions of the offender, creating goal conflict; that is, the goal of the police and prosecutor is to get the transgressor off the street, which is antithetical to the "caretaker" role of the corrections worker, who often wants to rehabilitate and return the offender to the community. The criminal justice process does not allow much in the way of alternative means of coping with offenders. Eventually, the nonsystem adherent believes that the offender will become a mere statistic, more important on paper than as a human being.[19]

Because the justice process lacks sufficient program and procedural flexibility, these adherents argue, its workers can either circumvent policies, rules, and regulations, or they can adhere to organizational practices they know are, at times, dysfunctional. (As evidence, they can point to the many cases of *informal* treatment of criminal cases that occur, such as when a police officer "bends" someone's constitutional rights in order to return stolen property to its rightful owner; or the "unofficial probation" by a juvenile probation officer who, without a solid case but with strong suspicion, warns a youth that any further infractions will result in formal court-involved proceedings.)

Or a True Criminal Justice System?

That all of the foregoing perspectives on the justice system are grounded in truth is probably evident by now. In many ways, the police, courts, and corrections components work and interact to function like a process, network, or even a non-system. Those factors, all of which include the disunity of the justice operation, however, may yet constitute a true system. As Willa Dawson stated, "Administration of justice can be regarded as a system by most standards. It may be a poorly functioning system but it does meet the criteria nonetheless. The systems approach is still in its infancy."[20] J. W. La Patra added that "I do believe that a criminal justice system does exist, but that it functions very poorly. The CJS is a loosely connected, nonharmonious, group of social entities."[21]

To be fair, however, perhaps this method of dealing with offenders is best after all. It may be that having a well-oiled machine—in which all activities are coordinated, goals and objectives are unified, and communication between participants is maximized, all serving to grind out "justice" in a highly efficacious manner—may not be what we truly want or need in a democracy.

We hope that we have not belabored the subject; however, it is important to establish early in this book the type of system and its components that you, as a potential criminal justice administrator, may encounter. You can reconcile for yourself the differences of opinion described earlier. In this book, however, we adhere to the notion that even with all of its disunity and lack of fluidity, what criminal justice officials administer in the United States is a system. Nonetheless, it is good to look at its operation and shortcomings and, as stated earlier, force ourselves to confront problems with the criminal justice system (CJS) and possible areas for improvement.

Now that we have a systemic view of what criminal justice managers actually administer, it would be helpful to look briefly at how they may go about doing it. To begin in *tabula rasa* fashion, we first consider the legal and historical bases that provide for the United States to be a democracy regulated by a government and by a system of justice: We include the consensus-conflict continuum, with the social contract on one end and maintainance of the status quo/repression on the other. Next we distinguish between administration and work in the public and private sectors because the styles, incentives, and rewards of each are, by their very nature, quite different. This provides the foundation for the final point of discussion, a brief look at the decision-making process in criminal justice agencies.

The Foundations of Justice and Administration: Legal and Historical Bases

Given that our system of justice is founded on a large, powerful system of government, these questions must be addressed: From whence is that power derived? How can governments presume to maintain a system of laws that effectively serves to govern its people and, furthermore, a legal system that exists to punish persons who willfully suborn those laws? We now consider the answers to those questions.

The Consensus versus Conflict Debate

U.S. society has innumerable lawbreakers. Most of them are easily handled by the police and do not challenge the legitimacy of the law while being arrested and incarcerated for violating it. Burglars do not argue that the crime for which they were arrested was unreasonable or morally wrong. Nor do they challenge the system of government that enacts the laws or the justice agencies that carry them out. The stability of our government for more than 200 years is a testimony to the existence of a fair degree of consensus as to its legitimacy.[22] Thomas Jefferson's statements in the Declaration of Independence hold as true today as the day he wrote them, accepted as common sense:

> We hold these truths to be self-evident, that all men are created equal, that they are endowed by their Creator with certain inalienable Rights, that among these are Life, Liberty and the pursuit of Happiness—That to secure these rights, Governments are instituted among Men, deriving their just powers from the consent of the governed. That whenever any Form of Government becomes destructive of these ends, it is the Right of the People to alter or abolish it.

The principles of the Declaration were almost a paraphrase of John Locke's *Second Treatise on Civil Government,* which justified the acts of government on the basis of his theory of *social contract.* According to Locke, in the state of nature, people were created by God—free, equal, independent, and with inherent inalienable rights to life, liberty, and property. Each person had the right of self-protection against those who would infringe on those liberties. In Locke's view, although most people were good, some would be likely to prey on their fellows, who in turn would constantly have to be on guard against such evildoers. To avoid this brutish existence, people joined together, forming governments to which they surrendered their rights of self-protection. In return, they received governmental protection of their lives, liberty, and property. As with any contract, each side has benefits and considerations; people give up their rights to protect themselves and receive protection in return. Governments give protection and receive loyalty and obedience in return.[23]

Locke believed that the chief purpose of government was the protection of property, which people joined together to form the commonwealth. Once the people unite into a commonwealth, they cannot withdraw from it, nor can their lands be removed from it. But property holders within a commonwealth cannot be made members of that commonwealth; only their express consent can make them so. They must accept that property only on the condition that they submit to the government of the commonwealth. This is Locke's famous theory of *tacit consent*: "Every Man . . . doth hereby give his *tacit Consent,* and is as far forth obliged to Obedience to the Laws of the Government."[24] Locke's theory essentially describes an association of landowners.[25]

Another theorist connected with the social contract theory is Thomas Hobbes, who argued that all people were essentially irrational and selfish. He maintained that people had just enough rationality to recognize their situation and to come together to form governments for self-protection, agreeing "amongst themselves to submit to some Man, or Assembly of men, voluntarily, on confidence to be protected by him against all others."[26] Therefore, they existed in a state of consensus with their governments, consenting to their existence.

Jean-Jacques Rousseau, a conflict theorist, differed substantively from both Hobbes and Locke, arguing that "Man is born free, but everywhere he is in chains."[27] Like Plato, Rousseau associated the loss of freedom and the creation of conflict in modern societies with the development of private property and the unequal distribution of resources. Rousseau described conflict between the ruling group and the other groups in society, where Locke had described consensus in the ruling group and the need to use force and other means to ensure the compliance of the other groups.[28]

Thus, the primary difference between the consensus and conflict theorists, with respect to their view of government vis-a-vis the governed, concerns their evaluation of the legitimacy of the actions of ruling groups in contemporary societies. Locke saw those actions as consistent with natural law, describing societies as consensual and arguing that any conflict in them was illegitimate and as such could be repressed by force and other means. Rousseau evaluated the actions of ruling groups as irrational and selfish, creating conflicts among the various groups in society.[29]

This debate is important because it plays out the competing views of humankind toward its ruling group; it also has relevance with respect to the kind of justice system (or process) we have. The systems model has been criticized for implying a greater level of organization and cooperation among the various agencies of justice than actually exists. The word *system* conjures an idea of machine-like precision in which wasted effort, redundancy, and conflicting actions are nearly nonexistent. Our current justice system does not possess such a level of perfection. As mentioned earlier, conflicts among and within agencies are rife, goals are not shared by its three components, and the system may move in different directions. Therefore, the systems approach is part of the *consensus model* point of view, which assumes that all parts of the system work toward a common goal.[30] The *conflict model,* holding that agency interests tend to make actors within the system self-serving, provides the other approach. Persons subscribing to this view note the pressures for success, promotion, and general accountability, which together result in fragmented efforts of the system as a whole, leading to a criminal justice nonsystem.[31]

This debate has relevance for criminal justice administrators. Assume a consensus-conflict continuum, where we place social contract (the people totally allowing government to use its means to protect them) on one end and class repression on the other. That our administrators of criminal justice agencies do *not* allow their agencies to "drift" too far to one end of the continuum or the other is of paramount importance. Americans cannot allow the compliance or conflict that would result at either end. The safer point is more toward the middle of the continuum, where people are not totally dependent on their government for protection and maintain enough control to prevent totalitarianism.

Crime Control Through Due Process

Both the systems and nonsystems models of criminal justice provide a view of agency relationships. Another way to view American criminal justice is in terms of its goals. Two primary goals exist within this context: (1) the need to enforce the law and maintain social order, and (2) the need to protect people from injustice.[32] The first, often referred to as the crime control model, values the arrest and conviction of criminal offenders. The second, because of its emphasis on individual rights, is commonly known as the due process model. Due process—found in the Bill of Rights, particularly in the Fourteenth Amendment—is a central and necessary part of our system, requiring a careful and informed consideration of the facts of each individual case. Due process seeks to ensure that innocent people are not convicted of crimes.

The dual goals of crime control and due process are often suggested to be in constant and unavoidable opposition to one another. Many critics of criminal justice, as it exists in the United States, argue that our attempt to achieve "justice" for offenders too often occurs at the expense of due process. Other more conservative observers believe that our system is too lenient with its clients, coddling offenders rather than protecting the innocent.

We are never going to be in a position to avoid ideological conflicts such as these. Some observers, however, such as Frank Schmalleger, believe it is realistic to think of the U.S. system of justice as representative of *crime control through due process*.[33] This model of crime control is infused with the recognition of individual rights, which provides the conceptual framework for this book.

Public- versus Private-Sector Administration

That people derive positive personal experience from their work has long been recognized.[34] Because work is a vital part of our lives and is an activity that carries tremendous meaning in terms of our personal identity and happiness, the right match of person to job has long been recognized as a determinant of job satisfaction.[35] Factors such as job importance, accomplishment, challenge, teamwork, management fairness, and rewards become very important.

People in both the public (i.e., government) and private (e.g., retail business) sectors derive positive personal consequences from their work. The means by which they arrive at those positive feelings and are rewarded for their efforts, however, are often quite different. Basically, whereas private businesses and corporations can use a panoply of *extrinsic* (external) rewards to motivate and reward their employees, people working in the public sector must achieve job satisfaction primarily through *intrinsic* (internal) rewards.

Extrinsic rewards include such perquisites as financial compensation, including salary and benefits package; private office; key to the executive washroom; bonuses; trips; company car; awards (including such designations as the employee of the month or the insurance industry's "million-dollar roundtable"); expense account; membership in country clubs and organizations; and job title. The title assigned to a job can affect one's general perceptions of the job regardless of actual job content. For example, the role once known disparagingly as "grease monkey" in a gasoline service station has commonly become known as "lubrication technician"; garbage collectors have become "sanitation engineers"; and so on. Much of our society's enhancement of job titles is to add job satisfaction and extrinsic rewards to what may often be lackluster positions.

Corporations often devote tremendous sums of time and money to bestowing extrinsic rewards, incentives, and job titles to employees to enhance their job satisfaction. These rewards, of course, cannot and do not exist in the public sector nearly to the extent that they exist in the private sector.

As indicated earlier, public-sector workers must instead seek and obtain job satisfaction primarily from within—through intrinsic means. These workers, unable to become wealthy and to occupy positions that are filled with perks, instead need jobs that are gratifying and that intrinsically make them feel good about themselves and what they accomplish. Criminal justice work is often characterized by practitioners as intrinsically rewarding, providing a sense of worth in making the world a better place in which to live. These employees also seek appreciation from their supervisors and co-workers and generally require challenges.

These views can easily be translated to individual views concerning the workplace. In other words, some people work primarily for a paycheck and other external rewards. For example, some police officers merely put in time on the job. They would probably have been glad to "patrol" around a flagpole all month if such was required to earn their pay.

To be successful, administrators should attempt to understand the personalities, needs, and motivations of their employees and attempt to meet those needs and provide motivation to the extent possible. The late Sam Walton, the multibillionaire founder of Wal-Mart Stores, provided a unique example of attempting to do this. One night, Walton could not sleep, so he went to a nearby all-night bakery (in Bentonville, Arkansas), bought four dozen doughnuts, and took them to a distribution center where he chatted with graveyard-shift Wal-Mart employees. From that chat, he discovered that two more shower stalls were needed at that location.[36] Walton obviously solicited—and valued—employee input and was concerned about their morale and working conditions. Although Walton was known to be unique in his business sense, these elements of administration can be applied by public administrators.

Policymaking in Justice Administration

Imagine the following scenario. Someone with criminal justice operations in his or her purview (e.g., a city or county manager, or a municipal or criminal justice planner) is charged with the responsibility of formulating an omnibus policy with respect to crime reduction. He or she might begin by trying to list all related variables as they contribute to the crime problem: poverty; employment; demographics of people residing within the jurisdiction; environmental conditions (such as housing density and conditions and areas where living conditions are at their worst); mortality, morbidity, and suicide rates; educational levels of the populace; and so on.

Next the administrator would request from each justice administrator within the jurisdiction more specific information to determine where problems might exist in the practitioners' view of the police, courts, and corrections subsystems. For example, a police executive would contribute information concerning calls for service, arrests, and crime data (including offender information and crime information—time of day, day of week, methods, locations, targets, and so on). The status of existing programs, such as community policing and crime prevention, would also be provided. From the courts, information would be sought concerning the sizes of court dockets (civil and criminal) and backlogs ("justice delayed is justice denied"). Included in this report would be input from the prosecutor's office concerning the quality and quantity of police reports and arrests, as well as data on case dismissals and conviction rates at trial. From corrections administrators, he or she would be acutely interested in the average officer caseload and recidivism and revocation rates. Budgetary information would certainly be solicited from all subsystems, as well as miscellaneous data regarding their personnel levels, level of training, and so on. Finally, he or she would attempt to formulate a crime policy, setting forth goals and objectives needed for addressing the jurisdiction's needs.

As an alternative, the policymaker could approach this task in a far less complex manner, simply setting, either explicitly or without conscious thought, the relatively simple goal of "keeping crime down." This goal might be compromised or complicated by only a few other goals, such as a bullish economy. This person could in fact disregard most of the other variables discussed previously as being beyond the ken of his or her current needs and interests, and would for the time being not even attempt to consider them as being immediately relevant. The criminal justice practitioners would not be pressed to attempt to cull out these vast amounts of information and critical analyses. If pressed for time (as is often the case in these real-life scenarios), the planner would readily admit that these variables were being ignored.[37]

Because executives and planners of the alternative approach expect to achieve their goals only partially, they expect to repeat endlessly the sequence just described as conditions and aspirations change and as accuracy of prediction improves. Realistically, however, the first of these two approaches assumes intellectual capacities and sources of information that people often do not possess; further, the time and money that can be allocated to a policy problem is limited. Public agencies are in effect usually too hamstrung to practice the first method; it is the second method that is practiced. Curiously, however, the literature on decision making, planning, policy formulation, and public administration formalizes and "preaches" the first approach.[38] The second method is much neglected in this literature.

In the United States, probably no part of government has attempted a comprehensive analysis and overview of policy on crime (the first method). Thus, making crime policy is at best a very rough process. For example, without a more comprehensive process, we cannot possibly understand how a variety of problems—education, housing, recreation, employment, race, and policing—might encourage or discourage juvenile delinquency. What we normally engage in is a comparative analysis of the results of similar past policy decisions. This explains why justice administrators often feel that outside experts or academics are not helpful to them—why it is safer to "fly by the seat of one's pants."

Theorists often urge the administrator to go the long way to the solution of his or her problems, following the scientific method, when the administrator knows that the best available theory will not work. Theorists, for their part, do not realize that the administrator is often in fact practicing a systematic method.[39] So, what may appear to be mere muddling through is both highly praised as a sophisticated form of policy and decision making as well as soundly denounced as no method at all. Society needs to bear in mind that justice administrators possess an intimate knowledge of past consequences of actions that "outsiders" do not. While seemingly less effective and rational, this method, according to policymaking experts, has merit. Indeed, this method is commonly used for personal problem solving in which the means and ends are often impossible to separate, aspirations or objectives undergo constant development, and drastic simplification of the complexity of the real world is urgent if problems are to be solved in reasonable periods of time.[40]

Summary

This chapter presented the foundation for the study of justice administration. We also established the legal existence of governments, our laws, and the justice agencies that administer them. We demonstrated that each of the three components of the justice system is independent, fragmented, and often working at odds with one another toward the accomplishment of the system's overall mission.

Questions for Review

1. What is an organization?

2. Do the three justice components (police, courts, and corrections) constitute a true system, or are they more appropriately described as a process or a true nonsystem? Defend your response.

3. What are the legal and historical bases for a justice system and its administration in the United States? Why is the conflict versus consensus debate important?

4. What are some of the substantive ways in which public- and private-sector administration are similar? How are they dissimilar?

5. Which method—a rational process or one that some view as just muddling through—appears to be used in criminal justice policymaking today? Which method is probably best, given real-world realities?

Notes

1. For a more thorough explication of these terms and roles, particularly as applied in policing, see Richard N. Holden, *Modern Police Management* (Englewood Cliffs, N.J.: Prentice Hall, 1986).

2. Michael E. O'Neill, Ronald F. Bykowski, and Robert S. Blair, *Criminal Justice Planning: A Practical Approach* (San Jose, Calif.: Justice Systems Development, Inc., 1976), p. 5.

3. Ibid., p. 12.

4. Ibid.

5. Steven M. Cox and John E. Wade, *The Criminal Justice Network: An Introduction* (2d ed.) (Dubuque, Iowa: Wm. C. Brown, 1989), p. 1.

6. Ibid., p. 4.

7. Ibid., p. 12.

8. Ibid., pp. 13–14.

9. Philip H. Ennis, "Crime, Victims, and the Police," *Transaction* 4 (June 1967):36–44.

10. The President's Commission on Law Enforcement and the Administration of Justice, *The Challenge of Crime in a Free Society* (Washington, D.C.: U.S. Government Printing Office, 1967), p. 7.

11. Alfred Cohn and Roy Udolf, *The Criminal Justice System and Its Psychology* (New York: Van Nostrand Reinhold, 1979).

12. Burton Wright and Vernon Fox, *Criminal Justice and the Social Sciences* (Philadelphia: W. B. Saunders, 1978).

13. "Justice on Trial: A Special Report," *Newsweek* (March 8, 1971):16.

14. Ibid., p. 18.

15. Alan R. Coffey and Edward Eldefonso, *Process and Impact of Justice* (Beverly Hills, Calif.: Glencoe Press, 1975), p. 32.

16. The President's Commission, *The Challenge of Crime in a Free Society,* p. 5.

17. Coffey and Eldefonso, *Process and Impact of Justice,* p. 35.

18. Ibid., p. 39.

19. Ibid., p. 41.

20. Willa Dawson, "The Need for a System Approach to Criminal Justice," in Donald T. Shanahan (ed.), *The Administration of Justice System—An Introduction* (Boston: Holbrook, 1977).

21. J.W. La Patra, *Analyzing the Criminal Justice System* (Lexington, Mass.: Lexington Books, 1978).

22. Alexander B. Smith and Harriet Pollack, *Criminal Justice: An Overview* (New York: Holt, Rinehart and Winston, 1980), p. 9.

23. Ibid., p. 10.

24. Ibid., p. 366.

25. Thomas J. Bernard, *The Consensus-Conflict Debate: Form and Content in Social Theories* (New York: Columbia University Press, 1983), p. 78.

26. Thomas Hobbes, *Leviathan* (New York: E. P. Dutton, 1950), pp. 290–291.

27. Jean-Jacques Rousseau, "A Discourse on the Origin of Inequality," in G. D. H. Cole (ed.), *The Social Contract and Discourses* (New York: E. P. Dutton, 1946), p. 240.

28. Bernard, *The Consensus-Conflict Debate*, pp. 83, 85.

29. Ibid., p. 86.

30. Frank Schmalleger, *Criminal Justice Today* (5th ed.) (Upper Saddle River, N.J.: Prentice Hall, 1999), p. 18.

31. One of the first publications to express the nonsystems approach was the American Bar Association's *New Perspective on Urban Crime* (Washington, D.C.: ABA Special Committee on Crime Prevention and Control, 1972).

32. Schmalleger, *Criminal Justice Today*, pp. 27–28.

33. Ibid.

34. Fernando Bartolome and Paul A. Lee Evans, "Professional Lives versus Private Lives: Shifting Patterns of Managerial Commitment," *Organizational Dynamics* 7 (1982):2–29; Ronald C. Kessler and James A. McRae Jr., "The Effect of Wives' Employment on the Mental Health of Married Men and Women," *American Sociological Review* 47 (1979):216–227.

35. Robert V. Presthus, *The Organizational Society* (New York: Alfred A. Knopf, 1962).

36. Joseph A. Petrick and George E. Manning, "How to Manage Morale," *Personnel Journal* 69 (October 1990):87.

37. This scenario is modeled on that set out by Charles E. Lindblom, a Harvard economist, in "The Science of 'Muddling Through,'" *Public Administration Review* 19 (Spring 1959): 79–89.

38. Ibid., p. 80.

39. Ibid., p. 87.

40. Ibid., p. 88.

ORGANIZATION AND ADMINISTRATION: PRINCIPLES AND PRACTICES

We are born in organizations, educated by organizations, and most of us spend much of our lives working for organizations. We spend much of our leisure time paying, playing, and praying in organizations. Most of us will die in an organization, and when the time comes for burial, the largest organization of all—the state—must grant official permission.

—Amitai Etzioni

Introduction

It is no surprise that "Dilbert"—one of today's most popular cartoon strips and television programs—portrays downtrodden workers, inconsiderate bosses, and dysfunctional organizations. Scott Adams's cartoon "hero," a mouthless engineer with a perpetually bent necktie, is believed by many Americans to be a documentary on today's workplace. They believe that the Dilbert principle—the most ineffective workers are systematically moved to the place where they can do the least damage—is alive and well. Although a sizable majority of U.S. workers routinely indicate that their workplace is a pleasant environment, more than 70 percent also experience stress at work because of red tape, unnecessary rules, poor communication with management, and other causes. Indeed, what gives Adams grist for the Dilbert mill is the way managers mishandle their employees and downsizing.[1] This chapter examines organizations and the employees within them and how they should be managed and motivated.

The chapter offers a general discussion of organizations, focusing on their definition, theory and function, and structure. Included are several approaches to managing and communicating within organizations. We then focus on one of the most important aspects of leadership, personnel administration. We review historical schools of thought concerning management and examine organizational leadership theories. We also consider a chronology of management fads that have evolved over the last four decades. We conclude with a discussion of several motivational techniques for employees based on findings by major theorists in the field.

Defining Organizations

Like *supervision* and *management,* the word *organization* has a number of meanings and interpretations that have evolved over the years. We think of organizations as entities of two or more people who cooperate to accomplish an objective(s). In that sense, certainly the concept of organization is not new. Undoubtedly, the first organizations were primitive hunting parties. Organization and a high degree of coordination were required to bring down huge animals, as revealed in fossils from as early as 40,000 B.C.[2]

An organization may be formally defined as "a consciously coordinated social entity, with a relatively identifiable boundary, that functions on a relatively continuous basis to achieve a common goal or set of goals."[3] The term *consciously coordinated* implies management. *Social entity* refers to the fact that organizations are comprised of people who interact with one another and with people in other organizations. *Relatively identifiable boundary* alludes to the organization's goals and the public served.[4]

Using this definition, we can consider many types of formal groups as full-blown organizations. Four different types of formal organizations have been identified by asking the question, "Who benefits?" Answers include (1) mutual benefit associations, such as police labor unions; (2) business concerns, such as General Motors; (3) service organizations, such as community mental health centers, where the client group is the prime beneficiary; and (4) commonweal organizations, such as the Department of Defense and criminal justice agencies, where the beneficiaries are the public at large.[5] The following analogy is designed to help the reader to understand organizations.

An organization corresponds to the bones that structure or give form to the body. Imagine that the fingers are a single mass of bone rather than four separate fingers and a thumb made up of bones joined by cartilage to be flexible. The mass of bones could not, because of its structure, play musical instruments, hold a pencil, or grip a baseball bat. A criminal justice organization is analogous. It must be structured properly if it is to be effective in fulfilling its many diverse goals.[6]

It is important to note that no two organizations are exactly alike. Nor is there one best way to run an organization.

Organizational Theory and Function

Elements of an Organization

Max Weber (1864–1920), known as the "father of sociology," explored in depth the organization structure as well as the dynamics related to bureaucracy. He argued that if a bureaucratic structure is to function efficiently, it must have the following elements:

1. *Rulification and routinization.* Organizations stress continuity. Rules save effort by eliminating the need for deriving a new solution for every situation. They also facilitate standard and equal treatment of similar situations.
2. *Division of labor.* This involves performing functions that have been marked off as part of a systematic division of labor and the provision of the necessary authority to carry out these functions.
3. *Hierarchy of authority.* The organization of offices follows the principle of hierarchy; each lower office is under the control and supervision of a higher one.
4. *Expertise.* Specialized training is necessary. It is thus normally true that only a person who has demonstrated adequate technical training is qualified to be a member of the administrative staff.
5. *Written rules.* Administrative acts, decisions, and rules are formulated and recorded in writing.[7]

Bureaucracies are often criticized on two grounds. First, they are said to be inflexible, inefficient, and unresponsive to changing needs and times. Second, they are said to stifle individual freedom, spontaneity, and self-realization of their employees.[8] James Q. Wilson referred to this widespread discontent with modern organizations as the "bureaucracy problem," where the key issue is "getting the frontline worker . . . to do 'the right thing.'"[9] In short, then, bureaucracies themselves can create problems.

Organizational Inputs/Outputs

Another way to view organizations is as systems that take *inputs,* process them, and thus produce *outputs.* These outputs are then sold in the marketplace or given free to citizens in the form of a service. A police agency, for example, processes reports of criminal activity and, like other systems, attempts to satisfy the customer (crime victim). Figure 2.1 demonstrates the input/output model for the police and private business. There are other types of inputs by police agencies; for example, a robbery problem might result in an input of newly created

BUSINESS ORGANIZATION

Inputs	**Processes**	**Outputs**
Customer takes photos to shop to be developed.	Photos are developed and packaged for customer to pick up.	Customer picks up photos and pays for them.

Feedback
Analysis is made of expenses/revenues and customer satisfaction.

LAW ENFORCEMENT AGENCY

Inputs	**Processes**	**Outputs**
A crime prevention unit is initiated.	Citizens contact unit for advice.	Police provide spot checks and lectures.

Feedback
Target hardening results; property crimes decrease.

COURT

Inputs	**Processes**	**Outputs**
A house arrest program is initiated.	Certain people in pre- and post-trial status are screened and offered the option.	Decrease in number of people in jail, speeding up court process.

Feedback
Violation rates are analyzed for success; some offenders are mainstreamed back into the community more smoothly.

Figure 2.1

The organization as an input/output model. (*Figure 2.1 continues on p. 24.*)

PROBATION/PAROLE AGENCIES

Inputs	**Processes**	**Outputs**
Parole guidelines are changed to shorten length of incarceration and reduce overcrowding.	Qualified inmates are contacted by parole agency and given new parole dates.	A higher number of inmates are paroled into the community.

Feedback
Parole officer's caseload and revocation rates might increase; less time to devote per case.

Figure 2.1

(continued)

robbery surveillance teams, the processing would be their stakeouts, and the output would be the number of subsequent arrests by the team. Feedback would occur in the form of conviction rates at trial.

Organizational Structure

All organizations have an organization structure or table of organization, be it written or unwritten, very basic or highly complex. An experienced manager uses this organization chart or table as a blueprint for action. The size of the organization depends on the demand placed on it and the resources available to it. Growth precipitates the need for more people, greater division of labor, specialization, written rules, and other such elements.

In building the organization structure, the following principles should be kept in mind:

1. *Principle of the objective.* Every part of every organization must be an expression of the purpose of the undertaking. You cannot organize in a vacuum; you must organize for something.

2. *Principle of specialization.* The activities of every member of any organized group should be confined, as far as possible, to the performance of a single function.

3. *Principle of authority.* In every organized group, the supreme authority must rest somewhere. There should be a clear line of authority to every person in the group.

4. *Principle of responsibility.* The responsibility of the superior for the acts of his or her subordinate is absolute.

5. *Principle of definition.* The content of each position, the duties involved, the authority and responsibility contemplated, and the relationships with other positions should be clearly defined in writing and published for the information of all concerned.

6. *Principle of correspondence.* In every position, the responsibility and the authority should correspond.

7. *Span of control.* No person should supervise more than six direct subordinates whose work interlocks.[10]

A related, major principle of hierarchy of authority is *unity of command,* which refers to placing one and only one superior officer in command or in control of every situation and employee. When a critical situation occurs, it is imperative that someone be responsible and in command. The unity of command principle ensures that multiple and/or conflicting orders are not issued to the same police officers by several superior officers. For example, a patrol sergeant might arrive at a hostage situation, deploy personnel, and give all appropriate orders, only to have a shift lieutenant or captain come to the scene and countermand the sergeant's orders with his or her own orders. This type of situation would obviously be counterproductive for all concerned. All officers must know and follow the chain of command at such incidents. Every person in the organization should report to one and only one superior officer. When the unity of command principle is followed, everyone involved is aware of the actions initiated by superiors and subordinates.

An organization should be developed with careful evaluation, or the agency may become unable to respond efficiently to client needs. For example, the implementation of too many specialized units in a police department (e.g., community relations, crime analysis, media relations) may obligate too many personnel to these functions and result in too few patrol officers. As a rule of thumb, at least 55 percent of all sworn personnel should be assigned to patrol.[11]

A simple structure indicating the direct line of authority in a chain of command is shown in Figure 2.2.

The classic pyramidal design is shown in Figure 2.3. The pyramidal structure has the following characteristics:

1. Nearly all contacts take the form of orders going *down* and reports of results going *up* the pyramid.

2. Each subordinate must receive instructions and orders from only one boss.

3. Important decisions are made at the top of the pyramid.

4. Superiors have a limited "span of control," supervising only a limited number of people.

5. Personnel at any level (except at the top and bottom) have contact only with their boss above them and their subordinates below them.[12]

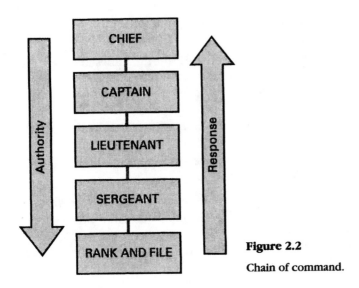

Figure 2.2

Chain of command.

Figure 2.3

Organization pyramid. (*Source:* Adapted from L. R. Sayles and G. Strauss, *Human Behavior Organizations,* Englewood Cliffs, N.J.: Prentice Hall, 1966, p. 349).

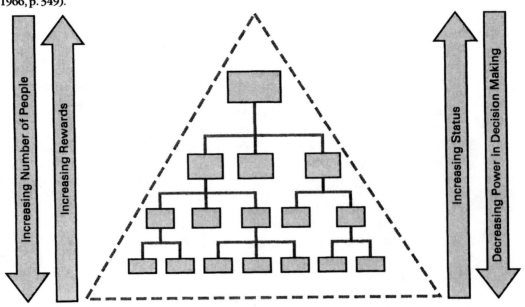

Managing the Organization

The success of any organization normally depends on the quality of work life within the agency. Peter Drucker, often referred to as the "business guru,"[13] observed that "nothing quenches motivation as quickly as a slovenly boss. People expect and demand that managers enable them to do a good job. . . . People have . . . a right to expect a serious and competent superior."[14] Unfortunately, as Drucker was implying, leaders are both good and bad because many people— untrained, uncaring, unfit, and/or unwilling to have the mantle of leadership thrust upon them—do not succeed (at least in the eyes of their subordinates).

We now look at leaders and what they can do to motivate their subordinates.

What Is Management?

Probably since the dawn of time, when cave dwellers clustered into hunting groups and some particularly dominant person assumed a leadership role over the party, administrators have received, from those around them, advice on how to do their jobs. Even today, manuals for managers, bosses, and upwardly mobile executives abound, offering quick studies in how to govern others. Although many have doubtless been profitable for their authors, most of these how-to primers on leading others enjoy only a brief, ephemeral existence.

To understand management, we must first define the term. This is an important and fairly complex undertaking, however. Perhaps the simplest definition is to say that management is "getting things done through people." Ralph Stogdill, in a review of 3,000 leadership studies, noted that "there are almost as many definitions of leadership as there are persons who have attempted to define the concept."[15] Among the most recent definitions are the following:

- "The process of influencing the activities of an individual or a group in efforts toward goal achievement in a given situation."[16]
- "Working with and through individuals and groups to accomplish organizational goals."[17]
- "The activity of influencing people to strive willingly for group objectives."[18]
- "The exercise of influence."[19]

Others have said that the manager is viewed variously as a

team captain, parent, steward, battle commander, fountain of wisdom, poker player, group spokesperson, gatekeeper, minister, drill instructor, facilitator, initiator, mediator, navigator, candy-store keeper, linchpin, umbrella-holder and everything else between nurse and Attila-the-Hun.[20]

In criminal justice organizations, leadership might best be defined as "the process of influencing organizational members to use their energies willingly and appropriately to facilitate the achievement of the [agency's] goals."[21]

We discuss management in greater detail in later chapters.

Organizational Communication

Definition and Characteristics

Communication is one of the most important dynamics of an organization. Indeed, a major role of today's administrators and other leaders is that of communication. Managers of all types of organizations spend an overwhelming amount of their time engaged in the process of—and coping with problems in—communication.

Today we communicate via facsimile machines, video camcorders, cellular telephones, satellite dishes, and so on. We converse orally, in written letters and memos, through our body language, via television and radio programs, and through newspapers and meetings. Even private thoughts—which take place four times faster than the spoken word—are communication. Every waking hour, our minds are full of ideas and thoughts. Psychologists say that nearly 100,000 thoughts pass through our minds every day, conveyed by a multitude of media.[22]

Communication becomes exceedingly important and sensitive in nature in a criminal justice organization because of the nature of information that is processed by practitioners—particularly police officers, who often see people at their worst and when they are in the most embarrassing and compromising situations. To "communicate" what is known about these kinds of behaviors could be devastating to the parties concerned. A former Detroit police chief lamented several decades ago that "many police officers, without realizing they carry such authority, do pass on rumors. The average police officer doesn't stop to weigh what he says."[23] Certainly the same holds true today, and includes court and corrections personnel, especially in view of the very high-tech communications equipment now in use.

Studies have long shown that communication is the primary problem in administration, and lack of communication is employees' primary complaint about their immediate supervisors.[24] Mark Twain once said, "The difference between the right word and the almost right word is the difference between lightning and lightning bug."[25]

Managers are in the communications business. It has been said that

> Of all skills needed to be an effective manager/leader/supervisor, skill in communicating is *the* most vital. In fact, more than 50 percent of a [criminal justice] manager's time is spent communicating. First-line supervisors usually spend about 15 percent of their time with superiors, 50 percent of their time with subordinates, and 35 percent with other managers and duties. These estimates emphasize the importance of communications in everyday ... operations.[26]

Several elements compose the communication process: encoding, transmission, medium, reception, decoding, and feedback.[27]

> *Encoding:* To convey an experience or idea to someone, we translate, or encode, that experience into symbols. We use words, other verbal behaviors and gestures, or other nonverbal behaviors to convey the experience or idea.

Transmission: This element involves the translation of the encoded symbols into some behavior that another person can observe. The actual articulation (moving our lips, tongue, etc.) of the symbol into verbal or nonverbal observable behavior is transmission.

Medium: Communication must be conveyed through some channel or medium. Media for communication may be our sight, hearing, taste, touch, or smell. Some other media are television, telephone, paper and pencil, and radio. The choice of the medium is important as well. For example, a message that is tranmitted via formal letter from the chief executive officer will carry more weight than if the same message is conveyed via a secretary's memo.

Reception: The stimuli, the verbal and nonverbal symbols, reach the senses of the receiver and are conveyed to the brain for interpretation.

Decoding: The individual who receives the stimuli develops some meaning for the verbal and nonverbal symbols and decodes the stimuli. These symbols are translated into some concept or experience of the receiver. Whether the receiver is familiar with the symbols, or whether interference such as any physical noise or physiological problem occurs, determines how closely the message that the receiver has decoded approximates the message that the sender has encoded.

Feedback: When the receiver decodes the transmitted symbols, he or she usually provides some response or feedback to the sender. If somone appears puzzled, we repeat the message or we encode the concept differently and transmit some different symbols to express the same concept. Feedback that we receive acts as a guide or steering device and lets us know whether the receiver has interpreted our symbols as we intended. Feedback is obviously a crucial element in guaranteeing that the proper meaning that the sender intended was in fact conveyed to the receiver.

Communication Within Criminal Justice Organizations

Organizational systems of communication are usually created by establishing formal systems of responsibility and explicit delegations of duties, such as implicit statements of the nature, content, and direction of the communication that are necessary for the group's performance. Most criminal justice administrators prefer a formal system, regardless of how cumbersome it may be, because they can control it and because it tends to create a record for future reference. Several human factors affect the flow of communication, however. Employees typically communicate with those persons who can help them to achieve their aims; they avoid communicating with those who do not assist, or may retard, their accomplishing those goals; and they tend to avoid communicating with people who threaten them and make them feel anxious.[28] Other barriers to effective communication are discussed later.

Communication within a criminal justice organization may be downward, upward, or horizontal. There are five types of *downward* communication within a criminal justice organization:

1. Job instruction—communication relating to the performance of a certain task.
2. Job rationale—communication relating a certain task to organizational tasks.
3. Procedures and practices—communication about organization policies, procedures, rules, and regulations (discussed in Chapter 3).
4. Feedback—communication appraisal of how an individual performs the assigned task.
5. Indoctrination—communication designed to motivate the employee.[29]

Other reasons for communicating downward—implicit in this list—include opportunities for administrators to spell out objectives, change attitudes and mold opinions, prevent misunderstandings from lack of information, and prepare employees for change.[30]

Upward communication in a criminal justice organization may be likened to a trout trying to swim upstream: It is a much harder task than floating downstream, with many currents of resistance. Several factors deter upward communication. First, the physical distance between superior and subordinate impedes upward communication. Communication is often difficult and infrequent when superiors are isolated and seldom seen or spoken to. In large criminal justice organizations, administrators may be located in headquarters that are removed from the operations personnel. The complexity of the organization may also cause prolonged delays of communication. For example, if a correctional officer or patrol officer observes a problem that needs to be taken to the highest level, normally this information must first be taken to the sergeant, then to the lieutenant, captain, deputy warden or chief, and so on. Individuals at each level will reflect on the problem, put their own interpretation on it (possibly including how the problem might affect them professionally or even personally), and possibly even dilute or distort it. Thus, delays in communication are inherent in a bureaucracy, and problems may not be brought to the attention of the chief executive for a long time. The more levels the communication passes through, the more it is filtered and the more accuracy is lost.

There is also the danger that administrators have a "no news is good news" or "slay the messenger" attitude, thereby discouraging the reception of information. Unless the superior does in fact maintain an open door atmosphere, subordinates are often reluctant to bring, or will temper, bad news, unfavorable opinions, and mistakes or failures to the superior.[31] Administrators may also believe that they know and understand what their subordinates want and think, and that complaints from subordinates are indications of disloyalty.

For all of these reasons, administrators may fail to take action on undesirable conditions brought to their attention, which will cause subordinates to lose faith in their leaders. Many time-consuming problems could be minimized or eliminated if superiors would take the time to listen to their subordinates.

Horizontal communication thrives in an organization when formal communication channels are not open.[32] The disadvantage to horizontal communication is that it is much easier and more natural to achieve than vertical communication and, therefore, it often replaces vertical channels. The horizontal channels are usually of an informal nature—including the grapevine, discussed later. The advantage is that horizontal communication is essential if the subsystems within a criminal justice organization are to function in an effective and coordinated manner. Horizontal communication among peers may also provide emotional and social bonds that build morale and feelings of teamwork among employees.

The Grapevine

In addition to the several barriers discussed earlier, the so-called grapevine—termed as such because it zigzags back and forth like a grapevine across organizations—can also serve to confound effective communication. Communication also includes rumors, and probably *no* type of organization in our society has more grapevine "scuttlebutt" than that which exists in police agencies. Departments even establish "rumor control" centers during major riots. Compounding the usual barriers to communication is the fact that policing is a 24-hour, seven-day occupation, so that rumors are easily carried from one shift to the next.

The grapevine's most effective characteristics are that it is fast; it operates mostly at the workplace, and it supplements regular, formal communication. On the positive side, it can be a tool for management to get a feel for employees' attitudes, to spread useful information, and to help employees vent their frustrations. The grapevine can also carry untruths and be malicious, however. Without a doubt, the grapevine is a force for adminstrators to reckon with on a daily basis.

Oral and Written Communication

Our society places considerable confidence in the written word within complex organizations. Writing establishes a permanent record, but transmitting information in this way does not necessarily ensure that the message will be clear to the receiver. Often, in spite of the writer's best efforts, information is not conveyed clearly. This may be due in large measure to shortcomings with the writer's skills. Nonetheless, criminal justice organizations seem to increasingly rely on written communication, as evidenced by the proliferation of written directives found in most agencies.

This tendency for organizations to promulgate rules, policies, and procedures has been caused by three contemporary developments. First is the *requirement for administrative due process* in employee disciplinary matters, encouraged by federal court rulings, police officer bill of rights legislation, and labor contracts. Another development is *civil liability.* Lawsuits against local governments and their criminal justice agencies and administrators have become commonplace.

Agency-written guidelines prohibiting certain acts provide a hedge against successful civil litigation.[33] In the same vein, written communication is also preferred as a medium for dealing with citizens or groups outside the criminal justice agency. This means of communication provides the greatest protection against the growing number of legal actions taken against agencies by activists, citizens, and interest groups. Finally, a third stimulus is the *accreditation movement*, particularly police agencies pursuing the status and practical effects of becoming accredited. Agencies that are either pursuing accreditation or have become accredited must possess a wealth of policies and procedures.[34]

In recent years, electronic mail (e-mail) has proliferated as a communication medium in criminal justice organizations. E-mail can provide an easy to use and almost instantaneous communication with anyone else possessing a personal computer—in upward, downward, or horizontal directions. For all its advantages, however, e-mail messages can lack security and be ambiguous—not only with respect to content meaning, but also with regard to what they represent. Are such messages, in fact, mail, to be given the full weight of an office letter or memo, or should they be treated more as offhand comments?[35]

Other Barriers to Effective Communication

In addition to the barriers discussed earlier, several other potential barriers exist to effective communication. Some people, for example, are not good listeners. Unfortunately, listening is one of the most neglected and the least understood of the communication arts.[36] We allow other things to obstruct our communication, including time, inadequate or too great a volume of information, the tendency to say what we think others want to hear, failure to select the best word, prejudices, and strained sender-receiver relationships.[37] Also, subordinates do not always have the same "big picture" viewpoint that superiors possess, and also do not always communicate well with people in higher positions who are perhaps more fluent and persuasive than they are.

Cultural Empathy

It is important to note that most communication—at least 90 percent—is *nonverbal* in nature, involving posture, facial expressions, gestures, tone of voice ("it's not what you say, but how you say it"), and so on.[38] These meanings are not taught, but people learn to interpret nonverbal messages by growing up in a particular culture. Not every culture shares the same nonverbal cues, however.

For example, in some cultures the avoidance of eye contact by looking to the ground is meant to convey respect and humility. Making exaggerated hand gestures may be a normal means of communication in some cultures, and social distance for conversation for some societies may be much closer than in the United States. Someone from Nigeria, for example, may stand less than 15 inches from you while conversing, whereas about two feet is a comfortable conversation zone for Americans. These few examples demonstrate why criminal justice practitioners must possess cultural empathy and understand the cultural cues of citizens from other nations.

Historical Approaches to Management

According to Gerald Lynch,[39] the history of management can be divided into three approaches and time periods: (1) scientific management (1900–1940), (2) human relations management (1930–1970), and (3) systems management (1965–present).

Scientific Management

Frederick W. Taylor, who first emphasized time and motion studies, is known today as the "father of scientific management." Spending his early years in the steel mills of Pennsylvania, Taylor became chief engineer and later discovered a new method for making steel, which allowed him to retire at age 45 to write and lecture. He became interested in methods to achieve greater productivity from workers and was hired in 1898 by Bethlehem Steel, where he measured the time it took workers to shovel and carry pig iron. Taylor recommended giving workers hourly breaks and going to a piecework system, among other adjustments. Worker productivity soared; the total number of shovelers needed dropped from about 600 to 140, and worker earnings increased from $1.15 to $1.88 per day. The average cost of handling a long ton (2,240 pounds) dropped from $0.072 to $0.033.[40]

Taylor, who was highly criticized by unions for his management-oriented views, proved that administrators must know their employees. He published a book, *The Principles of Scientific Management,* on the subject in 1911. His views caught on, and soon emphasis was placed entirely on the formal administrative structure: Such terms as *authority, chain of command, span of control,* and *division of labor* were generated.

In 1935, Luther Gulick formulated the theory of POSDCORB, an acronym for planning, organizing, staffing, directing, coordinating, reporting, and budgeting (Figure 2.4). This philosophy was emphasized in police management for many years. Gulick emphasized the technical and engineering side of management, virtually ignoring the human side.

The application of scientific management to criminal justice agencies was heavily criticized. It viewed employees as passive instruments whose feelings were completely disregarded. In addition, employees were considered to be motivated by money alone.

Human Relations Management

Beginning in 1930, people began to realize the negative effects of scientific management on workers. A view arose in policing that management should instill pride and dignity in officers. The movement toward human relations management

PLANNING: working out in broad outline what needs to be done and the methods for doing it to accomplish the purpose set for the enterprise;

ORGANIZING: the establishment of a formal structure of authority through which work subdivisions are arranged, defined, and coordinated for the defined objective;

STAFFING: the whole personnel function of bringing in and training the staff and maintaining favorable conditions of work;

DIRECTING: the continuous task of making decisions, embodying them in specific and general orders and instructions, and serving as the leader of the enterprise;

COORDINATING: the all-important duty of interrelating the various parts of the organization;

REPORTING: informing the executive and his assistants as to what is going on, through records, research, and inspection;

BUDGETING: all that is related to budgeting in the form of fiscal planning, accounting, and control.

Figure 2.4

Gulick's POSDCORB. (*Source:* Luther Gulick and Lyndall Urwick, *Papers on the Science of Administration.* New York: Institute of Public Administration, 1937.)

began with the famous studies conducted during the late 1920s through the mid-1930s by the Harvard Business School at the Hawthorne plant of the Western Electric Company.[41] These studies, which are discussed in more detail later in this chapter, found that worker productivity is more closely related to *social* capacity than to physical capacity, that noneconomic rewards play a prominent part in motivating and satisfying employees, and that employees do not react to management and its rewards as individuals but as members of groups.[42]

In the 1940s and 1950s, police departments began to recognize the strong effect of the informal structure on the organization. Agencies began using such techniques as job enlargement and job enrichment to generate interest in policing as a career. Studies indicated that the supervisor who was "employee centered" was more effective than one who was "production centered." Democratic or participatory management began to appear in police agencies. The human relations approach had its limitations, however. With the emphasis being placed on the employee, the role of the organizational structure became secondary; the primary goal seemed to many to be social rewards, with little attention seemingly given to task accomplishment. Many police managers saw this trend as unrealistic. Employees began to give less and expect more in return.[43]

Systems Management

In the mid-1960s, the features of the human relations and scientific management approaches were combined in the *systems management* approach. Designed to bring the individual and the organization together, this approach attempted to help managers use employees to reach desired production goals. The systems approach recognized that it was still necessary to have some hierarchical arrangement to bring about coordination; that authority and responsibility were essential; and that overall organization was required.

The systems management approach combined the work of Maslow,[44] who developed his hierarchy of needs, in which he classified the needs of people at different levels; McGregor,[45] who stressed the general theory of human motivation; and Blake and Mouton,[46] who developed the "managerial grid," which emphasized two concerns—for task and for people—that managers must have. (These theories are discussed in greater detail later.) In effect, the systems management approach emphasizes that to be effective, managers must be interdependent with other individuals and groups and have the ability to recognize and deal with conflict and change. More than mere technical skills are required; managers require knowledge of several major resources: people, money, time, and equipment.[47] Team cooperation is required to achieve organizational goals.

Several theories of leadership also have evolved over the past several decades, the most common being trait theory, style theory, and situational leadership. The following sections discuss each briefly.

Primary Leadership Theories

Trait Theory

Trait theory was very popular until around the 1950s. This theory was based on the contention that good leaders possessed certain character traits that poor leaders did not. Those who developed this theory, Stogdill and Goode, believed that a leader could be identified through a two-step process. The first step involved studying leaders and comparing them to nonleaders to determine which traits only the leaders possessed. The second step sought people who possessed these traits to be promoted into managerial positions.[48]

A study of 468 administrators in 13 companies found certain traits in successful administrators. They were more intelligent and better educated; had a stronger power need; preferred independent activity, intense thought, and some risk; enjoyed relationships with people; and disliked detail work more than did their subordinates.[49] Figure 2.5 shows traits and skills commonly associated with leader effectiveness, according to Yuki. Following this study, a review of the literature on trait theory revealed the traits most identified as being associated with leadership ability. Those traits were intelligence, initiative, extroversion, sense of humor, enthusiasm, fairness, sympathy, and self-confidence.[50]

Traits	Skills
Adaptable to situations	Clever (intelligent)
Alert to social environment	Conceptually skilled
Ambitious and achievement oriented	Creative
Assertive	Diplomatic and tactful
Cooperative	Fluent in speaking
Decisive	Knowledgeable about group task
Dependable	Organized (administrative ability)
Dominant (desire to influence others)	Persuasive
Energetic (high activity level)	Socially skilled
Persistent	
Self-confident	
Tolerant of stress	
Willing to assume responsibility	

Figure 2.5

Traits and skills commonly associated with leadership effectiveness.
(*Source:* Gary Yuki, *Leadership in Organizations.* Englewood Cliffs, N.J.:
Prentice Hall, 1981, pp. 70, 121–125.)

Trait theory has lost much of its support since the 1950s, largely because of the theory's basic assumption that leadership cannot be taught. A more important reason, however, is simply the growth of new, more sophisticated approaches to the study of leadership. Quantifiable means to test trait theory were limited. What does it mean to say that a leader must be intelligent? By whose standards? As compared with persons within the organization or within society? How can such traits as sense of humor, enthusiasm, fairness, and the others listed earlier be measured or tested? The inability to measure these factors was the real flaw in and reason for the decline of this theory.

When the trait theorists could not empirically document characteristics found in leaders, researchers in the 1940s and 1950s began examining leaders and the situations in which leaders actually functioned.

Style Theory

A study at Michigan State University investigated how leaders motivated individuals or groups to achieve organizational goals. The study determined that leaders must have a sense of the task to be accomplished as well as the environment in which the followers work. Three principles of leadership behavior emerged from the Michigan study:

1. Leaders must assume the leadership role and give task direction to their followers.

2. The closeness of supervision directly affects employee production. High-producing units had less direct supervision; highly supervised units had

lower production. Conclusion: Employees need some degree of freedom to make choices. Given this, they produce at a higher rate.

3. Leaders must be employee oriented. It is the leader's responsibility to facilitate employees' accomplishment of goals.[51]

In the 1950s, Edwin Fleishman began studies of leadership at Ohio State University. After focusing on leader behavior rather than personality traits, he identified two dimensions of basic principles of leadership that could be taught: *initiating structure* and *consideration* (Figure 2.6).[52] Initiating structure referred to supervisory behavior that focused on the achievement of organizational goals, and consideration was directed toward a supervisor's openness toward subordinates' ideas and respect for their feelings as persons. Moderate initiating structure and high consideration were assumed to yield higher job satisfaction and productivity than high initiating structure and low consideration.[53]

The major focus of the style theory is a manager's adoption of a single managerial style based on his or her position in regard to initiating structure and consideration. Three pure leadership styles were thought to be the basis for all managers: autocratic, democratic, and laissez-faire.

Autocratic leaders are leader centered and have a high initiating structure. They are primarily authoritarian in nature and prefer to give orders rather than invite group participation. They have a tendency to be personal in their criticism. This style works best in emergency situations in which strict control and rapid decision making are needed. The problem with autocratic leadership is the organization's inability to function when the leader is absent. It also stifles individual development and initiative, because subordinates are rarely allowed to make an independent decision.[54]

The *democratic,* or participative, leadership style tends to focus on working within the group and striving to attain cooperation from group members by eliciting their ideas and support. Democratic managers tend to be viewed as consideration oriented and strive to attain mutual respect with subordinates. Democratic leaders operate within an atmosphere of trust and delegate much authority.

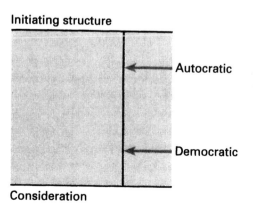

Initiating structure

Consideration

? ← Laissez-faire

Figure 2.6

Style theory. (*Source:* Richard N. Holden, *Modern Police Management.* Englewood Cliffs, N.J.: Prentice Hall, 1986, p. 40.)

This style is useful in organizations where the course of action is uncertain and problems are relatively unstructured. It often taps the decision-making abilities of subordinates. In emergency situations requiring a highly structured response, however, democratic leadership may prove too time consuming and awkward to be effective. Thus, although workers may appreciate the strengths of this style, its weaknesses must be recognized as well.[55]

The third leadership style, *laissez-faire,* is a hands-off approach in that the leader is actually a nonleader. The organization in effect runs itself, with no input or control from the manager. This style has no positive aspects, as the entire organization is soon placed in jeopardy. In truth, this may not be a leadership style at all; instead, it may be an abdication of administrative duties.

Situational Leadership

Style theory assumes that each administrator will adopt one of the styles discussed previously (autocratic, democratic, or laissez-faire) almost exclusively. Further, style theory assumes that all administrators will select a style that they believe works and stay with it, due to managerial rigidity. This assumption has led many researchers to abandon its tenets for a theory that is more flexible: situational leadership.

Early work in situational leadership (see Figure 2.7) was conducted by Fred Fiedler. Fiedler held that personality characteristics relevant to leadership are stable over time and across situations. Some personality attributes are believed to contribute to effective leadership in other situations. Through some studies he conducted, Fiedler also concluded that leadership capacity is not likely to be improved through either training or experience.[56]

Fiedler's work was known as *contingency theory* because he argued that there is no single best approach to leadership and that the influence of the situation determines the appropriate leadership style.

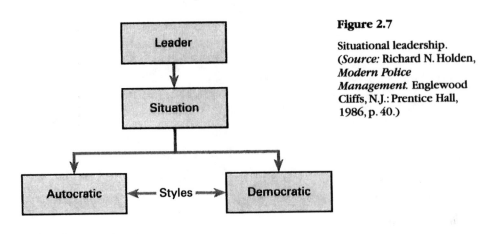

Figure 2.7

Situational leadership.
(*Source:* Richard N. Holden, *Modern Police Management.* Englewood Cliffs, N.J.: Prentice Hall, 1986, p. 40.)

The Managerial Grid

In 1964, Robert R. Blake and Jane S. Mouton developed their managerial grid from the studies done by Fleishman and others at Ohio State University. The Ohio team used two variables, focus on task (initiating structure) and focus on relationships (consideration), to develop a management quadrant describing leadership behavior.

The managerial grid includes five leadership styles based on concern for output (production) and concern for people (Figure 2.8). Using a specially developed testing instrument, people can be assigned a numerical score depicting their concern for each variable. Numerical indications such as 9,1, 9,9, 1,1, and 5,5 are then plotted on the grid using the scales on the horizontal and vertical axes. The grid is read like a map, right and up. Each axis is numbered 1 to 9, with 1 indicating the minimum effort or concern and 9 the maximum. The horizontal axis represents the concern for production and performance goals, and the vertical axis represents the concern for human relations or empathy.

The points of orientation are related to styles of management. The lower-left-hand corner of the grid shows the 1,1 style (representing a minimal concern for task or service and a minimal concern for people). The lower-right-hand corner of the grid identifies the 9,1 style. This type of leader would have a primary concern for the task or output and a minimal concern for people. Here, people are seen as tools of production. The upper-left-hand corner represents the 1,9 style, often referred to as "country club management," with minimum effort given to output or task. The upper right, 9,9, indicates high concern for both people and production—a "we're all in this together," "common stake" approach of mutual respect and trust. In the center—a 5,5, "middle-of-the-road" style—the leader has a "give a little, be fair but firm" philosophy, providing a balance between output and people concerns.[57]

These five leadership styles can be summarized as follows:[58]

- Authority-compliance management (9,1)
- Country club management (1,9)
- Middle-of-the-road management (5,5)
- Impoverished management (1,1)
- Team management (9,9)

Types of Leadership Skills

In 1974, Robert Katz identified three essential skills that leaders should possess: technical, human, and conceptual. Katz defined a skill as the capacity to translate knowledge into action in such a way that a task is accomplished successfully.[59] Each of these skills (when performed effectively) results in the achievement of objectives and goals, which is the primary nature of management.

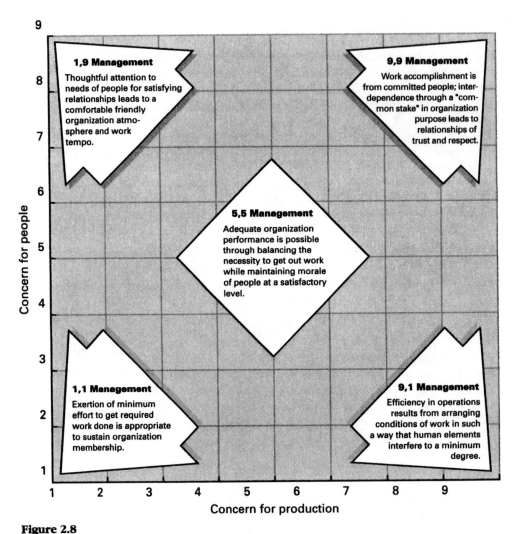

Figure 2.8

Managerial grid. (Reprinted by permission of *Harvard Business Review*
[Nov.–Dec. 1964]. An exhibit from "Breakthrough in Organizational
Development" by Robert R. Blake, Jane S. Mouton, Louis B. Barnes, and Larry
E. Greiner. Copyright 1964 by the President and Fellows of Harvard
College; all rights reserved.)

Technical skills are those a manager needs to ensure that specific tasks are
performed correctly. They are based on proven knowledge, procedures, or techniques. A police detective, a court administrator, and a probation officer have all
developed technical skills directly related to the work they perform. Katz wrote
that a technical skill "involves specialized knowledge, analytical ability within that
specialty, and facility in the use of the tools and techniques of the specific

discipline."[60] This is the skill most easily trained for. A court administrator, for example, has to be knowledgeable in such areas as computer applications, budgeting, caseload management, space utilization, public relations, and personnel administration; a police detective must possess technical skills in interviewing, fingerprinting, and surveillance techniques.[61]

Human skills involve working with people, including being thoroughly familiar with what motivates employees and how to utilize group processes. Katz visualized human skills as including "the executive's ability to work effectively as a group member and to build cooperative effort within the team he leads."[62] Katz added that the human relations skill involves tolerance of ambiguity and empathy. *Tolerance of ambiguity* means that the manager is able to handle problems when insufficient information precludes making a totally informed decision. *Empathy* is the ability to put oneself in another's place. An awareness of human skills allows a manager to provide the necessary leadership and direction, ensuring that tasks are accomplished in a timely fashion and with the least expenditure of resources.[63]

Conceptual skills, Katz said, involve "coordinating and integrating all the activities and interests of the organization toward a common objective."[64] Katz considered such skills to include "an ability to translate knowledge into action." For example, in a criminal justice setting, a court decision concerning the admissibility of evidence would need to be examined in terms of how it affects detectives, court cases, the forensic laboratory, the property room, and the work of the street officer.

Katz emphasized that these skills can be taught to actual and prospective administrators; thus, good administrators are not simply born but can be trained in the classroom. Furthermore, all three of these skills are present in varying degrees for each management level. As one moves up the hierarchy, conceptual skills become more important and technical skills less important. The common denominator for all levels of management is *human* skills. In today's unionized, litigious environment, it is inconceivable that a manager could neglect human skills.

Management Fads

Paul Whisenand and Fred Ferguson[65] placed much of this theorizing into a chronology, resulting in an interesting history of four decades of management fads. These fads began in the 1950s when "seat-of-the-pants" management was becoming outdated and Frederick Taylor insisted that running a company should be more a science than an art. These four decades of fads are described here. It should be emphasized that several of these so-called "fads" (such as computerization, Theory X and Y, management by objectives, the managerial grid, and management by walking around) were not short-lived fads at all but have stood the test of time and are still in use today, in differing degrees.

The 1950s

1. *Computerization:* The first corporate mainframes were displayed as proud symbols of success.
2. *Theory X and Y:* Propounded by MIT professor Douglas McGregor, this theory held that workers are more productive if they have an influence in their work.
3. *Quantitative Management:* Trust the numbers; running a business is more like a science than an art.
4. *Diversification:* The problem of cyclical ups and downs could be countered by buying other businesses.
5. *Management by Objectives:* Peter Drucker popularized the process of setting an executive's goals through negotiation.

The 1960s

6. *T-Groups:* Encounter seminars were used to teach interpersonal sensitivity.
7. *Centralization, Decentralization:* This concerns whether headquarters or line managers should make decisions.
8. *Matrix Management:* Managers report to different superiors according to the task.
9. *Conglomeration:* Disparate businesses are placed under a single corporate umbrella.
10. *The Managerial Grid:* This is a process for determining whether a manager's chief concern is people or production.

The 1970s

11. *Zero-based Budgeting:* This year's budget is based on throwing out last year's numbers and starting from scratch.
12. *The Experience Curve:* This method uses past experience to generate profits by cutting prices, gaining market share, and boosting efficiency.

The 1980s

13. *Theory Z:* Japanese management techniques such as quality circles and job enrichment are adopted.
14. *Demassing:* Trimming the workforce and demoting managers leads to greater efficiency.
15. *Restructuring:* This technique involves sweeping out businesses that don't measure up, often while taking on considerable debt.
16. *Corporate Culture:* Attending to the values, goals, rituals, and heroes that characterize a company's style is thought to improve overall performance.
17. *Management by Walking Around:* By leaving the office to visit the troops instead of relying on written reports, managers obtain more relevant information.

Why did such a proliferation of theories occur? Whisenand and Ferguson speculated the reason to be the intense pressure on managers to perform miracles, resulting in a mad scramble for instant solutions.[66]

Where today's criminal justice administrator is concerned, a return to the basics appears to be "in?" now, with such values as integrity, innovation, quality, service, and a people orientation. These basics have been practiced for centuries and normally resulted in successful managers and organizations.[67]

Motivating Employees

One of the most fascinating subjects throughout the history of humankind is that of motivating people. Some have sought to do so through justice (Plato), others through psychoanalysis (Freud), some through conditioning (Pavlov), some through incentives (Frederick Taylor), and still others through fear (any number of dictators, czars, pharaohs, and despots). Since the Industrial Revolution, managers have been trying to get a full day's work from their subordinates. Today, this issue remains a primary concern in the workplace.

The flap in the early 1990s caused by Japanese businessmen who stated that American workers were lazy certainly raised our collective ire. Many U.S. businesspeople and managers would probably agree that better worker motivation is needed. As Donald Favreau and Joseph Gillespie stated: "Getting people to work, the way you want them to work, when you want them to work, is indeed a challenge."[68]

Many theories have attempted to explain motivation. Some of the best known are those resulting from the Hawthorne studies and those developed by Abraham Maslow, Douglas McGregor, and Frederick Herzberg, all of which are discussed here along with the expectancy and contingency theories.

The Hawthorne Studies

As mentioned earlier, one of the most important studies of worker motivation and behavior, launching intense interest and research in those areas, was Western Electric Company's study in the 1920s. In 1927, engineers at the Hawthorne Plant of Western Electric Company near Chicago conducted an experiment with several groups of workers to determine the effect of illumination on production. The engineers found that when illumination was increased in stages, production increased. To verify their findings, they reduced illumination to its previous level; again, production increased. Confused by their findings, they contacted Elton Mayo and his colleague Fritz Roethlisberger from Harvard to investigate.[69]

First, the researchers selected several experienced women assemblers for an experiment. Management removed the women from their formal group and isolated them in a room. The women were compensated on the basis of the output of their group. Next, researchers began a series of environmental changes, each discussed with the women in advance of its implementation. For example, breaks were introduced and light refreshments were served. The normal six-day week was reduced to five days and the work day was cut by one hour. *Each* of these changes resulted in increased output.[70] To verify these findings, researchers returned the women to their original working conditions: Breaks were eliminated, the six-day work week was reinstituted, and all other work conditions were reinstated. The result was that production again increased!

Mayo and his team then performed a second study at the Hawthorne plant. A new group of 14 workers—all males who worked in simple, repetitive telephone coil winding duties—were given variations in rest periods and work weeks.[71] The men were also put on a reasonable piece rate; that is, the more they produced, the more money they would earn. The assumption was that the workers would strive to produce more since it was in their own economic interest.

The workers soon split into two informal groups on their own, each group setting its own standards of output and conduct. The workers' output did not increase. Neither too little nor too much production was permitted, and peers exerted pressure to keep members in line. The values of the informal group appeared to be more powerful than the allure of bigger incomes:

1. Don't be a "rate buster" and produce too much work.
2. If you turn out too little work, you are a "chiseler."
3. Don't be a "squealer" to supervisors.
4. Don't be officious; if you aren't a supervisor, don't act like one.[72]

Taken together, the Hawthorne studies revealed that people work for a variety of reasons, not just for money and subsistence. They seek satisfaction for more than their physical needs at work and from their co-workers. For the first time, clear evidence was gathered to support workers' social and esteem needs. As a result, this collision between the human relations school, begun in the Hawthorne studies, and traditional organizational theory sent researchers and theorists off in new and different directions. At least three major new thrusts evolved: inquiries into (1) what motivates workers (leading to the work of Maslow and Herzberg), (2) leadership (discussed earlier), and (3) organizations as behavioral systems.

Maslow's Hierarchy of Needs

Abraham H. Maslow (1908–1970), founder of the humanistic school of psychology, conducted research on human behavior at the Air University, Maxwell Air Force Base, Alabama, during the 1940s. His approach to motivation was unique in that the behavior patterns analyzed were those of motivated, happy, and production-oriented people—achievers, not underachievers. He studied biographies of historical and public figures, including Abraham Lincoln, Albert Einstein, and Eleanor Roosevelt. He also observed and interviewed some of his contemporaries—all of whom had no psychological problems and no signs of neurotic behavior.

Maslow hypothesized that if he could understand what made these people function, it would be possible to apply the same techniques to others, thus achieving a high state of motivation. His observations were coalesced into a *hierarchy of needs.*[73]

Maslow concluded that because human beings are part of the animal kingdom, their basic and primary needs or drives are physiological: air, food, water, sex, and shelter. These needs are related to survival. Next in order of prepotency are needs related to safety or security: protection against danger, murder, criminal assault, threat, deprivation, and tyranny. At the middle of the hierarchy is belonging, or social needs: being accepted by one's peers, and association with members of groups. The next level on the hierarchy consists of the needs or drives related to ego: self-esteem, self-respect, power, prestige, recognition, and status. Located at the top of the hierarchy is self-realization or actualization: self-fulfillment, creativity, becoming all that one is capable of becoming.[74] Figure 2.9 depicts this hierarchy.

Unlike the lower needs, the higher needs are rarely satisfied. Maslow suggested that to prevent frustration, needs should be filled in sequential order. A satisfied need is no longer a motivator. Maslow's research also indicated that once a person reaches a high state of motivation (i.e., esteem or self-realization levels), he or she will remain highly motivated, will have a positive attitude toward the organization, and will follow a "pitch in and help" philosophy.

McGregor's Theory X/Theory Y

Douglas McGregor (1906–1967), who served as president of Antioch College and then on the faculty of the Massachusetts Institute of Technology, was one of the great advocates of humane and democratic management. At Antioch, McGregor tested his theories of democratic management. He noted that behind every managerial decision or action are assumptions about human behavior. He chose the simplest terms possible with which to express them, designating one set of assumptions as Theory X and the other as Theory Y.[75]

Theory X managers hold the traditional views of direction and control, such as the following:

- The average human being has an inherent dislike of work and will avoid it if possible. This assumption has deep roots, beginning with the punishment of Adam and Eve, their banishment into a world where they had to work for a living. Management's use of negative reinforcement and the emphasis on "a fair day's work" reflect an underlying belief that management must counter an inherent dislike for work.[76]

- Because of this human characteristic of dislike of work, most people must be coerced, controlled, directed, or threatened with punishment to get them to put forth adequate effort toward the achievement of organizational objectives. The dislike of work is so strong that even the promise of rewards is not generally enough to overcome it. People will accept the rewards and demand greater ones. Only the threat of punishment will work.[77]

Self-Realization Needs	Job-Related Satisfiers
Reaching Your Potential Independence Creativity Self-Expression	Involvement in Planning Your Work Freedom to Make Decisions Affecting Work Creative Work to Perform Opportunities for Growth and Development

Esteem Needs	Job-Related Satisfiers
Responsibility Self-Respect Recognition Sense of Accomplishment Sense of Competence	Status Symbols Merit Awards Challenging Work Sharing in Decisions Opportunity for Advancement

Social Needs	Job-Related Satisfiers
Companionship Acceptance Love and Affection Group Membership	Opportunities for Interaction with Others Team Spirit Friendly Co-workers

Safety Needs	Job-Related Satisfiers
Security for Self and Possessions Avoidance of Risks Avoidance of Harm Avoidance of Pain	Safe Working Conditions Seniority Fringe Benefits Proper Supervision Sound Company Policies, Programs, and Practices

Physical Needs	Job-Related Satisfiers
Food Clothing Shelter Comfort Self-Preservation	Pleasant Working Conditions Adequate Wage or Salary Rest Periods Labor-Saving Devices Efficient Work Methods

Figure 2.9

Maslow's hierarchy of human needs. (*Source:* A. H. Maslow, *Motivation and Personality*, 2d ed. New York: Harper & Collins, 1970.)

• The average human being prefers to be directed, wishes to avoid responsibility, has relatively little ambition, and wants security above all. This assumption of the "mediocrity of the masses" is rarely expressed so bluntly. Although much lip service is paid to the "sanctity" of the worker and human beings in general, many managers reflect this assumption in practice and policy.

(*Note:* Theory X managers would be autocratic and classified as a 9,1 on the managerial grid.)

Theory Y managers naturally take the opposite view of the worker:

• The expenditure of physical and mental effort in work is as natural as play or rest. The average human being does not inherently dislike work; it may even be a source of satisfaction, to be performed voluntarily.
• External control and the threat of punishment are not the only means for bringing about effort toward organizational objectives.
• Commitment to objectives is a function of the rewards associated with their achievement. The most significant of such rewards—satisfaction of ego and self-actualization needs—can be direct products of effort directed toward organizational objectives.
• Under proper conditions, the average human being learns not only to accept but to seek responsibility. Under this view, the avoidance of responsibility, lack of ambition, and the emphasis on security are general consequences of experience, not inherent human characteristics.
• The capacity to exercise a high degree of imagination, ingenuity, and creativity in the solution of organizational problems is widely, not narrowly, distributed in the population.
• Under the conditions of modern industrial life, the intellectual potentialities of the average human being are only partially utilized.

Herzberg's Motivation-Hygiene Theory

During the 1950s, Frederick Herzberg conducted a series of studies in which he asked workers, primarily engineers, to describe the times when they felt particularly good and particularly bad about their jobs. The respondents identified several things that were sources of satisfaction and dissatisfaction in their work. Then, from these findings, Herzberg isolated two vital factors found in all jobs: maintenance or hygiene factors and motivational factors.

Maintenance factors are those things in the work environment that meet an employee's hedonistic need to avoid pain. Hygiene factors include the necessities of any job (e.g., adequate pay, benefits, job security, decent working conditions, supervision, interpersonal relations). Hygiene factors do not satisfy or motivate; they set the stage for motivation. They are, however, the major source of dissatisfaction when they are inadequate.[78]

Motivational factors are those psychosocial factors in work that provide intrinsic satisfaction and serve as an incentive for people to invest more of their time, talent, energy, and expertise in productive behavior. Examples include achievement, recognition, responsibility, the work itself, advancement, and potential for growth. The absence of motivators does not necessarily produce job dissatisfaction.[79]

Although these needs are obviously related, they represent totally different dimensions of satisfaction.

Expectancy and Contingency Theories

In the 1960s, the *expectancy theory* was developed, holding that employees will do what their managers or organizations want them to do if the following are true:

1. The task appears to be possible (employees believe they possess the necessary competence).
2. The reward (outcome) offered is seen as desirable by the employees (intrinsic rewards come from the job itself; extrinsic rewards are supplied from others).
3. There is a perception in the minds of employees that performing the required behavior or task will bring the desired outcome.
4. There is a good chance that better performance will bring greater rewards.[80]

The expectancy theory will work for an organization that specifies what behaviors it expects from people and what the rewards or outcomes will be for those who exhibit those behaviors. Rewards may be pay increases, time off, chances for advancement, a sense of achievement, or other benefits. Managers and organizations can find out what their employees want and see to it that they are provided with the rewards they seek.

Walter Newsom[81] said that the reality of the expectancy theory can be summarized by the "nine C's": (1) capability (does a person have the capability to perform well?); (2) confidence (does a person believe that he or she can perform the job well?); (3) challenge (does a person have to work hard to perform the job well?); (4) criteria (does a person know the difference between good and poor performance?); (5) credibility (does a person believe the manager will deliver on promises?); (6) consistency (do subordinates believe that all employees receive similar preferred outcomes for good performance, and vice versa?); (7) compensation (do the outcomes associated with good performance reward the employee with money or other types of rewards?); (8) cost (what does it cost a person, in effort and outcomes foregone, to perform well?); and (9) communication (does the manager communicate with the subordinate?).

Later, in the 1970s, Morse and Lorsch built on McGregor's and Herzberg's theories with their theory of motivation called *contingency theory*. This theory sought to determine the fit between the organization's characteristics and its tasks, and the motivations of individuals. The basic components of the contingency theory are that (1) among people's needs is a central need to achieve a sense of competence; (2) the ways in which people fulfill this need will vary from person to person; (3) competence motivation is most likely to be fulfilled when there is a fit between task and organization; and (4) a sense of competence continues to motivate people even after competence is achieved. In essence, we all want to be competent in our work. Contingency theory contends that people performing highly structured and organized tasks perform better in Theory X organizations, and that those who perform unstructured and uncertain tasks perform better under a Theory Y approach. This theory tells managers to tailor jobs to fit people or to give people the skills, knowledge, and attitudes they will need to become competent.[82]

Summary

Most young people entering the labor force would probably like to retain their individuality, feel free to express themselves, have a sense of being an important part of the team, and realize both extrinsic and intrinsic rewards from their work. The reality is, however, that a majority of people entering the job market will work within the structure of an organization that will not meet all of their personal needs.

We have seen that many organizations have a highly refined bureaucracy. Whether an organization will meet one's individual needs depends largely on its administrative philosophy. Therefore, our discussions in this chapter covered the structure and function of organizations and, just as important, how administrators and subordinates function within them. Also shown to be of major importance is the need for effective communication within organizations.

The main point to be made is that administrators must know their people. In addition to covering several prominent theories that have withstood the test of time, we pointed out some approaches that have not succeeded. One can learn much from a failed approach or even from a poor boss who failed to appreciate and understand subordinates and practiced improper or no motivational techniques.

Questions for Review

1. Define *organization*. What is its function and structure?
2. What are the three historical approaches to management? Distinguish between the historical approach to management and the more "enlightened" contemporary view.
3. What are some of the skills that strong leaders commonly possess (using the Katz model) and some of the common weaknesses in leadership?
4. What are the major leadership fads from past decades, beginning with the 1950s?
5. What are three major theories concerning the motivation of employees?

6. What does *communication* mean? What is its importance in organizations? Explain some of the major barriers to effective communication and why it can be particularly problematic in criminal justice agencies.

7. Objectively assess what kind of leader you would be likely to be (if helpful, use the management grid). Is it an effective style? What are some of the possible advantages and disadvantages of that style (if any)?

Notes

1. Steven Levy, "Working in Dilbert's World," *Newsweek* (August 12, 1996): 52–57.

2. David A. Tansik and James F. Elliott, *Managing Police Organizations* (Monterey, Calif.: Duxbury Press, 1981), p. 1.

3. Stephen P. Robbins, *Organizational Theory: Structure, Design, and Applications* (Englewood Cliffs, N.J.: Prentice-Hall, 1987).

4. Larry K. Gaines, Mittie D. Southerland, and John E. Angell, *Police Administration* (New York: McGraw-Hill, 1991), p. 5.

5. Peter W. Blau and W. Richard Scott, *Formal Organizations* (Scranton, Pa.: Chandler, 1962), p. 43.

6. Gaines, Southerland, and Angell, *Police Administration*, p. 9.

7. Max Weber, *The Theory of Social and Economic Organization*, trans. A. M. Henderson and Talcott Parsons (New York: Oxford University Press, 1947), pp. 329–330.

8. James Q. Wilson, *Varieties of Police Behavior* (Cambridge, Mass.: Harvard University Press), pp. 2–3.

9. Ibid., p. 3.

10. Adapted from Lyndall F. Urwick, *Notes on the Theory of Organization* (New York: American Management Association, 1952).

11. Gaines, Southerland, and Angell, *Police Administration*, p. 9.

12. Leonard R. Sayles and George Strauss, *Human Behavior in Organizations* (Englewood Cliffs, N.J.: Prentice Hall, 1966), p. 349.

13. See, for example, Samuel C. Certo, *Principles of Modern Management: Functions and Systems* (4th ed.) (Boston: Allyn and Bacon, 1989), p. 103.

14. Quoted in Charles R. Swanson, Leonard Territo, and Robert W. Taylor, *Police Administration* (2d ed.) (New York: Macmillan, 1988), p. 127.

15. Quoted in Wayne W. Bennett and Karen Hess, *Management and Supervision in Law Enforcement* (St. Paul, Minn.: West, 1992), p. 61.

16. Paul Hersey and Kenneth H. Blanchard, *Management of Organizational Behavior* (3d ed.) (Englewood Cliffs, N.J.: Prentice Hall, 1977).

17. Ibid.

18. Quoted in Bennett and Hess, *Management and Supervision in Law Enforcement*, p. 61.

19. Ibid.

20. Roger D. Evered and James C. Selman, "Coaching and the Art of Management," *Organizational Dynamics* (Autumn 1989): 16.

21. Swanson, Territo, and Taylor, *Police Administration* (2d ed.), p. 61.

22. Ibid., p. 86.

23. Louis A. Radelet, *The Police and the Community: Studies* (Beverly Hills, Calif.: Glencoe), p. 92.

24. *Interpersonal Communication: A Guide for Staff Development* (Athens, Ga.: Institute of Government, University of Georgia, August 1974), p. 15.

25. Quoted in Swanson, Territo, and Taylor, *Police Administration* (2d ed.), p. 161.

26. Bennett and Hess, *Management and Supervision in Law Enforcement*, p. 85.

27. See R. C. Huseman, Ibid., pp. 21–27. Material for this section was also drawn from Charles R. Swanson, Leonard Territo, and Robert W. Taylor, *Police Administration: Structures, Processes, and Behavior* (4th ed.) (Upper Saddle River, N.J.: Prentice Hall, 1998).

28. Charles R. Swanson, Leonard Territo, and Robert W. Taylor, *Police Administration: Structures, Processes, and Behavior* (3d ed.). New York: Macmillan, 1993, p. 203.

29. D. Katz and R. L. Kahn, *The Social Psychology of Organizations* (New York: John Wiley & Sons, 1966), p. 239. As cited in P. V. Lewis, *Organizational Communication: The Essence of Effective Management* (Columbus, Ohio: Grid, 1975), p. 36.

30. Lewis, *Organizational Communication*, p. 38.

31. Swanson, Territo, and Taylor, *Police Administration* (3d ed.), p. 206.

32. See R. K. Allen, *Organizational Management Through Communication* (New York: Harper & Row, 1977), pp. 77–79.

33. Swanson, Territo, and Taylor, *Police Administration*, p. 248.

34. Stephen W. Mastrofski, "Police Agency Accreditation: The Prospects of Reform," *American Journal of Police*, 5:3 (1986):45–81.

35. Alex Markels, "Managers Aren't Always Able to Get the Right Message Across With E-Mail," *The Wall Street Journal*, August 6, 1996, p. 2.

36. Robert L. Montgomery, "Are You a Good Listener?" *Nation's Business* (October 1981): 65–68.

37. Bennett and Hess, *Management and Supervision in Law Enforcement*, p. 101.

38. G. Weaver, "Law Enforcement in a Culturally Diverse Society", *FBI Law Enforcement Bulletin*, September 1992.

39. Ronald G. Lynch, *The Police Manager: Professional Leadership Skills*, (3d ed.) (New York: Random House, 1986), p. 4.

40. Certo, *Principles of Modern Management: Functions and Systems*, p. 35.

41. See Elton Mayo, *The Human Problems of an Industrial Civilization* (New York: Macmillan, 1933).

42. Paul M. Whisenand and Fred Ferguson, *The Managing of Police Organizations* (3d ed.) (Englewood Cliffs, N.J.: Prentice Hall, 1989), pp. 218–219.

43. Lynch, *The Police Manager: Professional Leadership Skills*, pp. 5–6.

44. Abraham H. Maslow, *Motivation and Personality* (New York: Harper & Row, 1954).

45. Douglas McGregor, *The Human Side of Enterprise* (New York: McGraw-Hill, 1960).

46. Robert R. Blake and Jane S. Mouton, *The Managerial Grid* (Houston: Gulf Publishing Company, 1964).

47. Lynch, *The Police Manager: Professional Leadership Skills*, pp. 7–8.

48. Richard Holden, *Modern Police Management* (Englewood Cliffs, N.J.: Prentice Hall, 1986), p. 38.

49. Thomas A. Mahoney, Thomas H. Jerdee, and Alan N. Nash, "Predicting Managerial Effectiveness," *Personnel Psychology* (Summer 1960):147–163.

50. Joe Kelly, *Organizational Behavior: An Existential Systems Approach* (rev. ed.) (Homewood, Ill.: Richard D. Irwin, 1974), p. 363.

51. Bennett and Hess, *Management and Supervision in Law Enforcement*, pp. 65–66.

52. Edwin Fleishman, "Leadership Climate, Human Relations Training and Supervisory Behavior," *Personnel Psychology* 6 (1953):208–222.

53. Stephen M. Sales, "Supervisory Style and Productivity: Review and Theory," in Larry Cummings and William E. Scott, (eds.), *Readings in Organizational Behavior and Human Performance* (Homewood, Ill.: Richard D. Irwin, 1969), p. 122.

54. Holden, *Modern Police Management*, pp. 39–40.

55. Ibid., pp. 41–42.

56. Fred Fiedler, *A Theory of Leadership Effectiveness* (New York: McGraw-Hill, 1967).

57. Donald F. Favreau and Joseph E. Gillespie, *Modern Police Administration* (Englewood Cliffs, N.J.: Prentice Hall, 1978), p. 80.

58. Bennett and Hess, *Management and Supervision in Law Enforcement*, p. 66.

59. Robert L. Katz, "Skills of an Effective Administrator," *Harvard Business Review* 52 (1975): 23.

60. Ibid., p. 23.

61. Dan L. Costley and Ralph Todd, *Human Relations in Organizations* (St. Paul, Minn.: West, 1978).

62. Ibid., p. 24.

63. James M. Higgins, *Human Relations: Concepts and Skills* (New York: Random House, 1982).

64. Ibid., p. 27.

65. Adapted from Whisenand and Ferguson, *The Managing of Police Organizations* (3d ed.), pp. 4–5.

66. Ibid., p. 6.

67. Ibid., pp. 7–8.

68. Favreau and Gillespie, *Modern Police Administration*, p. 85.

69. W. Richard Plunkett, *Supervision: The Direction of People at Work* (Dubuque, Iowa: Wm. C. Brown, 1983), p. 121.

70. Elton Mayo, *The Social Problems of an Industrial Civilization* (Boston: Division of Research, Graduate School of Business Administration, Harvard University, 1945), pp. 68–86.

71. Favreau and Gillespie, *Modern Police Administration*, pp. 100–101.

72. Frederick J. Roethlisberger and William J. Dickson, *Management and the Worker* (Cambridge, Mass.: Harvard University Press, 1939), p. 522.

73. Favreau and Gillespie, *Modern Police Administration*, p. 87.

74. Ibid.

75. Ibid., p. 88.

76. Ibid., p. 89.

77. Ibid.

78. Harry W. More and W. Fred Wegener, *Behavioral Police Management* (New York: Macmillan, 1992), pp. 163–164.

79. Frederick Herzberg, "One More Time: How Do You Motivate Employees," in Walter E. Netemeyer (ed.), *Classics of Organizational Behavior* (Oak Park, Ill.: Moore, 1978).

80. Randall S. Schuler, *Personnel and Human Resources Management* (St. Paul, Minn.: West, 1981), pp. 41–43.

81. Walter B. Newsom, "Motivate, Now!" *Personnel Journal* (February 1990):51–55.

82. Warren Richard Plunkett, *Supervision: The Direction of People at Work*, pp. 131–132.

THE POLICE

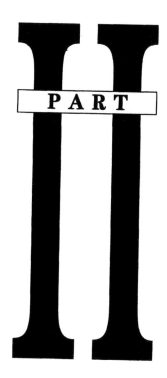

PART II

This part consists of three chapters. Chapter 3 examines police organization and operation. Chapter 4 covers police personnel roles and functions, and Chapter 5 discusses police issues and practices. The introductory section of each chapter provides specific chapter content. Case studies in police administration appear at the end of Chapter 5.

POLICE
ORGANIZATION
AND OPERATION

Blessed are the peacemakers.

—Matthew 5:8

Introduction

To perform smoothly (as smoothly as society, resources, politics, and other influences will permit), police agencies are organized to enhance the accomplishment of their basic mission and goals. In this chapter, we consider first how police agencies are defined and operate as bona fide organizations. We then present the contemporary organization of police departments, including an overview of the bureaucratic model that has evolved and recent challenges to it.

We then discuss the need to develop appropriate policies, procedures, rules, and regulations. Next we examine the influence of recent research on contemporary policing functions to learn what works. Then, after briefly discussing police innovation, we also identify and then debunk myths of police practices. Finally, we explore the "back-to-the-basics" community oriented policing and problem-solving concept that is being instituted across the country. We define these terms, show how the concept breaks from the traditional mode of policing, and examine the roles of chief executives, mid-level managers, and first-line supervisors under this strategy. Essentially, the goal of this chapter is to set the stage for later analyses of personnel and problems in the field.

Police Agencies as Organizations

Missions and Goals

An *organization* is a group of people working together to accomplish a desired goal.[1] Certainly police agencies fit this definition. First, the organization of these agencies includes a number of specialized units (e.g., patrol, traffic, investigation, records). The role of chief executives, mid-managers, and first-line supervisors is to ensure that these units work together to reach a common goal. Allowing each unit to work independently would lead to fragmentation, conflict, and competition and would subvert the entire organization's goals and purposes. Second, police agencies consist of people who interact within the organization and with external organizations.

Through mission statements, policies and procedures, and management style, among other factors, police administrators attempt to ensure that the organization meets its overall goals of investigating and suppressing crime and that the organization works amiably with similar organizations. As the organization becomes larger, the need for people to cooperate to achieve the organizational goals increases. The formal organizational charts discussed later in this chapter assist in this endeavor by spelling out areas of responsibility and lines of communication and defining the chain of command.

Police administrators modify or design the structure of their organizations to fulfill their mission. An organizational chart reflects the formal structure of task and authority relationships determined to be most suited to accomplish the police mission. The major concerns in organizing are (1) identifying what jobs need to be done, such as conducting the initial investigation, performing the latent or followup investigation, and providing for the custody of evidence seized at crime scenes; (2) determining how to group the jobs, such as those responsible for patrol, investigation, and the operation of the property room; (3) forming levels of authority, such as officer, detective, corporal, sergeant, lieutenant, and captain; and (4) equalizing responsibility and authority. For example, a sergeant who supervises seven detectives must have sufficient authority to discharge that responsibility properly, or he or she cannot be held accountable for any results.[2]

Specialization in Police Agencies

The larger an agency, the greater the need for specialization and the more vertical (taller) its organizational chart becomes. Some 2,300 years ago, Plato observed that "each thing becomes ... easier when one man, exempt from other tasks, does one thing."[3] *Specialization,* or the division of labor, is one of the basic features of traditional organizational theory.[4] Specialization produces different groups of functional responsibilities, and the jobs allocated to meet these different responsibilities are held by people who are considered to be especially well qualified to perform those jobs. Thus, specialization is crucial to effectiveness and efficiency in large organizations.[5]

Specialization makes the organization more complex, however, by complicating communication, increasing the units from which cooperation must be obtained, and creating conflict among different units. Specialization creates an increased need for coordination because it adds to the hierarchy, which can lead to narrowly defined jobs that stifle the creativity and energy of their incumbents. Police departments are aware of these potential shortcomings of specialization, however, and attempt through various means to inspire their employees to the extent possible. For example, personnel can be rotated to various jobs and given additional responsibilities that challenge them. In addition, in a medium-sized department serving a community of 100,000 or more, a police officer with 10 years of police experience could have had the responsibilities of dog handler, motorcycle officer, detective, and/or traffic officer while being a member of special weapons or hostage negotiation teams. Officers can be empowered through a community oriented policing and problem-solving strategy (discussed later) or involved in organizational decision making as part of total quality management.

In sum, the advantages to specialization in large police departments include the following:

- *Placement of responsibility:* The responsibility for the performance of given tasks can be placed on specific units or individuals. For example, the traffic division investigates all accidents and the patrol division handles all calls for service.
- *Development of expertise:* Those who have specialized responsibilities receive specialized training. Homicide investigators can be sent to forensic pathology classes; special weapons and tactics teams train regularly to deal with terrorists or hostage situations.
- *Group esprit de corps:* Groups of specially trained persons share a camaraderie and depend on one another for success, which leads to cohesion and high morale.
- *Increased efficiency and effectiveness:* Specialized units have a high degree of proficiency in job task responsibility. For example, a specially trained financial crimes unit normally is more successful with complex fraud cases than is a general detective division.[6]

Contemporary Police Organization

The Traditional Bureaucratic Model

By the 1950s, some police chiefs began to demonstrate that good administration could make a difference in a police organization's efficiency.[7] These administrators stressed military organization; for them, efficiency meant close supervision and strong internal discipline. This movement improved police service and probably appealed to most police officers, most of whom were military veterans. Given the backgrounds of police recruits and the demands being made by communities at the time, the move from political patronage to the military model was probably the wisest change possible.[8]

Frederick Taylor's scientific management theory was in vogue in the 1950s, but its task-oriented approach to worker productivity was not universally popular. Ronald Lynch[9] stated the major criticisms of the scientific management theory as it relates to policing:

1. Officers were considered passive instruments; their personal feelings were completely disregarded. Any differences, especially regarding motivation, were ignored; all officers were treated basically alike.
2. The employee was considered to be an "economic man" who could be motivated through wage incentives or fear of job loss.
3. The focus was on technical efficiency, not the effectiveness of the organization.
4. The efficiency of operation was to be obtained only through division of labor (breaking the job down into small parts), specialization of police activities, rigid structure of line and staff departments, and the use of a span of control whereby supervisors had only a few subordinates.

The scientific management theory, as many police officers know, is alive and well today in some police agencies where employees are still motivated by fear and administrators practice a "do as I say and not as I do" philosophy.

A *bureaucracy* is an organization with specialized functions, adherence to fixed rules, and a hierarchy of authority. Police organizations in the United States are *bureaucracies,* as are virtually all large organizations in modern society, such as the military, universities, and private corporations. To a large extent, the structure and management process of most police agencies are similar. The major agency differences result from size, between large and small departments: The former are more complex, reflect more specialization, have a taller hierarchical structure, and use authoritarian style of command to a greater degree.

The administration of most police organizations is based on the traditional, pyramidal, quasimilitary organizational structure containing to one extent or another the elements of a bureaucracy noted previously. According to Thomas Johnson, Gordon Misner, and Lee Brown (former chief of police in New York City), the appropriateness of the tall, hierarchical, quasimilitary organizational structure of bureaucracies is often being challenged, especially by large numbers of college-educated police personnel. Indeed, Johnson, Misner, and Brown express surprise at the large numbers of people who are disillusioned with it.[10] The reasons for this disillusionment are several and include the quasimilitary discipline of police organizations; the inability of management to match talent and positions; the organizational restrictions on personal freedom of expression, association, and dress; communication blockage in the tall structure; the outmoded methods of operation that organizations cling to; the lack of management flexibility and real challenge of the job; and the narrow job descriptions in the lower ranks of police organizations.

Attempts to Reform the Traditional Model

Attempts to reform the traditional tall hierarchical structure of police organizations and their inherent rank structure have been described as "attempts to bend granite."[11] Because the rank structure controls the incentives of pay, status, and power, it seriously hinders attempts to provide counterincentives for the officer on the street. Some attempts have been made, however, to replace the traditional structure, including the following:

1. Using expanded pay scales or salary incentives for the patrol officer (with step or ladder increases).
2. Creating the Master Police Officer designation. Recommended in 1967 by the President's Crime Commission, it would afford patrol officers pay and status while working on the street.
3. Adopting skill attainment plans, which provide incentive pay for the patrol officer rank on the basis of longevity, certification in a skill, an academic degree, or a job assignment requiring a particular skill.
4. Separating autonomy from rank to address the current situation in which patrol officers with college backgrounds can be overruled by superiors with less education. The patrol officer with the most knowledge would be in charge of a situation. For example, an evidence technician with the rank of patrol officer should have authority over ranking officers at a crime scene.
5. Implementing a career development plan, a rare system that includes formal job rotation, special assignment to positions that have career value, leaves of absence to pursue education or experience in other agencies, and exchange programs with other departments.[12]

In the 1940s and 1950s, some police departments began to recognize the needs of the employees within the organization. Agencies began using such techniques as job enlargement and job enrichment to generate interest in policing as a career. Studies indicated that the supervisor who was *employee centered* was more effective than one who was *production centered.* Democratic or participatory management began to be used in police agencies as private industry began to move away from the pyramid-shaped, tall organizational structure to a flatter structure.

This human relations approach had its limitations, however. By emphasizing the employee, the organizational structure became secondary. The primary goal of this approach seemed to many to be social rewards rather than task accomplishment. Employees began to give less and expect more in return.[13]

A number of agencies have experimented with other approaches with mixed results.[14] Indeed, when some police agencies have attempted to flatten the organizational structure and replace paramilitary police uniforms with blazers, they have most often returned to the traditional style. In the late 1960s, the military model was replaced by one that stressed bureaucratic accountability. In the

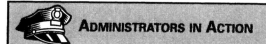

ADMINISTRATORS IN ACTION

Capital Ideas: DC Chief Unveils Blueprint for Top-to-Bottom Overhaul

For the fourth time in as many years, the Washington, D.C., Metropolitan Police Department is about to undergo a departmental reorganization, and hopes are high that the latest overhaul will produce far greater success than any of the earlier efforts. . . .

Chief Charles H. Ramsey unveiled a plan that he said would dramatically change the structure of the department, with an emphasis on decentralization and geographic accountability.

"I'm going to expose you to a concept, to an idea, that is fundamentally going to change the way we do business," said Ramsey, who came to Washington six months ago from the Chicago Police Department, where he was hailed as the architect of the city's community policing effort. "What we're going to do is rebuild the Metropolitan Police Department. . . . [and] unlike before, we're not going to hire consultants."

[The plan that] accompanied the announcement, is described as "a significant departure from the way police departments . . . have been organized. The new structure represents nothing short of the wholesale transformation of the MPDC from a bureaucratic, incident-driven agency to a streamlined, customer-driven service organization—one that is focused on forging alliances to more effectively fight crime and solve problems."

"In recent years," the document continues, "police departments across the country have struggled with trying to implement the philosophy of community policing with the same organizational structures we have used for years. The result: our structure has become fundamentally out of sync with the way work gets done in the organization." The new plan purports to do away with the "traditional, vertical structure" that is common in policing and rely instead on a more "lateral" structure that is based less on function than on geography.

Ramsey told *The Washington Post,* "It struck me one day that I can't fix this place. I really underestimated the problems. They really are systemic. We're not structured in a way to get work done."

Ramsey's plan calls for moving 400 detectives and officers in specialized, headquarters-based investigative units to seven police districts. The specialized units, which include homicide, traffic and sex crimes, will then be disbanded. Detectives in the seven districts will work in one of two squads: property crimes and violent crimes. . . .

Ramsey's plan also includes sending teams of officers and residents into the community to provide training in problem-solving.

Among other components of the latest reorganization of D.C.'s 3,555-member police force are:

¶ Four bureaus will be eliminated: patrol services, support services, technical services and human resources. In their place will be "a more logical and streamlined command system which promotes team work, communication and geographic accountability for fighting crime."

The seven full-service districts will be organized into three Regional Operations Command centers, ROCS, each headed by an assistant chief who will oversee the center from a field office rather than from headquarters. Each ROC will have a youth investigations unit, a canine unit, crime analysis capability and an executive officer.

¶ Additional officers and supervisors will be added to the city's 83 police service areas (PSAs), which were created in July 1997 as a first step toward refocusing the department in a community-policing mode. Each PSA will have a manager of captain's rank who will have 24-hour-a-day accountability and will report to the district commander. Crime scene technicians will also be reassigned to the PSAs.

¶ The city's seven police districts will be expanded to provide a full range of police services including violent-crime investigators, property-crime investigators, focused mission teams, operational support and customer services. To accomplish this, personnel will be shifted from centralized units.

¶ A Special Services Group will be created that will include emergency response, special events and major narcotics—functions described as having unique training, resource and operational needs. The group will report to the Assistant Chief in charge of Operations.

¶ A new citywide operations command will be established within the Office of the Executive Assistant Chief to provide a 24-hour command presence to respond to and oversee major incidents.

¶ Administrative and technical functions, including human services, business services, training and operational support services, will be unified under a new corporate support structure led by an assistant chief in order to streamline the delivery of those services in those areas.

¶ The Mayor's security detail will be slashed from 15 officers to eight.

Source: "Capital Ideas: DC Chief Unveils Blueprint for Top-to-Bottom Overhaul," *LEN,* October 15, 1998. Reprinted with permission from *Law Enforcement News,* John Jay College of Criminal Justice (CUNY), 555 W. 57th St., New York, NY 10019.

1970s, experts on police organization, such as Egon Bittner, contended that the military-bureaucratic organization of the police, emphasizing chain of command, adherence to rules, and unquestioned authority, created obstacles to communication and the development of a truly professional police system.[15] Paul Whisenand listed four reasons why bureaucratic organization is beginning to disappear: (1) It is too rigid to adapt to change; (2) it is incapable of meeting the demands of sustained growth; (3) it cannot integrate the greater diversity of contemporary society; and (4) bureaucracy is not designed to accommodate "new concepts of man, power, and human values."[16]

Michel Crozier[17] described a four-part "vicious circle" that develops in bureaucracies: (1) Bureaucracies require impersonal rules; (2) centralization of decision making limits supervisors in the field (they cannot adjust to problems, as they must "go by the book"); (3) often one level of the organization is not aware of what is happening at another level; and (4) unofficial power relationships control areas not covered by rules.

The alternative is to combine a few features of the military model (police officers taking orders from superiors during critical incidents) and a few features of the bureaucratic model with other characteristics to create a reasonably professional organization.[18] Until that occurs, large police agencies will probably continue to experience the lethargy described by a Pennsylvania state trooper as "being herd-bound."[19]

Disenchantment with the traditional bureaucratic structure of police organizations may exist, but that structure continues to prevail. Many administrators still consider it the best structure when rapid leadership and division of labor are required in times of crises. The traditional structure—assuming each police supervisor can effectively supervise only seven employees—requires this tall organizational structure. The traditional structure actually causes a chain reaction in policing: Narrow spans of control make police departments taller, and taller organizations are complex and may react slowly during crisis situations because the number of different levels present within the chain of command hampers effective communication. Police agencies with tall hierarchical organization must therefore develop policies and procedures to overcome these problems. Many police departments have redesigned their organizations to reflect larger spans of control or management, resulting in flatter organizational structures.[20]

A Basic Police Organizational Structure

An organizational structure has been developed to help departments carry out the many complex responsibilities of policing. The highly decentralized nature and the different sizes of police departments in the United States, however, cause the structure of police agencies to vary. It is possible, however, to combine the traits of most departments and to make certain general statements about all agencies to characterize a "typical" police organization.

As mentioned earlier, the police have traditionally been organized along military lines with a rank structure that normally includes the patrol officer, sergeant, lieutenant, captain, and chief. Many departments, particularly larger ones, employ additional ranks, such as corporal, major, and deputy chief, but there is a legitimate concern that these departments will become top heavy. The military rank hierarchy allows the organization to designate authority and responsibility at each level and to maintain a chain of command. The military model also allows the organization to emphasize supervisor-subordinate relationships and to maintain discipline and control. We discuss the military model again later.

Every police agency, regardless of size, has a basic plan of organization. In addition, every such agency, no matter how large or small, has an organizational chart. A visitor to the police station or sheriff's office may even see this organizational chart displayed prominently on a wall. Even if it is not on paper, such a chart exists. A basic organizational chart for a small agency is shown in Figure 3.1.[21]

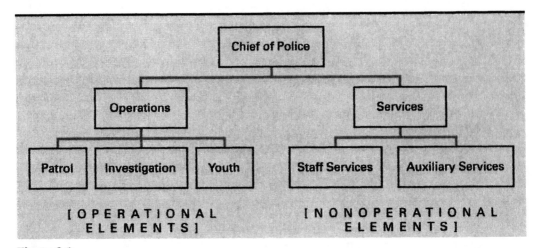

Figure 3.1

Basic police organizational structure.

Operational or line elements involve policing functions in the field and may be subdivided into primary and secondary line elements. The patrol function—often called the "backbone" of policing—is the primary line element because it is the major law enforcement responsibility within the police organization. Most small police agencies, in fact, can be described as patrol agencies with the patrol forces responsible for all line activities.[22] Such agencies provide routine patrol, conduct criminal and traffic investigations, and make arrests. These agencies are basically generalists. In a community that has only one employee—the marshal—he or she obviously must perform all the functions just listed. This agency's organizational chart is a simple horizontal one with little or no specialization.

Investigative and youth activities are the secondary operational elements. These functions would not be needed if the police were totally successful in their patrol and crime prevention efforts—an obviously impossible goal. Time and area restrictions on the patrol officers, as well as the need for specialized training and experience, require some "spin-off" from the patrol activity.

The nonoperational functions and activities can become quite numerous, especially in a large community. These functions fall within two broad categories: *staff services* (also known as administrative) and *auxiliary* (or *technical*) *services*. Staff services are usually people oriented and include recruitment, training, promotion, planning and research, community relations, and public information services. Auxiliary services involve the types of functions that a nonpolice person rarely sees, including jail management, property and evidence, crime laboratory services, communications (dispatch), and records and identification. Many career opportunities exist for persons interested in police-related work but, for some reason, cannot or do not want to be a field officer.

The Chicago Police Department's organizational structure (Figure 3.2) demonstrates the extent to which specialization exists in a large police department (discussed more fully later), and represents the horizontal chain of command in a large organization. This organizational structure is designed to

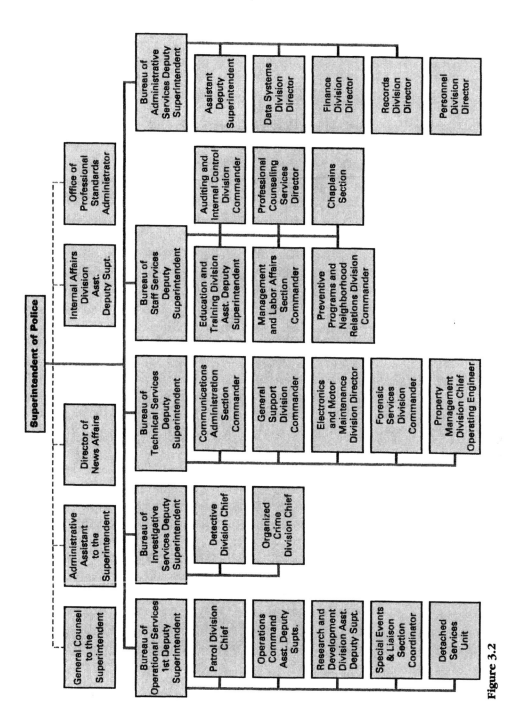

Figure 3.2

Chicago Police Department organization for command.

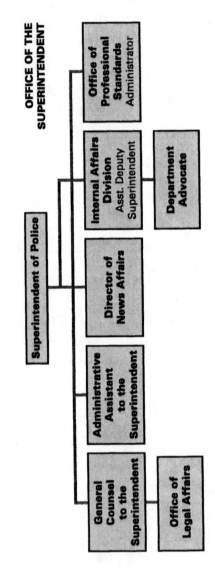

Figure 3.2
(*continued*)

BUREAU OF OPERATIONAL SERVICES

Figure 3.2
(*continued*)

BUREAU OF INVESTIGATIVE SERVICES

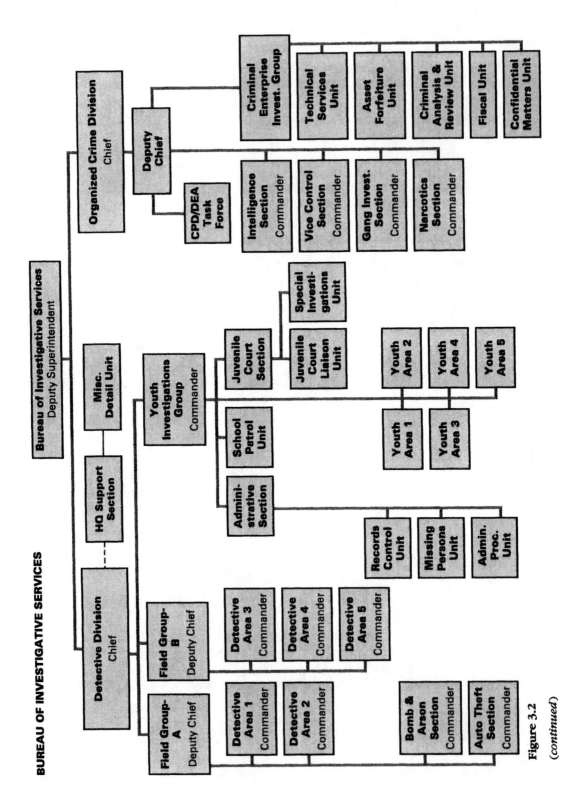

Figure 3.2

(continued)

BUREAU OF TECHNICAL SERVICES

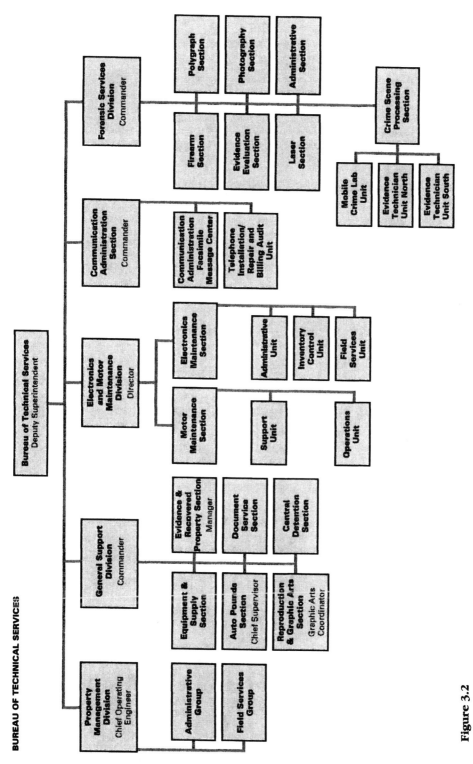

Figure 3.2

(continued)

67

BUREAU OF STAFF SERVICES

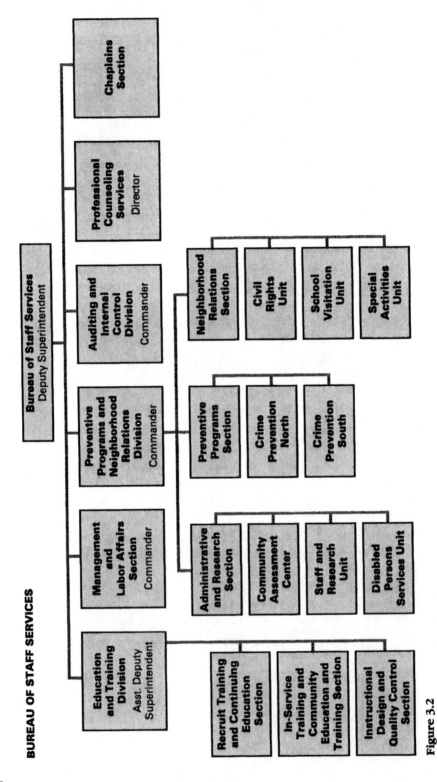

Figure 3.2

(*continued*)

BUREAU OF ADMINISTRATIVE SERVICES

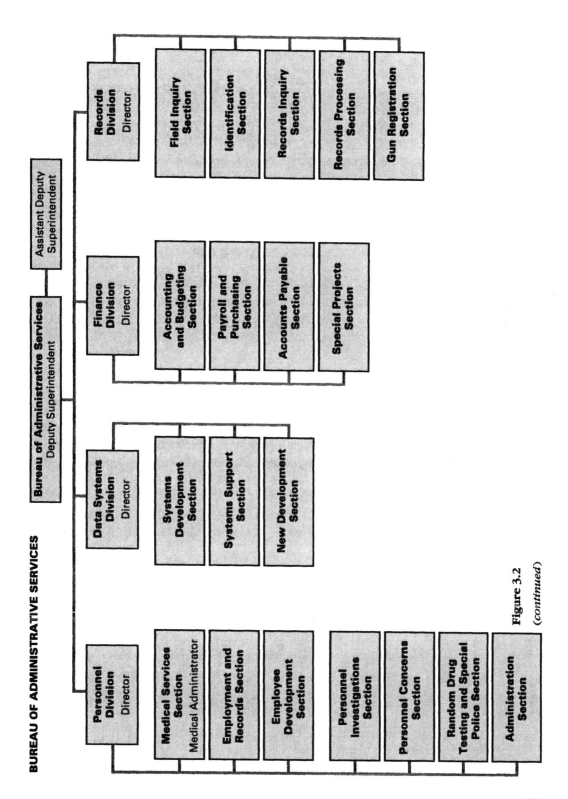

Figure 3.2
(*continued*)

fulfill five functions: (1) apportion the workload among members and units according to a logical plan; (2) ensure that lines of authority and responsibility are as definite and direct as possible; (3) specify a unity of command throughout, so there is no question as to which orders should be followed; (4) place responsibility and authority, and if responsibility is delegated, the delegator is held responsible; and (5) coordinate the efforts of members so that all will work harmoniously to accomplish the mission.[23] In sum, this structure establishes the so-called chain of command and determines lines of communication and responsibility.

In addition to these generally well-known and visible areas of specialization, other branches involved in policing include crime prevention, drug education, juvenile delinquency, and child abuse units.

Policies, Procedures, Rules, and Regulations in Policing

In policing, policies, procedures, rules, and regulations are very important to define role expectations for all officers. Police officers are granted an unusually strong power in a democratic society and because they possess such extraordinary powers, police officers pose a potential threat to individual freedom. Thus, because police agencies are intended to be service oriented in nature, they must work within well-defined, specific guidelines designed to ensure that all officers conform consistently to behavior that will enhance public protection.[24]

Related to this need for policies, procedures, rules, and regulations is the fact that police officers possess a broad spectrum of discretionary authority in performing their duties. This fact, coupled with the danger posed by their work and the opportunities to settle problems informally, work against having narrow, inflexible job requirements.

Thus, the task for the organization's chief executive is to find the middle ground between unlimited discretion and total standardization. The police role is much too ambiguous to become totally standardized, but it is also much too serious and important to be left completely to the total discretion of the patrol officer. As Gary Sheehan and Gary Cordner put it, the idea is for the chief executive to "harness, but not choke, their employees."[25]

Organizational *policies* are more general than procedures, rules, or regulations. Policies are basically guides to the organization's philosophy and mission rather than action and help to interpret those elements to the officers.[26] Policies should be committed to writing, then controlled, adjusted, and deleted according to the changing times and circumstances of the department and community.

Procedures are more specific than policies; they serve as guides to action. According to Wilson and McLaren, a procedure is "more specific than a policy but less restrictive than a rule or regulation. It describes a method of operation while still allowing some flexibility within limits."[27]

Most organizations are awash in procedures. Police organizations have procedures that cover investigation, patrol, booking, radio, filing, roll-call, arrest, sick leave, evidence handling, promotion, and other areas. These procedures are not totally inflexible, but they do describe in rather detailed terms the preferred methods for carrying out policy.

Some procedures are mandated by the U.S. Supreme Court. A good example is the Court's 1985 decision in *Tennessee v. Garner.* This decision resulted in a new policy concerning the use of deadly force. Officers are allowed to use deadly force only when a "suspect threatens the officer with a weapon or there is probable cause to believe that [the suspect] has committed a crime involving the infliction or threatened infliction of serious physical harm."[28]

Some police executives have attempted to run their departments via flurries of temporal memos containing new procedures or rules and regulations. This path is often fraught with difficulty. As Loen observed, an abundance of standardized procedures can stifle initiative and imagination, as well as complicate jobs.[29] On the positive side, procedures can decrease the time wasted in figuring out how to accomplish tasks and thereby increase productivity.[30] As they must with policies, chief executives must seek the middle ground in drafting procedures and remember that it is next to impossible to have procedures that cover all possible exigencies.

Rules and regulations are specific managerial guidelines that leave little or no latitude for individual discretion; they require action (or in some cases, inaction). Some require officers to wear their hats when outside their patrol vehicles, check the patrol vehicle's oil and emergency lights before going on patrol, not consume alcoholic beverages within four hours of going on duty, and arrive in court 30 minutes before sessions open or at roll call 15 minutes before scheduled duty time. Rules and regulations are not always popular, especially if they are perceived as unfair or unrelated to the job. Nonetheless, these rules and regulations contribute to the total police mission of community service.

Rules and regulations should obviously be kept to a minimum because of their coercive nature. If they become too numerous, they can hinder action and give the message that management believes that it cannot trust the rank and file to act responsibly on their own. Once again, the middle range is the best. As Thomas Reddin, former Los Angeles police chief, stated,

> Certainly we must have rules, regulations and procedures, and they should be followed. But they are no substitutes for initiative and intelligence. The more a [person] is given an opportunity to make decisions and, in the process, to learn, the more rules and regulations will be followed.[31]

The Influence of Research on Police Functions

The Mid-1970s: Crises Stimulate Progress

Little research concerning police functions and methods was conducted until 1964.[32] In fact, little substantive research examining police methods actually occurred until the mid-1970s. Two reasons account for this lack of inquiry into policing. First, the police tended to resist outside scrutiny. Functioning in a bureaucratic environment, they—like other bureaucracies—were sensitive to outside research. Many police administrators perceived research studies as a threat to personal careers and the organization's image, and they were concerned as to the legitimacy of the research. Administrators were naturally reluctant to invite trouble. Given these obstacles, sociologists were often reluctant to attempt to penetrate the walls of what appeared to be a closed fortress.

Second, few police administrators saw any benefit to the research for them. They had no need to challenge traditional methods of operation. The "if it ain't broke, don't fix it" attitude prevailed, particularly among old-school administrators. Some ideas—additional police personnel and vehicles equaled more patrolling and therefore less crime, a quicker response rate, and a happier private citizen—were etched in stone. The methods and effectiveness of detectives and their investigative techniques and the old myths of good policing were not even open to debate.

Then, as the police faced crises, things began to change. As Herman Goldstein stated,

> Crises stimulate progress. The police came under enormous pressure in the late 1960s and early 1970s, confronted with concern about crime, civil rights demonstrations, racial conflicts, riots and political protests.[33]

Five national studies investigated police practices, each with a different focus: the President's Commission on Law Enforcement and the Administration of Justice (1967), the National Advisory Commission on Civil Disorders (1968), the National Advisory Commission on the Causes and Prevention of Violence (1969), the President's Commission on Campus Unrest (1970), and the National Advisory Commission on Criminal Justice Standards and Goals (1973). A 1985 national survey probed the effect of budget limits or cuts on police forces in the 1970s and 1980s. It found that 44 percent of police and sheriff's departments had the same number or fewer personnel than they had five years earlier.[34] As a result, police administrators came under increasing pressure to use personnel and equipment in the most efficient fashion—to do more with less. This pressure may explain why police administrators became more willing to challenge traditional assumptions and beliefs and to open the door to researchers. That willingness to allow researchers to examine traditional methods led to the growth and development of two important policing research organizations, the Police Foundation and the Police Executive Research Forum (PERF). The results of the research have been significant. As Joan Petersilia of the RAND Corporation observed, "Although systematic research on policing began [only recently], it is already influencing major changes in the way police departments operate and in public perceptions of policing."[35]

George Kelling and a research team at the Police Foundation conducted the best-known study of the assumptions concerning patrolling in Kansas City, Missouri, in 1973. The researchers divided the city into 15 beats, which were then categorized into five groups of three matched beats each. Each group was composed of neighborhoods that were similar in terms of population, crime characteristics, and calls for police services. Patrolling techniques used in the three beats varied: There was no preventive patrolling in one (police responded only to calls for service); preventive patrol activity in another was two or three times the typical amount; and the third beat maintained the usual level of service. Citizens were interviewed and crime rates measured during the one-year period of the Kansas City Preventive Patrol Experiment. The results showed no significant differences in the crime rates or citizen perceptions of safety as a result of the type of preventive patrol an area received. Similar results were obtained in studies in St. Louis and Minneapolis. These studies also found that the police can stop routinely patrolling their beats for up to a year without necessarily being missed by the residents and without a rise in crime rates in the patrol area.[36]

Police response time has also been analyzed. According to the long-standing assumption concerning police response time, the ability to arrest perpetrators decreased proportionately as response time increased. Thus, conventional wisdom held, the more police on patrol in rapid vehicles, the more quickly they can reach the crime scene and make arrests. In 1977, the National Institute of Justice (NIJ) funded a project to analyze the effect of response time on the outcome of police services (arrests, citizen injury, witness availability, and citizen satisfaction). Again, the site of the research was Kansas City, Missouri. Over a two-year period, the police department collected information on crimes in 56 of its 207 beats; observers rode with police officers and collected travel-time data. The results indicated that police response time was unrelated to the probability of making an arrest or locating a witness, and neither dispatch nor travel time was strongly associated with citizen satisfaction. The time it takes to *report* a crime, the study found, is the major determining factor of whether an on-scene arrest takes place and whether witnesses are located.[37]

Rethinking "Sacred Cow" Traditions

On the basis of these two major studies of patrol methods and effectiveness, many police executives are rethinking their "sacred cow" traditions that have kept the old myths in a protective shroud. For example, one chief of police stated that,

> Evidence from the Kansas City study, and others since then, has definitely impacted the way in which I allocate resources. The research findings certainly got me focused on looking at the effectiveness of my own policies and made me do some evaluations of my own. Also, once I understood that preventive patrol does not necessarily reduce crime, I became more flexible in using that manpower in other ways. The Kansas City experiment really opened up the doors for researchers, previously thought to be mostly academic, done for other academics.[38]

Researchers examined another sacred cow—the methods of criminal investigations used by police and their effectiveness. Police departments have always ranked criminal investigation—attempting to link a crime with a suspect—as one of their most critical duties. A mystique, largely perpetuated by the movies, that most crimes can be solved, that most cases involving unknown criminals are solved through good detective work, and that detectives should be assigned to follow-up investigation of all but the most minor criminal cases has historically surrounded the area of investigation.[39]

Countless present and former patrol officers can attest to the elitism and aloofness often displayed by detectives as a result of this mystique. It often seems that a kind of invisible "leash" is attached to the necks of patrol officers, to be jerked by some detectives when a patrol officer unilaterally takes an investigation too far.

Until 1975, however, the criminal investigation function itself had never been investigated. The National Institute of Justice hired the RAND Corporation to study the investigative function. The study surveyed 150 large police agencies by interviewing and observing investigators in more than 25 police departments. At about the same time, the Stanford Research Institute (SRI) conducted another study of investigations. It found that in Alameda County, California, in more than 50 percent of the burglaries in which the burglar was arrested, the arrest was made within 48 hours of the report of the burglary. Both the RAND and SRI study results suggested that detectives actually played a relatively minor role in solving burglaries, and that the information provided by patrol officers from their preliminary investigations was an important determining factor in whether a follow-up investigation would result in an arrest.[40]

As a result of these findings, NIJ funded more studies of the investigation process in the late 1970s in Santa Monica, California; Cincinnati, Ohio; and Rochester and Syracuse, New York. Several consistent findings emerged: Many serious crimes are not solved; patrol officers are responsible, directly or indirectly, for most arrests (either arresting the suspect at the scene or obtaining helpful descriptions from victims or witnesses); and only a small percentage of all arrests for Part I offenses result from detectives with specialized training and skills.[41]

In 1983, PERF published the results of its own look at the investigative function, including the following:

> Changes have occurred in investigative management as a result of the earlier studies; all of them had a profound influence on investigative management today. For instance, there has been a greater emphasis on case screening and on improving the role of patrol officers in investigations—policy changes that were recommended by many of the earlier studies.[42]

These studies proved that if not all cases can be solved, not all cases should be pursued as vigorously as others. The SRI research produced "predictors of case closure," an index to be used by the police for estimating the solvability of burglaries. Included are such elements as the estimated range of time when the crime occurred, whether a witness reported the offense and an eyewitness was present, if usable fingerprints were retrieved, and if a suspect was described or named. Using this yardstick, police can better manage the burglary caseload and determine which burglaries have little or no chance of being solved. Obviously, the solvability factors of this predictor prevent the expenditure of tremendous amounts of time and resources on dead end investigations.

Other Major Findings

Other major research findings have shaken old assumptions about policing. The following points are now accepted in most quarters as part of the common wisdom of the police:

1. The police do much more than deal with crime; they deal with many forms of behavior that are not defined as criminal.
2. In the past, too much emphasis has been placed on criminal law (using arrests only) in order to get the police job done. Arrest and prosecution are simply not effective ways to handle much of what constitutes police business.
3. Police use a wide range of methods—formal and informal—to do their jobs. Law enforcement is only one method among many.
4. The police (contrary to the desires of earlier advocates of the "professional" model, such as Fuld, Fosdick, Vollmer, and Wilson) are not autonomous. The sensitive function they perform requires that they be accountable, through the political process, to the community.
5. Individual police officers exercise a great deal of discretion in deciding how to handle the tremendous variety of circumstances they confront.[43]

We now know that two-person patrol cars are no more effective than one-person cars in reducing crime or apprehending criminals. Furthermore, injuries to police officers are not more likely to occur in one-person cars. Also, most officers on patrol do not stumble across felony crimes in progress—only "Dirty Harry" does.[44]

Although the results of research studies reported here should not be viewed as being conclusive—different results could be obtained in different communities—they do demonstrate that traditional police methods should be viewed cautiously. The "we've always done it this way" mentality, still pervading policing to a large extent, may not only be an ineffective means of organizing and administering a police agency, but may also be a costly squandering of valuable human and financial resources.

A police agency can perform different types of research provided that it has the desire to do it and the personnel to implement it. For example, research into the best way to create a beat could be conducted. Traditionally, many city beats have been configured without a rational basis: Boundaries often have been determined by a conveniently located major street or river in town. It would be far better if the geographical boundaries for beats were drawn after analyzing where most crimes have been committed and with a view to make the workload more equal among available officers. In the same vein, it would be a better use of resources to assign personnel according to the time of day and day of week when most crimes and calls for service occur rather than to set goals such as reducing response time, which has not been found to increase arrests. Other types of in-house research that can be performed involve comparing the number of arrests to convictions, the number of personnel hours worked to incidents handled, vehicles to personnel, and error rate to reports.[45] Additional quantitative information that can be generated for practical advantage includes the number of crimes that are cleared by arrest, the number of officers per 1,000 population, types of crimes committed and value of items taken, and crime projections.

Innovation in Police Organizations

Research has shown that neither agency size, technological approach to policing, population variables, nor type of local government substantially constrains the organizational structure of police agencies. In other words, none of these factors determines, to any substantial degree, how agencies are structured.[46] This finding is important, because it means that police leadership can use innovative approaches to shape police organizations far more effectively than traditional theory allows. Although changing police organizations may sometimes appear to be similar to bending granite,[47] as mentioned earlier, it can be accomplished by leaders with vision and the skills to articulate and implement it.

Indeed, Jerome Skolnick and David Bayley examined police departments in six cities—Santa Ana, Newark, Oakland, Denver, Houston, and Detroit. Although some of these departments once had reputations for corruption, insensitivity to citizens' needs, gross inefficiency, and even repression and brutality, Skolnick and Bayley reported that innovative administrators kindled the hope that these agencies, despite their bureaucracies, could be transformed into more responsive servants of their communities.

Skolnick and Bayley undertook this study in part because of the "almost unrelievedly negative findings" about policing methods in the United States.[48] They observed innovations that incorporated community oriented policing and problem solving (discussed later). Additionally, they associated successful innovation with four critical ingredients: (1) the chief executive's active commitment to policing that is oriented toward crime prevention, (2) the chief's ability to motivate personnel to "enlist in the cause" of new methods, (3) the leadership's commitment to protect the integrity of these innovations and to prevent their decline in quality as a result of everyday demands, and (4) the support and patience of the public.[49]

Also during the course of this study, Skolnick and Bayley identified six obstacles to police innovation: (1) tradition and bureaucratic inertia, (2) public resistance to change and support for traditional police services, (3) resistance by labor unions, (4) the costs of innovation, (5) a lack of vision by police executives, and (6) the inadequate capacity of police departments to evaluate their own effectiveness.[50]

Community Oriented Policing and Problem Solving

Since the 1980s, community oriented policing and problem solving—COPPS— has emerged as the dominant direction for thinking about policing. This approach

Bill Bratton: The Bruce Springsteen of Policing

William Bratton spent the 1980s and 1990s transforming police department after police department using methods he had first applied successfully in the Fenway district of Boston in the late 1970s. In Fenway, Sergeant Bratton was sent down from headquarters to experiment with new command strategies, the success of which launched him into the executive ranks of the Boston Police Department. After rising as high as Deputy Superintendent (at the age of 32), Bratton left the Boston Police Department for a succession of police agencies where he produced ever more impressive results. In Bratton's first solo command, as Chief of the Massachusetts Bay Transit Authority Police from 1983 to 1986, crime went down by 27 percent. . . . Bratton then went on to modernize and reinvigorate the Metropolitan Police, Massachusetts' third largest police agency, as its superintendent from 1986 to 1989. At his next stop, the New York Transit Police from 1990 to 1992, overall felonies were reduced by 22 percent, robberies by 40 percent, fare evasion by 50 percent, and riders came back to the system after years of fearful aversion. As New York City Police Commissioner from 1993 to 1996, Bratton oversaw a department that topped the performances of all the agencies he has led previously, catapulting Bratton to national recognition.

The future of policing is here, courtesy of William Bratton. In "Turnaround," Bratton tells us how he transformed big-city policing. The book is must reading for every officer, police supervisor and agency

leader in this country. "Turnaround" should be shackled to the wrist of every social science professor who ever pronounced crime intractable, and to the ankle of every business and public administration savant who doubted that government agencies could be re-engineered into powerful and effective vehicles for meeting their mandates.

Bratton's Fenway debut was not flawless. He came to Fenway with the systems-control mentality acquired from a stint in the Boston police commissioner's office, where rapid response, random patrols and reactive investigation ("the three R's") were key operational principles. Also, the year was 1977 and Bratton was but a year removed from the investigator/patrol officer's world where policing was defined by cracking the big crimes and catching the bad guys. So some of Bratton's first moves did little to win over Fenway's diverse community. Residents, many of whom were poised to flee the area's declining quality of life, did not want after-the-fact policing by officers otherwise hermetically sealed in their vehicles. They did not want big police busts when that meant largely ignoring the minor violators who created the hundreds of little bothers residents endured daily. Neither the inputs Bratton so methodically applied nor the outputs his officers so eagerly sought ranked as high priorities with the community. . . .

The rapid adjustments in Fenway were made possible by a flexibility that Bratton demonstrated from his first days as a police manager and has refined over the years.

What is truly special, and what sets Bratton apart, is his fundamental understanding of why Plan A wasn't working, and why Plan B likely would work. Bratton credits his college education with broadening his vision of the police role, and with sensitizing him to how different groups of citizens view police. Police can be seen as protectors or as occupiers, Bratton learned....

Bratton's book also underscores the importance of lifelong learning for police professionals. Many of the concepts Bratton has applied so effectively to policing were unknown when Bratton went to Boston State College as a mid-career student on a scholarship in the early 1970s....

One secret to Bratton's success as a leader of police agencies is his commitment to making life easier for the men and women on the line. He says: "Equipment helps cops do their jobs, and it makes them feel good. I fought for these resources.... If people feel you'll fight for them, they'll work for you.... They'll take risks to move the organization forward. 'He's meeting me halfway, so I'll do it for him.' And once your people see that your ideas work, and they are praised and rewarded for carrying them out, their work becomes easier and gets done better...."

Bratton's management approach relies heavily on trust and respect for employees. "Pick good people and let them do their jobs" is Bratton's credo. He knows that all organizations have corrupt, inept or irresponsible employees, but refuses to manage to the least common denominator. Railing against screw-ups, Bratton understands, speaks not only to the unlawful employee (who is not likely to change) but also to the innovative employee (who likely will change, but for the worse, into a by-the-book minimalist)....

Another Bratton tactic for shaking up moribund police agencies was leapfrogging promotions, elevating commanders two, three and even four ranks to the agency's top positions. This practice is much more than the "cleaning house" and "bringing in one's own people" done reflexively by most newly installed public executives....

Big-city police departments, and large public organizations in general, are necessarily unwieldly creatures—segmented, centrifugal, inertial. In their daily existence, organizations spew forth a miasma of information. The job of the agency executive is to extract those nuggets of data most germane to effective management. This data, furthermore, must be obtained from units whose chiefs, on the whole, will resent, feel threatened by and/or resist outright management's data-mining efforts. To a great extent, the failures of public management leadership are due to an understandable, but nonetheless irresponsible lack of perseverance in combating inertia, overcoming the squirreling of data by units, and making renegade unit heads accountable. Bratton is the outstanding police leader of the 20th century because he developed methods, the most recent and successful being Compstat, for overcoming inertial and centrifugal police organizations.

Source: "Bill Bratton: The Bruce Springsteen of Policing," *LEN,* June 15/30, 1998. Reprinted with permission from *Law Enforcement News,* John Jay College of Criminal Justice (CUNY), 555 W. 57th St., New York, NY 10019.

to crime detection and prevention provides police officers and supervisors with new tools for addressing recurrent problems that plague communities and consume a majority of police agency time and resources. The California Department of Justice provided the following definition for COPPS:

> Community-oriented policing and problem solving is a philosophy, management style, and organizational strategy that promotes proactive problem solving and police-community partnerships to address the causes of crime and fear as well as other community issues.[51]

Two principal and interrelated components emerge from this definition: community engagement (partnerships) and problem solving. With its focus on collaborative problem solving, COPPS seeks to improve the quality of policing. This is no simple task, however, and several steps must be taken for administrators to accomplish this goal: (1) Police must be equipped to define more clearly and to understand more fully the problems that they are expected to handle; (2) police must develop a commitment to analyzing problems; and (3) police must be encouraged to conduct an uninhibited search for the most effective response to each problem.[52] The SARA process discussed later provides police with the tools necessary to accomplish these steps.

COPPS broadens officers' understanding of problems and moves them from viewing incidents separately and individually to recognizing that incidents are often related and are symptoms of deeper problems. COPPS also teaches officers why and how crimes repeatedly occur and what strategies they may employ to reduce crime. Once the causes of crimes are identified, police are better prepared to address those underlying conditions.

The SARA Process

SARA (Figure 3.3) provides officers with a logical step-by-step framework to identify, analyze, respond to, and evaluate crime, fear of crime, and neighborhood disorder. This approach, with its emphasis on in-depth analysis and collaboration, replaces officers' short-term reactive responses with a process vested in longer-term outcomes. Next we briefly discuss each component of the SARA process.

Scanning: Problem Identification
Scanning means identifying problems. It initiates the problem-solving process by conducting a preliminary inquiry to determine if a problem really exists and

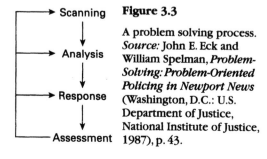

Figure 3.3

A problem solving process. *Source:* John E. Eck and William Spelman, *Problem-Solving: Problem-Oriented Policing in Newport News* (Washington, D.C.: U.S. Department of Justice, National Institute of Justice, 1987), p. 43.

whether further analysis is needed. A problem may be defined as a cluster of two or more similar or related incidents that are of substantive concern to the community and to the police (Figure 3.4). If the incidents to which the police respond do not fall within the definition of a problem, then the problem-solving process is not applicable.

Numerous resources are available to police for identifying problems, including calls for service data—especially repeat calls, crime analysis information, police reports, and officers' own experiences. Other sources of information include other government agencies, public and private agencies, businesses, media reports, and information obtained from the public. Scanning helps officers to determine whether problems really exist before moving on to more in-depth analyses.

Analysis: Determining the Extent of the Problem

Analysis is the heart of the problem-solving process. It is the most difficult and important step in the SARA process. Without analysis, long-term solutions are limited and problems are likely to persist.

Here, officers gather as much information as possible from a variety of sources. A complete and thorough analysis consists of officers identifying the seriousness of the problem, all persons affected, and the underlying causes. Officers should also assess the effectiveness of current responses.

Many tools are available to assist with analysis. Crime analysis may be useful in collecting, collating, analyzing, and disseminating data related to crime, incidents not requiring a report, criminal offenders, victims, and locations. Mapping and geographic information systems (GIS) can identify patterns of crime and "hot spots." Police offense reports can also be analyzed for suspect characteristics, victim characteristics, and information about high-crime areas and addresses. Computer-aided dispatch (CAD) is also a reliable source of information, as it collects data on all incidents and specific locations from which an unusual number of incidents require a police response.

Response: Formulating Tailor-Made Strategies

Once a problem has been clearly defined, officers may seek the most effective responses. The importance of developing long-term solutions to problems is of paramount importance with COPPS; however, officers cannot ignore the fact that

Figure 3.4

Problem analysis triangle. *Source:* Bureau of Justice Assistance, U.S. Department of Justice, *Comprehensive Gang Initiative: Operations Manual for Implementing Local Gang Prevention and Control Programs* (Draft, October 1993), pp. 3–10.

more serious situations may require immediate action. For example, in the case of an open-air drug market involving rival gang violence, police may initially increase the number of patrols in the area to arrest offenders and gain control of public space and to secure the safety of residents and officers. Once this is accomplished, longer-term responses may be considered that include the collaborative efforts of officers, residents, and other agencies.

Administrators must bear in mind that responses to substantial problems rarely involve a single agency or tactic or quick fix. For example, arrest is often viewed as the only response to a problem even though it is rarely sufficient to provide more permanent resolutions. More appropriate responses often involve the police and public and other appropriate channels including business, private and social service organizations, and other government agencies.

Patrol officers have many options when responding to problems. Officers should not expect to eliminate every problem they take on, however. With some social problems, such as gangs and homelessness, elimination is impractical and improbable.

Another important prevention tool for COPPS is crime prevention through environmental design (CPTED). CPTED teaches officers how building space, architectural design, lighting, and other such features of the environment contribute to criminal opportunities. Both situational crime prevention and CPTED provide officers with tools necessary to employ comprehensive prevention strategies.

Assessment: Evaluating Overall Effectiveness

The final stage of the SARA process is assessment. Here, officers evaluate the effectiveness of their responses and may use the results to revise their responses, collect more data, or even redefine the problem. For some problems, assessment is very simple (observing a location to see if a problem resurfaces). For example, in one East Coast city, when asked how he determined that his COPPS efforts in a local park were successful, one officer simply mentioned that more families were using the park.

In most cases, however, assessments should be comprehensive and include such measures as before/after comparisons of crime and call for service data, environmental crime prevention surveys, and neighborhood fear reduction surveys. The nature of the problem will often dictate the methods of assessment.

Change Begins with the Supervisor

Robinette[53] asserted that the traditional police supervisor, shift commander, or mid-level executive is largely unprepared by training and experience for the requirements of the COPPS strategy. Most officers do not see their supervisors as sources of guidance and direction, but rather as authority figures to be satisfied (by numbers of arrests and citations, the manner in which reports are completed, the officers' ability to avoid citizen complaints, and so on). This view of supervisors varies greatly from the characteristics listed earlier.

Organizational change begins or ends with an agency's supervisors. The link between a street officer and the organization is through his or her sergeant.

Indeed, the quality of an officer's daily life is often dependent on the supervisor. There is some cause for supervisors' reluctance to change, however.

A difficult hurdle that supervisors must overcome is the idea that giving line officers the opportunity to be creative and take risks does not diminish the role or authority of the supervisor. Risk taking and innovation require mutual trust between supervisors and line officers. It means changing from being a "controller," primarily concerned with rules, to being a "facilitator" and "coach" for officers engaged in COPPS work. As noted, supervisors must learn to encourage innovation and risk taking among their officers. They must also be well skilled in problem solving, especially in the analysis of problems and evaluation of efforts. Conducting workload analyses and finding the time for officers to solve problems and engage the community are important aspects of supervision. Supervisors must also be prepared to intercede and remove any roadblocks to officers' problem-solving efforts.

Supervisors should also understand that not all patrol officers or detectives will enjoy or be good at COPPS work. Supervisors should assist officers with managing their beats and utilizing time for COPPS activities. Some agencies accomplish this by assigning a specialized team to COPPS. We believe this risks creating the illusion that COPPS is composed of "privileged prima donnas" who get benefits that other officers do not. Also, supervisors should not contribute to the COPPS initiative becoming a mere public-relations campaign: The emphasis is always on results.[54]

To gain time for officers to engage in COPPS functions, departments should review their patrol plans to determine whether units are fielded in proportion to workload. Delaying response time to calls for service can also provide more time for officers. Response time research has determined that rapid responses are not needed for most calls. Furthermore, dispatchers can set citizens' expectations of when an officer will arrive. Slower police response to nonemergency calls has been found satisfactory to citizens if dispatchers tell citizens an officer might not arrive at their home right away. Managers have also garnered more time for officers by having nonsworn employees handle noncrime incidents.[55]

Implementing COPPS

Gaining the support of supervisors and officers is the first step in implementing COPPS. To make COPPS a part of officers' routine daily activities, however, requires an entire organizational transformation that cannot be accomplished overnight.

Four key components of implementation profoundly affect the way agencies do business: leadership and management, organizational culture, field operations, and external relations.[56]

Leadership and Management
COPPS requires changing the philosophy of leadership and management throughout the entire organization. This begins with the development of a new *vision/values/mission statement.* All *policies and procedures* should be

reviewed to ensure that they comport with the department's COPPS objectives. *Leadership* should be promoted at all levels, and a shift in *management style* from controller to facilitator is necessary. The organization should invest in *information systems* that will assist officers in identifying patterns of crime and support the problem-solving process. Progressive leaders will need to prepare for the new millennium by developing long-term *strategic planning* and continuous *evaluation processes,* but at the same time they must be flexible and comfortable with change. *Finances and resources* will no longer be firmly established within boxes in the organizational chart. Rather, they will be commonly shared across the organization, with other city departments and the public engaged in neighborhood problem solving.

Organizational Culture

Human resources is the "heart and soul" of organizational culture. For employees, it answers the question, "What's in it for me?" Any major change in an organization requires that a review of all human resources is conducted. Community engagement and problem solving require new skills, knowledge, and abilities for everyone in the organization. Therefore, such areas as *recruiting, selection, training, performance evaluations, promotions, honors and awards,* and *discipline* should be reviewed to ensure they promote and support the organization's transition to COPPS. Agencies must also work closely with the various *labor organizations,* which will be concerned with any proposed changes in shifts, beats, criteria for selection, promotion, discipline, and so on. It is wise to include labor representatives in the planning and implementation process from the beginning.

Field Operations

The primary concern with field operations is structuring the delivery of patrol services to assist officers in dealing with the root causes of persistent community problems. The first issue raised is whether a *specialist versus generalist* approach will be used. It is not uncommon, especially in larger police agencies, to begin COPPS implementation with an experimental district comprised of a team of specially trained officers. The experience of many agencies over the past 15 years, however, suggests that department-wide implementation should occur as quickly as possible. This will eliminate the common criticism that COPPS officers do not do "real police work" and receive special privileges. This attitude, if allowed to fester, can quickly impair any implementation efforts. The need for available time presents a supervisory challenge that begins with *managing calls for service,* which looks at call prioritization and differential response methods. A *decentralized approach* to field operations involves assigning officers to a beat and shift for a minimum of one year, to learn more about a neighborhood's problems.

External Relations

Collaborative responses to neighborhood crime and disorder are essential to the success of COPPS. These responses require new relationships and the sharing of information and resources between the police and community, local government agencies, service providers, and businesses. Agencies must educate and inform their external partners about police resources and neighborhood problems using surveys, newsletters, community meetings, and public service announcements. The *media* also provide an excellent opportunity for police to educate the community. Press releases about collaborative problem-solving efforts should be sent to the media, and news conferences should be held to discuss major crime reduction efforts.

The Chief Executive and Mid-Level Manager

Major changes in philosophy and practices are required within a police organization before a major shift such as COPPS can be made. We briefly examine how the chief or sheriff and the captain and lieutenant are all key figures in effecting such a major transformation.

First, the police organization needs a viable change agent: The person at the top is responsible for setting both the policy and tone of the organization. The chief executive must be both visible and credible and create a climate conducive to change. Employees must be involved in the change process. Gauging the pace and degree of change is also necessary. It is essential, however, that chief executives communicate the idea that COPPS is department-wide in scope and encourage and guide all officers to engage in problem solving.

Mid-level managers also play a crucial role in the implementation of a COPPS philosophy. They must not view COPPS as a threat to their power. Middle managers are essential to the process of innovation, much of which can originate only in middle management.[57] As George Kelling and William Bratton observed,[58] ample evidence exists that when a clear vision of the business of the organization is put forward, when mid-level managers are included in planning, when their legitimate self-interests are acknowledged, and when they are properly trained, mid-level managers can be on the leading edge of innovation and creativity.[59]

Mid-level managers and first-line supervisors are discussed in greater detail in Chapter 4.

Summary

Today, Robert Peel, the founder of modern policing in England in 1829, would be amazed. His persistent efforts to organize and deploy a full-time police force have resulted in a proliferation of police around the globe. In this chapter, we explored the contemporary organization of the police in general; the policies, procedures, rules, and regulations that guide them; and the results of research into policing methods. We hope that this body of police research will continue to provide impetus for policing to meet the needs of our shifting society.

Contemporary police organization, an area that presently bears close observation, was also discussed. The organization is an area that needs further research and change. The popularity of community oriented policing and problem solving is currently causing changes in the traditional administration of police agencies. We expect that careful analysis of the findings of research studies will result in changes to the traditional bureaucratic model of policing as well.

Questions for Review

1. What are the distinctions among policy, procedure, and rules and regulations? Why are they necessary in law enforcement agencies? What are their relationship and role vis-a-vis police discretion?

2. How do law enforcement agencies constitute bureaucracies? Can such a form of organization ever be eliminated?

3. What is the basic police organizational structure? Draft an organizational chart with the level of specialization you might find in your home town or county police agency.

4. What are some of the major recent findings concerning policing? How have they affected the field?

5. What role do innovation and values play in police organizations?

6. Explain what is meant by *community oriented policing and problem solving.* How does this concept differ from past policing methods? What improvements does it offer? Under this strategy, what important roles are played by chief executives, mid-level managers, and first-line supervisors?

Notes

1. Larry K. Gaines, Mittie D. Southerland, and John E. Angell, *Police Administration* (New York: McGraw-Hill, 1991), pp. 5–6.

2. Stephen P. Robbins, *The Administration Process* (Englewood Cliffs, N.J.: Prentice Hall, 1976).

3. *The Republic of Plato,* trans. Allen Bloom (New York: Basic Books, 1968), p. 7.

4. See Luther Gulick and L. Urwick, eds., *Papers on the Science of Administration* (New York: Augustus M. Kelley, 1969).

5. Charles R. Swanson, Leonard Territo, and Robert W. Taylor, *Police Administration* (3d ed.) (New York: Macmillan, 1993), p. 134.

6. Orlando W. Wilson and Roy C. McLaren, *Police Administration* (3d ed.) (New York: McGraw-Hill, 1972), p. 79.

7. Egon Bittner, *The Functions of the Police in a Modern Society,* Public Health Service Publication 2059 (Washington, D.C.: U.S. Government Printing Office, 1970), p. 53.

8. John J. Broderick, *Police in a Time of Change* (Prospect Heights, Ill.: Waveland Press, 1987), p. 231.

9. Ronald G. Lynch, *The Police Manager: Professional Leadership Skills* (3d ed.) (New York: Random House, 1986), p. 4.

10. Thomas A. Johnson, Gordon E. Misner, and Lee P. Brown, *The Police and Society: An Environment for Collaboration and Confrontation* (Englewood Cliffs, N.J.: Prentice Hall, 1981), p. 53.

11. Dorothy Guyot, "Bending Granite: Attempts to Change the Rank Structure of American Police Departments," *Journal of Police Science and Administration* 7 (1979):253–284.

12. Ibid., pp. 273–274.

13. Lynch, *The Police Manager,* pp. 5–6.

14. Geoffrey P. Alpert and Roger G. Dunham, *Policing Urban America* (Prospect Heights, Ill.: Waveland Press, 1988), p. 71.

15. Bittner, *The Functions of the Police in a Modern Society,* p. 51.

16. Paul M. Whisenand and Fred Ferguson, *The Managing of Police Organizations* (Englewood Cliffs, N.J.: Prentice Hall, 1973), p. 9.

17. Michel Crozier, *The Bureaucratic Phenomenon* (Chicago: University of Chicago Press, 1964), p. 190.

18. Broderick, *Police in a Time of Change* (2d ed.), p. 233.

19. In Ray Graham and Jeffrey R. Cameron, "The Integrated Approach to Career Development," *The Police Chief* (June 1985):26–30.

20. Swanson, Territo, and Taylor, *Police Administration* (3d ed.), p. 142.

21. For further discussion about basic police organization structures, see George D. Eastman and Esther M. Eastman (eds.), *Municipal Police Administration* (7th ed.) (Washington, D.C.: International City Management Association, 1971), p. 17.

22. Ibid., p. 18.

23. President's Commission on Law Enforcement and Administration of Justice, *Task Force Report: The Police* (Washington, D.C.: U.S. Government Printing Office, 1967), p. 46.

24. Robert Sheehan and Gary W. Cordner, *Introduction to Police Administration* (2d ed.) (Cincinnati, Ohio: Anderson, 1989), pp. 446–447.

25. Ibid., p. 449.

26. Ibid.

27. Wilson and McLaren, *Police Administration,* p. 130.

28. 471 U.S. 1 (1985).

29. Raymond O. Loen, *Manage More by Doing Less* (New York: McGraw-Hill, 1971), pp. 86–89.

30. Sheehan and Cordner, *Introduction to Police Administration* (2d ed.), p. 453.

31. Thomas Reddin, "Are You Oriented to Hold Them? A Searching Look at Police Management," *The Police Chief* (March 1966): 17.

32. Peter K. Manning, "The Researcher: An Alien in the Police World," in Arthur Niederhoffer and Abraham S. Blumberg (eds.), *The Ambivalent Force: Perspectives on the Police* (2d ed.) (Hinsdale, Ill: Dryden Press, 1976), pp. 103–121.

33. Herman Goldstein, *Problem-Oriented Policing* (New York: McGraw-Hill, 1990), p. 9.

34. Joan Petersilia, "The Influence of Research on Policing," in Roger C. Dunham and Geoffrey P. Alpert (eds.), *Critical Issues in Policing: Contemporary Readings* (Prospect Heights, Ill.: Waveland Press, 1989), p. 230.

35. Ibid.

36. Ibid., pp. 231–232.

37. Ibid., p. 235.

38. Ibid., p. 236.

39. Ibid., p. 237.

40. Ibid.

41. Ibid., p. 238.

42. John E. Eck, *Solving Crimes: The Investigation of Burglary and Robbery* (Washington, D.C.: Police Executive Research Forum, National Institute of Justice, 1983), p. xxiii.

43. Goldstein, *Problem-Oriented Policing,* pp. 8–11.

44. Jerome H. Skolnick and David H. Bayley, *The New Blue Line, Police Innovation in Six American Cities* (New York: Free Press, 1986), p. 4.

45. Gaines, Southerland, and Angell, *Police Administration,* p. 349.

46. Robert H. Langworthy, *The Structure of Police Organizations* (New York: Praeger, 1986).

47. Guyot, "Bending Granite: Attempts to Change the Rank Structure of American Police Departments," pp. 253–284.

48. Skolnick and Bayley, *The New Blue Line,* p. 4.

49. Ibid.

50. Ibid., pp. 220–224.

51. California Department of Justice, *COPPS: Community-Oriented Policing and Problem Solving*. Office of the Attorney General, Crime Violence Prevention Center (Sacramento, Calif.: 1995).

52. Herman Goldstein, "Problem-Oriented Policing." Paper presented at the Conference on Policing: State of the Art III, National Institute of Justice, Phoenix, Arizona, June 12, pp. 5–6.

53. H. M. Robinette, "Supervising Tomorrow." *Virginia Police Chief* (Spring 1993), p. 10.

54. Police Executive Research Forum, *Supervising Problem-Solving* (Washington, D.C.: Author, training outline), 1990.

55. John Eck and William Spelman, "A Problem-Oriented Approach to Police Service Delivery." In Dennis Jay Kenney (ed.), *Police and Policing: Contemporary Issues* (New York: Praeger, 1989), pp. 95–111.

56. Ronald W. Glensor and Kenneth J. Peak, "Implementing Change: Community-Oriented Policing and Problem Solving." *FBI Law Enforcement Bulletin* 7 (1996):14–20.

57. Eck, J. and W. Spelman, "Solving Problems: Problem Oriented Policing in Newport News." Research in Brief, Washington D.C.: U.S. Department of Justice, National Institute of Justice (January 1987).

58. Rosabeth Moss Kanter, "The Middle Manager as Innovator," *Harvard Business Review* (July-August 1982):95–105.

59. Kelling and Bratton, "Implementing Community Policing: The Administrative Problem," p. 11.

POLICE PERSONNEL ROLES AND FUNCTIONS

The police are the public and the public are the police.

—Robert Peel

Introduction

To say that one of the most important and challenging positions one can hold in our society, or in any democratic society, is that of a police administrator, manager, or supervisor is probably accurate. Given the weight of contemporary police decisions and the omnipresent threat of liability in the event of failure to make proper decisions, the administrative role assumes a much higher level of importance than in past decades.

For reasons as much related to the internal aspects of the police organization as they are to external factors, changing times have required a higher caliber of leader. The requirements that officers march and salute militarily and refrain from expressing opinions about politics, religion, or police matters—rules found in many departments as late as the 1970s and 1980s—are clearly outmoded today. The Theory X—"do as I say and not as I do"—philosophy of the past engendered many officer complaints and brought about the creation of many police unions; thus, the difficult nature of today's police administration is in large part due to the iron hand rule of the past. It is also directly a result, however, of a changing, more difficult and litigious society. (Negligence, liability, and other related issues will be discussed more thoroughly in Chapter 14.)

This chapter examines today's police executives and the many roles they fulfill. This examination is initiated by adapting Mintzberg's model of chief executive officers: In this section, we also consider whether a dominant administrative style exists among police managers and identify the agreed upon observable skills of good police managers. Later we explore the assessment center, a means used for hiring and promoting people into executive and mid-level positions. Several appropriate methods of assessing chief executive performance are described as well.

Then we consider the roles and functions of various management levels in police organizations: executives (chiefs and sheriffs), middle managers (captains and lieutenants), and primary supervisory officers (sergeants). Figure 4.1 shows the hierarchy of managers within the typical police organization and the inverse relationship between rank and number of personnel. In other words, as rank increases, the number of persons at that hierarchical rank decreases.

We conclude this chapter with a comprehensive examination of how patrol forces are distributed and deployed. Included in this discussion are methods for determining patrol force size, workload analysis, and shift scheduling.

Figure 4.1

Hierarchy of managers within the typical police organization. (*Source:* Larry K. Gaines, Mittie D. Southerland, and John E. Angell, *Police Administration.* New York: McGraw-Hill, 1991, p. 11.)

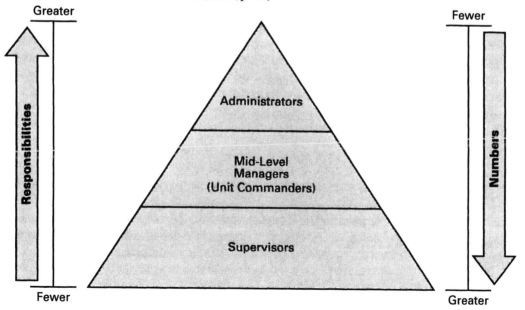

Roles of the Police Executive: The Mintzberg Model of CEOs

A police chief executive fills many roles. Henry Mintzberg[1] described a set of behaviors and tasks of chief executive officers in any organization. Following is an overview of the role of the chief executive officer (CEO)—that is, the chief of police or sheriff—as adapted to policing, using the Mintzberg model as an analytical framework.

The Interpersonal Role

One role of the chief executive officer is the *interpersonal* role, which comprises (1) figurehead, (2) leadership, and (3) liaison duties. As a *figurehead,* the CEO performs various ceremonial functions. He or she rides in parades and attends civic events, speaks before school and university classes and civic organizations, meets visiting officials and dignitaries, attends academy graduation and swearing-in ceremonies and certain weddings and funerals, and visits injured officers in the hospital. Like the mayor, whose public responsibilities include cutting ribbons and kissing babies, the police CEO performs these duties simply because of his or her title and position within the organization; they come with being a figurehead. Although chiefs or sheriffs certainly cannot be expected to attend the grand opening of every retail or commercial business and other events to which they are invited, they are certainly obligated from a professional standpoint to attend many civic functions and ceremonies.

The *leadership* role requires the CEO to motivate and coordinate workers while having to resolve different goals and needs within the department and the community. A chief or sheriff may have to urge the governing board to enact a code or ordinance that, whether popular or not, is in the best interests of the jurisdiction. For example, a chief in a western state recently led a drive to pass an ordinance that prohibited parking by university students in residential neighborhoods surrounding the campus. This was a highly unpopular undertaking, but the chief was prompted because of the hardships suffered and complaints by the area residents. The CEO also may provide leadership by taking stands on bond issues (seeking funds to hire more officers or build new buildings, for example) and advising the governing body on the effects of proposed ordinances.

The *liaison* role occurs when the CEO of a police organization interacts with other organizations and coordinates work assignments. It is not uncommon for executives from a geographical area—the police chief, sheriff, ranking officer of the local highway patrol office, district attorney, campus police chief, and so on—to meet informally each month at breakfast to discuss common problems and strategies. Chief executives also serve as liaisons to regional law enforcement councils, narcotics units, crime labs, dispatching centers, and so on. They also meet with representatives of the courts, juvenile system, and other criminal justice agencies.

The Informational Role

Another role identified by the Mintzberg model is the *informational* one. In this capacity, the CEO engages in tasks relating to (1) monitoring/inspecting, (2) dissemination, and (3) spokesperson duties. In the *monitoring/inspecting* function, the CEO constantly reviews the department's operations to ensure that things are operating smoothly (or as smoothly as police operations can be expected to operate). This function is often referred to as "roaming the ship"; many CEOs who isolated themselves from their personnel and the daily operations of the agency can speak from sad experience of the need to be alert and make a presence. For example, a Midwestern sheriff of a small county was voted out of office in part because it was revealed that two deputies on the graveyard shift were engaged in a Batman and Robin style of police work that included using an M-16 automatic rifle and a police dog. The deputies had received no formal training in the use of either tool. The sheriff, unaware of these covert activities and preferring to administer by looking the other way, was eventually caught in a tidal wave of opposition. Many police executives use daily staff meetings to acquire information about their jurisdictions, especially criminal and other activities during the previous 24 hours.

Dissemination tasks include distributing information to members of the department via memoranda, special orders, general orders, and policies and procedures described in Chapter 3. The *spokesperson* function is related but is more focused on providing information to the news media. This is a difficult task for the chief executive since news organizations, especially television and print media, are competitive businesses that seek to obtain the most complete news in the shortest amount of time, which often translates to wider viewership and therefore greater advertising revenues for them. From one perspective, the media must appreciate that frequently a criminal investigation can be seriously compromised by premature or excessive coverage. From the other perspective, the public has a legitimate right to know what is occurring in the community, especially matters relating to crime. Therefore, the prudent police executive attempts to have an open door and professional relationship with the media in which each side knows and understands its responsibilities. The prudent chief executive also remembers the power of the media and does not alienate them. As an old saying goes, "Never argue with someone who buys his ink by the barrel." Unfortunately, many police executives (a good number who involuntarily left office) can speak of the results of failing to develop an appropriate relationship with the media.

The Decision-Maker Role

In the decision-maker role, the CEO of a police organization serves as (1) an entrepreneur, (2) a disturbance handler, (3) a resource allocator, and (4) a negotiator. In the capacity of *entrepreneur,* the CEO must sell ideas to the members of the governing board or the department—perhaps helping them to understand a new computer or communications system, the implementation of a policing strategy or different work methods, all of which are intended to improve the organization. Sometimes the roles blend, as when several police executives band together (in the entrepreneurial and liaison functions) to lobby the state attorney general and the legislature for new crime-fighting laws.

As a *disturbance handler,* the executive's tasks range from resolving minor disputes between staff members to dealing with major events such as riots, continued muggings in a local park, or cleaning up the downtown area. Sometimes the executive must solve intradepartmental disputes, which can reach major proportions. For example, the chief executive must intervene when friction develops between different units, as when the patrol commanders' instruction to street officers to increase arrests for public drunkenness causes a strain on the resources of the jail division's commander.

As a *resource allocator,* the CEO must clearly understand the agency's budget and its budgetary priorities. The resource allocator must consider requests for funds from various groups. Personnel, for example, will ask for higher salaries, additional officers, and better equipment. Citizens may complain about speeding motorists in a specific area, which would require the allocation of additional resources to that area or neighborhood. In the resource allocator role, the CEO must be able to prioritize requests and be able to defend his or her choices.

As a *negotiator,* the police manager resolves employee grievances and, although not normally sitting himself or herself at the bargaining table—appointing a representative instead—tries to represent the best interests of both the city and labor during collective bargaining. A survey by the Police Executive Research Forum (PERF) found that 7 out of 10 municipal police departments of more than 75 employees now have some form of union representation. This puts the CEO in a negotiating position where the police agency has collective bargaining. In the resource allocator role, the CEO must consider rank and file's requests for raises and increased benefits as part of budget administration. If funds available to the jurisdiction are limited, the CEO must negotiate with the collective bargaining unit to reach an agreement. At times, contract negotiations reach an impasse or deadlock.

Labor relations, including unionism and collective bargaining, are discussed more fully in Chapter 14.

Is There a Dominant CEO Leadership Style?

Several studies have attempted to identify the management styles of police leaders. A study by Jack Kuykendall and Peter Unsinger[2] involved 155 police executives in California and Arizona, with staffs ranging in number from 3 to over 1,700. About half of the managers were from agencies with more than 100 employees. The basic purpose of the study was to determine whether the executive emphasized accomplishing *tasks* (therefore using primarily one-way communication with subordinates) or having positive relationships with *people* (with the leader engaging in a lot of two-way communication with subordinates).

Executives' styles were measured using a survey instrument to determine whether they fit into one or more of the following four categories: (1) the *telling* style—a high-task, low-people orientation where the leader is characterized by one-way communication, telling followers what, when, where, and how to do various tasks; (2) the *selling* style, which emphasizes both task accomplishment and people relationships, using two-way communication and emotional support to get workers to "buy into" decisions; (3) the *participating* style, which emphasizes relationships and low task orientation, involves two-way communication, and encourages shared decision making; and (4) the *delegating* style, which has low task and people orientations, basically letting people "run their own show."[3]

Kuykendall and Unsinger found that police managers used the selling style more frequently than others but tended to be flexible as to style. None of the managers used all four styles, however. The delegating style was used least often. Data showed that about 80 percent of the executives tended to be effective, shifting to a particular style that suited a specific situation. Police executives commonly used two styles with great frequency. More than three-fourths (78 percent) of the executives tended to use participating-selling or telling-selling combinations.

Today the management process in a police setting is affected by the administrator's management style, the people being managed, and the situation. Therefore, one's management style must be flexible. The style a commander uses at the scene of a hostage situation should be much different from that used by a supervisor at a shoplifting scene. A less experienced employee requires a more authoritarian style of management than does a more experienced employee. Management style is always contingent on the situation and the people being managed.[4]

Observable Skills of Good Managers

In addition to assuming several roles and using several management styles, the police executive must develop certain basic management skills. First is *technical* skill, which involves specialized knowledge, analytical ability, and facility in the use of tools and techniques of the specific discipline. This is the skill most easily trained for. Examples in policing include budgeting, computer usage, and fundamental knowledge of some specialized equipment, such as radar or breathalyzer machines. Second is the *human* skill, which is the executive's ability to work effectively as a group member and build cooperation. This includes being sensitive to the needs and feelings of others, tolerating ambiguity, and being able to empathize with different views and cultures. Finally, *conceptual* skills involve coordinating and integrating all the activities and interests of the organization into a common objective: in other words, being able to translate knowledge into action.[5]

These skills can be taught just as other skills can. This proves that good administrators are not simply born but can be trained in the classroom and can learn by practicing the skills on the job.

Police Executives

Prior to examining the role and functions of contemporary police executives, we digress a bit and consider how persons are selected for these positions. Given the obvious responsibilities put on those occupying these positions, the means employed to test applicants or to promote individuals become important.

Promoting and Hiring the Best: The Assessment Center

Because a person has been functioning effectively at one level in an organization does not guarantee that he or she will perform effectively at a higher level. For several reasons, many excellent "street cops" have been unsuccessful after being promoted to higher positions. Perhaps they wanted to remain one of the troops and could not maintain the personal distance, perspective, or disciplinary authority needed at times. Or perhaps they could not see the big picture but still identified most strongly with favorite assignments (for example, after being promoted to deputy chief, an officer who had worked in and strongly identified with the investigative division wanted to provide disproportionate resources to this division). For these reasons, every reasonable means must be utilized to select the best person for the job while identifying those who do not have the ability, temperament, or desire for it.

To obtain the most capable people for executive positions in policing—and to avoid personnel, liability, and other kinds of problems that can arise from poor personnel choices—the assessment center method has surfaced as an elaborate yet efficacious means of hiring and promoting personnel. This method, which originated in Germany during World War I and is now used increasingly to select people for all management or supervisory ranks, may include interviews; psychological tests; in-basket exercises; management tasks; group discussions; simulations of interviews with subordinates, the public, and news media; fact-finding exercises; oral presentation exercises; and written communication exercises.[6]

First, behaviors important to the successful performance of the position are identified. Job descriptions listing responsibilities and skills should exist for all executive, middle management, and supervisory positions (such as chief, captain, lieutenant, sergeant, and so on). Then each candidate's abilities and skill levels should be evaluated using several of the techniques mentioned. (*Note:* Unlike local police chiefs, sheriffs are normally elected, not hired or promoted into their position; thus, the assessment center is of little use for that position.)

Individual and group role-playing provide a hands-on atmosphere during the selection process. For example, candidates may be required to perform in simulated police-community problems (such as having candidates conduct a "meeting" to hear concerns of local minority groups), react to a major incident (such as having candidates explain what they will do and in what order in a simulated shooting or riot situation), hold a news briefing, or participate in other such exercises. They may be given an in-basket situation where they take the role of the new chief or captain who receives an abundance of paperwork, policies, and problems to be prioritized and dealt with in a prescribed amount of time. Writing abilities may also be evaluated. For example, candidates may be given 30 minutes to develop a use-of-force policy for a hypothetical or real police agency. This type of exercise not only illustrates candidates' written communications skills and understanding of the technical side of police work but also shows how they think cognitively and build a case.

During each exercise, several assessors analyze candidates' behavior and perform some type of evaluation; and when the assessment center process ends, they submit their individual rating information to the person making the hiring or promotional decision. Typically selected because they have held the position for which candidates are now vying, assessors must not only know the types of problems and duties incumbent in the position but also should be keen observers of human behavior.

Although operating assessment centers is obviously more costly than using conventional testing procedures, they are well worth the extra investment. As with other occupations, in policing "what goes around, comes around." Monies invested at the early stages of a hiring or promotional process to avoid selecting the wrong person can save untold dollars and problems for many years to come. Good executives, middle managers, and supervisors make fewer mistakes and are probably sued less often.

The Responsibilities of the Police Manager

What are the actual duties of a contemporary police manager? Ronald Lynch stated the primary tasks simply yet directly, saying that police managers

> listen, talk, write, confer, think, decide—about men, money, materials, methods, facilities—in order to plan, organize, direct, coordinate, and control their research service, production, public relations, employee relations, and all other activities so that they may more effectively serve the citizens to whom they are responsible.[7]

Contemporary police managers certainly are not without their problems. Many police administrators see their primary duties as involving internal personnel matters and see themselves as being personnel managers who happen to wear a uniform. Many such managers forgot long ago how to process a DUI arrest, but they know quite well how to investigate and discipline an officer.

Chiefs or sheriffs in a 10-person agency face the same problems and expectations as their big-city counterparts. The difference between managing large and small departments is a matter of scale. Executives of large departments have many of the same problems that executives of small departments have—just more of them. Yet the chief of a small department must perform the managerial duties as well as those of a working officer.

Chiefs of Police

Political and Community Expectations

The *chief of police* (also known as *commissioner* or *superintendent*) is generally considered to be one of the most influential and prestigious persons in local government. Indeed, in earlier times they often amassed great power and influenced the level of crime in a community. The use of participatory management, the advent of city managers and public safety directors, the attrition rate of police chiefs, the increased power of local personnel (or human relations) departments, and the influence of police unions, however, have eroded much of this traditional power in recent times. Furthermore, mayors, city managers and administrators, members of the agency, citizens, special-interest groups, and the media all have differing role expectations of the chief of police that often conflict.

The mayor or city manager likely believes that the chief of police should be an enlightened administrator whose responsibility is to promote departmental efficiency, reduce crime, improve service, and so on. Other, wiser mayors and managers will appreciate the chief who simply keeps the lid on while keeping morale high and citizens' complaints low. All too many mayors and managers view the police chief in much the same way as the owners of professional sports franchises often view their coaches: as scapegoats for not solving problems beyond their control.[8]

The mayor or city manager also may properly expect the chief to communicate with city management about police-related issues and to be part of the city management team; to communicate city management's policies to police personnel; to establish agency policies, goals, and objectives, and put them in writing; to develop an administrative system of managing people, equipment, and the budget in a professional and businesslike manner; to set a good example, both personally and professionally; to administer disciplinary action consistently and fairly when required; and to select personnel whose performance will ably and professionally adhere to the organization's objectives.

Members of the agency also have expectations of the chief executive and these expectations may differ from those of the mayor or manager. The rank and file may be less concerned with the city's wish for efficiency and cost-effectiveness than with a chief who will be their advocate, supporting them when necessary and representing the agency's interests when dealing with judges and prosecutors who may be indifferent or hostile. Citizens tend to expect the chief of police to provide efficient and cost-effective police services while keeping crime and tax rates down (often an area of built-in conflict) and preventing corruption and illegal use of force.

Special interest groups expect the chief to advocate policy positions that they favor. For example, Mothers Against Drunk Driving (MADD) insists on strong anti-DUI measures by the police and oppose any movement to reduce expenditures related to enforcing these measures. Finally, the media expect the chief to cooperate fully with their efforts to obtain fast and complete crime information. Some media organizations (in the author's personal experience and observation) have participated in a human version of a "feeding frenzy" for news at times, which can involve the chief in a lively or controversial news story when the opportunity presents itself.

Qualifications, Selection, and Tenure

Qualifications for the position of police chief vary widely, depending on the size of the agency and the region of the country. Small agencies, especially those in rural areas, may not have any minimum educational requirement for the job. In the early 1970s, the National Advisory Commission on Criminal Justice Standards and Goals surveyed police chiefs and their superiors to determine qualities believed to be essential for the job. Education was found to be an important consideration; many agencies' common requirement today is a high school education plus several years of experience as a police supervisor. Large and medium-size agencies frequently require a college education plus several years of progressively responsible police management experience.[9]

Police chief executives also need several types of important management skills. The National Advisory Commission asked police chiefs and their superiors to rate, on a scale of 1 to 10, the importance of 14 desirable management skills. The ability to motivate and control personnel and relate to the community received overall greater importance. A survey today would probably yield similar results. In fact, PERF asked almost 500 police chiefs to indicate the areas in which they needed more training for better decision making: They listed management, legal problems and issues, personnel management, the use of computers, and strategic planning as their priorities.[10]

Although it is perhaps more economical to select a police chief from within the organization, the debate as to whether it is better to promote from within or hire from outside will probably not be resolved soon; each method has obvious advantages and disadvantages. A study of police chiefs in the West both promoted from within and hired from outside indicated only one significant difference in qualification: educational attainment. The outsiders were more highly educated. No difference was found regarding background; attitudes; salary; tenure in current position or in policing; or size of agency, community, and current budget.[11]

Job security of police chiefs ranges from full civil service protection in a small percentage of agencies to appointment and removal at the discretion of the mayor or city manager. Increasingly, a term of office is fixed, such as in four- or five-year contracts. Traditionally, however, the tenure of police chiefs has been short. A federal study in the mid-1970s found that the average length in office by chiefs of police was 5.4 years.[12] Another PERF study in the mid-1980s found the average to be practically unchanged, 5.5 years. The average tenure of a metropolitan police chief has dropped from 5.5 years to between 3.5 and 4.5 years.[13] Those who are appointed from within the agency tend to have longer tenure than those appointed from outside.

This short tenure of police chiefs has several negative consequences. It prevents long-range planning, results in frequent new policies and administrative styles, and prohibits the development of the chief's political power base and local

ADMINISTRATORS IN ACTION

Survey Says Big-City Chiefs Are Better-Educated Outsiders

Police chiefs from large jurisdictions are more educated than ever and are more likely to be chosen from outside the agencies they head, but still spend less than five years in the position—about the same length of time served by their predecessors 20 years ago, according to survey data released recently by the Police Executive Research Forum.

The survey, which canvassed 358 city and county police chiefs in jurisdictions of 50,000 or more residents, was the first of its kind ever conducted by PERF . . .

PERF found that more than half of the chiefs reported that their predecessors served only five years or less in their positions. The average tenure for chiefs in jurisdictions larger than 500,000 was 4.9 years, the survey said, about the same as in 1975 and 1982, when in both years it was just over five years. . . .

"There's been the thought that police chief tenure has been declining because chiefs have become somewhat more [politically] vulnerable, and therefore, tenure has declined. It's probably declined somewhat, but it hasn't been a terribly dramatic shift," according to Jim Burack, PERF counsel.

However, a big shift has occurred in the willingness of local officials to look beyond their own police agencies when hiring a new police chief, Burack noted. . . .

PERF found that 43 percent of currently serving chiefs came from departments other than the one they now lead.

"There seems to be more of an openness today in accepting chiefs from outside the agency," Burack said.

In general, the chiefs said the most significant factors that led them to accept their current posts were "career advancement/promotion" opportunities (84 percent); "desire for greater challenge" (83 percent); "salary/benefit considerations" (69 percent); and "consideration of family members" (38 percent). Roughly one in four (26 percent) said they kept a jurisdiction's "political/social community climate (i.e., too liberal/conservative)" in mind as they made their decision. . . .

PERF found the chiefs' positions are still held overwhelmingly by white males. Ninety-nine percent of the chiefs polled were male; only two were women. Ten percent of the respondents were black, compared to more than 80 percent who were white.

Perhaps the most marked change over the years has been in the education level of police chiefs. In 1975, according to the IACP survey, only about 15 percent had bachelor's degrees, and a mere 4.3 percent had more advanced degrees. Now, 87 percent hold bachelor's degrees, while almost 47 percent have master's degrees, according to PERF. Nearly 5 percent have law degrees or doctoral-level degrees, the survey found.

The top categories of college degrees earned by police chiefs were criminology/justice administration/criminal justice (43 percent) and public policy/political science/government (26 percent). Just under 8 percent said they held business degrees.

Chiefs also are continuing to stay on top of developments in the profession through a variety of executive training programs, such as the one offered at the FBI Academy in Quantico, Va. Half of those polled said they had undergone leadership training at the FBI Academy. . . .

And chiefs indicated they received a lot of gratification from the job, with 44 percent saying they are "completely satisfied" with their current positions and another 49 percent indicating they were "somewhat satisfied." Asked if they'd still aspire to be a police chief "if you had it to do over again," 86 percent indicated that they would indeed.

Source: "Survey Says Big-City Chiefs Are Better-Educated Outsiders," *LEN,* April 30, 1998. Reprinted with permission from *Law Enforcement News,* John Jay College of Criminal Justice (CUNY), 555 W. 57th St., New York, NY 10019.

influence. In addition, the agency must expend financial and time resources to hire a new chief.

Across the country, police executives are in the eye of the storm. Rising crime, limited budgets, unionization, and conflicting public demands have caused many U.S. police executives to be heavily scrutinized. The toll has been high, with many of the nation's largest city police departments facing turmoil or turnover at the top during the 1990s.

Because of such political influence and control over police executives, city charters across the country began to be amended decades ago to insulate chiefs from politicians. Now the mood and temper of the public has changed. "There has to be civilian control of the police," asserted Patrick V. Murphy, director of the U.S. Conference of Mayors' police policy board and a former New York police commissioner.[14] This situation leaves chiefs with little job protection, however. Few chiefs are willing to battle various constituencies—city councils, unions, and various local organizations—to implement major reform without some job security.

The various community constituencies battle more viciously when chiefs attempt to implement major change, such as community policing, which unions and some officers might resist. The message being sent from chiefs is that, without some job protection, do not expect too much real reform or many long-tenured chiefs.[15]

Sheriffs

Contemporary Nature and Functions

Unfortunately, because of television and movie portrayals, much of the public perceives the county sheriff as a stupid, cruel, overweight, corrupt person wearing a Stetson hat and sunglasses while talking with a Southern drawl (see, e.g., *Smoky and the Bandit, Mississippi Burning, The Dukes of Hazzard, Walking Tall,* and many others). This image is both unfair and highly inaccurate. County sheriffs and their offices are dedicated to maintaining order while providing valuable services to unincorporated areas, operating detention facilities, and performing important civil process functions and other duties as delineated later.

The position of sheriff has a long tradition. Because sheriffs tend to be elected, most of them are aligned with a political party. Therefore, it is possible that the only qualification a person brings to the office is the ability to get votes. In some areas of the country, the sheriff's term of office is limited to two years with successive terms prohibited (thus, the office has been known to be rotated between the sheriff and undersheriff). In most counties, however, the sheriff has a four-year term of office and can be reelected. The sheriff enjoys no tenure guarantee, although the federal study referred to earlier found that sheriffs (averaging 6.7 years in office) had longer tenure in office than chiefs of police (5.4 years).[16] This politicization of the office of sheriff can obviously result in high turnover rates of personnel who do not have civil service protection. The uncertainty as to tenure is not conducive to long-range (strategic) planning.

Largely due to the political nature of the office, sheriffs tend to be older, less likely to have been promoted through the ranks of the agency, less likely to be college graduates, and less likely to have specialized training than police chiefs. Research has also found that sheriffs in small agencies have more difficulty with organizational problems (field activities, budget management) and that sheriffs in large agencies find dealing with local officials and planning and evaluation to be more troublesome. Because of the diversity of sheriff's offices throughout the country, it is difficult to describe a "typical" sheriff's department. Those offices run the gamut from the traditional, highly political, limited-service office to the modern, fairly nonpolitical, full-service police organization. It is possible, however, to list functions commonly associated with the sheriff's office.

1. Serving and/or implementing civil processes (divorce papers, liens, evictions, garnishments and attachments, and other civil duties, such as extradition and transportation of prisoners).
2. Collecting certain taxes and conducting real estate sales (usually for nonpayment of taxes) for the county.
3. Performing routine order-maintenance duties by enforcing state statutes and county ordinances, arresting offenders, and performing traffic and criminal investigations.
4. Serving as bailiff of the courts.
5. Maintaining and operating the county correctional institutions.[17]

Other general duties are found, of course, from one region to another.

Sheriffs often see themselves as police officials and regard their jail administration duties as a liability. Sheriffs are frequently untrained and uninterested in corrections management, although that is one of their primary functions. Sheriffs must respond to numerous problems. An example is the problem of what to do with prisoners released because jails are overcrowded.

Rating Chief Executive Performance

How good is your police chief or sheriff? The answer probably depends on whom you ask. To some, the police chief executive or CEO is the best thing that ever happened to the community or county; to others, he or she is the worst thing. Rating the CEO's performance in this complex job involves several potential "traps." CEOs are human; they do make mistakes, but citizens' perceptions of them and their performance are often wrong. Therefore, it is difficult to assess accurately how the CEO is performing; no litmus test or simple fill-in-the-boxes exercise exists. Several broad, general guidelines can be applied, however, when evaluating these CEOs.

Inappropriate Evaluation Criteria

As pointed out by Jerald Vaughn, former police chief and author of a report for PERF,[18] inappropriate criteria can be used to evaluate CEOs, such as the following:

1. *Personal popularity.* The longer the CEO's tenure, the greater the chance that people within and outside the department will have complaints about something the CEO did or did not do.

2. *Department morale.* Morale is a fragile thing. Peter Drucker wrote that morale does not mean that "people get along together"; the test is performance, not conformance.[19] Like soldiers and other workers in bureaucratic organizations, police officers can become chronic and notorious complainers. The "grapevine" normally keeps people stirred up, and a certain amount of griping will occur even when things are running smoothly. Thus, the morale of a department is not necessarily the result of the CEO's leadership.

3. *Controversy surrounding the CEO.* Some CEOs may become involved in controversial local issues. Controversy and conflict can be productive, causing people to challenge old ideas and methods. CEOs are highly visible and influential; they should be allowed to speak out and provide leadership on matters that concern public safety.

4. *A rising crime rate.* The former chief of Madison, Wisconsin, David Couper, observed that social and economic factors have a large influence on community crime levels.[20] To blame the chief executive for the crime rate is to miss the point. When a serious crime rate or public concern about crime exists, however, the chief executive should develop programs and strategies to combat it rather than merely watching crime statistics soar and engage in mere bean counting.

5. *Single issues: "Run the bum out of town".* Occasionally, a single, critical event or issue, such as a police beating or shooting of a citizen or promotional policies, will arise that can mushroom into a call to oust the CEO.

Sometimes the chief executive survives the incident if his or her total performance is reviewed. On other occasions, the passion of the moment may prevail. Indeed, in some incidents the chief may deserve to be relieved of command; however, more often a multidimensional review of the chief's total performance should be made. The ouster of the chief does not ensure that the basic problem causing the upheaval will be eliminated.

Appropriate Evaluation Criteria

A police executive's evaluation should focus only on qualities, characteristics, and behavior required to do the job. Honesty and integrity are probably the chief's most important qualities, followed by leadership effectiveness. The direction of the department, its commitment to professional and ethical standards, and its basic values emanate from the chief's leadership role. The chief's ability to motivate people without shoving them and to inspire people both inside and outside the department should also be considered. Any assessment of the chief executive must consider leadership effectiveness. The chief's ability to be a good follower and take a subordinate position to the mayor and city manager/council is also important. It is important that the chief know where the lines are drawn: when it is time to quit leading and start following.

The management skills of CEOs should be considered in an evaluation. CEOs manage a significant amount of resources—human and financial, equipment, and physical facilities. CEOs must make timely and responsible decisions, as well as realize the impact and legal ramifications of those decisions. The chief executive must also delegate authority and decision making to others rather than taking on too much, which often results in a sluggish operation. Finally, a chief executive must be innovative and creative in thinking. Today's CEO must be willing to keep up with the challenges facing law enforcement and the need to move the agency into a new era of research, experimentation, and risk taking.[21]

Several other areas of the chief executive's performance must be evaluated. The first relates to the department's values. Under the CEO's leadership, do the department's values reflect a commitment to the rights of individuals and its employees? The department's view toward the use of force should be considered. Does the CEO manage force carefully and aggressively to ensure that the public is not subjected to unlawful or unwarranted physical force by police? Written directives are a key to the organization's foundation. Does the CEO require the agency to have clear policies, rules, and procedures to guide employees? Does the CEO see that those directives are constantly updated and enforced fairly and consistently? Has the CEO introduced or implemented crime strategies to make the community safer?

The labor climate of the organization is another valid area for consideration when evaluating the chief's performance. This is a very difficult area for today's police executive. Civil service, unions, appeal boards, the courts, and the changing profile of today's police officer have made managing labor relations a constant challenge.[22]

NJSP "Profiling" Uproar Costs Chief His Job

After nearly a year of complaints by civil rights groups and black community leaders, the latest fallout from allegations that the New Jersey State Police engaged in illegal racial profiling has claimed the career of the agency's superintendent, Col. Carl A. Williams, who was fired Feb. 28, just days after he asserted that marijuana and cocaine traffickers are disproportionately members of minority groups.

Gov. Christine Todd Whitman, who dismissed the man she had appointed in 1994 after a decorated career, nonetheless defended the agency, reiterating her belief that there was no widespread racial profiling practiced by the State Police. The Governor said of Williams: "I don't think he's a racist, but I don't believe he saw how insensitive his comments were. That's part of the problem."

Minority Musings

The remarks were made during an interview with *The Newark Star-Ledger,* in which Williams ridiculed the notion that race should not be considered as a factor when searching for possible drug couriers.

"Two weeks ago the President of the United States went to Mexico about drugs," Williams told the newspaper. "He didn't go to Ireland. He didn't go to England. Today, with this drug problem, the drug problem is cocaine or marijuana. It is mostly a member of a minority group that's involved with that."

Critics who have long called for the removal of Williams, including black state legislators, religious leaders and civil rights advocates, hailed Whitman's action as a step in the right direction.

William Buckman, a Mount Holly attorney whose case led to a 1996 finding by a Gloucester County judge that black drivers were stopped nearly five times as often as white drivers on the southern half of the New Jersey Turnpike, said only Whitman or the Justice Department can force the State Police to adopt the kind of changes necessary. "Race is a major component of New Jersey State Police thinking," he told *The New York Times.*

The dismissal of Williams came just weeks after the agency's own documents revealed that African Americans constituted nearly two-thirds of 109 arrests made during the first two months of 1997. While the State Police tried to put a positive spin on the statistics, pointing out that nearly all of the arrests ended in convictions, it did little to convince civil libertarians that the agency had not been targeting black motorists. . . .

Allegations of racial profiling have been as vigorously denied by the State Police over the years as they have been asserted by members of the black community. The issue moved to the frontburner last year after a number of incidents, including the first-ever lawsuit brought by an active member of the force alleging that the agency is involved in the illegal practice, and the shooting of four unarmed minority men in their van by two white troopers on the turnpike on April 23. . . .

Two former troopers had testified that they had been trained and coached to make race-based profile stops through a Drug Interdiction Training Unit that was formed in 1987 to teach techniques for discovering drugs in vehicles. The unit was disbanded in 1992. "The utter failure of the State Police hierarchy to monitor and control a crackdown program like DITU or investigate the many claims of institutional discrimination manifests its indifference, if not acceptance," the judge concluded....

Aggressive methods taught by the DITU have been passed along to younger troopers, they said. In a maneuver called "lights across the highway," for example, the trooper parks the cruiser perpendicular to the flow of traffic, with the headlights on high beam. In the instant that the light floods the interior of a passing car, the occupant's complexion, features and clothing are easily identified. "It's a relatively quick decision-making process," a trooper said. "Oh, there's a good stop. He looks good!" ...

Source: "NJSP 'Profiling' Uproar Costs Chief His Job," *LEN,* February 28, 1999. Reprinted with permission from *Law Enforcement News,* John Jay College of Criminal Justice (CUNY), 555 W. 57th St., New York, NY 10019.

Finally, the CEO's understanding of where the department stands with the community and the public's major concerns should be evaluated. Knowing community perceptions should be a paramount concern of the chief executive. No other sector of government in our society has more frequent and direct contact with the public than the police. As Darlene Walker and Richard Richardson observed,

> Whatever the citizen thinks of the police, they can hardly be ignored. Whereas other police bureaucrats are often lost from the public's view, locked in rooms filled with typewriters and anonymity, police officers are out in the world—on the sidewalks and in the streets and shopping malls, cruising, strolling, watching, as both state protectors and state repressors.[23]

Public opinion surveys provide vital information and feedback to the police executive concerning public perception of officer performance and the department's standing and communication with the public. The mood of the public should be a vital consideration when making public policy decisions.[24]

Mid-Level Managers: Captains and Lieutenants

Few police administration books contain information about the middle-management members of a police department, the captains and lieutenants. This is unfortunate because they are too numerous and too powerful within police organizations to ignore. Opinions vary toward these mid-management personnel, however, as we discuss later.

Leonhard Fuld, one of the early progressive police administration contributors, said in 1909 that the captain is one of the most important officers in the organization. Fuld believed that the position had two broad duties—policing and administration. The captain was held responsible for preserving the public peace and protecting life and property within the precinct. Fuld defined the captain's administrative duties as being of three kinds: clerical, janitorial, and supervisory.[25]

Normally, captains and lieutenants are commissioned officers, with the position of captain being second in rank to the executive manager. Captains have authority over all officers of the agency below the chief or sheriff and are responsible only to those higher ranking officers. Lieutenants, who report to captains, are in charge of sergeants and all officers within assigned responsibility. Captains and lieutenants may perform the following duties:

- Inspect assigned operations
- Review and make recommendations on reports
- Help develop plans
- Prepare work schedules
- Oversee records and equipment
- Oversee recovered or confiscated property
- Enforce all laws and orders[26]

One problem of police organizations is that they tend to become top-heavy. Such organizations, having too many leaders and not enough followers, often do not function well, because this structure can generate autocracy in its worst form, stifle creative thought or suggestions from the lower ranks, frustrate communication, and pose a hindrance to accomplishing goals and objectives. Top administrators, the people who make the key decisions, must be close to the point at which the job is accomplished. Middle management, including captains and lieutenants, often poses a major barrier between the administrator and the officer in the field.

Too often, middle managers become glorified paper pushers, especially in the present climate that requires a myriad of reports, budgets, grants, and so on. The agency should determine what managerial services are essential and whether lieutenants are needed to perform them. Some communities, such as Kansas City, Missouri, have eliminated the rank of lieutenant. They found that this move had no negative consequences and some positive effects.[27]

Obviously, when a multilayered bureaucracy is created, a feudal kingdom and several fiefdoms will occupy the building. As Richard Holden observed, however, "if feudalism was so practical, it would not have died out in the Middle Ages."[28] It is important to remember that the two crucial elements to organizational effectiveness are top administrators and operational personnel. As stated, middle management can pose a threat to the agency by creating a barrier between these two primary elements. Perhaps a lesson may be learned from the Roman Catholic Church, which serves many millions and employs many thousands of people with only five levels in its hierarchy.[29] Research has shown an inverse relationship between the size of the hierarchy in an organization and its effectiveness.[30] Normally, the closer the administrator is to the operations, the more effective the agency.

First-Line Supervisors: The Role of Patrol Sergeant

Seeking the Gold Badge

Some time during the career of a patrol officer (provided that he or she acquires the minimal years of experience), the opportunity for career advancement is presented—a chance to wear the sergeant's "gold badge." This is a difficult position to occupy because at this middle level, first-line supervisors are caught between upper management and the rank-and-file officers. People who can successfully work with yet command people are in short supply and long demand.

Because most rank-and-file officers will retire with the same rank—patrol officer—at which they entered the occupation, the initial promotional opportunity to attain the rank of sergeant is normally attractive. Practically no lateral entry from agency to agency exists at the lower ranks; therefore, patrol officers are not able to transfer to another police agency with a promotion. Their promotional opportunities are limited to their present agency, and the waiting period for sergeant's vacancies to arise through retirement or otherwise, especially in smaller agencies, can seem interminable.

Intracity and departmental politics certainly influence the promotional process: Mayors, city managers, and police administrators have been known to predetermine who will be promoted even before testing and interviewing begin. Another administrative consideration that affects promotion decisions is the knowledge that good patrol officers do not automatically become good mid-level supervisors. Many good patrol officers promoted to the rank of sergeant cannot divorce themselves from being one of the troops and are unable to flex their supervisory muscles when necessary. In short, a good sergeant must wear two hats, one as a people-oriented, democratic leader with concern for subordinates and the other as a task-oriented and authoritarian leader who must make difficult decisions to which subordinates may object. Unfortunately, many supervisors (within and outside of the police field) today believe that their subordinates are motivated more by the desire for financial rewards than anything else. Over the years, however, a number of studies, including the Hawthorne studies mentioned previously, have shown that intrinsic rewards, such as appreciation, sympathetic help, and being made to feel a part of the organization, take precedence over income.

Fuld argued in 1909 that when considering the first-line supervisor, the ideal sergeant needs to possess four qualifications: (1) the ability to write and prepare reports, (2) a thorough knowledge of police business, (3) a capacity for being discrete and intelligent, and (4) a rudimentary knowledge of criminal law.[31]

Getting That First Promotion

It is not uncommon for 60 to 65 percent or more of those who are eligible to do so to take the test for promotion; and it is common for more than half of all persons promoted to sergeant in an agency to be persons working outside the patrol division and not as patrol officers at the time. Senior administrators believe that this is better than bringing the patrol officer's mentality to the sergeant's role. Competition for the sergeant's openings in most departments is obviously quite keen, but the material rewards are actually quite slight. Those who are promoted often lose opportunities for overtime that are available to patrol officers. Conventional wisdom among many officers is that their immediate supervisors take home less money than they do. Still, the opportunity to test for sergeant normally draws a crowd. Many officers test simply for the experience, because of pressure from peers, out of curiosity, or just to get off the streets for a short while.

Becoming a sergeant in a good-sized U.S. police agency is governed by departmental and civil service procedures that are intended to guarantee legitimacy and impartiality in the process. As mentioned earlier, sponsorship or political pull may still have some influence, although it may not be the blatant "hook" of past decades.[32] Officers are often told it is best to rotate into different assignments to gain exposure to a variety of police functions and supervisors before testing for sergeant. The promotional system, then, favors officers who are skilled at test taking as well as those skilled at cultivating relationships outside the patrol division.[33]

Sergeants are chosen from a final rank-ordered list of names often based on scores from written and oral tests as well as such factors as years of experience, minority status, supervisory ratings, military experience, and departmental commendations. The testing process often is regarded by officers as a capricious gauntlet that tests inappropriate skills and knowledge, gives unfair advantage to certain groups (e.g., women, minorities, college graduates, veterans), and emphasizes "trick" or subtle questions. The test is also seen as a mildly embarrassing process that dishonors more than it honors. As Van Maanen observed, however, "One could hardly expect a favorable impression of a testing procedure that screens out over 95 percent of its takers."[34]

Transition to Sergeant

After becoming a sergeant, several dynamics at work make the transition difficult. The new sergeant confronts a solitary process with little, if any, formal training in the new position and must therefore seek advice and counsel. New sergeants are often given unpopular relief assignments with few officers that the sergeant knows and no officers permanently assigned to him or her. Thus, the sergeant is able to develop little loyalty from subordinates.

The new sergeant eventually adapts to the role and develops individual characteristics that the officers he or she supervises come to know well.

Distribution and Deployment of Patrol Forces

Police administrators realize that the largest, most costly, and most visible function in their agency is that of patrol. Yet the patrol function often receives the least amount of planning or analysis. Patrol beats, for example, are often designed by using convenient streets, railroad tracks, rivers, and so forth, rather than by thoughtful planning and analysis of officer workload by geographical area. Few police agencies pay regular attention to evaluating and adjusting patrol plans to meet service demands. Instead, patrol is often the first division in which an administrator seeks to reduce personnel in order to enhance specialized units or to create new programs. This practice often leaves the patrol division in need of personnel and often results in morale problems and unnecessary delays in responding to calls for service (CFS). Consequently, supervisors are left to manage the demands of patrol by reacting to crises rather than through thoughtful planning.

An important part of police leadership lies in how to best allocate resources. The methods, issues, and considerations involved in resource allocation are discussed next.

Determining the Size of the Patrol Force

The collection and analysis of data are the foundation of proper patrol deployment. Unfortunately, as we have mentioned earlier, most police agencies do not adhere to such rational and scientific approaches. Three crude methods are used by police departments to determine resource needs.[35]

Intuitive: This method involves basically educated guesswork based on the experience and judgment of police managers. It is probably the most commonly used method for small agencies, where the numbers of incidents and officers available are so few that more analytical analyses may not be necessary.

Workload: This method requires comprehensive information, including standards of expected performance, community expectations, and the prioritization of police activities. Although rarely used by an entire police agency, it is most often used for determining resource needs for patrol or specific programs such as crime prevention.

Comparative: This is a commonly used method in policing in which agencies make decisions based on a comparison of agencies by numbers of officers per 1,000 residents. Data to be used are available in the *Uniform Crime Reports* (UCR), published annually by the Federal Bureau of Investigation (FBI). The UCR provides numbers of full-time, sworn police officers per 1,000 residents in the United States in communities of all sizes.

Another method for determining allocation needs is to set an objective related to the amount of time an agency wants officers to be committed to CFS and available for other functions. There is no established guideline, but agencies often set an objective that would restrict officers' time that is committed to CFS at 30 to

40 percent of total time available per shift.[36] The following is a guide for agencies when determining allocation needs using this formula:

Step 1: Set an objective for patrol performance (e.g., 30 to 40 percent committed to CFS).

Step 2: Select a time period to be analyzed.

Step 3: Determine CFS workload for this time period.

Step 4: Calculate the number of units needed based on the workload and the selected objective.

Step 5: Calculate the number of on-duty officers needed per shift.

Step 6: Multiply by the relief factor to obtain the total number of officers needed.

To illustrate, Table 4.1 shows the basic data for calculating the number of patrol officers needed in a city's patrol force. Assume that, after discussion of how busy patrol units should be, and given that the agency is engaged in the community oriented policing and problem-solving (COPPS) strategy (discussed in Chapter 3), it is determined that there should be the following objective: "There should be sufficient units on duty so that the average unit utilization on CFS will not exceed 30 percent." Assume further that a mix of 70 percent one-officer and 30 percent two-officer units will be established for each shift. The data were collected during a four-week (28-day) period.

TABLE 4.1   An Example of Data for Determining Patrol Force Size

	MIDNIGHTS	*DAYS*	*EVENINGS*
1. Workload data			
Calls for service	1,027	1,614	2,059
Average time (minutes)	32 min.	28	33
Assists	225	273	463
Average time (minutes)	22 min.	20	18
Traffic accidents	109	129	150
Average time (minutes)	63 min.	58	60
2. Hours of work for entire 4-week period	745	969	1,421
Average hours of work per shift	26.6	34.6	50.8
3. Units needed for 30%	11	14	21
4. Number of 1-officer units	8	10	15
Number of 2-officer units	4	4	6
5. Number of officers needed per shift	14	18	27
6. Total number of officers needed (relief factor = 2.2)	31	40	59

Source: U.S. Department of Justice, National Institute of Justice, *Patrol Deployment* (Washington, D.C.: U.S. Government Printing Office, 1985), p. 34.

The first section of Table 4.1 shows the *total* number of calls for service, assists, and traffic accidents by shift for the four weeks, along with the average times for these activities for each shift. With these activities and average times, the total amount of work for the patrol force amounts to about 769 hours for the midnight to 8 A.M. shift; 969 hours for the 8 A.M. to 4 P.M. shift; and 1,421 hours for the 4 P.M. to midnight shift. Since a 28-day period was being studied, the average work *per shift* amounted to 26.6 hours, 34.6 hours, and 50.8 hours, respectively. (As an example, for midnights, $1,027 \times 32 = 32,864$; $225 \times 22 = 4,950$; $109 \times 63 = 6867$, for a grand total of 44,681 minutes, or 745 hours, of work; 745 hours of work divided by 28 shifts = 26.6 hours of average work per shift.)

To calculate the number of patrol units needed to meet the desired objective—average unit utilization on CFS will not exceed 30 percent—we use the following formula:

$$\frac{Average\ Hours\ of\ Work\ Per\ Shift}{(Shift\ Length)\ (Unit\ Utilization)} = Number\ of\ Units\ Needed$$

Again, using the midnight shift as an example, the calculation would be as follows:

$$\frac{26.6\ hours}{(8\ hours)\ (30\%)} = 11.08\ units$$

The answer must be rounded to 11 units, since fractions of units are not possible. Similar calculations for the day and evening shifts give results of 14 units and 21 units, respectively. Table 4.1 shows the officers needed for these shifts under the decision of a 70 percent/30 percent split between one-officer and two-officer units.

The final line in Table 4.1 multiplies the number of officers needed by the department's relief factor of 2.2 (to cover officers' absences due to days off, sick leave, vacations, training, and so on) to give a total of 35 officers for the midnight shift, 42 officers for the day shift, and 59 officers for the evening shift. A total of 136 officers would be required to meet the objective of an average 30 percent unit utilization. If an objective other than unit utilization had been selected, the same steps would have been followed to determine the number of units needed, but the calculations would have been different.

The 30 percent unit utilization objective is subject to criticism, as there is no universal rule to guide the choice of a percentage. The use of a relief factor of 2.2 is also subject to debate. Another commonly accepted relief factor is 1.66 for determining the number of police officers that are needed to staff a shift annually.

Workload Analysis

The primary objective of a workload analysis is to provide information concerning patterns of service demand for the purpose of determining allocation needs, developing efficient and effective shift schedules, and developing deployment schemes. Allocations can be attained by calculating for every day the percentage of the total workload occurring during each shift and then assigning a comparable percentage of available officers to shifts. The same process can be used for distributing personnel in each area. Table 4.2 shows an example of two plans for allocating patrol resources.

Option one in Table 4.2 is the traditional approach to deployment used by many agencies, with equal staffing on all three shifts. Under option two (assuming that 20 officers are sufficient for the evening shift), the department reduces the total number of officers required by matching allocations to CFS demands. The savings are obvious. As a bonus, the surplus of officers can either be transferred to an understaffed section of the department or redeployed as a special operations unit for enhancing crime prevention and directed patrol activities.[37]

Deployment by Time and Location

Two of the most important factors in allocating personnel are location and time. The location of problems helps police to divide the community into geographic beats or divisions of approximately equal workload. By analyzing the varying times of incidents, appropriate shifts may be determined. Mobility and geographic barriers are also important factors when considering allocation needs.

Table 4.3 shows how personnel workload can be determined by CFS per shift by calculating for every day the percentage of the total workload occurring during each shift and then assigning a comparable percentage of the available officers to the shifts.

Figure 4.2 shows an example of CFS demands for each hour of the day, and Figure 4.3 is a sample of CFS workload demands by day of the week, the latter showing days of the week broken down into 168 hours.

TABLE 4.2   Two Plans for Allocating Patrol Resources

| | | DEPLOYMENT OPTIONS | |
| | Percentage of Total Calls for Service | Option One | Option Two |
SHIFT	by Shift	Equal Staffing	Efficiency[a]
Midnight	20	20	9
Day	35	20	16
Evening	45	20	20
Total personnel deployed[b]		60	45

[a]The efficiency option assumes that the 20 officers assigned to the evening shift are sufficient to respond to all calls for service and provide adequate preventive patrol during the peak demand period.

[b]This total reflects only the number of officers deployed and not the total complement actually needed, because the relief factor was not considered.

Source: Adapted from U.S. Department of Justice, National Institute of Law Enforcement and Criminal Justice, *Improving Patrol Productivity, Volume I: Routine Patrol* by Gay et al. (Washington, D.C.: U.S. Government Printing Office, July 1977), pp. 26–29.

TABLE 4.3   Sample Distribution of Personnel by Hourly Workload

HOURS BY SHIFT	CALLS FOR SERVICE	PERCENTAGE OF TOTAL HOURLY WORKLOAD	PERCENTAGE OF PERSONNEL ASSIGNED
0700–0759	58	2.11	Day Shift
0800–0859	77	2.80	
0900–0959	90	3.28	29.27
1000–1059	100	3.64	
1100–1159	107	3.90	
1200–1259	117	4.26	
1300–1359	123	4.48	
1400–1459	132	4.80	
1500–1559	158	5.75	Evening Shift
1600–1659	153	5.57	
1700–1759	165	6.01	47.03
1800–1859	172	6.26	
1900–1959	161	5.86	
2000–2059	164	5.97	
2100–2159	164	5.97	
2200–2259	155	5.64	
2300–2359	159	5.79	Midnight Shift
2400–0059	118	4.30	
0100–0159	101	3.68	23.68
0200–0259	90	3.28	
0300–0359	60	2.18	
0400–0459	45	1.64	
0500–0559	37	1.35	
0600–0659	40	1.46	
Total	2,746	99.98*	99.98*

*Total does not equal 100% because of rounding.

Source: U.S. Department of Justice, National Institute of Justice, *Patrol Deployment* (Washington, D.C.: U.S. Government Printing Office, 1985), p. 29.

Car Plans

After patrol personnel have been assigned according to time and location needs, the supervisor must deploy them to beats or patrol car districts. The car plan in use will normally be dictated by the number of officers on duty and available for field patrol. If two-officer units are used, adjustments will of course be necessary.

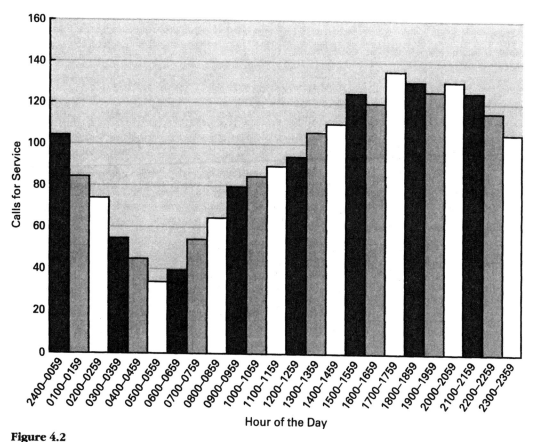

Figure 4.2

Sample 24-hour graph of workload distribution. *Source:* U.S. Department of
Justice, National Institute of Justice, *Patrol Deployment* (Washington, D.C.:
U.S. Government Printing Office, 1985), p. 27.

Using one-officer units, a nine-car plan will be required to cover nine beats, unless
two of the beats use two-officer patrol units, in which case 10 officers would be
required. Patrol districts should ideally be grouped into beats so that each will
contain as nearly as practicable an equal percentage of the total police work. Each
beat in a 10-car plan would theoretically contain 10 percent of the work, each
beat in a 5-car plan would ideally contain 20 percent of the work, and so on.

Use of Computer Models

Computer-based analysis and allocation models assist administrators who often
struggle with shift-related issues such as fixed versus rotating schedules, one- versus two-officer cars, and compressed schedules. These automated systems are
capable of performing a number of staff distribution functions and can simplify
the process of determining allocation needs and designing beats. The Statistical

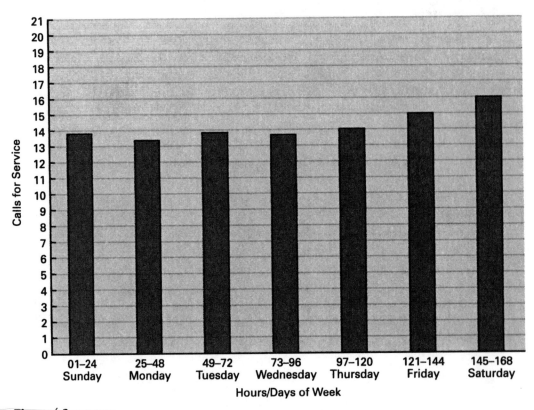

Figure 4.3

Sample workload by day of week. (*Source:* U.S. Department of Justice,
National Institute of Justice, *Patrol Deployment* (Washington, D.C.: U.S.
Government Printing Office, 1985), p. 28.

Package for Social Sciences (SPSS) can also be used to analyze workload and
develop schedules. This package is personal computer based, inexpensive, and
simple to run with some training.

Shift Scheduling

General Recommendations

The question of whether to work around-the-clock shifts is not an option for the
police. Police organizations are bound by their 24-hour responsibility to public
problems to deploy officers to beats in shifts. What is most important is that
departments develop shifts that assure the safety and longevity of officers and
provide efficient and effective services to the public. Primary concerns are the
physical and emotional health and productivity of officers. O'Neill and Cushing[38]
provided the following advice for administrators when creating shifts:

1. A system of steady shifts with selection based, at least in part, on fair and equitable criteria such as seniority grade. Shift selection could provide for 75 percent of the positions to be filled by seniority and 25 percent of the positions filled at management's discretion.

2. A steady midnight shift in which the work week is limited to four consecutive days. Officers' court dates would be scheduled for the day preceding their first night of work, and this would be considered a work day.

3. Redeployment of personnel so that only the required minimum number of officers and supervisors are on duty from 2 A.M. to 6 A.M. This would more accurately reflect the demand for service by assigning more officers to shifts where they are needed most.

4. In general, no changing of shifts within a time period should be permitted without making allowances for proper rest. There should be no changing of shifts for purely disciplinary reasons. Officers should be permitted to bid for another shift at least twice during a year, and vacancies should be announced.

Traditionally, the patrol division has utilized a three eight-hour shift plan. For example, day shift officers would be assigned to work from 8 A.M. to 4 P.M., "swing" or evening shift officers work from 4 P.M. to 12 A.M., and night ("graveyard") shift officers are deployed from 12 A.M. to 8 A.M. In recent years, however, alternative 9-, 10-, and 12-hour shifts have become popular. Regardless of the shift schedule that is employed, police administrators should ensure that it provides proper staffing levels and supervision and improves patrol effectiveness.

Permanent versus Rotating Shifts

The issue of permanent versus rotating shifts has been argued at length in police management literature, and both methods have advantages and disadvantages. The advantages of having personnel work a permanent or fixed shift include its simplicity of scheduling, assignment of officers according to workload, fewer physiological problems for personnel, fringe benefits for senior officers (such as better choices of days off), easier court scheduling, and the fact that studies have long indicated that most officers prefer to work fixed shifts.[39] Another reason for giving strong consideration to permanent shift assignments concerns the requirements of COPPS. Shift rotation can greatly frustrate the officers' attempts to solve neighborhood problems on their beats; thus, frequent officer rotation can be a death knell for COPPS's effectiveness.

The disadvantages of fixed shifts include the time-honored tradition of placing rookie officers on the graveyard shift (thus, it has the greatest number of least experienced personnel), stress on younger officers who may be assigned to higher workload shifts, and officers lacking the experience gained by working various shifts.

Rotating shifts offer some advantages, however, including giving officers an opportunity to experience the varying kinds of work from shift to shift and having different times of day off for their personal or family needs. But disadvantages of rotating shifts include disruptions in officers' home lives and their pursuit of higher education as well as fatigue. The physical adjustment to rotating shifts may be the equivalent of jet lag. Because rotating shift work has been blamed for officers' poor performance, bad attitudes, absenteeism, and accidents, many administrators favor the fixed schedule.

Research on shift work suggests that administrators should carefully weigh the benefits and hazards of various shift schemes. Human beings are naturally day oriented or diurnal in their activity patterns. Shift work disrupts the body's complex biological clock, known as the circadian rhythm, and can result in stress-related illnesses, fatigue-induced accidents, family crisis, and lower life expectancy. There is a higher probability of accidents and errors when officers are fatigued during shifts.

There are two principal forms of shift scheduling. The first is a flat system of scheduling, in which an equal number of officers is assigned to each shift. The obvious problem with this type of scheduling is that demands vary across shifts. Most jurisdictions may find the weekend late evening and early morning hours to be the busiest, thus presenting the most danger to officers. The day shift may also be busy but will often involve noninvestigative theft and burglary reports or traffic- and accident-related incidents that present little threat to officers. Also, a high percentage of typical day shift calls can be assigned to differential responses (defined earlier).

Compressed Work Schedules

Compressed work schedules have gained considerable momentum recently, with the strong support of police employees and labor organizations. The trend for law enforcement began in the 1970s, with many agencies moving toward 4/10 plans (officers working four days per week, 10 hours per day).

Benefits and concerns appear with each type of compressed work schedule. Of utmost concern to administrators who are considering a compressed schedule is ensuring that the schedule meets the needs of both the department and employees. Following are some of the types of compressed work schedules that have been implemented and tested by agencies across the United States:

5-day, 8-hour schedule [5-2 (8)]: The 5-2 (8) work schedule remains the most commonly used by police agencies. In some jurisdictions, an overlapping 7 P.M. to 3 A.M. shift is added to assist evening (swing) and night (graveyard) officers during what is traditionally the busiest time of their shifts—when bars and taverns empty, fights and domestic disturbances begin to occur, and buildings and residences are more often burglarized under cover of darkness.

4-day, 10-hour schedule [4-3 (10)]: Under the 4-3 (10) shift plan, officers work four 10-hour days per week, with three days off. This shift configuration also has a built-in overlap during shifts (see Table 4.4), which can be utilized to ensure that more employees are available during peak workload times. Officers generally favor the shorter work week because of the added time for leisure, educational pursuits, moonlighting, and so on. Many police executives have decided against implementing the 4-3 (10) plan for a host of reasons, however, including the fatigue factor, the greater need to control officers' moonlighting, the need for more equipment to accommodate extra personnel during overlapping periods of duty, and the potential need for greater salary budgets to pay employees at overtime rates for exceeding eight hours per day.[40] In addition, this schedule makes training for 10-hour blocks problematic.

Table 4.4 depicts in simple terms the 8- and 10-hour shift configurations.

Table 4.5 presents a comparison of the 5-2 (8) and the 4-3 (10) shift schedules, using average types and amounts of days off that are taken by officers in a typical year. Several important aspects of the two shifts may be noted. First, 5-2 (8) personnel are on duty 1,760 hours per year and can be scheduled to work for 220 shifts; 4-3 (10) personnel are on duty for 1,680 hours per year and work 168 shifts. What is *not* shown in the table is that while both 5-2 (8) and 4-3 (10) personnel will earn about the same hourly wage (because they work about the same number of hours per year), 4-3 (10) personnel will earn much more compensation per shift worked as well as per overtime hour and shift.

3-day, 12-hour schedule [3-4 (12)]: Unlike 9- and 10-hour plans, the 3-4 (12) shift plan fits neatly into a 24-hour day for scheduling. Normally, officers are assigned to work three days a week, with four days off for three weeks, and four days a week with three days off for the fourth week of a 28-day cycle. Proponents claim the benefits of increased productivity and employee morale as justification for 3-4 (12) shifts.[41] Management voices concerns regarding increased fatigue and potential increased costs associated with The Fair Labor Standards Act (FLSA), discussed later, as primary issues. Nonetheless, the 12-hour plan is enjoying increased support, with many agencies now using and praising it.[42] It is touted by many agencies as resulting in higher officer morale and productivity, with reduced sick leave time taken.

TABLE 4.4   A Basic 8- and 10-Hour Duty Shift Configuration

TYPE OF SHIFT	EVENING DAY	NIGHT (SWING)	(GRAVEYARD)
Three	8 A.M.–4 P.M.	4 P.M.–12 P.M.	12 P.M.–8 A.M.
8-hour	or	or	or
shifts*	7 A.M.–3 P.M.	3 P.M.–11 P.M.	11 P.M.–7 A.M.
4–10 hour shift†	7 A.M.–5 P.M.	3 P.M.–1 A.M.	9 P.M.–7 A.M.

*Swing or relief officers may work all three shifts to cover as needed.
†This shift has built-in overlapping of personnel.

Source: M. J. Levine and J. T. McEwen, *Patrol Deployment* (Washington, D.C.: U.S. Department of Justice, 1985).

TABLE 4.5 Comparisons of Scheduling Availability for the 8- and 10-Hour Duty Shifts

---

5-2 (8) SHIFT SCHEDULING AVAILABILITY

Base = 8 hrs./day × 365 days per year = 2,920 hours

From the base, we subtract the following time off (averages are used; actual amount of time off taken per year will vary from agency to agency, officer to officer):

Days		Hours
Days off	2 days/week × 8 hrs./day × 52 wks./yr. =	832 hrs.
Vacation	16 days/week × 8 hrs. =	128
Holidays	3 days/year =	24
Sick/Injury	7 days/year =	56
Training	5 days/year =	40
Compensatory	8 days/year =	64
Compassionate	1 day/year =	8
Other (military, discipline)	1 day/year =	8
	Total:	1,160 hrs.

Hours and shifts for which personnel may be expected to be on duty are as follows: 2,920 hrs. (base) − 1,160 hrs. off duty = 1,760 hrs. (or 220 eight-hour shifts).

Note that an officer is available for duty only *60 percent* of the time.

4-3 (10) SHIFT SCHEDULING AVAILABILITY

Base = 10 hrs./day × 365 days per year = 3,650 hours

From the base, we subtract the following time off (averages are used; actual amount of time off taken per year will vary from agency to agency, officer to officer):

Days		Hours
Days off	3 days/week × 10 hrs./day × 52 wks./yr. =	1,560 hrs.
Vacation	16 days/week × 10 hrs. =	160
Holidays	3 days/year =	30
Sick/Injury	7 days/year =	70
Training	5 days/year =	50
Compensatory	8 days/year =	80
Compassionate	1 day/year =	10
Other (military, discipline)	1 day/year =	10
	Total:	1,970 hrs.

Hours and shifts for which personnel may be expected to be on duty are as follows: 3,650 hrs. (base) − 1,970 hrs. off duty = 1,680 hrs. (or 168 10-hour shifts).

Note that an officer is available for duty only *46 percent* of the time.

5-day, 9-hour schedule [5-2 (9)]: The 9-hour work schedule requires five working days followed by two days off, five work days followed by three days off, and a final work day with another three days off. The 5-2 (9) schedule is becoming popular with nonuniformed assignments, such as detectives and administration.

There is no single shift scheduling configuration that fits all needs, nor would we recommend one shift pattern over the others. Administrators should decide on the shift that accomplishes a balance between organizational objectives and employee needs. Maintaining staffing levels, productivity, fatigue, equipment, and overtime costs should be evaluated carefully before deciding on a compressed schedule.

ADMINISTRATORS IN ACTION

Durham Officials, Cops All Like Week-off Plan

To the delight of officers, the Durham, N.C. Police Department has reinstated a work-schedule system—one that had been scrapped nearly three years ago—which will give officers one week off every three weeks.

The schedule . . . replaces a previous arrangement under which officers worked 12-hour shifts followed by two- or three-day breaks. Under the new schedule, officers will work 12-hour shifts for 14 of 21 days, then get a week off.

Officials said the change will expand the number of officers on patrol, give them more time to adjust to shift changes and allow them to spend more time with their families. . . .

A similar schedule had been in place for nearly 15 years when, in April 1995, it was scrapped by then-Police Chief Jackie McNeil, who said shorter breaks would allow him to assign officers to beats more frequently, thereby aiding community-policing efforts. Officers greeted the change with pickets and filed grievances, claiming the arrangement deprived them of time with their families and jeopardized part-time jobs.

Sgt. Phil Wiggins, president of the Durham chapter of the Fraternal Order of Police, which represents city officers in labor negotiations, said officers are thrilled with the new scheduling policy.

"We feel it has a lot of benefits all the way around. The time off gives us time to adjust, then come back a bit more refreshed and not have to worry about the job every day," he told Law Enforcement News. . . .

A survey conducted by the FOP showed that 98 percent of the officers "liked the way it was," Wiggins said. . . .

Source: "Durham Officials, Cops All Like Week-Off Plan," *LEN,* January 15, 1998. Reprinted with permission from *Law Enforcement News,* John Jay College of Criminal Justice (CUNY), 555 W. 57th St., New York, NY 10019.

Split and Overlapping Shifts

So-called "split shifts"—in which officers work a few hours, are relieved for a period, and then return to complete their tours of duty—normally should not be used because of their adverse effects on morale. There are times, however, when such arrangements are desirable for officers wishing to further their education or attend to other personal needs during the middle of their shifts. Indeed, split shifts may be sought after by such personnel.[43]

Also, on occasion, because of inordinately high workloads at certain peak periods, it may be desirable to institute overlapping shifts to meet these needs. For example, if certain problems arise at about 8 P.M. each evening, a 6 P.M. to 2 A.M. shift might be implemented. Like split shifts, overlapping shifts should also be avoided because of possible adverse effects on morale and effectiveness, unless the problem in question is very serious at the end of one shift and the beginning of another. Such overlapping shifts should be eight consecutive hours in length (avoiding officers' working split shifts).[44]

Labor Considerations

The Fair Labor Standards Act (FLSA) (at 29 U.S.C. 203 et seq.) provides minimum pay and overtime provisions covering both public- and private-sector employees. In 1985, the U.S. Supreme Court brought local police employees under the coverage of the FLSA. In this major (and very costly) decision, *Garcia v. San Antonio Transit Authority*, the Court held, 5 to 4, that Congress imposed the requirements of the FLSA on state and local governments.

Criminal justice operations, working 24 hours per day, seven days per week, often require overtime and participation in off-duty activities such as court appearances and training sessions. The FLSA comes into play when overtime salaries must be paid. It provides that an employer must generally pay employees time and a half for all hours worked over 40 hours per week. Overtime must also be paid to personnel for all work in excess of 43 hours in a seven-day cycle or 171 hours in a 28-day period. Public safety employees may accrue a maximum of 480 hours of "comp" time, which, if not utilized as leave, must be paid off upon separation from employment at the employee's final rate of pay or at the average pay over the last three years, whichever is greater.[45] Furthermore, employers usually cannot require employees to take compensatory time in lieu of cash. The primary issue with the FLSA is the rigidity of application of what is compensable work. The act prohibits an agency from taking "volunteered time" from employees.

Today, an officer who works the night shift must receive pay for attending training or testifying in court during the day. Further, officers who are ordered to remain at home in anticipation of emergency actions must be compensated. Notably, however, the FLSA's overtime provisions do not apply to persons employed in bona fide executive, administrative, or professional capacities. In criminal justice, the act has generally been held to apply to detectives and sergeants but not to those of the rank of lieutenant and above.

Summary

Clearly, police management carries tremendous responsibility. Our initial discussion of the roles and functions of police managers has noted the awesome trust and challenges inherent in this position. Police managers must decide what the best leadership method is and how to perform each role in the best way. They are concerned with their standing with the governing board and the rank and file. They must decide how to best deploy and schedule their officers. Police managers must face these issues daily.

Questions for Review

1. What are some of a police executive's primary roles? (Use the three major categories of the Mintzberg model of chief executive officers in developing your response.)
2. Is there a dominant management style of police executives? If so, is it the best style? Defend your responses.
3. What are some elements of the police chief's position that make it attractive or unattractive? Are contemporary hiring requirements adequate?
4. How do chiefs and sheriffs differ in role and background?
5. How is the performance of chiefs and sheriffs evaluated? Are there other, better criteria that could be used? What personal traits are most important for persons occupying or seeking these offices?
6. How do the role and function of sergeants differ from those of upper or middle management?
7. What criteria are used to determine the size of the patrol force?
8. What are some advantages and disadvantages of fixed and rotating shifts in policing? Eight-hour and 10-hour work shifts?

Notes

1. Henry Mintzberg, "The Manager's Job: Folklore and Fact," *Harvard Business Review* 53 (July/August 1975):49–61.
2. Jack Kuykendall and Peter C. Unsinger, "The Leadership Styles of Police Managers," *Journal of Criminal Justice* 10 (1982):311–322.
3. Paul Hershey and Kenneth H. Blanchard, *Management of Organizational Behavior* (Englewood Cliffs, N.J.: Prentice Hall, 1977), pp. 161–172.
4. Larry K. Gaines, Mittie D. Southerland, and John E. Angell, *Police Administration* (New York: McGraw-Hill, 1991), pp. 10–11.
5. Robert Katz, "Skills of an Effective Administrator," *Harvard Business Review* (January/February 1955):33–41.

6. R. J. Filer, "Assessment Centers in Police Selection," in C. D. Spielberger and H. C. Spaulding (eds.), *Proceedings of the National Working Conference on the Selection of Law Enforcement Officers* (Tampa, Fla.: University of South Florida, March 1977), p. 103.

7. Ronald G. Lynch, *The Police Manager* (3d ed.) (New York: Random House, 1986), p. 1.

8. Clemens Bartollas, Stuart J. Miller, and Paul B. Wice, *Participants in American Criminal Justice: The Promise and the Performance* (Englewood Cliffs, N.J.: Prentice Hall, 1983), p. 35.

9. Ibid., p. 42.

10. Donald C. Witham, *The American Law Enforcement Chief Executive: A Management Profile* (Washington, D.C.: Police Executive Research Forum, 1985), p. xii.

11. Janice K. Penegor and Ken Peak, "Police Chief Acquisitions: A Comparison of Internal and External Selections," *American Journal of Police* 11 (1992):17-32.

12. National Advisory Commission on Criminal Justice Standards and Goals, *Police Chief Executives* (Washington, D.C.: U.S. Government Printing Office, 1976), p. 7.

13. Gordon Witkin, "Police Chiefs at War," *U.S. News and World Report* (June 8, 1992), p. 33.

14. Witkin, "Police Chiefs at War," p. 33.

15. Ibid.

16. National Advisory Commission, *Police Chief Executives,* p. 7.

17. Bartollas, Miller, and Wice, *Participants in American Criminal Justice,* pp. 51-52.

18. Jerald R. Vaughn, *How to Rate Your Police Chief* (Washington, D.C.: Police Executive Research Forum, 1987), pp. 7-14.

19. Peter Drucker, *Management, Tasks, Responsibilities, and Practices* (New York: Harper & Row, 1974).

20. David C. Couper, *How to Rate Your Local Police* (Washington, D.C.: Police Executive Research Forum, 1973).

21. Vaughn, *How to Rate Your Police Chief,* pp. 15-20.

22. Ibid., pp. 23-29.

23. N. Darlene Walker and Richard J. Richardson, *Public Attitudes Toward the Police* (Chapel Hill, N.C.: Institute for Research in Social Science, 1974), p. 1.

24. Mervin F. White and Ben A. Menke, "On Assessing the Mood of the Public Toward the Police: Some Conceptual Issues," *Journal of Criminal Justice* 10 (1982):211-230.

25. Leonhard F. Fuld, *Police Administration* (New York: G. P. Putnam's Sons, 1909), pp. 59-60.

26. Wayne K. Bennett and Karen M. Hess, *Management and Supervision in Law Enforcement* (St. Paul, Minn.: West, 1992), pp. 44-45.

27. Richard N. Holden, *Modern Police Management* (Englewood Cliffs, N.J.: Prentice Hall, 1986), pp. 294-295.

28. Ibid., p. 295.

29. Ibid., p. 117.

30. Thomas J. Peters and Robert H. Waterman, Jr., *In Search of Excellence* (New York: Warner Books, 1982), pp. 306-317.

31. Fuld, *Police Administration,* p. 56.

32. Arthur Niederhoffer, *Behind the Shield* (New York: Doubleday, 1967), p. 79.

33. John Van Maanen, "Making Rank: Becoming an American Police Sergeant," in Roger G. Dunham and Geoffrey P. Alpert (eds.), *Critical Issues in Policing: Contemporary Readings* (Prospect Heights, Ill.: Waveland Press, 1989), pp. 146-161.

34. Ibid., p. 151.

35. Roy R. Roberg and Jack Kuykendall, *Police Organization and Management: Behavior, Theory, and Processes* (Pacific Grove, Calif.: Brooks/Cole, 1990), p. 284.

36. M. J. Levine and J. T. McEwen, *Patrol Deployment* (Washington, D.C.: U.S. Department of Justice, 1985), p. 35.

37. C. H. Levine, *Cutback Management in the Criminal Justice System: A Manual of Readings* (Washington, D.C.: University Research Corporation, 1982).

38. J. L. O'Neill and M. A. Cushing, *The Impact of Shift Work on Police Officers* (Washington D.C.: Police Executive Research Forum, 1991), pp. 71–73.

39. See G. D. Brunner, "Law Enforcement Officers' Work Schedules: Reactions." *The Police Chief* (January 1976):30–31.

40. Nathan F. Iannone, *Supervision of Police Personnel* (5th ed.) (Englewood Cliffs, N.J.: Prentice-Hall, 1994).

41. T. M. Schissler, "Shift Work and Police Scheduling," *Law and Order* (May 1996):61–64.

42. See, for example, G. B. Talley, "12-Hour Shifts: Comments From the Field." *The Police Chief* (December 1995):29.

43. Iannone, *Supervision of Police Personnel.*

44. Ibid.

45. Charles R. Swanson, Leonard Territo, and Robert W. Taylor, *Police Administration* (3rd ed.) (New York: Macmillan, 1993).

POLICE

ISSUES

AND

PRACTICES

Since this is a time of increasing crime, increasing social unrest and increasing public sensitivity to both, it is a time when police work is peculiarly important, complicated, conspicuous, and delicate.
—The President's Commission on Law
Enforcement and Administration
of Justice, 1967

Introduction

In the infancy of policing, it has been stated that "a size 3 hat and a size 43 jacket" were the only qualifications for entering police work. Given the nature and responsibilities of the job, that description certainly does not apply today.

This chapter begins with a look at the important issue of ethics in policing, followed by a discussion of community oriented policing and problem solving (COPPS), which was introduced in Chapter 3. Three case studies review formal COPPS initiatives. The chapter also examines the need for policy development regarding the use of force (including warning shots, weapons, pursuits, and special weapons and tactics) and special operations (including crowd control, hostage negotiation, and disasters) in which police engage. Then we discuss a growing trend for national accreditation of law enforcement agencies, which is similar to a report card. After discussing the increasingly important administrative function of providing adequate training for officers, we conclude with a brief look at administrative approaches to police stress and burnout.

Unlike the two preceding chapters, in this chapter we address several administrative matters that are literally life and death in nature, again underscoring the extremely challenging nature of contemporary police administration. Grave issues such as those listed earlier require policies and procedures that are well thought out, written, explained, and implemented.

Several case studies concerning problems of police administration are provided at the end of this chapter. Also note that other police issues concerning the development and use of technology are discussed in Chapter 16.

Ethics in Policing

Philosophical Foundations

The term *ethics* is rooted in the ancient Greek idea of character. Ethics involves doing that which is right or correct and is generally used to refer to how people should behave in a professional capacity. Ethical rules of conduct essentially should transcend everything a person does. A central problem with understanding ethics is that there is always a question as to "whose ethics" or "which right." How individuals view a particular controversy largely depends on their values, character, or ethics.

Another area for examination is that of deontological ethics, which does not consider consequences but instead examines one's duty to act. The word *deontology* comes from two Greek roots, *deos* meaning duty, and *logos* meaning study. Thus, deontology means the study of duty. When police officers observe a violation of law, they have a duty to act. Immanuel Kant, an eighteenth-century philosopher, expanded the ethics of duty by including the idea of good will.

Types of Ethics

Ethics usually involves standards of fair and honest conduct and what we call conscience, the ability to recognize right from wrong, and acting in ways that are good and proper. There are absolute ethics and relative ethics. *Absolute ethics* has only two sides; something is either good or bad, black or white. The original interest in police ethics focused on such unethical behaviors as bribery, extortion, excessive force, and perjury.

Relative ethics is more complicated and can have a multitude of sides with varying shades of gray. What is considered ethical behavior by one person may be deemed highly unethical by someone else. Not all police ethical issues are clear cut, however, and communities *do* seem willing at times to tolerate extralegal behavior if there's a greater public good, especially in dealing with such problems as gangs and the homeless. This willingness on the part of the community can be conveyed to the police.

As a community accepts relative ethics as a part of community policing, it may send the wrong message to the police: that there are few boundaries placed on police behavior, and that, at times, "anything goes" in their fight against crime. As Kleinig pointed out,[1] giving false testimony to ensure that a public menace is "put away," or illegally wiretapping an organized crime figure's telephone, might sometimes be viewed as "necessary" and "justified" though wrong. The ethical problem here is that even if the action could be justified as morally proper, it remains illegal. But for many persons, the protection of society overrides other concerns. This viewpoint—the "principle of double effect"—holds that when one commits an act to achieve a good end, and an inevitable but intended effect is negative, then the act might be justified.

These special areas of ethics can become problematic and controversial, as when police officers can use deadly force and lie and deceive people in their work. Police could justify a whole range of activities that others may term unethical simply because the activities resulted in the greatest good for the greatest number—the *utilitarian* approach. If the ends justified the means, perjury would be ethical when committed to prevent a serial killer from being set free to prey on society. In our democratic society, however, the means are just as important, if not more important, than the desired end. The community cannot tolerate completely unethical behavior from its officers, but it *will* seemingly tolerate extralegal behavior if there's a greater public good, especially with gang members and the homeless.

It is important for police administrators, supervisors, and officers to appreciate and come to grips with police ethics. Indeed, in the last few years, ethical issues in policing have been affected by three critical factors: (1) the growing level of temptation stemming from the illicit drug trade; (2) the potentially compromising nature of the police organizational culture—a culture that exalts loyalty over integrity, with a "code of silence" that protects unethical, corrupt officers; and (3) the challenges posed by decentralization (flattening the organization and pushing decision making downward) through the advent of COPPS.[2] The latter concept is characterized by more frequent and closer contacts with the public, resulting (in the minds of many observers) in less accountability and, by extension, more opportunities for corruption.

Police Values

Value statements are attempts to articulate police ethics and to delineate what police should do and how they should do it. Values guide the organization and employees' behavior.[3] Value statements for police departments are not new. O. W. Wilson wrote value statements for the Wichita Police Department and the Chicago Police Department when he was chief in the 1950s.

With the advent of community policing, an increasing number of departments are developing value statements to guide police behavior.[4] Value statements can serve as broad policies and provide officers with general direction when performing their duties, and they can also be viewed as goals and objectives. Values serve to provide a general understanding of and commitment to a police department's mission.[5] If everyone has a full understanding of the department's position relative to a given issue or problem, officers have better parameters to guide their decisions and actions. Conversely, if a police administrator fails to integrate the agency's values into the police culture, police officers will learn values from other officers—values that may be inconsistent with or contradictory to the department's values.

As an illustration, the Hayward, California, police department adopted a mission statement and organizational values to reflect its commitment to COPPS:

> We, the members of the Hayward Police Department, are committed to being responsive to our community in the delivery of quality services. We recognize our responsibility to maintain order, while affording and respecting dignity of life through a community partnership which promotes safe, secure neighborhoods.

What Works: Community Policing and Problem Solving in Action

The COPPS concept is being used in communities of all sizes. Following are three case studies—in Philadelphia; Reno, Nevada; and Lakewood, Colorado—where a return to the basics—taking police officers out of their patrol vehicles and placing them in closer contact with their communities to unite for solving problems—has paid huge dividends.

Note that all of the case studies used a common approach: the SARA model (scanning, analysis, response, and assessment, all of which were discussed in Chapter 3). They also employed a common theme: working with the community to identify and address problems. In all cases, police responded to community needs and took advantage of opportunities for collaboration. The case studies also demonstrate the rich variety of police problem-solving strategies that can be employed to address these kinds of problems. These techniques go far beyond the traditional reactive, incident-driven police responses.

Case Studies

Cleaning Up Queen Village in Philadelphia

Scanning: Residents and police officers working in the Queen Village area of Philadelphia[6] were concerned about the prevalence of crime and drug trafficking. Both agreed that the neighborhood's physical appearance was a major contributing factor to the crime, drug trafficking, and fear in the community. Together, they decided to improve the physical environment and remove the drug dealers.

Analysis: To begin, officers conducted an environmental survey of the neighborhood to identify and collect information on the physical conditions that were contributing to the problem. Officers also noted that six blocks had poor lighting because of broken lights or overgrown trees.

Response: Officer B., an eight-year veteran, was placed in charge of addressing the problems identified in the environmental survey. The officer immediately began removing the abandoned vehicles, securing and demolishing abandoned or dilapidated buildings, and clearing up vacant lots. Vehicle owners were identified through state motor vehicle records and ordered to remove or repair the vehicles within 30 days. The officer coordinated the removal of unclaimed vehicles by working with several salvage companies in the city. In total, 32 vehicles were removed.

Officer B. then turned his attention to the problem of abandoned and dilapidated housing. Some houses had become litter strewn, drug infested, and crime ridden. Large crowds gathered daily to hang out, drink, and sell drugs. They also presented a hazard to children who were observed by patrol officers to be playing in the houses. Officer B. began working on one such house where there was obvious evidence of drug dealing. He coordinated his efforts with the city's licensing and inspection departments, responsible for inspecting buildings and enforcing building code violations. After an unsuccessful attempt at contacting the owner, it was discovered from records that $3,000 in real estate taxes were due.

Because the house had to be demolished, the situation was referred to the city's contractual services department, which hired wrecking companies. Officer B. contacted the director of contractual services and a bid was quickly accepted and the building demolished. Officer B. worked with the city's building and inspections department and residents to clean up other abandoned lots in the area.

Assessment: No formal evaluation of the results was conducted; however, Officer B. reported that residents were pleased with the physical improvements to their neighborhood. He continued to monitor the problems during his patrol of the area.*

Mobile Home Park Problems in Reno, Nevada

Scanning: Panther Valley is a small secluded community of approximately 3,500 residents located in a northeast section of Reno, Nevada. It is comprised of middle- to low-income single family residences, a small industrial park, and a campground that was converted into a residential trailer park. The trailer park contains 150 trailer spaces that are rented on a weekly or monthly basis. Residents of the park represent the area's lowest socioeconomic status.

A short time after the conversion of the campground, the number of calls for service that were related to disturbances, thefts, burglaries, and drug activity significantly increased. Residents living outside the park also complained about its deteriorated condition and its residents, whom they suspected were responsible for the increased crime in the area. Officers assigned to Panther Valley became aware of its problems when crime and complaints from residents increased.

Sgt. J. T., swingshift supervisor for North Patrol, approved a request to work on the problems in Panther Valley as a problem oriented policing (POP) project.

Analysis: A crime analysis for the area found there were significant increases in the number of burglaries, vandalism, larcenies, assaults, and family disturbances. There were also increased calls for service related to vehicles speeding, juvenile disturbances, and drug activity.

Sgt. J. T. and Officer H. conducted an extensive environmental survey of the area and identified several factors that contributed to the park's deteriorated condition. Abandoned vehicles cluttered the narrow streets, creating hazardous conditions for children who used them as a playground. Most of the teenagers living in the park were unsupervised and suspected of being responsible for the majority of drug activity and vandalism. Trailer spaces were improperly marked or illegible, creating a slower response by police and fire personnel. Poor lighting existed throughout the park, making it convenient to conduct drug transactions and other crimes. Public bathrooms were inoperable and had become "offices" for narcotic activity. Residents, afraid to use the public bathrooms, often urinated and defecated in the open spaces around the park.

The park swimming pool was not used because of major structural problems; it became a dumping ground for refuse because of the lack of garbage containers in the park. Residents also deposited garbage in the unrented trailer spaces throughout the park.

Response: Officer H. contacted the manager of the trailer park, learning that new owners were in the process of purchasing it. He discussed the problems with the manager and suggested they conduct a series of meetings with residents to discuss crime-related incidents and environmental factors contributing to the park's poor condition. The following responses ensued:

- New tenant rules were established for residents, including their responsibility to keep their spaces clean and uncluttered by abandoned vehicles.
- Several of the problem residents were quickly evicted from the park.
- Ten abandoned vehicles were towed from the park. A local salvage company removed the vehicles for scrap metal.
- A general cleanup of trash and refuse was completed by park residents.
- The public bathrooms were repaired and repainted, and proper lighting was installed by the manager.
- Arrangements were made through the Job Corps vocational training program to use students to repair a number of plumbing and lighting problems that existed.
- The swimming pool was cleaned and repainted, and a new filtering system was installed. The pool was opened to the entire community.
- Speed bumps were installed to slow vehicles.

Assessment: These efforts resulted in a significant reduction in crime and calls for service. Neighborhood meetings greatly improved the relationship between the park manager and residents. Follow-up inspections conducted by the health department and city building inspector noted significant improvements. As a result of this collective effort, the overall environment and quality of life in Panther Valley was improved.

Mall Gang Problems in Lakewood

The following case study illustrates how the gang problem triangle (which looks at offender, victim, and place) can be helpful in addressing gang-related problems.

Lakewood, Colorado,[7] is a mostly middle-class suburb on the west side of Denver. The biggest retail center in town is the Villa Italia Mall, with a 1,252,000-square-foot interior containing four department stores and 6,300 parking spaces outside. Recently, patrons began reporting auto thefts in large numbers. There had also been an increase in the number of black and Hispanic youths wearing clothes associated with gangs—distinctive colors and sports team paraphernalia. The police agreed that the auto theft problem might be related to the gang presence.

Scanning: This problem became visible because of the efforts of the mall's general manager and the reports made to police officers. Rather that merely increasing patrols in the mall or making investigations of auto theft cases a high priority, the gang problem triangle suggests that other, less obvious strategies may be even more effective.

Analysis: Working with mall security, the police first learned more about the potential offenders. Few of the auto thieves had been caught, but security and police officers had talked to many of the apparently gang-involved youths (possible offenders) in the mall itself. Most of the problems inside the mall were caused by 14- to 15-year-old youths who were not yet gang members. Apparently, these "wannabes" intimidated mall patrons and picked fights with members of rival gangs. Most (about two-thirds) came from Denver and were Hispanic. The police talked to the victims, learning that most were mall employees, not patrons. Most of the auto thefts were reported on weekdays, and the autos stolen were mostly Jeep Cherokees and large General Motors cars. Typically, the thief would break out a wing or side window, break the steering column lock, and hotwire the ignition. The cars were usually dumped, intact but empty of gas, across town. Almost all were recovered within a few days of being stolen.

The thefts also formed an interesting pattern in time and space (place), the highest risk times being during school hours. Most of the cars were parked in the northeast corner of the lot.

Response: With this information, police and mall security officers developed a number of ideas, several of which involved ways to recruit effective "controllers" (people who try to prevent these youths from committing crimes). For example, because so many thefts were occurring during school hours by school-age youths, clearly the schools played an important role. Officers and guards began acting as truant officers (controllers), stopping youths in the mall on weekdays and taking them back to school. After a few days of this, the number of underage youths in the mall was greatly reduced. The bus company changed its routes so that the youths would not be dropped off at this location, forcing would-be thieves to either try to steal cars from better guarded sections of the parking lot or elsewhere.

The victimization pattern suggested several possibilities for "guardianship" (people or things that exercise control over a crime problem). For example, employees could be encouraged to use portable bars that lock the steering column externally. Or they could be asked to park closer to the mall entrance, effectively guarded by the increased traffic. Further, mall security could beef up its patrols in the far corners of the lot. Other possible alternatives included allowing employees to go out and check their cars once or twice during their shifts, or even staggering shifts to increase the number of people in the high-risk area during the worst times. One mall store was persuaded to mount a closed-circuit television camera on the roof and train it on the high-risk section. This camera caught several youths in the act of breaking into and stealing cars.

Assessment: The police and mall security are still assessing activities at the mall and working on a complete response to their gang problems, but truancy, fights, and auto thefts are already down. As the number of effective controllers, guardians, and managers increases, most likely the problem will continue to subside.

Note that all three elements of the gang problem triangle (offender, victim, and place) were needed to form a complete picture of what was going on. In gathering this information, the connection between the gang problem inside the mall and the parking lot was clarified. Also note that most of the potential solutions required the assistance of others outside the criminal justice system: schools, private security, a department store, or a neighborhood.

Managing the Use of Force

Violence By and Against the Police

In recent years, there have been several widely publicized shootings and beatings of minorities by police officers. Amadou Diallo, a 22-year-old unarmed West African street vendor, was shot 19 times by four New York police officers who mistook him for a serial rapist. Abner Louima, a Haitian emigre, was beaten and sodomized by four Brooklyn officers in August 1997. These cases and others (including Malice Green in Detroit and Rodney King in Los Angeles) have raised the collective ire of citizens, resulted in public demonstrations and protests, fostered calls for the firing of police executives, and even provoked widespread rioting. If any good comes from such unfortunate incidents, perhaps it is that the public and police leadership realized that they must be cognizant of the potential for excessive force by officers.

A relatively new issue for administrators involves domestic violence by police officers. The 1996 Domestic Violence Offender Gun Ban bars anyone—including police and military personnel—from carrying firearms if they have a misdemeanor conviction for domestic violence. Hundreds of police officers across the nation have lost their jobs as a result of this law.[8]

No one denies that a police officer who physically assaults a spouse or child should be terminated from his or her position. Critics of the law, however,

ADMINISTRATORS IN ACTION

NYPD Under Fire Over Killing of Unarmed Man

Statistics may in fact show that New York City's plummeting crime rate has been achieved with significantly less firepower than has been used by police in years past, yet the numbers trotted out by New York's Mayor and Police Commissioner have done little if anything to quell a barrage of questions, protests and demands for substantial changes in the Police Department's hiring and training methods in the aftermath of the killing of an unarmed African immigrant who died in a hail of police gunfire on Feb. 4, 1999.

Amadou Diallo was hit 19 times by four white police officers, members of an elite crime-fighting unit, who fired 41 rounds at the 22-year-old street peddler from Guinea in West Africa. His death has become a rallying point for civil libertarians, black activists and others, including some city officials, trying to push through objectives such as a residency requirement for police and the intensified hiring of minorities to bring the department to a level reflective of the city's racial makeup—the latter goal one that is not at odds with stated NYPD aims.

It remains unclear why the officers fired at Diallo as he stood in the vestibule of his Bronx apartment building at 12:44 A.M. that night. Officers Sean Carroll, 35, Edward McMellon, 26, Kenneth Boss, 27, and Richard Murphy, 26, who have kept silent regarding the incident, were assigned to the Street Crimes Unit, a plainclothes squad that focuses primarily on taking illegal guns off the street. In the past two years, the unit has grown from 138 officers to a current staffing level of 380, and the swift expansion has left some law enforcement observers concerned about both the training and supervision of hundreds of newly assigned officers.

The four involved in the shooting were apparently patrolling the victim's neighborhood in an unmarked car investigating a pattern of 40 serial rapes and robberies in Manhattan and the Bronx when they came upon Diallo, said police. One official who spoke to *The New York Times* on condition of anonymity said the officers described the victim as "acting suspicious." They did not communicate over their radios before approaching him, so investigators do not know what prompted the officers' interest in Diallo in the first place. Nor is it known why they began shooting. . . .

What is clear, however, is that the shooting has reopened a fissure between the city's black community and the police department, one that had barely begun to heal—if it had at all—in the wake of the police beating of Haitian immigrant Abner Louima just two years ago. The Diallo shooting has also prompted ugly allegations to reemerge about innocent black and Hispanic residents stopped, frisked and generally hassled in their own neighborhoods by overzealous officers.

The Street Crimes Unit makes up just 2 percent of the NYPD's sworn ranks, yet the unit's members seize 40 percent of illegal guns confiscated in the city. In 1997, Street Crimes officers frisked 18,023 people, and 27,061 last year. Those encounters resulted in only 4,899 arrests in 1997 and 4,647 in 1998, which critics say means that nearly 40,000 people were stopped and frisked because the Street Crimes officer mistakenly believed they were carrying guns. . . .

Established in 1971, the Street Crimes Unit was not considered a choice assignment until 1994, when a "zero tolerance" policy toward quality-of-life offenses was adopted by Giuliani and then-Police Commissioner William J. Bratton. Officers inside the unit said that under Bratton they were instructed to be more aggressive. The unit also increased its use of decoy cops to capture criminals who preyed on cabdrivers, tourists and prostitutes.

Before the expansion two years ago, however, candidates for the all-volunteer unit underwent intensive screening, with nearly half of them rejected. Most of the training was done on the job, with experienced officers mentoring those who were newly assigned. The interview process was shortened after 1997, police commanders say, and the influx of new recruits made it impossible to send each of them out with veteran partners. . . .

In response to criticisms, city officials have been quick to point out that police-involved shootings have actualy declined in the past year. Giuliani used graphs to show that NYPD officers fired 856 shots in 1998, compared with 1,040 the year before. The number of fatal shootings by officers last year was 19—the lowest figure since 1985. . . .

In the days and weeks immediately following the Diallo shooting, protests and counter-protests were held throughout Manhattan and the Bronx by activists and police alike. . . .

There is a growing perception in minority communities that some police officers are "out of control" and are targeting blacks and Hispanics. . . .

But the Diallo shooting has brought more to the forefront than just angry accusations and dissension. It has opened the door to a renewed focus on boosting minority representation within the ranks, mainly through what the NYPD and city officials hope will be more city residents at roll call.

There can be little argument about the department's lack of racial diversity. Although the NYPD has experienced record expansion of its ranks in recent years, it remains overwhelmingly white— 67.4 percent in a city with a white population of 43.4 percent, according to the department and 1990 census figures. All but 26 of 449 captains are white, and there are only 9 black and 10 Hispanic inspectors and chiefs among the 237 who occupy the topmost echelons of the NYPD. . . .

Giuliani dismissed an earlier recommendation, made by a panel he had appointed in 1997 in the wake of the Louima case, that the city impose residence requirements on police. The Mayor and Safir instead unveiled a package of proposals aimed at attracting city residents to the force by sweetening the pot.

In an effort to attract more New Yorkers, the NYPD will grant a residency credit on promotional exams for lieutenants and captains—the same five-point bonus given to applicants on the police officer entrance test. As an incentive to keep officers already living in the city from moving to suburban counties, the department plans to offer them down payments to buy homes in the five boroughs. The benefit could take the form of an interest-free loan or an outright cash grant....

[*Author's note:* On February 25, 2000, a jury acquitted the four NYPD officers of second degree murder and five lesser charges.]

Source: "NYPD Under Fire Over Killing of Unarmed Man," *LEN*, March 15, 1999. Reprinted with permission from *Law Enforcement News*, John Jay College of Criminal Justice (CUNY), 555 W. 57th St., New York, NY 10019.

including many politicians, police associations, and unions, argue that the law is too broad. Assume, as in one actual case, that a female police officer tells her 15-year-old son he cannot leave the house to go "hang out" with some kids she knows to be using drugs. Her son calls her names and attempts to leave, at which time she grabs him by the arm and sits him down. The youth is not injured except for a bruise on his arm, but he calls the police, a report is filed, and the female officer is convicted of misdemeanor assault in a trial by judge with no right to trial by jury. Because of the domestic violence law, she loses her right to carry a gun; thus, her career is ended.[9]

The issue is not whether abusive police officers should be terminated but whether the law, as it is written, is effective and legal. Congress is now considering several proposals that would amend the law to soften its impact on the police, and in August 1998 the District of Columbia Circuit Court of Appeals declared the law unconstitutional. Because police agencies typically have no unarmed positions, unless the law is amended it in effect ends the careers of officers who are affected by it.

With regard to violence used against the police, for their part many police officers see the United States as a mean and dangerous place. As William A. Westley wrote in 1969 in *Violence and the Police*, "The policeman's world is spawned of degradation, corruption and insecurity. He sees man as ill-willed, exploitative, mean and dirty; himself a victim of injustice . . . he walks alone, a pedestrian in Hell."[10] The job for many police officers is like a daily foray into a combat zone. Indeed, the inner-city streets have been deemed a "domestic Vietnam."[11] Instead of facing Viet Cong or some other foreign enemy, however, the foes of these officers include gangs, homicidal killers, and drug addicts. Police adversaries are more heavily armed and more arrogant than ever. About 80 police officers are killed each year in the line of duty.

Levels of Force

Police officers in the United States are allowed to perform three actions that no civilian can do: (1) use deadly force, (2) restrain the freedom of others, and (3) engage in high-speed pursuits.

Police can exercise several forms of force ranging from a simple verbal command, a light touch on the arm to encourage someone to move along or comply with an order, the use of a baton or Mace to control someone, to the use of the lateral-vascular neck restraint (the so-called chokehold or sleeper hold that has been criticized following several deaths when it was applied), to the use of lethal or deadly force. These levels of legitimate force are especially important in policy-making and on the street. As stated in police circles, "You don't bring a baton to a knife fight, and you don't bring a knife to a gunfight."

Prior to the 1970s, police officers had tremendous discretion regarding their use of firearms; police departments often had poorly defined or nonexistent policies regarding this issue. Investigations into police shootings were sometimes conducted in a half-hearted manner, and police agencies did not always keep records of all firearm discharges by officers.[12]

In 1985, the U.S. Supreme Court ruled that shootings of any unarmed, nonviolent fleeing felony suspect violated the Fourth Amendment to the Constitution.[13] As a result, almost all major urban police departments enacted restrictive policies regarding deadly force. Supreme Court decisions also made it easier for a private citizen to sue and collect damages as a result of a questionable police shooting.[14]

A study concerning justifiable homicides by the police in 57 cities conducted by the International Association of Chiefs of Police (IACP) was instructive on the use of weapons. Certainly, police administrators need to consider these findings when they develop policy for the carrying, caliber, training, and rewarding of police use of their weapons. The following variables were associated with high justifiable homicide rates: awarding incentives for firearms marksmanship; in-service officer survival training; the issuance of on-duty weapons larger than .38 caliber; the issuance of shotguns; a high supervisory/officer ratio; the use of semi-automatic handguns by SWAT units; in-service SWAT training; the absence of policy for the management of stakeout and decoy units; and exertion-type pre- and in-service firearms training.[15] What these variables appear to demonstrate is that homicides by police occur with more frequency when there is organizational and peer support—a hardware milieu—for firearms use and training.

Warning Shots, Weapons, and Pursuits: Policy and Procedure

We now consider several specific types of uses of force and whether policy is needed to provide instruction and uniformity in their use.

- Should a departmental policy on high-speed pursuits exist? This is a commonly overlooked form of force used by the police, one that many observers believe will soon be controlled by a Supreme Court decision similar to *Tennessee v. Garner.* Many people believe that the propelling of a 5,000-pound vehicle down a public street at 80 miles per hour to attempt to catch someone who may have committed a misdemeanor is overkill and requires regulation. Such pursuits present a tremendous danger to the public and have already resulted in numerous lawsuits and settlements.

- Most police department policies prohibit firing warning shots in the line of duty because police cannot control where the bullet will end up. In some situations, however, the use of a warning round—into a tree or the dirt—may be necessary to halt a serious brawl or disturbance.

ADMINISTRATORS IN ACTION

Doing Something About Excessive Force

By D. P. Van Blaricom

Citizen complaints and civil litigation against the police frequently allege that officers used "excessive force" in making arrests and in other custodial confrontations. Like many terms used in everyday language, however, the precise meaning of excessive force is elusive and often subject to wide interpretation that can depend upon an individual observer's perspective and predisposition toward the police. Virtually all force may be objectionable to some, whereas others will view nearly all force as being reasonable. Reality is somewhere in between those two extremes, but the question, of course, is where?

What Is It?

The U.S. Supreme Court has mandated standards of care for police use of force in their landmark decisions of *Tennessee v. Garner* (1985) and *Graham v. Connor* (1989). Garner focused on deadly force and essentially replaced the so-called "fleeing felon" rule with a requirement of "probable cause to believe that a criminal suspect poses a threat of serious physical harm to the officer or others" before an officer may shoot. In the Graham decision four years later, the Court imposed an "objective reasonableness" standard on all uses of force and decided that the amount used is to be considered within "the totality of circumstances." ...

After the Court has written the rules of the game, how does the chief policy-maker of a law enforcement agency translate legal language into appropriate police conduct out on the street? Constitutional lawyers can and will argue the precise meaning of "objective reasonableness" in great detail, but those tedious analyses are unlikely to be of practical effect in the real world of policing.

What Can Be Done About It?

There is an administrative duty upon the chief policy-maker of any law enforcement agency to control all police use of force and to prevent excessive force. At a minimum, there must be: (1) adoption of well written policies and procedures; (2) training of officers in those policies and procedures; (3) supervision of officers in the field; (4) awareness of current developments in tactics and equipment; and (5) monitoring of uses of force to hold officers and their supervisors accountable.

While not an easy task, anything less may be shown to have been "deliberate indifference" to controlling use of force, and may create civil liability for accused officers, the chief policy-maker and the law enforcement agency. Jury awards in the millions of dollars are not unusual in egregious cases and that money could have been far more wisely spent in training and equipment that would have better served the police and public alike by preventing excessive force in the first place. Most are well aware of the "if it ain't broke, don't fix it" philosophy of management, but the correct approach for today's policing environment is a preventive maintenance plan of "fix it before it's broke," somewhat akin to maintaining airliners before they fall out of the sky.

¶ **Adoption of Well Written Policies and Procedures.** This is where the chief policy-maker tells the troops what is expected and how they are to perform in an acceptable manner. It is axiomatic in an organizational setting that if you do not tell people what is expected of them, they are unlikely to divine it on their own. Use of force must be given priority policy guidance in accordance with its critical importance to all concerned....

¶ **Training Officers in the Adopted Policies and Procedures.** Training is where the chief policy-maker's intentions are translated into action and serves to answer questions as to what particular guidelines mean in actual practice....

The U.S. Supreme Court's decision in *City of Canton v. Harris* (1989) established the "deliberate indifference" to training standard, wherein "the need for more or different training is so obvious and the inadequacy so likely to result in the violation of constitutional rights." Accordingly, a failure to provide adequate training in such a fundamental police function as use of force can be a significant source of civil liability.

¶ **Supervision of Officers in the Field.** The first-line supervisors are the most critical link in the chain of command, and they are the people who really know what is going on out there. If supervisors are well trained and committed to the agency's policy, incidents of excessive force will be minimal, but if they are not, excessive force will be used with impunity by those who are inclined to do so. Furthermore, a street climate of tolerance to excessive force will soon result in escalating incidents after a demonstrated and recognized lack of discipline....

¶ **Awareness of Current Developments in Tactics and Equipment.** A variety of tactics have been devised and equipment developed to reduce the need to use force and to provide for physical control with lesser levels of force. Every chief policy-maker should investigate these alternatives as they become available and determine whether or not to introduce them into the continuum of force options available to officers....

¶ **Monitoring Uses of Force to Hold Officers and Their Supervisors Accountable.** Any chief policy-maker whose law enforcement agency is too large for personal interaction with every street officer needs an early-warning system for identifying excessive-force incidents....

Indicators of potentially aberrant individual behavior include frequent use-of-force reports, arrests for obstructing or resisting (potential "contempt of cop" charges to cover bad arrests), medical attention required by arrestees, and citizen complaints of force that are either sustained or not sustained. Such statistics are easily maintained by a simple computer program for routine analysis and identification of potentially brutal officers before they become an irretrievable loss to their agencies....

The 2-Percent Factor

An enduring mystery about policing is why 98 percent of the officers who are doing a difficult job well will tolerate the 2 percent whom we would all be better off without. Some have labeled that phenomenon the "code of silence," but regardless of how described, the well known fact is that a few officers will use excessive force when it suits them to do so, and the rest tend to ignore, excuse or explain it away.

This is not acceptable, and it is the responsibility of the chief policymakers of each and every law enforcement agency to recognize excessive force for what it is and then do something about it. A failure to do so will result in unnecessary injuries to the citizens whom officers have sworn to protect, and many of those incidents will be followed by civil litigation that we can ill afford, either in monetary awards or much-needed public confidence.

Source: "Doing Something About Excessive Force," *LEN,* January 15, 1998. Reprinted with permission from *Law Enforcement News,* John Jay College of Criminal Justice (CUNY), 555 W. 57th St., New York, NY 10019.

- Police policy does not allow officers to attempt to shoot to wound an assailant or other persons they must fire upon. Only Roy Rogers and his peers always managed to wing their adversaries. The police technically do not shoot to kill, however; rather, policy requires that they direct their fire with the expressed purpose of stopping aggressive behavior—normally into an assailant's "center of mass." Only snipers, normally operating at a considerable distance from their targets, must actually shoot to kill.
- Department policy should absolutely mandate that all officers be qualified with their off-duty weapons. Furthermore, experts suggest that the same policy should prohibit them from carrying off-duty, low-caliber weapons that are often ineffective and cause more problems than they solve.
- Should department policy allow officers to carry and use lead-filled "slappers" and blackjacks? These tools have historically been intended to inflict considerable damage to the head. Finding an "expert" to train officers to certify their abilities is extremely difficult if not impossible.
- Department policy should provide for disciplinary action when accidental discharges of police weapons occur. Few truly accidental discharges of weapons happen; most are the result of officer negligence. The problem with such discharges is that no one knows where the bullet is going. When such policies exist and are enforced, they normally reduce the number of such occurrences greatly.

To develop policy and procedures for the use of force by police officers, administrators should consider the information contained in Figure 5.1. The high incident (HI) police activities and behaviors indicated in the upper-left quadrant of the figure occur with a considerable degree of frequency and result in a high liability (HL) factor. The two combined result in the high probability of legal problems for the individual officer, the supervisor, the department, and the employing jurisdiction. Such activities or behaviors include high-speed pursuits, lateral-vascular neck restraint, drug raids, and the execution of felony warrants.[16]

Administrators must be alert to recent court decisions affecting police practices and undertake annual reviews of the policies to update them or develop new ones in response to current rulings.

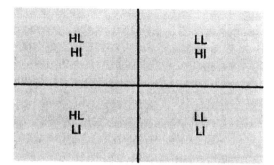

"HL" = high liability
"HI" = high incidence of occurrence
"LL" = low liability
"LI" = low incidence of occurrence

Figure 5.1

Guidelines for
developing use-of-force
policies.

Police administrators should consider the creation of a red flag warning system to alert them when an officer receives three citizen complaints within a one-year period. This system should cue the administration to review the officer's personnel file closely and possibly to have the officer seek counseling or take other measures to address the problem. Other actions may indicate the need for inquiry and intervention, for example, in the case of an officer who makes numerous arrests following routine stops for traffic violations rather than issuing citations.

Managing Special Operations: Strategies and Tactics

Several unique types of incidents tend to test the mettle of police administrators. Examples of such problems include crowd and riot control, hostage situations, and major disasters. These types of occurrences thoroughly challenge administrators' ability to analyze and react to them rapidly. In police organizations, leadership qualities are often measured by a person's reaction under duress. In this section, we consider briefly these types of situations and some of their important elements as they affect administrators.

Crowd and Riot Control

As riots in several cities during the 1990s have demonstrated, police executives must be prepared for such civil disturbances. These incidents serve as constant reminders that the powder keg can blow at any time when something happens to kindle the flame.

Seeing that officers were trained in forming a line and doing the "stomp-and-drag" maneuver, also known in police circles as the "hat and bat" routine, worked well in the 1960s and 1970s and is still appropriate for some types of problems. This formation, however, makes officers targets for snipers, and they must quickly disperse if fired upon. Today's field force plan calls for greater use of small-unit tactics, with a sergeant commanding only five or six officers. Spotters are placed high on building tops to observe citizen activities. The teams take control of and occupy areas of the city as they move. Meanwhile, some officers must be kept in reserve for other duties, because a police agency's calls for service ("I want to see an officer" type of communications) commonly triple during a major disturbance.

When such incidents occur, the first step in mobilizing personnel is to discontinue all nonessential police tasks, such as routine patrolling and response to miscellaneous calls for service. Off-duty and reserve officers should be called to duty quickly. Many jurisdictions have mutual aid agreements and compacts that allow officers from contiguous jurisdictions to respond and assist, and military and federal law enforcement personnel may also be needed. Normally, the decision to involve military personnel is a serious one; our system of government eschews a military state. Thus, requests for the imposition of martial rule must come from the chief executive of the local government or from some other official source, such as a magistrate or sheriff. The governor may make the decision to send military support independently.[17] This course of action is one of last resort. Local policing has long been recognized as the primary law enforcement body in the country, and laws have been passed with that concept in mind.

Hostage Negotiation

One of the most difficult situations for police executives to plan and train personnel for is the hostage situation. Of all the problems the police confront, few are as emotionally charged or complex as incidents in which hostages have been taken. The barricade-and-hostage incident presents a no-win situation in which the media and public will carefully scrutinize police strategies, procedures, and competence.[18] A hostage situation may be defined as "when one or more persons seize another person(s) by force and hold them captive against their will for the purpose of bargaining to have certain demands met by authorities."[19] Hostage takers may be divided into four categories: (1) traditional (or criminals trapped at the scene of a crime or while escaping from a crime scene), (2) terrorists, (3) prisoners, and (4) people who are mentally disturbed.

The police have several available options when facing hostage situations. They can assault or attack without attempting to negotiate; they can neither attack nor assault but instead attempt to wait out the hostage takers; they can negotiate but make no concessions to demands; they can negotiate and give in to demands; or they can negotiate and lie about giving in to demands.[20]

The job of the specially trained hostage negotiator is to seek peaceful resolution of a dangerous situation by talking and listening. The negotiator attempts to engage in a dialogue with the hostage taker, barricaded suspect, or person threatening suicide. The purpose of the dialogue is to calm the person, become a sympathetic listener, determine the person's motivation, and negotiate a peaceful solution.[21] The negotiator must obviously be a patient person who can ferret out any relevant information about hostages, weapons, and conditions that can be passed on to the SWAT team in the event that negotiations fail.

The success rate of skillful hostage negotiators is high. Negotiations often take hours and sometimes days, but eventually most hostage takers and barricaded subjects are convinced to surrender, rewarding the negotiator's patience and skills.

Special Weapons and Tactics Teams

Since the 1970s, a large number of police departments have developed special weapons and tactics (SWAT) teams to cope with a variety of special problems. According to a report by the Los Angeles Police Department (LAPD), the SWAT concept was initiated there in late 1967[22] in response to the increased incidence of urban violence, including snipers, political assassins, and urban guerrilla warfare. LAPD's SWAT team was activated almost 200 times from 1967 to 1974.[23]

Special weapons teams are trained to protect police officers from sniper attack during crowd control, to provide high ground and perimeter security for visiting dignitaries, to rescue hostages, to provide for the nonviolent apprehension of desperate barricaded suspects, to provide control assault firepower in certain nonriot situations, to rescue officers or citizens endangered by gunfire, and to neutralize guerrilla or terrorist operations directed against government personnel or the general public.

The special weapons team often wears distinctive clothing (black overalls and baseball caps) and is well equipped with automatic rifles, shotguns, flash bang grenades (emitting a loud bang and a bright flash), gas masks and canisters, smoke devices, ropes, pry bars, and walkie talkies. Members of teams often have different position designations, such as leader, scout, marksman or sniper, observer, and rear guard. In large cities, they are accompanied by a mobile command post that carries communications systems, armored vests, steel helmets, ballistic shields, extra ammunition, battering rams, and other provisions including robots equipped with cameras.[24]

Given the tremendous firepower and aggressive behavior of these assault teams, their operations must be supervised with great care. As former police chief and author Anthony Bouza said: "Operations that use dynamite, 'thunderflash stun grenades,' and aggressive SWAT teams can experience spectacular failures. There are the thumpers and Rambos who must be controlled, especially in such popular operations as drug raids, where they like to think they've been granted *carte blanche*."[25]

Major Disasters

Almost every citizen of the United States, regardless of the geographical area of his or her residence, lives under threat of some act of nature: a tornado, flood, earthquake, hurricane, or a devastating fire. In addition, disasters such as plane/train crashes, chemical spills, power plant explosions, structure collapses, major auto accidents, and terrorist attacks result from human action. Many police officers may never encounter such disasters personally during their careers, but all must be prepared for whatever befalls their jurisdiction. Because such events occur so infrequently, it is not uncommon for the police to be caught unprepared when they do take place.

The administrator is responsible for ensuring that an adequate disaster plan is developed and kept current. Many jurisdictions stage mock disasters to give their personnel experience in coping with them: These mock exercises also teach them to establish a command post and communications network, use first aid techniques, and coordinate interagency logistics and mobilization.

Accreditation of Police Agencies

Police executives have long been criticized for resisting outside examination and generally being reluctant to change. In this section, as in prior chapters, we see that this is not necessarily the case. We now review police accreditation, a movement that has begun sweeping the country.

The Commission on Accreditation for Law Enforcement Agencies (CALEA), a private, nonprofit organization located in Fairfax, Virginia, was formed in 1979. Today its manual contains 436 standards organized into 40 chapters or topic areas. Each standard has three parts: the standard statement, the commentary, and the levels of compliance (see Table 5.1, which presents examples of CALEA standards on the use of force).

The levels of compliance denote the relative importance assigned to each standard, based on agency size: A (1–24 personnel), B (25–74), C (75–299), and D (300 or more). For each of these four agency size categories, the levels of compliance indicate whether a given standard is mandatory (M), other-than-mandatory (O), or not applicable (N/A).[26]

As of mid-1999, 455 police agencies in the United States were CALEA accredited.[27] For two reasons, many police agencies have felt impelled to devote personnel and financial resources to seek accreditation during the last decade. First, most of the standards identify topics and issues that must be covered by written policies and procedures. Therefore, successful accreditation provides a "liability shield" against successful litigation.[28] Second, the process provides a nationwide system for change.[29]

One of the most important parts of the accreditation process is self-assessment. Each agency undergoes a critical self-evaluation and is later assessed by an on-site team of law enforcement professionals to determine whether it has complied with the applicable standards for a department of its size.[30] The accreditation process is voluntary for all agencies (although in this era of greater police accountability, many believe the time is coming when the public will demand that their local agency be accredited, or will want to know why their agency is *not* accredited).

TABLE 5.1 Example of a CALEA Standard on the Use of Force

1.3 Use of Force

1.3.1 *A written directive states personnel will use only the force necessary to accomplish lawful objectives.*

Commentary: None. (M M M M)

1.3.2 *A written directive states that an officer may use deadly force only when the officer reasonably believes that the action is in defense of human life, including the officer's own life, or in defense of any person in immediate danger of serious physical injury. Definitions of conditional terms, such as those for reasonable belief, serious physical injury, or similarly used terms that are used to qualify the directive, shall be included.*

Commentary: The intent of this standard is to establish a clear cut agency policy on the use of deadly force that provides officers with guidance in the use of force in life-and-death situations and to prevent unnecessary loss of life.

The agency should review this directive with all sworn employees (see 1.3.11). The agency also may wish to cross-reference this policy with other critical policies, such as vehicle pursuits (see 41.2.2) and roadblocks (see 61.3.4). (M M M M)

1.3.3 *A written directive governs the discharge of "warning" shots.*

Commentary: Generally, warning shots should be prohibited due to the potential for harm. If permitted, the circumstances under which they are utilized should be narrowly defined. (M M M M)

1.3.4 *A written directive governs the use of authorized less-than-lethal weapons by agency personnel.*

Commentary: None. (M M M M)

1.3.5 *A written directive specifies procedures for ensuring the provision of appropriate medical aid after use of lethal or less-than-lethal weapons, or other use of force incidents as defined by the agency.*

Commentary: The intent of this standard is to minimize the severity posed by obvious injuries or nonvisible trauma commonly associated with some weaponless or hand-to-hand tactics. Such tactics may include neck holds, hard punches to the head, heart, or other vital organs, or restricting respiratory function. "Appropriate medical aid" does not place the burden on the agency to have each injured person immediately evaluated at a medical facility. "Appropriate medical aid" may include increased observation to detect obvious changes in condition, flushing chemical agents from the eyes, applying first aid, evaluation by paramedics, or for more serious or life threatening incidents, immediate aid by medical professionals. "Other use of force incidents as defined by the agency" may

(table continues)

TABLE 5.1 (continued)

include procedures for the provision of medical aid to a person injured prior to contact with the agency, but the scope of this standard is limited to actions taken by agency personnel causing, or likely to cause injury. (M M M M)

1.3.6 *A written report is submitted whenever an employee:*
   a. *discharges a firearm, for other than training or recreational purposes;*
   b. *takes an action that results in, or is alleged to have resulted in, injury or death of another person;*
   c. *applies force through the use of lethal or less-than-lethal weapons; or*
   d. *applies weaponless physical force at a level as defined by the agency.*

Commentary: The intent of this standard is to establish use of force reporting systems within the agency for effective review and analysis (see 1.3.7 and 1.3.13). The reporting systems should help identify trends, improve training and officer safety, and provide timely information for the agency addresing use of force issues with the public. Early and accurate reporting helps establish agency credibility.

Software programs such as the I.A.C.P. national database on use of force incidents may be used to generate the necessary reporting elements of this standard or the agency may choose to use a variety of reporting methods to document use of force incidents, based on severity or other established criteria.

This standard does not require reporting the pointing of weapons or using weaponless, hand-to-hand control techniques that have little or no chance of producing injuries when gaining control over, or subduing non-compliant or resisting persons. These techniques include, but are not limited to, physical touching, gripping or holding, frisking, pain compliance measures, pressure point application, come-alongs, handcuffing, or other custodial procedures. It should be noted, however, that some agencies have had success documenting this type of information, using a standard checklist report format associated with the arrest report.

In deciding the threshold of when to generate a use of force report and how extensive the report needs to be, the agency should carefully examine all incidents wherein its employees have caused, or are alleged to have caused death or injury to another, have accidentally or intentionally discharged a firearm, or have applied weaponless force upon another to the extent it is likely to cause or lead to unforeseen injury, claim of injury, or allegations of excessive force, e.g. the use of neck holds, four point restraints (commonly referred to as the "hog-tie" restraint), punches, or kicks. The agency should also consider who is required to write reports when multiple employees were engaged in the same use of force incident.

If physically able, the primary employee involved should be required to verbally report his/her involvement within a specified time period. The verbal report should be committed to writing as soon as practical, thereafter. Written procedures should state by whom, when, and how the report will be submitted. The standard is not intended to document the display of weapons by officers. (M M M M)

1.3.7 *The agency has a procedure for reviewing the report required by standard 1.3.6.*

Commentary: The intent of the review is to determine whether there are policy, training, weapon/equipment, or discipline issues which should be addressed. (M M M M)

1.3.8 *A written directive requires the removal from line duty assignment, pending administrative review, any employee whose actions or use of force results in a death or serious physical injury.*

Commentary: The purpose of this standard is twofold: to protect the community's interest when officers may have exceeded the scope of their authority in their actions or in their use of force and to shield officers who have not exceeded the scope of their authority from possible confrontations with the community.

The agency should consider removing from line-of-duty status all officers involved in a critical or traumatic incident, not limited to shootings, and may include incidents such as a fatal motor vehicle collision involving the employee. During the period of administrative leave, the agency should consider provisions for post-incident debriefing or counseling for those employees involved. In some critical incidents, the employee's family may require assistance also.

The removal process may have a detrimental effect on employees involved. Agencies may wish to routinely include a review of these procedures during in-service training sessions (see 1.3.11) to enhance understanding of this procedure. (M M M M)

1.3.9 *A written directive requires that only weapons and ammunition authorized by the agency be used by agency personnel in law enforcement responsibilities. The directive shall apply both on and off duty, and must address:*

   a. *the types and specifications of all lethal and less-than-lethal weapons approved for use;*

   b. *the types and specifications of ammunition approved for use;*

   c. *the procedure for review, inspection, and approval of all weapons intended for use by each employee in the performance of duty, prior to carrying, by a qualified weapons instructor or armorer, and a process to remove unsafe weapons; and*

   d. *the procedure for maintaining a record on each weapon approved by the agency for official use.*

Commentary: The intent of this standard is to establish strict agency control over all firearms, weapons, and ammunition it allows members to carry and use in the performance of their official duties, both on and/or off duty. Clear guidelines should be established for exact types and specifications of each category and include the proficiency levels associated with each weapon.

For firearms, the agency should establish an approval process. Each firearm should be identified, meet the agency's established criteria and be safe and in good working order. The user should demonstrate his or her proficiency in using the firearm on an approved qualifying course before being approved, in writing, by the agency, to carry and use the firearm. A certified firearms instructor or armorer should inspect and approve the firearm and oversee the proficiency testing.

(table continues)

TABLE 5.1 (continued)

A complete record of all weapons approved by the agency should be maintained. For firearms, the record should list the type, description, identifying model, and serial numbers of each firearm, as well as the identity of the owner or assignee. The record should also include the name of the official making the approval, the date of approval, the course fired, and all scores used to qualify the user on the demonstration of proficiency. All approvals should be conditional upon periodic requalification pursuant to procedures established to comply with standard 1.3.11. (M M M M)

1.3.10 *A written directive requires that only agency personnel demonstrating profi-
         ciency in the use of agency-authorized weapons be approved to carry such
         weapons.*

Commentary: The intent of this standard is to cover the carrying and use, both on and off duty, of all weapons, such as handguns, shotguns, chemical sprays, or striking weapons (see 1.3.9). Demonstrated proficiency includes achieving minimum qualifying scores on a prescribed course; attaining and demonstrating a knowledge of the laws concerning the use of authorized weapons and knowledge of agency policy(s) on the use of force, escalating force, and deadly force; and being familiar with recognized safe-handling procedures for the use of these weapons. The instruction and qualification of all weapons should be provided by a certified weapons instructor. (M M M M) . . .

Issues Related to Police Training

Given public concern about police use of force, the dramatic increase in liability lawsuits, the expanded use of the COPPS strategy, the popularity of new police technology, and other developments, police training has come under the spotlight. In this section, we examine how police administrators may be deemed negligent for failure to train their officers adequately.

Liability and Negligence

The serious implications that the training function has for police is perhaps best demonstrated by a very unfortunate incident that occurred in Colorado, which points out how negligence can be found in the supervision and training of personnel. While holding a shotgun in one hand and attempting to handcuff a prisoner with the other, a police officer accidentally killed the person when the shotgun he was pointing at the prisoner's head discharged. At trial, the officer stated that he had seen the technique in a police training film. The training officer, however, testified that the film was intended to show how *not* to handcuff a prisoner; unfortunately, no member of the training staff made that important distinction to the training class. In *Sager v. City of Woodlawn Park*,[31] the court ruled that improper training resulted in the prisoner's death.

Another case involving training negligence is *Popow v. City of Margate*.[32] An innocent bystander was killed on his front porch at night by a police officer in foot pursuit. The court held the city negligent because the officer had had no training in night firing, shooting at moving targets, or use of firearms in a residential area. In *Beverly v. Morris,*[33] a police chief was held liable for improper training and supervision of his officers following the blackjack beating of a citizen by a subordinate officer.

These cases are but a few of the body of legal precedent relating to inadequate police training. The need for police agencies to provide adequate training for their officers to safeguard both the officers and the public is evident. The cost of negligence in training can be quite high in both human and financial terms.

Ongoing Training

Once police officers leave the basic training academy, it is critical for administrators to see that these neophytes continue to receive adequate annual in-service training throughout their careers. This training can be accomplished in several ways. News items, court decisions, and other relevant information can be covered daily at roll-call prior to the beginning of each shift. Short in-service courses are available, ranging from a few hours' to several weeks' duration. Computer-assisted training modules, videotapes, and even laser-disc training formats are now available.

Stress and Burnout in Police Organizations

Much has been written about the causes and management of stress of criminal justice system employees, particularly in policing.[34] The ways that administrators can assist stressed individuals by understanding and recognizing the symptoms of stress and then helping them to deal with this ominous problem has received far less attention.

Police officers have comparatively high levels of stress and burnout. For these individuals, many of whom often deal with people who are at their worst, no retreat or "fight/flight" choice is available. Police are on the firing line, so to speak, and they need to understand the causes of stress, paying particular heed to the emotional and physical signals they experience and what they can do to manage stress.

Several studies have found that officer stress and burnout are more related to problems occurring *within* the organization.[35] Therefore, the administrator's management style can have a direct impact on the stress problem. For example, it is well known that the lack of opportunity to participate in the decision-making processes that affect one's job is a major source of stress and eventual burnout.[36]

Implications for Administrators and Supervisors

Much of the stress that patrol officers suffer results from the fact that doing a good job on the street does not necessarily bring departmental rewards and praise. The street officer finds that his or her performance evaluation is often based on a search for failure to follow department rules or negative reports from citizens. Thus, officers may believe that they are being penalized for mistakes but not rewarded for being effective law enforcers and providing service to the community.[37]

Advanced training for administrators and first-line supervisors on how to supervise, which includes understanding how employees are motivated, provides positive reinforcement for good behavior, and describes the causes and prevention of stress, would be a major contribution to improving the morale of officers. Furthermore, administrators and supervisors should also strive to act as educators and advisors to the officers who work under them, especially in ways to relate to the public. Finally, the most important role of the supervisor could be that of role model. Modeling appropriate behaviors is one of the most effective ways of teaching behaviors. Rookie officers are likely to treat people in the manner that they see their supervisors treating them.[38]

Administrators and supervisors must also recognize that the number of situations officers deal with—especially those that place them in contact with death and brutality—will likely result in all officers at one time or another having very strong emotional reactions that interfere with their performance. Besides acute symptoms that arise from traumatic events, such as shootings and disasters, day-to-day stresses build up and result in adverse consequences such as divorce, substance abuse, and even suicide. These are all symptoms of stress that push the officers beyond the zone of stablility.[39]

If a professional such as a psychiatrist, psychologist, or counselor is made available, officers may well resist discussing their personal problems, for a number of reasons: They have an image of strength to protect, and admitting to problems they cannot handle might hurt this image; and they may feel that outsiders do not understand what it is like to be a police officer and cannot be of much help. Therefore, much remains to be done in providing counseling services for police officers. An alternative choice is to provide peer counseling.[40]

Police psychologists recommend that systematic programs to combat stress should minimally (1) develop a behavioral profile of each officer, to indicate different reactions or patterns—"red flags"; (2) train supervisors to recognize early warning signs (e.g., withdrawal, accidents, drinking, depression) and to know when to intervene; (3) provide a flexible counseling program for groups as well as for families and individuals (utilizing the peer counseling method); (4) train employees to use biofeedback, relaxation, and other methods of handling stress; and (5) encourage the police organization to reduce department-induced stress, for example, by changing to the use of objective performance criteria and decreasing busywork and other stressors.[41]

Summary

This chapter opened with a discussion of police ethics and the growing trend of police administrators to implement the COPPS strategy, which seeks to proactively improve the quality of life in their communities.

ADMINISTRATORS IN ACTION

Honoring Policing's "Point Walkers"

By Steve Scarano

. . . Policing isn't the most physically dangerous occupation, the insurance industry reports; apparently firefighting, agriculture and mining top the list. But, as an army general once told my officer *street survival* class (now there's a concept for society to ponder), except for soldiering there isn't another job where deliberate violence (not danger) is a predictable (sort of) occupational hazard. *Predictable,* by the way, speaks to the kind of certainty unrelated in any way to a pencil mark on an appointment planner. In a certain sense, there is a battle going on and society has chosen its modern centurions to fight it. "And, if the Republic survives," news commentator Paul Harvey has observed about them, "from somewhere out there on a pinnacle of history yet unreached, tomorrow's historians, looking back, will thank God that we had at least a few of the likes of you on our side."

Those centurions are heroes for today. "We want them to take care of the problem. We just don't want to see how its done," remarked Professor Charles H. Webb of California State University-Long Beach. Indeed, the officers themselves have chosen. Newspaper reporter Carole Hemingway believed that a single action doesn't necessarily make one a hero. Rather, a lifetime of facing the uncertainties courageously and mostly privately is heroic. Having witnessed many swearing-in ceremonies and a few commendations for "valor" during a half-lifetime of policing,

my observation is that an officer's moment of heroism comes when he or she makes the decision to pin on the badge.

Whether or not these good people are "winning" the war is fodder for both researchers and those on "the thin blue line." What we do know is that many of them—one is too many and should offend our collective senses—have gone down fighting, some of them to stay and others to get up again with their scars inside and out. Last year, according to preliminary statistics available prior to the completion of the FBI's annual report, we said goodbye to 61 who were murdered and another 72 who were accidentally killed nationwide. In California last year, eight officers were accident victims and eight were assassinated. (What else do you call it?) Already this year we have lost two California officers to murder while doing society's combat. Somebody remarked that "a society that makes war against its police had better learn to make friends with its criminals." . . .

Retired San Diego police Lieut. John Morrison suggested that cops are walking the point for society, and that "a few of us . . . know that there are some things you just can't do without suffering casualties, and our job is one of them." Morrison, a Vietnam veteran, saw that "You can't be a cop because you didn't get some other job. You can only be a cop because you want it." He goes on to recall his own sergeant, who told him that "there are only three rules in war. Rule No. 1 is 'young men die.' Rule No. 2 is 'you can't change rule one.' And Rule No. 3 is 'somebody's got to walk the point.' "

Who are these men and women who will "walk the point" for us? Paul Harvey called them a composite of what all people are, a mingling of saint and sinner, dust and deity. To much of society, crimes and victims have a way of getting reduced to a 30-second sound byte of broadcast time or to whole-number-and-fraction stick figures on a researcher's graph or a sliver of pie chart on a government agency's year-end report. To the police officer, however, victims are way too real, and so we take our losses emotionally as well when we end the shift wearing some of the people's pain.

Sociologists have described the police as a "closed society," associated with feelings of isolation and a "code of silence." Well, my 27 years of hindsight suggest that if you put service-oriented young men and women in a 24-hour fishbowl, in which they are unceasingly second-guessed by the media, the courts, the public they serve, and even themselves, it can be, shall we say, a real challenge. There is an expectation that the cops will stand unflinching

for a 20- or 30-year career and never be comfortable with saying "Ouch! Some of this hurts!" or "I just don't know the answer this time." Rick Baratta, former general manager of the Peace Officers' Research Association of California, remarked: "It's a good job, really. Except for the wear and tear on the soul, and a little more—always a little more." . . .

Former FBI Director Clarence Kelley said society expects of its police "honesty, courtesy, ability, intelligence, discipline, training, understanding and humaneness . . . all of the time . . . plus the ability to act quickly, often with inadequate information but always with wisdom." Former Chief Justice Warren Burger acknowledged that officers "often have only minutes—or even seconds—to make decisions . . . that perplex experienced judges for weeks." . . .

Source: "Honoring Policing's 'Point Walkers,'" *LEN,* February 14, 1999. Reprinted with permission from *Law Enforcement News,* John Jay College of Criminal Justice (CUNY), 555 W. 57th St., New York, NY 10019.

The chapter also explored the issues of the use of force and special operations by the police, accreditation, adequate training, and administrative approaches to coping with officer stress and burnout.

Questions for Review

1. What are the two primary types of ethics? What is their relationship to policing?
2. What types of issues involving the use of force should be addressed in policy? What are some essential considerations for each policy?
3. Why are police accreditation and training important and worth the time and money invested?
4. Why is the issue of police training particularly important at present? Give examples of problems and consequences if training is inadequate.
5. What can police administrators do to recognize and treat officer stress?
6. How did the 1996 Domestic Violence Offender Gun Ban affect policing in general, and administrators in specific?

Notes

1. J. Kleinig, *The Ethics of Policing* (New York: Cambridge University Press, 1996), p. 55.
2. T. J. O'Malley, "Managing For Ethics: A Mandate For Administrators," *FBI Law Enforcement Bulletin* (April 1997): 20–25.
3. Robert Wasserman and Mark H. Moore, *Values in Policing. Perspectives on Policing, No. 8* (Washington, D.C.: National Institute of Justice, 1988).
4. Ibid.
5. S. R. Covey, *Principle-Centered Leadership* (New York: Summit Books, 1991).
6. U.S. Department of Justice, Bureau of Justice Assistance, *Problem-Oriented Drug Enforcement: A Community-Based Approach for Effective Policing* (Washington, D.C.: Police Executive Research Forum, October 1993), pp. 53–54.
7. U.S. Department of Justice, Bureau of Justice Assistance, and the Police Executive Research Forum, *Comprehensive Gang Initiative: Operations Manual for Implementing Local Gang Prevention and Control Programs* (Draft 1993), pp. 4–10 through 4–14.
8. "Beat Your Spouse, Lose Your Job." *Law Enforcement News*, December 31, 1997, p. 9.
9. Adapted from Jerry Hoover, "Brady Bill Unfair in Broad Approach to Police Officers," *Reno Gazette Journal*, (September 25, 1998): 11A.
10. William A. Westley, *Violence and the Police: A Sociological Study of Law, Custom, and Morality* (Cambridge, Mass.: MIT Press, 1970).
11. Gordon Witkin, Ted Gest, and Dorian Friedman, "Cops Under Fire," *U.S. News and World Report* (December 3, 1990): 32–44.
12. Mark Blumberg, "Controlling Police Use of Deadly Force: Assessing Two Decades of Progress," in Roger G. Dunham and Geoffrey P. Alpert (eds.), *Critical Issues in Policing: Contemporary Readings* (Prospect Heights, Ill.: Waveland Press, 1989), pp. 442–464.
13. In *Tennessee v. Garner*, 471 U.S. 1, 105 S.Ct. 1694, 85 L.Ed.2d 1 (1985).
14. *Monell v. Department of Social Services*, 436 U.S. 658, 98 S.Ct. 2018 (1978).
15. International Association of Chiefs of Police, *A Balance of Forces: A Study of Justifiable Homicide by the Police* (Gaithersburg, Md.: Author, 1981).
16. John Sullivan, personal communication, May 20, 1993.
17. Thomas F. Adams, *Police Field Operations* (Englewood Cliffs, N.J.: Prentice Hall, 1985), pp. 310–311.
18. B. Grant Stitt, "Ethical and Practical Aspects of Police Response to Hostage Situations," in Roslyn Muraskin (ed.), *Issues in Justice: Exploring Policy Issues in the Criminal Justice System* (Bristol, Ind.: Wyndham Hall Press, 1990), pp. 20–45.
19. Ibid., p. 21.
20. Joseph Betz, "Moral Considerations Concerning the Police Response to Hostage Takers," in Frederick Elliston and Norman Bowie (eds.), *Ethics, Public Policy and Criminal Justice* (Cambridge, Mass.: Oelgeschlager, Gunn & Hain, 1982), pp. 110–132.
21. Robert Sheehan and Gary W. Cordner, *Introduction to Police Administration* (2d ed.) (Cincinnati, Ohio: Anderson, 1989), p. 387.
22. Los Angeles Police Department, *Special Weapons and Tactics* (Los Angeles: Author, 1974), p. 101.
23. Center for Research on Criminal Justice, *The Iron Fist and the Velvet Glove: An Analysis of the U.S. Police* (Berkeley, Calif.: Author, 1975), p. 49.
24. Ibid., pp. 48–49.

25. Anthony V. Bouza, *The Police Mystique* (New York: Plenum Press, 1990), p. 277.

26. Commission on Accreditation for Law Enforcement Agencies, Inc., "Standards for Law Enforcement Agencies: The Standards Manual of the Law Enforcement Agency Accreditation Program," (3d ed), 1994, pp. xiii–xv.

27. Personal communication, staff member at the Commission on Accreditation for Law Enforcement Agencies, Inc., June 16, 1999.

28. Gary W. Cordner, "Written Rules and Regulations: Are They Necessary?" *FBI Law Enforcement Bulletin* 58 (1988):18.

29. Russell Maas, "Written Rules and Regulations: Are They Necessary?" *Law and Order* (May 1990):36.

30. Charles R. Swanson, Leonard Territo, and Robert W. Taylor, *Police Administration* (3d ed.) (New York: Macmillan, 1993), p. 51.

31. 543 F.Supp. 282 (D.Colo., 1982).

32. 476 F.Supp. 1237 (1979).

33. 470 F.2d 1356 (5th Cir. 1972).

34. See Kenneth J. Peak, *Policing America: Methods, Issues, Challenges* (3d ed.) (Upper Saddle River, N.J.: Prentice Hall, 2000), Chapter 11; W. Clinton Terry III, *Policing Society: An Occupational View* (New York: Wiley, 1985), Part 7; Roger G. Dunham and Geoffrey P. Alpert, *Critical Issues in Policing: Contemporary Readings*, Section VIII; Harry W. More Jr., *Critical Issues in Law Enforcement* (Cincinnati, Ohio: Anderson, 1985), Chapter 8.

35. See, for example, Laura Weber Brooks and Nicole Leeper Piquero, "Police Stress: Does Department Size Matter?" *Policing: An International Journal of Police Strategies and Management* 21 (1998):600–617.

36. Paul W. Brown, "Probation Officer Burnout: An Organizational Disease/An Organizational Cure," *Federal Probation* 50 (1986):4–7; Cary Cherniss, *Professional Burnout in Human Services Organizations* (New York: Praeger, 1980).

37. Wayne Anderson, David Swenson, and Daniel Clay, *Stress Management for Law Enforcement Officers* (Englewood Cliffs, N.J.: Prentice Hall, 1995), p. 283.

38. Ibid., pp. 283–284.

39. Ibid., p. 289.

40. Ibid.

41. Ben Daviss, "Burnout," *Police Magazine* (May 1982):58.

CASE STUDIES

Intruding Ima
and the Falsified Report*

An eight-year employee of your police agency, Officer Ima Goodenough, is a patrol officer who often serves as field training officer. Goodenough is generally capable and experienced in both the patrol and detective divisions. She takes pride in being of the "old school" and has evolved a clique of approximately 10 people that she gets along with, while mostly shunning other officers.

As an officer of the old school, she typically handles calls for service without requesting cover units or backup. She has had six complaints of brutality lodged against her during the past three years. For Ima and her peers, officers who call for backup are "wimps." She has recently been involved in two high-speed pursuits during which her vehicle was damaged when she attempted to run the offender off the road.

Ima will notify a supervisor only when dealing with a major situation. She is borderline insubordinate when dealing with new supervisors. She feels that, generally speaking, the administration exists only to "screw around with us"— the field officers. You, her shift commander, have been fed up with her deteriorating attitude and lackadaisical performance for some time and have been wondering if you will soon have occasion to take some form of disciplinary action against her.

You have also learned that Ima has a reputation among her supervisors as being a "hot dog." Some of her past and present supervisors have even commented that she is a "walking time bomb" who is unpredictable and could "blow" at any time.

One day while bored on patrol, Ima decides to go outside her jurisdiction, responding to a shooting call that is just across the city limit and in the county. She radios the dispatcher that she is out "assisting," then walks into the home where paramedics are frantically working on a man lying on the floor with a head wound. Nearby on the floor is a large, foreign-made revolver. Ima holds and waves the revolver in the air, examining it. A paramedic yells at her, "Hey! Put that down, this may be an attempted homicide case!" Ima puts the revolver back on the floor. Meanwhile, you have been attempting to contact Ima via radio to get her back into her jurisdiction. Later, when the sheriff's office complains to you about her actions at their crime scene, you require that she write a report of her actions. She completes a report describing her observations at the scene, but denies touching or picking up anything.

---

*Contributed by former Washoe County, Nevada, Sheriff Richard C. Kirkland, and Reno Police Department Lt. Linda Ditz.

Looking at Ima's personnel file, you determine that her performance evaluations for the past eight years are "standard"—average to above average. She has never received a suspension from duty for her actions. While verbally expressing their unhappiness with her for many years, it appears that Ima's supervisors have not expressed that disdain in writing.

Questions for Discussion

1. What are the primary issues involved in this situation?
2. Do you believe that there are sufficient grounds for bringing disciplinary action against Goodenough? If so, what would be specific charges? What is the appropriate punishment?
3. Do you believe that grounds exist for termination?
4. Does the fact that her supervisors have rated her as standard have any bearing on this matter or create difficulties in bringing a case for termination?

"Racin' Ray," the Graveyard-Shift Gadabout*

Members of the Hooterville County sheriff's department have been involved in several vehicle pursuits within the past year. One such incident resulted in the death of a 14-year-old juvenile who crashed during a pursuit in which he was joyriding in his parents' vehicle. This tragedy sparked a massive public outcry and criticism of the police department for using excessive force. A lawsuit against the department and individual officers involved in the pursuit is pending.

The sheriff immediately changed the department's policy regarding pursuits. The policy now requires that a supervisor cancel any pursuit that does not involve a violent felony crime or other circumstances that would justify the danger and potential liability. All officers have been trained in the new policy. A separate policy prohibits the firing of warning shots unless "circumstances warrant."

Last night at 1:00 A.M., Deputy Raymond "Racin' Ray" Roadhog was patrolling an industrial park in his sector. Deputy Roadhog, freshly graduated from the state police academy and field training, engages in pursuits at every opportunity; also, unbeknown to the sheriff and other supervisors, he occasionally takes along his personal German Shepherd dog for use in building checks and has an M-16 automatic rifle in his trunk. He was providing extra patrol in response to reports of vandalism and theft of building materials in that area of the county. Generally, after 6:00 P.M., no one should have any reason to be in any construction area. A parked vehicle attracts his attention because private vehicles are not normally parked in the area at this time.

---

*Contributed by Deputy Chief Ronald W. Glensor, Ph.D., Reno, Nevada, Police Department.

As Roadhog approaches the vehicle with his cruiser's lights off and spot-light on, he notices the brake lights on the vehicle flash on and off. Roadhog, immediately getting out of his vehicle for a better view, calls dispatch for backup assistance in the event that there is a burglary or theft in progress.

At this point, the vehicle takes off at a high rate of speed, in Roadhog's direc-tion. Roadhog, being out of his vehicle and seeing the vehicle coming at him from about 30 yards, fires a warning shot into the ground. When about 15 yards away, the vehicle veers away from him, then leaves at a high rate of speed. As the escap-ing vehicle crosses the path of his spotlight, Roadhog sees that there are two young people inside, a man driving and a woman in the passenger's seat. Road-hog yells for the driver to halt, then lets loose another warning shot, this time into a nearby fire hydrant. He then takes off in pursuit of the vehicle.

The officer radios dispatch to inform him of his observations and of his present pursuit. You, the shift commander—a patrol lieutenant—hear this radio transmission.

Questions for Discussion

1. What are the central issues involved?

2. Is the deputy in compliance with the use-of-force policy?

3. Are you going to "shut down" Roadhog's pursuit? Explain.

4. Should the deputy have fired warning shots?

5. Assuming that all of the earlier information comes to light, will the sheriff be likely to begin disciplinary action against Roadhog?

6. Do the policies appear to be sound as written? Are additional policies needed?

Dismal City P.D.'s Command to "Do More With Less"*

Dismal City, USA, is a rapidly growing community of 50,000 residents located in the southern part of the state along the ocean. The city gains a population of 10,000 to 20,000 visitors a day during the summer months, when ocean recreation is a popular activity.

The city's demographics are changing rapidly. Its Hispanic and Asian popula-tions are growing at a tremendous rate. Most of these new residents work outside the city, however. The downtown area has slowly degenerated over the past few years resulting in increased crime and disorder.

A property tax cap has resulted in reduced revenues to local jurisdictions, and the recent recession has also taken a substantial toll on the city's budget.

---

*Contributed by Deputy Chief Ronald W. Glensor, Ph.D., Reno, Nevada, Police Department.

The result has been significant reductions in staffing. The city's two attempts to have voters approve bond issues for increased taxes and police officers have failed. The police department has experienced its share of budget cuts and reduced staffing levels. The chief recently retired due to continued problems with the city council, the budget, and low morale in the agency. As a result of these matters, relations between the community and the department have been tense.

The police department has experienced a continued reduction in staffing over the past five years. Reductions are not expected to continue, but increases are also not expected. The morale of the department is at its worst and is fueled by the increase in workload and what is perceived as an uncaring chief. The increase in violent crime only aggravates the problems, as officers believe that their safety is in jeopardy as a result of the lower staffing levels. Furthermore, the increase in Hispanic and Asian residents creates an additional burden, as the department consists largely of white male officers. The department has no bilingual officers.

You have been hired as the new chief and will begin work in two weeks. The city manager and council have asked for a meeting with you to discuss the future of the department. At this meeting they explain the situation to you and request a staff report within one month of your reporting to work. The manager and several council persons recently attended a conference that presented several workshops on the implementation of community policing. They are convinced that this trend, now apparently sweeping the nation, would result in a more efficient police department.

The manager and governing board enthusiastically seek your views on community policing, its potential for Dismal City, and how you might approach its implementation. They inform you that the police officers' union has heard rumors of this idea and has made it clear that they probably would not want anything to do with changing the organization at a time when resources are strained.

Questions for Discussion

1. In your report, how would you respond concerning whether or not community policing is the panacea for the city's financial and demographic woes? Will it help the department?

2. Do you envision any problems with "traditional thinking" supervisors and community policing? If so, how would you handle their concerns?

3. How would you improve the relations between labor and management?

4. Would the community need to be involved in the design and implementation of community policing? If so, how?

5. How might community policing provide more effective delivery of services?

6. Would you anticipate that the officers' workload would be reduced or increased under this strategy?

7. What types of information would you use to evaluate the progress of your community policing initiative for city hall?

THE COURTS

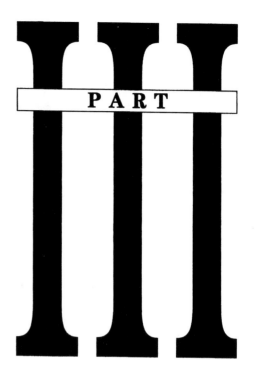

PART

III

This part consists of three chapters, all of which focus on the courts. Chapter 6 examines court organization and operation, Chapter 7 covers personnel roles and functions, and Chapter 8 discusses court issues and practices. The introductory section of each chapter provides specific chapter content. Case studies in court administration appear at the end of Chapter 8.

COURT
ORGANIZATION
AND
OPERATION

The place of justice is a hallowed place.

—Francis Bacon

Courts and camps are the only places to learn the world in.
—Earl of Chesterfield

Introduction

Courts have existed in some form for thousands of years. Indeed, the ancient trial court of Israel, and the most common tribunal throughout its Biblical history, was the "court at the gate," where elders of each clan determined controversies within the kin group. Then, in the fourth century B.C., courts in Athens, Greece, dealt with all premeditated homicides and heard constitutional cases. Since then, the court system has survived the dark eras of the Inquisition and the Star Chamber (which, in England during the 1500s and 1600s, without a jury enforced unpopular political policies and meted out severe punishment, including whipping, branding, and mutilation). The U.S. court system developed rapidly after the Revolution and attended to the establishment of law and justice on the western frontier.

Federal, state, and local courts in the United States employ about 390,000 judicial and legal personnel; the annual payroll for these workers is about $5.5 billion. The largest percentage of these employment and payroll expenditures is at the local level (55.5 percent and 57.6 percent, respectively).[1]

We will examine the courts from several perspectives. First we address the questions of whether courts are organizations in the usual sense of the term with a bureaucratic structure and function. Then we examine typical courtroom decor and decorum. Next we discuss whether the adversary system and other procedural mechanisms of our courts maintain serious impediments to finding the truth. Then we consider the courts in general as policymaking bodies. We next ponder the effects of today's litigious society, in which we have little reservation about suing our neighbors, which foists on the courts a veritable avalanche of suits, petitions, writs, briefs, and motions.

We then examine a relatively new and promising concept, alternative dispute resolution, which has developed to counter the escalating court dockets. Finally, we look at the citizen or "consumer" relationship with our court system, a subject that serves as a bridge to the following chapter.

Courts as Organizations

A Nonbureaucratic Work Group

In the view of Edward Clynch and David Neubauer, many academics have erroneously characterized courts as bureaucracies.[2] Bureaucracies have differentiated and separate divisions tied together by a distinctive authoritarian structure or hierarchy. They also have well-defined organizational rules governing the disposition of particular tasks, including individually defined, specialized ones.[3] These characteristics do not apply to courts.

Here we examine how courts are very different from the typical organization and how court administration is made more complex because of this uniquely informal structure and organization. Indeed, courts are relatively autonomous single work units that do not function in a bureaucratic manner. A trial court is an entity that does not report to a single authority figure in a chain of command. It often ignores formal rules in favor of shared decision making among judges, prosecutors, and defense attorneys.[4] Rather than being bureaucracies, trial courts are informal work groups in which interaction among members occurs on a continuing basis. Court participants have discretion in carrying out their tasks. They are mutually interdependent but have the independent ability to modify formal rules and procedures so that people can complete their assignments successfully. A common professional bond exists because most of the participants are lawyers. A bureaucratic management style is usually inappropriate for the courts. In fact, the more a judge insists on being treated with great deference, the more that work group's cohesion diminishes. More important, participants' roles are interchangeable: Defense attorneys may become prosecutors or judges, and so on.[5]

Formal authority is modified in trial courts in many ways. For example, while the judge has the authority to make the major decisions—setting bail, determining guilt, and imposing sentence—he or she often relies on input from others. Also, because they know more about cases coming to court, the judges' subordinates (prosecutors and defense attorneys) can influence his or her decisions by selective information flow.[6]

For these informal work groups to be effective, group norms must be enforced. Group members must comply with the norms of behavior: If they do, they are rewarded, and if not, they are subject to being sanctioned. Defense attorneys who do not file unnecessary motions or avoid pushing for "unreasonable" plea bargains may be rewarded by receiving greater amounts of information, such as being allowed to read the police reports of their cases. Prosecutors may receive more time to talk with witnesses or defense counsel. Conversely, sanctions for defense attorneys who violate group norms may include less access to case information, not being appointed to represent indigents in future cases, or their clients being punished with harsher sentences. Furthermore, prosecutors may not receive requested continuances (most requests for continuances come from the district attorney's office).[7] In sum, it is important to remember: "Courts are not an occasional assemblage of strangers who resolve a particular conflict and then dissolve, never to work together again."[8]

Unifying Court Names and Functions

Turning now to the *functional* organization of the courts, Figure 6.1 shows an organization structure for a county district court serving a population of 300,000. Note the variety of functions and programs that exist and those that are in addition to the basic court role of hearing trials and rendering dispositions.

Overall, court organization has "demonstrated little logic or planning, because adding certain new courts serves various political goals."[9] States that do not have a unified court system often have a confusing maze of overlapping courts and jurisdictions, which can cause considerable confusion for litigants, victims, witnesses, and lawyers alike. Figure 6.2 shows the various names of state courts of last resort and the numbers of judges for each. Figure 6.3 presents the same types of information for state intermediate courts of appeals, and Figure 6.4 shows the names for major trial courts in different states.

Perhaps the best example of how courts should be organized statewide is a system that has become unified on a statewide basis. Kansas, which unified its court system in 1977, serves as a good example of how a change in court organization results in success. Kansas has a supreme court (seven justices; exclusive appellate and original jurisdiction); an intermediate court of appeals (seven justices; hears appeals from district courts); a district court (70 district, 64 associate district, and 76 district magistrate judges; general original jurisdiction in all civil and criminal matters, hearing appeals from lower courts); and municipal courts (384 judges; handle city ordinance violations, with no jury trials).[10]

This is actually about as simple as court unification can be. Witness the Kansas court system *prior to* unification in 1977: a supreme court; 29 district

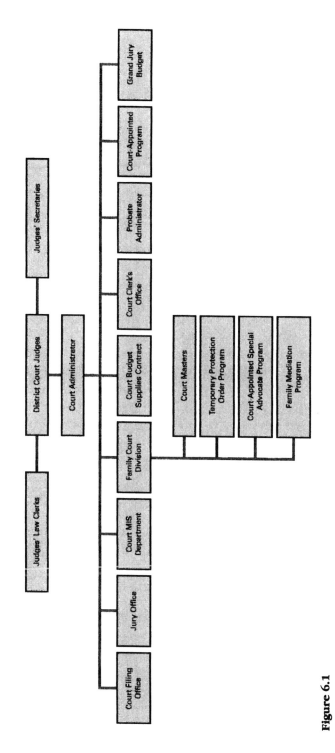

Figure 6.1

Organization structure for a district court serving a population of 300,000.

Supreme Court	Alabama (9), Alaska (5), Arizona (5), Arkansas (7), California (7), Connecticut (7), Delaware (5), Florida (7), Georgia (7), Hawaii (5), Idaho (5), Illinois (7), Indiana (5), Iowa (9), Kansas (7), Kentucky (7), Louisiana (8), Michigan (7), Minnesota (9), Mississippi (9), Missouri (7), Montana (7), Nebraska (7), Nevada (5), New Hampshire (5), New Jersey (7), New Mexico (5), North Carolina (7), North Dakota (5), Ohio (7), Oklahoma[a] (9), Oregon (7), Pennsylvania (7), Rhode Island (5), South Carolina (5), South Dakota (5), Tennessee (5), Texas[a] (9), Utah (5), Vermont (5), Virginia (7), Washington (9), Wisconsin (7), Wyoming (5)
Court of Appeals	District of Columbia (9), Maryland (7), New York (7)
Supreme Judicial Court	Maine (7), Massachusetts (7)
Court of Criminal Appeals	Oklahoma (3),[a] Texas (9)[a]
Supreme Court of Appeals	West Virginia (5)

[a]Two courts of last resort in these states.

Figure 6.2

Courts of last resort in the states.

Figure 6.3

Intermediate courts of appeal.

Appeals Court	Massachusetts (14)
Appellate Court	Connecticut (9), Illinois (42)
Appellate Division of Superior Court	New Jersey (28)
Appellate Divisions of Superior Court	New York (48)
Appellate Terms of Supreme Court	New York (15)
Commonwealth Court	Pennsylvania (9)
Court of Appeals	Alaska (3), Arizona (21), Arkansas (6), Colorado (16), Georgia (9), Idaho (30), Indiana (5), Iowa (6), Kansas (10), Kentucky (14), Michigan (24), Minnesota (16), Missouri (32), Nebraska (6), New Mexico (10), North Carolina (12), North Dakota (3)[b], Ohio (65), Oklahoma (12)[a], Oregon (10), South Carolina (6), Tennessee (12)[a], Utah (7), Virginia (10), Washington (23), Wisconsin (15)
Court of Appeal	California (88), Louisiana (55), Texas (80)
Court of Civil Appeals	Alabama (3)
Court of Criminal Appeals	Alabama (5), Tennessee (9)
Court of Special Appeals	Maryland (13)
District Court of Appeals	Florida (57)
Intermediate Court of Appeals	Hawaii (3)
Superior Court	Pennsylvania (15)

[a]Civil only
[b]Temporary

Circuit Court	Alabama, Arkansas,ᵃ Florida, Hawaii, Illinois, Indiana,ᵇ Kentucky, Maryland, Michigan, Mississippi,ᵃ Missouri, Oregon, South Carolina, South Dakota, Tennessee,ᵃ Virginia, West Virginia, Wisconsin
Court of Common Pleas	Ohio, Pennsylvania
District Court	Colorado, Idaho, Iowa, Kansas, Louisiana, Minnesota, Montana, Nebraska, Nevada, New Mexico, North Dakota, Oklahoma, Texas, Utah, Wyoming
Superior Court	Alaska, Arizona, California, Connecticut, Delaware,ᵃ District of Columbia, Georgia, Maine, Massachusetts, New Hampshire, New Jersey, North Carolina, Rhode Island, Vermont,ᵃ·ᵈ Washington, New Yorkᶜ
Supreme Court	New York

ᵃArkansas, Delaware, Mississippi, and Tennessee have separate Chancery Courts with equity jurisdiction.
ᵇIndiana uses Superior and Circuit Courts.
ᶜNew York also uses County Courts.
ᵈVermont also uses District Courts.

Figure 6.4

Major trial courts in different states.

courts (no intermediate court of appeals); 93 county courts handling civil cases involving less than $1,000, felony preliminaries, misdemeanors, traffic cases of less than $2,500, and jury trials; 8 city courts hearing civil matters of less than $3,000, felony preliminaries, misdemeanors, traffic cases of less than $2,500, and jury trials; 5 magistrate courts hearing civil cases under $3,000, felony preliminaries, misdemeanors, and traffic cases under $2,500; 109 probate courts; 109 juvenile courts; 4 common pleas courts handling civil cases involving less than $3,000, felony preliminaries, misdemeanors, and traffic cases involving less than $2,500; and 384 municipal courts, hearing city ordinance violations, including traffic cases, resulting in less than one-year imprisonment.[11]

Note the several different titles and types of courts in the pre-1977 Kansas court system, with similar yet different roles and jurisdiction. Imagine the confusion, redundancy, and fragmentation that is found in a nonunified state having much greater population and geographic area. It is obvious that the earlier Kansas system's fragmentation, duplication, and confusion were discontinued by the creation of a statewide unified system. No matter where in the state a citizen resides, he or she is able to understand what the local "district" court does.

Court unification contains three components: (1) a simplified state trial court structure; (2) judicial system policy- and rule-making authority vested in the supreme court or judicial council, with overall system governance vested in the state supreme court chief justice; and (3) state funding of all or a substantial portion of the judicial system, with the budget prepared by the administrative office of the courts. The American Bar Association endorses such a unified court structure, which characteristically has uniform jurisdiction, uniform standards of justice (such as rules of procedure, management systems, education and training, etc.), clearly vested policymaking authority (preferably in the state supreme court), and clearly established administrative authority (normally by the chief justice as the administrative head of the state court system).[12]

Court Decor and Decorum

Practically everything one sees and hears in an American courtroom is intended to convey the meaning that the courtroom is a hallowed place in our society. Alexis de Tocqueville, in his study of the United States more than a century ago, observed the extent to which our legal system permeates our lives:

> Scarcely any political question arises in the United States that is not resolved, sooner or later, into a judicial question. Hence all parties are obliged to borrow, in their daily controversies, the ideas, and even the language, peculiar to judicial proceedings. (T)he spirit of the law, which is produced in the schools and courts of justice, gradually penetrates beyond their walls into the bosom of society, where it descends to the lowest classes, so that at last the whole people contract the habits and the tastes of the judicial magistrate.[13]

The physical trappings and demeanor one finds in the courts convey this sense of importance. Normally, citizens are struck by the unique decor commonly found in the courtroom: high ceilings, ornate marble walls, expensive furnishings.

Citizens who observe court proceedings will note the traditional decorum that is accorded this institution. All people must rise when the judge enters the courtroom, permission must be granted before a person can approach the elevated bench, and a general air of deference is granted the judge. A vitriolic message that could lawfully be directed to the president of the United States will result in the utterer's being jailed for contempt of court when directed toward a judge.

The design of the courtroom, although dignified and intended to convey a message of singularity, provides a safe, functional space that is conducive to efficient and effective court proceedings. The formal arrangement of the participants and furnishings reflects society's view of the appropriate relationships between the defendant and judicial authority. The courtroom must accommodate judges, court reporters, clerks, bailiffs, witnesses, plaintiffs, defendants, attorneys, juries, and spectators, as well as police officers, social workers, probation officers, guardians ad litem, interpreters, and the press. Sometimes space must be allotted for evidence, exhibits, recording equipment, and computers.[14]

The trend during the past 25 years has been toward building smaller, more specialized courtrooms; however, in recent years, several large and complex civil cases have highlighted the need for extremely large courtrooms to accommodate as many as 250 participating attorneys and to seat several judges. Criminal trials, such as those with multiple drug defendants, can be quite large in size as well.

Judges and court staff now may require audiovisual equipment and computer terminals to access automated information systems. The latter are becoming increasingly important to trials and caseload management. A computer equipped with a keyboard tray and a silent printer is often placed at the court clerk's station for typing the transcript. Provision must also be made for the projection of slides, movies, X-rays, and overhead materials. A telephone and silent alarm are almost indispensable for emergency communications.

Courts: Seekers of Truth or Impediments to the Truth?

Ralph Waldo Emerson stated that "every violation of truth ... is a stab at the health of human society."[15] Certainly most people would probably agree that the traditional, primary purpose of our courts is to provide a forum for seeking—and through the adversarial process, obtaining—the truth. Indeed, the U.S. Supreme Court declared that fact in 1966 in *Teban v. United States ex rel. Shott,*[16] stating that "the basic purpose of a trial is the determination of truth."

Today, however, the perception of our court system, in the words of a state supreme court justice, as a "domain of fiddlers preoccupied with dissonance while citizens' houses are threatened by fire"[17] is held by more and more people. Increasing numbers of Americans have the impression that truth is being compromised and even violated with regularity in the trial, plea bargaining, and appellate apparatus of our justice system, thereby stabbing at the health of human society, in the words of Emerson.

These observers see many impediments to truth that should be eliminated in the judicial process. High on their list of impediments is the adversary system itself. Although many people would argue that such a system is vital to a free democratic society, under this system the courtroom becomes a battleground where participants often have little regard for guilt or innocence; rather, concern centers on whether or not the state is able to prove guilt beyond a reasonable doubt. To many people, this philosophy flies in the face of what courts were intended to accomplish. For example, former Chief Justice Warren Burger believed that "the responsibility of an ethical lawyer ... is essentially the same whether the client announces an intention to bribe or threaten witnesses or jurors or to commit or procure perjury. No system of justice worthy of the name can tolerate a lesser standard."[18]

In the adversary system, the desire to win can become overpowering. As one state supreme court justice put it, prosecutors "are proud of the notches on their gun."[19] Defense counsel enjoy winning equally. The attention can shift from the goal of finding truth to being effective game players.

Should this system be modified or replaced? That is an important and difficult question. As one law professor observed: "Lawyers are simply not appropriate to correct the defects of our adversary system. Their hearts will never be in it; it is unfair to both their clients and themselves to require them to serve two masters."[20]

Other impediments to finding the truth must be rooted out of the system. It has been argued that activities prohibited under both the Fourth and Fifth Amendments to the Constitution—the exclusion of evidence and the right against self-incrimination, respectively—should be restrained to assist the courts in getting at the truth. Rules of discovery should be modified to no longer be a "lawyer's favorite weapon in jousting for a position of trial advantage."[21] The battle between expert witnesses that often creates a circus atmosphere must be revamped as well.

These changes may come sooner rather than later. In the words of one jurist: "The public ox will not be gored indefinitely. The criminal justice system as we know it today is simply too costly, too cumbersome, too protracted, and most importantly, too encompassed with truth retardants. The predominant master must be the truth."[22]

The Influence of Courts in Policymaking

The judicial branch has the responsibility to determine the legislative intent of the law and to provide public forums—the courts—for resolving disputes. This is accomplished by determining the facts and their legal significance in each case. If the court determines the legal significance of the facts by applying an existing rule of law, it is engaging in pure dispute resolution.[23] "But if to resolve the dispute the court must create a new rule or modify an old one, that is law creation."[24]

Determining what the law says and providing a public forum involve the courts in policymaking. *Policy* can be defined as choosing among alternative choices of action, particularly in the allocation of limited resources "where the chosen action affects the behavior and well-being of others who are subject to the policymaker's authority."[25] The policy decisions of the courts affect virtually all of us in our daily lives. And in recent decades, the courts have been asked to deal with issues that previously were within the purview of the legislative and judicial branches. Because many of the Constitution's limitations on government are couched in vague language, the judicial language branch must eventually deal with potentially volatile social issues, such as those involving the prisons, abortion, and the schools.[26]

U.S. Supreme Court decisions have dramatically changed race relations, resulted in the overhaul of juvenile courts, increased the rights of the accused, prohibited prayer and segregation in public schools, legalized abortion, and allowed for destruction of the American flag. State and federal courts have together overturned minimum residency requirements for welfare recipients, equalized school expenditures, and prevented road and highway construction from damaging the environment. They have eliminated the requirement of a high school diploma for a firefighter's job and ordered increased property taxes to desegregate public schools.[27] The only governmental area that has not witnessed judicial policymaking since the Civil War is foreign affairs.[28] Cases in which courts make policy determinations usually involve government, the Fourteenth Amendment, and the use of equity—the remedy most often used against governmental violations of law. Recent policymaking decisions by the judicial branch have not been based on the Constitution but, rather, on federal statutes concerning the rights of the disadvantaged, consumers, and the environment.[29]

Perhaps nowhere have the nation's courts had more of an impact than in the prisons. Among these accomplishments of judicial intervention have been extending recognized constitutional rights of free speech, religion, and due process to prisoners; abolishing the South's plantation model of prisons; accelerating the professionalization of American correctional managers; encouraging a new generation of correctional administrators more amenable to reform; reinforcing the adoption of national standards; and promoting increased accountability and efficiency of prisons. The only failure of judicial intervention has been its inability to prevent the explosion in prison populations and costs.[30]

The courts have become particularly involved in administrative policy because of public-interest-group litigation. For example, legislation was enacted allowing citizen lawsuits when certain federal regulatory agencies, such as the Environmental Protection Agency (EPA), failed to perform certain duties as required by statute. Thus, a citizens' environmental group was allowed to sue the EPA.

It may appear that the courts are overbroad in their review of issues. It should be remembered, however, that judges "cannot impose their views . . . until someone brings a case to court, often as a last resort after complaints to unresponsive legislators and executives."[31] And plaintiffs must be truly aggrieved, or have *standing.* The independence of the judicial branch, particularly at the federal court level where judges enjoy lifetime appointments, allows the courts to champion the causes of those who make up the underclass: those with fewer financial resources, votes, or a positive public profile.[32] It is also important to note that the judiciary is the "least dangerous branch," having no enforcement powers, and that the decisions of the courts can be overturned by legislative action. Even decisions based on the Constitution can be overruled by subsequent constitutional amendment. Thus, the judicial branch depends on a perception of legitimacy surrounding its decisions.[33]

An Overwhelmed Legal System

According to government figures, lawyers in the United States today hold about 700,000 jobs, 78,000 of which are as judges; and about 70 percent of all lawyers practice privately, either in law firms or in solo practices. Many lawyers do not practice but use their legal training in other positive ways in administrative, managerial, and business positions in banks, insurance firms, real estate companies, government agencies, and other organizations.[34]

The United States has become a society that engages in "hair-trigger suing." The number of civil suits in federal courts has soared 300 percent since 1960, and in the state courts civil suits have increased by more than 4 million. Currently, nearly 20 million lawsuits are filed in state courts alone each year. The fear of being sued has become almost endemic to our society, changing the way we interact and do business.[35]

Contrast this with Japan, which has about 15,000 *bengoshis,* or lawyers, for a population that is half that of the United States. The Japanese have a distaste for confrontation; their legal system therefore discourages litigation by imposing barriers, and litigious persons are not held in high esteem. To become a lawyer, one must win a spot in the Legal Training and Research Institute, which accepts only 2 percent of its applicants each year. Thus, only 400 lawyers are added annually.[36]

Greed Brings Frivolous Lawsuits

Although lawsuits have resulted in better administration, training, safety, protection, and many other positive outcomes for everyday living, the fact remains that the prospect of suing also brings out the inherent greed found in many Americans. Egged on by similarly avaricious attorneys and the prospect of huge financial windfalls, we are suing one another with unprecedented frequency. Many of today's cases would have been laughed out of court not long ago. But the number and type of lawsuits faced by the courts today are no laughing matter. Following are some of the types of actions that have been taken to the doors of our courts by people seeking to obtain "justice":[37]

- Two fans of the Washington Redskins filed a suit to overturn a loss by the team, contending that a crucial call by a referee violated the rules and robbed them of their "right" to see a victory.
- A young Colorado man sued his parents for $350,000, charging that they gave him inhumane and inadequate care as a child, making it impossible for him to fit into society as an adult.
- A 41-year-old California man, upset at being stood up on a date, sued his would-be companion for $38 to compensate him for getting dressed up and driving 40 miles for nothing.
- A young Portland man (the plaintiff), employed as a checkout clerk in a grocery store, sued another young man for $100,000. The suit charged that the defendant "continually and repeatedly" sought out the plaintiff on the premises of the grocery store, and after locating him, directed his "gas" toward the plaintiff, humiliating the plaintiff and inflicting severe mental stress on him.

We who think of ourselves as rational can only hope that few or none of these litigants prevailed at the bar. Lawsuits of this ilk—smacking of blatant frivolity—do not always fail, however. Following are some examples of jury awards of this nature:

- A jury awarded $200,000 to a Chicago couple who were "bumped" from a flight to Florida, causing the "humiliation, indignity, and outrage" of missing the birth of a horse.
- A 36-year-old Philadelphia real estate manager who spent 11 years as a student and teacher in transcendental meditation groups sued because he was never able to achieve the "perfect state of life" they promised. He alleged that he had been told he would learn to "fly" through self-levitation, but he learned only to "hop with the legs folded in the lotus position." A jury awarded him nearly $138,000 in damages.
- In New Hampshire, the parents of a 9-year-old won $3,020 from their 88-year-old neighbor, who refused to return their son's ball after it rolled into her yard.[38]

We can also hope that at least some of these verdicts were overturned or reduced on appeal. Nonetheless, jurors today are often sympathetic to "aggrieved" individuals, especially when the defendant is a large corporation with "deep pockets." In 1962, there was just one personal-injury verdict of more than $1 million; now it is not uncommon to have more than 500 such verdicts each year.[39]

Decreasing Litigation: Alternative Dispute Resolution (ADR)

ADR Advantages

Several methods are now being proposed to reduce the number of lawsuits in this country. One is to limit punitive damages, with only the judge being allowed to levy them. Another is to force losers to pay the winners' legal fees. The process of discovery also warrants examination. This process involves exchange of information between prosecutors and defense attorneys, to ensure that the adversary system does not give one side an unfair advantage over the other. Many knowledgeable people believe that the process of discovery wastes much time and could be revamped.[40]

Another proposal that is already in relatively widespread use is alternative dispute resolution (ADR). Realizing that the exploding backlog of both criminal and civil cases pushes business cases to the back of the queue, many private corporations are attempting to avoid courts and lawyers by using alternative means of resolving their legal conflicts. Some corporations have even opted out of litigation altogether. About 600 top corporations have signed pledges with other companies to consider negotiation and other forms of ADR prior to suing other corporate signers.[41]

ADR is appropriate when new law is not being created. It can provide the parties involved with a forum to reach a resolution that may benefit both sides. Litigation is adversarial; ADR can resolve disputes in a collaborative manner that allows the parties' relationship to be maintained. Furthermore, ADR proceedings are normally confidential, with only the final agreement made public. ADR is also much more expedient and less costly than a trial.[42]

ADR Options: Arbitration and Mediation

The two most common forms of ADR used today are arbitration and mediation. *Arbitration* is similar to trial, though less formal. An arbitrator is selected or appointed to a case, and civil court rules generally apply. Parties are usually represented by counsel. The arbitrator listens to testimony by witnesses for both sides; then, after hearing closing remarks by counsel, the arbitrator renders a verdict. Arbitration may be mandatory and binding, meaning that the parties abandon their right to go to court once they agree to arbitrate. The arbitration award is usually subject to appeal. The types of disputes commonly resolved through arbitration include collective bargaining agreements, construction and trademark disputes, sales contracts, warranties, and leases.[43]

Mediation is considerably less formal and more "friendly" than arbitration. Parties agree to negotiate with the aid of an impartial person who agrees to facilitate in the settlement negotiations. A mediation session usually begins with a joint meeting with the mediator and both parties. Each side then presents his or her position and identifies the issues and areas of dispute. The mediator works with the parties until a settlement is reached or the negotiations become deadlocked. In the latter case, the matter may be continued in court. Mediation is not binding or adversarial; instead, it encourages the parties to resolve the dispute among themselves. Mediation is commonly used when the parties in dispute have a continuing relationship, such as landlord-tenant disputes, long-term employment/labor disputes, and persons with continuing business relationships.[44]

The leading ADR firm is Judicial Arbitration & Mediation Services, Inc. (JAMS), based in Orange, California, and started in 1979. It employs a panel of about 200 former judges. Washington-based Endispute, Inc., and the Philadelphia-based Judicate, Inc., are rapidly growing in the field as well. These private arbitration and mediation firms charge $300 to $350 per hour, a huge savings from the $300 per hour that a battery of lawyers might each charge litigants.[45]

Given the increasing number of lawsuits in this country, it appears that ADR is the wave of the future. As one law professor noted, "in the future, instead of walking into a building called a courthouse, you might walk into the Dispute Resolution Center."[46]

Citizens in Court

Judges define justice by interpreting and enforcing laws, thus handing out justice. Whether justice is done depends, however, on the interests or viewpoints of the affected or interested parties. A victim may not agree with a jury's verdict. A "winner" in a civil case may not feel that he or she received an adequate sum of money for the suffering or damages involved. Thus, in light of the fact that "justice" is not always agreed upon, we must make another distinction and also say that the courts must *appear* to do justice. The court's responsibility is to provide a fair hearing, with rights accorded to all parties to speak or not to speak, to have the assistance of counsel, to cross-examine the other side, to produce witnesses and relevant documents, and to argue their viewpoint. This process, embodied in the due process clause, must appear to result in justice.[47]

The low esteem with which the public regards the courts diminishes the cooperation required from the public in reporting crime and in testifying as witnesses. Certainly, many people in today's society are fed up with accounts of what they perceive as coddling of offenders and the ravages of the "law's delay," which often allows convicted murderers to spend more than a decade awaiting final judgment. People tell their neighbors of long waits at the courthouse, waiting to take care of business or having been summoned for jury service. They hear victims and witnesses talk of having been treated badly at the hands of the justice system.

Citizen groups interested in reforming the system have undertaken studies of the courts. Leading this court-watching effort have been such organizations as Mothers Against Drunk Driving, the League of Women Voters, and the National Council of Jewish Women. They observe court hearings, examine state juvenile codes, tour correctional institutions, interview justice personnel, and publish their findings. Many times these groups have probably had unrealistic expectations, as courts do not prevent crime or enact legislation and only see a small fraction of offenders (see the discussion of the "crime control model" in Chapter 1). These groups may also have an insufficient understanding of the problems or operations of the courts.

Americans complain about trial delays, high costs, and even unjust decisions. They want to know what judges are doing about these problems. Americans are asking themselves, "Do we have enough people power in this country? Or have the public officials, including judges, stopped listening to the people?"[48] Americans will increasingly judge their judges. They are going to want the courts to circulate questionnaires and listen to local groups. Succinctly, according to Abrahamson, judges must begin looking at judging from the perspective of the consumer.[49] Still, it is important that courts not be swayed by public opinion.

In this vein, certainly court unification, discussed earlier, has made the courts more "user friendly." But many citizens still probably wonder whether the courts exist to ferret out the truth and to protect the innocent, or instead survive today primarily to maintain the adversarial system of justice and create or preserve jobs for what many perceive as being an all too "chummy" courtroom work group. Perception is reality to people, and the courts must heed these concerns as they enter the twenty-first century.

Summary

In this chapter, we reviewed the distinctive nature of the courts. Courts, which have thus far resisted attempts to be bureaucratized, have comparatively little formalized, hierarchical structure or chain of command but are composed of informal work groups and are largely autonomous.

Several areas of concern were highlighted as well. One increasing concern, even among jurists, is whether several elements of due process afforded the accused, the adversarial system itself, and the omnipresent will to win by some court participants are affecting the courts' historical search for truth. Another growing dilemma, because of the lawsuit proclivity permeating our country, concerns how long the courts will be able to cope with the increasing civil and criminal litigation. A final concern relates to citizens' knowledge of court operations. The mystique surrounding the courts and the fear of being involved with court processes that has been engendered in citizens, and their perception of "justice delayed," indicate a need for improved community relations.

Questions for Review

1. Discuss how the courts differ from other traditional bureaucracies in their organization. How and why do courts shun the usual characteristics found in a bureaucracy?
2. What are the effects of society's litigious nature on court administration?
3. In what ways does alternative dispute resolution hold promise for reducing the current avalanche of lawsuits?
4. How does the public view the courts today? What specific areas does the public believe need improvement?
5. In what ways are courts unique in terms of their decor and decorum?

Notes

1. Kathleen Maguire and Ann L. Pastore (eds.), *Sourcebook of Criminal Justice Statistics 1998*. U.S. Department of Justice, Bureau of Justice Statistics (Washington, D.C.: U.S. Government Printing Office, 1999), p. 20.
2. Edward J. Clynch and David W. Neubauer, "Trial Courts as Organizations: A Critique and Synthesis," in Stan Stojkovic, John Klofas, and David Kalinich (eds.), *The Administration and Management of Criminal Justice Organizations: A Book of Readings* (3d ed.) (Prospect Heights, Ill.: Waveland Press, 1999), pp. 69–88.
3. Peter M. Blau and Marshall W. Meyer, *Bureaucracy in Modern Society* (New York: Random House, 1971), Chapter 2.
4. Clynch and Neubauer, "Trial Courts as Organizations," p. 43.
5. Ibid., pp. 46–48.
6. Ibid., pp. 49–50.
7. Ibid., pp. 51–52.
8. James Eisenstein and Herbert Jacob, Felony Justice (Boston: Little, Brown, 1977), p. 20.
9. Henry R. Glick, *Courts, Politics, and Justice* (New York: McGraw-Hill, 1983), p. 41.
10. William E. Hewitt, Geoff Gallas, and Barry Mahoney, *Courts That Succeed* (Williamsburg, Va.: National Center for State Courts, 1990), p. vii.
11. Ibid., p. vii.
12. American Bar Association, Judicial Administration Division, *Standards Relating to Court Organization*, Vol. 1 (Minneapolis, Minn.: American Bar Association, 1990), pp. 6–7.
13. Alexis de Tocqueville, *Democracy in America* Vol. 1 (H. Reeve, trans.), 1875, pp. 283–284.
14. Don Hardenbergh, "Planning and Design Consideration for Trial Courtrooms," *State Court Journal* 14 (Fall 1990):32–38.
15. Stephen Whicher and R. Spiller (eds.), *The Early Lectures of Ralph Waldo Emerson* (Philadelphia: University of Pennsylvania Press, 1953).
16. 382 U.S. 406 (1966), at 416.
17. Thomas L. Steffen, "Truth as Second Fiddle: Reevaluating the Place of Truth in the Adversarial Trial Ensemble," *Utah Law Review* 4 (1988):799.

18. In *Nix v. Whiteside*, 475 U.S. 157 (1986), at 174.

19. Steffen, "Truth as Second Fiddle," p. 821.

20. W. Alschuler, "The Preservation of a Client's Confidences: One Value Among Many or a Categorical Imperative?" 52 U.Colo.L.Rev. 349 (1981), at 354.

21. Ibid., p. 835.

22. Ibid., pp. 842–843.

23. Howard Abadinsky, *Law and Justice: An Introduction to the American Legal System* (2d ed.) (Chicago: Nelson-Hall, 1991), p. 123.

24. Richard A. Posner, *The Federal Courts: Crisis and Reform* (Cambridge, Mass.: Harvard University Press, 1985), p. 3.

25. Harold J. Spaeth, *Supreme Court Policy Making: Explanation and Prediction* (San Francisco: W. H. Freeman, 1979), p. 19.

26. Jethro K. Lieberman, "What Courts Do and Do Not Do Effectively," in Sheldman Goldman and Austin Sarat (eds.), *American Court Systems: Readings in Judicial Process and Behavior* (New York: Longman, 1989), pp. 18–32.

27. Abadinsky, *Law and Justice* (2d ed.), p. 124.

28. Spaeth, *Supreme Court Policy Making*, p. 19.

29. Abadinsky, *Law and Justice* (2d ed.), p. 125.

30. Malcolm M. Feeley and Edward L. Rubin, *Judicial Policy Making and the Modern State: How the Courts Reformed America's Prisons* (New York, N.Y.: Cambridge University Press, 1998).

31. Stephen L. Wasby, *The Supreme Court in the Federal System* (3d ed.) (Chicago: Nelson-Hall, 1989), p. 5.

32. Abadinsky, *Law and Justice* (2d ed.), p. 126.

33. Ibid., p. 131.

34. Bureau of Labor Statistics, U.S. Department of Labor, *Occupational Outlook Handbook, 1998–99 Edition*, Bulletin 2500 (Washington, D.C.: U.S. Government Printing Office, 1998), pp. 137–139.

35. Michele Galen, Alice Cuneo, and David Greising, "Guilty!" *Business Week* (April 13, 1992): at 62.

36. Ibid., pp. 62, 64.

37. David F. Pike, "Why Everybody Is Suing Everybody," *U.S. News and World Report* (December 4, 1978):50–54.

38. Bob Cohn, "The Lawsuit Cha-Cha," *Newsweek* (August 26, 1991): 58.

39. Galen, Cuneo, and Greising, "Guilty!" pp. 62, 64.

40. Cohn, "The Lawsuit Cha-Cha," p. 59.

41. Galen, Cuneo, and Greising, "Guilty!" p. 63.

42. American Bar Association, "Dispute Resolution: A 60-Minute Primer" (Washington, D.C.: Author, 1994), pp. 1–2.

43. Ibid., p. 3.

44. Ibid., p. 4.

45. Quoted in Ibid.

46. Ibid., p. 64.

47. H. Ted Rubin, *The Courts: Fulcrum of the Justice System* (Santa Monica, Calif.: Goodyear, 1976):3.

48. Shirley S. Abrahamson, "The Consumer and the Courts," *Judicature* 74 (August/September 1990):93–95.

49. Ibid.

COURT
PERSONNEL
ROLES
AND FUNCTIONS

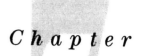

Chapter

7

The justice or injustice of the cause is to be decided by the judge.
—Samuel Johnson

Introduction

The administration of the judicial process is probably the least known and understood area of justice administration. Therefore, in this chapter we delineate the role of judges and other court staff members in ensuring that cases are processed in a timely and fair manner.

We base this discussion on the general observation, supported by the relevant literature,[1] that judges and lawyers are normally not well trained in handling the administrative tasks of their courts, nor do they often have the time required to accomplish them. Furthermore, few judges today would probably "like to spend all day or most of the day handling union grievances or making sure that employees know what their benefits are."[2]

A major function of the courtroom work group is to assure that there is a smooth flow of cases through the courts. Since case management is an underlying purpose of judicial administrators, it is strongly implicated in this chapter.[3]

We begin by considering the need for judicial independence and the relationship of that long-standing doctrine to the courts. We define and distinguish the terms *judicial administration* and *court administration*, then discuss the historically important role of court clerks—the original administrators of the court process—including the unique role played by those who work in rural environs. Following is the "heart and soul" of this chapter: the relatively new position of the specially trained court administrator. We then review some criteria that judges can employ to determine whether their court administrators are functioning effectively and efficiently. We close the chapter with a program of court administration and a view of courts that fail and succeed.

Defining Judicial Administration

The purpose of judicial independence is to mitigate arbitrariness in judging. But what is the purpose of judicial administration? That is more difficult to define. Consequently, as Russell Wheeler noted, "many court administrators today find themselves under the inevitable strain of not knowing for certain what their purpose is."[4]

Most works on judicial administration point to Roscoe Pound as the chief thinker in the field of judicial administration, as a result of his 1906 essay, "The Causes of Popular Dissatisfaction with Administration of Justice." However, the field should properly regard as just as much a founding document a major essay by Woodrow Wilson written 19 years earlier (in 1887), entitled "The Study of Administration." Wilson stressed that the vocation of administration was a noble calling, not a task for which every person was competent.[5] He emphasized that policy and administration are two different matters and, in extremely foresighted fashion, wrote that judges were responsible for judging and "establishing fundamental court policy," and that a third task was for a "trained executive officer, working under the chief judge or presiding judge," to "relieve judges generally" of "the function of handling the numerous business and administrative affairs of the courts."[6] Courts have *not* always regarded administration as a noble calling, but they have always been a bastion in defense of the distinction Wilson drew between policy and administration.[7]

Wilson's essay certainly gives intellectual respectability to the field of administration. It also poses two troubling aspects, however. First, although it is accurate in the abstract to state that a wall exists between administration and policy, almost every administrator and policymaker knows, as Wheeler phrased it, that "the wall is full of many gaps and is easily scaled."[8] Policy decisions inevitably intertwine with administrative decisions. Second, trying to honor this policy-administration dichotomy would leave the administrator adrift when confronted with inevitable policy decisions.

The difficulty of defining judicial administration became obvious during the 1970s, when it became vocationally attractive. Various people and commissions tried to define it but still seemed capable of only listing the duties of the office.

For example, the National Advisory Commission on Criminal Justice Standards and Goals stated in 1973 that "the basic purpose of court administration is to relieve judges of some administrative chores and to help them perform those they retain."[9] Furthermore, in 1974, the American Bar Association specified a variety of functions for the court administrator to perform "under the authority of the judicial council and the supervision of the chief justice."[10]

The problem of definition continued into the 1980s. One law professor who had done a large amount of research in the field felt in 1986 that the safest approach was "not ... to attempt a definition" but simply "to accept that it is a sub-branch of administration—more precisely of public administration."[11]

To assist in this dilemma and provide more clarity, a very good working definition of judicial administration is one advanced by Russell Wheeler and Howard Whitcomb. This definition allows an analysis from a variety of perspectives: "The direction of and influences on the activities of those who are expected to contribute to just and efficient case processing—except legal doctrinal considerations, insofar as they dispose of the particular factual and legal claims presented in a case."[12] This definition also nicely separates the judicial and nonjudicial functions of the court and implies that there is a set of people who share a role norm and that judicial administration constitutes *all* of the factors that direct and influence those people.[13]

Notably, however, the term *court administration* might be conceived of loosely as the specific activities of those persons who are organizationally responsible for manipulating these various judicial administration directions and influences.[14] This term is more commonly used in this chapter, as we focus on the development of the role and functions of the *individual trial court administrator.* This will become clearer as the chapter unfolds and the judge's and court administrator's relationship is discussed.

Judges As Administrators

Our Constitution intended the judiciary to play a key role in the application of its provisions: The overriding duty of judges is to protect the individual from the state. Our courts were created to provide the final defense of freedom: to be, in the words of James Madison, "an impenetrable bulwark against every assumption of power in the legislative or executive."[15] For this reason, our society for the most part accords its jurists a high level of esteem, as noted in Chapter 6.

Factors That Shape Judges' Attitudes

What makes judges behave and decide matters as they do? What elements of their education and experience might affect their views toward judicial administration? A considerable body of literature has investigated the forces that shape the attitudes of judges prior to their appointment.[16] One study reported that most judges were recruited from the locality in which they serve, bringing to the bench certain biases, values, and perceptions peculiar to their own locality.[17]

A judge's experience *after* his or her appointment may also have a significant bearing on the decision-making process, including both the sentencing and judicial administration functions.

Adapting to the Judgeship

Judges are required to be competent administrators, a fact of judicial life that comes as a surprise to many new judges. One survey of 30 federal judges found that 23 (77 percent) acknowledged having major administrative difficulties upon first assuming the bench. Half complained of heavy caseloads, stating that their judgeship had accumulated backlogs and that other adverse conditions compounded the problem. One federal judge maintained that it takes about four years to "get a full feel of a docket."[18]

Most trial judges experience psychological discomfort upon assuming the role as well. Seventy-seven percent of new federal judges acknowledged having psychological problems in at least one of five areas: maintaining a judicial bearing both on and off the bench, dealing with the loneliness of the judicial office, sentencing criminals, forgetting the adversary role, and responding to local pressure. One aspect of the judicial role is that of assuming a proper mien, or "learning to act like a judge." One judge remembered his first day in court: "I'll never forget going into my courtroom for the first time with the robes and all, and the crier tells everyone to rise. You sit down and realize that it's all different, that everyone is looking at you and you're supposed to do something."[19]

Like police officers and probation and parole workers, judges complain that they "can't go to the places you used to. You always have to be careful about what you talk about. When you go to a party, you have to be careful not to drink too much so you won't make a fool of yourself."[20] And the position can be a lonely one:

> After you become a . . . judge some people tend to avoid you. For instance, you lose all your lawyer friends and generally have to begin to make new friends. I guess the lawyers are afraid that they will some day have a case before you and it would be awkward for them if they were on too close terms with you.[21]

Judges frequently describe sentencing criminals as the most difficult aspect of their job. A federal judge reported that "Sentencing criminals is another problem which often troubles me. I have often said to the other judges that this is the hardest part of being a judge. You see so many pathetic people and you're never sure of what is a right or a fair sentence."[22]

Judges often meet together on a regular basis, and, in matters involving sentencing criminals, the new judge may frequently be guided by the experience of an older colleague. In most jurisdictions, however, there is almost no exchange of information between the novice trial judge and appellate judges. Novice trial judges typically feel that there may be an impropriety in discussing a judicial problem with an appellate judge; furthermore, trial judges often presume that there is nothing appellate judges can do to help them with their day-to-day problems.[23]

Consequently, many new judges rely on their court staff—particularly their court administrators—to assist them with the difficult early months of their judgeships. Another major source of socialization for novice judges is local lawyers. When the case subject matter is new to them, judges frequently ask opposing lawyers for information about "what the law says." Or, when they have a new or difficult case with which they need help, they occasionally contact a local attorney who specializes in the subject matter of the case at bar. Bench books and seminars are also helpful in socializing and training judges after appointment or election to the bench.[24]

The National Judicial College (NJC) in Reno, Nevada, is a major resource for judges, especially those who are newly elected to the office. The NJC is a full-time institution offering nearly 40 training sessions per year for more than 3,300 state judges, including judges from around the world. The NJC's annual budget is $8 million. (See the accompanying box; the Web site for the National Judicial College is provided in Appendix I.)

Judges as Court Managers

The Administrative Office of the United States Courts coordinates and administers the operations of the federal courts. In the states, judges assume three types of administrative levels: statewide jurisdiction, as that found with state supreme court chief justices; that which merely involves a local trial judge being responsible for administering the operations of his or her individual court; and that of a "presiding" or "chief" judge's position, wherein the judge supervises several courts within a judicial district.

Having a judge preside over several courts within a district developed as early as 1940, when Dean Roscoe Pound recommended that a chief or presiding judge of a district or a region be responsible for and have the authority for case and judge assignment.[25] Today these judges assume "general administrative duties over the court and its divisions" and are typically granted authority over all judicial personnel and court officials.[26] The duties of the presiding judge are numerous and include managing personnel and dockets and assigning cases and judges; coordinating the development of all judicial budgets; convening *en banc* court meetings; coordinating judicial schedules; creating and using appropriate court committees (to investigate problems, handle court business, etc.); dealing with outside agencies and the media; drafting local court rules and policies; maintaining the courts' facilities; and issuing orders for keeping, destroying, and transferring records.[27]

A basic flaw in this system is that the chief or presiding judge is actually a "first among equals" with his or her peers. The title of chief judge is often assigned by seniority; therefore, there is no guarantee that the chief judge will have the interest, temperament, or skills needed to manage a large court system. And

Judges Must Train to Take the Bench

At the National Judicial College (NJC) in Reno, Nevada, classroom bells—not gavels and bailiffs—rule the day. And the underlying message rings loud: Wearing a black robe alone does not a judge make. In times when the legal profession and the courts are coming under increased scrutiny and public criticism, the weight of judicial robes can be heavy.

At the judicial college, the goal is not only to coach lawyers on how to be judges, but to teach veteran judges how to be better arbiters of justice. For many lawyers, the move to the other side of the bench is an awesome transition. "Judges aren't born judges," said U.S. Supreme Court Justice Sandra Day O'Connor, who attended the NJC upon her election as an Arizona Superior Court judge in 1974. She recalled anxieties the first time she assumed the bench. "It was frightening, really. There was so much to think about and to learn. . . ."

Justice Anthony M. Kennedy, who is on the judicial college's faculty, described the college as

> an institutional reminder of the very basic proposition than an independent judiciary is essential in any society that is going to be based on the rule of law. Judicial independence cannot exist unless you have skilled, dedicated, and principled judges. This leads to so many different areas—judicial demeanor, how to control a courtroom, basic rules of civility, how to control attorneys. These are difficult skills for judges to learn. They're not something judges innately have. Judges have to acquire these skills.

Founded in 1963, the college presented its first course the following year in Boulder, Colorado. It is the only full-time institution in the country that provides judicial training primarily for state judges. It is affiliated with the American Bar Association, which pays about 10 percent of the college's annual budget. Other money comes from an endowment fund, donations, and program tuition and fees.

Courses run from two days to three weeks. Tuition and fees range from $530 to $2,060. Since its inception, the college has issued more than 66,000 certificates to judges from all 50 states and 150 foreign countries. Regular curriculum includes courses on courtroom technology; dealing with jurors; courtroom disruptions; domestic violence; managing complex cases; death penalty issues; mediation; family law; forensic, medical, and scientific evidence; and opinion writing.

As legal issues become increasingly complex and courts become overloaded with cases, judicial training becomes more critical. As stated by Joseph R. Weisberger, chief justice of the Rhode Island Supreme Court and an NJC instructor for 30 years, "It is the judiciary that transforms constitutional rights and liberties from a piece of parchment and printed words into living, breathing reality."

Adapted from Sandra Chereb, Associated Press, "Judges Must Train to Take the Bench," in the *Reno Gazette-Journal,* May 28, 1996, pp. 1B, 5B. Used with permission of The Associated Press.

where the chief judge is elected, there is always the possibility that a popular person will be elected, one who is not willing to "rock the boat."[28]

From a court administrator's standpoint, the office of and person serving as presiding judge are of utmost importance. As one judge put it, "the single most determinative factor of the extent of the administrator's role, aside from his personal attributes, is probably the rate of turnover in the office of the presiding judge."[29] As we will see later, the method of selection of judges is also an important process and consideration.

As mentioned, although judges are ultimately responsible for court administration, they have historically been ineffective managers overall. Judges are often confronted with issues about which they have little knowledge or experience. As one author stated:

> Until recently, judges typically proceeded without the advice of professional managers or the benefit of modern techniques of careful research, planning, evaluation and training. Even today, with court administrators having served for over 10 years in many courts, judges are often slow to heed their advice and continue to rely on intuitions and predilections born of legal training and disposition to follow precedents.[30]

Much of this lack of knowledge of behind-the-scenes court processes can be explained by the environment in which courts function. Judges primarily exist to hear cases; furthermore, they are often not given the necessary authority to govern all court operations. Moreover, they typically are not trained in court management. Lawyers learn early in law school training to treat each case individually; then, when becoming judges, they are unaccustomed to handling a large number of cases or analyzing caseloads or patterns of dispositions. As we will see in Chapter 8, however, case management is a judge's primary duty.

Court Clerks

Key Individuals

Not to be overlooked in the administration of the courts is the court clerk, also referred to as the prothonotary, registrar of deeds, circuit clerk, register of probate, and even auditor. Most courts have de facto court administrators in these clerks, irrespective of whether or not they have appointed administrators. These are key individuals in the administration of local court systems. They docket cases, collect fees and costs, oversee jury selection, and maintain court records. These local officials, elected in all but six states, can amass tremendous power.[31]

From the beginning in English North America, court clerks were vital members of society. The early "clerks of writs" or "clerks of the assize" existed in early Massachusetts, where people were litigious primarily because of land boundaries. There was a hostility toward lawyers carried over from England, and the clerk was the intermediary between the litigants and the justice of the peace. Their list of fees was twopence for summonses, threepence for attachment and replevin, and fourpence to take bond in order to prosecute a suit.

During the late seventeenth century, American courts became more structured and formalized. Books were available that superimposed English court usage in the colonies, and clerks, judges, and attorneys were provided proper forms that had to be used. In fact, the forms used by clerks 200 years ago are very similar to those in use today.[32]

Clerks have traditionally competed with judges for control over local judicial administration. In fact, one study found that the majority (58.9 percent) of elected clerks perceived themselves as colleagues, thus being coequal with the judges.[33] Court clerks have not as a rule been identified with effective management, however:

> Generally they are conservative in nature and reflect the attitudes and culture of the community. Their parochial backgrounds coupled with their conservative orientation, in part accounts for this resistance to change. This resistance often compels judicial systems to retain archaic procedures and managerial techniques.[34]

Clerks in Rural Courts: The Forgotten Majority

Much of the United States is rural in nature. Approximately 2,450 general jurisdiction and 14,100 limited jurisdiction courts exist in the United States;[35] nearly four-fifths of them exist in rural counties. These courts serve about 46 million people. A *rural court* is any trial court of general jurisdiction having fewer than two full-time judges authorized.[36] An enormous difference in court administration exists between urban courts and rural courts.

The small scale of rural courts affects the type of people who serve as clerks. Urban courts pay high salaries to obtain specially trained and educated court administrators, but rural clerks often have less training and education and receive lower salaries.[37]

While ultimately accountable for caseflow management, the clerk actually has little power to control the calendar. In most rural courts, lawyers actually review the proposed calendar before it is final. These clerks are challenged by such conditions as a single court reporter who is responsible for courtroom work in a large area, the lack of a local crime laboratory, having to bring expert witnesses from outside, and the limitation of the trial judge being available only a few days each month.

Other duties of rural court clerks include keeping tradition by maintaining records concerning the land grants of the town ancestors; the naturalization of the people who broke the sod; and births, deaths, marriages, and divorces in the community.

Court Administrators

Development and Training

One of the most recent and innovative approaches to solving the courts' management problems has been the creation of the position of court administrator. This relatively new criminal-justice position began to develop in earnest during the 1960s. Since that time, the number of practicing trial court administrators has increased tenfold and continues to grow. Actually, this concept has its roots in early England where, historically, judges have abstained from any involvement in court administration. This fact has not been lost on contemporary court administrators and proponents of this occupation: "It seems to be a very valuable characteristic of the English system that the judges expect to *judge* when they are in the courthouse . . . it does not allow time for administrative distractions."[38]

The development of the position of court administrator has been sporadic. In the early 1960s, there were probably 30 people in the United States who really worked as court administrators. By 1970, there were still fewer than 50 such specially trained employees.[39] Estimates differ concerning the expansion of the administrator's role during the 1980s. While one expert maintained that by 1982 there were probably between 2,000 and 3,000 people in the ranks of court managers,[40] another argued that there were only about 500.[41] At any rate, most estimators agree that more than twice as many of these positions were created between 1970 and 1980 than in the preceding six decades.[42]

We also know that by the 1980s every state had established a statewide court administrator, normally reporting to the state supreme court or the chief justice of the state supreme court. State court administrators' primary functions may be consolidated into three categories: preparing annual reports summarizing caseload data, preparing budgets, and troubleshooting.[43]

Today few, if any, metropolitan areas are without full-time court administrators[44] (the court organization chart shown in Chapter 6 demonstrates the breadth of responsibilities held by court administrators). An underlying premise and justification for this role is that by having a trained person performing the tasks of court management, judges are left free to do what they do best: decide cases. Indeed, since the first trial court administrative positions began to appear, "there was little doubt or confusion about their exact purpose."[45]

As court reformers have called for better trained specialists (as opposed to politically appointed persons) for administering court processes, the qualifications that are required for these persons have come under debate. The creation of the Institute for Court Management in 1970 was a landmark in the training for this role, legitimizing its standing in the legal profession. Many judges still believe that a law degree is essential, however, whereas others prefer a background in business administration. There will probably never be total agreement concerning the skills and background necessary for this position, but the kind of specialized training that is offered by the institute and a few graduate programs in judicial administration across the country would seem ideal.

Court administrators are trained specifically to provide the courts with the expertise and talent they have historically lacked. This point was powerfully made by Bernadine Meyer:

> Management—like law—is a profession today. Few judges or lawyers with severe chest pains would attempt to treat themselves. Congested dockets and long delays are symptoms that court systems need the help of professionals. Those professionals are managers. If court administration is to be effective, judicial recognition that managerial skill and knowledge are necessary to efficient performance is vital.[46]

General Duties

Turning to individual trial court administrators, a recent survey of these practitioners revealed that they actually perform six major duties:

1. *Reports:* Eighty percent of all trial court administrators reported primary responsibility for the preparation and submission to the judges of periodic reports of the activities and state of business of the court.
2. *Personnel administration:* Seventy-nine percent of all court administrators have as a primary duty serving as personnel officer for court's nonjudicial personnel.
3. *Research and evaluation:* These duties were performed by 78 percent of all respondents, to improve court business methods.
4. *Equipment management:* Three-fourths of all administrators are engaged in procurement, allocation, inventory control, and replacement of furniture and equipment.
5. *Preparation of court budget:* This major task is performed by 74 percent of all administrators.
6. *Training coordinator:* About 73 percent of trial court administrators surveyed provide training for nonjudicial personnel.[47]

Other duties that are assumed by the trained court administrator include jury management (reported as a primary duty by 42 percent of trial court administrators), case-flow or calendar management (42 percent), public information (56 percent), and management of automated data processing (59 percent).[48]

A few critics of this branch of the judicial reform movement feel that trial court administrators have in fact made little difference in the courts' efforts to function more effectively and dispense a higher quality of justice.[49]

Conflict Between Judicial Administrators

A Difficult Dichotomy

The nature of the administrative relationship between court administrators and clerks has been an area of concern. Administrators often view clerks as a threat and as an intrusion into their business. Clerks therefore have assumed a central role in resisting the creation of court administrator positions, but court administrators often depend on receiving information that only clerks can provide.[50]

Some conflicts occur between judges and court administrators. Sometimes judges usurp the administrators' role and make most management decisions unilaterally, defeating the purpose of having an administrator. Judges should delegate sufficient responsibility to administrators so that the former are getting what they need and the latter are doing what they were trained to do. On the other hand, judges sometimes totally abdicate their responsibilities, delegating too much of the court's work to the administrator and exercising virtually no oversight of the latter's performance. Abdication is particularly common when judges and administrators are in separate buildings or cities. In this instance, court administrators will in effect not be supervised.[51]

Tension and conflict may arise between judges and court administrators because some judges are reluctant to delegate responsibility for major aspects of court operations: budgeting and case scheduling, for example. In fact, some studies have shown that because of conflicts with clerks and judges, court administrators have not been given full responsibility over court duties of a nonjudicial nature; they are often allowed to perform only minor tasks.[52] In many courts, however, court administrators have been given full responsibility, including the latitude to be extremely innovative. Unfortunately, substantial confusion still exists over the proper role of the court administrator.[53] And in practice, the line separating the administrative and the adjudicatory functions of the courts has not been well established.

The rift that can exist between judges and court managers is also related to the fact that judges and courts resist bureaucracy. Thomas Leitko stated the problem in general terms:

> The integration of professionals into a professional bureaucracy has always been problematic. Because professionals identify more with their occupations than with their organizations, because they often control their own certification and performance standards, and because they have separate sources of legitimacy within their organizations, they often have functioned somewhat autonomously from and at odds with administrators.[54]

Judges resist measures of performance; their productivity is an intensely personal and private matter to them. The ultimate and perhaps only test of judicial performance occurs when the voters are asked to retain or reject them or during the appointment process. Not even other judges serve as performance evaluators. There are no merit salary programs or incentive or performance appraisal systems. Judges need autonomy and discretion. Conversely, for court administrators, accountability is the bottom line. Measures of performance are external to the individual administrator; supervisors evaluate their subordinates and people are hired, fired, and promoted with accountability in mind.[55]

Nonetheless, the two roles must support and cooperate with one another, even mesh together. The concept that judges should stick to judging and administrators to managing is counter-productive. There must be a mutual commitment to three fundamental values: the importance of joint policy formulation, respect for individual expertise, and mutual trust and support for achievement.[56]

In an ideal situation, the administrative and judicial activities operating within a court would be coordinated and equally balanced between the judge and the administrator. There would be activities that are clearly administrator centered, those that are judge centered, and those that involve joint decision making or information sharing—a "shared role" in the latter instance. Figure 7.1 depicts on a continuum how all court administration activities would be distributed and performed, and where collaboration between judge and administrator would be required.

Unfortunately, the relationship between court administrators and judges can involve a "clash between two cultures." Judges and administrators not only differ typically in background, education, and training, but they also approach their job roles from very different perspectives. Judges have the organizational power but

Figure 7-1

Continuum of administrative-judicial activities. (*Source:* E. Keith Stott Jr., "The Judicial Executive: Toward Greater Congruence in an Emerging Profession." *The Justice System Journal* 7[2] [1982]: pp. 152–179.)

Administrator-centered		Judge-centered
←		→
Administration		
		Adjudication

Administrator makes the decisions without consulting the judge	Joint decision making or information sharing; "a shared role"	Judge makes the decisions without consulting the administrator

Examples of Activities

Budgeting	Agency relationships	Case decisions
Training for nonjudicial personnel	Legislative relationships	Directing meetings of judges
Purchasing	Public information	Assigning judges
Accounting	Planning committees	Training for judges
Statistics	Research on rules and procedures	Selecting law-trained support personnel
Report preparation	Probation	Supervising screening and instructing of jurors
Systems analysis and research	Case processing	Record creation
Record keeping	Financial policy	
	Personnel rules	

lack the operational knowledge to perform all of the courts' operations, and court managers have the knowledge of court operations but lack the power. Obviously, if judges and court administrators can develop a team approach, they will merge these two strengths.[57]

Sources of Disagreement

Larry Mays and William Taggart examined court administrators' perceptions of the sources of conflict in court management. First, they asked respondents to indicate who had primary responsibility—a court administrator or a judge—for performing four administrative functions: budgeting, personnel, case scheduling, and jury management. At least half of the managers reported having the primary responsibility for each of these four functions. The degree of managerial control was not uniform across functions, however. The most prevalent function assigned to court administrators concerned the budget, for which nearly 9 of 10 respondents claimed responsibility. Less than two-thirds claimed primary responsibility for jury management and case scheduling.

The major source of conflict for both elected and appointed court managers was case-flow management (also known as calendar management), one of the crucial elements in any court's administrative scheme. Respondents commented on postponement of cases, judges rescheduling the calendar, docketing, judicial assignments, and backlogs.[58] This finding generally concurred with other researchers, that (1) case-flow management was one of the 10 least-delegated duties of presiding judges; and (2) case-flow management ranked last in a list of the 10 administrative duties most often mentioned in conjunction with court administration.[59] One explanation for this finding is that case-flow management has been believed to be one function that "judges would be reluctant to delegate," since it is a duty that "might be considered judicial in nature."[60] At the same time, however, Mays and Taggart found that case-flow management ranks high among the areas giving court administrators the greatest problems. Thus, it seems ironic that although case-flow management is described by many authors [61] as one of the primary functions of court managers, it is also grudgingly delegated by judges and is a leading source of conflict within the courtroom work group.

Mays and Taggart found that two of the five major areas of judge-administrator conflict in court management revolved around financial issues and personnel matters, two of the five major sources of conflict. Financial issues included accounting problems and methods, unbudgeted expenditures, procurement policies, and budget cutbacks. Among the personnel issues most often cited by respondents were employee evaluations, salary disputes, lack of adequate staffing, and the competency of staff.[62]

Court administrators must live by rules not of their own making. Internal court procedures and policies allow judges and others to hire, fire, direct, and compensate the manager's own employees. Both internal and external sources of conflict are evident in the areas of budgeting and personnel. Mays and Taggart learned that court administrators appear to feel constrained by legislative control, by the state administrative offices of the courts, and by the power judges wield, which court administrators often perceive as interference.[63]

Finally, other sources of conflict between judges, court administrators, and clerks were policy and planning issues and what may be called "authority to administer." In this regard, court administrators mentioned such issues as authority not being clearly established, delegation of responsibility without authority, lack of major policymaking authority, and changes that must be initiated by the judge(s). The latter concern is understandable. Court administrators do not enjoy constitutional status (as do elected clerks in the majority of the states), and most are appointed to their positions by a judge or a panel of judges and serve at the pleasure of their appointer(s). Thus, their authority is derived, or is an extension of the judge's (or judges'). This "reflected glory" can leave appointed administrators unsure of their power base and direction.[64] They must constantly "check with judges" to determine their wants and needs.[65] In fact, only 37.1 percent of court administrators perceive themselves as colleagues with the judges.[66]

Several court administrators have expressed that their judges either failed to provide support or leadership or, at worst, questioned the need for a court administrator position. Many administrators sense that their relationship is tenuous; nearly 4 in 10 (41.4 percent) consider their position as that of a court employee.[67] Other researchers have concluded that judges view their court administrators as administrative aides [68]—an attitude that could easily result in the discontinuation of such positions in tight fiscal times.

It is perhaps ironic that the more court managers attempt to control the administrative processes, the wider the gap may become between themselves and judges and lawyers. These two groups can have widely divergent perspectives on *what* is to be done and *how* it is to be accomplished.[69]

How Judges Evaluate Administrators

Like other mortals, judges and court administrators often see the world through "rose-colored glasses." As one Arizona judge observed:

> Judges and court administrators are not likely to view themselves in a negative light. As part of an organization that creates a certain amount of respect and awe for itself, it is not surprising that the [judge] and the court administrator may believe that they are better than they actually are. As a result, their top members frequently believe that the awe displayed toward them is intrinsic to their person, and not to the office . . .[70]

This view of the world is a pervasive impediment to objective assessment and clear decision making. Judges need to be able to determine whether their court administrators are performing competently and effectively.

According to John Greacen,[71] there are basically five strategies for judges to follow in determining the quality of work performed by their administrators:

1. *Look for the indications of good management.* A well-managed organization will have a number of plans and procedures in place, including personnel policies, recruitment and selection procedures, an orientation program for new employees, performance evaluation procedures, a discipline and grievance process, case management policies, financial controls, and other administrative policies (such as facilities and records management).

2. *Judges should be getting regular information.* Critically important reports and data on the court's performance, plans, activities, and accomplishments should be provided to judges on a routine basis. Judges should be notified of the numbers of case filings and terminations, pending cases, financial information, staff performance, long- and short-range plans, and other statistical data.

3. *Judges should be watching carefully.* Judges observe a lot of the staff's activities. They alone can make an assessment of their administrator's strengths and weaknesses. How does the administrator respond to problems and crises? Does he or she show initiative?

4. *Judges must often ask others about the performance of the administrator.* This includes soliciting input from lawyers, other judges, and other court staff members.

5. *Judges would be well advised to watch for danger signs.* Some people are basically retired in place, "putting in their time." If communication, energy, and new ideas seem to have dwindled or discontinued, there may be problems ahead.

Court Administration Reform: A Model Program

Imagine that you are in a crowded main lobby of a courthouse; it is packed, with sweltering heat. Tempers are short, lines are long, and people appear frustrated; some are even angry. Many have been waiting several hours simply to pay a traffic-violation fine.

Inside the courtrooms, matters are little better. Cases are dismissed for want of a speedy trial because records are lost; continuances abound for the same reason. The calendar is in a shambles. In the office areas the same conditions prevail. Large sums of money frequently disappear; boxes of money orders, checks, and even cash are piled up because no one knows what they are intended to pay or where they go. There are also huge piles of case files in 20 or more locations around the courthouse; dozens of cubic feet of warrants are stacked in boxes in bathrooms and closets because they cannot be matched to case files. The data-entry section is at least 5,000 cases behind and getting deeper. There is a large backlog of criminal cases. There are no written procedures; no forms management program; no employee performance reviews. Turnover is 50 percent and absenteeism is rampant. There is no training program. Public relations is a disaster, and complaints to the mayor and city council abound. This court does not work.[72]

Imagine that you return to the same court on a sweltering summer day three years later. Now, inside the lobby there is a cool white tile floor and ceiling fans, and citizens cool off during an average 15-minute wait until being served by well-trained, motivated court staff members (citizens give them a 90 percent favorable rating). An express box now allows many to pay fines without waiting. In the courtrooms, action is fast paced but flowing smoothly. The calendar is prompt and accurate; missing files now average less than 1 in 1,000. Dismissals due to speedy trial violations are now rare, and continuances are under control. No funds have disappeared from court offices in years, and cash security is tight. All payments are deposited within 24 hours; computer case records are updated within 48 hours. Loose paperwork is no problem, and each section has written procedures, lines of authority, flowcharts, and job standards. Comprehensive training is now provided to employees, who leave at an annual rate of only 4.5 percent and have comparatively little absenteeism. The public, attorneys, and media recently gave the court high marks for efficiency, and complaints to the politicians are nominal. The court now works very well.[73]

How has the total program of court administration turned itself around? Some courts and their administrators, such as that in Tucson, Arizona, and administrator Ron Zimmerman, have done so. They have provided useful information for others to follow as a model. First, there must be an atmosphere of trust and confidence between the administration and the judiciary. The presiding judge must delegate authority to the court administrator sufficient to get the job of reform going. In turn, the court administrator must respect the ultimate authority of the presiding judge. Second, the leadership must recognize that the currency of case filing is *the* priority for a high-volume court. All case files acted upon today must be processed (computer update, manual logging, mailing distribution, calendaring) and filed tomorrow.[74]

Third, all judicial administrators and staff must understand the fundamentals of court productivity. First, the clerk/judge ratio is of compelling importance. Zimmerman observed that "it makes no difference how many competent, hardworking judges a court may have if it does not have enough clerks to process the cases arriving daily from the bench." Zimmerman further noted that nine support staff for each full-time judge seems appropriate. The daily productivity of judges must be quantified according to the types of cases handled; then the average time to complete the case must be measured to determine how many hours of clerical time are involved in the actual actions received daily. With this information, the number of clerk positions needed may be calculated. Another factor contributing to court productivity is the ratio of total filings (complaints) per operations clerk. Zimmerman determined that a clerk can be expected to handle no more than 3,000 case filings per year. Thus, if each judge is found to handle all work derived from 15,000 complaints, each judge needs 4.66 clerical staff members to handle his or her work output.[75]

In Tucson, totally reorganizing court operations meant revamping a large, open bay of desks and pandemonium into three operating divisions and a support branch:

- **Court services** (including calendaring, motions, records, and domestic violence)
- **Public services** (counter transactions, mail and insurance, public telephones, and case initiation)
- **Case management** (warrant team, misdemeanor team, traffic team, arraignment team)
- **Administrative support branch** (bonds, restitution, enforcement team, fiscal-audit, and appeals).[76]

The supervision of court staff had been lacking, but more people were elevated to supervisory positions, allowing for greater decentralized decision making.

Following the inception of this structure, Tucson courts reduced their case-processing backlogs from 25,000 to 40,000 cases to zero; the number of dismissals for lack of a speedy trial became statistically insignificant; and judicial backlogs were reduced from several thousand to zero. Furthermore, the average time to service persons at the counter dropped from more than 10 minutes to 2.5 minutes each. The court calendar was also reformatted for easier readability and maintenance. A new case-tracking and management system was installed, including automatic reporting to the state motor vehicle division, automatic surcharge calculation, revenue distribution, and court scheduling.[77]

These changes required more than four years to accomplish, and the job is still not complete. Many years of failure to plan can require such an elongated effort, however. The benefits of changing from chaos to excellence are obvious. The message provided by a program of reform is that planning and, perhaps just as important, simplification are needed.[78]

Summary

The evolution of judicial administration is not simply the history of the court administrator's office. Conversely, the appointment of the first court administrator did not establish the beginning of judicial administration. Today, the court administrator's functions are quite different from the "housekeeping chores" seen in earlier times, involving policymaking as well. Judicial administration possesses a basic body of practical knowledge, a rudimentary theoretical perspective, and a concern for professional ethics.

It was also shown that several obstacles still exist in the total acceptance of court administration as an integral part of the judiciary. The extent of actual and potential areas of conflict between judges and administrators were seen as a major source of problems.

Court administration is a rapidly developing field. While it still has its detractors, it is apparent that it has come far from its roots and is evolving into a bona fide element of the American justice system.

Questions for Review

1. Why is the term *judicial administration* multifaceted? Provide a good working definition for this term.
2. Why do judges need assistance in keeping the courts' processes flowing smoothly? Include in your response a consideration of the socialization of judges and their accountability.
3. What are some criteria to be used for evaluating judges? How might you set up an evaluation process?
4. How have court clerks traditionally assumed and performed the role of court administrator?
5. What are some of the unique problems with being a court clerk in a rural area?
6. Why does the debate concerning the efficacy of court administrators continue? Discuss whether, given their history and relationships with judges, they have been completely successful or still have areas that need improvement.
7. What are some common areas of conflict between judges and court administrators?
8. What criteria may judges employ to evaluate the effectiveness of their administrators?

Notes

1. See, for example, Edward B. McConnell, "What Does the Future Hold for Judges?" *Judges Journal* 30 (Summer 1991):11; Russell R. Wheeler and Howard R. Whitcomb, *Judicial Administration: Text and Readings* (Englewood Cliffs, N.J.: Prentice Hall, 1977), p. xiii.; and Edward C. Friesen Jr., Edward C. Gallas, and Nesta M. Gallas, *Managing the Courts* (Indianapolis, Ind.: Bobbs-Merrill, 1971), p. 13.
2. Robert C. Harrall, "In Defense of Court Managers: The Critics Misconceive Our Role," *Court Management Journal* 14 (1982):52.
3. James Eisenstein and Herbert Jacob, *Felony Justice: An Organizational Analysis of Criminal Courts* (Boston: Little, Brown, 1977).
4. Russell Wheeler, *Judicial Administration: Its Relation to Judicial Independence* (Williamsburg, Va.: National Center for State Courts, 1988), p. 19.
5. Woodrow Wilson, "The Study of Administration," *Political Science Quarterly* 2 (1887):197; reprinted in *Political Science Quarterly* 56 (1941):481.
6. Quoted in Paul Nejelski and Russell Wheeler, *Wingspread Conference on Contemporary and Future Issues in the Field of Court Management* 4 (1980).

7. Russell Wheeler, *Judicial Administration,* p. 21.

8. Ibid., p. 22.

9. National Advisory Commission on Criminal Justice Standards and Goals, Courts (Washington, D.C.: U.S. Government Printing Office, 1973), p. 171.

10. American Bar Association, *Standards on Court Organization,* Standard 1.41 (1974).

11. Ian R. Scott, "Procedural Law and Judicial Administration," *Justice System Journal* 12 (1987):67–68.

12. Wheeler and Whitcomb, *Judicial Administration,* p. 8.

13. Ibid.

14. Ibid., p. 9.

15. Quoted in Doug Bandow, "Making Judges Accountable," *USA Today Magazine* (January 1988):55–57.

16. See, for example, Joel B. Grossman, "Social Backgrounds and Judicial Decision-Making," 79 Harv.L.Rev. 1551 (1966); Walter F. Murphy and Joseph Tanenhaus, *The Study of Public Law* (New York: Random House, 1972), Chapter IV.

17. Robert Carp and Russell Wheeler, "Sink or Swim: The Socialization of a Federal District Judge," *Journal of Public Law* 21 (1972):359–393.

18. Ibid., p. 370 (direct quote from the original).

19. Ibid., p. 372.

20. Ibid.

21. Ibid.

22. Ibid., p. 373.

23. Ibid., p. 378.

24. Ibid., pp. 382–383.

25. Roscoe Pound, "Principles and Outlines of a Modern Unified Court Organization," *Journal of the American Judicature Society* 23 (April 1940):229.

26. See, for example, the Missouri Constitution, Article V. Sec. 15, paragraph 3.

27. Forest Hanna, "Delineating the Role of the Presiding Judge," *State Court Journal* 10 (Spring 1986):17–22.

28. David W. Neubauer, *America's Courts and the Criminal Justice System* (6th ed.) (Belmont, Calif.: West/Wadsworth, 1999), p. 112.

29. Robert A. Wenke, "The Administrator in the Court," *Court Management Journal* 14 (1982): 17–18, 29.

30. Mark W. Cannon, "Innovation in the Administration of Justice, 1969–1981: An Overview," in Philip L. Dubois (ed.), *The Politics of Judicial Reform* (Lexington, Mass.: D.C. Heath, 1982), pp. 35–48.

31. Marc Gertz, "Influence in the Court Systems: The Clerk as Interface," *Justice System Journal* 2 (1977):30–37.

32. Robert B. Revere, "The Court Clerk in Early American History," *Court Management Journal* 10 (1978):12–13.

33. G. Larry Mays and William Taggart, "Court Clerks, Court Administrators, and Judges: Conflict in Managing the Courts," *Journal of Criminal Justice* 14 (1986):1–7.

34. Larry Berkson, "Delay and Congestion in State Systems: An Overview." In Larry Berkson, Steven Hays, and Susan Carbon (eds.), *Managing the State Courts: Text and Readings* (St. Paul, Minn.: West, 1977), p. 164.

35. Kathryn L. Fahnestock and Maurice D. Geiger, "Rural Courts: The Neglected Majority," *Court Management Journal* 14 (1982):4–10.

36. Ibid., p. 6.

37. Ibid., pp. 6, 8.

38. Ernest C. Friesen and I. R. Scott, *English Criminal Justice* (Birmingham, England: University of Birmingham Institute of Judicial Administration, 1977).

39. Harvey E. Solomon, "The Training of Court Managers," in Charles R. Swanson and Susette M. Talarico (eds.), *Court Administration: Issues and Responses* (Athens, Ga.: University of Georgia, 1987), pp. 15–20.

40. Ernest C. Friesen, "Court Managers: Magnificently Successful or Merely Surviving?" *Court Management Journal* 14 (1982):21.

41. Solomon, "The Training of Court Managers," p. 16.

42. Harrall, "In Defense of Court Managers," p. 51.

43. Neubauer, *America's Courts and the Criminal Justice System* (6th ed.), p. 112.

44. Ibid.

45. Geoffrey A. Mort and Michael D. Hall, "The Trial Court Administrator: Court Executive or Administrative Aide?" *Court Management Journal* 12 (1980):12–16, 30.

46. Bernadine Meyer, "Court Administration: The Newest Profession," *Duquesne Law Review* 10 (Winter 1971):220–235.

47. Mort and Hall, "The Trial Court Administrator," p. 15.

48. Ibid.

49. Ibid., p. 12.

50. Neubauer, *America's Courts and the Criminal Justice System* (5th ed.), p. 385.

51. John M. Greacen, "Has Your Court Administrator Retired? Without Telling You?" National Association for Court Management, conference papers from the Second National Conference on Court Management, *Managing Courts in Changing Times*, Phoenix, Ariz., September 9–14, 1990, pp. 1–20.

52. Larry Berkson, "Delay and Congestion in State Systems," p. 165.

53. E. Keith Stott, "The Judicial Executive: Toward Greater Congruence in an Emerging Profession," *Justice System Journal* 7 (1982):152–179.

54. Quoted in R. Dale Lefever, "Judge-Court Manager Relationships: The Integration of Two Cultures," *The Court Manager* 5 (Summer 1990):8–11.

55. Ibid., p. 10.

56. Ibid.

57. Ibid., p. 9.

58. Mays and Taggart, "Court Clerks, Court Administrators, and Judges," p. 3.

59. Burton W. Butler, "Presiding Judges' Perceptions of Trial Court Administrators," *Justice System Journal* 3 (1977):181.

60. Mort and Hall, "The Trial Court Administrator," p. 14.

61. See W. LeBar, "The Modernization of Court Functions: A Review of Court Management and Computer Technology," *Journal of Computers and Law* 5 (1975):97–119; Butler, "Presiding Judges' Perceptions of Trial Court Administrators;" J. M. Scheb, "Florida Conference Examines Education of Court Administrators," *Judicature* (1981):465-468; David Saari, *American Court Management: Theories and Practice* (Westport, Conn.: Quorum Books, 1982).

62. Mays and Taggart, "Court Clerks, Court Administrators, and Judges," p. 4.

63. Ibid..

64. Ibid., p. 5.

65. Saari, *American Court Management*, p. 62.

66. Mays and Taggart, "Court Clerks, Court Administrators, and Judges," p. 6.

67. Ibid.

68. For example, Mort and Hall, "The Trial Court Administrator."

69. Mays and Taggart, "Court Clerks, Court Administrators, and Judges," p. 7.

70. James Duke Cameron, Isaiah M. Zimmerman, and Mary Susan Downing, "The Chief Justice and the Court Administrator: The Evolving Relationship," 113 *Federal Rules Decisions* 443 (1987).

71. Ibid., pp. 5–20.

72. Adapted from Ron Zimmerman, "From Chaos to Excellence: Four Tough Years," *State Court Journal* 12 (Summer 1988):13–18.

73. Ibid.

74. Ibid., pp. 14–15.

75. Ibid., p. 15.

76. Ibid., pp. 15–16.

77. Ibid., p. 16.

78. Ibid., p. 18.

COURT

ISSUES

AND

PRACTICES

Chapter

Justice is such a fine thing that we cannot pay too dearly for it.
—Alain Rene LeSage

Introduction

Having looked at courts as organizations and explored the roles and functions of their personnel, next we examine their contemporary issues and practices. First we look briefly at drug courts, then we discuss in more detail the thorny issue of case delay, a subject that was touched on in earlier chapters. We look at the means by which caseloads are managed, the practical effects of delay, and the potentially exacerbating problems of records and paperwork. We then address a matter that is becoming more difficult and commonplace: the management of "notorious" cases involving celebrity defendants. Next is an examination of the problem of gender bias in the courts. Then, after a review of the expanding role that the courts are forced to play in resolving society's delicate and controversial health-related issues, followed by the legal basis for, and recent growth in, the use of interpreters in the courtroom, the chapter concludes with a brief discussion of stress on the bench. Three case studies concerning problems of court administration are provided at the end of the chapter.

Drug Courts

The courts in the United States are becoming increasingly clogged with drug-related cases, and many of our jails and prisons are overflowing with drug offenders. Nationwide, nearly 1.1 million arrests are made each year for drug offenses.[1] To cope with this massive problem, innovative drug courts are beginning to crop up around the country. As of mid-1998, there were 275 such courts operating and 155 drug courts being planned. Of the estimated 90,000 clients enrolled in drug courts, more than 70 percent had either graduated or were still enrolled. The average positive urinalyses of participants was 15 percent.[2]

To qualify for the program, a defendant must typically be charged with possessing or purchasing drugs; may not have a history of violent crime, a drug-trafficking arrest, or more than two previous nondrug felony convictions; and the state's attorney must agree to diversion. Program participants must have regular drug tests and return to court an average of once a month for a review of their progress. They will participate in and receive counseling, acupuncture, education courses, and vocational services along with strict monitoring.[3]

The Miami, Florida, drug court is one of the best known in the nation, with judges often handling an average of 80 cases a day. The judge explains the program to defendants, making it clear that it is difficult to complete. The judge also emphasizes that everyone involved in the program will assist and push the participants to complete it. Even with this large caseload, the judge talks with every defendant, offering a few words of encouragement for an offender who is improving, or chiding one who has been turning in "dirty" urine. The year-long program consists of three phases: detoxification, stabilization, and aftercare. It is much more complex—and initially more costly—than prosecution. The program cost per client per year, however, is roughly the cost of jailing an offender for about nine days. An evaluation of the program indicates a major benefit: Whereas typical recidivism rates range up to 60 percent, only 11 percent of the defendants who completed the program were rearrested in Dade County on any criminal charges in the year after graduation.[4]

Several research findings related to drug courts have found positive results. Such courts achieve cost savings for the justice system, particularly in the use of jail space and probation services. Several studies have shown that offenders referred to treatment by the courts have a powerful incentive to remain in treatment in order to avoid being jailed again. Other research suggests that the longer an addict remains in treatment, the better the chances for long-term recovery.[5]

The Dilemma of Delay

The principle that "justice delayed is justice denied" says much about the long-standing goal of processing court cases with due dispatch. Charles Dickens condemned the practice of slow litigation in nineteenth-century England, and

Shakespeare mentioned "the law's delay" in *Hamlet.* More recently, delay in processing cases remains one of the most visible problems of America's courts. The public often hears of cases that have languished on court dockets for years. Over half of all persons polled rated the efficiency of the courts as a "serious" or "very serious" social problem.[6] The overload in our bloated court system has been building for years. The most immediate source of pressure for the courts is the intensifying drug war; with increasing drug arrests, backlogs are growing.

Case backlog and trial delay affect many of our country's courts. The magnitude of the backlog and the length of the delay vary greatly, however, depending on the court involved. It is best to view delay not as a problem but as a symptom of a problem.[7] Generally, the term *delay* suggests abnormal or unacceptable time lapses in the processing of cases. Yet some time is needed to prepare a case. What is a concern is *unnecessary* delay. There seems to be no agreed upon definition concerning what unnecessary delay is, however.

Consequences of Delay

The consequences of delay can be severe. Delay can jeopardize the values and guarantees inherent in our justice system. Delay deprives defendants of their Sixth Amendment right to a speedy trial. Lengthy pretrial incarceration pressures can cause a defendant to plead guilty.[8] In contrast, delay can strengthen a defendant's bargaining position. Prosecutors are more apt to accept such pleas to lesser charges when dockets are crowded. Delays cause pretrial detainees to clog the jails, police officers to appear in court on numerous occasions, and attorneys to expend unproductive time appearing on the same case.[9]

One contributing factor to court delay is the little incentive that exists to process cases speedily. Although at least 10 states require cases to be dismissed and defendants to be released if they are denied a speedy trial,[10] the U.S. Supreme Court has refused to give the rather vague concept of a "speedy trial" any precise time frame.[11] The problem with time frames, however, is twofold: First, more complex cases legitimately take a long time to prepare; second, these time limits may be waived because of congested court dockets. In sum, there is no legally binding mechanism that works.

Suggested Solutions to the Delay Problem

The best known legislation addressing the problem is the Speedy Trial Act of 1974 and amended in 1979. It provides firm time limits: 30 days from the point of arrest to indictment and 70 days from indictment to trial. Thus, federal prosecutors have a total of 100 days between time of arrest and trial.

Overall, speedy trial laws have had only a limited impact in speeding up the flow of cases through the criminal courts.[12] Unfortunately, as Neubauer noted, "State laws have failed to provide the courts with adequate and effective enforcement mechanisms."[13]

Over the years, a number of proposals have emerged to help alleviate the courts' logjam, ranging from judicial jury selection and limits on criminal appeals to six-person juries. The latter was actually suggested more than two decades ago as a means of relieving congestion of court calendars and reducing court costs for jurors.[14] Thirty-three states have specifically authorized juries of fewer than 12, but most allow smaller juries only in misdemeanor cases. In federal courts, defendants are entitled to a 12-person jury unless the parties agree in writing to a smaller one.[15]

Some reform-minded persons concerned with delays suggest that the courts' greatest need is for better management and efficiency. In considering how the courts may function better, however, we must bear in mind that justice must be served. Where justice ends and expediency begins can be a difficult distinction to comprehend. Courthouse officials both "do justice" and move cases. It is the job of the court work group—some members of whom are actually the courts' greatest foes of efficiency—to assist the courts in performing both functions.

Case Scheduling

A key part of court administration is the ability to set a certain date for trial. One study found that courts with low backlogs and little delay were those that set a date for trial early in the history of a case.[16] Lawyers knew they had to be prepared by that date. If the judge sets a date that is uncertain, and if lawyers know that court dates are fluid and easily continued, they do not prepare.

Scheduling people for trials is problematic because of forces outside the administrator's control: slow or inaccurate mail delivery, notices of court appearances arriving on the day after the scheduled hearing, an illegible address preventing a key witness or defendant from ever being contacted about a hearing or trial, a jailer's inadvertent failure to include a defendant on a list for transportation. If just one key person fails to appear, the matter must be rescheduled. Furthermore, judges have limited ability to control the actions of personnel from law enforcement, probation, or court reporter's offices, all of whom have scheduling problems of their own.[17]

There are two primary methods by which cases are scheduled in the courts: the individual calendar system and the master calendar system.

Individual Calendar System

The simplest procedure for scheduling cases is the individual calendar. A case is assigned to a single judge, who must see all aspects of it through: arraignment, pretrial motions, and trial. The primary advantage is continuity: All parties to the case know that a single judge is responsible for its conclusion. There are other important advantages as well. Judge shopping is minimal, and administrative responsibility for each case is fixed. Also, it is easier to pinpoint delays, because one can easily compare judges' dockets to determine where cases are moving along and where they are not.

This system, however, is often affected by major differences in "case stacking," because some judges are fast, others are slow. Also, if a judge draws a difficult case, others must wait. Because most cases will be pleaded, however, case stacking is not normally a major problem unless a judge schedules too many cases for adjudication on a given day. Conversely, if a judge is too conservative and stacks too few cases for hearing or adjudication each day, delay will also result. If all cases settle, the judge has dead time, with a large backlog and nothing to do all day.

Master Calendar System

The master calendar system is a more recent development. Here judges specialize (usually on a rotating basis) in given stages of a case: preliminary hearings, arraignments, motions, bargaining, and trials. A judge is assigned a case from a central or master pool; once he or she has completed that phase of it, the case is returned to the pool. The primary advantage of this system is that judges who are good in one particular aspect of litigation (such as preliminary hearings) can be assigned to the job they do best. The disadvantage is that it is more difficult to pinpoint the location of or responsibility for delays. Judges also have less incentive to keep their docket current because when they dispose of one case, another appears. Also, the distribution of work can be quite uneven. If, for example, three judges are responsible for preliminary hearings and one is much slower than the others, an unequal shifting of the workload will ensue. In other words, the two harder-working judges will be penalized by having to work more cases.

Which System Is Best?

Each of the calendaring systems described here has advantages and disadvantages, but a running debate has developed over which is best. This probably depends on the nature of the court. Small courts, such as U.S. district courts, use the individual calendar system more successfully. But due largely to their complex dockets, metropolitan and state courts almost uniformly use the master calendar system. Research also indicates that courts using the master calendar experience the greatest difficulty. Typical problems include the following: (1) Some judges refuse to take their fair share of cases; (2) the administrative burden on the chief judge is often great; and (3) as a result of numbers 1 and 2, a significant backlog of cases may develop. In those courts where the master calendar system was discontinued in favor of the individual system, major reductions in delay were realized.[18]

Managing Notorious Cases

A Historical Phenomenon

The U.S. Supreme Court stated the following in 1966 in *Sheppard v. Maxwell:*

> Murder and mystery, society, sex and suspense were combined in this case in such a manner as to intrigue and captivate the public fancy to a degree perhaps

unparalleled in recent annals. Throughout . . . the nine-week trial, circulation-conscious editors catered to the insatiable interest of the American public in the bizarre. In this atmosphere of a "Roman Holiday" for the news media, Sam Sheppard stood trial for his life.[19]

The existence of notorious cases has always been a part of, and caused problems in, the courtrooms. The Salem witch trials, the trial of Aaron Burr, the Scopes trial, the Lindbergh kidnapping trial, the Sacco and Vanzetti trials, and those involving the Chicago 7, the Manson "family," and Alger Hiss point up the historical nature of trials that remain in our collective memories long after their conclusion. More recently, the trials of O. J. Simpson, Susan Smith, Mike Tyson, William Kennedy Smith, Oliver North, Marion Barry, Bernhard Goetz, Imelda Marcos, John Gotti, Manuel Noriega, and the police officers who were tried for assaulting Rodney King were clearly "notorious." Some of these trials gained nationwide notoriety through media depictions even after the actual trial was ended.

Certainly the work of the judge and the court administrator are greatly affected when such celebrated cases come up on the docket. In the following section, we examine the role of each in this arena and several of the attendant problems that must be addressed.

Administrative Issues

One issue in handling a notorious case is the selection of the judge. In these cases it is particularly important that the judge be experienced and have good legal skills, possess a good reputation in the legal community, be temperate and in command in the courtroom, and be seen as fair and unbiased. He or she should also possess good health and the ability to deal with the media. These trial judges should be individually handpicked by presiding judges for this assignment.[20]

Court administrators and other court staff members will necessarily devote considerable thought and planning efforts to these cases. They must anticipate all possible problems and concerns that might arise, including media requests; courtroom and courthouse logistics for handling crowds, the media, and security; managing the jury; and managing the court's docket of other existing cases. The judge must take firm control and insist on timely preparation by attorneys, adhering to dates set for court processes and avoiding granting continuances unless absolutely necessary.

A notorious trial may require that a larger courtroom be used so that larger than usual numbers of people from the press and the public, as well as defendants and attorneys, may be accommodated. Planning is essential for providing adequate space for judge's chambers, jury rooms, witness rooms, clerk's office, security personnel, parking, and lunchroom facilities.[21] The care, comfort, and safety of the prospective and actual jurors must be provided for. Jurors want to be kept informed of all case details relating to their task and time frames relating to the proceedings.

If the judge decides to sequester the jury, the court administrator must consider security issues (protecting the jury from outside interference and providing for conjugal visits, room searches, transportation, and so on) and jurors' personal needs (meals, entertainment, medical supplies).[22]

A number of other issues must be considered. Are identification and press passes needed? Are entry screening devices necessary? What seating arrangements will the case require? Should court observers be allowed to exit and reenter at will? Do purses, briefcases, and other such items need to be searched by hand? Is it necessary that all mail and telephone calls coming to the courthouse be monitored? Is a special command center desirable for coordination and communication?[23]

Meanwhile, there will be filings of new cases and other calendars while the notorious case is pending. Once a notorious case begins, the active trial and motion responsibilities of the trial judge should be transferred to another judge(s). The judge presiding over a notorious trial must avoid distractions and disruptions, taking care not to overlook any of the several important matters that accompany such a trial.[24]

Perhaps the most important task in managing notorious cases and avoiding and resolving problems is communication with the media. Some judges have established an open door policy in dealing with the media, setting aside a certain time when reporters may discuss the case. This method will go a long way toward ensuring that the media are receiving accurate information rather than relying on rumor and other sources of inaccurate information.[25]

The Problem of Gender Bias

Another concern exists for administrative judges: accusations of gender bias in the courts. Although it might be difficult to imagine that such a problem exists in the courts as they enter the twenty-first century, several of the nation's legislatures and state supreme courts have deemed this issue to be such a concern that they are convening special task forces to determine what can be done. Certainly there are data, records, and other information that court administrators can examine and bring to the courts' attention when gender bias occurs.

Gender bias has been described as "a problem with several aspects."[26] The term includes society's perception of the relative worth of women and men, what is perceived as women's and men's work, and myths and misconceptions about the economic and social realities of women's and men's lives."[27]

More specifically, gender bias in the courts can take the following forms:

1. In juvenile law, the American Bar Association has found that although the "crimes" that females are accused of are categorized as less serious and harmful to society than those of males, girls are often held in detention for longer periods and are less likely to be placed in community programs than are boys.[28]

2. Early studies noted the casual response of the legal profession and the judiciary to the plight of battered women. Some researchers interpreted this

finding as evidence of faint echoes of the common-law view of a wife as her husband's property, lingering in the minds of some judges and attorneys.[29]

3. There is extensive literature created by the antirape movement showing that judicial myths regarding the nature of male and female sexuality and attitudes toward the "proper" roles of women served to punish rape victims by defining rape and spousal abuse as "victim-precipitated" crimes.[30]

4. The looming "disaster" in family law that most disturbs those interested in equal justice is the underclass of women and children being created through inadequate child support and alimony awards. Social scientists studying the consequences of no-fault divorce in California uncovered the unwitting contribution that courts were making to the "feminization of poverty."[31]

In courtrooms across the country, women still find themselves judged on the basis of factors that trial researchers and feminists consider antiquated and prejudicial. Bias and stereotyped images, they say, influence jury selection, the treatment of female witnesses, and attitudes toward women attorneys and judges. The New York Task Force on Women in the Courts termed gender bias "pervasive" because of the tendency of some judges and attorneys to accord less credibility to the claims and testimony of women. These findings were nearly identical to those of a New Jersey study. These and other studies consistently turn up stereotypes that women jurors are more likely than male jurors to acquit in criminal cases (except in cases involving a child or threat to family); female jurors are less likely to favor female defendants or plaintiffs; and in civil cases, female jurors are more likely than males to vote in favor of the plaintiff, but vote for smaller awards than men do.[32]

The need to educate judges about the findings of researchers and the concerns of women lawyers was first articulated in 1969 by Sylvia Roberts, a pioneer Title VII litigator from Louisiana. Still, progress has been slow in coming. Little has yet to be written on the topic. Courses and workshops are now included in numerous judicial education programs for state and federal court judges, however.[33]

Roberts said women should adopt the Taoist philosophy of the Chinese ancients and "think of ourselves as water on stone."[34] Although the stone is hard and the water is merely splashing around it, the stone eventually wears away and the landscape is transformed. They will continue to act as water on stone, and perhaps through their consistent efforts the stone will eventually give way.

Other Courtroom Challenges

Health-Related Cases

Although not highly visible, another pervasive issue of concern in the courts is the role the judiciary is being asked to play in shaping the country's health care policy. The types of policy decisions judges must confront—many involving weighty medical ethics questions—were reflected in a recent two-week period:

A company attempted to drastically cut its insurance coverage for employees with AIDS; a woman convicted of child abuse was required to accept implantation of a long-term birth control drug; a woman was sentenced for child endangerment after passing an illegal drug to her infant through her breast milk, killing the child; a petition was filed to drop criminal charges because of the deteriorating health of the 85-year old defendant.

There is also growing judicial difficulty in determining causality and damages in cases involving silicone gel breast implants, life-sustaining medical treatment, new reproductive technologies (such as in vitro fertilization and surrogate parenthood), elder abuse and neglect, and possibly even claims of brain cancer attributable to currents in cellular telephones.[35]

These types of cases may create unique administrative problems and challenges for court processing. For example, they may be raised on an emergency basis and require an expedited decision. And, because there may not be expert witnesses available in these cases, the judge may have to spend a considerable amount of time developing necessary expertise.

The role of the courts in health-related issues is likely to expand as the onslaught of new litigation brings many additional health care–related issues before the courts.

The Growth in Scientific Testimony

Another problem facing courts today is that of complex testimony rendered by experts who speak in esoteric language and often disagree with each other in their findings. "Exhibit C" in today's courtroom might be a brain scan from a neuroscientist's laboratory instead of a murder weapon. The demand for expert testimony has tripled in the past decade: Scientists now make approximately 400,000 appearances per year to give depositions, attend briefings, and testify in court. Scientific evidence is used in nearly 30 percent of all court cases, and outcomes now often turn on the ability of judges and jurors with little or no scientific background to comprehend the complexities of such specialized subjects as physics, toxicology, and organic chemistry.[36]

Many persons now question whether courts and juries can properly digest the material and produce accurate decisions. Scientists shudder when a rapist is released by a jury despite a 99 percent probability that semen in evidence was the defendant's; they recoil when a judge fails to understand that animal studies can have strong implications for human beings and will not admit such research into evidence. Attorneys and clients are befuddled and outraged when two cases with identical scientific evidence yield opposite verdicts. Growing concern over such inconsistencies has led scientific societies, legal scholars, and even the U.S. Justice Department to call for changes to improve the quality of science-based verdicts.[37]

The most publicized dilemma for the courts is how to guarantee the quality and credibility of scientific testimony. Because lawyers seek the experts most likely to help win a case, many scientists regard courtroom testimony as suspect and simply refuse to participate. One federal judge observed that "an expert can be found to testify to the truth of almost any factual theory, no matter how frivolous."[38]

One solution is the court-appointed witness, chosen by a judge to act as a neutral voice in the midst of scientific disputes. The American Association for the Advancement of Science has pledged to aid judges in their quest for court experts by screening scientists and providing lists of suitable candidates. A Federal Judicial Center study revealed that although 80 percent of judges think appointing neutral experts can be useful, only 20 percent have ever done so. Most judges express concerns about affecting the outcome of a trial and worry that they lack the scientific expertise to choose an expert.[39]

The Justice Department is considering offering seminars to help judges better understand scientific methods, but with 400 cases on the average federal judge's calendar, attending such seminars may be difficult if not impossible. An alternative plan is for other groups to prepare primers on subjects such as DNA evidence and statistical methodology to guide judges through the relevant issues and debates. Pretrial crash courses for jurors and juror notebooks are also possibilities.[40]

Notwithstanding these efforts, studies suggest that judges and jurors base their decisions on a wide range of human impulses other than scientific rationality: sympathy, dread, the desire for revenge, and so on.[41] In the end, a verdict may not turn on their perception of scientific evidence but, instead, on their gut feelings of guilt and innocence.

Interpreters in the Courtroom

Legal Basis

Another area of court administration involves the use of interpreters in the courtroom. This matter is grounded on the Sixth Amendment, which allows criminal defendants to confront witnesses who testify against them, and the Fifth and Fourteenth Amendments, which guarantee due process and afford "fundamental fairness" to defendants.

Since the late 1960s, there has been a veritable explosion in the use of foreign-language interpreting in America's courtrooms. The major event that engendered the current trend toward greater use of interpreters in the courts, however, was the passage of Public Law 95-539, the federal Court Interpreters Act of 1978. The act provides for court-appointed interpreter services:

> In any criminal or civil action initiated by the United States in a United States District Court . . . if the presiding judicial officer determines on such officer's own motion or on the motion of a party that such party . . . (1) speaks only or primarily a language other than the English language; or (2) suffers from a hearing impairment . . . so as to inhibit such party's comprehension of the proceedings or communication with counsel or the presiding judicial officer, or . . . such witness's comprehension of questions and the presentation of such testimony. Note that the guarantee covers civil as well as criminal matters, and that the judge determines whether a given defendant or witness is in need of an interpreter's services.

Although specifically applicable to federal courts, this legislation has served to stimulate measures in state and municipal courts as well. Many states provide for courtroom interpreters by statute, while courts of lower jurisdiction are increasingly assigning foreign-language interpreters to non-English-speaking or hearing-impaired defendants, witnesses, and litigants.[42]

Role of Court Administrators

The need for interpreting arises in a multitude of languages, ranging from the commonplace such as Spanish (in 96.6 percent of all interpreter appearances), Italian, and German, to the "exotic" languages, such as the languages of Asia, Africa, and the Middle East. Court interpreters are commonly found on duty at criminal trials for initial appearances, bail hearings, preliminary hearings, pretrial and in-trial motions, pleas and changes of plea, sentencing, trials, and probation department recommendation.[43] At trial, court interpreters must swear to interpret to the best of their ability, and as accurately as possible, the proceeding at hand.[44]

Interpreting is a highly complicated process. The interpretation of speech can become a gross distortion of what has been said. Appeals based on errors in interpreting or translating have increased dramatically in recent years.[45] Several appeals have been successful when it was shown that interpreters were unqualified. For this reason, at the federal level, court interpreters must be certified by a court administrator, the director of the Administrative Office of the U.S. Courts. The test for certification is quite rigorous. In 1986, only 4 percent of those taking the exam passed it in its entirety.[46]

Stress on the Bench

As a result of their work, judges have had to endure threats, assaults, and even mail bombs. More than 3,000 such incidents against the federal judiciary were reported to the U.S. Marshals Service in one recent 14-year period.[47]

Such incidents are, of course, highly stressful for judges. Very little has been written concerning danger and related stress and burnout among members of the judiciary or other actors of the court. Judges, however, are not immune to their causes and effects. Grave consequences for all concerned can occur when judges develop psychological problems. Such a case occurred in New York, demonstrating how vulnerable even placid, seemingly in control professionals are prone to suffer psychological problems and display irrational behavior.

For several weeks, a wealthy Manhattan divorcee received menacing telephone calls demanding payment for some supposedly compromising photos and tapes. With the caller's voice electronically disguised, she could not identify the extortionist. When the FBI finally unmasked the caller after tailing him for more than a month, even scandal-hardened New York was stunned. The accused blackmailer was the chief judge of New York's Supreme Court. He was later arraigned on charges of attempting to extort money from the woman and threatening her

14-year-old daughter. It was later determined that the judge had had an affair with the victim, who had recently ended the relationship. The judge was ingloriously shackled to a psychiatric-ward bed for nearly three days before being placed under house arrest with an electronic monitoring bracelet. Hours later he resigned from the bench, with an apology, from the court he had served with distinction for two decades.[48]

Although this is an isolated case, psychiatrists and psychologists say it is not uncommon for professionals to crumble at or near the pinnacle of their careers. It has been said that "When their sense of power is pierced, these individuals often try to recapture it through very inappropriate means," and "when a judge has his jurist's robes on, that may compensate for the inadequacy in other parts of his life."[49]

Although on-the-job stress may not be the sole contributing factor in this instance or in similar cases, it may well be a major precipitating element. Job-related stress can often lead to problems in other areas of one's life, including interpersonal relationships and low self-esteem.

Summary

In this chapter, we discussed several challenges to the courts. We also laid bare several major problems and issues confronting the courts, generated from both internal and external means. The core problem today is that of case delay, since all of the courts' activities revolve around this key dilemma. We also examined several challenges involving gender bias, health, and language interpretation issues.

It is obvious that today's court managers carry a tremendous responsibility to be innovative, open to new ideas, accountable, and well trained and educated for the challenges that lie ahead. Certainly, legislators and policymakers must also become more aware of the difficulties confronting the courts and be prepared to provide additional resources for meeting the increasing caseloads, issues, and problems of the future.

Questions for Review

1. Describe the two primary methods of case scheduling employed by the courts. Which of the two methods is used most frequently in the United States? What are its advantages and disadvantages?
2. What is a "notorious" court case? What are some of the administrative problems that accompany the trying of such cases, and how have they wrought changes in court operations?
3. Explain the court administrator's role in dealing with non-English-speaking defendants. Why is this a potentially serious matter?

4. What are the philosophy, role, and methods of a drug court?
5. How may the courts be viewed as being guilty of gender bias? What might judges and administrators do to address the problem?
6. What kinds of court functions might contribute to stress among judges?

Notes

1. United States Department of Justice, Federal Bureau of Investigation, *Crime in the United States, 1998* (Washington, D.C.: Author, 1999), p. 211.
2. U.S. Office of Justice Programs, Drug Courts Program Office, *Looking at a Decade of Drug Courts* (Washington, D.C.: Author, 1998).
3. U.S. Department of Justice, National Institute of Justice Program Focus, "Miami's Drug Court: A Different Approach," June 1993, p. 3.
4. Ibid., p. 13.
5. Office of National Drug Control Policy, *Understanding Drug Treatment.* (Washington, D.C.: The White House, 1990.)
6. David W. Neubauer, *America's Courts and the Criminal Justice System* (5th ed.)(Belmont, Calif.: Wadsworth, 1996), p. 374.
7. David W. Neubauer, Maria Lipetz, Mary Luskin, and John Paul Ryan, *Managing the Pace of Justice: An Evaluation of LEAA's Court Delay Reduction Programs* (Washington, D.C.: U.S. Government Printing Office, 1981).
8. David W. Neubauer, *America's Courts and the Criminal Justice System* (6th ed.) (Belmont, Calif.: West/Wadsworth, 1999), p. 121.
9. Ibid.
10. See *Barker v. Wingo,* 407 U.S. 514 (1972).
11. Ibid., at p. 522.
12. Raymond Nimmer, *The Nature of System Change: Reform Impact in the Criminal Courts* (Chicago: American Bar Foundation, 1978).
13. Neubauer, *America's Courts and the Criminal Justice System* (6th ed.), p. 124.
14. National Advisory Commission on Criminal Justice Standards and Goals, *Courts.*
15. Neubauer, *America's Courts and the Criminal Justice System* (6th ed.), p. 338.
16. Ibid., p. 379.
17. Steven Flanders, *Case Management and Court Management in the United States District Courts* (Washington, D.C.: Federal Judicial Center, 1977).
18. Neubauer, Lipetz, Luskin, and Ryan, *Managing the Pace of Justice,* p. 27.
19. 86 S.Ct. 1507, 1519 (1966).
20. Timothy R. Murphy, Genevra Kay Loveland, and G. Thomas Munsterman, *A Manual for Managing Notorious Cases* (Washington, D.C.: National Center for State Courts, 1992), pp. 4–6. See also Timothy R. Murphy, Paul L. Hannaford, Kay Genevra, *Managing Notorious Trials* (Williamsburg, Va.: National Center for State Courts, 1998).
21. Ibid., p. 23.
22. Ibid., p. 53, 73.
23. Ibid., pp. 89–94.
24. Ibid., p. 22.
25. Ibid., pp. 27–30.

26. Lynn Hecht Shafran, in Marilyn Roberts, "National Conference on Gender Bias in the Courts," *State Court Journal* 13 (Summer 1989):12.

27. Ibid.

28. American Bar Association, *Little Sisters and the Law* (Washington, D.C.: Author, 1977).

29. Ibid.

30. Ibid.

31. Norma J. Wikler, "Water to Stone: A Perspective on the Movement to Eliminate Gender Bias in the Courts," *State Court Journal* 13 (Summer 1989):13–18.

32. Kathleen Mulvihill, "Female Stereotypes Persist in U.S. Courts, Recent Studies Show," *The Christian Science Monitor* (July 27, 1987):7.

33. Ibid., p. 14.

34. Marilyn Roberts, "National Conference on Gender Bias in the Courts," *State Court Journal* 13 (Summer 1989):12.

35. U.S. Department of Justice, National Institute of Justice Journal, Research in Action, "Health and Criminal Justice: Strengthening the Relationship," November 1994, pp. 25–26.

36. Joannie M. Schrof, "Courtroom Conundrum," *U.S. News and World Report* (October 26, 1992):67–69.

37. Ibid.

38. Ibid., p. 68 (direct quote from the original).

39. Ibid., p. 69.

40. Ibid.

41. Ibid.

42. Susan Berk-Seligson, *The Bilingual Courtroom: Court Interpreters in the Judicial Process* (Chicago: University of Chicago Press, 1990), p. 1.

43. Ibid., pp. 3–4, 8–9.

44. Ibid., pp. 55, 57.

45. Berk-Seligson, *The Bilingual Courtroom,* pp. 199–200.

46. J. Leeth, *The Court Interpreter Examination* (Washington, D.C.: National Resource Center for Translation and Interpretation, Georgetown University, no date).

47. Frederick S. Calhoun, "Hunters and Howlers: Threats and Violence Against Federal Judicial Officials in the United States, 1789–1993" (Washington, D.C.: U.S. Marshals Service, 1998).

48. David Gelman, Susan Miller, and Bob Cohn, "The Strange Case of Judge Wachtler," *Newsweek* (November 23, 1992):34–35.

49. Ibid., pp. 34, 35.

CASE STUDIES

The Court Administrator
and the Prudent Police Chief*

You are the court administrator in a system that has the following procedure for handling traffic matters:

1. All persons who are given a traffic citation are required to appear in court at 9:00 A.M. on either Monday or Wednesday within two weeks of their arrest. They are given a specific date to appear.

2. At the initial appearance, the arresting agency is represented by a court officer who has previously filed copies of all the citations with the clerk of the court.

3. The clerk, prior to the return date on the citation, prepares a file for each citation.

4. The clerk calls each case, and those persons appearing are requested by the court to enter a plea. If the plea is "not guilty," the matter is set for trial at a future date.

5. One case is scheduled per hour. On the trial date, the prosecutor and arresting officer are required to appear, ready for trial.

6. Those persons who fail to appear either at the return date or at trial are not required to appear, but have the option of staying home and simply forfeiting their bond, which has been posted in advance of their initial appearance.

7. Statistics show that 75 percent of those persons pleading not guilty in this jurisdiction fail to appear for trial.

The chief of police in the court's jurisdiction is very concerned about overtime for officers. He communicates with you, the court administrator, about this concern and explains that all police officers who appear in court for trial are entitled to the minimum two hours of overtime when they are not appearing during their regular shift. He views this as a tremendous and unnecessary expense to the city, in view of the fact that most of the officers are not needed because the defendants do not appear. He recognizes that defendants have a right to post bond under the law and simply forfeit it at the initial appearance or on the trial date. He is interested, however, in devising some system to save the city the tremendous cost for all the officers' overtime. He explains that other municipalities are faced with similar problems.

---

*Contributed by Hon. Burton A. Scott, former Associate Dean of the National Judicial College, Reno, Nevada.

Questions for Discussion

1. What kind of a system would you propose to address the problem, and how would you go about accomplishing this end? In creating a modified system, you are to work within the existing law, with no changes in statutes or ordinances.

2. After you have completed designing a system and explaining how you would go about obtaining the cooperation of the judges, prosecutors, clerk's office, and other law enforcement agencies, as well as that of the defense bar, discuss any proposed changes in the law you think might improve the system further.

3. How would you go about accomplishing other *significant* changes for improvement in the procedures and operation of this system? Consider the creation of an ongoing mechanism or committee that would propose, discuss, adopt, and carry out changes for the benefit of the system as a whole.

Chief Judge Cortez's Embattled Court*

You have just been hired as the new court administrator for a medium-sized court with approximately 90 employees. Once on the job, you discover that you have been preceded by two heavy-handed court administrators who together lasted less than a year on the job because of their inability to handle employee conflicts and to achieve a minimal level of productivity. They were more or less forced to resign because of a lack of employee cooperation and increasing talk of unionization.

There is general turmoil and distrust throughout the organization. Employees do not trust each other, and, as a group, they do not trust management. The courthouse runs on gossip and inertia. There is very little official communication throughout the organization. Prior court administrators made no attempt to solicit employee opinions or ideas.

The judges are all aware of the problem, but they have formed no clear consensus as to how to respond to it. In fact, there is turmoil and conflict among the judges themselves. They engage in "turf protection" with operating funds and the court's cases, and often take sides in office squabbles. As a result, they are unable to come to any clear consensus or to provide the court administrator with any guidance.

The chief judge, Dolores Cortez, has served in that capacity for 10 years and is known to be exceedingly fair, compassionate, and competent; however, she is approaching retirement (in six months) and appears unwilling to take a firm

---

*Contributed by Dennis Metrick, Management Analyst, Court Services Department, Administrative Office of the Courts, Phoenix, Arizona.

stand on, or a strong interest in, addressing intraoffice disputes and difficulties. In fact, she is not altogether convinced that there is a problem. Furthermore, in past years she has been quite reluctant to intervene in arguments between individual judges.

Questions for Discussion

1. As the "new kid on the block," how would you respond to this organization problem? What is the first problem you would address, and how would you address it? What additional problems require your attention?
2. As court administrator, how would you respond to the inability of the judges to develop a consensus? How could the decision-making process be improved?
3. What techniques could be employed to improve communication throughout the organization, lessen tension and strife, and generally create a more harmonious work environment?
4. What would be your general approach to Judge Cortez? To her successor?

An Unmanageable
Case-Management Quandary*

You are court administrator for a court of 50 employees. This court, which used to dispose of about 700 cases per month, now hears an average of 100 criminal and 400 civil cases per month. Case filings have doubled in the past seven years.

The present "hybrid" case management system has evolved over a long period of time through tradition and expediency. A growing caseload and increasing difficulties in avoiding a backlog have prompted the judges to rethink their present system, however. Criminal cases that used to reach final disposition in a month now require two to three months. The situation shows no signs of improving in the foreseeable future.

Again, the court has a mixed calendar system. Two judges are assigned to hear criminal cases and motions for a one-month period, while the remaining four judges hear all manner of civil matters on a random basis upon the filing of the civil complaint. The judges are responsible for the management of these cases until final disposition.

At the end of the one-month period, the two judges hearing criminal cases return to the civil division and two other judges rotate onto the criminal bench. Any pending criminal cases or motions are then heard by these two incoming criminal judges.

---

*Contributed by Dennis Metrick, Management Analyst, Court Services Department, Administrative Office of the Courts, Phoenix, Arizona.

One of the judges hears all juvenile-related matters in addition to any assignment in the criminal and civil divisions. The court collects statistics on the number of court filings and motions filed in each division on a month-to-month basis.

Questions for Discussion

1. In a general way, discuss both the merits and difficulties posed by this case management approach. Relate your response to the general advantages and disadvantages of both the individual and the master calendar systems.
2. What specific problems could arise in the criminal division? Why?
3. What specific problems could be created by the permanent assignment of a judge to the juvenile division? What are some of the advantages?
4. What comments would you make with regard to the court's statistical report? Are other data needed for management purposes? If so, what kind?

CORRECTIONS

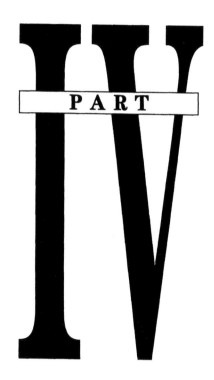

Each of the four chapters in this part focuses on corrections administration. Chapter 9 examines corrections organization and operation, including prisons and jails. Chapter 10 covers personnel roles and functions, and Chapter 11 discusses the administration of community corrections through probation and parole. Chapter 12 reviews corrections issues and practices. Introductory sections of each chapter provide specific chapter content. Case studies in corrections administration appear at the end of Chapter 12.

CORRECTIONS ORGANIZATION AND OPERATION

Chapter

9

Prisons are built with stones of Law.

—William Blake

The founders of a new colony ... recognized it among their earliest practical necessities to allot a portion of the virgin soil as a cemetery, and another portion as the site of a prison.

—Nathaniel Hawthorne

Introduction

The subculture of prisons and jails has been the subject of television and movie fare in the United States for several decades. Most of these dramas about prison and jail life have portrayed prison administrators and their personnel and organizations as cruel, bigoted, corrupt, and morally base. Furthermore, prison literature such as Jack Henry Abbott's *In the Belly of the Beast,* Eldridge Cleaver's *Soul on Ice,* George Jackson's *Soledad Brother,* and Malcolm Braly's *On the Yard,* among others, have presented similar views. These television programs, movies, and books reflect the public's interest in and often contribute to its lack of knowledge about our correctional institutions. As this chapter discusses, corrections has become a boom industry—with about 5.8 million adults under some form of correctional supervision (either in prisons or in jails or on probation or parole)[1]—and promises to continue being so well into the twenty-first century. Indeed, futurists believe corrections to be the most rapidly growing criminal justice career area for the future.[2]

This chapter first focuses generally on the organization, operation, and some unique aspects of correctional institutions. Then we consider the issue of the increasing amount of inmate civil litigation. Next we examine the causes and effects of prison crowding. Some approaches and limitations to helping inmates who have serious emotional and behavioral problems or violent personalities, who are addicted to narcotics or alcohol, or who practice deviant sexual behaviors are reviewed.

We also examine local jails, including issues such as crowding, programs, and a relatively new jail design and philosophy. We conclude the chapter by examining research findings concerning the effects of incarceration, including solitary confinement and life on death row, and some issues for correctional administrators and society at large to consider.

Correctional Organizations

General Features

The correctional organization is a complex, hybrid that utilizes two distinct, yet related, management subsystems to achieve its goals: One is concerned primarily with managing correctional employees, and the other is concerned primarily with delivering correctional services to a designated offender population. The correctional organization, therefore, employs one group of people—correctional personnel—to work with and control another group—offenders.[3]

An interesting feature of the correctional organization is that every correctional employee who exercises legal authority over offenders *is a supervisor,* even if the person is the lowest-ranking member in the agency or institution. Therefore, two distinct, yet related, supervisory roles exist. One involves supervising employees, referred to as *first-level supervision*; the other involves supervising offenders, or *line* or *field supervision.* In most organizations, line personnel normally provide labor that is used to convert materials into products or units of production. In correctional organizations, line supervisors provide the type of correctional service being delivered to the correctional client, be the client an inmate, probationer, or parolee. The product or unit of production is the pattern of supervisory interaction between the line employee and the offender.[4]

Another feature of the correctional organization is that everything a correctional supervisor does may have civil or criminal ramifications, both for himself or herself and for the agency or institution. Therefore, the legal and ethical responsibility for the correctional supervisor is greater than it is for supervisors in other types of organizations.

Finally, two different philosophies exist about what correctional organizations should be: (1) *custodial* organizations, which emphasize the caretaker functions of controlling and observing inmates; or (2) *treatment* organizations, which emphasize rehabilitation of inmates. These different philosophies contain potential conflict for correctional personnel.[5]

Open Systems

Traditionally, many correctional organizations have been administered as a *closed system*. This limits the organization's responsibility to only the structural boundaries of the official organization.[6] These institutions experience a degree of difficulty in communicating with the outside world and are often loathe to provide information to the outside world concerning their activities and methods.[7] Historically, this closed perspective contributed to the problem of political alienation and fragmentation of correctional services.[8]

Today, however, most correctional administrators and policy-makers recognize that their organizations are intricate components of government systems and of society itself. These *open systems* recognize that problems and solutions are generated by forces outside the organization that must be managed. For example, the decision to close a state prison in a small community may result in significant political pressure not to close it because that community's economy depends on the prison. Local pressure can also prevent locating a prerelease center in an established residential area.[9]

In short, the contemporary correctional organization is an intricate part of the social, political, and economic setting in which the organization functions. Therefore, the organization must be administered as an open system.

Administration and Management of Correctional Institutions

According to Vernon Fox, correctional administration is "the organization and management of the delivery system that brings the basic necessities and treatment programs of the correctional institutions or agencies to the correctional client."[10]

Correctional administration and management are both concerned with internal organizational issues such as personnel, budgets, and programs. Administration's major concerns are obtaining personnel, securing funds, and interfacing programs with other agencies. Management's primary concern is using available personnel and resources to implement programs. Most of an administrator's time and energy are expended on activities outside the organization, while most of management's time is spent on activities within the organization.[11]

Correctional administrators are responsible for developing policy; managers are responsible primarily for implementing it. Therefore, administrators are concerned with long-range planning that affects the entire organization, and managers are responsible for day-to-day planning. Finally, correctional administration is highly political, whereas management positions tend to be less so.[12]

Levels of Correctional Administration

Figure 9.1 represents the levels of correctional organizations, including top administration, executive management, middle management, supervisory management, and line or field supervision. In the figure, top administration refers to the "person in charge" of an agency, institution, or unit of government. Today, the head of each prison, generally appointed by the commissioner of corrections, is a warden, director, or superintendent, which is the more common title.[13] This person is responsible for the entire operation of the organization and is more often than not a political appointee.

The line between the levels of top administration and executive management is blurred in many organizations. Top administration usually makes major decisions, often merely approving recommendations made by executive management. Executive titles are often the same as those of top administration, with the addition of *assistant, deputy,* or *vice* (e.g., deputy or assistant warden, assistant commander). Executive management is normally responsible for developing and reviewing long-range plans; evaluating key management personnel; developing policies, rules, regulations, and standards for the organization; and performing other functions designated by top administrators.[14]

Middle management in correctional administration may refer to a variety of positions and to a number of levels within the organizational structure. Middle management positions include *department head, captain, lieutenant, sergeant, team leader, manager, program head, coordinator, shift commander,* and so on. Middle management, which may be organized into departments or divisions, is normally concerned with managing the delivery of one or more services. Examples include custody, treatment, food services, maintenance, prison industries, personnel, research, and education. Each division is ultimately responsible to an executive manager (such as an assistant warden for custody or treatment). Major functions of middle managers are developing plans, implementing rules and regulations, maintaining records, supervising subordinate supervisors, periodically evaluating personnel, accounting for unit resources (funds, property, equipment), and processing grievances.[15]

The lowest level of correctional administration is the first-level supervisor of employees, often referred to by titles such as *unit manager, supervisor, corporal, team leader,* or *section leader.* These people are responsible for the day-to-day operations of specific areas within organizational units. They make first-level job assignments; maintain close contact with operational employees; make detailed and short-range operating plans; provide counseling, motivation, control, and training to employees; and implement agency policies, rules, and regulations at the employee level. In short, the first-level supervisor translates organizational policy, goals, and objectives into action.[16]

Line or field correctional supervision is not normally designated as part of administration and management; however, this area exercises legal supervisory

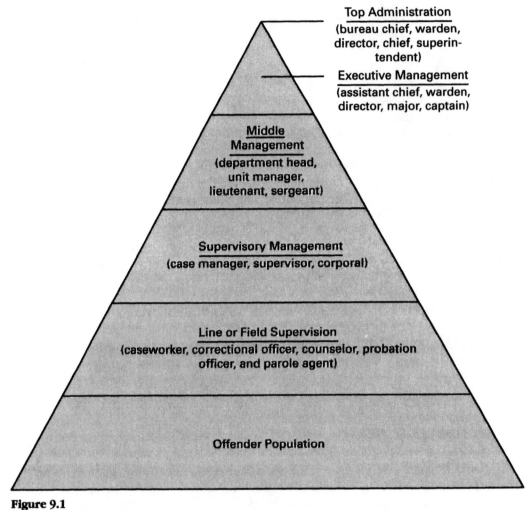

Figure 9.1

Levels of correctional organization. (*Source:* William G. Archambeault and
Betty J. Archambeault, *Correctional Supervisory Management: Principles
of Organization, Policy, and Law.* Englewood Cliffs, N.J.: Prentice Hall,
1982, p. 53. Used with permission.)

authority over members of an offender population. Employees at this level
must skillfully apply basic supervisory techniques and the ability to influence offenders. These people—be they correctional officers, counselors, or others—
must carry out all of the administrators' plans by interpreting and applying
institutional policy; planning, organizing, and supervising inmate activities and
work functions; ensuring maintenance of the physical plant and equipment;
avoiding circumstances that might lead to litigation; and engaging in decision

making. These workers are the "point of delivery" for all correctional services within the organization: The organization's effectiveness is closely linked to its performance.[17]

Prisons as Organizations

Until the beginning of the twentieth century, prisons were administered by state boards of charities, boards comprised of citizens, boards of inspectors, state prison commissions, or individual prison keepers. Most prisons were individual provinces. Wardens, who were given absolute control over their domain, were appointed by governors through a system of political patronage.

Every state now has some form of centralized department of corrections that is empowered to set and carry out policies for all correctional institutions within its jurisdiction. At the top of this department of corrections is the secretary or commissioner of corrections, who works directly with the governor to establish policy and institutional procedures, negotiates operating budgets for the various institutions, and makes major personnel decisions.

In the past, individuals were attracted to the position of warden because it carried many fringe benefits such as lavish residences, unlimited inmate servants, food and supplies from institutional farms and warehouses, furnishings, and a personal automobile. Now most wardens or superintendents are civil service employees who have earned their position through seniority and merit.[18]

Because the traditional prison was autocratic, with the central goal of maintaining custody of inmates, the organization was highly stratified and rigid, organized along military lines with authority and status related to rank. Decisions were made at the top. During the past few decades, many correctional institutions have been reorganized, adding another layer of hierarchy, commonly referred to as *noncustodial personnel.* These personnel are the *professional* staff of the prison, which includes psychiatrists, psychologists, medical personnel, chaplains, teachers, counselors, and dieticians.

Thus, the warden or superintendent may be assisted by one or more associate or deputy wardens: normally, one in charge of custody, including discipline, security, inmate movement, and control, and a second in charge of business matters, programs, records, library services, mail and visitation, recreation, and release procedures. A prison industries manager is in charge of prison industries, farms, production, and supplies. A medical supervisor is in charge of prison health services and sanitation.[19] This reorganization has produced a more vertical type of organization, forcing actual decision making downward within the organization, among deputies and their personnel. Organizing and managing a prison is obviously a major task, one that rivals such responsibilities in many large industries and businesses.

Figure 9.2 shows an organization structure for a state maximum security prison serving a statewide population of about 2 million and an inmate population of about 5,000.

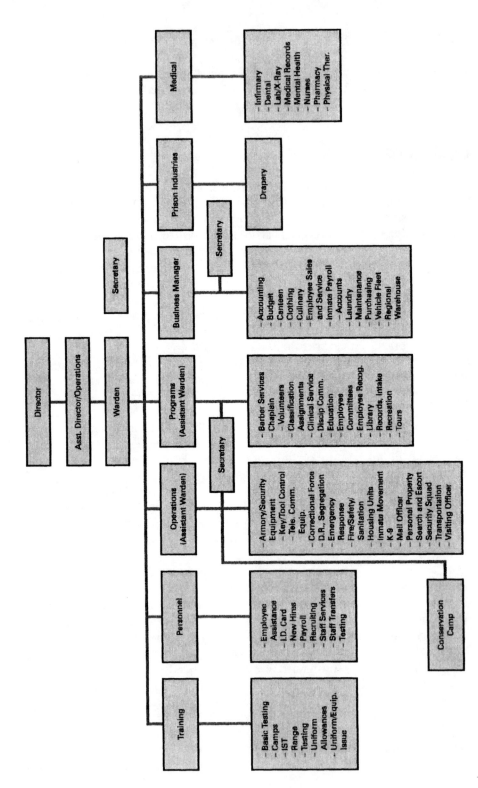

Figure 9.2

Organization structure for a maximum security prison.

Development and Status of Inmate Civil Litigation

Rights of Prison Inmates

Incarceration in prisons and jails entails stringent restrictions on freedom of movement and the loss of numerous privileges; however, inmates nonetheless enjoy several important constitutional rights. Legal circumstances of prison inmates have changed tremendously since 1871, when the Virginia Supreme Court told Woody Ruffin, a convicted murderer, that he was a "slave of the state" with no rights that need be recognized.[20]

The demise of the *hands-off doctrine,* by which courts deferred to the expertise of correctional administrators in the operation of their institutions, began in the mid-1960s. In *Cooper v. Pate,*[21] the U.S. Supreme Court held that state inmates could bring lawsuits against prison authorities under Title 42, Section 1983 of the Civil Rights Act. This decision began a new era for inmates and represented the beginning of what has been an explosion in inmate litigation. During the 1971–1972 Supreme Court term, following the deadly prison riot at Attica, New York, additional court decisions expanded prisoners' rights and remedies. One of the major decisions was *Wolff v. McDonnell*[22] (1974), in which the U.S. Supreme Court stated that "there is no Iron Curtain drawn between the Constitution and the prisons of this country."

A Resurgence of the Hands-Off Doctrine?

The turning point in this expansion of inmates' rights was the case of *Bell v. Wolfish*[23] in 1979, which considered, among other issues, double-bunking in the Metropolitan Correctional Center in New York City. The Court seemed to revert to the original hands-off doctrine, declaring in a 6 to 3 decision that jail management should be left to corrections personnel. In other words, the Court believed that deference should be extended to persons noted for their expertise in correctional matters, and administrative decisions should not be invalidated by the Court unless extreme circumstances required it.

Prisoner Litigation

In recent years, the attention of the media and legislators has focused on conditions *within* prisons. The current rhetoric advocates such issues as restoring fear to prisoners, caning, making a prisoner "smell like a prisoner," and returning executions to the county seat.[24] Some authors see federal and state court intervention as an erosion of the power of prison wardens,[25] but others believe that any progress corrections has made in the past quarter century in the direction of improved living conditions for inmates has been due, at least in part, to litigation.[26] Courts continue to be involved in reforming correctional institutions.

The volume of inmate litigation increased significantly following the *Cooper v. Pate* decision in 1964. In 1966, 218 petitions were filed, and the number increased to 16,741 in 1981.[27] In 1980, inmates of state and federal correctional institutions filed 23,287 petitions alleging both civil and criminal violations and seeking compensatory damages, injunctions, and property claims.[28] By 1990, the number of such petitions had swollen to nearly 43,000, and more than 64,000 petitions were filed in 1996.[29]

Prisoners sue primarily because they are either unwilling to accept their conviction or because they wish to hassle their keepers.[30] Prisoner litigants fall into two categories. First are those who file a single suit during their entire period of incarceration (usually requiring the assistance of others to do it). One study found that 71 percent of all litigants filed only one action but accounted for about half of all litigation.[31] The other group is composed of inmates who make law a prison career: "jailhouse lawyers."[32]

There is an irony connected to this litigation explosion. Until the 1970s, conditions in many prisons were almost insufferable for both staff members and inmates. The former often had to battle the same vermin and insects and eat the same food (some of which was poisoned with lead peeling from the kitchen walls), and for at least eight hours per day, generally had to endure the same conditions as the inmates. The irony here, of course, was that many administrators and staff had to hope to be sued by inmates for violating their Eighth Amendment rights and lose before working conditions could improve.

The Due Deference Doctrine

As noted earlier, the Supreme Court's decision in *Bell v. Wolfish* (1976), the "cornerstone of the future edifice of correctional law,"[33] represented to many a reinstatement of the hands-off doctrine. From that point to the present, *federal* courts have generally deferred to the expertise of prison administrators in cases involving day-to-day operations (court activism concerning overcrowding notwithstanding). From 1979 to 1986, federal courts initiated a pattern of deciding cases with greater deference to correctional officials. Cases decided from 1987 to 1994 made it even more difficult for prisoners to prevail in Section 1983 litigation.[34]

This reluctance of the courts to become involved in prison matters marked the emergence of the *due deference doctrine,* which refers to the courts' policy not to interfere in matters pertaining to prison administration. This doctrine has not been developed sufficiently, however, to determine for the courts when they should or should not intervene. Frequently, the result has been, as in *Bell,* that courts accept jurisdiction over prisoners' claims but fail to provide remedies to them.[35]

The media brought to light many past abuses that occurred inside prisons, but media attention may now be turning in another direction. Media reports of trivial lawsuits filed by inmates (such as an inmate's suit for being sold a jar of creamy peanut butter when he had ordered chunky style, and a cruel and unusual punishment claim by an inmate when a guard refused to refrigerate his ice cream) have become commonplace. The expense to defend against such lawsuits, coupled with the fact that the United States has the world's largest and costliest prison system,[36] fosters public resentment against prisons and prisoners.

The judiciary, too, may be growing weary of inmate complaints and court intervention in corrections. As indicated earlier, more control over prisons has gradually been given back to the states, and the courts are displaying more tolerance for minor violations of prisoners' constitutional rights. Such a shift was also exemplifed in *Turner v. Safley,*[37] in which the U.S. Supreme Court stated that "when a prison regulation impinges on inmates' constitutional rights, the regulation is valid if it is reasonably related to legitimate penological interests." Some authors have characterized *Turner* as another reformulation of the hands-off doctrine. This decision was strengthened with a later decision, *Wilson v. Seiter.*[38] When an inmate claims that the conditions of his or her confinement violate the Eighth Amendment, he or she must show a culpable state of mind on the part of prison officials. Finally, a more recent case of this nature emphasized the Supreme Court's desire to give "deference and flexibility to state officials trying to maintain a volatile environment."[39] This decision made it "more difficult to bring constitutional suits challenging prison management."[40]

Taken together, then, recent U.S. Supreme Court decisions have stated clearly that the *federal* doors to prison litigation have all but closed. Under due deference, the federal courts appear to distinguish substantive prisoner rights claims from frivolous complaints against prison administrators.[41] This "judicial retreat" or gradual return to the *Bell* decision troubles some observers, however, as it may reverse what has been termed "the most important development in the prisoner's environment,"[42] which substitutes the rule of law and rational/legal decision making for arbitrary prison administration decision making.[43]

The Increase in the Prison Population

Rehabilitative Versus Lock-'Em-Up Philosophies and Truth in Sentencing Laws

Several factors affect the prison population—now at about 1.3 million men and women,[44] with an average annual growth rate of about 7 percent.[45] First is the nation's drug problem. Data show that the number of persons admitted to state prisons for drug offenses has for several years exceeded the number entering for violent, property, or public-order crimes.[46] Other commonly cited factors include truth in sentencing laws, violence on television and in the movies, and a general deterioration of morals and of the family. In sum, the nation has become more punitive in nature.

Truth in sentencing for prison inmates began in 1984 in the state of Washington. The concept, which involves restriction or elimination of parole eligibility and good-time credits, quickly spread to other states after a determination in 1996 that prisoners were serving on average about 44 percent of their court sentences. To ensure that offenders serve larger portions of their sentences, Congress authorized[47] additional funding for more state prisons and jails if states met eligibility criteria for truth in sentencing programs. To qualify, states must require violent offenders to serve at least 85 percent of their prison sentences. By 1998, 27 states and the District of Columbia qualified; 14 states have abolished early parole board release for all offenders.[48]

A philosophical shift toward criminals and the purpose of incarceration is contributing to prison crowding. In response to the apparent failure of the *rehabilitative philosophy* and policies, the prevailing philosophy sees prisons as places to incarcerate and punish inmates in an effort to deter crime. This philosophy has resulted in get-tough sentencing practices (including mandatory sentencing laws) that contribute to rising prison populations. Legislators have essentially removed the word *rehabilitation* from the penal code while focusing on fixed sentences, resulting in the quadrupling of the number of prisoners and the need for $4.5 billion for new lockups in the early 1990s.[49] This shift from rehabilitating inmates to just deserts is based on the fact that offenders make "free will" decisions to commit crimes and therefore no longer deserve compassion and correction. This philosophy has brought an exclusionary era of repressive social control that attempts to banish, expel, and stigmatize the criminal.[50]

Americans are, however, becoming more rehabilitation oriented. A recent survey found that about 48 percent of all Americans believe that it is more important to try to rehabilitate people who are in prison than merely to punish them (14.6 percent).[51] These findings agree with the "conventional wisdom" concerning how to administer prison programs.

Robert Martinson's well-publicized finding that "almost nothing works" in correctional treatment programs served to "ignite a firestorm of debate that has lasted" nearly two decades.[52] Although Martinson's methodology was brought into serious question and he later attempted to recant his findings, his assessment clearly had a major impact. Legislators and corrections administrators became unwilling to fund treatment programs from dwindling budgets, while academics and policymakers claimed that the medical model of correctional treatment programs failed to accomplish their end. Paul Louis and Jerry Sparger noted that "perhaps the most lasting effect of the 'nothing works' philosophy is the spread of cynicism and hopelessness" among prison administrators and staff members.[53]

With the demise of the rehabilitative philosophy and the birth of the national call for just deserts in the 1970s, an even greater widening of the gap between the two perspectives occurred in the 1980s. Ted Palmer[54] identified these modified positions as the "skeptical" and "sanguine" camps. The skeptical believed that relatively few prison programs work and that successful ones account for only negligible reductions in recidivism. Furthermore, they believed that rehabilitation programs have not been given an adequate chance in correctional settings because they were either poorly designed or implemented. The sanguine perspective is that although the existing rehabilitation programs have not been very effective to date, evidence indicates that many programs provide positive treatment for selected portions of the offender population.

A recent reassessment of Martinson's "nothing works" statement by such researchers as Palmer has given new hope for rehabilitation. Palmer rejected Martinson's indictment of correctional treatment modalities and demonstrated that many of the programs initially reviewed by Martinson were actually quite successful.[55] Other research has supported Palmer's position.[56]

Although the rehabilitation philosophy has some support, the idea that "nothing works" is presently adhered to in the United States. That philosophy is not expected to be replaced in the foreseeable future. It is good to remember, however, the attempts made to rehabilitate criminals in earlier times, since we may one day return to those policies. Palmer has made three points about rehabilitation: (1) It need not be attached to a medical model, (2) it need not be linked to indeterminate sentencing, and (3) it need not demean its participants or interfere with extant reform movements.[57]

Unfortunately, this just deserts or "lock-'em-up" philosophy combined with the addition of more prisons—and more prisoners (now with nearly 1.8 million persons incarcerated in U.S. prisons and jails)[58]—have not caused a major decrease in crime. They have simply resulted in record numbers of inmates. As succinctly put by Malcolm Feeley, "there is no evidence of imprisonment's deterrent effect."[59]

According to Ted Gest, the logic of the lock-'em-up campaign is defeated by a combination of demography and justice-system inefficiency. Each year, a new crop of youths in their upper teens constitute the majority of those arrested for serious crimes. As these "seasoned" offenders are arrested and removed from the crime scene, a new crop replaces them. "The justice system is eating its young. It imprisons them, paroles them, and rearrests them with no rehabilitation in between," according to Dale Secrest.[60] Law enforcement seems to offer little deterrent to crime; even California, which uses an aggressive law enforcement approach to deal with criminals, reaches only a small fraction of those who commit more than a million serious crimes annually in the state.[61]

Large-scale long-term imprisonment unquestionably keeps truly serious offenders behind bars, preventing them from committing more crimes. The long-term incarceration of this class of criminals who would commit an average of 15 or more crimes per year creates the greatest need for more prison space.

Programs to Address Inmates' Problems

A Daunting Task

It is clear that

> offenders enter prison with a variety of deficits. Some are socially or morally inept; others are intellectually or vocationally handicapped; some have emotional hangups that stem from ... psychological problems; still others have a mixture of varying proportions of some or even all of these.[62]

Having to deal with inmates suffering from such serious and varied problems obviously does not bode well for correctional institutional treatment in general. Prison culture makes the environment inhospitable to programs designed to rehabilitate or reform, and, as noted, the failure of rehabilitative programs has shifted focus from them. High recidivism rates indicate that existing correctional strategies have not been successful and that these strategies cannot operate in a vacuum. As we will see later, the prison director's philosophy and practices with respect to inmate treatment and programs may in large measure impact the success rate of a particular institution.

There is also evidence of contemporary success in correctional settings with respect to narcotics addiction, sexual offenses, violent offenders, and alcoholism.

One survey determined that 56.1 percent of all male arrestees over age 18 used illicit drugs during the year prior to their arrest;[63] 46.8 percent were under the influence of drugs or alcohol during the commission of the offense for which they were arrested.[64] Drug-addicted offenders are currently subjected to one of three types of treatment: punitive, medical, or communal approaches. The punitive modality, the most widely used model since the early 1920s, consists largely of subjecting the inmate to withdrawal. It is based on the premise that drug addiction is a crime, not a disease, that requires punishment. The treatment of drug addiction as a medical problem consists of detoxification, rebuilding physical health, counseling, and social services. The communal approach, using group encounters and seminars conducted by former addicts who serve as positive role models, has been used by various penal facilities.[65]

A survey of correctional administrators revealed approximately 86,000 sexual offenders in federal and state prisons. The 48 states participating in the survey, the Federal Bureau of Prisons, and the District of Columbia reported that they provided individual and/or group counseling for these offenders.[66] The treatment of sexual offenders is based on the premise that intervention should be focused on the offender as a total person, not just on the deviant behavior.[67] The offender is encouraged to articulate fears, anxieties, wishes, fantasies, and ambitions to relieve mental and emotional distress. Rapists, voyeurs, and exhibitionists may also benefit from group therapy, which stresses touching and close physical contact. Child molesters, or pedophiles, may be similarly treated as whole personalities. Research has shown that the main concern, regardless of the sexual offender's specific problem, is to individualize treatment.[68] Treatment efforts in prisons are unlikely to produce positive outcomes, however, because of the nature of the environment.[69]

No uniform, simple treatment modality exists for a wide range of violent offenders. The treatment for offenders diagnosed as having antisocial personality disorders by psychotherapeutic intervention is seldom successful.[70] A complicating factor is that alcoholism is prevalent among those offenders;[71] therefore, each case requires formulation of an individual treatment plan. Alcoholism is generally recognized as a disease with medical, social, and psychological dimensions.[72] Psychological treatment to address this problem varies according to the offender's personality. The regimen used by Alcoholics Anonymous is frequently employed in the institutional setting.[73] Research has indicated that if the violent offender appears to possess the values of a subculture of violence, peer influences seem to work best in treatment; however, if deep-seated psychological factors appear to be present, a one-to-one relationship, in which the therapist is supportive, kind, and permissive but firm, may be utilized.[74]

Prison Industries: Ventures with the Private Sector

Prison industries that used inmate labor to manufacture goods for private firms were thriving enterprises in the first quarter of the twentieth century. The sale of open market prison-made products was banned in the 1930s and 1940s by Congress and the states, however, in response to protests from competing manufacturers and labor unions. In 1979, legislation was enacted to restore private sector involvement in prison industries to its former status. Within 15 years, the U.S. Department of Justice had certified 32 correctional agencies to operate private sector prison industries, employing more than 1,000 inmates (who earned more than $30 million) in joint ventures. By the mid-1990s, private companies employed inmates for data entry and information processing, electronic component assembly, garment manufacturing, contract packaging, metal fabrication, telemarketing, and handling travel reservations.[75]

Correctional administrators report that joint ventures provide meaningful, productive employment that helps to reduce inmate idleness. Other positive outcomes include the supply to companies of a readily available and dependable source of labor, with a cost-competitive, motivated workforce that can continue to work after release from prison; financial incentives, including low-cost industrial space and equipment purchase subsidies offered by corrections officials; a safe work environment as a result of the presence of security personnel and metal detectors; and the partial return to society of inmate earnings to pay state and federal taxes, offset incarceration costs, contribute to the support of inmates' families, and compensate victims.

Different types of business relationships have developed to meet the needs of both correctional institutions and private companies (Figure 9.3). In one, prisoners are employed by the state division of correctional industries, which in turn charges the companies a burden rate for their labor. This approach is called the *personnel* or *manpower model,* because it resembles the nationwide temporary personnel service company of that name. For example, in South Carolina, companies that operate feeder plants inside correctional facilities supervise inmate workers with their own staff, but the prisoners are employed by the state, which charges the companies for the inmates' labor.

In the *employer model,* in which the company employs the inmates, private companies own and operate their prison-based businesses, with prison officials providing the space in which the companies operate as well as a qualified labor pool from which the companies hire employees. An example is Trans World Airlines, which owns and operates several prison-based businesses and supervises and employs their inmate workforce.

Model	Workers employed by	Workers supervised by	Workers trained by	Benefits for company	Benefits for prison
Personnel	Prison	Company	Prison	Workforce Rent/utility Money for equipment Administrative support	Employment Overhead rate Wage deductions Payback on equipment
Employer	Company	Company	Company	Workforce Rent Utilities	Employment Wage deductions
Customer	Prison	Prison	Prison	Product or service	Payment for finished goods

Figure 9.3

Principal characteristics of three types of joint ventures.

A third partnering approach is the *customer model,* in which the company contracts with the prison to provide a finished product at an agreed-upon price. The correctional institution owns and operates the business that employs the inmate workforce. For example, a correctional facility in Minnesota provides a variety of light assembly, sorting, packaging, and warranty repair services for dozens of private firms in the area.

To be sure, these joint ventures provide challenges and problems. Absenteeism and rapid turnover of employees, limited opportunities for training, and logistics can be problems. Furthermore, the AFL-CIO remains concerned with joint ventures and views them as a challenge to unionized and nonunionized civilian workforces. Also, a debate about the proper role of inmates in today's labor force is ongoing. Many entrepreneurs and prison administrators feel these ventures are very valuable to inmates because of the benefits described earlier. Because workers must have a good disciplinary record to participate in these programs, show up for their jobs on time, and work hard during their shifts, these ventures develop valuable work habits that are not reflected in financial statements. Indeed, many inmates have been hired by companies after their release.

Jails as Organizations

Across the United States, approximately 3,316 jails are locally administered, holding approximately 593,000 inmates—about 57 percent of whom are awaiting trial.[76] As with prisons, no "typical" organizational structure exists for jails; their organization and hierarchical levels are obviously determined by several factors: size, budget, level of crowding, local views toward punishment and treatment, and even the level of training and education of the jail administrator. An organizational structure for a jail serving a county with a population of about 250,000 is suggested in Figure 9.4.

The administration of jails is frequently one of the major tasks of county sheriffs. Several writers have concluded that sheriff and police personnel primarily see themselves as law enforcers first and view the responsibility of organizing and operating jails as a millstone.[77] Therefore, their approach is often said to be at odds with advanced corrections philosophy and trends.

The "New Generation" Jail

As noted previously, the federal courts in the mid-1960s began to abandon their traditional "hands-off" philosophy toward prison and jail administration. This change was largely in response to the deplorable conditions and inappropriate treatment of inmates. The courts became more willing to hear inmate allegations of constitutional violations ranging from inadequate heating, lighting, and ventilation to the censorship of mail. One of every five cases filed in federal courts was on behalf of prisoners,[78] and 20 percent of all jails were a party in a pending lawsuit.[79]

In response to this deluge of lawsuits and to improve conditions, many local jurisdictions constructed new jail facilities. The court-ordered pressures to improve jail conditions afforded an opportunity for administrators to explore new ideas and designs. As described earlier, the term *new generation* was coined to characterize a style of architecture and inmate management totally new and unique to local detention facilities, and a new generation in correctional thought.[80] The concept was endorsed by the American Correctional Association and the Advisory Board of the National Institute of Corrections. W. Walter Menninger, Director of Law and Psychiatry at the Menninger Foundation in Topeka, Kansas, observed:

> Careful studies of these new generation facilities have found significant benefits for inmates, staff and society at large. There are fewer untoward incidents and assaults, (a) greater level of personal safety for both staff and inmates, greater staff satisfaction, more orderly and relaxed inmate housing areas, a better maintained physical plant. Finally, these facilities are cost effective to construct and to operate.[81]

There are several reasons for the fact that the new generation jail is not expanding. First, new jails are not typically built until old jails either wear out or become too small. Second, there is often a public perception that such facilities are "soft on crime." Finally, for many people, these facilities simply do not have the *appearance* of being jails.[82] To the extent possible, symbols of incarceration were to be removed in these new jails, which were to have no bars in the living units; windows were to be provided in every prisoner's room; and carpets, padded and movable furniture, and colorful wall coverings were to be used to reduce the

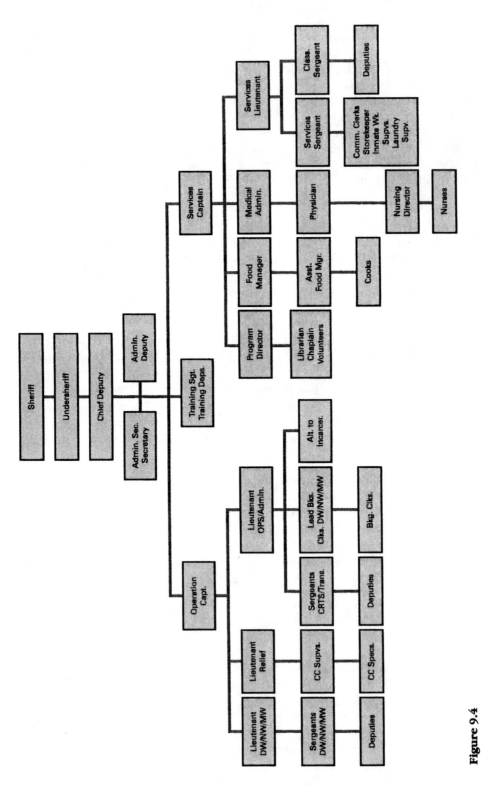

Figure 9.4

Organizational structure for a jail serving a county with a population of 250,000. (DW = day watch; NW = night watch; MW = mid-watch; CC = conservation camps)

facility's institutional atmosphere. Inmates were to be divided into small groups of approximately 40 to 50 for housing purposes. Officers were to interact with inmates rather than remain inside an office or behind a desk. Finally, interior features of the facility were to be designed to reduce the "trauma" of incarceration.[83]

The most important features of many of these facilities were one-person cells for inmates, direct staff supervision, and "functional inmate living units," which located all "sleeping, food, and hygiene facilities . . . in one self-contained, multi-level space."[84] A corrections officer was to be assigned to each unit to ensure direct and continuous supervision.

The first facility of the "new generation" style opened in the 1970s in Contra Costa County, California. This facility quickly became a success and was deemed cost-effective to build and safer for inmates and staff.

Making Jails Productive

The 1984 Justice Assistance Act removed some of the longstanding restrictions on interstate commerce of prisoner-made goods. By 1987, private sector work programs were under way in 14 state correctional institutions and two county jails.[85] Today, many inmates in U.S. jails are involved in productive work. Some simply work to earn privileges, and others earn wages applied to their custodial costs and compensation to crime victims. Some hone new job skills, improving their chances for success following release. At one end of the continuum is the trusty who mows the grass in front of the jail and thereby earns privileges for doing so; at the other end would be those jail inmates working for private industry for real dollars.[86]

Some jails have undertaken training programs for their inmates, following the recommendations of the American Jail Association. For example, one state-of-the-art facility in the West trains inmates to operate a plastic-sign engraving machine and has plans to teach dog grooming at the local animal control center. The engraving equipment, as well as the facility's 24 computers for inmate use, cost taxpayers nothing; they were purchased through commissary funds. This jail's inmates can also earn a GED, and the facility is considering programs in auto detailing, food service, book mending, mailing service, painting, printing, carpet installation, and upholstering.

Research in Correctional Institutions

Recent Research Findings

Many writers have painted a horrible landscape of prisons, describing them as being devoid of even the most basic elements of humanity[87] and detrimental to the humanity of the offender.[88] They generally issue a scathing indictment of prisons.[89] The following research findings should establish whose assessment is more nearly correct. Although appearing similar on the outside, prisons have been proven via research to vary widely in terms of their security, programming, and living conditions. According to James Bonta and Paul Gendreau, however, "Careful empirical evaluations have failed to uncover these pervasive negative effects of incarceration that so many have assumed. Even Goffman did not collect data directly from prisons."[90]

Prison and Jail Crowding

Many correctional administrators see crowding as *the* major barrier to humane housing of offenders. As mentioned earlier, this problem has resulted in court intervention in 37 states. Researchers have viewed the problem as a complex phenomenon, with most agreeing that crowding is a psychological response to high population density, which is often viewed as stressful.[91] Bonta and Gendreau found that the inmates' age played an important role, and that the relationship between misconduct and population density was more pronounced in institutions housing young offenders.[92] They also found evidence that prison variables other than overcrowding may influence aggressive behavior; for example, crowded prisons may be poorly managed.[93]

In summary, crowded prisons and jails may cause physiological and psychological stress among many inmates, although disruptive behavior depends on other factors such as age, institutional parameters (sudden shifts in the inmate membership), and the chronicity of the situation.[94] We discuss possible administrative approaches to crowding in Chapter 10.

Spatial and Social Densities

The average number of square feet per inmate in a jail is referred to as *spatial density*; the average number of inmates per living unit is the *social density*. Organizing and managing jails becomes more difficult when a larger number of inmates are living in high-density situations. Maintaining high population densities can affect routine activities such as food service, visitation, recreation, medical care and sick call, inmate property management, and inmates' movements to and from court or consultations with attorneys. A high spatial density facility is identified as one in which more than 40 percent of the inmates have less than 60 square feet per person in housing where confined for 10 hours or more set by the American Correctional Association.[95]

The standard for the highest social density residence category is an average of five persons per housing unit. By that definition, 27.6 percent of all jails, housing 61.1 percent of all jail inmates nationwide, are high social density facilities. Higher population densities are more common in jails holding 500 to 999 inmates; of those, 43.8 percent have at least 40 percent of their inmates residing in less than 60 square feet for more than 10 hours per day.[96]

Inmate suicide rates are higher in small jails and highest in small jails with lower population densities.[97] Seventy percent of all jail suicides occur in facilities with average daily populations of fewer than 250 inmates.[98] These facilities account for 37 percent of all jail inmates[99] and 52 percent of all jail admissions nationwide.[100]

Health Risks from Incarceration

Does incarceration threaten the health of the confined? A number of researchers have failed to find negative effects on inmate health as a result of incarceration.[101] In fact, two studies have even found a significantly lower incidence of hypertension among inmates than in the general population.[102] Indeed, the evidence indicates that many prisons may actually be conducive to good health. In a number of cases, complaints either decrease with time served[103] or remain unchanged.[104] Interestingly, we may conclude that because most prisons afford regular and nutritious diets, access to recreational exercise, and opportunity to sleep, along with available medical care, the offender may receive a fortuitous benefit from being isolated from highly risky lifestyles in the community.[105]

In the United States, deaths due to homicide are actually less likely inside than outside prisons.[106] The findings for a 20-year period indicate that inmate suicides occurred at a rate of 17.5 per 100,000 inmates, compared with 11 per 100,000 people in the general population.[107] Self-mutilations occur at an even higher rate.[108]

Effects of Long-Term Incarceration

Today more than 70,000 men and women are serving life sentences in the state and federal prisons.[109] What happens to such people? Although few of them will actually spend an entire lifetime incarcerated, the advent of mandatory sentencing laws, increases in violent crimes, decreases in early paroles, and commission of new crimes by inmates create the opportunity for long-term incarceration.

Cognitive tests have been administered to long- and short-term inmates; their results indicated no differences in intellectual performance. Long-termers showed increased hostility and social introversion[110] and decreased self-evaluation and evaluation of work.[111] Other studies have found no evidence of psychological deterioration; in fact, these studies reported an improvement in intelligence over time and a decrease in hostility.[112]

Timothy Flanagan compared misconduct rates of short- and long-term inmates, finding that even after controlling for age, the misconduct rate among the long-term inmates was approximately half that of the short-term offenders.[113] Additional studies assessing lifers found no deterioration in health, psychiatric symptoms, or intellect.[114] Even long-termers themselves have reported that the earlier portion of their sentences was more stressful and that with time they had learned to cope effectively.[115] Similar findings have occurred with respect to female offenders; in fact, long-term women inmates were more bothered by boredom and lack of activity than by anxiety.[116]

In summary, the evidence indicates little support for the notion that long-term imprisonment has detrimental effects on inmates' health. As a caution, however, Flanagan suggested that lifers may experience negative changes in areas that are as yet unmeasured,[117] such as family separation issues and vocational skill training needs.[118]

Effects of Solitary Confinement

Solitary confinement, also referred to as *punitive segregation,* has been described as "the most individually destructive, psychologically crippling, and socially alienating experience that could conceivably exist within the borders of [Canada]."[119] This statement also applies in the United States. Is this scathing denouncement an accurate depiction? Is solitary confinement per se "cruel and unusual" punishment?

Studies using volunteers have found few detrimental effects for subjects placed in solitary confinement for periods of up to 10 days. Perceptual and motor abilities were not impaired, physiological levels of stress were lower than for control groups, and various attitudes toward the experience and the self did not worsen.[120] Studies using prison inmates have also found no detrimental effects. In general, inmates found the first 72 hours to be the most difficult, but after that they adjusted quite well. Researchers concluded that there was "no support for the claim that solitary confinement . . . is overwhelmingly aversive, stressful, or damaging to the inmates."[121] Note, however, that two studies (that did not use control groups) found indications of pathology for inmates incarcerated for periods of up to a year.[122]

Effects of Death Row

Today about 3,200 prisoners are under sentence of death in 38 states.[123] Very little research concerning how inmates adjust to death row is available. The first such study, of 19 inmates awaiting execution in Sing Sing, was done in 1962. Expecting to find intense anxiety and depression, researchers found none.[124] Another study that investigated eight men awaiting execution found that five men showed no observable deterioration, but three displayed symptoms ranging from paranoia to insomnia.[125] A study of 34 death row inmates showed increased feelings of depression and hopelessness: Severe disturbances (psychosis) were not observed.[126]

Robert Johnson interviewed 35 men on death row and found them concerned over their powerlessness, fearful of surroundings, and feeling emotionally drained.[127] Similar studies using unstructured interviews found that most inmates exhibited well-intact defenses regarding their alleged guilt[128] and that *all* slept well and felt relatively good about themselves.[129]

Although limited in number, these studies demonstrate a lack of evidence of severe psychological reactions to a tragic fate. In fact, there are indications that the family and friends of condemned inmates suffer more than the inmates themselves.[130]

Pressing and Important Issues Relating to Correctional Institutions

In view of numerous factors—the contemporary tough law-and-order stance toward offenders, the amount of violent crime, jail and prison crowding, recidivism rates, new prison and jail construction costs, and the paucity of programming for inmates—society must contemplate the message it is sending to correctional administrators. If society's primary purpose of incarceration is *custody* and *incapacitation* for a set period, we have clearly succeeded. Recalling that nearly half of all Americans support rehabilitative efforts, however, if society really wishes to *rehabilitate* them, it is failing to do so, according to research data.

We now know that the specter of imprisonment appears to do little to prevent crime. Most offenders today come from communities where conditions fall below the living standards that most Americans would recognize.[131] We must wonder whether the threat of incarceration really holds any deterrent benefit for many members of our society.

John DiIulio complained that those who know the most about what prisons do have rarely taken part in the debates over their purpose. He noted that people who have actually spent their lives working with prisoners have ideas on the subject, but more attention is given to outside researchers whose focus is on the inmates rather than the correctional organization.[132] Should correctional administrators crusade for greater latitude in punishing and treating their charges? Have the courts and society at large played too large a role in this traditionally "laissez-faire" area? Are correctional administrators in a position to make a difference in preventing, punishing, or rehabilitating criminals? Do administrators know what works better than those of us in the outside world? These are pressing and important issues to consider.

Summary

This chapter presented an overview of correctional organization, prison litigation, industries, and the treatment and custody operations. Increases in violent crime and the general finding that institutionalization can be more of a positive than negative experience led us to conclude that serious offenders neither accept nor abide by society's norms. Again, we must question whether the threat of incarceration holds any deterrent value whatsoever for many persons in our society.

Questions for Review

1. What is the typical organization of the modern prison?
2. In what ways are correctional organizations unique?
3. Why is it important that correctional organizations adhere to the open system of management?
4. What factors are presently contributing to the increase in the prison population in the United States?
5. What is the "new generation" jail, and how might it help reduce the effects of overcrowding and increase the quality of life in institutions?
6. What options for attempting to work with inmates' emotional or behavioral problems are available to administrators?
7. Is society interested in attempting to rehabilitate offenders? Why or why not?
8. Defend the recent trend for prisons to enter into joint ventures with private companies. What are some of the inherent problems now confronted by these ventures? What are the three types of ventures that now exist?
9. In what major ways do jails differ from prisons?
10. Discuss some major recent findings in corrections research regarding the effects of incarceration and death row on prison inmates. What are the implications for correctional administrators?

Notes

1. Extrapolated from data presented in U.S. Department of Justice, Bureau of Justice Statistics Executive Summary, *Correctional Populations in the United States* (Washington, D.C.: Author, March 1999), p. 1, and U.S. Department of Justice, Bureau of Justice Statistics Bulletin, *Prison and Jail Inmates at Midyear 1998* (Washington, D.C.: Author, March 1999), p. 1.
2. George F. Cole, personal communication, April 18, 1991.
3. William G. Archambeault and Betty J. Archambeault, *Correctional Supervisory Management: Principles of Organization, Policy, and Law* (Englewood Cliffs, N.J.: Prentice Hall, 1982), p. 5.
4. Ibid.
5. Ibid., p. 6.
6. Jim L. Munro, "Towards a Theory of Criminal Justice Administration: A General Systems Perspective," *Public Administration Review* (November/December 1977):621–631.
7. See Ken Peak, "Correctional Theory in Theory and Praxis," *Criminal Justice Review* 10 (1985).
8. Richter H. Moore Jr., "The Criminal Justice Non-system," in R. Moore, T. Marks, and R. Barrow (eds.), *Readings in Criminal Justice* (Indianapolis, Ind.: Bobbs-Merrill, 1976), pp. 5–13.
9. Archambeault and Archambeault, *Correctional Supervisory Management,* pp. 44–45.
10. Vernon Fox, *Introduction to Corrections* (2d ed.) (Englewood Cliffs, N.J.: Prentice Hall, 1977), p. 406.

11. Archambeault and Archambeault, *Correctional Supervisory Management*, p. 48.
12. Ibid., p. 49.
13. Ibid., p. 54.
14. Ibid.
15. Ibid., p. 55.
16. Ibid., p. 56.
17. Ibid., p. 59.
18. James A. Inciardi, *Criminal Justice* (6th ed.) (Fort Worth, Tex.: Harcourt Brace, 1999), p. 454.
19. Ibid., p. 455.
20. *Ruffin v. Commonwealth*, 62 Va. 790, 796 (1871).
21. 378 U.S. 546 (1964).
22. 418 U.S. 539 (1974).
23. 441 U.S. 520 (1979).
24. Adam Nossiter, "Making Hard Time Harder: States Cut Jail TV and Sports," *New York Times* (September 17, 1994): A1, A10.
25. Todd Clear and George F. Cole, *American Corrections* (Belmont, Calif.: Wadsworth, 1994).
26. Susan P. Sturn, "The Legacy and Future of Corrections Litigation," *University of Pennsylvania Law Review* 142:639–738. Also, for an excellent resource concerning major cases in corrections, see Rolando V. del Carmen, Susan E. Ritter, and Betsy A. Witt, *Briefs of Leading Cases in Corrections* (2d ed.) (Cincinnati, Oh.: Anderson, 1998).
27. A. E. D. Howard, "The States and the Supreme Court," 31 *Catholic University Law Review* 375 (1982), at 379.
28. Timothy J. Flanagan and Kathleen Maguire (eds.), *Sourcebook of Criminal Justice Statistics 1991.* U.S. Department of Justice, Bureau of Justice Statistics (Washington, D.C.: U.S. Government Printing Office, 1992), p. 555.
29. Ibid. Also see Kathleen Maguire and Ann L. Pastore (eds.), *Sourcebook of Criminal Justice Statistics 1995.* U.S. Department of Justice, Bureau of Justice Statistics (Washington, D.C.: U.S. Government Printing Office, 1996), p. 177.
30. Jim Thomas, Kathy Harris, and Devin Keeler, "Issues and Misconceptions in Prisoner Litigation," *Criminology* 24 (1987): 901–919.
31. Jim Thomas, "Repackaging the Data: The 'Reality' of Prisoner Litigation," *New England Journal of Criminal and Civil Confinement* 15 (1989).
32. Ibid., p. 50.
33. Charles H. Jones, "Recent Trends in Corrections and Prisoners' Rights Law," in Clayton A. Hartjen and Edward E. Rhine (eds.), *Correctional Theory and Practice* (Chicago: Nelson-Hall, 1992), pp. 119–138.
34. Darrell L. Ross, "Emerging Trends in Correctional Civil Liability Cases: A Content Analysis of Federal Court Decisions of Title 42 United States Code Section 1983," *Journal of Criminal Justice* 25 (1997): 501–514.
35. Ibid., p. 120.
36. Francis X. Cline, "Prisons Run Out of Cells, Money and Choices," *New York Times* (May 28, 1993): B7.
37. 107 S. Ct. 2254 (1987), at 2254.
38. 111 S. Ct. 2321 (1991).
39. *Sandin v. Conner*, 115 S. Ct. 2321 (1995), at 2293.
40. Linda Greenhouse, "High Court Makes It Harder for Prisoners to Sue," *New York Times* (June 20, 1995): A11.

41. Ibid., pp. 121–122.

42. James Jacobs, *Stateville: The Penitentiary in Mass Society* (Chicago: University of Chicago Press, 1977).

43. Jones, "Recent Trends in Corrections and Prisoners' Rights Law," p. 122.

44. U.S. Department of Justice, Bureau of Justice Statistics Bulletin, *Prison and Jail Inmates at Midyear 1998,* p. 1.

45. U.S. Department of Justice, Bureau of Justice Statistics Executive Summary, *Correctional Populations in the United States,* p. 2.

46. Ibid.

47. See the Violent Offender Incarceration and Truth-in-Sentencing Incentive Grants program, Public Law 103–322, 108 Stat. 1796 (1994).

48. U.S. Department of Justice, Bureau of Justice Statistics Special Report, *Truth in Sentencing in State Prisons* (Washington, D.C.: Author, January 1999), pp. 1–3.

49. Ted Gest, "The Prison Boom Bust," *Newsweek* (May 4, 1992): 28–31.

50. John P. Conrad, "The Redefinition of Probation: Drastic Proposals to Solve an Urgent Problem." In Patrick D. McAnany, Doug Thomson, and David Fogel (eds.), *Probation and Justice: Reconsideration of Mission* (Cambridge, Mass.: Oelgeschlager, Gunn, and Hain, 1984), p. 258.

51. Kathleen Maguire and Ann L. Pastore (eds.), *Sourcebook of Criminal Justice Statistics 1997.* U.S. Department of Justice, Bureau of Justice Statistics. (Washington, D.C.: U.S. Government Printing Office, 1998), p. 137.

52. T. Paul Louis and Jerry R. Sparger, "Treatment Modalities Within Prison," in John W. Murphy and Jack E. Dison (eds.), *Are Prisons Any Better? Twenty Years of Correctional Reform,* pp. 147–162.

53. Ibid., p. 149.

54. Ted Palmer, "The 'Effectiveness' Issue Today: An Overview," *Federal Probation* 42 (1983): 3–10.

55. Paul Gendreau and Robert R. Ross, "Correctional Treatment: Some Recommendations for Effective Intervention," *Juvenile and Family Court Journal* 34 (1984):31–39.

56. See D. A. Andrews, "Program Structure and Effective Correctional Practices: A Summary of the CAVIC Research," in Robert R. Ross and Paul Gendreau (eds.), *Effective Correctional Treatment* (Toronto, Ontario, Canada: Butterworth, 1980); R. Peters, *Deviant Behavioral Contracting with Conduct Problem Youth* (Kingston, Ontario, Canada: Queen's University, 1981).

57. Ibid.

58. U.S. Department of Justice, Bureau of Justice Statistics Bulletin, *Prison and Jail Inmates at Midyear 1988,* p. 1.

59. Gest, "The Prison Boom Bust," p. 29.

60. Ibid.

61. Ibid.

62. Robert Levinson, "Try Softer," in Robert Johnson and Hans Toch (eds.), *The Pains of Imprisonment* (Beverly Hills, Calif.: Sage Publications, 1982), p. 246.

63. Kathleen Maguire and Ann L. Pastore (eds.), *Sourcebook of Criminal Justice Statistics, 1997* (Washington, D.C.: Government Printing Office, 1998), p. 252.

64. Ibid., p. 472.

65. Louis and Sparger, "Treatment Modalities Within Prison," pp. 152–153.

66. CEGA Publishing, *Corrections Compendium* (Lincoln, Neb.: Author, July 1991), pp. 10–15.

67. Alexander B. Smith and Louis Berlin, *Treating the Criminal Offender* (New York: Plenum Press, 1988).

68. Murray L. Cohen, Theohans Seghorn, and Wilfred Calmas, "Sociometric Study of the Sex Offender," *Journal of Abnormal Psychology* 74 (1971):249–255.

69. Louis and Sparger, "Treatment Modalities Within Prison," p. 155.

70. Stanley L. Brodsky (ed.), *Psychologists in the Criminal Justice System* (Urbana, Ill.: University of Illinois Press, 1973); Fritz A. Henn, Marijan Herjanic, and Robert H. Vanderpearl, "Forensic Psychiatry: Profiles of Two Types of Sex Offenders," *American Journal of Psychiatry* 133 (1976):654–696.

71. Samuel B. Guze, *Criminality and Psychiatric Disorders* (New York: Oxford University Press, 1976).

72. See, for example, U.S. Department of Justice, Bureau of Justice Statistics, *Report to the Nation on Crime and Justice: The Data* (Rockville, Md.: National Criminal Justice Reference Service, 1983); C. R. Bartol and A. M. Bartol, *Criminal Behavior: A Psychosocial Approach* (Englewood Cliffs, N.J.: Prentice Hall, 1986); Marvin Wolfgang, *Patterns in Criminal Homicide* (Philadelphia: University of Pennsylvania Press, 1958).

73. Louis and Sparger, "Treatment Modalities Within Prison," p. 157.

74. Ibid., p. 154.

75. U.S. Department of Justice, National Institute of Justice, Program Focus, "Work in American Prisons: Joint Ventures with the Private Sector," November 1995, pp. 2–3.

76. U.S. Department of Justice, Bureau of Justice Statistics Bulletin, *Prison and Jail Inmates at Midyear 1998*, pp. 1, 7.

77. For example, see James M. Moynahan and Earle K. Stewart, *The American Jail: Its Development and Growth* (Chicago: Nelson-Hall, 1980), p. 100; Clemens Bartollas, Stuart J. Miller, and Paul B. Wice, *Participants in American Criminal Justice: The Promise and the Performance* (Englewood Cliffs, N.J.: Prentice Hall, 1983), p. 59.

78. J. Moore, "Prison Litigation and the States: A Case Law Review," *State Legislative Report* 8 (1981):1.

79. National Sheriffs' Association, *The State of Our Nation's Jails, 1982* (Washington, D.C.: Author, 1982), p. 55.

80. Linda L. Zupan, *Jails: Reform and the New Generation Philosophy* (Cincinnati, Ohio: Anderson, 1991), p. 71.

81. Quoted in William R. Nelson and M. O'Toole, *New Generation Jails* (Boulder, Colo.: Library Information Specialists, Inc., 1983), pp. 35–36.

82. Matt Leone, personal communication, March 16, 1997.

83. Zupan, *Jails: Reform and the New Generation Philosophy*, p. 67.

84. R. Wener and R. Olson, *User Based Assessments of the Federal Metropolitan Correctional Centers: Final Report* (Washington, D.C.: U.S. Bureau of Prisons, 1978), p. 4.

85. U.S. Department of Justice, National Institute of Justice Research in Brief, *Making Jails Productive* (Washington, D.C.: Author, 1987), p. 1.

86. Ibid., p. 16.

87. Cf. Gresham Sykes, *The Society of Captives: A Study of a Maximum Security Prison* (Princeton, N.J.: Princeton University Press, 1958).

88. Milton G. Rector, "Prisons and Crime," *Crime and Delinquency* 28 (1982):505–507.

89. Jessica Mitford, *Kind and Unusual Punishment* (New York: Alfred A. Knopf, 1973).

90. James Bonta and Paul Gendreau, "Reexamining the Cruel and Unusual Punishment of Prison Life," *Law and Human Behavior* 14 (1990):347–372.

91. Irwin Altman, "Crowding: Historical and Contemporary Trends in Crowding Research," in A. Baum and M. Y. M. Epstein (eds.), *Human Response to Crowding* (Hillsdale, N.J.: Lawrence Erlbaum, 1978), pp. 3–29.

92. Bonta and Gendreau, "Reexamining the Cruel and Unusual Punishment of Prison Life," p. 353.

93. See Gerald G. Gaes, "The Effects of Overcrowding in Prison," in Michael Tonry and Norval Morris (eds.), *Crime and Justice,* Vol. 6 (Chicago: University of Chicago Press, 1985), pp. 95–146.

94. Bonta and Gendreau, "Reexamining the Cruel and Unusual Punishment of Prison Life," p. 355.

95. U.S. Department of Justice, Bureau of Justice Statistics Special Report, *Population Density in Local Jails, 1988,* p. 4.

96. See *Manual of Standards for Adult Correctional Institutions,* (College Park, Md.: American Correctional Association, August 1977); and *Federal Standards for Correction* (Washington, D.C.: U.S. Department of Justice, 1980).

97. U.S. Department of Justice, Bureau of Justice Statistics Special Report, *Population Density in Local Jails: 1988,* pp. 2, 7.

98. Ibid., p. 9.

99. Ibid.

100. Ibid.

101. See Seth B. Goldsmith, "Jailhouse Medicine: Travesty or Justice?" *Health Services Report* 87 (1972):767–774; R. A. Derro, "Administrative Health Evaluation of Inmates of a City-County Workhouse," *Minnesota Medicine* 61 (1978):333–337.

102. See L. Culpepper and J. Floom, "Incarceration and Blood Pressure," *Social Services and Medicine* 14 (1980):571–574; Lloyd F. Novick, Richard Della-Penna, Melvin S. Schwartz, Elaine Remlinger, and Regina Lowenstein, "Health Status of the New York City Prison Population," *Medical Care* 15 (1977):205–216.

103. Doris L. MacKenzie and Lynne Goodstein, "Long-term Incarceration Impacts and Characteristics of Long-term Offenders: An Empirical Analysis," *Criminal Justice and Behavior* 13 (1985):395–414.

104. J. S. Wormith, "The Effects of Incarceration: Myth-Busting in Criminal Justice," paper presented at the 94th Annual Conference of the American Psychological Association. Washington, D.C., August 1986.

105. Bonta and Gendreau, "Reexamining the Cruel and Unusual Punishment of Prison Life," p. 357.

106. R. Barry Ruback and Christopher A. Innes, "The Relevance and Irrelevance of Psychological Research: The Example of Prison Crowding," *American Psychologist* 43 (1988): 683–693.

107. W. T. Austin and Charles M. Unkovic, "Prison Suicide," *Criminal Justice Review* 2 (1977): 103–106.

108. Robert R. Ross and H. B. McKay, *Self Mutilation* (Lexington, Mass.: Lexington Books, 1979).

109. U.S. Department of Justice, Bureau of Justice Statistics, *Prisoners in 1998* (Washington, D.C.: Author, 1999), p. 13.

110. K. J. Heskin, F. V. Smith, P. A. Banister, and N. Bolton, "Psychological Correlates of Long-Term Imprisonment: II. Personality Variables," *British Journal of Criminology* 13 (1973): 323–330.

111. K. J. Heskin, F. V. Smith, P. A. Banister, and N. Bolton, "Psychological Correlates of Long-Term Imprisonment: III. Attitudinal Variables," *British Journal of Criminology* 14 (1974): 150–157.

112. N. Bolton, F. V. Smith, K. J. Heskin, and P. A. Banister, "Psychological Correlates of Long-Term Imprisonment: IV. A Longitudinal Analysis," *British Journal of Criminology* 16 (1976): 36–47.

113. Timothy J. Flanagan, "Time Served and Institutional Misconduct: Patterns of Involvement in Disciplinary Infractions among Long-Term and Short-Term Inmates," *Journal of Criminal Justice* 8 (1980):357-367.

114. W. Rasch, "The Effects of Indeterminate Sentencing: A Study of Men Sentenced to Life Imprisonment," *International Journal of Law and Psychiatry* 4 (1981):417-431.

115. MacKenzie and Goodstein, "Long-Term Incarceration Impacts and Characteristics of Long-Term Offenders," p. 414.

116. Doris L. MacKenzie, James W. Robinson, and C. S. Campbell, "Long-term Incarceration of Female Offenders: Prison Adjustment and Coping," *Criminal Justice and Behavior* 16 (1989):223-238.

117. Timothy J. Flanagan, "Lifers and Long-termers: Doing Big Time." In Robert Johnson and Hans Toch (eds.), *The Pains of Imprisonment*, pp. 115-128.

118. Deborah G. Wilson and Gennaro F. Vito, "Long-term Inmates: Special Needs and Management Considerations," *Federal Probation* 52 (1988):21-26.

119. M. Jackson, *Prisons of Isolation: Solitary Confinement in Canada* (Toronto, Ontario, Canada: University of Toronto Press, 1983), p. 243.

120. Bonta and Gendreau, "Reexamining the Cruel and Unusual Punishment of Prison Life," p. 360.

121. P. Suedfield, C. Ramirez, J. Deaton, and G. Baker-Brown, "Reactions and Attributes of Prisoners in Solitary Confinement," *Criminal Justice and Behavior* 9 (1982):303-340.

122. B. M. Cormier and P. J. Williams, "Excessive Deprivation of Liberty as a Form of Punishment," paper presented at the meeting of the Canadian Psychiatric Association, Edmonton, Alberta, Canada, 1966; Stuart Grassian, "Psychopathological Effects of Solitary Confinement," *American Journal of Psychiatry* 140 (1983):1450-1454.

123. U.S. Department of Justice, Bureau of Justice Statistics Executive Summary, *Correctional Populations in the United States*, p. 2.

124. Harvey Bluestone and Carl L. McGahee, "Reacting to Extreme Stress: Impending Death by Execution," *American Journal of Psychiatry* 119 (1962):393-396.

125. Johnnie L. Gallemore and James H. Panton, "Inmate Responses to Lengthy Death Row Confinement," *American Journal of Psychiatry* 129 (1972):81-86.

126. James H. Panton, "Personality Characteristics of Death Row Prison Inmates," *Journal of Clinical Psychology* 32 (1976):306-309.

127. Robert Johnson, "Life under Sentence of Death," in Johnson and Toch (eds.), *The Pains of Imprisonment*, pp. 129-145.

128. Charles E. Smith and Richard Reid Felix, "Beyond Deterrence: A Study of Defenses on Death Row," *Federal Probation* 50 (1986):55-59.

129. Julius Debro, Komanduri Murty, Julian Roebuck, and Claude McCann, "Death Row Inmates: A Comparison of Georgia and Florida Profiles," *Criminal Justice Review* 12 (1987):41-46.

130. John O. Smykla, "The Human Impact of Capital Punishment: Interviews of Families of Persons on Death Row," *Journal of Criminal Justice* 15 (1987):331-347.

131. Joan Petersilia, "When Probation Becomes More Dreaded Than Prison," *Federal Probation* 54 (March 1990):23-27.

132. John J. DiIulio Jr., *Governing Prisons: A Comparative Study of Correctional Management* (New York: Free Press, 1987) p. 165.

CORRECTIONS PERSONNEL ROLES AND FUNCTIONS

Chapter

The mood and temper of the public in regard to the treatment of crime and criminals is one of the most unfailing tests of the civilization of any country.

—Winston Churchill

The vilest weeds like poison-weeds/Bloom well in prison-air.

—Oscar Wilde

Introduction

This chapter focuses on the administrative methods and problems of correctional organizations. First, we analyze several facets and challenges of prison administration, including the wardens' difficult and changing roles and attitudes toward the use of prison amenities; administering prisons; carrying out death sentences; dealing with overcrowding; and using confidential information and inmate self-help groups. We then turn to the front-line personnel in prisons: the correctional officers, including a view of their stereotyped roles and functions as well as their professional orientation. Finally, we examine the "cousin" of prisons, the jails. In this section we highlight how jail staff, inmates, and facilities are in reality quite different from those found in prisons.

Two basic principles constitute the philosophy of prison "keepers": First, whatever the reasons a person is sent to prison, he or she is not to suffer pains beyond the deprivation of liberty—confinement itself is the punishment; second, regardless of the crime, the prisoner must be treated humanely and in accordance with his or her behavior. Even the most heinous offender is to be treated with respect and dignity and given privileges if institutional behavior warrants it.[1] Our analysis of institutional management is predicated on these two principles.

The Warden

A Most Difficult Position

A prison director stated to one of the author's administration classes that the job of prison warden is the most difficult in all of corrections.[2] This assessment is probably unarguable because the warden must take the director's policies and put them into effect throughout the institution.

Of course, both staff and inmates will be very sensitive to the warden's granting of what each side perceives to be a strengthened position for the other side. For example, if a policy gives the staff more power over inmates, the inmates will be unhappy, perhaps even rebellious. Conversely, if a policy that the staff believe affords too much additional freedom to inmates, the staff will feel sold out. Furthermore, the prison director, typically appointed by and serving at the pleasure of the state's governor, can use political pressures to influence the warden.

Clearly, the warden's position is difficult at best. These correctional executives also oversee the fastest growing agencies in state government; administer increasingly visible operations; and are held accountable by politicians, auditors, the press, organized labor, and numerous other stakeholders.[3] Wardens work within a field that has become more demanding, consumes an increasing share of public funds, and involves responsibility for the lives and safety of others.

A Profile

A national survey by Flanagan, Johnson, and Bennett[4] of 641 prison wardens at state-level adult institutions provided the following demographic information: 86 percent were male, the mean age of respondents was 47 years old, the majority (80 percent) were white, about half possessed a graduate degree or had done some graduate work, 54 percent had been correctional officers, and they had been in their current positions for an average of 5.7 years. Sixty-one percent of the respondents reported being "very satisfied" with their position, and two-thirds stated that if free to go to any kind of job they wanted, they would keep their current job. More than three-fourths (76.2 percent) believed that if they had to decide all over again whether to take their present job, they would do so, and two-thirds (67.9 percent) said they would strongly recommend a warden's job to friends. Taken together, the responses suggest that prison wardens are a highly satisfied occupational group.

Wardens who responded that the central office, inmates, and the media exerted more influence on prisons had lower job satisfaction scores. This finding was not surprising to Flanagan and colleagues, who observed that

> Correctional professionals are, in the final analysis, in the business of *control.* Because control (of inmates, of staff, and of the entire prison) is the *sine qua non* of the warden's job, it is perhaps not surprising that perceived loss of control and lower job satisfaction would be closely associated.[5]

Changes Brought by the Civil Rights Movement and the War on Drugs

Since the 1960s, correctional administration in the United States has been shaped by major social, economic, and political events outside the justice system. Two examples are the civil rights movement of the 1960s and the more recent "war" on drugs. Prior to the civil rights movement, correctional administrators were generally free to operate prisons as they saw fit.[6] Since that time, the federal government has become involved in virtually every aspect of prisoner operations, including the day-to-day activities of prison administrators. These executives are now under intense scrutiny from the judicial system, Congress, the media, and a disgruntled public.[7]

The war on drugs changed prison operations by causing unprecedented growth, decreasing the average time served (resulting in a less stable, more rapidly changing prison population), and dramatically changing the demographic and ethnic composition of prisons. The public desire for a more punitive correctional environment has placed pressures on corrections to "get tough," causing prisons to be transformed from places where offenders are held *as punishment* to places *for punishment.* In reaction to this tougher milieu, correctional administrators are being ordered to purge their facilities of air conditioning, educational programs, weights, drug treatment programs, and "free" medical services.[8]

Wardens' Use of Amenities: "Soft on Crime" or Pragmatism?

Recent changes in the social and political climate in U.S. society have revived support for the "principle of least eligibility," which holds that prisoners should be least eligible for the benefits that accrue to other citizens.[9] An example of this principle is that inmates should not receive freely any goods or services for which law-abiding citizens have to pay. Recently, a prison warden was brought to South Carolina from Texas to effect a "get-tough" policy. The new warden's reforms included removing air conditioning and televisions from cells, discontinuing intramural sports, requiring inmates to wear uniforms, abolishing furloughs for inmates convicted of violent crimes, and banning long hair and beards. Other states are making conditions in prisons more restrictive as well. Arizona, for example, instituted a grooming policy and dress code, halted the annual prison rodeo, and reinstated double-bunking, all of which resulted in dramatic decreases in escapes and prison costs.[10]

Still, today's prisons include such amenities as aerobics, theater groups, conjugal visits, in-cell cable television, and even catered prime-rib dinners.[11] Some observers believe that such "absurd" amenities may actually contribute to the crime problem (representing for some an improvement in their lifestyle) and make prison operations so expensive that more prisons cannot be built.[12]

A national survey of 6,451 wardens by Johnson, Bennett, and Flanagan[13] found that the respondents tended to reduce or eliminate such amenities as martial arts instruction, cosmetic surgery, conjugal visits, cosmetic dentistry, sexually oriented reading material, condom distribution, boxing, disability benefits, and tobacco smoking/chewing. (No information was provided concerning the extent to which these amenities were being offered in the respondents' institutions.) Conversely, the wardens least favored the reduction in or elimination of basic literacy programs, high school equivalency (GED) diploma programs, vocational training, jogging, library services, ball games, AIDS treatment, and physical therapy. Little interest was demonstrated by respondents for reducing or eliminating televisions and VCRs, radios, tape and CD players, musical instruments, special diets, telephone calls, mail privileges, weight-lifting equipment, and air conditioning. The survey also revealed that the following amenities *had* been reduced or eliminated at the respondents' institutions in the previous year (shown in descending order): college education programs, tobacco smoking, conjugal visitation, martial arts instruction, boxing, tobacco chewing, nonregulation clothing, and weight lifting.[14]

The survey also found that wardens believed incapacitation to be the most important goal of prisons, followed by deterrence, rehabilitation, and retribution. Wardens who selected rehabilitation as the most important goal of prisons were less inclined to favor reduction of prison amenities than those who ranked rehabilitation lower, whereas wardens who identified retribution as the most important goal of prisons were more supportive of reducing prison amenities than those who ranked retribution lower. Wardens who had formerly been correctional officers were almost equally divided regarding support for amenities. Conversely, among wardens with no correctional officer experience, 35 percent reported that they would reduce a large number of amenities, and 65 percent indicated they would reduce fewer amenities.[15] Also, more than 60 percent of the wardens who indicated that inmates exert a great deal of influence showed little support for amenity reduction. On the other hand, 54 percent of the wardens reporting that inmates exert little influence in their institution reported moderate to high support for elimination of prison amenities.[16]

The researchers concluded that there is little evidence that wardens are "soft on crime" or excessively sympathetic to the plight of prisoners. Why, then, do wardens appear to be so unwilling to reduce or eliminate prison programs and services? The answer is a pragmatic one: Several prison programs and amenities—such as watching television, hobby crafts, and the like—soak up otherwise uncommitted time within the prison week. A major problem in prisons is that of excess time and too few constructive activities for inmates. Programs and activities, therefore, help inmates—and staff—to manage boredom and tedium in the prison environment.[17]

Programs and amenities thus serve a critical *control* function within prisons. Correctional officials can grant access to them in exchange for obedience to prison rules and can restrict that access as punishment for rule violations. Indeed, the entire prison disciplinary structure is founded on punishments that amount to restriction of privileges.[18] Amenities that draw the loudest criticism from persons outside the prison, such as cable television, actually enhance the control of prison staff in that they are better able to direct the times, channels, and content of television programming.

In contrast, political leaders view prisons through an *ideological* prism. The political gain to be derived from railing against "coddling criminals" is considerable and has struck a chord with American voters for nearly three decades.[19] The perspective that prisons should be places *for* punishment gives rise to the principle of least eligibility and calls into question any service or program that prisons might provide. When coupled with the budget constraints present in many states, prison programs become an easy target for criticism and elimination.[20]

Clearly, the dilemma for wardens—and society at large—is how to reconcile the need to make prison life as unattractive as possible to deter free-world people from crime while giving corrections executives the ability to maintain order in their facilities by keeping inmates busy.

Administering Prisons

Throughout the nineteenth and the early part of the twentieth centuries, studies of prisons generally focused on the administrators rather than on the inmates. Beginning in the 1940s, however, an ideological shift from focus on prison administration to inmates occurred. The central reason for the shift seems to have been that these institutions were poorly managed or were what prison researcher John J. DiIulio Jr. referred to as "ineffective prisons."[21] Many writers expressed grave doubts about the efficacy of correctional administrators and expressed the idea that prison managers could do nothing to improve conditions behind bars.

It is not surprising that when contemporary researchers attempt to relate prison management practices to the quality of life behind bars, the results are normally quite negative: Prisons that are managed in a tight, authoritarian fashion are plagued with disorder and inadequate programs, and those that are managed in a loose, participative fashion are equally troubled; and those with a mixture of these two styles are not any better.[22]

In a three-year study of prison management in Texas, Michigan, and California, however, DiIulio found that levels of disorder (rates of individual and collective violence, and other forms of misconduct), amenity (availability of clean cells, decent food, etc.), and service (availability of work opportunities and educational programs) did not vary with any of the following factors: a "better class" of inmates, higher per capita spending, lower levels of crowding, lower inmate-to-staff ratios, greater officer training, more modern plant and equipment, and more routine use of repressive measures. DiIulio concluded that "all roads, it seemed, led to the conclusion that the quality of prison life depended mainly on the quality of prison management."[23]

DiIulio also found that prisons managed by a stable team of like-minded executives, structured in a paramilitary, security-driven, bureaucratic fashion, had better order, amenity, and service than those managed in other ways, *even when* the former institutions were more crowded, spent less per capita, had higher inmate/staff ratios, and so on: *"The only findings of this study that, to me at least, seem indispensable, is that ... prison management matters"* [emphasis his].[24]

Studies analyzing the causes of major prison riots found that they were the result of a breakdown in security procedures—the daily routine of numbering, counting, frisking, locking, controlling contraband, and searching cells—that are at the heart of administration in most prisons.[25] Problems in areas such as crowding, underfunding, festering inmate-staff relations, and racial animosities may make a riot more *likely,* but poor security management will make riots *inevitable.*[26]

DiIulio offered six general principles of good prison leadership:

1. Successful leaders focus, and inspire their subordinates to focus, on results rather than processes, on performance rather than procedures, on ends rather than means. In short, managers are judged on results, not on excuses.

2. Professional staff members—doctors, psychiatrists, accountants, nurses, and other nonuniformed staff—receive some basic prison training and come to think of themselves as correctional officers first. As an example, in a recent disturbance at a federal penitentiary, middle-aged secretaries in skirts toted guns on the perimeter.

3. Leaders of successful institutions follow the management by walking around (MBWA) principle. These managers are not strangers to the cellblocks and are always on the scene when trouble erupts.

4. Successful leaders make close alliances with key politicians, judges, journalists, reformers, and other outsiders. (The need to practice openness is discussed later.)

5. Successful leaders rarely innovate, but the innovations they implement are far-reaching and the reasons for them are explained to staff and inmates well in advance. Line staff are notoriously sensitive to what administrators do "for inmates" versus "what they do for us." Thus, leaders must be careful not to upset the balance and erode staff loyalty.

6. Successful leaders are in office long enough to understand and, as necessary, modify the organization's internal operations and external relations. DiIulio used the terms "flies," "fatalists," "foot soldiers," and "founders." The flies come

and go unnoticed and are inconsequential. Fatalists also serve brief terms, always complaining about the futility of incarceration and the hopelessness of correctional reform. The foot soldiers serve long terms, often inheriting their job from a fly or fatalist and make consequential improvements whenever they can. Founders either create an agency or reorganize it in a major and positive way.[27]

To summarize, to "old" penologists, prison administrators were admirable public servants, inmates were to be restricted, and any form of self-government was eschewed. To "new" penologists, prison administrators are loathsome and evil, inmates are responsible victims, and complete self-government is the ideal. DiIulio calls for a "new old penology," or a shift of attention from the society of captives to the government of keepers. He asserted that tight administrative control is more conducive to decent prison conditions than loose administrative control. This approach, he added, will "push administrators back to the bar of attention," treating them at least as well as their charges.[28]

Contemporary Challenges to Prison Administrators

An Array of Demands

As indicated earlier, today's prison administrator is faced with a fascinating array of challenges: These include locating correctional facilities; designing and building them (cheaper and quicker); containing health care costs; managing overcrowding; developing alternatives to incarceration; addressing issues of gangs, AIDS, and staff safety and training; continuing to satisfy old court orders and consent decrees (while avoiding new court oversight due to increasing institution populations); and enhancing security and programs (while facing a reduction in resources).[29]

In the 1970s and 1980s, a solid correctional administrator focused on managing the institution, but in the new millennium he or she must spend large amounts of time in the public policymaking arena. The "tough on crime" stance adopted by the political process has required administrators to enter the political domain more than ever before.

Prisons experience the same problems that other sectors of the economy face: rising food, construction, and health care costs (the latter exacerbated by individuals who are living longer as well as those whose health has deteriorated as a result of alcoholism, drug use, and AIDS) in addition to personnel expectations with regard to salary and benefits (with greater union activism in those areas).

As discussed earlier, society's litigious nature has permeated the prison walls. Today's correctional administrators must spend time and money defending against inmate lawsuits. Inmates sue not only for alleged confinement abuses but also about tattoos, pornography, voting rights, accessibility to lottery tickets, too little dessert, clothing style, air quality, and so on. Death penalty cases are on appeal indefinitely, negligent supervision suits abound, and employees are increasingly seeking assistance from the courts to resolve their differences.[30]

Corrections has been the subject of little research, which has provided few if any findings leading to new methodologies to control or change the behavior of inmates. As a result, correctional administrators today develop or apply programs that are generally advertised as being inexpensive and that therefore inevitably hold political attraction. Also, correctional administrators in the twenty-first century must deal with the Willie Horton legacy: On any given day an offender may reoffend, causing public and political opinion within a jurisdiction to change completely. Politicians who have learned the lesson of Willie Horton well perceive that the tough on crime stance is a political cornerstone.[31]

Many people working in correctional administration feel that the public image of the field is negative. A corrections consultant wrote that the low level of public esteem commences with the media:

> The public view of corrections in this country is, frankly, horrible. People are inundated with stories about explosions in offender populations, monopoly-money costs for new prison and jail construction, and vexatious prison and jail litigation. The big stories that reach the public about corrections are almost universally negative.[32]

Correctional administrators have also been chastised for not being politically adept. A "fortress corrections" mentality is said to have become a philosophy within the field: Many staff, from the top to the bottom, do not understand the public's right to information, and paranoia about the media is rampant among corrections personnel. Most often, prison-media relations involve the institution announcing that a suicide occurred in the middle of the night or even avoiding the press in the hope that the newspapers and TV will not find out about it: "The myth persists that if one holds onto negative information tightly enough, one will be able to hide in plain sight."[33]

The corrections field has also been reproached by its own for the manner in which it communicates its research:

> There are no widely read professional journals in the field. The lack of serious research efforts is criminal considering the magnitude of public policy questions arising from corrections. There is good research, but most of that is never published. Thus, we re-create each other's mistakes too often. That picture does not connote professionalism. We have a very poor self-image. We don't like ourselves a lot and we don't think well of ourselves. I defy [anyone] to identify an occupation in which such a high percentage of people acknowledge going into the field "by accident."[34]

"Death Work": Carrying Out Executions

One of the major duties of prison administrators, at least in a majority of the states, is to carry out the wishes of the people and see that condemned persons are executed in a manner that is professional and does not shock the conscience.

The discharge of the death penalty requires a number of people who are trained in individual tasks. Robert Johnson, who has referred to this entire undertaking as "death work,"[35] has studied and witnessed the process personally. Although no "typical" process for bringing executions to fruition exists, following is a general description of the key events.

Preparation for execution gains momentum when a date draws near and the prisoner is moved to the death house, a short walk from the death chamber. The process culminates in the so-called "death watch," a 24-hour period that ends with the prisoner's execution. This final period is generally supervised by the execution team, which reports directly to the warden of the institution. The warden or a representative by law presides over the execution.[36]

Although the public image of the executioner is often one of a sinister, solitary figure who wears a black hood, today that impression is largely inaccurate and misleading. Although occasionally a state will advertise for someone to fill a vacancy for the "state executioner" position, most executions are carried out by a highly trained team. To minimize the possibility of error, the execution team is carefully drilled in the mechanics of execution. The process has been broken down into distinct tasks and practiced repeatedly.

During the actual death watch, a member of the execution team is with the prisoner at all times. The officer keeps the inmate calm and attempts to serve his or her immediate needs. At this stage, the execution team views the prisoner as a person with a potentially explosive personality, so surveillance is constant and intense. During the last five or six hours, two officers are assigned to guard the prisoner. They attempt to maintain a conversation with the inmate, keeping tabs on his or her state of mind and trying to avoid subjects that might cause depression or anger. As the execution time approaches, the mood normally becomes more somber and subdued. A last meal is served, although prisoners who are about to be executed normally eat little or nothing at all, and then the prisoner boxes all of his or her worldly goods, which are inventoried by staff, for delivery to family or friends.[37]

The prisoner then showers, dons a fresh set of clothes, and is placed in an empty tomblike death cell. At this point the prisoner normally exhibits a numb resignation and waits peacefully (possibly having been given a sedative) to be escorted to his or her death. The warden and the remainder of the execution team then come and the former then reads the court order, or death warrant. Meanwhile, official witnesses are prepared for their role. Normally, from 6 to 12 citizens serve as witnesses to the execution.[38]

The steps that are taken from this point, with regard to the actual execution, depend, of course, on the actual method used. For example, 32 states employ lethal injection, 11 use electrocution, 7 utilize lethal gas, 4 use hanging, and 3 authorize use of a firing squad (numbers do not total 50 states because 15 states authorize more than one method of execution, generally at the election of the condemned prisoner or depending on the date of their receiving a capital sentence).[39]

Staff-Inmate Relationships

A common misconception held by the public is that prison administrators, through their correctional officers, have complete control over inmates. Historically, prisoners were expected to do as they were told. Even the courts, stating that they did not have the expertise or the jurisdiction to determine how the prison should be managed, deferred to the wardens.[40]

Now, however, inmates have power. Without their consent and cooperation, the modern correctional institution could not function. According to Victor D. Lofgreen, today's "mega-prison" has changed from a correctional facility with programs and activities aimed at rehabilitating offenders to a racially segregated, gang-controlled warehouse for convicts to do their time. By depending on inmate labor and leadership in order to function, the prisons give power to the inmate groups. In addition, correctional officers are under constant scrutiny by administrators and are subject to litigation by inmates. In sum, "the modern prison has become a combat zone."[41]

Lofgreen described a model of the life cycle of the power relationship between the staff and inmates in an adult prison (Figure 10.1). The model demonstrates the change in the balance of power in the prison from staff to inmates over time, from total staff domination to total inmate domination. In Stage I, that of *staff dominant-inmate submissive*, administration and staff are in clear, visible, and total control of the institution, with inmates in a lockdown status, usually following a rebellion or major shakedown. A correctional facility cannot operate very long under these circumstances. The institution depends on inmate laborers to function as cooks, laundry personnel, maintenance, and so on. Therefore, to provide enough personnel for these tasks, the institution moves into

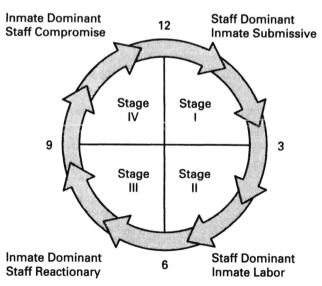

Inmate Dominant
Staff Compromise

12

Staff Dominant
Inmate Submissive

Stage IV   Stage I

9   3

Stage III   Stage II

Inmate Dominant
Staff Reactionary

6

Staff Dominant
Inmate Labor

Figure 10.1

Model of the life cycle of the inmate–staff power relationship in an adult prison. (*Source:* Victor D. Lofgreen, "A Model of the Dynamic Power Relationship Between Staff and Inmates in a Secure Correctional Facility," paper presented at the Annual Meeting of the Academy of Criminal Justice Sciences, 1991, Reno, Nevada. Used with permission.)

Stage II, the *staff dominant–inmate labor* stage. As soon as possible following a disturbance, staff begin to classify inmates and identify those who can be trusted to work. Over time other inmates are released from lockdown and return to their work assignments. The institution regains its equilibrium and inmates are given increased autonomy, freedom of movement, and privileges. A balance of power is created between the two groups, with each side cooperating with the other (although the inmates know they could take control of the prison whenever they wished).[42]

After reaching this state of equilibrium, however, a phenomenon occurs whereby each time the administration extends a privilege to the inmates, the inmates expect it to be a permanent offering. They meet any attempt by administration to withdraw privileges with extreme resistance. Eventually, if administration and staff continue to award new privileges in order to motivate inmates, the latter will have the most power. Inmates may expect to be catered to, and even pressure officers to participate in activities that violate institutional rules or law. In this stage of development, known as the *inmate dominant—staff reactionary* stage, or Stage III, inmates are in a position of superiority over the administration and staff.[43]

Through this progression, the institution becomes more and more unstable. Certain inmates are protected, and others are punished unfairly. At some point, the lack of consistent treatment and favoritism toward certain inmates causes a major loss of credibility in prison administration. Inmates and officers are confused, not knowing what to expect. This is Stage IV, *inmate dominant—staff compromise.* The tension and anxiety lead to a major disturbance. When the disturbance occurs, the institution is again thrown into an emergency lockdown status (Stage I). Order is restored and the process begins again. This cycle may take 2 or 20 years, depending on how long it takes the inmate subculture to compromise administration and staff. The goal of the administrator is to develop an institutional culture that creates a balance between the power of the staff and the inmates.[44]

By managing change in a deliberate manner, it is possible for the correctional administrator to keep the balance of power between Stages II and III for an extended period of time. Lofgreen recommended that administration occasionally "move inmates to a periodic scheduled lockdown to prevent the accumulation of contraband and maintain staff power over the inmates."[45]

Overcrowding: Possible Solutions

As discussed in Chapter 9, overcrowding may well be the primary problem affecting prisons and jails today. According to some observers, however, a larger problem may be that corrections facilities have admitted defeat in the battle against overcrowding. The heart of the problem, it is argued, lies in the fact that density and crowding, although related, are not the same. "The major factors responsible for crowding effects lies within the dynamic properties of social interactions" rather than in density per se.[46]

In other words, the real pains of crowding come not from inmate density but from the fact that prisoners feel crowded and suffer its ill effects as a result: Crowding interferes with their preferred ways of living. Social interactions, marked by poor coping behavior, cause various difficulties. Therefore, improving the quality of prison life should be the first order of reform. Some reformers maintain that other changes, such as building new prisons and using alternative forms of punishment (see Chapter 11), are important but play a secondary role in reducing prison crowding. These strategies should be pursued *after* the crowding problem has been solved.[47]

Inmates feel crowded when they live under conditions of high density (many bodies), low resources (little to do), and limited control over their lives (few if any ways to escape unpleasant encounters). These conditions magnify the pressures of prison life. The key to avoiding problems of crowding, it is argued, is to provide more resources and expand the inmates' capacity to choose how resources are deployed. Prisoners will thus be treated as bona fide "consumers of correctional services."[48] Administrators could conduct consumer surveys to determine prisoners' perceptions of their needs and the means to meet those needs. Services that inmates do not want or use could be modified or discarded; others could be retained for program development.[49] Prisoners themselves might even find sources of services through a variety of existing self-help organizations (described later).

Administration and inmates can work together to develop decent prisons. More areas of stable private space can be developed for prisoners in densely populated, close-custody institutions. Functional units offer a means for doing so. These subdivide larger prisons into smaller "institutions" or "mini-prisons." Cubicles can be used in dormitories, shops, and classrooms. "Small prisons with private spaces for inmates are very desirable for the physical and psychological welfare of the inmates as well as from a prison management perspective."[50] These functional units "rearrange the distribution of currently available resources with the likely result that if we are not doing more with less, at least we are doing it for the same costs."[51]

No new space is needed to house functional units; only existing space is needed. These, Johnson added, are eminently practical means to convert a crowded prison from an interpersonal wasteland to a civilized social environment.[52]

Prison Rule Violators

Institutional administrators must develop, implement, and enforce rules and procedures for their organizations. These rules regulate inmate conduct to ensure orderly operation of the institution and to protect all who live and work there; they help to manage confined populations that outnumber staff by 3 to 1. Administrators respond to the more serious violations through administrative hearings and consider the merits of the charges and appropriate penalties.

Characteristics of Prison Rule Violators

A national survey of state prison inmates found that over half (53 percent) had been charged with violating prison rules at least once since entering prison on their current sentence.[53] This finding is consistent with that of a similar survey in 1979, which found that prison rule violators were likely to be young, unmarried, and currently incarcerated for a property offense or a robbery. They were also more likely than other inmates to be recidivists, to have been arrested for the first time at an early age, to have used drugs regularly, and to have completed less than 12 years of formal education. Furthermore, inmates housed in larger prisons or maximum security prisons had higher percentages of rule violations than did prisoners in other types of facilities.[54]

A slightly higher percentage of male inmates (53 percent) than female inmates (47 percent) were charged with rule breaking. As noted, marital status seemed to influence violations: About 60 percent of inmates who had never married were charged with violating prison rules, compared with about 41 percent of married inmates. Age was the prisoner characteristic that related most directly to prison rule violation: The younger the age, the larger the percentage of inmates charged with rule violations. About 60 percent of the inmates age 18 to 24 were charged with infractions. White and black rule violators reported nearly identical distributions of punishments received for rule violations.[55]

Obtaining Confidential Information

Accurate information is necessary for the orderly and effective operation of every organization. Correctional institutions are certainly no exception. To have such information, prison and jail administrators and staff members observe conditions, listen to complaints, and monitor the results of their actions. The unique nature of these organizations, however, creates a need for information beyond that of normal business. Timely information is crucial for staff and administration to avert riots, escape plots, or other threats to security. It is also essential that inmates involved in criminal activities that occur often in these institutions be identified and prosecuted successfully.[56]

Inmates themselves are obvious sources of information. One of the strongest taboos in the inmate subculture, however, is to "snitch" on other inmates or cooperate with prison officials. That philosophy works against obtaining needed information. Inmate informants can become targets of death threats, which are sometimes carried out. Protecting informants can become a serious problem for the administration.

Three types of inmate informants are employed: "snitches," the innocent witness or victim, and coconspirators. The idea of using snitches—trusted inmates who provide a regular flow of information—is attractive. This system often causes more problems than it solves, however. Inmates soon learn who the snitches are. The snitch system can also become undependable: Some clever informants take great delight in working as double agents.[57] The negative side of this system was ingloriously demonstrated at the 1980 New Mexico Penitentiary riot, where 33 inmates were murdered, some after being mutilated with blowtorches. Many inmates were also raped repeatedly. Among the first to be dragged from their cells and murdered were, of course, known snitches.

Instead of using designated snitches regularly, information can be sought from inmates when crimes and serious rule violations are investigated or in response to threats to safety and security in the prison. Although many inmates will report that they didn't see anything when crimes were committed, many serious crimes and incidents in prison have been solved as a result of cooperation from inmates. Coconspirators present special problems. Many serious crimes would never be solved without inside information from coconspirators wishing to help themselves. Correctional administrators need to consider, however, that the coconspirator may actually be the principal offender, who is willing to sacrifice partners who played a minor role in order to obtain immunity. Unless conclusive evidence corroborates the information, determining whether inmates are innocent witnesses or coconspirators may be difficult.[58]

Legal problems arise when confidential information is to be presented to a disciplinary committee. Correctional administrators need a basic working knowledge of the law surrounding the use of confidential information as evidence to ensure that due process is allowed inmates and to avoid lawsuits as a result of inappropriate use. Information used as a basis for punishing an inmate must meet at least some minimal standard of reliability. The disciplinary committee must be shown that the informant had firsthand knowledge and must receive information to help it determine the informant's reliability. *Mendoza v. Miller*[59] explained three ways to establish an informant's reliability. First, the investigator can swear an oath that the investigative report is true and then appear before the disciplinary committee to answer questions. Second, the informant's information can be corroborated by other evidence (this is possible when there is more than one informant). Third, the committee can verify firsthand knowledge of the informant based on the past record.[60]

Administrative Use of the Inmate Self-Help Movement

The Seventh Step Program at Kansas State Prison in Lansing was a spinoff of Alcoholics Anonymous and was the original prisoner self-help organization. Like many self-help groups, it was based on the personal experiences of its founder, Bill Sands. Designed to help long-term, hard-core recidivists to return to the mainstream of life, Sands's program was simple:

> Such classes should be conducted by ex-convicts rather than correctional authorities. For two good reasons. One, because such a man knows what must be done, knows what it feels like to be out in the world, branded with a felony record; and two, because the men inside prisons refuse, for the most part, to take moral lessons from the so-called do-gooders.[61]

According to Mark Hamm, inmates have demonstrated a strong and sustained interest in self-help organizations during the past two decades. He asserted that this "movement" has captured the attention of correctional administrators concerned with the plight of special offender populations. From the familiar Alcoholics Anonymous to the little-known Schizophrenics Anonymous, Taking Pounds Off Sensibly, Women Who Love Too Much, Partners Without Partners, Mended-Hearts, Widow-to-Widow, Tough Love, and support groups for stutterers and diabetics to Hell's Angels seeking spiritual enlightenment to groups of transsexuals coping with their transitions, the self-help movement involves activities that reach into many areas of our social world. The American Veterans in Prison, Vietnam Veterans of America, and the Disabled American Veterans organizations also provide help for inmates.[62]

Historically, correctional treatment focused on past problems and errors and attempted to build a better tomorrow; however, several authors have observed that too often the immediate struggle for survival in prison distracts an inmate's attention from these "official" treatment programs.[63] As a result, inmates have increasingly turned to gangs, religious fellowships, and self-help organizations as alternatives to state-provided programs.[64]

Prisoner self-help groups provide certain opportunities for both administrators and inmates. These groups provide a support system that meets prisoners' social and/or cultural needs.[65] Some groups also provide leadership training, prisoner-administration politics, and organizational development and management. They also can relieve administration of some of the burden it carries for providing rehabilitative programs. These groups are of little threat to the corrections administration.[66]

A number of ethnic self-help groups, including Black Awareness for Community Development, Chicanos Organizados Pinton Aztlan, Afro-American Coalition, Affirmative Action Latin Group, and the Native American Brotherhood, have been organized. These groups seek to develop strong ties between minority communities on the outside and try to elicit support from religious and university communities. Because group leaders have tended to provoke and challenge them, correctional administrators have often taken a dim view of ethnic self-help groups.[67]

Overall, however, Hamm suggested that inmate self-help groups can work in concert with administrators to improve confinement conditions. For the future, the challenge for administrators will be to understand the potential of these groups, how they may contribute to institutional stability, and the extent to which they might facilitate community integration. Hamm cautioned, however, that administrators will not tolerate threats from these groups, regardless of their noble intentions.[68]

Correctional Officers: "Thy Brother's Keeper"

Between the institutional director and the inmates is the correctional staff—members who, in the words of Gordon Hawkins, are "the other prisoners."[69] Their role and nature are particularly important, given that they provide the front-line supervision and control of inmates, and correctional administrators may be promoted from this level.

In close association with inmates, correctional officers know that brute force and the system of rewards and punishments (especially in light of recent court decisions) are inadequate as control mechanisms. The officers know that a day of reckoning when all IOUs come due, when they may become hostages of the inmates, may eventually come, and when the decision as to whether the officers live or die may turn on their treatment of, and their reputation among, the inmate population. Thus, to be successful, officers may feel compelled to engage in *quid pro quos—tradeoffs or deals*—overlooking small infractions by inmates, in return for their general compliance with rules and orders. Gresham Sykes noted that "it is apparent, then, that the power of custodians is defective . . . the ruled are rebellious . . . the rulers are reluctant." He also asserted that "it is a paradox that they [the officers] can ensure their dominance only by allowing it to be corrupted."[70]

Comparison of Correctional Officers and Inmates

One guard stated: "We're all doing time, some of us are just doin' it in eight-hour shifts."[71] Richard Hawkins and Geoffrey Alpert compared officers and inmates: Both groups are likely to be drawn from lower- and working-class backgrounds; both are likely to be in their present roles because of lack of employment opportunities; both groups are largely invisible; both are closely watched and experience some depersonalization (e.g., they wear uniforms and are subject to psychological testing and probing into their pasts); both develop feelings of powerlessness; and both are fighting for their individual rights (conditions of incarceration and employment, respectively).[72]

Most applicants for positions as correctional officers probably had little knowledge of the job when they applied. A job description for the position might read something like this:

> [They] must prevent rape among two hundred convicts enraged by their powerlessness and sexual deprivation . . . prevent violence among the convicts . . . shake down all cells for contraband . . . know what is going on in the convicts' head and report it to their supervisors . . . account for all material entering or leaving each cellblock . . . maintain sanitation in each cell . . . give individual attention to all . . . convicts . . . [and] prevent the suicide or running amok of the raped, the depressed, and the terrified . . . and look out for their own physical and psychological survival.[73]

In most assignments, correctional officers experience stimulus overload, are assailed with the sounds of "doors clanging, inmates talking or shouting, radios and televisions playing, and food trays banging . . . (and odors) representing an institutional blend of food, urine, paint, disinfectant, and sweat."[74]

Correctional officers are not allowed to provide informal counseling or to aid in the rehabilitative effort. Due process rights for prisoners have made corrections jobs even more difficult.[75] Therein lies what Hawkins and Alpert referred to as "the big bitch" of correctional officers: They are losing power and influence while inmates are gaining them as they are accorded more due process rights.[76] This frustration can be vented in physical ways. Although certainly not frequent today, beatings and even sexual attacks by some officers have been documented.[77]

Requirements of Correctional Officers

The issue of what specific skills and level of education are needed to do the work of a correctional officer has rarely been raised. An issue of the Department of Labor's *Dictionary of Occupational Titles*[78] reported that the skill complexity level is the same for correctional officers and road construction flagpersons, school bus monitors, and morgue attendants!

Several federal commissions have strongly recommended higher educational standards among correctional officers, although none of them provided evidence that better educated persons necessarily made better officers.[79] The question of whether higher education is required for correctional officers is important. Education has a tendency to raise a person's aspirations and expectations. As one person put it, "Better educated people expect to do better."[80]

Considerable evidence suggests that higher education is marginally beneficial for correctional officers but may actually lead to lower job satisfaction. One observer noted that "except for the somewhat disappointing finding that [correctional officers] with more education are less satisfied with their jobs, the overall picture shows that education is not related to any attitudinal variable examined thus far."[81] Other researchers have commented that "more highly educated officers were significantly less satisfied with their jobs"[82] than were less educated ones. Other studies have determined that as officers' educational levels increased, so did their desire to become administrators; the less likely they were to feel a sense of accomplishment working as correctional officers or to want to make a career of corrections; the more likely they were to express dissatisfaction with the pace of career advancement; the more interest they had in counseling;[83] and the less willing they were to engage in rehabilitation activities.[84]

Two Canadian researchers studied the behavioral skills that effective correctional officers possessed: They compared the correctional officers, supervisors, and inmates with regard to correctional officers' tasks.[85] Correctional officers and supervisors attributed more importance to the "responsibility/leadership" skills (including writing reports, enforcing rules and regulations, working independently without excessive supervision, working effectively with others, providing inmates with appropriate information on different aspects of their incarceration, and providing clear direction to inmates on how to improve unacceptable behavior before applying negative consequences)[86] than the inmates did. Staff members perceived these job skills as the primary elements in their jobs, but inmates were obviously less concerned with them.

Results of Research Concerning Correctional Officer Characteristics

We now examine the professional orientation of correctional officers with respect to two broad aspects of their job: their individual views of and performance on the job, and their philosophy and views as members of organizations.

Attitudes

Recent studies indicate a consensus that "many officers see correctional work as an intrinsically worthwhile endeavor."[87] The attitudes of correctional officers[88] toward race, gender, education, chronological age, and age of entry into correctional work have been examined. Studies have not found any significant relationship between race and punitive attitudes toward inmates.[89] One study found no differences in officers' professional orientation according to race or by region (rural or urban).[90] Another researcher determined that nonwhite officers expressed an optimistic attitude toward inmates.[91] Finally, although one researcher found no significant differences regarding support for custody, black officers reported significantly greater support for rehabilitation.[92]

No studies have reported that officer gender was of significant concern to inmates.[93] One study did find a significant negative relationship between education and custody orientation, however.[94] Although chronological age was not found to be related to punitive attitude, a significant relationship between being older and support for a counseling orientation was discovered.[95] Similarly, older officers have been found significantly more optimistic regarding inmates.[96] Officers who entered corrections at a later age were significantly more likely to express support for rehabilitation.[97]

In summary, the results of studies into individual attitudes of corrections officers regarding the impact of race and age and the importance of gender and education are conflicting.[98]

A number of organizational conditions, such as institutional security classification, frequency of inmate contact, shift, correctional seniority, role conflict, job stress, perceptions of danger, and supervisory support have been studied. One study detected a significantly greater punitiveness among officers in minimum security units,[99] but another found significantly more optimism toward inmates in minimum security units.[100] A study investigating whether frequency of inmate contact affected officers' attitudes did not uncover a significant relationship in the degree of optimism regarding inmates.[101]

Not surprisingly, officers assigned to the night or "graveyard" shift, when inmates are normally "locked down," have reported a significantly more custodial and less rehabilitative orientation.[102] Although seniority has not been significantly related to attitudes toward inmates,[103] one study determined that seniority was significantly negatively related to beliefs in inmates' rehabilitation potential (as seniority increased, officers' expectation that rehabilitation was possible decreased).[104] Similarly, other studies found a significant positive relationship between seniority and custody orientation,[105] and that as seniority increased, optimism toward inmates' rehabilitation decreased.[106]

Jail Administration

Prisoners

Most, if not all, of the research findings on prison administrators and staff members previously presented can be extended to workers in jails. Jails differ from prisons, however, in several ways. Although about one-half million people are incarcerated in the nation's 3,300 jails every day,[107] social scientists, like the general public, have shown little interest in them or in the administration and operation of jails. In a legal sense, however, the jail is the point of entry into the criminal justice system. Jails hold persons booked for criminal activity and held for court appearances if they cannot arrange bail and those who are serving sentences for misdemeanors of up to one year.

John Irwin, a noted penal expert and author who served time in several jails and prisons, has some interesting views on jails and those who live and work in them. They are detached because they are not well integrated into conventional society, have few ties to social networks, and carry unconventional values and beliefs. They are disreputable because they are perceived as irksome, offensive, threatening, and capable of arousal.[108]

Irwin referred to jail prisoners as "rabble," meaning "disorganized" and "disorderly"—the "lowest class of people." He also referred to jail administration as "managing rabble."[109] Certain significant physical characteristics and management processes of jails, he wrote, reflect the fact that jails are intended to hold only the rabble. First, because not many of the rabble are expected to appear in court or even to stay in jail, security has been the fundamental concern in the construction of jails. The result has been massive buildings, complicated locking systems, and elaborate surveillance techniques. Second, Irwin maintained that because the rabble cannot be expected to behave themselves in jails, they must be controlled.[110] Hans Mattick agreed, but noted that

> Some jail administrators go overboard when it comes to the smaller details of jail security. Instead of relying on good peripheral security and the rational internal deployment of staff, they deplete the time and energies of their limited staffs by harassing the inmates in the details of daily living by frequent head counts, strip searches, cell "shakedowns," and the censorship of prisoner mail. In general, this is a wasteful use of scarce personnel. There is also a general tendency to treat *all* prisoners, except "trusties," as maximum security cases.[111]

Irwin believed that security-oriented measures caused jail inmates in general to experience more punishment per day than convicts in a state prison. Jailed persons, he said, suffered sudden interruption of their affairs, abrupt initiation into the jail, restriction of activities to a very small area, virtually no opportunities for recreation and expression, and a reduced health regimen that can lead to physical deterioration and occasionally to serious illness.[112] (*Note:* These characteristics do indeed indicate a harsher incarceration for those in jails as compared with prisons, especially with regard to health-related issues. See the discussion of research on prison inmates in Chapter 9.)

Although a large number of U.S. jails are undoubtedly similar to those described by Irwin and Mattick, a number of state-of-the-art jail facilities are progressive, treatment oriented to the extent possible, and generally "softer" than those described.

Career Paths for Jail Personnel

Because no single jail administrator is responsible for statewide jail management, detention officers (or "jailers") may manage their jails according to vastly different perceptions and philosophies concerning their staffing and operation. Most jails are supervised by a sheriff's office, where career advancement may be quite limited. When jails are separate units of local government with their own director, they tend to attract more qualified administrators with greater career commitments. A separate jail-related career path for correctional workers in jail administration is currently needed.

In some facilities, however, detention officers may transfer to patrol on the basis of seniority. Many of them, after receiving their basic training, want to do "real police work" and go out on patrol: They eschew the confined, nonpolice duties of detention that many agencies first require of new personnel. Many good officers, unwilling to serve a period of several years working in detention, resign. Police administrators should attempt to create two separate career paths, one in patrol and one in detention, so that persons beginning one path can remain and be promoted in it and hopefully retire from it.

Training of Jail Personnel

Jail administrators need to be thoroughly trained in all aspects of their jobs. Jail workers have been criticized for being untrained and apathetic, although many are highly effective and dedicated. One observer wrote that

> Personnel is still the number one problem of jails. Start paying decent salaries and developing decent training and you can start to attract bright young people to jobs in jails. If you don't do this, you'll continue to see the issue of personnel as the number one problem for the next 100 years.[113]

Training should be provided on the booking process; inmate management and security; general liability issues; policies related to AIDS; problems of inmates addicted to alcohol and other drugs; communication and security technology; and issues concerning suicide, mental health problems, and medication.

Jail Overcrowding

Justice administrators across the country have identified crowding as the most serious problem facing criminal justice today.[114] Nearly a third of the nation's jails are under court order to limit their populations or improve conditions, suggesting the seriousness of the problem. Overcrowding increases tensions for staff and inmates and wear and tear on facilities and equipment, creates overtime budgetary problems, and exacerbates the problems related to meeting program and service standards. Judges, prosecutors, probation and parole officers, and other officials often find jail crowding a severe constraint when jailing offenders seems necessary but space is unavailable. Finally, court functions suffer overall when crowding affects the movement of inmates to and from scheduled appearances.[115]

Alleviating the Problem

Justice administrators and policymakers can affect jail crowding, however. As one judge said, they can use "a lot of little ways" to halt or reverse jail population increases without releasing serious offenders.[116] *Police administrators* can invoke policies concerning arrest practices—whether to arrest, transport to jail, book or detain for bail setting—that are critical determinants in jail populations. Stationhouse release before booking, field citations, and court-authorized bail schedules also eliminate unnecessary confinement.

Jail administrators can reduce overcrowding by ensuring ready access for pretrial release screening and bail review. *Prosecutors* can engage in early case screening to reduce unnecessary length of confinement by eliminating or downgrading weak cases as soon as possible. Prosecutors can also use "vertical case screening," which assigns the same attorney or team of attorneys to a case from start to finish. "Horizontal case screening" (reassigning cases from one assistant prosecutor to another while the matter is before the court) may cause stagnation in case flow.

Judges make more decisions affecting jail populations than anyone else: They can issue summonses instead of arrest warrants; provide guidelines authorizing direct release by police, jail, and pretrial staff; and provide bail setting outside normal court hours. Courts may defer service of jail sentences when the jail is at capacity.

Defense attorneys can perform early screening for indigency, defender appointment, and defendant contact, which can decrease length of confinement and yield substantial savings of jail space.

Probation and parole agencies can provide nonjail alternatives for sentencing and enhance case-processing efficiency by streamlining presentence investigation (PSI) procedures and expediting revocation decisions.[117]

Summary

This chapter has examined several elements of correctional administration, including administrative aspects of both prisons (including amenities, carrying out death sentences, and crowding) and local jails. Also explored were correctional officers' roles and functions and their professional orientation.

Certainly, substantial pressures are now put on prison and jail administrators. They must maintain custody of and offer some degree of treatment to inmates while protecting inmates against themselves and others. At the same time, they must avoid decisions and behaviors that might lead to costly liability while attempting to prevent or remedy overcrowding.

Questions for Review

1. What is meant by the term *new old penology?*
2. What are some of the major elements of well-administered prisons? Enumerate the major principles of good prison administration.
3. Describe the life cycle of the inmate-staff power relationship. Why is it rare for a prison to pass through all phases of the cycle?
4. What can prison administrators do to alleviate crowding? How can they provide relief from overcrowding without adding new space?
5. What are some problems and methods of dealing with prison rule violators and snitches for correctional administrators?
6. What makes an effective correctional officer? Given research findings concerning their attitudes toward offenders, do these officers believe that rehabilitation of prisoners is possible?
7. How does jail administration differ from prison administration?

Notes

1. John J. DiIulio Jr., *Governing Prisons: A Comparative Study of Correctional Management* (New York: Free Press, 1987), p. 167.
2. Personal communication, Ron Angelone, Director, Nevada Department of Prisons, April 27, 1992.
3. F. T. Cullen, E. J. Latessa, R. Kopache, L. X. Lombardo, and V. S. Burton Jr., "Prison Wardens' Job Satisfaction," *The Prison Journal* 73 (1993):141–161.
4. Timothy J. Flanagan, W. Wesley Johnson, and Katherine Bennett, "Job Satisfaction Among Correctional Executives: A Contemporary Portrait of Wardens of State Prisons for Adults," *The Prison Journal* 76 (December 1996): 386.
5. Ibid., p. 395.

6. S. Sturm, "The Legacy and Future of Corrections Litigation," *University of Pennsylvania Law Review* 142 (1993):639–738.

7. Flanagan, Johnson, and Bennett, "Job Satisfaction Among Correctional Executives: A Contemporary Portrait of Wardens of State Prisons for Adults," pp. 385–397.

8. W. Wesley Johnson, Katherine Bennett, and Timothy J. Flanagan, "Getting Tough on Prisoners: A National Survey of Prison Administrators," *Crime and Delinquency* 43 (1997):24–41.

9. David J. Rothman, *The Discovery of the Asylum* (Boston: Little, Brown, 1971).

10. Robert James Bidinotto, "Must Our Prisons Be Resorts?" *Reader's Digest,* (November 1994): 65–71.

11. Ibid.

12. Ibid.

13. Johnson, Bennett, and Flanagan, "Getting Tough on Prisoners."

14. Ibid., p. 31.

15. Ibid., pp. 31, 34.

16. Ibid., p. 35.

17. Ibid., p. 37.

18. Timothy J. Flanagan, "Discretion in the Prison Justice System: A Study of Sentencing in Institutional Disciplinary Proceedings," *Journal of Research in Crime and Delinquency* 19 (1982):216–237.

19. Timothy J. Flanagan and Dennis R. Longmire (eds.), *Americans View Crime and Justice* (Thousand Oaks, Calif.: Sage, 1996).

20. Johnson, Bennett, and Flanagan, "Getting Tough on Prisoners," p. 39.

21. In George F. Cole and Marc C. Gertz (eds.), *The Criminal Justice System: Politics and Policies* (7th ed.) (Belmont, Calif.: West/Wadsworth, 1998) pp. 448–457.

22. Ibid., p. 449.

23. DiIulio, *Governing Prisons,* p. 256.

24. Ibid.

25. Bert Useem, *States of Siege: U.S. Prison Riots, 1971–1986* (New York: Oxford University Press, 1988).

26. John J. DiIulio Jr., "Well-Governed Prisons Are Possible," in Cole and Gertz (eds.), *The Criminal Justice System,* p. 450.

27. John J. DiIulio Jr., *No Escape: The Future of American Corrections* (New York: Basic Books, 1991), Chapter 1.

28. DiIulio, "Well-Governed Prisons Are Possible," p. 456.

29. Chase Riveland, "Being a Director of Corrections in the 1990s," *Federal Probation* 55 (June 1991):10-11.

30. Ibid. p. 10.

31. Ibid., p. 11.

32. Jeffrey A. Schwartz, "Fortress Corrections," *Corrections Today* 51 (August 1989):216–223.

33. Ibid., p. 222.

34. Ibid., pp. 222–223.

35. See Robert Johnson, *Death Work: A Study of the Modern Execution Process* (2d ed.) (Belmont, Calif.: West/Wadsworth, 1998).

36. Robert Johnson, "This Man Has Expired," *Commonweal* (January 13, 1989):9-15.

37. Ibid.

38. Ibid.

39. U.S. Department of Justice, Bureau of Justice Statistics, *Sourcebook of Criminal Justice Statistics–1997* (Washington, D.C.: Author, 1998), p. 539.

40. See *Banning v. Looney,* 213 F.2d 711 (10th. Cir., 1954).

41. Victor D. Lofgreen, "A Model of the Dynamic Power Relationship Between Staff and Inmates in a Secure Correctional Facility," paper presented at the Annual Meeting of the Western Social Science Association, Reno, Nev., 1991, p. 6.

42. Ibid., pp. 8–10.

43. Ibid., pp. 12–14.

44. Ibid., pp. 14–16.

45. Ibid., p. 18.

46. Verne C. Cox, Paul B. Paulus, and Garvin McCain, "Prison Crowding Research: The Relevance for Prison Housing Standards and a General Approach Regarding Crowding Phenomena," *American Psychologist* 39 (October 1984):1148–1160.

47. Robert Johnson, "Crowding and the Quality of Prison Life: A Preliminary Reform Agenda," in Clayton A. Hartjen and Edward E. Rhine (eds.), *Correctional Theory and Practice* (Chicago: Nelson-Hall, 1992), pp. 139–145.

48. See Robert Johnson, *Hard Time: Understanding and Reforming the Prison* (Monterey, Calif.: Brooks/Cole, 1987).

49. Johnson, "Crowding and the Quality of Prison Life," p. 142.

50. Cox, Paulus, and McCain, "Prison Crowding Research," p. 1156.

51. Robert B. Levinson, "Try Softer," in Robert Johnson and Hans Toch (eds.), *The Pains of Imprisonment* (Prospect Heights, Ill.: Waveland Press, 1988), pp. 241-256.

52. Johnson, *Hard Time,* p. 170.

53. U.S. Department of Justice, Bureau of Justice Statistics Special Report, *Prison Rule Violators* (Washington, D.C.: Author, 1989), p. 1.

54. Ibid., p. 2.

55. Ibid., pp. 1–2.

56. Perry Johnson, "The Snitch System: How Informants Affect Prison Security," *Corrections Today* (July 1989):26,28,72.

57. Ibid., p. 28.

58. Ibid., p. 72.

59. *Mendoza v. Miller* (7th Cir. 1985).

60. Van Vandivier, "Do You Want to Know a Secret? Guidelines for Using Confidential Information," *Corrections Today* (July 1989):30, 32, 73.

61. Bill Sands, *My Shadow Runs Fast* (Englewood Cliffs, N.J.: Prentice Hall, 1964).

62. Mark S. Hamm, "Current Perspectives on the Prisoner Self-Help Movement," *Federal Probation* 52 (June 1988):49–56.

63. John Irwin, "Adaptation to Being Corrected," in Daniel Glaser (ed.), *Handbook of Criminology* (Chicago: Rand McNally, 1974); Johnson, *Hard Time,* 1987; G. G. Kassebaum, D. A. Ward, and D. M. Wilner, *The Effectiveness of a Prison and Parole System* (Indianapolis, Ind.: Bobbs-Merrill, 1971).

64. E. M. Abdul-Mu'Min, "Prisoner Power and Survival," in Robert M. Carter, Leslie T. Wilkins, and Daniel Glaser (eds.), *Correctional Institutions* (New York: Harper and Row, 1985; John Irwin, *Prisons in Turmoil* (Boston: Little, Brown, 1980).

65. Ibid.

66. Hamm, "Current Perspectives on the Prisoner Self-Help Movement," p. 50.

67. Milton Burdman, "Ethnic Self-Help Groups in Prison and on Parole," *Crime and Delinquency* (April 1974); Patrick D. McAnany and Edward Tromanhauser, "Organizing the Convict: Self-Help for Prisoners and Ex-Cons," *Crime and Delinquency* (January 1977).

68. Hamm, "Current Perspectives on the Prisoner Self-Help Movement," p. 55.

69. Gordon Hawkins, *The Prison* (Chicago: University of Chicago Press, 1976).

70. Ibid., p. 201.

71. Cited in Eric D. Poole and Robert M. Regoli, "Alienation in Prison: An Examination of the Work Relations of Prison Guards," *Criminology* 19 (1981):251–270.

72. Hawkins and Alpert, *American Prison Systems*, p. 338.

73. Adapted from Carl Weiss and David James Friar, *Terror in the Prisons* (Indianapolis, Ind.: Bobbs-Merrill, 1974), p. 209.

74. Ben M. Crouch, *The Keepers: Prison Guards and Contemporary Corrections* (Springfield, Ill.: Charles C. Thomas, 1980), p. 73.

75. Hawkins and Alpert, *American Prison Systems*, p. 340.

76. Ibid., p. 345.

77. See Lee H. Bowker, *Prison Victimization* (New York: Elsevier, 1980), Chapter 7.

78. United States Department of Labor, *Dictionary of Occupational Titles* (4th ed.) (Washington, D.C.: U.S. Government Printing Office, 1977).

79. Robert Rogers, "The Effects of Educational Level on Correctional Officer Job Satisfaction," *Journal of Criminal Justice* 19 (1991):123–137.

80. Ivan Berg, *Education and Jobs: The Great Training Robbery* (New York: Praeger, 1970), p. 128.

81. Susan Philliber, "Thy Brother's Keeper: A Review of the Literature on Correctional Officers," *Justice Quarterly* 4 (1987):9–37.

82. Nancy Jurik and Michael C. Musheno, "The Internal Crisis of Corrections: Professionalization and the Work Environment," *Justice Quarterly* 3 (1986):457–481.

83. Rogers, "The Effects of Educational Level on Correctional Officer Job Satisfaction," p. 134.

84. David Robinson, Frank J. Porporino, and Linda Simourd, "The Influence of Educational Attainment on the Attitudes and Job Performance of Correctional Officers," *Crime and Delinquency* 43 (1997):60–77.

85. Cindy Wahler and Paul Gendreau, "Perceived Characteristics of Effective Correctional Officers by Officers, Supervisors, and Inmates Across Three Different Types of Institutions," *Canadian Journal of Criminology* (April 1990):265–277.

86. Ibid., pp. 268–269.

87. Johnson, *Hard Time*, p. 138.

88. Kenneth B. Melvin, Lorraine K. Gramling, and William M. Gardner, "A Scale to Measure Attitudes toward Prisoners," *Criminal Justice and Behavior* 12 (1985):241–253.

89. James B. Jacobs and Lawrence Kraft, "Integrating the Keepers: A Comparison of Black and White Prison Guards," *Social Problems* 25 (1978):304–318; Ben M. Crouch and Geoffrey P. Alpert, "Sex and Occupational Socialization Among Prison Guards: A Longitudinal Study," *Criminal Justice and Behavior* 9 (June 1982):159–176.

90. John Klofas, "Discretion among Correctional Officers: The Influence of Urbanization, Age and Race," *International Journal of Offender Therapy and Comparative Criminology* 30 (1986):111–124.

91. Nancy C. Jurik, "Individual and Organizational Determinants of Correctional Officer Attitudes toward Inmates," *Criminology* 23 (August 1985):523–539.

92. Francis T. Cullen, Faith E. Lutze, Bruce G. Link, and Nancy T. Wolfe, "The Correctional Orientation of Prison Guards: Do Officers Support Rehabilitation?" *Federal Probation* 53 (March 1989):33–42.

93. Jurik, "Individual and Organizational Determinants of Correctional Officer Attitudes toward Inmates"; Cullen, Lutze, Link, and Wolfe, "The Correctional Orientation of Prison Guards."

94. Eric D. Poole and Robert M. Regoli, "Role Stress, Custody Orientation, and Disciplinary Actions: A Study of Prison Guards," *Criminology* 18 (August 1980):215–226.

95. Toch and Klofas, "Alienation and Desire for Job Enrichment among Correction Officers."

96. Jurik, "Individual and Organizational Determinants of Correctional Officer Attitudes toward Inmates."

97. Cullen, Lutze, Link, and Wolfe, "The Correctional Orientation of Prison Guards."

98. John T. Whitehead and Charles A. Lindquist, "Determinants of Correctional Officers' Professional Orientation," *Justice Quarterly* 6 (March 1989):69–87.

99. Carol F. W. Smith and John R. Hepburn, "Alienation in Prison Organizations," *Criminology* (August 1979):251–262.

100. Jurik, "Individual and Organizational Determinants of Correctional Officer Attitudes toward Inmates."

101. Ibid.

102. Cullen, Lutze, Link, and Wolfe, "The Correctional Orientation of Prison Guards: Do Officers Support Rehabilitation?"

103. Jacobs and Kraft, "Integrating the Keepers: A Comparison of Black and White Prison Guards"; Cullen, Lutze, Link, and Wolfe, "The Correctional Orientation of Prison Guards."

104. Boaz Shamir and Amos Drory, "Some Correlates of Prison Guards' Beliefs," *Criminal Justice and Behavior* 8 (June 1981):233–249.

105. Poole and Regoli, "Role Stress, Custody Orientation, and Disciplinary Actions."

106. Jurik, "Individual and Organizational Determinants of Correctional Officer Attitudes toward Inmates."

107. U.S. Department of Justice, Bureau of Justice Statistics, *Prison and Jail Inmates at Midyear 1998* (Washington, D.C.: Author, 1999), p. 1.

108. John Irwin, *The Jail: Managing the Underclass in American Society* (Berkeley, Calif.: University of California Press, 1985), p. 2.

109. Ibid., p. 8.

110. Ibid., p. 43.

111. Hans Mattick, "The Contemporary Jails of the United States: An Unknown and Neglected Area of Justice," in Daniel Glaser (ed.), *Handbook of Criminology* (Chicago: Rand McNally, 1974).

112. Irwin, *The Jail,* pp. 45–46.

113. Quoted in Advisory Commission on Intergovernmental Relations, *Jails: Intergovernmental Dimensions of a Local Problem* (Washington, D.C.: Author, 1984), p. 1.

114. U.S. Department of Justice, National Institute of Justice Research in Brief, *Systemwide Strategies to Alleviate Jail Crowding* (Washington, D.C.: Author, 1987), p. 1.

115. Ibid., p. 2.

116. Ibid.

117. Ibid., pp. 2–4.

COMMUNITY CORRECTIONS: PROBATION AND PAROLE

Chapter 11

Even I/Regained my freedom with a sigh.

—Lord Byron

Introduction

Community corrections, it has been stated, is "the last bastion of discretion in the criminal justice system."[1] Only a few decades ago, community-based corrections was enthusiastically viewed as a humane, logical, and effective approach for working with and changing criminal offenders. The President's Task Force endorsed this model in 1967, saying that it

> includes building or rebuilding solid ties between the offender and the community, obtaining employment and education, securing in the large sense a place for the offender in the routine functioning of society. This requires...efforts directed towards changing the individual offender (and) mobilization and change of the community and its institutions.[2]

Changes in national ideological thought and other matters have combined to present difficulties for these lofty ideals. These factors also have compelled us to increasingly use incarceration instead of community-based corrections.

This chapter, which examines probation and parole, begins with what is perhaps the core of this chapter: the consideration of tough alternatives to imprisonment. Then we examine the problem of large caseloads. The types of administrative systems and issues that are related to the administration of probation and parole are considered. Next we analyze the relatively new alternatives to incarceration and conventional probation and parole, known as *intermediate sanctions:* intensive supervision (of probation), electronic monitoring/house arrest, shock incarceration, and boot camps.

Why Alternatives to Imprisonment?

Sanctions or mechanisms of social control for enforcing society's standards are most likely to deter if they injure "the social standing by the punishment" and make "the individual feel a danger of being excluded from the group."[3] The United States bases assumptions about what punishes on the norms and living standards of society at large. This view overlooks several very important facts: First, most serious offenders neither accept nor abide by those norms; and second, most incarcerated people today come from communities where conditions fall far below the living standards that most Americans would accept.[4] The national shame is that for many people who go to prison, the conditions inside are not all that different from, and might even be better than, the conditions outside.

Social isolation is the second presumably punitive aspect of imprisonment. When a person goes to prison, however, he or she seldom feels isolated but is likely to find friends, if not family, already there.[5]

Furthermore, it seems plausible that prison life is not perceived as being as difficult as it once was. Inmates' actions speak loudly in this respect: More than 50 percent of today's inmates have served a prior prison term. Knowing what prison is like, these inmates evidently still believe the "benefits" of committing a new crime outweigh the costs of being in prison.[6] We must wonder how punitive the prison experience is for such offenders.

Finally, the stigma of having a prison record is not the same as it was in the past, because so many of the offenders' peers and family members also have done time. One survey found that 40 percent of youths in state training schools had parents who had also been incarcerated.[7] Imprisonment also confers status in some neighborhoods. Gang members have repeatedly stated that incarceration was not a threat because they knew their sentence would be minimal. To many people, serving a prison term is a badge of courage. It also is their source of food, clothing, and shelter.[8]

We have thus begun our discussion of community sanctions with these unfortunate statistics concerning the effectiveness of prisons to punish criminal behavior. These statistics demand that society determine whether it is time to seriously consider alternatives to incarceration. Probation and parole administrators might question whether conventional probation and parole are effective alternatives to prison sentences in all cases or whether other alternatives—such as intensive supervision programs—should be implemented.

The Burden of Large Probation and Parole Caseloads

Obviously, the quality of service that a probation or parole officer can provide to his or her clients is quite likely related to that officer's caseload. *Caseload* refers to the average number of cases supervised in a given period. Each case represents an offender on probation or parole who is supervised by an individual officer. As John Conrad observed:

> There is much that a good probation/parole officer can do for the people on his or her caseload. A parole officer who makes it clear that, "fellow, if you don't watch your step I'm gonna run your ass right back to the joint," is not in a position to be helpful as a counselor or facilitator. With the best intentions, a[n] officer struggling with the standard unwieldy caseload of 100 or more will deal with emergencies only, and sometimes will not be able to do that very well.[9]

Today about 3.4 million adults are on probation in the United States.[10] Although ideal caseloads for probation officers range from 25 to 50, many probation officers actually have caseloads of 200 or more. Because the quality of their contact with probationers is affected directly by the officers' ability to have face-to-face contact with them regularly, probation is often judged unfairly as being ineffective as a deterrent to crime. Probation departments are often the last to be given additional funding to create new positions to handle increasing numbers of offenders. Few agencies or courts consider the negative implications of giving understaffed and underfunded probation departments increasing numbers of persons to supervise.[11]

Regarding parole caseloads, parole officers supervise about 705,000 parolees in the United States.[12] As with probation, while the optimal caseload is about 25 to 50 parolees, in some jurisdictions the parolee/parole officer ratio is as high as 300 to 1.

Probation and parole administrators can probably do very little about excessively high caseloads. Being at the end of the justice system process, they have little control over the number of people whom the police arrest, prosecutors formally charge, juries convict, or judges sentence to prison.

Probation Systems

Types of Systems

Figure 11.1 depicts an organization structure for a regional parole and probation organization. Probation is the most frequently used sanction of all. It costs offenders their privacy and self-determination and usually includes some element of the

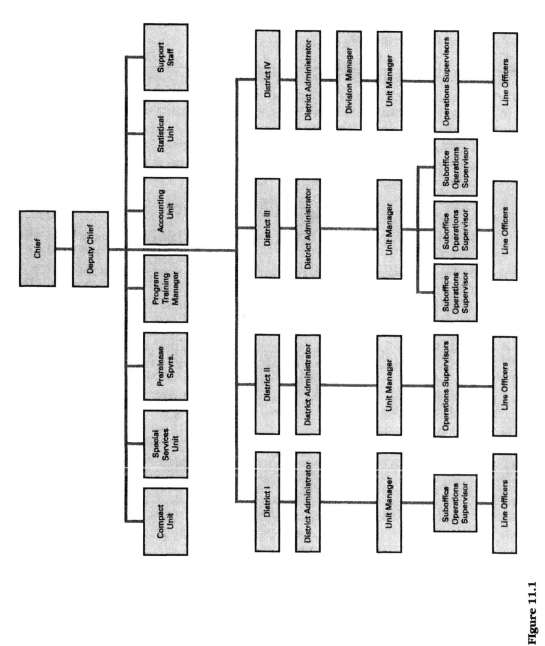

Figure 11.1

Organization structure for a regional adult parole and probation agency.

other sanctions: jail time, fines, restitution, or community service.[13] Probation in the United States is administered by more than 2,000 different agencies. Its organization is a patchwork that defies simple explanation. Texas alone has more than 100 county adult probation departments, but in about three-fourths of the states, adult probation is part of the executive branch of state government. By contrast, more than half of the agencies providing juvenile probation services are administered on the local level.[14]

Furthermore, according to Howard Abadinsky, the administration of probation systems can be separated into six categories, one of which will be employed:

1. *Juvenile:* Separate probation services for juveniles are administered on a county or municipal level or on a statewide basis.
2. *Municipal:* Independent probation units are administered by the lower courts under state laws and guidelines.
3. *County:* Under laws and guidelines established by the state, a county operates its own probation agency.
4. *State:* One agency administers a central probation system, which provides services throughout the state.
5. *State combined:* Probation and parole services are administered on a statewide basis by one agency.
6. *Federal:* Probation is administered as an arm of the federal courts.[15]

Regarding this patchwork nature of probation systems, two central organizational issues have been raised concerning the administration of probation services: Should probation be part of the judicial or the executive branch of government? Does the lack of uniformity in administering probation make justice less equitable statewide?[16] These important and lingering issues concerning probation administration and organization have been considered for more than a quarter century by the President's Task Force on Corrections.[17]

Abadinsky argued that probation administered by the judiciary on a *county* level promotes *diversity:*

> Innovative programming can be implemented more easily in a county agency since it has a shorter line of bureaucratic control than would a statewide agency. A county agency can more easily adapt to change, and the successful programs of one agency can more easily be adopted by other probation departments . . . and unsuccessful programs avoided. Although the judiciary is nominally responsible for administering probation, the day-to-day operations are in the hands of a professional administrator—the chief probation officer.[18]

One problem with the county-level administration of probation services, however, is the increased dissimilarity in operations. The officer/client ratios may differ in large measure from one county to another, as would probably not be the case if monitored by a statewide agency whose personnel can easily be shifted from one county to another. These officer caseloads range widely from county to county.

This brings us to the second issue concerning whether this lack of uniformity in providing probation services makes justice less equitable statewide. This issue has led states with county-based probation systems to create statewide bodies for better coordination and uniformity of services.

Probation Departments' Need for an Organization Plan

As early as 1924, a probation executive wrote that "without a consistent, orderly, and practical plan of organization, and without adequate, competent, and sensible methods of supervising the staff, a probation department cannot function properly."[19] Studies discussed later indicate that these are problems for probation departments as they enter the new millennium: What are my resources? How can I use them to maximize our supervision and services? These questions constantly challenge the probation administrator but are seldom addressed directly, according to Patricia L. Hardyman, who performed a major study of probation administration. The answers would enable the probation administrator to better control limited resources, select supervision strategies, and pursue attainable outcomes.[20]

Each year millions of dollars are invested in building and acquiring the capital to build office space for probation departments. This investment does not include the human resources invested by community volunteers and the families of probationers, yet little is known about how these resources are translated into activities or the outcomes and impacts.[21]

Systems Theory

As with the administration of a police, court, or prison organization, the probation department administrator's goals may affect the services provided to the client, which in turn may have an impact on the client's request for services. This systematic interaction between an organization's resources, structure, and community has been referred to as its *sociotechnical environment*,[22] meaning that the principles of the system are organized to execute the basic production technologies of the organization. Each probation administrator needs to recognize that the organization is a system of inputs, processes, and outputs. For probation, for example, inputs would be clients coming into the office for counseling and supervision (the processes); outputs would be the probationer's obtaining employment, acquiring a skill, observing a curfew, and so on. This understanding of probation, using systems theory, provides a means to learn how probation departments function and interact with their environment, and to examine the resources, activities, and outcomes in a way that will identify the goals, describe the day-to-day activities, and link the department's activities to resources and outcomes.

According to systems theory, probation may be conceptualized as a network of interwoven resources, activities, and outcomes.[23] According to Hardyman, *resources* include the probation department's funding level, goals, policies and procedures, and organization structure and caseloads; the probation staff's characteristics; the services available to probationers; and the rates of unemployment, poverty, and crime in the county. *Activities* are supervision techniques, rewards, leadership styles, contacts, and direct/indirect services provided by the probation department. *Outcomes,* according to systems theory, are the number of probationers who were arrested, incarcerated, and/or received a technical violation during the follow-up period, and the needs of probationers and the community that were considered.[24]

Hardyman's study of probation administrators focused on their management style—the fundamental determinant of the nature of the probation organization—and was instructive in terms of the impact of their style on the department's operation. Few departments, even those with hierarchical organizational structure, had a pure management style: Administrators vacillated among a variety of styles, including laissez-faire, democratic, and authoritarian. The degree to which administrators included the probation officers in the decision-making process and communicated with officers varied. The *authoritarian* administrator created emotional and physical distance between the officers and themselves. Officers in such systems reported feeling that they had little control over their cases and that policies and procedures were developed and enforced by those persons who were unconcerned with their plight.[25]

Surprisingly, the most common management style used by probation administrators was *laissez-faire.* Hardyman found that many probation administrators simply did not participate in the day-to-day activities and supervision strategies of the staff. They remained remote but made final decisions on critical policies and procedures.[26]

Hardyman found that few probation administrators across the country operated with the *democratic* style. Those who did, of course, listened more to the concerns and suggestions of the line supervisors and officers. The administrator still made final decisions, but information was generally sought from the line staff and their opinions were considered. Officers working under this style obviously had a greater sense that their opinions mattered and that the administrator valued their input. An additional benefit of the democratic style was that the administrators had power both by virtue of their position and their charisma, which inspired teamwork and task accomplishment.[27]

Hardyman also found several negative aspects of probation administration. Chaos was extremely high in urban laissez-faire probation departments. She observed shouting matches between staff members, and officers reported conflicting departmental policies and standards of supervision. She noted a lack of communication between the administrator and the staff and an inability to create and finish projects. Changes were viewed as imposed from above and were therefore resisted; officers were convinced that their administrators would not listen. Even in democratic probation departments with open and friendly environments, projects to address current crises were abandoned, and line staff and administrators frequently disagreed. None of the probation departments studied was proactive.[28]

Rethinking Probation: Community Supervision, Community Safety

By Donald G. Evans

Reorganizing probation has been a primary objective during the past decade. Efforts to do so have moved probation from its roots of "advise, assist and befriend" models of supervision to monitoring and disciplining offenders and offering to protect victims and the community. The results of this shift in philosophy leave much to be desired. Fortunately, there is within the field of probation a growing movement to rethink probation and find a purpose suitable for the times. . . .

[There are] critical issues in building public confidence in probation and how probation can contribute to enhancing the community's sense of public safety. Probation probably should stop focusing on offenders and focus more on victims and community safety. . . .

An effective probation service should provide: an adequate and appropriate response to criminal justice policy; a clear and coherent accountability mechanism (performance-based); effective leadership and agency management; an effective stewardship of resources; confidence to legislators, courts and the community that you are doing what you say you are doing; links to other community organizations and criminal justice agencies; and services to victims of crime.

[Probation administrators should] sharpen their focus and be clear about what they are prepared to commit to. It is possible to have clear focus and it is up to probation to decide who would create that focus. Will the focus come from outside the profession or will it come from within? Enlightened probation professionals can rethink probation and find a focus for the next century, but it will take intellectual effort, practical experience and a clear set of values.

Clearly, there is remarkable innovation going on in the probation field, but it is varied and scattered. There is very little coherence to the efforts and, as a result, it appears that the bulk of probation work is still fairly traditional. In fact, it appears that clarity of purpose is needed or else probation, in its attempts to adapt to the various environmental winds, will find itself drifting without a rudder. . . . A starting point for rethinking probation would be to consider the following focus: public (community) safety through crime reduction, reparation and community-building.

Source: "Rethinking Probation: Community Supervision, Community Safety," *Corrections Today,* in "Probation Departments' Need for an Organizational Plan" section, April 1999. Reprinted with permission of The American Correctional Association, Lanham, MD.

Parole Systems

Models for Providing Services

The administration of parole is much less complex than probation; consequently, less information is available concerning its needs, problems, and practices. (It should also be noted that in about 20 states, probation officers also serve as parole officers; thus, much of the information presented in the foregoing section applies to parole as well.) One agency per state administers the parole function on a statewide basis, although with a slight deviation: In a number of states, persons paroled from a local jail come under the supervision of a *county* probation and parole department.[29]

A parole agency can provide three basic services: parole release, parole supervision, and executive clemency. In a number of states that have abolished parole release (such as California), parole officers continue to supervise offenders released not by a parole board but on *good time.*

The National Advisory Commission on Criminal Justice Standards and Goals delineated two basic models for administering parole services:

1. *The independent model:* A parole board is responsible for making release (parole) determinations as well as supervising persons released on parole (or good time). It is independent of any other state agency and reports directly to the governor.

2. *The consolidated model:* The parole board is a semiautonomous agency within a large department that also administers correctional institutions. Supervision of persons released on parole (or good time) is under the direction of the commissioner of corrections, not the parole board.[30]

Both models sometimes combine probation services with parole services in a single statewide agency.

The President's Task Force on Corrections summarized the advantages of the independent model:

1. The parole board is in the best position to promote the idea of parole and to generate public support and acceptance of it. Because the board is accountable for parole failures, it should be responsible for supervising parolees.

2. The parole board that is in direct control of administering parole services can evaluate and adjust the system more effectively.

3. Supervision by the parole board and its officers properly divorces parole release and parolees from the correctional institution.

4. An independent parole board in charge of its own services is in the best position to present its own budget request to the legislature.[31]

The advantages of including both parole services and institutions in a consolidated department of corrections were summarized by the Task Force as follows:

1. The correctional process is a continuum. All staff, both institutional and parole, should be under a single administration rather than be divided, which avoids competition for public funds and friction in policies.

2. A consolidated correctional department has consistent administration, including staff selection and supervision.

3. Parole boards are ineffective in performing administrative functions: Their major focus should be on case decision, not on day-to-day field operations.

4. Community-based programs that fall between institutions and parole, such as work release, can best be handled by a single centralized administration.[32]

Critics of the independent model contend that it tends to be indifferent or insensitive to institutional programs and that the parole board places undue emphasis on variables outside the institution. Critics of the consolidated model contend that in it the parole board is pressured to emphasize institutional factors in making parole decisions.[33] Clearly, the trend in this country, beginning in the late 1960s, is in the direction of consolidation.

In the past, whether institution staff or independent agencies should make parole decisions has been controversial. The arguments for staff deciding when to release inmates are based on the following: The staff knows the inmates better, independent agencies and parole boards are too far removed from institutions to know what goes on within them, and giving this responsibility to independent boards downgrades the professional competence of staff and is unnecessarily complicated. These arguments are countered by those contending that independent agencies granting parole will eliminate irrational decision making by staff, that staff often lengthen stays for the violation of trivial and meaningless rules, and that staff may be secretive about the criteria for release and hold release over the heads of inmates.[34]

The Demise of Federal Parole

The U.S. Sentencing Commission established a new set of sentencing guidelines that were instituted on November 1, 1987. The guidelines also abolished parole for federal prisoners. Supervised release from prison was *not* discontinued entirely, however. In effect, something equivalent to parole is still in place, but the sentencing court is now the controlling authority over the inmate rather than a federal parole commission. The court has the authority to impose sanctions on released prisoners if they violate conditions of their release.

Many, if not most, prisoners sentenced under the new guidelines are still in prison (and have attempted a substantial amount of litigation attacking the new sentencing guidelines, most of which has been rejected by the courts). Prison wardens have undoubtedly experienced a higher inmate population that is serving longer terms because of this legislation. As a result, they must expend greater effort toward seeking alternatives to incarceration.

Intermediate Sanctions

As this and preceding chapters indicate, the overall health of corrections is not good. The criminal justice community, including probation agencies, is said to be involved in guerrilla warfare, meaning that the highest-risk probationers are out of control and generally reside in "out-of-control communities."[35] As one author observed, offenders may be smiling because "revolving door justice" has become an all-too-frequent fact of prison and jail life.[36] Institutional and community systems are being utilized beyond capacity. The United States is not soft on crime, but because prisons are not in a position to effect great change,[37] the search for solutions must involve change for corrections in the community.

The demand for prison space has created a reaction throughout corrections. Many state systems have attempted to solve the problem by building more prisons or expanding existing ones; however, these reactive efforts have resulted in financial, legal, and administrative problems.[38] With the cost of prison construction now exceeding $200,000 in maximum security institutions, cost-saving alternatives are becoming more attractive if not necessary. Opening the gates of jails and prisons and liberating inmates is, of course, one solution to the overcrowding problem. But it is not a serious alternative. A real alternative to incarceration must have three elements to be effective: It must incapacitate offenders enough so that it is possible to interfere with their lives and activities to make committing new offenses extremely difficult; it must be unpleasant enough to deter offenders from wanting to commit new crimes; and it has to provide real and credible protection for the community.[39]

As mentioned in Chapter 10, in addition to overcrowding, two interrelated developments characterize the state of corrections today and reflect major correctional problems: ideological restatement and, as a result, intermediate initiatives. In response to the criticisms and failures of rehabilitative philosophy and policies, the prevailing ideology of incapacitation, punishment, and deterrence has resulted in get-tough sentencing practices that contribute to rising prison populations. This shift from rehabilitating inmates to giving them their just deserts focuses on the fact that offenders make free will decisions to commit crimes and therefore no longer deserve compassion and correction. This ideology has wrought an exclusionary era of repressive social control, which attempts to banish, expel, and stigmatize the criminal deviant.[40] This is a vicious cycle, however. We have seen that these actions do little to deter crime.

Alternatives to Incarceration: Intensive Supervision, Electronic Monitoring/House Arrest, Shock Probation, Boot Camps

Probation and parole do not operate in a vacuum; their operations are affected in large measure by what occurs in the rest of the justice system and actions of other justice administrators. As the number of crimes continues to increase, the availability of incarceration facilities decreases. The implications of this problem are not lost on offenders: If they commit more crimes, they cause more over-crowding, spend less time in an institution, and are quickly released to commit a new round of offenses.[41]

Much of the experimentation with community-based alternatives to imprisonment reflects the current crisis in our prisons. The tension between the get-tough philosophy and the realities of prison overcrowding has led to a "search for intermediate punishments . . . an attempt to find mid-range solutions."[42] This in turn has brought about the emergence of a new generation of techniques, making community-based corrections, according to Barry Nidorf, a "strong, full part-ner in the fight against crime and a leader in confronting the crowding crisis. It is no longer considered a weak stepchild of the justice system."[43] Economic reality dictates that cost-effective measures be developed, and this is motivating the development of intermediate sanctions.[44]

A 1999 survey by the Association of State Correctional Administrators[45] found that 86 percent of all states used intensive supervision, 83 percent used electronic monitoring and 34 percent used house arrest (see Table 11.1 and Figure 11.A for other programs that are provided by state corrections agencies; data for shock incarceration and boot camps are presented later). Table 11.1 shows the number of persons under supervision by program type.

The growing interest in these four techniques is not based solely on the need to develop less expensive alternatives to prisons, although the economic realities cannot be overlooked.[46] Today's probation and parole administrators must have an arsenal of risk-control tools at their disposal. Community corrections agencies are using the following programs.

Intensive Supervision

In the compelling and sobering article, "When Probation Becomes More Dreaded Than Prison," Joan Petersilia, then director of the criminal justice program for the RAND Corporation, questioned whether community sanctions are punitive enough to convince the public that the punishment fits the crime. Petersilia considered that intensive supervision probation/parole programs (ISPs) offer some hope of relieving prison overcrowding without draining the public purse.[47]

Petersilia acknowledged that intensive supervision programs are still on trial. In several states, however, *given the option of serving prison terms or partici-pating in ISPs, many offenders have chosen prison.*[48] Many offenders may pre-fer to serve a short prison term than spend five times as long in an ISP.

Consider the alternatives now facing offenders in one western state:

> *ISP:* The offender serves two years under this alternative. During that time, a probation officer visits the offender two or three times per week and phones on the other days. The offender is subject to unannounced searches of his or her home for drugs and have his or her urine tested regularly for alcohol and drugs. The offender must strictly abide by other conditions as set by the court—not carrying a weapon, not socializing with certain persons—and must perform community service and be employed or participate in training

TABLE 11.1   Persons Under Jail Supervision, by Confinement Status and Type of Program, Midyear 1995–98

CONFINEMENT STATUS AND TYPE OF PROGRAM	NUMBER OF PERSONS UNDER JAIL SUPERVISION			
	1995	1996	1997	1998
Total	541,913	591,469	637,319	664,847
Held in jail	507,044	518,492	567,079	592,462
Supervised outside a jail facility[a]	34,869	72,977	70,239	72,385
Electronic monitoring	6,788	7,480	8,699	10,827
Home detention[b]	1,376	907	1,164	370
Day reporting	1,283	3,298	2,768	3,089
Community service	10,253	17,410	15,918	17,518
Weekender programs	1,909	16,336	17,656	17,249
Other pretrial supervision	3,229	2,135	7,368	6,048
Other work programs[c]	9,144	14,469	6,631	7,089
Treatment programs[d]	—	10,425	6,693	5,702
Other	887	517	3,342	4,493

—Not available.
[a]Excludes persons supervised by a probation or parole agency.
[b]Includes only those without electronic monitoring.
[c]Includes persons in work release programs, work gangs/crews, and other work alternative programs administered by the jail jurisdiction.
[d]Includes persons under drug, alcohol, mental health, and other medical treatment.

Source: U.S. Department of Justice, Bureau of Justice Statistics, *Prison and Jail Inmates at Midyear 1998* (Washington, D.C.: Author, March 1999), p. 5.

or education. In addition, he or she will be strongly encouraged to attend counseling and/or other treatment, particularly if he or she is a drug offender.]or[

Prison: The alternative is a sentence of two to four years, of which the offender will serve only about three to six months. During this term, the offender is not required to work or to participate in any training or treatment but may do so voluntarily. Once released, the offender is placed on a two-year routine parole supervision and must visit his or her parole officer about once a month.[49]

Note that the ISP does not represent freedom. In fact, it may stress and isolate repeat offenders more than imprisonment does.

When choosing punishment of offenders, policymakers must consider the attitudes of this country's serious offenders. Obviously, imprisonment no longer represents a horrible punishment and therefore has lost much of its deterrent power. If fear of prison does not prevent criminal behavior, other methods should be tried. This country must get over its preoccupation with imprisonment as the only suitable sanction for serious offenses.[50]

No common standard exists for deciding how many contacts with probationers are necessary in an intensive supervision program. A review of ISP programs in 37 states identified a wide range from two contacts per month by probation officers with probationers in Texas to as many as 32 contacts per month in Idaho.[51] To clarify, however, ISP has the following characteristics:

- Small client-officer caseloads; no more than a 10 to 1 ratio.
- A weekly face-to-face contact between officer and client.
- Regular field visits at a probationer's workplace, perhaps monthly or bimonthly.
- The inclusion of preventive conditions such as regular drug and alcohol testing.
- Swift and certain administrative review and revocation procedures for violating one or more probation conditions.[52]

The effects of ISP have been the subject of a great deal of interest and research.[53] Its value in reducing recidivism has been questioned since the late 1980s.[54]

An evaluation of ISPs in the mid-1990s by Joan Petersilia and Susan Turner[55] expressed similar misgivings. Petersilia and Turner noted that a growing number of jurisdictions had come to believe that the use of ISPs with serious offenders within the community could both relieve prison overcrowding and lessen the risks to public safety that such offenders pose—all at a cost savings. Some of this enthusiasm was generated by early reports from programs such as that of the Georgia Department of Corrections, which seemed to indicate a number of benefits of the program.

(*Note:* Georgia's program is what many believe to be a model ISP. Georgia, known by some as the chain gang capital of the world, has historically had one of the highest imprisonment rates in the country. It launched an ISP program in the mid-1980s. The program could accommodate about 1,400 offenders annually; its cost, with 33 trained two-person surveillance teams, was about one-fifth as much as caring for and feeding a prisoner and was paid entirely by the state's probationers. The state cited a 78 percent success rate.[56])

The RAND study noted the claim by many ISPs to have saved at least $10,000 each year for each offender who otherwise would have been sentenced to prison.[57] In many places where ISPs were adopted, however, the results were mixed. Some sites (such as Illinois and New Jersey) reported cost savings, but others (Massachusettts and Wisconsin) did not; some (such as Iowa) reported reducing recidivism, while others (Ohio and Wisconsin) did not. The ambiguous results of these programs indicate that assumptions about the ability of ISPs to relieve prison overcrowding, lower costs, and control crime may not have been well founded. Petersilia and Turner stated that "It appears not that the ISPs themselves have failed, but that the objectives set for them may have been overly ambitious, raising expectations they have been unable to meet."[58]

Electronic Monitoring/House Arrest

Like ISPs, the use of electronic monitoring began in the mid-1980s. In the early 1980s, Jack Love, a judge in New Mexico, saw a Spiderman comic in which evil-doers placed an electronic monitor on Spiderman to track his whereabouts. Love persuaded a friend to develop the idea and the technology; the rest is history.[59] Electronic monitoring has become another form of intermediate sanction. It applies to offenders whose crimes are less serious than those requiring long-term incarceration but are more serious than those committed by persons serving standard probation.

Two basic types of electronic monitoring devices are available. Continuously signaling devices attached to the offender constantly monitor his or her presence at a particular location. A receiver-dialer apparatus is attached to the offender's telephone and detects signals from the transmitter. A central computer accepts reports from the receiver-dialer over telephone lines, compares them with the offender's curfew schedule, and alerts corrections officials to unauthorized absences.[60]

The second type involves the use of programmed contact devices that contact the offender periodically to verify his or her presence. Various manufacturing companies use a different method to assure that the offender is the person responding to the call and is in fact at the monitored location as required. One system uses voice verification technology. Another requires a wristlet, a black plastic module that is strapped to the offender's arm. When the computer calls, the wristlet is inserted into a verifier box connected to the telephone to verify that the monitored offender answers the telephone. Use of the telephone requires corrections officials to verify that certain technologies are not in use on the offender's telephone. For example, call forwarding and a portable telephone would make it easy for the offender to respond to calls while away from home, and call waiting might interfere with the equipment's efforts to call the central computer.[61]

As with ISPs, the use of electronic monitoring has generated controversy. It has led to some debate concerning the purpose of correctional supervision in the community. Indeed, a conference of the American Probation and Parole Association stated the conflict in its title, "Supervision in the 1990s: Surveillance vs. Treatment."[62] The American Civil Liberties Union (ACLU) agrees with probation administrators that the system is an effective, inexpensive method to supervise probationers but is concerned that the state can use these devices to monitor its citizens in the last bastion of privacy, the home. Unlike old-fashioned probation, electronic monitoring empowers the government to control a population with more oversight and authority, which represents an increase in police power. The ACLU argues that the prospects for greater incursions into privacy are ominous. For example, videocameras have already been used to monitor drunk drivers in Maryland; cameras are installed in an offender's home and a jailer calls the offender once or twice a day and asks him or her to step in front of the camera, take a self-administered breath alcohol test, and display the results in front of the camera.[63]

The ACLU also believes that the devices that turn homes into jails are not the answer to prison overcrowding because the nation's penal institutions are

ASCA Survey Results: Community Corrections

The . . . fax back survey was on community corrections and restorative justice.Twenty-nine agencies responded. . . .

The first question asked agencies to report if they provided specific community corrections programs and services, including electronic monitoring and house arrest, and to tell how many offenders were assigned to each category.

Intensive/special supervision was the most widely recognized community corrections program, with 25 agencies (86%) reporting the use of it. An average of 817 inmates were assigned to intensive/special supervision. . . . Iowa had the highest number of offenders assigned to intensive/special supervision with 2,755.

Electronic monitoring was the second most widely used program in community corrections, with 24 agencies (82.7%) reporting its use. Offenders spend most of their time at home with a small transmitter attached to their wrist or ankle.An average of 214 offenders per reporting agency were assigned to electronic monitoring. . . .

Seventy-two percent, or 21 agencies, provide community service programs which assign offenders to work for government or private nonprofit agencies. Fifteen agencies (51.7%) provide community work crews and day reporting centers. Much like community service, community work crews are assigned to work detail within the community, under supervision. An average of 630 offenders were assigned to community work crews at the time of the survey. Illinois reported the highest number of offenders serving the community, with 2,402. . . .

Fifteen agencies (51.7%) reported that community corrections has day reporting centers within agencies.An average of 292 inmates were assigned to day reporting centers, where offenders are required to report to a central location every day. Offenders usually follow a daily schedule that includes work, treatment, obeying curfews, and if applicable, partaking in random drug testing. . . . An average of 3,492 offenders were assigned to house arrest. . . . Florida reported the highest population under house arrest, with 13,895. . . .

Restorative justice is often defined as a process whereby all the parties with a stake in a particular offense come together with the intention to collectively resolve the consequences of the offense and its implications on the future.

In the second question, we asked agencies to report what types of restorative justice programs they offered. Fifteen agencies (51.7%) reported that they provide victim impact/empathy panels. Thirteen agencies (44%) reported that they offer victim-offender reconciliation/mediation programs.These programs bring victims and offenders together through mediation to discuss the crime, the consequences of the crime, and what types of things both parties can do to "make things right."

Twelve agencies (41%) reported court diversion programs, and 34% of the respondents (10 agencies) reported alternatives-to-violence programs. . . .

The third question asked the average cost per day of operating community correction services. The highest average cost

Figure 11.A

Percentage of agencies with particular programs.

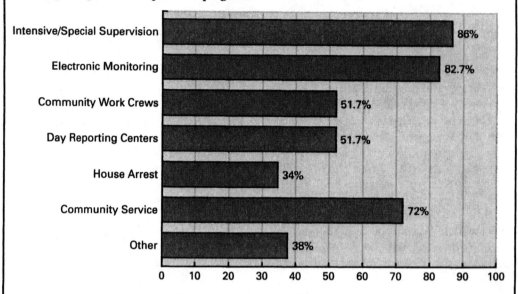

per day was for day reporting centers with a $21.76 daily cost....

The second highest average cost per day ($19.17) came from the community work crews....

The average daily cost of house arrest was $11.84....

Intensive/special probation was reported with an average daily cost of $9.31. ... Electronic monitoring averaged a cost of $8.22....

The fourth question asked what criteria would rule out participation in community corrections. A variety of reasons ranged from sentencing guidelines to statutory prohibitions. In Missouri, sex offenders are excluded from community service. Other jurisdictions would pro-hibit participation within community corrections programs if there were a violent history or past program failure in the record....

The fifth question asked if particular programming/services were offered. ...

Twenty-five agencies (86%) reported alcohol/drug treatment programs. Sixty-five percent of the respondents provide employment/job placement. Eighteen agencies (62%) provide sex offender treatment and counseling services, while 17 agencies (58%) provide education programs. Mental health services are provided by 55% of the respondents, and 41% provide vocational training.

The last question asked agencies whether victim notification was part of community corrections. Twenty-five agencies (86%) reported that victim notification is part of community corrections.

Source: Association of State Correctional Administrators, "ASCA Survey Results: Community Corrections," *ASCA Newsletter,* April 1999, p. 4.

overcrowded by the thousands, not by the hundreds. The ACLU concurs with federal judge Henry Bramwell, who wrote in the *Howard Law Journal* that

> the poor and the minority defendant is usually one who has committed a violent crime, is without means, and has little or no recognition in his community. As a result, the middle-class defendant gets alternative sentencing or part-time imprisonment, usually without incarceration, and the poor and minority defendant gets a heavy jail term. This certainly is not justice. Alternative sentencing and part-time imprisonment have strong class overtones.[64]

In contrast, Rolando Del Carmen maintains that electronic monitoring provides a more structured environment and better supervision and accomplishes a curfew situation for the probationer. He contended that judges can be prevented from "widening the net," a term for sanctioning (in this case, putting someone on electronic monitoring) people who would normally not have been punished (or, in this situation, would have been placed on regular probation): "You identify certain offenses where defendants are currently sent to jail, such as burglary, or where the penal code provides mandatorily that the defendant would have gone to prison. You want to hit that middle cohort instead of dipping down."[65]

Shock Incarceration

Another less costly intermediate alternative to incarceration that is supported by many correctional administrators is *shock probation*. This form of corrections combines a brief exposure to incarceration with subsequent release on probation. This option, adopted in at least 14 states,[66] allows sentencing judges to reconsider the original sentence to prison and, upon motion, to recall the inmate and place him or her on probation, under conditions deemed appropriate. The idea is that the "shock" of a short stay in prison will give the offender a taste of institutional life and will make such an indelible impression that he or she will be deterred from future crime and will avoid the negative effects of lengthy incarceration.[67]

Shock probation has not enjoyed widespread popularity, however, based on a concern that "any institutional stay interferes with therapeutic efforts,"[68] and even limited prison exposure can produce negative attitudes and promote resentment. Indeed, one study focusing on the length of incarceration reported that those spending three months in prison were as likely to recidivate as those serving 7 to 12 months.[69] On the other hand, it was found that offenders confined for 30 days or less had a lower reincarceration rate than those serving more than 30 days.[70] Such studies point to the conclusion that "the negative effects of exposure to prison begin to occur very quickly—much sooner than shock probation programs are designed to release offenders."[71]

Furthermore, shock probation is not always implemented as originally intended. In order to achieve true "shock" value, one would logically assume that these programs would be reserved for first-time offenders or those who have not yet been incarcerated. Many judges, however, refuse to be bound by these guidelines; in one state, for example, slightly more than one-third of those granted release had committed violent- and/or narcotics-related offences.[72]

As might be expected, higher success rates have been reported among groups for which the program was intended: "Young adults who commit non-violent probation-eligible offenses."[73]

Boot Camps

The use of boot camp programs, or shock incarceration, has become popular. Since 1993, 75 boot camp prisons have opened in 29 state correctional institutions, in addition to many programs developed and being considered in local (city and county) jails, including many for juveniles.[74] These programs place offenders in a quasi-military program similar to a military basic training program to instill discipline, routine, and unquestioning obedience to orders. Offenders serve a short institutional sentence and then are put through a rigorous regimen of drills, strenuous workouts, marching, and hard physical labor.

Proponents of the boot camp concept argue that many young offenders become involved in crime because they lack self-respect and are unable to structure their lives. Consequently, the boot camp model targets young first offenders who seem to be embarking on a path to sustained criminality.[75] Proponents also maintain that these youths can benefit from this militarylike atmosphere as well as exposure to relevant educational opportunities, vocational training, drug treatment, and general counseling.

These offenders may experience improvements in self-esteem, educational achievement, and physical fitness. Research to date has found, however, that this regimen and harsh atmosphere do little to overcome the problems that cause inner-city youths to get in trouble with the law in the first place. In fact, follow-up of boot camp graduates shows that they do no better than other offenders without this experience.[76] Only boot camps that are carefully designed, target the right offenders, and provide them with rehabilitative services and aftercare are likely to save the state money and reduce recidivism.[77] Too many boot camps overemphasize the value of discipline; in fact, in one California county, a special parole caseload had to be established for boot camp graduates because their failure rates were so high after leaving the program.

Figure 11.A (p. 286) shows percentages of state correctional agencies providing other types of restorative justice programs and services.

Summary

This chapter focused on probation and parole. It is clear that probation and parole agencies continue to bear the brunt of the combined effects of increased crime, tough mandatory sentencing laws leading to increased incarceration of offenders, a get-tough public and justice system attitude toward crime that permeates the country, and tremendously overcrowded prisons. Given this situation, it is probably a credit to probation and parole administrators that they have managed to cope under such circumstances and have even implemented several alternative methods, known as *intermediate sanctions,* to address these problems.

Questions for Review

1. What are the various types of probation systems being administered in the United States? Describe each.

2. Should probation services be placed within the judicial or executive branch of government? Defend your answer.

3. What are some of the major needs, problems, and concerns of probation administrators?

4. What are the two basic models of parole administration.

5. Why are intermediate sanctions being used so widely in probation and parole?

6. What do *intensive supervision* and *electronic monitoring/house arrest* mean?

7. How can shock probation further the goals of corrections? How can boot camps? What successes and problems have been found with these practices?

Notes

1. Todd R. Clear, "Punishment and Control in Community Supervision," in Clayton A. Hartjen and Edward E. Rhine (eds.), *Correctional Theory and Practice* (Chicago: Nelson-Hall, 1992), pp. 31–42.

2. See the President's Commission on Law Enforcement and Administration of Justice, *Task Force Report: Corrections,* (Washington, D.C.: U.S. Government Printing Office, 1967), p. 7.

3. Franklin E. Zimring and Gordon J. Hawkins, *Deterrence: The Legal Threat in Crime Control* (Chicago: University of Chicago Press, 1973).

4. Joan Petersilia, "When Probation Becomes More Dreaded Than Prison," *Federal Probation* 54 (March 1990):23.

5. Ibid.

6. Ibid., p. 25.

7. Allen Beck, Susan Kline, and Lawrence Greenfield, *Survey of Youth in Custody: 1987* (U.S. Department of Justice, Bureau of Justice Statistics, 1988).

8. Petersilia, "When Probation Becomes More Dreaded Than Prison," p. 24.

9. John Conrad, "The Pessimistic Reflections of a Chronic Optimist," *Federal Probation* 55 (June 1991):4–9.

10. U.S. Department of Justice, Bureau of Justice Statistics Executive Summary, *Probation and Parole Statistics* (Washington, D.C.: Author, August 1999), p. 1.

11. Dean J. Champion, *Corrections in the United States: A Contemporary Perspective* (Englewood Cliffs, N.J.: Prentice Hall, 1990), p. 37.

12. U.S. Department of Justice, Bureau of Justice Statistics, Executive Summary, *Probation and Parole Statistics* (Washington, D.C.: Author, August 1999), p. 1.

13. Barry J. Nidorf, "Community Corrections: Turning the Crowding Crisis into Opportunities," *Corrections Today* (October 1989):82–88.

14. Howard Abadinsky, *Probation and Parole: Theory and Practice* (5th ed.) (Englewood Cliffs, N.J.: Prentice Hall, 1994), p. 32.

15. Ibid.

16. Ibid., pp. 32–36.

17. See the *Task Force Report: Corrections*, pp. 35–37.

18. Abadinsky, *Probation and Parole* (5th ed.), p. 35.

19. E. P. Volz, "Staff Supervision and Organization." In *Proceedings of the National Probation Association—1924* (New York: National Probation Association, 1924), pp. 103–105.

20. Patricia L. Hardyman, "Management Styles in Probation: Policy Implications Derived from Systems Theory," in Clayton A. Hartjen and Edward E. Rhine (eds.), *Correctional Theory and Practice*, pp. 61–81.

21. David Duffee, "The Community Context of Probation," in Patrick McAnany, Doug Thompson, and David Fogel (eds.), *Probation and Justice: Reconsideration of Mission* (Cambridge, Mass.: Oelgeschlager, Gunn, and Hain, 1984).

22. Eric Trist, "On Socio-Technical Systems," in Kenneth Benne and Robert Chin (eds.), *The Planning of Change* (2d ed.) (New York: Holt, Rinehart and Winston, 1969), pp. 269–281.

23. Daniel Katz and Robert I. Kahn, *The Social Psychology of Organizations* (New York: John Wiley, 1966).

24. Hardyman, "Management Styles in Probation," p. 68.

25. Ibid., p. 70.

26. Ibid.

27. Ibid., p. 71.

28. Ibid., pp. 74–75.

29. Abadinsky, *Probation and Parole* (5th ed.), p. 32.

30. National Advisory Commission on Criminal Justice Standards and Goals, *Corrections* (Washington, D.C.: U.S. Government Printing Office, 1973), pp. 396–397.

31. *Task Force Report: Corrections*, p. 71.

32. Ibid.

33. National Advisory Commission, *Corrections*, pp. 396–397.

34. *Task Force Report: Corrections*, p. 65.

35. Donald Cochran, "Corrections' Catch 22," *Corrections Today* (October 1989):16–18.

36. Nidorf, "Community Corrections: Turning the Crowding Crisis into Opportunities," p. 82.

37. John P. Conrad, "The Redefinition of Probation: Drastic Proposals to Solve an Urgent Problem," in Patrick D. McAnany, Doug Thomson, and David Fogel (eds.), *Probation and Justice: Reconsideration of Mission*, p. 258.

38. Peter J. Benekos, "Beyond Reintegration: Community Corrections in a Retributive Era," *Federal Probation* 54 (March 1990):53.

39. Ibid.

40. Ibid., p. 53.

41. Nidorf, "Community Corrections," p. 84.

42. Belinda R. McCarthy, *Intermediate Punishments: Intensive Supervision, Home Confinement, and Electronic Surveillance* (Monsey, N.J.: Criminal Justice Press, 1987), p. 3.

43. Nidorf, "Community Corrections," p. 85.

44. Benekos, "Beyond Reintegration," p. 54.

45. Association of State Correctional Administrators, *Newsletter,* April 1999, Vol. XV, No. III, pp. 4–5.

46. McCarthy, *Intermediate Punishments,* p. 3.

47. Petersilia, "When Probation Becomes More Dreaded Than Prison," pp. 23–27.

48. Ibid., p. 23.

49. This information was compiled from ISP brochures and information from the Oregon Department of Corrections, by Joan Petersilia.

50. Petersilia, "When Probation Becomes More Dreaded Than Prison," p. 27.

51. James M. Byrne, "The Control Controversy: A Preliminary Examination of Intensive Probation Supervision Programs in the United States," *Federal Probation* 50 (1986):4–16.

52. Adapted from Vincent O'Leary and Todd R. Clear, *Directions for Community Corrections in the 1990s* (Washington, D.C.: National Institute of Corrections, 1984.

53. See, for example, Don Gottfredson and Marc Neithercutt, *Caseload Size Variation and Difference in Probation/Parole Performance* (Pittsburgh, Pa.: National Center for Juvenile Justice, 1974); J. Banks, A. L. Porter, R. L. Rardin, T. R. Silen, and V. E. Unger, *Issue Paper: Phase I Evaluation of Intensive Special Probation Project* (Atlanta, Ga.: School of Industrial and System Engineering, Georgia Institute of Technology, 1976); and D. Fallen, C. Apperson, J. Holt-Milligan, and J. Roe, *Intensive Parole Supervision* (Olympia, Wash.: Dept. of Social and Health Services, Analysis and Information Service Division, Office of Research, 1981).

54. R. Adams and H. J. Vetter, "Effectiveness of Probation Caseload Sizes: A Review of the Empirical Literature," *Criminology* 9 (1971):333–343; Edward Latessa and Gennaro F. Vito, "The Effects of Intensive Supervision on Shock Probationers," *Journal of Criminal Justice* 16 (1988), pp. 319–330.

55. U.S. Department of Justice, National Institute of Justice Research in Brief, "Evaluating Intensive Supervision Probation/Parole: Results of a Nationwide Experiment," May 1993.

56. Kathy Sawyer, "The Alternative to Prison," *The Washington Post National Weekly Edition* (September 2, 1985):6–7.

57. James Byrne, Arthur J. Lurigio, and Christopher Baird, "The Effectiveness of the New Intensive Supervision Programs," *Research in Corrections* 2 (1989).

58. U.S. Department of Justice, National Institute of Justice Research in Brief, "Evaluating Intensive Supervision Probation/Parole: Results of a Nationwide Experiment," May 1993, p. 2.

59. Keenen Peck, "High-Tech House Arrest," *The Progressive* (July 1988):26–28.

60. Annesley K. Schmidt, "Electronic Monitors: Realistically, What Can Be Expected?" *Federal Probation* 59 (June 1991):47–53.

61. Ibid., p. 47.

62. Ibid., p. 48.

63. Peck, "High-Tech House Arrest," p. 27.

64. Quoted in Peck, "High-Tech House Arrest," p. 27.

65. Ibid.

66. Harry E. Allen and Clifford E. Simonsen, *Corrections in America: An Introduction* (8th ed.) (Upper Saddle River, N.J.: Prentice Hall, 1998), p. 210.

67. Jeanne B. Stinchcomb and Vernon B. Fox, *Introduction to Corrections* (5th ed.) (Upper Saddle River, N.J.: Prentice Hall, 1999), p. 165.

68. Diane Vaughan, "Shock Probation and Shock Parole: The Impact of Changing Correctional Ideology," in David M. Petersen and Charles W. Thomas (eds.), *Corrections: Problems and Prospects* (2d ed.) (Englewood Cliffs, N.J.: Prentice Hall, 1980), p. 216.

69. Joseph A. Waldron and Henry R. Angelino, "Shock Probation: A Natural Experiment on the Effect of a Short Period of Incarceration," *Prison Journal* 57 (1977): 45–52.

70. Gennaro F. Vito and Harry E. Allen, "Shock Probation in Ohio: A Comparison of Outcomes," *International Journal of Offender Therapy and Comparative Criminology* 3 (1978): 123–132.

71. Wayne Logan, "Description of Shock Probation and Parole," in Dale G. Parent, *Shock Incarceration: An Overview of Existing Programs* (Washington, D.C.: U.S. Department of Justice, 1989), p. 53.

72. Vaughn "Shock Probation," p. 223.

73. Logan, "Description of Shock Probation and Parole," p. 52.

74. Doris MacKenzie, James Shaw, and Voncile Gowdy, *An Evaluation of Shock Incarceration in Louisiana* (Washington, D.C.: U.S. Department of Justice, 1993), p. 2.

75. Todd R. Clear and George F. Cole, *American Corrections* (4th ed.)(Belmont, Calif.: Wadsworth), 1997.

76. Doris L. MacKenzie, "Boot Camp Prisons and Recidivism in Eight States," *Criminology* 33 (3)(1995):327–358.

77. Doris Layton MacKenzie and Alex Piquero, "The Impact of Shock Incarceration Programs on Prison Crowding," *Crime and Delinquency* 40(2), (April 1994):222–249.

CORRECTIONS ISSUES AND PRACTICES

Chapter

Boredom is beautiful.

—Nevada Prison Warden

*I never saw a man who looked/With such a wistful eye/
Upon that little tent of blue/Which prisoners call the sky.*

—Oscar Wilde

Introduction

The preceding three chapters addressed several issues related to prisons. In this chapter, we discuss additional challenges for contemporary correctional administrators. We focus briefly on coed prisons and smoke-free facilities. Next we examine several pressing issues concerning sex and violence (the latter as it exists both by and against staff and inmates), and drug abuse, interdiction, and treatment. Then we discuss inmate gangs, followed by a review of prison riots and inmate classification. We then consider how the costs of corrections can be hidden or completely ignored. Next is an overview of two relatively new correctional issues and practices: the privatization and accreditation of prisons. The chapter concludes with a review of stress and burnout among corrections personnel, including coping strategies.

Case studies concerning problems in corrections administration are provided at the end of this chapter.

Recent Innovations in Correctional Facilities

Coed Prisons

Segregation of prisoners according to their gender dates back several centuries to the Walnut Street Jail and the Auburn Penitentiary in New York. Reasons for this policy included the improvement of inmate morality, a reduction in inmate promiscuity, and increased privacy for inmates of both sexes. In recent years, however, prisoners of both sexes have expressed interest in co-correctional, or coed, prisons.[1] In some of these institutions, men and women prisoners are housed in the same prison supervised by male and female staff and can participate in all activities together. Unlike the practice in Denmark and other countries, U.S. prisons do not allow inmates in coed prisons to share the same quarters or have sexual encounters.

The ratio of male to female inmates is recommended to be 50–50.[2] When women are in the minority, they feel conspicuous and tend to be treated as a minority group by their male counterparts.[3] Also, jealousies among the dominant sex may arise because of greater competition for social encounters and more intimate relationships.

A major public misconception about co-correctional prisons is that they allow unchecked promiscuity and male and female inmates to share quarters, resulting in numerous illegitimate births.[4]

Coed prisons have experienced several positive results. Staff enthusiasm has increased, and their parolees have found employment more easily. One institution realized a 40 percent reduction in the number of violent discipline charges, a 73 percent reduction in the number of general discipline charges, and a 42 percent reduction in the number of grievances filed by inmates.[5]

The institutions also experience negative outcomes. A superintendent of a women's prison in a western state offered several caveats to co-correctional institutions. The look-but-don't-touch policy of these institutions can aggravate sexual frustrations of both sexes and may actually encourage homosexual relationships. Husbands or wives of the residents of a co-correctional institution may become jealous. The stresses and strains caused by sexual frustrations may well be detrimental to the programmatic planning designed for a given inmate. If an inmate is strongly attracted to a member of the opposite sex but can make no advances, treatment may be more difficult.[6] Finally, one survey of Minnesota correctional officers found that resistance to female correctional officers in male institutions came primarily from more experienced male officers—a likely obstacle for women seeking promotional opportunities in adult male prisons.[7]

Smoke-Free Correctional Facilities

Cigarette smoking has been recognized as the single most preventable cause of death in our society. The American Cancer Society estimates that more than 430,000 Americans die each year as a result of cigarette smoking, including 3,000 who die from secondhand smoke.[8] The Surgeon General has suggested that the simple separation of smokers and nonsmokers within the same airspace may significantly reduce this unnecessary risk.[9]

Largely as a result of these findings, smoking is becoming less socially acceptable, and Americans are fighting over where, when, and whether a person may smoke. This is an issue for correctional institutions as well. The American Correctional Association conducted a survey in 1987 on implementing smoking restrictions in correctional institutions. The results indicated that most correctional institution administrators had very serious reservations about the effect of such policies. Most believed that it would make their jobs more difficult and worsen the overall environment of their facilities.[10]

This issue has resulted in a number of lawsuits. Hearing of studies concerning secondhand smoke, inmates have not been reluctant to file lawsuits over their right to a smoke-free environment. Furthermore, a number of recent court decisions have held that inmates have no constitutional right to smoke while incarcerated. Once a few facilities made the decision to become smoke-free, others have followed.

Thus, an increasing number of correctional administrators have outlawed smoking in their facilities. When the decision is first announced, there is normally an outcry from all sectors about worker and prisoner rights and threats of rebellion. Administrators have had to hold their ground and refuse to capitulate on any point or relinquish any small area of their facilities to smokers. They have typically followed a certain "protocol" in implementing the plan: (1) requesting a legal opinion from the appropriate counsel's office concerning the constitutionality of the proposal and its chance for prevailing in the face of inmate challenges (it is more likely that a nonsmoking inmate's suit would prevail on the grounds that he or she is forced to share a cell with a smoking companion); (2) discussing the plan openly with employees to assuage their concerns and explain, among other things, that institutions that have instituted smoke-free programs have experienced no extraordinary inmate behavior; (3) announcing the decision well in advance of its implementation to allow time for people to adjust to the idea, smoke their cigarettes, and, perhaps most important, attend counseling and smoking cessation programs provided by the county health department.[11]

It has been found that following a few months of minor irritation and complaints, the policy has met with little resistance. Inmates eventually appreciate the benefits of the policy: improvement in their breathing, cleaner walls and ceilings, and an overall healthier environment. The administration spends less on repainting walls and replacing cigarette-burned carpets and air filters.[12] Perhaps the greatest advantage of all is the elimination of a potential fire hazard.

Sex and Violence in Correctional Institutions

Sexual Victimization

People serving terms in correctional institutions do not leave their sexuality at the front gate. Paul Tappan maintained that homosexuality is a universal concomitant of sex-segregated living and a perennial problem in camps, boarding schools, one-sex colleges, training schools, and, of course, correctional facilities. From a biological point of view, he argued, homosexuality is normal behavior in the latter institutions.[13]

Persons entering prisons and jails express their sexuality in many forms, some of which are innocuous and others very violent. If placed on a continuum, solitary or mutual masturbation, or the manufacturing of a sexual object (such as the so-called "Fifi bag," which involves a rolled-up magazine and other objects) would be at one end, consensual homosexual behavior in the middle, and gang rapes at the other end. The most frequent form of sexual release is solitary masturbation: "Nobody—inmate, staff, or visitor—is in a prison very long before seeing an inmate masturbating in a toilet, shower, or cell."[14] Estimates are that between 30 and 45 percent of inmates have experienced homosexual behavior, depending on the degree of custodial surveillance, the nature of the inmate population, and the average length of confinement in a given prison.[15]

As in the outside world, people in prison are often extremely dominant or submissive, and the latter can easily be exploited. As in the outside world, heterosexual rape does not result from sexual *need* but from hate and a desire to dominate, control, and conquer. This problem exists in women's institutions as well as in those for men. Women rarely sexually assault other women prisoners; however, when such attacks do occur, they can be quite brutal and involve the use of such objects as broom handles.[16]

Violent sexual incidents among male inmates fall into two categories. In the first, the aggressor violently coerces his target; the type of force is decided upon in advance. The primary cause of this violence is the need to uphold men's "rights" to use force to gain sexual access. The second category of incidents involves targets who react violently to propositions perceived as threatening. This type often resembles victim-precipitated homicide in the outside world because words or gestures perceived as offensive provoke retaliatory insults, threats, or violence.[17]

The actual extent of sexual aggression in prisons is difficult to assess. A few authors have contended that the problem of homosexual rape is *the* major problem inside correctional institutions; others (including many administrators) maintain that sexual violence is practically no problem at all. Indeed, although early studies of the prison[18] suggested a high rate of homosexual rapes, later studies[19] suggested that the actual incidence of homosexual rape is far lower. The latter researchers, however, do report widespread fear of sexual victimization among inmates. Norman Smith and Mary Ellen Batiuk argued that because the social setting of prisons is hostile, the fear of being sexually victimized permeates every social act (e.g., inmates are extremely conscious of the need to act macho, hide their emotions, and be careful of what they wear; they try to do nothing that can be interpreted as a weakness or "signal" of homosexual propensities).[20]

It is clear that today's violent gang- and clique-dominated prison society fosters increased fears of rape and other unwanted sexual activity. The fear is greatest—and most justified—among young white prisoners, 83 percent of whom are targets of rape and other aggressive sex, in contrast to about 15 percent of blacks and 2 percent of Hispanics. Most aggressors are black (80 percent), some are Hispanic (14 percent), but only a few are white (6 percent).[21]

> It's a way for the black man to get back at the white man. It's one way he can assert his manhood. Anything white, even a defenseless punk, is part of what the black man hates. It's part of what he's had to fight all his life just to survive, just to have a hole to sleep in and some garbage to eat. . . . It's a new ego thing. He can show he's a man by making a white guy into a girl.[22]

In his study of prison victimization, Lee Bowker commented that "like heterosexual rape on the streets, prison homosexual rape has effects that go beyond the immediate victims. Homosexual rape impacts all prisoners and fundamentally alters the social climate of correctional institutions."[23]

Inmate fear of sexual victimization is justified. In fact, many believe that homosexual attacks are quite common, even reaching epidemic proportions in some institutions:

> Sexual assaults are epidemic in some prison systems. Virtually every slight built young man committed by the courts is sexually approached within a day or two after his admission to prison. Many of these young men are overwhelmed and repeatedly "raped" by gangs of inmate aggressors.[24]

It is probably surprising that sexual aggression in correctional institutions is not more widespread. Even in men's prisons, estimates of the incidence of sexual assault among the general population run as low as 1 percent.[25] Still, it remains a serious problem for the weak and unprotected.

Is there anything correctional administrators can do to reduce or eliminate the problem of homosexual rapes, given the violent tendencies of many inmates? Programs that may reduce prison sexual violence are aimed at targets as well as aggressors. Such programs face difficulties, however. Aggressors with histories of violence ruthlessly exploit others, and targets often use force to protect themselves and to promote masculine images. Furthermore, threatened men are often reluctant to report such problems to the staff because existing official remedies can cause more problems than they solve.

Daniel Lockwood suggested that administrators consider offering human relations training, with the goals of increasing interpersonal skills, relieving interpersonal or intergroup tension, and developing individual and group problem-solving skills.[26]

Institutional Violence

Violence by Inmates

Personal safety for prisoners and staff members is at best uncertain; some risk of injury or material loss at the hands of aggressive or unbalanced fellow prisoners and prison gangs always exists.[27] Violent actions by inmates include homicides and very serious assaults inflicted with a variety of ingenuous homemade weapons.

As with incidents of homosexual rape, the extent of violence against other inmates in prisons is not known precisely, nor do we know whether institutional assaults occur with more or less frequency than they do in the community at large.[28] Prisons are unquestionably violent settings, however, particularly those penal institutions that house large proportions of young inmates, who account disproportionately for disruptive behavior.[29] The probabilities that violence will occur increase when large numbers of "state-raised" youths, prisoners who have extensive experience in juvenile institutions, are housed in an institution.[30] In addition to inmate age, the amount of violence in an institution is normally influenced by its population density and factors tied to prisonization (adopting the prison subculture's mores), such as deprivation and continuation of violent, aggressive, and unacceptable *previous* behavior patterns in the institutional setting.

Conventional prison violence is confined almost exclusively to male prisons, although violence (often comprised of angry outbursts in reaction to stressful situations) does occur in women's institutions. Former inmates have noted that whereas men may engage in short-term fights to prove their manhood and achieve a reputation but cause little permanent harm to victims, women inmates' fights often leave permanent scars, from earrings torn from pierced ears to facial scratches from fingernails.[31]

Prisoner violence frequently follows court efforts to improve prison conditions. This reaction has been referred to as the *paradox of reform*. Studies show that prisoners are often safer *before* the reforms and that high rates of violence and fear become a normal element of postreform prison life.[32]

Inmates assault correctional officers with some frequency. Peter Kratcoski determined that four factors were significantly related to these assaults: location (more than 70 percent of the assaults occurred in detention/high-security areas), shift (the majority of all such assaults occurred during the day), work experience (inexperienced trainees received a disproportionate number of assaults), and age of the assailant (most assaults against staff members were committed by inmates age 25 and younger). He also examined the type of situation. Only 3 percent of federal correctional officers were assaulted while attempting to break up inmate fights, but 32 percent of state correctional officers were assaulted during such situations. Policy dictates that an officer who is required to break up a fight must request backup assistance. An inexperienced officer may try to handle such a situation alone and be assaulted. The sex of correctional officers was not found to have a relationship to assaults.[33]

Violence Against Inmates

When they perceive a loss of control over prisoners, guards sometimes employ violent tactics.[34] In these situations, guards become more custodial and punitive toward prisoners. In addition to using more insults and obscenities, they may perform violent acts. Guards' attempts to maintain control may create relatively unstable conditions and may even produce rebellious prisoners and an unsafe working environment for guards.[35]

Administrative Approaches to Violence

Each of the four groups who are part of the prison community has a reason to prevent violence: (1) The administration wants to prevent violence, (2) inmates want to live without fear, (3) correctional officers desire a safe working environment and control over inmates, and (4) noncustodial staff want information about and the ability to control inmates. Indeed, two major administrative problems that can occur within an institution are a lack of control over staff and inmates and polarization between custodial and noncustodial staff.[36]

One approach that has been attempted to curb violence is the unit management concept, which has been described as one of a number of small, self-contained "institutions" operating in semiautonomous fashion within the confines of a larger facility.[37] This approach involves housing 50 to 100 inmates together in one physical area and keeping them together for as long as possible. These inmate groups (units) are supervised by a multidisciplinary management team normally comprised of at least a unit manager, a caseworker, a secretary, a correctional counselor, a correctional officer, an educator, and a psychologist or other mental health worker. These teams have disciplinary authority and are guided by a set of common policies and procedures.[38]

Drug Interdiction and Treatment in Prisons

As discussed previously, a major problem in prisons is drug abuse, which was a major problem for many inmates prior to their incarceration. A federal study found that 36 percent of all male jail inmates were under the influence of drugs at the time of committing the offense for which they were incarcerated.[39]

A related problem for correctional administrators is the availability of illegal drugs and their use by inmates *after* incarceration. This is not an insignificant matter, according to a study of 957 state confinement facilities for adults. About seven of every eight U.S. prisons conducted urine drug tests with about 565,500 inmates for one or more illegal drugs. Of those tests, 1.4 percent were positive for cocaine, 1 percent for heroin, 2.3 percent for methamphetamines, and 5.8 percent for marijuana.[40]

Drug interdiction methods include making physical checks, questioning inmates, having inmates exchange clothing, searching body cavities, and using patdowns. All persons entering prisons, random groups, and those suspected of carrying drugs were checked in these ways. About three-fourths (76 percent) of all federal and state confinement institutions tested inmates for drugs when use was suspected. The most intrusive technique was body cavity searches. Facilities that used body cavity searches showed lower rates of drug use among inmates than did facilities using other methods.

Questioning visitors to both state and federal facilities and searching their belongings were also widely used. More than 80 percent of federal facilities patted down all inmates and required them to exchange clothing. Almost 78 percent of state confinement facilities frisked all inmates, and 57 percent substituted prison clothes.

Inmates may acquire illegal drugs from visitors and staff members. Because of this potential security breach, about half of all state confinement administrators had policies to question or pat down staff when they report to work. About one-fourth of state facilities randomly frisked staff members. Most interdiction activities involving staff were conducted on suspicion of smuggling drugs.[41]

Correctional administrators have responded to the growing number of drug-involved offenders by increasing the number of available programs. Still, the number of drug-using inmates far exceeds the number enrolled in such programs. In addition to treatment benefits, these programs help provide good security, improve working conditions for staff, reduce staff conflict, and provide a resource for conflict resolution and the potential for positive publicity.[42]

Prison Gangs

It has been argued that because of weakened authority of correctional administration over inmates as a result of court decisions that recognize prisoners' rights and remedies, inmate gangs have formed to share and eventually dominate, through violent means, the power base once occupied by the "keepers."[43] For whatever reason, it is clear that gangs have gained a substantial foothold in the day-to-day activities and operation of prisons and even jails. Figure 12.1 provides examples of prison tattoos.

The formation of prison gangs began in 1950, at Washington Penitentiary in Walla Walla, when a group of prisoners organized themselves and became known as the Gypsy Jokers.[44] Then, in 1967, a tightly knit Chicano clique of youths from Los Angeles and a number of other prisoners began to take over San Quentin. Known as the "Mexican Mafia," they quickly gained a reputation for toughness, which was enhanced by the rumor that to become a member, one had to kill another prisoner.[45] Soon a rival Chicano group, La Nuestra Familia, formed. The rivalry between these two gangs became so deadly that the state segregated them: The Mexican Mafia went to San Quentin, and La Nuestra Familia went to Soledad.[46]

To protect themselves from violent crimes committed by these two groups, black and white inmates began to form gangs. Whites formed the Aryan Brotherhood, and blacks organized the Black Guerilla Family. Amid escalating racial

Peacock with tears
on either arm

Initials

[Will tell arresting
officer this stands for
girlfriend (Nancy Flores)]

Virgin Mary on back

Mongolian with earring
in left ear only

Female Mexican
with bandoliers and gun

Butterflies

Figure 12.1

Prison gang tattoos and symbols.

Rose put on
during initiation

Star on arm or
body is one hit.
Star on face
is two hits

Nuestra Familia

Sombrero and knife

Tear drops under
left eye only

Cross under left
eye only
(NF exclusively)

Male Mexican
with large mustache.
Gun and bandoliers.
Number of bullets
denotes how many
hits. Only used
by lieutenants,
captains, and generals

Nuestra Familia

Sombrero and knife

Figure 12.1 (continued)

tension, the Aryan Brotherhood formed an alliance with the Mexican Mafia, and the Black Guerillas allied with La Nuestra Familia.[47]

Statistics show that prison gangs exist in the federal prison system and in 32 state jurisdictions. In 29 of those 32 jurisdictions, administrators have identified 114 gangs by name. Overall, gang members compose about 3 percent of the total federal and state prison populations.[48]

With the emergence of prison gangs, two serious conditions have developed: the increased difficulty of prison officials to maintain order and discipline[49] and the rapid increase in inmate violence, often related to increases in drug trafficking, extortion, prostitution, protection, gambling, and contract inmate murders.[50] One study of prison gangs reported that they account for half or more of all prison problems.[51]

Gang members have a belligerent attitude toward all institutions and authority when they enter prison: Members are preoccupied with status and gang rivalry. They plan boycotts, strikes, and even riots. Despite administrative attempts to accommodate gangs in some prisons, they continue to seek to obtain "loot, sex, respect, revenge, [and] will attack any outsider."[52] The close confinement and limited space in prisons make ignoring gang threats impossible. Prisoners who want to circulate beyond their own cells often must join a clique or gang for protection.

Wardens and superintendents have been brought into gang-ridden prison systems specifically to do something with the gang problem. By transferring gang leaders and using other methods to segregate and isolate members, some have managed to greatly diminish gangs' power. The crowding problem; court decisions, court orders, and consent decrees; and other contemporary administrative limitations, however, have curtailed the power of correctional administrators to use such tactics.

Prison Riots

Prison riots have occurred throughout history, and they can be anticipated to continue in the future and to pose serious challenges to corrections administrators. In an effort to provide guidance to these administrators prior to, during, and after such incidents, a recent study sponsored by the National Institute of Justice and the Federal Bureau of Prisons examined eight disturbances across the country. The following is an overview of the major findings gleaned from that study.[53]

Before the Riot

Planning is an important aspect of riot preparation. A riot plan that describes the special responsibilities to be met, the resources to be used, and the contribution of each individual or group involved should be developed.

There are some simple means available to prison wardens and others to help to anticipate an impending riot. First, it is very important to know how to "read the yard." Wardens should walk the prison yard several times a day to see, for example, if inmates are banding together by racial groups to an unusual extent, are standing near doorways, or are playing their music very loudly (possibly to cover up their plotting, acts of violence, and so on). Also, inmate purchases of long-term goods at the prison canteen can be predictive.[54]

Who should take command during the incident must be decided according to such factors as knowledge of the facility, effects of the assignment on the chain of command, and breadth of experience and communication. The administrative framework is also a consideration. Some of these factors favor assigning command to the warden, who is likely to have greater knowledge of the facility. This would maintain the chain of command. If the warden is new or inexperienced, however, someone else, such as a state department of corrections administrator or the commissioner of corrections, may assume command instead. Another factor to be considered is who knows how to use resolution strategies, understands existing policies, and is familiar with agencies outside the prison (such as those providing medical care, added security, investigation, and so on).

A critical element of such a plan is the development of a use-of-force policy. Which staff members are authorized to order the use of force? What responses are appropriate in various situations? What weapons and less-than-lethal munitions (such as tear gas) are appropriate?

Training is also very important, because readiness can best be achieved through field practice and instruction. Demanding, unannounced onsite riot exercises are also highly beneficial: They integrate the activities of command, hostage negotiation teams, and tactical teams. A small group of administrators should receive extensive training in hostage negotiations and problem solving. They should be chosen on the basis of intelligence, verbal skills, and the ability to think quickly.

Planning cannot prevent all prison riots, but it can help administrators to avoid some disturbances, take action to prevent the small-scale disturbance from expanding, and terminate a riot should one occur in the least costly way.

During the Riot

During a riot, prison administrators have three main options to attempt to bring about resolution: forcibly retake the prison, negotiate an end, or wait and let the riot die of its own accord. Many times, however, the boundaries between these strategies are indistinguishable. For example, negotiations can be used to collect information for a tactical assault or to tire and demoralize the inmates; a waiting policy can be used to strengthen the administration's tactical capabilities or to force inmates to bargain seriously.

In general, a riot can be terminated at any time by using overwhelming force. Nevertheless, such a deployment of force can be costly (a lesson learned from the 1971 riot in Attica, New York, in which 39 people died). Therefore, commanders must develop strategies to minimize the risks to hostages, assault forces, and inmates. Force may be used, however, as a first response to a disturbance. Armed personnel may rush in to prevent inmates from becoming organized, fashioning weapons, fortifying positions, and recruiting additional participants. The greatest challenge in the early use of force is assembling the necessary personnel and equipment with sufficient speed. A riot control squad that is deployed too quickly runs the risk of being unsuccessful and even taken hostage.

A planned tactical strike maximizes the element of surprise in order to rescue hostages or retake the facility before inmates can react. Key elements in a tactical strike are intelligence information (concerning riot leadership, location of hostages, and so on), drills and rehearsals (simulating the planned mission), timing (determining a maximum opportunity for success), weaponry (including stun grenades), speed, and surprise. The disadvantages of using a tactical strike are that they may be unnecessary because negotiations may resolve the incident, and they may be too risky.

Negotiations involve a dialogue between inmates and authorities, with inmates hoping to use any hostages as bargaining chips with the state for publicity, amnesty, improved conditions, or other benefits. Administrators may be pitted against a single, unified group of inmates or individual inmates with no organization whatsoever. For negotiations to progress, an inmate or group of inmates with whom officials can talk with a measure of continuity must be identified. Those persons with command authority should refrain from talking directly with inmates. In some instances, bringing in an outside person (such as a popular inmate, legislator, lawyer, reporter) may prove useful in negotiations.

After the Riot

A riot's aftermath consists of short-term, medium-term, and long-term problems. Short-term problems include securing the prison (including searching for contraband and moving inmates to secure units), assessing damage, providing necessary medical care, and collecting evidence for prosecutions. Medium-term problems relate to providing continued support to employees in coping with their experience, repairing damage to the facility, normalizing institutional operations, and undertaking the administrative follow-up associated with a disturbance. Long-term problems are solved by assessing what caused the riot and developing new policy reflecting that assessment. The unique characteristics of each institution, its administration, its staff, and its inmate population, as well as other variables, will shape the aftermath of a riot.

Inmate Classification

Classification Systems

One of the most important and potentially far-reaching responsibilities for today's correctional administrators is inmate classification.

Relating human and environmental variables can improve prisoner adjustment and prison management.[55] As rehabilitation fell into disfavor and prison populations began to rise, traditional diagnostic techniques of classification were no longer appropriate or practical, and a shift in the function and structure of classification occurred.

Classification systems are intended to help administrators manage the prison population, treat inmates, and understand and predict their behavior.[56] More broadly, these four primary functions of classification are used to assign inmates to appropriate security levels, to place them in specific living quarters, to designate the required custody level for each, and to select program activities for each. Classification forms the basis for assigning inmates to settings to minimize problems cost effectively and to make policy decisions regarding the proper care and supervision of prisoners.[57]

The search for accurate and precise classification models has become a legal issue for correctional administrators. Courts have repeatedly found that traditional classification procedures and criteria were based on unsupported assumptions regarding inmate behavior and that criteria were not applied uniformly to all inmates.[58] In several cases,[59] courts have also held that classification methods cannot be "capricious, irrational, or discriminatory." For a classification model to be "coherent" and thus judicially acceptable, "placement and assignment must be clearly understandable, consistently applied and conceptually complete."[60]

The search for classification systems that meet these criteria has gone in several directions. Three of the most commonly used systems today are *Megargee's MMPI typology*, which uses a psychology inventory to classify inmates into groups with particular characteristics related to their criminality and projected troubles in prison; *Toch's Prison Preference Inventory*, which measures inmates' concerns about eight environmental attributes to determine individual needs; and *risk assessment*, currently the most common form of classification, which uses demographic, criminal, and behavioral characteristics to distinguish inmates according to the likelihood that they will be involved in institutional misconduct.[61]

These three systems serve different purposes, use different variables to classify inmates into groups, and are operationalized in quite different ways. Each predicts some adjustment outcomes but not others. According to an analysis of the three methods by Kevin Wright, no system emerges as clearly superior. Risk assessment appears to predict aggressive disciplinary infractions, whereas neither of the other two was useful in this regard. Risk assessment did not predict the probabilities of self-reported internal and physical problems, but the other two systems did. All three successfully predicted self-reports of external problems. Of the three, Toch's system predicted outcomes least successfully.[62]

Implications for Institutional Management

If for no other reason, classification is justified on the grounds that it provides a security strategy. With offenders receiving longer prison sentences than ever before and a national recidivism rate of more than 30 percent, the task of protecting the public must involve more than architectural design. Indeed, with the enactment of the 1987 federal sentencing guidelines and life-without-parole statutes in many states, classification of inmates has in effect become a continuous, lifelong process. Institutional managers must realize that the classification of offenders for security purposes is essential to the operation of an orderly and safe prison.

Classification eases the burden of a major consent decree regarding crowding and conditions of confinement, provides consistency and equity to inmates in placement and treatment, and allows funds and human resources to be planned and managed in a cost-efficient manner. Classification processes can prevent escapes and reduce the need for protective custody; furthermore, they can limit violent incidents to certain units of the institution.[63]

Calculating Correctional Costs

Correctional administrators and several organizations, including the U.S. Census Bureau and the American Correctional Association, report annual cost figures associated with housing prison inmates. At present, we are often given estimates that the cost to house an inmate in prison for a year is in the range of $16,000 to $20,000; however, the actual cost is probably much higher. For jails, estimated costs do not appear to be reliable.[64]

The problem is that expenditures that should be counted as costs of providing a particular service are overlooked. The total cost of a particular correctional service should include both *direct* costs, expenditures made by an agency of government to provide the service in question, and *indirect* costs, which are those borne by government or nongovernmental parties to support a particular correctional activity. Although the latter costs are real, their calculation is often difficult, speculative, and controversial.[65] Figure 12.2 shows the general kinds of costs that are associated with corrections.

The direct costs that other agencies incur in serving a correctional agency's mission must also be counted as direct correctional costs. For example, teachers in prisons and jails are sometimes paid by a school district, not by the correctional agency; the same holds true for doctors and other medical workers paid by local or state departments. In-hospital care is often charged to the public hospital, utility bills in correctional facilities are sometimes paid by departments of public works, and departments of transportation often provide the vehicles used to move prisoners. The failure to count these kinds of services provided by other agencies and levels of government will result in significantly underestimating the total direct cost of a correctional service.[66]

How much higher are the real costs of corrections likely to be? Studies indicate that the actual cost of operating public correctional programs is about 33 to 66 percent higher than is usually reported.[67]

Obviously, correctional administrators need good data and cost figures for planning and projecting and for accounting to the general public. To the extent possible, the shortcomings in determining the total direct cost of a correctional service must be addressed.

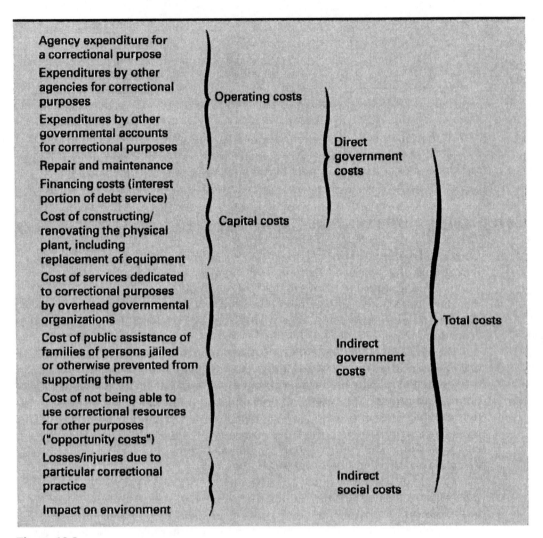

Figure 12.2

Components of corrections costs. (*Source:* Douglas C. McDonald, "The Cost of Corrections: In Search of the Bottom Line," in *Research in Corrections,* U.S. Department of Corrections, National Institute of Corrections, February 1989, p. 7.)

The Move Toward Privatization

Emergence of the Concept

"Punishment for Profit," "The Corporate Warden," "Incarceration Unlimited"— these headlines in business journals have proclaimed a new opportunity for venture capital: criminal punishment.[68] Attracted by the huge sums of money devoted each year to holding adult criminals behind bars, entrepreneurs have been trying to turn prisons into profit-making corporations. One commentator remarked: "There's a whole new industry developing, from the likely meeting of pinstripes and prison stripes."[69] These entrepreneurs are often cheered on by prison administrators, who think the government can stand the competition.[70]

Private vendors already supply health care services, educational and vocational training, and an array of other services to public institutions.[71] The largest and most prominent of the corporations attempting to operate correctional institutions privately is Corrections Corporation of America (CCA), formed in 1983.[72]

Corporations pursue contracts to construct and/or manage prisons and detention facilities. Most of the contracts awarded to these and other firms have been for small, low security facilities for the Immigration and Naturalization Service, the Federal Bureau of Prisons, or county jails, beginning as early as 1984.[73] "The private jail market is ripe," says one source, "and it's the brokers, architects, builders and banks—not the taxpayers—who will make out like bandits."[74]

Advantages and Disadvantages

Proponents for privatization of prisons and jails believe that it will offer a greater diversity of programs and facilities and increase the ability to handle special inmate populations or offer special rehabilitative or training programs.[75] The strongest argument, however, is the belief that private industry can respond more quickly than government bureaucracies and in a cost-effective manner to the current pressure for more prison space, because private industry is not bound by state civil service rules or by employee unions. Proponents maintain that a private prison will charge the state less per day to hold each inmate than the publicly operated facility will by reducing building and labor costs and using economies of scale. They also argue that the profit motive creates an inherent efficiency.[76] Finally, one study in Florida found that inmates released from private prisons had lower recidivism rates (10 percent) than those released from public institutions (19 percent), and that those released from private prisons who reoffended committed less serious subsequent offenses than did their public prison counterparts.[77]

Critics of the privatization of prisons suggest that the profit motive may restrict or eliminate services to underprivileged groups or those with special needs.[78] They are also concerned that reduced costs will come at the expense of reduced salaries and training for staff members. Indeed, one contracted site provided less than 50 hours of training, compared to the 320-hour program mandated for public employees.[79] Critics also question the hidden costs of privately operated prisons, such as the administration of contracts. They argue that the largest hidden cost would involve the necessary creation of a regulatory bureaucracy to oversee the private corporations' operations.[80]

Alexis Durham suggests that adequate effort has not been committed to evaluating these private corporations:

Only through exacting monitoring and evaluation can a reasoned assessment of achievements of privatization be made. Furthermore, only with the information produced by such evaluations can sensible correctional policy be developed. Thus it is crucial that adequate effort be committed to evaluating the initiatives of the private sector.[81]

Finally, opponents believe that for the state to abdicate its power of punishment to the lowest bidder will seal off prisons more completely from constitutional and societal controls.[82]

Corrections Accreditation

In Chapter 5, we discussed the development of accreditation standards for police agencies. Accreditation has been in existence longer and is far more advanced in the corrections field, however. In the 1970s, a national system of corrections accreditation was developed to generally upgrade correctional institutions and programs. This movement was preceded by years of experience on an international level, not with accreditation as such, but with its most essential element: the formulation of agreed-upon standards. International committees had been working off and on for many decades to develop standards, especially with the old League of Nations.

The effort to accredit correctional facilities became more organized and effective as a result of the efforts by the U.N. Commission on the Prevention of Crime and the Treatment of Offenders.[83] Although the Commission exists today, the American Corrections Association (ACA) has taken over the responsibility for day-to-day accreditation operations through its Division of Standards and Accreditation. The ACA does not actually grant accreditation, however; that function is performed by the Commission on Accreditation for Corrections (CAC), which was formed in 1974.

Any agency wishing to be accredited submits an application to the CAC and pays a fee for the services involved in the process. The agency then conducts a self-evaluation. For those items not in compliance, the CAC reviews the self-evaluation reports and audits the agency's evaluation by use of on-site visits by staff and a visiting committee of consultants. The agency must submit a plan for correcting any deficiency identified during the visit or by the self-evaluation. The process is rigorous.

This system of voluntary accreditation is believed to possess several benefits. In short, it provides the best means to ensure quality correctional services, to mobilize and capitalize on professional talent, and to infuse research findings into correctional practices. It also provides support for elected and appointed state and federal officials committed to improving corrections, correctional administrators with a sound rationale when appropriations for correctional services are requested, interested citizens with factual measurements of the correctional services in their communities or states, and overall professionalization of correctional services.[84]

Stress in Corrections

The Problem

A growing body of research has established what correctional officers already know: Correctional institutions are unpleasant and stressful places in which to work.[85] In fact, the incidence of high blood pressure is especially high among corrections workers.[86] And, as with the police, the internal work environment and management style contribute more to high stress levels than factors external to the occupation.[87]

Tremendous interest in correctional officer job satisfaction began in the 1980s, possibly because of the growing recognition of chronic labor supply problems. The turnover rate for correctional officers in 1961 was 24.8 percent.[88] A 1976 study concluded that correctional officers had the highest turnover rate of any workers in the justice system,[89] and a 1981 national survey revealed that the turnover rate was 24.5 percent.[90] More recently, attrition rates of correctional officers in a majority of the states have been found to be 25 percent or higher.[91] In the last several decades, a number of prominent panels and commissions have also been created to address the chronic labor supply problems in corrections.

It is not surprising that correctional officers report feelings of burnout, given the level of general dissatisfaction that has been reported with their jobs. Studies suggest that the nature of the correctional institution environment contributes more to officer burnout than do personal characteristics.[92] The more ineffective or powerless staff feel with inmates, the more emotionally and physically exhausted they become.[93] Officers who engage in stimulating activities (e.g., providing human services, such as acting as an inmate referral agent or advocate) experience less burnout than those who have no incentives (e.g., merely patrolling the cell block) or engage in boring activities.[94] In general, stress is more closely tied to the nature of the working environment, but the most important contributor is the staff's relationship with the inmates.[95]

Those who view a job as threatening have been found more likely to cope through the use of intrapsychic processes, such as avoidance (avoiding people in general), wishful thinking (hoping a miracle will happen), and/or minimization of the threat (attempting to gain sympathy and understanding from someone). The use of these mechanisms has been noted especially in workers in the correctional field.[96] Corrections officers experiencing higher diastolic blood pressure have been found to cope with greater reliance on all three of these mechanisms. Officers who attempt to cope by partially withdrawing from the situation by using these mechanisms, however, place their physical well-being and that of their co-workers at risk. Alternatively, they may quit their jobs[97] or be absent with greater frequency.[98]

The implications for correctional administrators appear rather straightforward. A study by the National Institute of Corrections found that a critical element in employee satisfaction is effective management and leadership, as evidenced by accessibility, familiarity with the institution's operations, fairness, and immediate feedback. Employees feel strongly about the need for staff empowerment, participative management, receiving recognition and respect, and feeling that their jobs are worthwhile. Other strategies for staff retention include awards, employee assistance programs, decentralization and delegation, and effective policies and practices concerning overtime and grievance processes.[99] Ongoing correctional staff training and research are needed to fend off stress-related problems.[100]

Probation and Parole Officers

Stress and burnout among probation and parole officers have been linked with longevity: Officers who experience stress and/or burnout are more likely to leave the position or try to avoid additional work.[101] Studies also suggest that officers under a democratic or laissez-faire management style tend to stay with the department longer, reducing staff turnover and producing more experienced officers. In turn, a stable, experienced staff is better able to handle the caseloads, and officers do not have to handle excessive or multiple caseloads due to vacant positions caused by turnover. Thus, the number of officers employed by a department and the length of time an employee remains with it are probably closely linked to management style. It is the responsibility of the manager to monitor and minimize stress and thereby reduce officer burnout.[102]

Most important, probation and parole administrators need to maintain an "open door" with their line officers and communicate openly and directly with their staff. The type and amount of communication within a department often mirrors the administrators' management style. Laissez-faire probation and parole administrators tend to communicate solely through memos and written operations manuals, while authoritarian leaders hold formal staff meetings and scheduled appointments as well as issuing written operations manuals. The democratic administrator prefers to meet informally with officers on an ad hoc basis, with formal decisions being announced via memos and operations manuals. Generally, large staff meetings are considered a waste of time.[103]

Summary

This chapter examined the major issues confronting today's correctional administrators: coed prisons and smoke-free facilities, sex and violence, drug use and interdiction, gangs, riots, inmate classification, the costs of corrections, privatization and accreditation of prisons, and stress and burnout among personnel. These issues do not lend themselves to our society's frequent demand for a "quick fix" and will continue to challenge these administrators for many years to come.

Questions for Review

1. What new and successful programs are at work in corrections?
2. What can be done to reduce sexual victimization and violence in correctional facilities?
3. To what extent is drug abuse a problem in correctional institutions? How may administrators interdict and treat this problem?
4. What can correctional administrators do to control gangs in prisons?
5. Why is inmate classification an important responsibility for correctional administrators?
6. What are some advantages and disadvantages of privatization?
7. What are some problems inherent in calculating the cost of correctional services? What actual costs tend to be ignored or undercounted? How might this problem be rectified?
8. What are some unique stressors for persons employed in corrections? Is it more difficult for these workers to manage job-related stress?

Notes

1. Clarice Feinman, *Women in the Criminal Justice System* (2d ed.) (New York: Praeger, 1986), pp. 64–65.
2. Sue Mahan, "Co-corrections: Doing Time Together," *Corrections Today* 48 (1986):134–165.
3. Ibid., p. 134.
4. Sally Chandler Halford, "Kansas Co-Correctional Concept," *Corrections Today* 46 (1984):44–54.
5. Ibid., p. 54.
6. Jacqueline K. Crawford, "Two Losers Don't Make a Winner: The Case Against the Co-Correctional Institution," in John Ortiz Smykla (ed.), *Coed Prison* (New York: Human Sciences Press, 1980), pp. 262–268.
7. Richard Lawrence and Sue Mahan, "Women Corrections Officers in Men's Prisons: Acceptance and Perceived Job Performance," *Women and Criminal Justice* 9 (1998):63–86.
8. American Lung Association Fact Sheet: Smoking.www.lungusa.org/tobacco/smoking_factsheet99.html, September 1999.
9. U.S. Department of Health and Human Services, *The Health Consequences of Involuntary Smoking: A Report of the Surgeon General* (Rockville, Md.: Author, 1986).
10. American Correctional Association, *Corrections Today* 49 (August 1987):14.
11. Brad L. Neiger, "Development of a Smoke-Free Jail Policy: A Case Study in Davis County, Utah," *American Jails* (Summer 1998): 23.
12. Ibid.
13. Paul W. Tappan, *Crime, Justice, and Correction* (New York: McGraw-Hill, 1960), pp. 678–679.
14. Gene Kassebaum, "Sex in Prison," *Psychology Today* (January 1972):39.
15. Joseph Fishman, *Sex in Prison* (New York: National Library Press, 1934); Donald Clemmer, *The Prison Community* (New York: Rinehart, 1958), pp. 249–273; Gresham Sykes, *The*

Society of Captives: A Study of a Maximum Security Prison (Princeton, N.J.: Princeton University Press, 1958); Peter C. Buffum, *Homosexuality in Prisons* (Washington, D.C.: U.S. Government Printing Office, 1972).

16. See Rose Giallombardo, *Society of Women: A Study of a Women's Prison* (New York: Wiley, 1966); David Ward and Gene Kassebaum, *Women's Prisons* (Chicago: Aldine, 1965), pp. 80–101; John H. Gagnon and William Simon, "The Social Meaning of Prison Homosexuality," *Federal Probation* 32 (March 1968): 23–29.

17. Daniel Lockwood, "Reducing Prison Sexual Violence," in Robert Johnson and Hans Toch (eds.), *The Pains of Imprisonment* (Prospect Heights, Ill.: Waveland Press, Inc., 1982): 257–265.

18. Donald Clemmer, *The Prison Community* (New York: Rinehart and Company, 1940); Gresham M. Sykes, *The Society of Captives: A Study of a Maximum Security Prison;* Alan J. Davis, "Sexual Assaults in the Philadelphia Prison System and Sheriff's Vans," *Trans-Action* 6 (1968): 8–16.

19. Clemens Bartollas, Stuart J. Miller, and Simon Dimitz, *Juvenile Victimization: The Institutional Paradox* (New York: Halsted, 1976); Lee Bowker, *Prison Victimization* (New York: Elsevier, 1980); Daniel Lockwood, *Prison Sexual Violence* (New York: Elsevier, 1980); Ulla Bondeson, *Prisoners in Prison Societies* (New Brunswick, N.J.: Transaction Publishers, 1989).

20. Norman E. Smith and Mary Ellen Batiuk, "Sexual Victimization and Inmate Social Interaction," *The Prison Journal* 69 (Fall/Winter 1989): 29–38.

21. Lockwood, *Prison Sexual Violence,* p. 29.

22. Leo Carroll, "Humanitarian Reform and Biracial Sexual Assault in a Maximum Security Prison," *Urban Life* 5 (January 1977): 422.

23. Bowker, *Prison Victimization,* p. 1.

24. Lockwood, *Prison Sexual Violence,* p. 29.

25. Ibid., p. 30.

26. Lockwood, "Reducing Prison Sexual Violence," pp. 261–262.

27. Lee H. Bowker, "Victimizers and Victims in American Correctional Institutions," in Johnson and Toch (eds.), *The Pains of Imprisonment,* pp. 63–76.

28. D. Jones, *The Health Risks of Imprisonment* (Lexington, Mass.: D. C. Heath, 1976); Sawyer F. Sylvester, John H. Reed, and David O. Nelson, *Prison Homicide* (New York: Spectrum, 1977); and Bowker, *Prison Victimization.*

29. Timothy J. Flanagan, "Correlates of Institutional Misconduct among State Prisoners," *Criminology* 21 (1983): 29–39.

30. John Irwin, *The Felon* (Englewood Cliffs, N.J.: Prentice Hall, 1970; Bartollas, Miller, and Dinitz, *Juvenile Victimization.*

31. Tom Howard, personal communication.

32. Ben M. Crouch and James W. Marquart, "Resolving the Paradox of Reform: Litigation, Prisoner Violence, and Perceptions of Risk," *Justice Quarterly* 7 (March 1990): 103–123.

33. Peter C. Kratcoski, "The Implications of Research Explaining Prison Violence and Disruption," *Federal Probation* 52 (March 1988): 27–32.

34. Lucien X. Lombardo, "Stress, Change and Collective Violence in Prison," in Johnson and Toch (eds.), *The Pains of Imprisonment,* pp. 77–93.

35. John R. Hepburn, "Prison Guards as Agents of Social Control," in Lynne Goodstein and Doris Layton MacKenzie (eds.), *The American Prison: Issues in Research and Policy* (New York: Plenum Press, 1989), pp. 191–206.

36. J. Forbes Farmer, "A Case Study in Regaining Control of a Violent State Prison," *Federal Probation* 52 (March 1988): 41–47.

37. Robert B. Levinson and Roy E. Gerard, "Functional Units: A Different Correctional Approach," *Federal Probation* 37 (December 1973): 8–16.
38. Farmer, "A Case Study in Regaining Control of a Violent State Prison," p. 46.
39. U.S. Department of Justice, Bureau of Justice Statistics Executive Summary, *Correctional Populations in the United States* (Washington, D.C.: Author, March 1999), p. 3.
40. U.S. Department of Justice, Bureau of Justice Statistics Special Report, *Drug Enforcement and Treatment in Prison: 1990* (Washington, D.C.: Author, 1992), p. 1.
41. Ibid., p. 2.
42. U.S. Department of Justice, Office of Justice Programs, National Institute of Justice, *Prison Programs for Drug-Involved Offenders* (Washington, D.C.: Author, 1989), pp. 1, 4.
43. James Jacobs, *Stateville: The Penitentiary in Mass Society* (Chicago: University of Chicago Press, 1997).
44. George M. Camp and Camille G. Camp, *Prison Gangs: Their Extent, Nature, and Impact on Prisons,* Grant 84-NI-AX-0001, U.S. Department of Justice, Office of Legal Policy (Washington, D.C.: U.S. Government Printing Office, 1985).
45. John Irwin, *Prisons in Turmoil* (Boston: Little Brown, 1980), pp. 189–190.
46. Ibid., p. 190.
47. Joel Samaha, *Criminal Justice* (St. Paul, Minn.: West, 1988), p. 558.
48. Ibid.
49. Jacobs, *Stateville: The Penitentiary in Mass Society.*
50. Irwin, *Prisons in Turmoil.*
51. George M. Camp and Camille G. Camp, *The Correctional Year Book* (South Salem, N.Y.: Criminal Justice Institute, 1987).
52. Irwin, *Prisons in Turmoil,* p. 192.
53. U.S. Department of Justice, National Institute of Justice, Research in Brief "Resolution of Prison Riots" (October 1995). See also Bert Useem, Camille Graham Camp, and George M. Camp, *Resolution of Prison Riots: Strategies and Policies* (New York, N.Y.: Oxford University Press, 1996).
54. Personal communication, John Slansky, October 28, 1993.
55. K. N. Wright, J. M. Harris, and Nancy Woika, *Improving Correctional Classification Through a Study of the Placement of Inmates in Environmental Settings,* Final Report, NIJ Grant 83-IJ-CX-0011 (Washington, D.C.: U.S. Government Printing Office, 1985).
56. Doris Layton MacKenzie, C. Dale Posey, and Karen R. Rapaport, "A Theoretical Revolution in Corrections: Varied Purposes for Classification," *Criminal Justice and Behavior* 15 (March 1988):125–136.
57. Kevin N. Wright, "The Relationship of Risk, Needs, and Personality Classification Systems and Prison Adjustment," *Criminal Justice and Behavior* 15 (December 1988):454–471.
58. James Austin, "Assessing the New Generation of Prison Classification Models," *Crime and Delinquency* 29 (1983):561–576.
59. See *Holt v. Sarver,* 1971; *Morris v. Travisono,* 1970; *Pugh v. Locke,* 1976; *Laman v. Helgemoe,* 1977; *Palmigiano v. Garraby,* 1977; *Ramos v. Lamm,* 1979.
60. Austin, "Assessing the New Generation of Prison Classification Models," pp. 562–563.
61. Ibid., pp. 455.
62. Wright, "The Relationship of Risk, Needs, and Personality Classification Systems and Prison Adjustment," p. 468.
63. Parker Evatt, Sammie Brown, and Lorraine T. Fowler, "Offender Classification: Don't Overlook This Important Security Strategy," *Corrections Today* (July 1989):34–37.
64. National Institute of Corrections, *Research in Corrections* 2 (February 1989): 4.
65. Douglas C. McDonald, "The Cost of Corrections: In Search of the Bottom Line," in National Institute of Corrections, *Research in Corrections* 2 (February 1989):6.

66. Ibid., p. 8.

67. Ibid., p. 11.

68. Craig Becker and Mary Dru Stanley, "The Downside of Private Prisons," *The Nation* (June 15, 1985):728–730.

69. Quoted in Becker and Stanley, "The Downside of Private Prisons," p. 728.

70. Kerry Elizabeth Knobelsdorff, "The Move to Hand Prisons Over to Private Businesses Draws Flak," *The Christian Science Monitor* (July 27, 1987):17–18.

71. Camille Camp and George Camp, "Correctional Privatization in Perspective," *The Prison Journal* 65 (1985):14–31.

72. Becker and Stanley, "The Downside of Private Prisons," p. 729.

73. Charles W. Thomas and Suzanna L. Foard, *Private Correctional Facilities Census* (Gainesville, Fla.: University of Florida, Center for Studies in Criminology and Law, 1991).

74. Quoted in Becker and Stanley, "The Downside of Private Prisons," p. 728.

75. Robert B. Levinson, "Okeechobee: An Evaluation of Privatization in Corrections," *The Prison Journal* 65 (1985):75–94; J. Mullen, "Corrections and the Private Sector," *The Prison Journal* 65 (1985):1–13.

76. Ted Gest, "Prisons for Profit: A Growing Business," *U.S. News and World Report* (July 2, 1984):45–46.

77. Kaduce Lonn Lanza, Karen F. Parker, and Charles W. Thomas, "A Comparative Recidivism Analysis of Releasees From Private and Public Prisons," *Crime and Delinquency* 45 (1999):28–47.

78. Christine Bowditch and Ronald S. Everett, "Private Prisons: Problems Within the Solution," *Justice Quarterly* 4 (September 1987):441–453.

79. Ibid., p. 447.

80. Ibid., p. 448.

81. Alexis M. Durham III, "Evaluating Privatized Correctional Institutions: Obstacles to Effective Assessment," *Federal Probation* 52 (June 1988): 65–71.

82. Becker and Stanley, "The Downside of Private Prisons," p. 730.

83. Paul Keve, *Corrections* (New York: Wiley, 1981), p. 478.

84. Adapted from E. Preston Sharp, "Why Accreditation?" *Proceedings of the 104th Annual Congress of Correction, Houston, Texas, August 18–22, 1974* (College Park, Md.: American Correctional Association, 1975), pp. 31–32.

85. Carroll Brodsky, "Long-Term Stress in Teachers and Prison Guards," *Journal of Occupational Medicine* 19 (1977):133–138; also see Carroll Brodsky, "Work Stress in Correctional Institutions," *Journal of Prison and Jail Health* 2 (1982):74–102.

86. B. Sheppard, "Mortality and Stress Survey of San Francisco Juvenile Probation Officers," pamphlet published by Local No. 21 AFL-CIO (San Francisco: AFL-CIO, 1982).

87. Kay Lancefield, C. J. Lennings, and Don Thomson, "Management Style and Its Effect on Prison Officers' Stress," *International Journal of Stress Management* 4 (1997): 205–219.

88. Walter Lunden, *The Prison Warden and the Custodial Staff* (Springfield, Ill.: Charles C. Thomas, 1965).

89. National Planning Association, American Institutes for Research, and the Bureau of Social Science Research, *A Nationwide Survey of Law Enforcement Criminal Justice Needs and Resources* (Washington, D.C.: Author, 1976).

90. "Corrections Officers," *Corrections Compendium* 6 (1982): 1–7.

91. Susan Philliber, "Thy Brother's Keeper: A Review of the Literature on Correctional Officers," *Justice Quarterly* 4 (1987): 9–37.

92. Lawrence H. Gerstein, Charles G. Topp, and Gregory Correll, "The Role of the Environment and Person When Predicting Burnout among Correctional Personnel," *Criminal Justice and Behavior* 14 (September 1987): 352–369.

93. See Cary Cherniss, *Staff Burnout: Job Stress in the Human Services* (Newbury Park, Calif.: Sage Publications, 1980); Lucien Lombardo, *Guards Imprisoned: Correctional Officers at Work* (New York: Elsevier/North Holland, 1981).

94. Ibid.

95. Gerstein, Topp, and Correll, "The Role of the Environment and Person When Predicting Burnout Among Correctional Personnel," p. 362.

96. Frances Cheek and Marie Miller, "The Experience of Stress for Correction Officers: A Double-Bind Theory of Correctional Stress," *Journal of Criminal Justice* 11 (1983): 105-120.

97. J. Foote, "Prison Guards Ever Under Pressure, First to Be Attacked," *San Francisco Examiner* (August 27, 1981):A1.

98. J. Reiterman, "Ticking Bombs in Prisons: Conditions Set Stage for Huge Explosion," *San Francisco Examiner* (August 17, 1981):A1.

99. George M. Camp, Camille G. Camp, and Michael V. Fair, *Managing Staff: Corrections' Most Valuable Resource* (Washington, D.C.: National Institute of Corrections, 1996). See also Risdon N. Slate and Ronald E. Vogel, "Participative Management and Correctional Personnel: A Study of the Perceived Atmosphere for Participation in Correctional Decision Making," *Journal of Criminal Justice* 25 (1997): 397-408; Elizabeth L. Grossi, Thomas Keil, and Gennaro F. Vito, "Surviving 'the Joint:' Mitigating Factors of Correctional Officer Stress," *Journal of Crime and Justice* 19 (1996): 103-120.

100. Gerstein, Topp, and Correll, "The Role of the Environment and Person When Predicting Burnout Among Correctional Personnel," p. 363.

101. John T. Whitehead and Charles Lindquist, "Job Stress and Burnout Among Probation/Parole Officers: Perceptions and Causal Factors," *International Journal of Offender Therapy and Comparative Criminology* 29 (1985): 109-119.

102. Patricia L. Hardyman, "Management Style in Probation: Policy Implications Derived from Systems Theory," in Clayton Hartjen and Edward E. Rhine (eds.), *Correctional Theory and Practice* (Chicago: Nelson-Hall, 1992), pp. 61-81.

103. Ibid., p. 73.

CASE STUDIES

Prisons, Politics, Poverty, and the Rebellious Rurals*

It is time to prepare the annual budget for the Department of Prisons for the legislature. The entire country is suffering a recession, and your state is no different. Tax revenues are down. All state agencies, including the Department of Corrections, have suffered a blanket 10 percent cut in their budgets during the current fiscal year. For the prison system, this meant the closure of a prison and the firing of over 100 staff members. Your state is overwhelmingly urban in distribution of population and political power.

The director of the prison system has just returned from the governor's cabinet meeting, where he has been told that the governor will recommend to the legislature an even lower budget amount for prisons next year. This is very troubling, given that the legislature will be considering a budget that will not even begin for another 18 months, and that the inmate population is sure to grow during that time.

Meetings within the prison system over the next several days result in a three-part proposal to live within the smaller budget:

1. Closing all minimum custody work camps in the rural areas of the state.
2. Operating the remaining institutions and facilities at the absolute limit of their capacity.
3. Proposing the enactment of an emergency release bill that would grant early parole (60 days) to inmates who are closest to discharge, to keep from exceeding prison capacity.

The early release proposal is approved by the governor and is now being presented to the legislature. At present, the state's prison system houses 12,000 inmates. According to population projections, it is estimated that 800 inmates would be eligible for release under this program: two-thirds from the minimum custody institutions, one-fourth from camps, and the remainder being medium or maximum custody inmates.

Upon learning of this plan, a tremendous outcry is heard from the rural areas of the state over the closure of their work camps and, consequently, the ensuing layoffs of many workers and the negative impact on their local economies. Furthermore, some legislators complain to the governor and prison director about the early release program (exhibiting their traditional "tough on crime" posture).

---

*Contributed by Ron Angelone, Director, Virginia Department of Corrections, and Glen Whorton, Chief of Classification and Planning, Nevada Department of Prisons.

A sticky political situation has developed, because the "rurals" carry a lot of clout when they band together on an issue.

Legislative hearings are imminent on this issue, and the media have begun to clamor for responses to the concerns of rural interest groups and "tough on crime" advocates, who include the staff members at the camps who are at risk of being laid off. The attacks on the program generally relate to one or more of the following categories:

1. "Why doesn't the department close prisons instead of camps, so that rural communities can continue to benefit from the economic influence of salaries and purchases, and the public works performed by the inmates?"
2. "Releasing inmates into the community early will place our citizens at risk."
3. "How does the department justify the practice of not operating institutions at their emergency capacities at all times, during good economic times as well as bad?"

You, the department's budget analyst, have been instructed by the director to prepare a response to these questions as well as a general position paper on the three-point plan.

Questions for Discussion

1. What is the rationale for the closure of the camps? Is it basically sound?
2. What would be the effect of closing prisons instead of camps, as desired by the rural people?
3. What is the risk to the community, and is the public's concern legitimate?
4. How can the department defend its practice of not operating prisons at their emergency capacity levels?
5. What, if any, action(s) should be taken by the director against the staff members in rural areas who appear to be engaging in political "mutiny"?
6. To what extent, if any, should the prison director play the political "game" and begin contacting state legislators to solicit their support of the foregoing proposal?

The Prison Director versus the Irate Inmate*

The director of the state Department of Prisons has received a grievance from an inmate who indicates that the classification staff at the maximum security prison have classified him incorrectly. Specifically, the inmate argues that he is serving a

---

*Contributed by Ron Angelone, Director, Virginia Department of Corrections, and Glen Whorton, Chief of Classification and Planning, Nevada Department of Prisons.

sentence for forgery, and his offense has been treated (for purposes of classification) as if it were murder. He also maintains that the staff have begun to retaliate against him because of his grievances regarding his classification placement. The inmate states that if he does not receive satisfaction in regard to the classification, he is going to file suits based on the conditions of confinement at the prison. This is troubling to the director, given the overcrowding that already exists, the physical deficiencies of the maximum security prison, and the type and extent of programs available there.

A review of the inmate's file indicates that he is incarcerated as a habitual offender with three life sentences. The root offense for the habitual offender findings was indeed forgery. He has been incarcerated only 18 months on the first life sentence. He has four prior felonies for similar offenses in other states. The inmate is 56 years old and in poor health. The file is replete with complaints about other inmates and staff. He has sued the central records staff on one previous occasion, claiming that staff misconduct resulted in the mishandling of a request for a speedy trial on a detainer that had been lodged against him. This suit was dismissed when it was discovered that the inmate had lied about having requested the trial. The file also includes numerous disciplinary violations related to refusing to work and possession of unauthorized property. There is no violence in the record or evidence of serious misconduct.

The file also discloses that the inmate is embroiled in a dispute with the chief of the prison medical division over his treatment for cancer. The inmate has recently claimed that staff physicians have completely ignored his medical condition and have refused to treat the cancer. The computerized inmate information system indicates that about four months ago, the inmate was taken to a local hospital and remained there for approximately one week. A call to the institution's doctor reveals that the inmate's cancer was surgically removed during that visit.

A review of classification documents reveals that the staff have correctly scored the inmate's offense on the objective classification instrument. The score for Murder II and Habitual Offender are the same. The instrument's computed score on the classification documents indicates that he is a medium custody inmate, however. He was assigned to a higher level of custody because of the extremely long sentence that he has to serve. This custody assignment, and the original transfer to the maximum security prison, were approved by the central classification staff, who review classification recommendations for the director.

You are the director's administrative aide, and enjoy the director's trust. She has asked that you prepare a position statement on this matter, representing all relevant viewpoints and possible pitfalls and developing recommendations. You are told, however, that "the bottom line is to do what's right for the inmate."

Questions for Discussion

1. What is the primary inmate-related issue that the director must deal with: classification or transfer? Were the classification staff technically correct in sending the inmate to a maximum security institution in the first place?

2. Can the inmate be safely transferred to a lower-level institution? If so, to medium or minimum? (Bear in mind that while being infirm and a relatively old inmate, he is nevertheless serving a lengthy sentence.)

3. If the inmate is transferred, have the director and staff lost any real power in the eyes of other inmates?

4. How does the director deal with these issues without giving an obviously litigious inmate more "ammunition" with which to harass staff or sue the department? Should the director ask the classification team to reconsider the case?

5. What are the staff-related issues the director has to deal with? What are the options in regard to dealing with those issues?

6. Are any broader policy issues presented in this situation? If so, what action do they suggest?

"Out of Town Brown" and the Besieged Probation Supervisor*

Joan Casey is a career probation officer. She majored in criminal justice as an undergraduate and plans to get her master's in criminology within the next few years. She holds memberships in several national correctional organizations, attends training conferences, and does a lot of reading on her own time to stay current in the field.

Joan began working for the Collier County Probation Department soon after she graduated from college and was promoted to a supervisory position within five years, a remarkable accomplishment considering her relative lack of seniority in the organization. She supervises an adult probation unit consisting of eight seasoned probation officers, all of whom have been in the workforce longer than she has. The unit is responsible for investigating approximately 80 offenders a month and preparing presentence investigation reports on them.

Collier County Probation Department has made the front page of the local newspapers twice in the past year. Both times it was a nightmare for the chief probation officer, Jack Brown, and the entire agency. "Collier County Soft on Crime!" screamed the first headline, and then, just a month later, "Northside Stalker Gets Probation!"

Brown called a management team meeting. It was short and to the point: "No more lousy publicity," he said, "or heads are gonna roll! Has everybody got it?" Everybody got it. No written policy concerning media relations exists, however, nor is any particular person authorized to release agency information.

---

*Contributed by Catherine Lowe, Director, California Center for Judicial Education and Research, Emeryville, California.

This week Brown is on annual leave, the assistant chief is out of state at an American Correctional Association meeting, and Joan Casey is the designated officer in charge. One of Joan's probation officers has recommended community-based treatment for a 16-year-old mentally retarded boy who was prosecuted as an adult. The youth murdered his stepfather with an axe after submitting to many years of physical and mental abuse. He had been an incest victim since he was 5 years old.

Joan is aware of the probation officer's recommendation and agrees with it. After all, she reasons, the boy is a low risk for recidivism, and he is as much a victim of this offense as was his stepfather.

It is 4:45 P.M. on Thursday. Joan's phone rings; her secretary has put through a call from a reporter at a local newspaper. The reporter is a strong crusader in the local war against crime. He has his own byline weekly column at the paper. He knows that the "kiddie-killer" will be sentenced tomorrow.

Questions for Discussion

1. What should Joan's response to the reporter be other than hanging up or telling him to call back?
2. If she elects to discuss her officer's recommendation, what should she say to justify it?
3. What should the chief probation officer do upon his return to work?
4. Was the probation officer's recommendation correct based on these facts?
5. Should a policy be immediately drafted for this situation? Should any personnel actions be taken?

"Cheerless Chuck" and the Parole Officer's Orientation Day*

"So, you're the new parole officer with a criminal justice degree from the university? Well, I hope you last longer than the last recruit I had. She meant well, but I guess her idealistic ideas about the job of parole officer couldn't handle the realities of the work.

"In a way, I understand what she went through. Same thing happened to me 12 years ago when I started this job. There I was, fresh out of college with a brand new diploma with 'Social Work' written on it. I figured that piece of paper made me a social worker, and I better get right to work fixing society. It didn't take me long to realize that the real world was different from what I had learned in

---

*Contributed by Matthew Leone, Assistant Professor of Criminal Justice, University of Nevada, Reno.

college. It was like I had been trained as a sailor, and I was about to set out on a voyage, but I couldn't take the time to steer the ship because I was so busy bailing water. The crises we deal with here make it darned difficult to do the work we all see needs to be done.

"Years ago, when I first started with the parole department, things were a lot better than they are now. Caseloads were lower, fewer people were getting parole who didn't deserve it, and the rest of the criminal justice system was in a lot better shape, which made our jobs a lot easier to do. Think about it. We vote in politicians who promise the public that they are going to 'get tough' on crime and the first thing they do is allot more money for law enforcement stuff: beat cops, car computers, helicopters, and so on. These things are great, but all they do is add more people into a system that is already overloaded. No one gets elected by promising to build more courts or add jail and prison space, or probation and parole officers. Eventually these added police officers arrest more people than the system can handle.

"The courts back up, which in turn messes up the prisons and the jails. The inmates stuck in these crowded places get tired of living like sardines, so they sue the prisons and jails. Remember, the Constitution prohibits cruel and unusual punishment. A lot of times inmates' complaints are legitimate, and they win. The judge orders the prison to lower its population to a reasonable level, which forces the parole board to consider more inmates for early release. They come knocking on our doors, hoping we can get them out of the mess that politics and budgets have created. Nobody mentions giving the parole department more officers, or a bigger budget for added administrative help. No, the bucks go to the flashy, visible things like cops and cars. Meanwhile, in the past 10 years our average caseload for a parole officer has increased 75 percent. We have more people who need supervision, and we are doing it on a budget that has not kept pace with the remainder of the criminal justice system.

"This wouldn't be so bad if the system was at least adding things to other areas, like the jail or the courts. The problem here is that we depend on the jail to hold our parolees who have violated their conditions. We catch some of them using booze or drugs, and we are *supposed* to bring them in to the county jail to wait for a hearing to decide if they are going back to prison, or back on the street. But the jail has its own set of problems. A couple of years ago the U.S. District Court slapped a population cap on our jail. If it goes over that population, the jail will not accept our violators. So we send them home. If they get into more serious trouble, we call it a new crime, the police arrest them, and the jail has to take them. Then they have to sit and wait for the court to catch up, since the courts are not in much better shape than the jail.

"I guess the job would be easier if the prisons were doing their jobs, too. I can't really blame them, since the prisons are funded in much the same way that parole is. We are not 'glamorous' places to send your tax dollars, but if the prisons were getting more money, they might be able to improve the quality of inmate they send to us. Maybe a little more vocational training and substance abuse counseling, so they could stay off the booze and drugs. Maybe then fewer of these parolees would wind up back behind bars a few years later.

"The worst part about the job is the caseload. We presently have so many on parole that I am lucky if I can get a phone call to each of them once a week, and maybe a home visit once a month. You can't tell me that a phone call and a home visit is really keeping these guys from committing crimes. The sad part about it is that with the proper budget and staff, we could really make a difference. We spend so much time bailing water out of the boat, we don't realize that there is no one steering, and we are just drifting in circles.

"By the way, my name is Charlie Matthews, but everyone calls me Chuck. I'm a supervisor here as well as the designated new-employee orientation specialist and all-round public relations person. I hope I've not depressed you too much on your first day, but now is a good time to drop your idealism and get to work 'bailing.' What're *your* views and ideas?"

Questions for Discussion

1. How would changes in politics directly and indirectly affect the parole system?
2. How does an old criminal justice planning adage that "you can't rock one end of the boat" seem to be applicable to what Chuck says about law enforcement getting so much new political funding?
3. What could you tell Chuck about existing means of dealing with bloated caseloads?
4. What kinds of administrative problems and practices might be responsible for this agency's situation?
5. Why do crowded jails and prisons make the job of parole officers more difficult?
6. How could practices of the jails and prisons change the success of the parole system?
7. Based on Chuck's assessment of the local situation, where do you believe the greatest misconceptions about courts and corrections exist?
8. Should Chuck be retained as orientation coordinator? Why or why not?

The Wright Way*

Randall Wright has been a shift supervisor at the Granite County Jail Facility for the past 10 years and has worked at the jail for a total of 18 years. Wright enjoys taking visitors on tours of the facility and takes pride in the fact that he knows every aspect of the jail's operation.

---

*Contributed by Ted Heim, Professor Emeritus, Department of Criminal Justice, Washburn University, Topeka, Kansas.

This summer, Wright is providing some of the supervision for an intern the facility has accepted from the local university's criminal justice program. The intern, Tom Sharpe, finds Wright to be an interesting and outspoken person. In their conversations about work in the jail, Tom asks Wright how he deals emotionally with his job, because he has read about stress in his textbooks.

"I'm glad you asked that, young fella," the veteran responds. "I have some good advice for you if you are going into any kind of correctional work." He continues, "First, I never take this job home with me. My wife and kids used to ask about what I do at work, but I have made it a strict policy never to discuss what happens here. My family wouldn't understand what goes on here. They might be concerned about what I do, so I decided long ago that it was best to dummy up about it all.

"Second, I find that you have to be realistic about your chances for having any positive influence on these birds who come through here. Oh, I have seen lots of guys who thought they could change the world come in here, and they are the ones who will come down hard. Me? Well, I'm a realist. Let's face it. We get the people everyone else has given up on, so what can we be expected to do? I tell visitors that 'We get the cream of the crap here,' and I mean it. Don't set your expectations very high, and you won't be disappointed.

"The job tends to get you down if you let it. I have found that you have to find a relief from all the frustrations you experience and the problems created by some of the SOBs who come through here. About once a week, the gang and I hold choir practice. Kelsey's Place down the street is where we go. After about five or six beers, this place and the world look a helluva lot better. People who don't work corrections don't understand the need to let off a little steam, but I can tell you that 'choir practice' keeps me going.

"One more bit of advice for you, Sharpe: Don't lose your sense of humor. I have always prided myself on my ability to laugh at almost any situation. Hell, the top brass around here and the politicians over at the courthouse are easy to laugh at. All you need to do when you're down is look at some of the orders these clowns put out and some of the things our glorious leaders tell the public about rehabilitation, efficiency, blah, blah, blah. I usually tell my staff to disregard new memos and such. Sometimes it's hard to stop laughing. It has all worked for me. Why, in just 9 years, 3 months, and 20 days I will be able to retire and walk away from this place."

Questions for Discussion

1. Assume that you are Wright's supervisor and, while standing in the hallway, you overhear this conversation. What would be your *immediate* reaction to his speech about on-the-job actions? What *long-term* actions—disciplinary or otherwise—would you take with Wright?

2. If you were Wright's supervisor, would you feel compelled to look into, leave alone, or halt the "choir practices"?

3. Assume that you are the student intern who just listened to this delivery. Of all the points made by Wright, which do you agree with? Disagree with? Would you now feel more or less compelled to enter the field? Do you value such a person's candor?

4. In your estimation, is Wright the sort of employee who should be supervising others? Greeting interns? Will an employee of this nature last until retirement?

5. Do you believe such cynicism is common in corrections? In criminal justice, generally? In most other occupations? Is it healthy or debilitating?

ISSUES SPANNING THE JUSTICE SYSTEM: ADMINISTRATIVE CHALLENGES AND PRACTICES

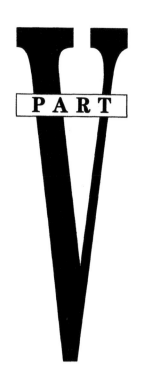

This part consists of five chapters, all of which focus on administrative problems or methods spanning the entire justice system. Chapter 13 examines the rights of criminal justice employees, and Chapter 14 reviews several unique challenges involving human resources (employee discipline, labor relations, and liability). Chapter 15 discusses financial administration, and Chapter 16 reviews the latest technological hardware and software now in use in criminal justice agencies. The book concludes with Chapter 17, which contemplates what the future holds for criminal justice administrators.

RIGHTS
OF CRIMINAL
JUSTICE
EMPLOYEES

Chapter

Uneasy lies the head that wears the crown.
—William Shakespeare

We all have enough strength to bear other people's troubles.
—Duc de la Rochefoucauld

Good orders make evil men good and bad orders make good men evil.
—James Harrington

Introduction

In the past few decades, the rights and obligations of criminal justice employees, like those of workers in the private sector, have changed dramatically. Changes in values, demographics, laws, and technology have blurred the line dividing the manager and those who are managed in enforcement, judicial, and correctional agencies. Today's criminal justice employees are far more sophisticated about employee rights.[1] For that reason, and because of attendant liability considerations (discussed in Chapter 14), contemporary criminal justice managers must be more aware of employees' legal rights.

After an overview of the relevant employment laws, we discuss recruitment and hiring issues, age discrimination, affirmative action, property rights, pay and benefits, and safe workplace matters. Then we examine constitutional rights of criminal justice employees as determined by the courts regarding freedom of speech and association, searches and seizures, self-incrimination, religious practices, sexual misconduct, residency requirements, moonlighting, misuse of firearms, alcohol and drugs in the workplace, sexual harassment, and the Americans With Disabilities Act.

An Overview

Law and litigation affecting criminal justice employees can arise out of federal and state constitutions, statutes, administrative regulations, and judicial interpretations and rulings. Even poorly written employee handbooks or long-standing agency customs or practices may create vested rights. The ripple effect begun by improper or illegal hiring, training, discipline, or discharge can lead not only to poor agency performance and morale, but also to substantial legal and economic liability. It should become apparent in the following overview—and court decisions that follow—that utilizing good common sense as well as a sense of fairness will help to prevent legal problems in the employment relationship.[2]

It should also be noted that the Civil Rights Act of 1991 may result in significant changes in public- and private-sector employment. It will take several years, however, for significant decisions to wind their way through the courts for a final determination of the intent and reach of the act by the Supreme Court. Therefore, in this section we focus on presenting the issues rather than on attempting to settle the law in these areas.

- *Fair Labor Standards Act* [at 29 U.S.C. 203 et seq.]: This act provides minimum pay and overtime provisions covering both public- and private-sector employees. Part 7(a) contains special provisions for firefighters and police officers. We discuss the FLSA more fully later.
- *Title VII of the Civil Rights Act of 1964 and Its Amendments* [42 U.S.C. 2000e]: This broadly based act established a federal policy requiring fair employment practices in both the public and private sectors. It prohibited unlawful employment discrimination in areas such as the hiring process; discharge; discipline; working conditions; and the provision of benefits based on race, color, religion, sex, and national origin. Its provisions extend to "hostile work environment" claims based on sexual, racial, or religious harassment.
- *Equal Pay Act* [29 U.S.C. 206(d)]: This act provides an alternative to Title VII for sex-based discrimination in wages and benefits, when people do similar work. It applies the simpler Fair Labor Standards Act procedures to claims. The Equal Pay Act does not mean "comparable worth"—an area that attempts to determine wages by requiring equal pay for employees whose work is of comparable worth even if the job content is totally different.
- *The Pregnancy Discrimination Act of 1978* [42 U.S.C. Section 2000e(k)]: This act is an amendment to the scope of sexual discrimination under Title

VII. It prohibits unequal treatment of women because of pregnancy or related medical conditions (e.g., nausea). The act requires that employers treat pregnant women like other temporarily disabled employees. The U.S. Supreme Court decided a major case in 1991 that limited employers' ability to exclude women who are pregnant or of childbearing age from certain jobs, under a fetal protection policy.[3]

- *Age Discrimination in Employment Act* [29 U.S.C. 623]: This act generally prohibits the unequal treatment of applicants or employees based on their age, if they are age 40 or over, in regard to hiring, firing, receiving benefits, and other conditions of employment.

- *Americans With Disabilities Act of 1990* (ADA) [42 U.S.C. 12112]: The goal of this legislation is to remove barriers that might prevent otherwise qualified individuals with disabilities from enjoying the same employment opportunities available to persons without disabilities. Although this act has only recently been implemented, the Rehabilitation Act of 1973 (see 29 U.S.C. 701) and its amendments have long prevented similar disability discrimination among public agencies receiving federal funds. The ADA is discussed more fully later.

- *42 U.S.C. 1983*: This major piece of legislation is the instrument by which an employee may sue an employer for civil rights violations based on the deprivation of constitutional rights. It is the most versatile civil rights action and is also the most often used against criminal justice agencies. Section 1983 is discussed more in Chapter 14.

In addition to the foregoing legislative enactments and state statutes that prohibit various acts of discrimination in employment, there are additional remedies that have tremendous impact on public-sector employees. Civil tort claims may be brought by public-sector employees against their employers for a wide variety of claims, ranging from assault and battery to defamation. Contractual claims may grow out of collective bargaining agreements. Bargained agreements may include procedures for assignments, seniority, due process protections (such as in the "Police Officers' Bill of Rights"), and grievances. Often the source of the right defines the remedy and the procedure to obtain that remedy. For example, statutes or legal precedents often provide for an aggrieved employer to receive back pay, compensatory damages, injunctive relief, or punitive damages.

The Employment Relationship

Recruiting and Hiring

Numerous selection methods for hiring police officers have been utilized over the years. Issues in recruitment, selection, and hiring also often involve internal promotions and assignments to special units, such as an "alert team" in a prison. Requirements concerning age (e.g., the FBI will hire no one older than 37 years of age), height, weight, vision, education, and possession of a valid driver's license have all been utilized over the years in criminal justice. In addition, tests are commonly used to determine intelligence, emotional suitability and stability (with psychological examinations and oral interviews), physical agility, and character (with polygraph examinations and extensive background checks).[4] More recently, drug tests have become frequently used as well (discussed more fully later).

The critical question for such tests is whether or not they validly test the types of skills needed for the job. A companion concern is whether or not the tests are used for discriminatory purposes or have unequal impact on protected groups. As a result of these considerations, a number of private companies have developed so-called "canned" examinations, providing valid, reliable test instruments for use by the public sector.

Disparate Treatment

It should be emphasized that there is nothing in the law which states that an employer must hire or retain incompetent personnel. In effect, the law does not prohibit discrimination. Thus, it is not unlawful to refuse to hire people who have a record of driving while intoxicated for positions that require driving. What *is* illegal is to treat people differently because of their age, gender, race, or other protected status: That is disparate treatment. It is also illegal to deny equal employment opportunities to such persons: That is disparate impact.[5] Federal equal opportunity law prohibits the use of selection procedures for hiring or promotion that have a discriminatory impact on the employment opportunities of women, Hispanics, blacks, or other protected classes.

An example of overt discriminatory hiring is reflected in a court decision in 1987 arising out of a situation in a sparsely populated county in Virginia. Four women sued because they were denied positions as courtroom security officer, deputy, or civil process server because of their gender. Sheriffs had refused to hire the women, justifying their decision by contending that being male was a *bona fide occupational qualifier* (BFOQ) for the position and because the positions were within the "personal staff" of the sheriff, thus exempting such positions from the coverage of Title VII. The Fourth Circuit overturned a lower court decision, finding that the sheriff did not establish that gender was a BFOQ for the positions and that the positions were not part of the sheriff's personal staff (the positions were not high level, policymaking, or advisory in nature). Thus, the refusal to hire the women violated Title VII.[6] There may, however, be a "business justification" for a hiring policy even though it has a disparate impact. For example, in one case an employer required airline attendants to cease flying immediately upon discovering they were pregnant. The court upheld the policy, on the ground that pregnancy could affect one's ability to perform routine duties in an aircraft, thereby jeopardizing the safety of passengers.[7]

A classic example of an apparently neutral employment requirement that actually had a disparate impact on gender, race, and ethnicity was the once prevalent height requirement used by most public safety agencies. Minimum height

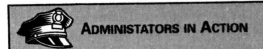

ADMINISTATORS IN ACTION

Plenty of Talk, Not Much Action: IACP Survey Says PDs Fall Short on Recruiting, Retaining Women

Police executives may extol the exceptional interpersonal skills that female officers bring to the job as crucial to community policing, but that fact has not prompted them either to recruit women in substantial numbers or to protect them from gender bias and sexual harassment once they are hired, according to a comprehensive analysis by the International Association of Chiefs of Police.

The study of women in policing . . . found that female officers are absent in nearly 20 percent of the 800 departments surveyed. Overall, women make up just 12 percent of the nearly 600,000 police officers in the country, a proportion that has not changed significantly in the past decade, despite an unprecedented level of hiring in law enforcement under the 1994 Federal grant program.

Among the other findings:

- Ninety-one percent of departments reported having no women in policy-making roles. Of the 17,000 police agencies in the country, just 123 have female chiefs.
- Gender bias was listed by 10 percent of the departments surveyed as among the reasons women do not get promoted. This finding was especially pertinent since all survey respondents were police chiefs or other top department executives.
- Women have won more than one-third of the lawsuits filed against police departments charged with gender bias and sexual harassment.

"I accept this report as a clear mandate," said the IACP's president, Chief Ronald S. Neubauer of St. Peters, Mo. "They want our help to improve and expand the roles of women in policing and they'll get it."

The Albuquerque Police Department, where women constitute nearly 13 percent of the sworn ranks, has been identified by police executives as a possible model for other agencies. In the past three years, female recruits there have increased from 8 percent of the academy class to 25 percent. . . .

Three years ago, the department found it was still having problems recruiting female candidates, despite its participation in job fairs and the competitive salary it offered. But significant changes were made that seem to have turned the situation around. For instance, a trainer was hired to help female candidates pass the physical conditioning tests. The department also switched to weapons that were better suited to women's smaller hands. It even found a body-armor manufacturer that was willing to construct bulletproof vests that accommodated bust sizes. . . .

Improvements in gender integration were also apparent after the department discovered that its in-house psychologists were disqualifying a disproportionate number of female candidates whose employment histories did not include law enforcement experience or other work traditionally listed by male applicants. . . .

While 25 percent of the respondents to the IACP survey said they still had concerns about the ability of female officers to handle physical conflicts, they indicated that they would still like to see more women in policing because of the superior skills they possess in other categories. In domestic violence situations, for example, women often have the ability to defuse potentially volatile incidents.

But even more difficult than recruiting women is keeping them on the force once they've joined. More than half of female officers—60 percent—who leave law enforcement do so between their second and fifth year on the job, according to the IACP survey. The organization has recommended implementing fairer screening procedures, instituting tougher sexual harassment policies and sustained recruiting drives designed to attract more women and keep them in policing....

While the reasons vary, family pressure is the most frequently cited factor in female officers leaving the job....

Besides making women aware of the kinds of personal obstacles they may face if they choose a career in policing . . . recruitment must be more aggressive.

The city of Portland, Ore., has broken with tradition in an effort to step up its recruitment drive, hiring an outside consultant to help fill 160 positions over the next few years....

The department has increased its recruiting efforts on college campuses and is also tapping into the military, another male-dominated environment, but one that has had success in recruiting, promoting and retaining women....

Source: "Plenty of Talk, Not Much Action," *LEN,* January 15/31, 1999. Reprinted with permission from *Law Enforcement News,* John Jay College of Criminal Justice (CUNY), 555 W. 57th St., New York, NY 10019.

requirements of "5 feet, 10 inches or above" were often advertised and effectively operated to exclude most women and many Asians and Hispanics from employment.[8] Such a requirement has gradually been superseded by a "height in proportion to weight" requirement. Nonetheless, other existing physical agility tests serve to discriminate against the lesser upper-body strength of women and smaller men. One is forced to wonder how many pushups a police officer must do on the job, or be able to do, to perform the duties adequately, or how many six-foot walls, ditches, and attics officers must negotiate. (Occasionally, the situation of pre-employment physical abilities testing becomes ludicrous. For example, the author once allowed a recruiter from a major western city to recruit students in an upper-level criminal justice course. The recruiter said the city's physical test included a six-foot wall. He quickly pointed out, however, that testing staff would boost all female applicants over it.)

Litigation is blossoming in this area. For example, in another western city, a woman challenged the police department's physical abilities test as discriminatory and not job-related, prompting the agency to hire a Canadian consultant who developed a job-related pre-employment agility test (currently used by the Royal Canadian Mounted Police and other agencies across Canada), based on data provided by officers and later computer analyzed for incorporation into the test. In other words, recruits are now tested on the physical demands placed on police officers in that specific community (no pushups or six-foot walls are included).[9]

Discrimination may also exist in criminal justice positions in promotions and job assignments. As an example of the former, a Nebraska female correctional center worker brought suit alleging that her employer violated her Title VII and equal protection rights by denying her a promotion. The woman was qualified for the position she sought promotion to (assistant center manager for programming), and she also alleged that the center treated women inequitably and unprofessionally, that assertiveness in women was viewed negatively, and that women were assigned clerical duties not assigned to men. The court found that she was indeed denied a promotion because of her sex, in violation of Title VII and the equal protection clause of the Fourteenth Amendment. She was awarded back pay ($7,500), front pay ($122 biweekly, until a comparable position became available), general damages, and court costs.[10]

With respect to litigation in the area of job assignments, four women matron/dispatchers who were refused assignments to correctional officer positions in Florida, even though they had been trained and certified as jail officers, were awarded damages. It was ruled that a state regulation prohibiting females in male areas of the jail was discriminatory without proof that gender was a BFOQ.[11] A particular assignment may validly exclude one sex, however. Thus, an assignment to work as a decoy prostitute could validly demonstrate a "business necessity" for women.[12]

How Old Is "Too Old" in Criminal Justice?

State and public agencies are not immune from age discrimination suits where arbitrary age restrictions have been found to violate the law. In Florida, a police lieutenant with the state highway patrol with 29 years of service was forced by statute to retire at age 62. The Equal Employment Opportunity Commission (EEOC) brought suit, alleging that Florida's statute violated the Age Discrimination in Employment Act (ADEA). The court held that age should not be a BFOQ, as youthfulness is not a guarantee of public safety. Rather, a physical fitness standard would better serve the purpose of ensuring the ability to perform the tasks of the position.[13]

Indeed, the U.S. Supreme Court rejected mandatory retirement plans for municipal firefighters and police officers.[14] Until 1985, the City of Baltimore had relied on a *federal* police officer and firefighter statute (5 U.S.C. 8335b), an exemption to the ADEA, to establish age limits for appointing and retiring its firefighters and police officers. The city also contended that age was a BFOQ for doing so. The U.S. Supreme Court held that while Congress had exempted federal employees from application of the ADEA, another agency cannot just "adopt" the same standards without showing an agency-specific need. Age is not a BFOQ for nonfederal firefighters (or, by extension, police officers). The Court also established a "reasonable federal standard" in its 1984 decision in *EEOC v. Wyoming*,[15] where it overturned a state statute providing for the mandatory retirement of state game wardens at age 55. It held that the ADEA did not require employers to retain unfit employees, only to make more individualized determinations about fitness.

Criminal Justice and Affirmative Action

Probably no single employment practice has caused as much controversy as affirmative action. The very words bring to mind visions of quotas and of unqualified people being given preferential hiring treatment.[16] Indeed, quotas have been at the center of legal, social, scientific, and political controversy for more than two decades.[17] The reality of affirmation is substantially different from the myth, however. As a general rule, affirmative action plans give preferred treatment only to affected groups when all other criteria (e.g., education, skills) are equal.[18]

The legal question (and to many persons, a moral one) that arises from affirmative action is: When does preferential hiring become *reverse* discrimination? The leading case here is *Bakke v. Regents of the University of California*,[19] 1978, where Allan Bakke was passed over for medical school admission at the University of California, Davis, partly because of the school's setting aside a number of its 100 medical school admissions slots annually for "disadvantaged" applicants. The Supreme Court held, among other things, that race could be used as a criterion in selection decisions, but it could not be the only criterion.

In a series of cases beginning in 1986,[20] the Supreme Court considered the development and application of affirmative action plans, establishing a two-step inquiry that must be satisfied before an affirmative action plan can be put in place. A plan must have a remedial purpose, to correct past inequities, and there must be a manifest imbalance or significant disparity to justify the plan. (The Court emphasized that such plans cannot completely foreclose employment opportunities to nonminority or male candidates, however.)

Generally, the validity of such plans is determined on a case-by-case basis. For example, the District of Columbia Circuit held in 1987 that an affirmative action plan covering the promotion of blacks to management positions in the police department was justified, as only 174 of the 807 positions (22 percent) above the rank of sergeant were filled by blacks, in a city where 60 percent of the labor market was black.[21] There, 21 past and present detectives of the Metropolitan Police Department who were passed over for promotion challenged the department's voluntary affirmative action plan designed to place "special emphasis" on the hiring and advancement of females and minorities in those employment areas where there existed an "obvious imbalance" in their numbers.[22]

The plaintiffs believed their failure to be promoted was attributable to illegal preferential treatment of blacks and women—reverse discrimination—violating their rights under Title VII and the due process clause of the Fifth Amendment. The court held that the nonminority and male employees of the department failed to prove that the plan was invalid. There was a considerable body of evidence of racial and sexual imbalance at the time the plan was adopted, and the plan did not unnecessarily trammel any legitimate interests of the nonminority or male employees since it did not call for displacement or layoff and did not totally exclude them from promotion opportunities.[23]

In summary, then, whenever a criminal justice employer wishes to implement and maintain job requirements, they must be job related. Furthermore, whenever a job requirement discriminates against a protected class, it should have a strong legitimate purpose and be the least restrictive alternative. Finally, attempts to remedy past hiring inequities by such means as affirmative action programs need substantial justification to avoid becoming reverse discrimination.[24]

Property Rights in Employment

The Fourteenth Amendment to the U.S. Constitution provides in part that

> No state shall make or enforce any law which shall abridge the privileges or immunities of citizens of the United States; nor shall any State deprive any person of life, liberty, or property without due process of law; nor deny to any person within its jurisdiction the equal protection of the law.

Furthermore, the Supreme Court has set forth four elements of a due process claim under Section 1983: A (1) person acting under color of state law (2) deprived an individual (3) of constitutionally protected property (4) without due process of law.[25]

A long line of court cases have established the legal view that public employees have a property interest in their employment. This flies in the face of the old view, that employees served "at will" or until their employers, for whatever reason, no longer needed their services. The Supreme Court has provided some general guidance on how the question of a constitutionally protected "property interest" is to be resolved:

> To have a property interest in a benefit, a person clearly must have more than an abstract need or desire for it. He must have more than a unilateral expectation of it. He must, instead, have a *legitimate claim of entitlement to it*. It is a purpose of the ancient institution of property to protect those claims *upon which people rely in their daily lives, reliance that must not be arbitrarily undermined* [emphasis added].[26]

The Court has also held that employees are entitled to both a pre-termination and post-termination notice,[27] and an opportunity to respond, and that state legislators are free to choose not to confer a property interest in public employment.

The development of a property interest in employment has an important ramification: It means that due process must be exercised by a public entity before terminating or interfering with an employee's property right. What has been established, however, is that a probationary employee has little or no property interest in employment. For example, in one case, the Ninth Circuit held that a probationary civil service employee ordinarily has no property interest and could be discharged without a hearing or even "good cause." But in that same decision, the court held that a woman who had passed her six-month probationary period, and who had then been promoted to a new position for which there was a probationary period, had the legitimate expectation of continued employment.[28]

On the other hand, an Indiana police captain was deemed to have a property interest in his position even though a state statute allowed the city manager to demote without notice. There, a captain of detectives, a Democrat, was demoted by a newly elected Republican mayor. The court determined that the dismissal of even a "policymaking" public employee for politically motivated reasons is forbidden unless the employee's position is "policymaking" in the sense that the position inherently encompasses tasks that render political affiliation an appropriate prerequisite for effective performance.[29]

Normally, however, policymaking employees (often called exempt appointments) possess an automatic exception to the contemporary property interest view. Generally these personnel, often elected agency heads, are free to hire and fire those employees who are involved in the making of important decisions and policy. Examples of this area include new sheriffs who appoint undersheriffs and wardens who appoint deputy wardens. These employees currently have no property interest in their positions and may be asked at any time to leave the agency or revert back to an earlier rank.

This property interest in employment is, of course, generally implied. An example of this implication may be found in a Utah case, where a property interest was found to exist based on an implied contract founded on an employment manual. Due process standards were therefore violated when the police department fired an officer without showing good cause or giving him a chance to respond to the charges against him.[30] In a Pennsylvania case, where a patrol officer was suspended for 30 days without pay for alleged violations of personnel policies and was not given an opportunity to file a written response to the charges, the court held that the officer's suspension resulted in a deprivation of property.[31]

Also, the property right in one's employment does not have to involve discipline or discharge to afford an employee protections. For example, the claim of a parole officer that he was harassed, humiliated, and interfered with in a deliberate attempt to remove him from his position established a civil rights action for deprivation of property.[32] This decision, against the Illinois Department of Corrections, resulted from allegations that the department engaged in "a deliberate and calculated effort to remove the plaintiff from his position by forcing him to resign, thereby making the protections of the personnel code unavailable to him." As a result, the plaintiff suffered anxiety, stress, and eventually went on disability status at substantially reduced pay.[33]

The key questions, then, once a property right is established, are: (1) What constitutes adequate grounds for interference with that right? and (2) what is adequate process to sustain that interference?[34]

Pay and Benefits

The Fair Labor Standards Act (FLSA), described earlier, has had a major impact on criminal justice agencies. One observer referred to the FLSA as the criminal justice administrator's "worst nightmare come true."[35] Initiated in 1938 to establish minimum wages and to require overtime compensation in the private sector, amendments were added in 1974 extending its coverage to state and local government employees and special work period provisions for police and fire employees. In 1976, however, the U.S. Supreme Court ruled that the extension of the act into the area of traditional local and state government functions was unconstitutional.[36] In 1985, the Court reversed itself, however, bringing local police employees under the coverage of the FLSA. In this major (and very costly) decision, *Garcia v. San Antonio Transit Authority*,[37] the Court held, 5 to 4, that Congress imposed the requirements of the FLSA on state and local governments.

Since criminal justice operations are open 24 hours per day, seven days per week, they often require overtime and participation in off-duty activities such as court appearances and training sessions. The FLSA comes into play when over-time salaries must be paid. It provides that an employer must generally pay employees time and a half for all hours worked over 40 per week. Overtime must also be paid to personnel for all work in excess of 43 hours in a seven-day cycle or 171 hours in a 28-day period. Public safety employees may accrue a maximum of 240 hours of "comp" time, which, if not utilized as leave, must be paid off upon separation from employment at the employee's final rate of pay or at the average pay over the last three years, whichever is greater.[38] Further, employers usually cannot require employees to take compensatory time in lieu of cash. The primary issue with the FLSA is the rigidity of application of what is compensable work. The act prohibits an agency from taking "volunteered time" from employees.

Today, an officer who works the night shift must receive pay for attending training or testifying in court during the day. Further, officers who are ordered to remain at home in anticipation of emergency actions must be compensated. Notably, however, the FLSA's overtime provisions do not apply to persons employed in a bona fide executive, administrative, or professional capacity. In criminal justice, the act has generally been held to apply to detectives and sergeants but not to those of the rank of lieutenant and above.

A companion issue with respect to criminal justice pay and benefits is that of equal pay for equal work. Disparate treatment in pay and benefits can be litigated under Title VII or statutes such as the Equal Pay Act or the equal protection clause. An Ohio case involved matron/dispatchers who performed essentially the same job as jailers but were paid less. This was found to be in violation of the Equal Pay Act and, since discriminatory intent was found, Title VII.[39]

In a related case, a court ruled that a Section 1983 claim by 133 southern Virginia state troopers could be filed where the plaintiffs did not receive a salary differential as did troopers in the northern part of the state. The plaintiffs argued that the salary differential was arbitrary, without any rational relationship to legitimate state interests, and as such was an unconstitutional denial of their rights to due process and equal protection under the Fourteenth Amendment. Conversely, the State of Virginia argued that based on the results of a statewide study and the need for higher salaries to attract qualified applicants in the north and prevent in-service troopers to leave for positions in private security, the differential was necessary.[40]

Other criminal justice employee benefits are addressed in Title VII, the ADEA, and the Pregnancy Discrimination Act (PDA). For example, it is illegal to provide less insurance coverage for a female employee who is more likely to use maternity leave, or one who is older and more likely to use more coverage. Also, an older person or a woman could not be forced to pay higher pension contributions because (it is believed) they would be paying in for a shorter period of time or would be expected to live longer. Regarding pregnancy, the PDA does not require an employer to discriminate in favor of a pregnancy-related condition. It demands only that the employer not treat pregnancy differently than any other temporary medical condition. For example, if an agency has a six-month leave policy for officers who are injured or ill from off-duty circumstances (on-duty circumstances would probably be covered by worker's compensation), that agency would have to provide six months' leave (if needed) for a pregnancy-related condition.[41]

Criminal Justice and a Safe Workplace

It is presently unclear what duties are owed by public employers to their employees in providing a safe workplace. Federal, state, and local governments are exempted from the coverage of the Occupational Safety and Health Act, in 29 U.S.C. 652. Nonetheless, criminal justice work is often dangerous, involving the use of force and often occurring in locations outside governmental control. Therefore, workplace safety issues in criminal justice are more likely to revolve around adequacy of training and supervision than physical plants.[42]

The Supreme Court has noted the unique nature and danger of public service employment. In one case, the Court specifically stated that an employee could not bring a Section 1983 civil rights action alleging a workplace so unsafe that it violated the Fourteenth Amendment's due process clause. In this matter, a sewer worker was asphyxiated while clearing a sewer line. The widow alleged that the city knew the sewer was dangerous and that the city had failed to train or supervise the decedent properly.[43]

Other federal courts, however, especially the federal circuits, have ruled inconsistently on the safe workplace issue. One federal circuit held that a constitutional violation could be brought if it was proven that the city actively engaged in conduct that was "deliberately indifferent" to the employee's constitutional rights.[44]

But the Fifth Circuit held differently in a Louisiana case, based on a failure to comply with a court order to have three officers on duty at all times in a prison disciplinary unit.[45] Here, a prison correctional officer in Baton Rouge was the only guard on a dangerous cellblock. While attempting to transfer a handcuffed inmate, the guard got into a scuffle with the inmate and was injured, although not severely. He claimed that he received insufficient medical attention and that, as a result, he became permanently disabled and that the Institute "consciously" and with wanton disregard for his personal safety conspired to have him work alone on the cellblock. He invoked 42 U.S.C. 1983 in his charges, claiming that the Institute acted in an indifferent, malicious, and reckless manner toward him, and that he suffered "class-based discrimination." The court held that the guard had no cause of action (no federal or constitutional grounds for litigation).

Liability for an employee's injury, disability, or death is a critical concern for criminal justice agencies. In particular, police and correctional officers often work under circumstances where violent actions occur. While state worker's compensation coverage, disability pensions, life insurance, and survivor pensions are designed to cover such tragedies, such coverage is typically limited and only intended to be remedial. On the other hand, civil tort actions in such cases can have a devastating impact on governmental budgets. Clearly, this is a difficult and costly problem to resolve. Certainly, it is also an area with moral dilemmas as well. Consider, for example, what should be done with a prison intelligence unit that knew of an impending disturbance but failed to alert its officers (who are subsequently injured). And might a police department, with knowledge that its new police vehicles have defective brakes, fail to take immediate action for fear that its officers will refuse to drive the vehicles, thus reducing the effective manpower?[46] These moral and legal dilemmas are not easily resolved in the criminal justice realm.

Constitutional Rights of Criminal Justice Employees

Freedom of Speech and Association

Most, if not all, criminal justice employees—especially police officers, judges, and probation or parole officers—see and know much about other citizens: They observe people in their most embarrassing and vulnerable moments. Therefore, because of their position in our society, information that criminal justice practitioners pass on by way of formal or informal conversation assumes a tremendous air of importance and gravity. In Chapter 2, we quoted a former midwestern police commissioner described the situation well, commenting: "I'm sorry to say that many police, without realizing they carry such authority, do pass on rumors. The average police officer does not stop to weigh what he or she says." That statement could probably be made about many other types of criminal justice employees as well. Given the delicate nature of their work, they must all guard against being indiscreet with the information they possess.

The 24-hour shift configuration found in criminal justice work serves to exacerbate the "grapevine." Even while on routine patrol, police officers witness many illegal or immoral acts—acts for which citizens would gladly pay the officer for his or her silence. Thus, police officers are often in the limelight with respect to speech-related activities. Criminal justice personnel can also become chronic complainers. Normally, passive grumbling is not unhealthy, but it can take a serious turn when a grapevine is running rampant, incomplete or inaccurate information is being disseminated, or when personnel go public to air their views.

Many criminal justice executives have attempted to harness what their employees say to the public. Executives develop and rely on policies and procedures designed to govern employee speech. As will be seen later, on occasion those restrictions will be challenged. A number of court decisions have attempted to define the limits of criminal justice employees' exercise of free speech.

Although the right of freedom of speech is one of the most fundamental of all rights of Americans, the Supreme Court has indicated that "the State has interests as an employer in regulating the speech of its employees that differ significantly from those it possesses in connection with regulation of the speech of the citizenry in general."[47] Thus, the state may impose restrictions on its employees that it would not be able to impose on the citizenry at large. These restrictions must be reasonable, however.[48]

There are two basic situations in which a police regulation may be found to be an unreasonable infringement on the free speech interests of officers.[49] The first is when the action is overly broad. A Chicago Police Department rule prohibiting "any activity, conversation, deliberation, or discussion which is derogatory to the Department" is a good example, as such a rule obviously prohibits all criticism of the agency by its officers, even in private conversation.[50] A similar situation arose in New Orleans, where the police department had a regulation that prohibited statements by a police officer that "unjustly criticize or ridicule, or express hatred or contempt toward, or . . . which may be detrimental to, or cast suspicion on the reputation of, or otherwise defame, any person."[51] The regulation was revised and later ruled constitutional.[52]

The second situation in which free speech limitations may be found to be unreasonable is in the way in which the governmental action is applied. Specifically, a police department may be unable to demonstrate that the statements by an officer being disciplined actually adversely affected the operation of the department. For example, a Baltimore regulation prohibiting public criticism of police department action was held to have been unconstitutionally applied to a police officer who was president of the police union and had stated in a television interview that the police commissioner was not leading the department effectively,[53] and that "the bottom is going to fall out of this city."[54]

A related area is that of political activity. As with free speech, government agencies may restrict the political behavior of their employees; the rationale being that without such restrictions, there is a danger that employees could be pressured by their superiors to support certain political candidates or engage in political activities, under threat of loss of employment or other adverse action. At the federal level, various types of political activity by federal employees are controlled by the Hatch Act: Its constitutionality has been upheld by the U.S. Supreme Court.[55] Many states have similar statutes, often referred to as "little Hatch Acts."

Although it may appear that Supreme Court decisions have laid to rest all controversy in this area, that has not been the case. Two recent cases show lower courts opting to limit the authority of the state to restrict political activities of their employees. In Pawtucket, Rhode Island, two firefighters ran for public office (mayor and city council member), despite a city charter provision prohibiting all political activity by employees (except voting and privately expressing their opinions). The Rhode Island Supreme Court issued an injunction against enforcing the charter provision, on the ground that the provision applied only to *partisan* political activities.[56] In a similar Boston case, however, the court upheld the police department rule on the basis that whether the partisan-nonpartisan distinction was crucial was a matter for legislative or administrative determination.[57]

In a Michigan case, a court declared unconstitutional, for being overly broad, two city charter provisions that prohibited contributions to or solicitations for any political purpose by city employees.[58] Clearly, although the Supreme Court seems to be supportive of governmental attempts to limit the political activities of their employees, lower courts seem just as intent to limit the Supreme Court decisions to the facts of those cases.

May a police officer be disciplined, even discharged, because of his or her political affiliations? The Supreme Court ruled on that question in a case arising out of the Sheriff's Department in Cook County, Illinois.[59] The newly elected sheriff, a Democrat, fired the chief deputy of the process division and a bailiff of the juvenile court, both of whom were nonmerit employees, because they were Republican. The Court ruled that it was a violation of the employees' First Amendment rights to discharge them from nonpolicymaking positions solely on the basis of their political party affiliation.[60]

Nonpolitical associations are also protected by the First Amendment. It is common, however, for police departments to prohibit officers from associating with known felons or others of bad reputation, on the ground that "such associations may expose an officer to irresistible temptations to yield in his obligation to impartially enforce the law, and . . . may give the appearance that the police are not themselves honest and impartial enforcers of the law."[61]

Rules against association, however, as with other First Amendment rights, must not be overly broad. A Detroit Police Department regulation prohibiting knowing and associating with known criminals or persons charged with crimes, except in connection with regular duties, was declared unconstitutional. The court held that it prohibited some associations that had no bearing on the officers' integrity or public confidence in the officer (e.g., an association with a fellow church member who had been arrested on one occasion years ago, and the befriending of a recently convicted person who wanted to become a productive citizen).[62]

Occasionally, a criminal justice employee will be disciplined for improper association even though it was not demonstrated that the association had a detrimental effect on the employee or the agency. For example, a Maryland court held that a fully qualified police officer who was a practicing nudist could not be fired simply on that basis.[63] On the other hand, a court upheld the discharge of an officer who had had sexual intercourse at a party with a woman he knew to be a nude model at a local "adult theater of known disrepute."[64]

Regulating Off-Duty Relationships

An individual has a fundamental liberty interest in being free to enter into certain intimate or private relationships. Freedom of association is not an absolute right, however. For example, a federal district court held that the dismissal of a married police officer for living with another man's wife was a violation of the officer's privacy and associational rights.[65] Other courts have found that off-duty sexual activity can affect job performance, however. Where a married city police officer allegedly had consensual, private, nonduty, heterosexual relations with single adult women other than his wife in violation of state law criminalizing adultery, the adultery was not a fundamental right. Thus, the officer's extramarital affairs were not protected and the intimate relationship affected the public's perception of the agency.[66]

In another case, a police officer became involved with a city dispatcher who was the wife of a sergeant in the same department. The adulterous officer became eligible for promotion and received a high score on the exam. The chief, confirming via an investigation that the officer had in fact been involved in an adulterous relationship with the dispatcher, refused on that basis to promote the officer, as he "would not command respect and trust" from rank-and-file officers and would adversely affect the efficiency and morale of the department. The Texas Supreme Court held that the officer's private, adulterous sexual conduct was not protected by state or federal law. The U.S. Supreme Court denied the appeal.[67]

Finally, the U.S. Court of Appeals for the Sixth Circuit held that a police department could conduct an investigation into the marital sexual relations of a police officer accused of sexual harassment.[68] In this case, there were allegations that the married officer had sexually harassed co-workers and had dated a gang member's mother. The department investigated the accusations, and the officer and his wife brought a Section 1983 action (discussed later), alleging that the investigation violated their constitutional rights to privacy and freedom of association. The court held that the agency's investigation was reasonable, and, further, that the police department would have been derelict in not investigating the matter.

In summary, police administrators have the constitutional authority to regulate employees' off-duty associational activities, including off-duty sexual conduct that involves a supervisory/subordinate relationship and associations that impact adversely the employees' ability to do their jobs or impair the effectiveness and efficiency of the organization.[69]

The First Amendment's reach also includes means of expression other than verbal utterances. For example, the Supreme Court upheld the constitutionality of a regulation of the Suffolk County, New York, Police Department that established several grooming standards (regarding hair, sideburn, and moustache length) for its male officers.[70] In this case, *Kelley v. Johnson,* the Court believed that to make officers readily recognizable to the public and to maintain the esprit de corps within the department, the agency justified the regulations and did not violate any right guaranteed by the Fourteenth Amendment.

Searches and Seizures

The Fourth Amendment to the U.S. Constitution protects "the right of the people to be secure in their persons, houses, papers, and effects, against unreasonable searches and seizures." In an important case in 1967, the Supreme Court held that the amendment also protected individuals' reasonable expectations of privacy, not just property interests.[71]

The Fourth Amendment usually applies to police officers when they are at home or off duty in the same manner as it applies to all citizens. Because of the nature of their work, however, police officers can be compelled to cooperate with investigations of their behavior where ordinary citizens would not. Examples would include equipment and lockers provided to the officers by the department. There, the officers have no expectation of privacy that affords or merits protection.[72] Lower courts have established limitations when searches of employees themselves are concerned, however. The rights of prison authorities to search their employees arose in a 1985 Iowa case, in which employees were forced to sign a consent form as a condition of hire. The court disagreed with such a broad policy, ruling that the consent form did not constitute a blanket waiver of all Fourth Amendment rights.[73]

Police officers may also be forced to appear in a lineup, a clear "seizure" of his or her person. Normally requiring probable cause, a federal appeals court upheld a police commissioner's ordering 62 officers to appear in a lineup during an investigation of police brutality, holding that "the governmental interest in the particular intrusion [should be weighed] against the offense to personal dignity and integrity." Again, the court cited the nature of the work, noting that police officers do "not have the full privacy and liberty from police officials that [they] would otherwise enjoy."[74]

Self-Incrimination

The Supreme Court has also addressed questions concerning the Fifth Amendment as it applies to police officers who are under investigation. In *Garrity v. New Jersey*,[75] a police officer was ordered by the attorney general to answer questions or be discharged. The officer testified that information obtained as a result of his answers was later used to convict him of criminal charges. The Supreme Court held that the information obtained from the officer could not be used against him at his criminal trial, because the Fifth Amendment forbids the use of coerced confessions.

In *Gardner v. Broderick*,[76] a police officer had refused to answer questions asked by a grand jury investigating police misconduct, as he believed his answers might tend to incriminate him. The officer was terminated from his position as a result. The Supreme Court ruled that the officer could not be fired for his refusal to waive his constitutional right to remain silent. The Court added that the grand jury could have forced the officer to answer or be terminated for his refusal, however, provided that the officer was informed that his answers would not be used against him later in a criminal case.

As a result of these decisions, it is proper to fire a police officer who refuses to answer questions that are related directly to the performance of his or her duties, provided that the officer has been informed that any answers may not be used later in a criminal proceeding. Although there is some diversity of opinion among lower courts on the question of whether or not an officer may be compelled to submit to a polygraph examination, the majority of courts that have considered the question have held that an officer can be required to take the examination.[77] (See *Gabrilowitz v. Newman,* 582 F.2d 100 [1st Cir. 1978].) Cases upholding the department's authority to order a polygraph examination for police officers include: *Eshelman v. Blubaum,* 560 P.2d 1283 (Ariz. 1977); *Dolan v. Kelly,* 348 N.Y.S.2d 478 (1973); *Richardson v. City of Pasadena,* 500 S.W.2d 175 (Tex. 1973); *Seattle Police Officer's Guild v. City of Seattle,* 494 P.2d 485 (Wash. 1972); *Roux v. New Orleans Police Department,* 223 So.2d 905 (La. 1969); and *Farmer v. City of Fort Lauderdale,* 427 So.2d 187 (Fla. 1983), *cert. den.,* 104 S.Ct. 74 (1984).

Religious Practices

Criminal justice work often requires that personnel are available and on duty 24 hours per day, seven days a week. Although it is not always convenient or pleasant, such shift configurations require that many criminal justice employees work weekends, nights, and holidays. It is generally assumed that one who takes such a position agrees to work such hours and abide by other such conditions (i.e., carrying a weapon, as in a policing position). It is usually the personnel with the least seniority on the job who must work the most undesirable shifts.

There are occasions when one's religious beliefs are in direct conflict with the requirements of the job, however. For example, there may be conflicts between one's work assignments and attendance at religious services or periods of religious observance. In these situations, the employee may be forced to choose between his or her job and religion. (The author is acquainted with a midwestern state trooper whose religion (adopted after his hiring date) posed another related cause of job-religion conflict—his religion banned the carrying or use of firearms. Here, the officer chose to give up his weapon and thus his job.) There have been a number of people who chose to litigate the work-religion conflict rather than cave in to agency work demands, however.

Title VII of the Civil Rights Act of 1964, discussed earlier, prohibits religious discrimination in employment. The act defines religion as including "all aspects of religious . . . practice, as well as belief, unless an employer . . . is unable to reasonably accommodate to an employee's . . . religious . . . practice without undue hardship on the conduct of the employer's business."[78] Thus, Title VII requires reasonable accommodation of religious beliefs, but not to the extent that the employee has complete freedom of religious expression.[79] For example, an Albuquerque firefighter was a Seventh Day Adventist and refused to work Friday or Saturday nights, as this would interrupt his honoring the Sabbath. He refused to trade shifts or take leave with (as vacation) or without pay, even though existing policy permitted his doing so, saying the *department* should have to make such arrangements for coverage or simply excuse him from his shifts. The department refused to do either, discharging him. The court ruled that the department's accommodations were reasonable and that no further accommodation could be made without causing an undue hardship to the department. His firing was upheld. The court emphasized, however, that future decisions would depend on the facts of the individual case.[80]

Recently, a court also held that the termination of a Mormon police officer for practicing plural marriage (polygamy), in violation of state law, was not a violation of his right to freely exercise his religious beliefs.[81]

Sexual Misconduct

To be blunt, there is ample opportunity for criminal justice employees to become engaged in affairs, incidents, trysts, dalliances, or other behavior that is clearly sexual in nature. History (and news accounts) have shown that wearing a uniform, occupying a high or extremely sensitive position, or being sworn to maintain an unblemished and unsullied lifestyle does not mean that all people will do so for all time. Some people are not bashful about their intentions: Several officers have told the author they aspired to police work because they assumed that wearing a uniform made them sexually irresistible.

Instances of sexual impropriety in criminal justice work can range from casual flirting while on the job to becoming romantically involved with a foreign agent whose principal aim is to learn delicate matters of national security. And there have been all manner of incidents between those extremes, including the discipline of female police officers who posed nude in magazines. Some major police departments have even been compelled to recruit officers for their sexual preference (i.e., homosexuality) in order to enhance their agency's diversity.

Clearly, this is a delicate area, one in which discipline can be and has been meted out as police managers attempt to maintain high standards of officer conduct. It has also resulted in litigation, as some officers believe that their right to privacy has been infringed.

Instances for which police officers may be disciplined for impropriety involving sexual conduct are generally cases involving adultery and homosexuality. Most court decisions of the 1960s and 1970s agreed that adultery, even when involving an off-duty police officer and in private, could result in disciplinary action,[82] as such behavior brought debilitating criticism upon the agency and undermined public confidence in the police. The views of the courts in this area seem to be moderating with the times, however. A case involving an Internal Revenue Service agent suggested that to uphold disciplinary action for adultery, the government would have to prove that the employing agency was actually discredited.[83] The U.S. Supreme Court more recently appeared to be divided on the issue of extramarital sexual activity in public employment, however. In 1984, the Sixth Circuit held that a Michigan police officer could not be fired simply because he was living with a woman to whom he was not married (a felony under Michigan law).[84]

The issue of homosexual activity as grounds for termination of public employees recently arose in an Oklahoma case, in which a state law permitted the discharge of schoolteachers for engaging in "public homosexual activity."[85] A lower court held the law to be unconstitutionally restrictive, and the Supreme

Court agreed.[86] Another federal court held that the firing of a bisexual guidance counselor did not deprive the counselor of her First or Fourteenth Amendment rights. The counselor's discussion of her sexual preferences with teachers was not protected by the First Amendment.[87]

Residency Requirements

In the 1970s and 1980s, interest in residency requirements for government employees heightened, especially in communities experiencing economic diffi-culties.[88] Many government agencies now specify that all or certain members in their employ must live within the geographical limits of their employing juris-diction. In other words, employees must reside within the county or city of employment. Such residency requirements have often been justified by employ-ing agencies, particularly in criminal justice, on the grounds that employees should become familiar with and be visible in the jurisdiction of employment, or that they should reside where they are paid by the taxpayers to work. Perhaps the strongest rationale given by employing agencies is that criminal justice employees must live within a certain proximity of their work in order to respond quickly in the event of an emergency.

Prior to 1976, there were numerous challenges to residency requirements, even after the Michigan Supreme Court ruling that Detroit's residency require-ment for police officers was not irrational.[89] Then, in 1976, when the U.S. Supreme Court held that Philadelphia's requiring firefighters to live in the city did not violate the Constitution, the challenges subsided. The cases now seem to revolve around the question of what constitutes residency. Generally, the police officer must demonstrate that he or she spends a substantial amount of time at the in-city residence.[90] Strong arguments have been made, however, that in areas where housing is unavailable or is exceptionally expensive, a residency require-ment is unreasonable.[91]

Moonlighting

The courts have traditionally supported criminal justice agencies placing limita-tions on the amount and kinds of outside work their employees can perform.[92] For example, police department restrictions on moonlighting range from a com-plete ban on outside employment to permission to engage in certain forms of work, such as investments, private security, teaching police science courses, and so on. The rationale for agency limitations is that "outside employment seriously interferes with keeping the [police and fire] departments fit and ready for action at all times."[93]

In a Louisiana case, however, firefighters successfully provided evidence that moonlighting had been a common practice for 16 years before the city banned it, no firefighters had ever needed sick leave as a result of injuries acquired while moonlighting, there had never been a problem locating off-duty firefighters to respond to an emergency, and moonlighting had never caused a level of fatigue that was serious enough to impair a firefighter's work. With this evidence, the court invalidated the city ordinance that had sought to prohibit moonlighting.[94]

Misuse of Firearms

Because of the need to defend themselves or others and be prepared for any exigency, police officers are empowered to use lethal force when justified. Although restricted in this use of force by the Supreme Court's 1985 decision in *Tennessee v. Garner*[95] (deeming the killing of unarmed, nondangerous suspects as unconstitutional), the possession of, and familiarity with, firearms remains a central aspect of the contemporary officer's role and function. Some officers take this responsibility to the extreme, however, becoming overly reliant on and consumed with their firepower.

Thus, police agencies typically attempt to restrain the use of firearms through written policies and frequent training of a "Shoot/Don't Shoot" nature. Still, a broad range of potential and actual problems remain with respect to the use and possible misuse of firearms, as the following will show.

As mentioned earlier, in the face of extremely serious potential and real problems and the omnipresent specter of liability suits, police agencies generally have policies regulating the use of handguns and other firearms by their officers, both on and off duty. The courts have held that such regulations need only be reasonable and that the burden rests with the disciplined police officer to show that the regulation was arbitrary and unreasonable.[96] The courts also grant considerable latitude to administrators in determining when their firearms regulations have been violated.[97] Police firearms regulations tend to address three basic issues: (1) requirements for the safeguarding of the weapon, (2) guidelines for carrying the weapon while off duty, and (3) limitations on when the weapon may be fired.[98]

Courts and juries are increasingly becoming more harsh in dealing with police officers who misuse their firearms. The current tendency is to "look behind" police shootings in order to determine if the officer acted negligently or the employing agency negligently trained and supervised the officer/employee. In one case, a federal appeals court approved a $500,000 judgment against the District of Columbia when a police officer who was not in adequate physical shape shot a man in the course of an arrest. The court noted that the officer had received no fitness training in four years and was physically incapable of subduing the victim. The court believed that had the officer been physically fit and adequately trained in disarmament techniques, a gun would not have been necessary. In his condition, however, the officer posed a "foreseeable risk of harm to others."[99]

Courts have awarded damages against police officers and/or their employers for other acts involving misuse of firearms, such as when an officer shot a person while intoxicated and off duty in a bar;[100] an officer accidentally killed an arrestee with a shotgun while handcuffing him;[101] an unstable officer shot his wife five times and then committed suicide with an off-duty weapon the department required him to carry;[102] and when an officer accidentally shot and killed an innocent bystander while pursuing another man at nighttime (the officer had had no instruction in shooting at a moving target, night shooting, or shooting in residential areas).[103]

Alcohol and Drugs in the Workplace

Alcoholism and drug abuse problems have "taken on a life of their own" in contemporary criminal justice. Employees must be increasingly wary of the tendency to succumb to these problems, while administrative personnel must be able to recognize (drug testing is discussed later) and attempt to counsel and treat these companion problems.

Indeed, in the aftermath of the early 1990s beating death of Malice Green by a group of Detroit police officers, it was reported that the Detroit Police Department had "high alcoholism rates and pervasive psychological problems connected with the stress of policing a city mired in poverty, drugs, and crime."[104] It was further revealed that while the Detroit Police Department had paid $850,000 to two drug-testing facilities, the department did not have the counseling programs many other cities offer their officers. A psychologist asserted that "There are many, many potential time bombs in that department."[105]

It is obvious, given the extant law of most jurisdictions and the nature of their work, that criminal justice employees must not be "walking time bombs," but must be able to perform their work with a "clear head," unbefuddled by alcohol or drugs.[106] Police departments and prisons will often specify in their manual of policy and procedures that no alcoholic beverages will be consumed within a specified period prior to reporting for duty.

Such regulations have been upheld uniformly as rational because of the hazards of the work. A Louisiana court went further, upholding a regulation that prohibited police officers from consuming alcoholic beverages on or off duty to the extent that it caused the officer's behavior to become obnoxious, disruptive, or disorderly.[107] Enforcing such regulations will occasionally result in criminal justice employees being ordered to submit to drug or alcohol tests. That issue—testing—is discussed next.

Drug Testing

The courts have had several occasions to review criminal justice agency policies requiring employees to submit to urinalysis to determine the presence of drugs or alcohol. For example, it was held as early as 1969 that a firefighter could be ordered to submit to a blood test when the agency had reasonable grounds to believe he was intoxicated, and that it was appropriate for the firefighter to be terminated from employment when he refused to submit to the test.[108]

In March 1989, the U.S. Supreme Court issued two major decisions on drug testing of public employees in the workplace. *Skinner v. Railway Labor Executives Association*[109] and *National Treasury Employees Union v. Von Raab*[110] dealt with drug testing plans for railroad and U.S. Customs workers, respectively.

Under the Fourth Amendment, government workers are protected from unreasonable search and seizure, including how drug testing can be conducted. The Fifth Amendment protects federal, state, and local workers from illegal governmental conduct.

In 1983, the Federal Railway Administration promulgated regulations that required railroads to conduct urine and blood tests on their workers following major train accidents or incidents. The regulations were challenged, one theory arguing that since railroads were privately owned, government action, including applying the Fourth Amendment, could not legally be applied. The Supreme Court disagreed in *Skinner,* ruling that railroads must be viewed as an instrument or agent of the government.

Three of the most controversial drug testing issues have been whether testing should be permitted when there is no indication of a drug problem in the workplace, whether or not the testing methods are reliable, and whether a positive test proves there was on-the-job impairment.[111] The *Von Raab* case addressed all three issues. There, the U.S. Customs Service implemented a drug-screening program that required urinalysis for employees desiring transfer or promotion to positions that were directly involved in drug interdiction, where carrying a firearm was necessary, or where classified material was handled. Only five of 3600 employees tested positive. The Treasury Employees Union argued that such an insignificant number of positives created a "suspicionless search" argument: In other words, drug testing was unnecessary and unwarranted. The Supreme Court disagreed, ruling that although only a few employees tested positive, drug use is such a serious problem that the program could continue.

Further, the Court found nothing wrong with the testing protocol. (An independent contractor was used: Succinctly, the worker, after discarding outer garments, produced a urine specimen while being observed by a member of the same sex; the sample was signed by the employee, labeled, placed in a plastic bag, sealed, and delivered to a lab for testing.) The Court found no "grave potential for arbitrary and oppressive interference with the privacy and personal security of the individuals" in this method.

Proving the connection between drug testing and on-the-job impairment has been an ongoing issue. Urinalysis, for example, cannot prove when a person testing positive actually used the drug. Therefore, tests may punish and stigmatize a person for extracurricular drug use that may have no effect on the worker's on-the-job performance.[112] In *Von Raab,* the Court indicated that this dilemma is still no impediment to testing. It stated that the Customs Service had a compelling interest in having a "physically fit" employee with "unimpeachable integrity and judgment."

Together, these two cases may set a new standard for determining the reasonableness of drug testing in the criminal justice workplace. They may legalize many testing programs that formerly would have been risky. *Von Raab* presented three compelling governmental interests that could be weighed against the employee's privacy expectations: the integrity of the workforce, public safety, and protection of sensitive information. *Skinner* stated that railroad workers also had diminished expectations of privacy because they are in an industry that is widely regulated to ensure safety.[113]

Sexual Harassment

Sexual harassment became a major workplace problem in the early 1980s and continued to be one through the 1990s. It can probably be predicted to continue as such into the next millennium. To borrow a term from early police authors A. C. Germann, Frank D. Day, and Robert R. Gallatti,[114] many "Neanderthals" in the business of police administration simply do not take the necessary steps to understand the breadth and weight of the matter. If these administrators do not learn the law of sexual harassment *in-house* (through training and education), they may eventually learn the law in the *courthouse*. Indeed, in the 1990s, there were a number of judgments in excess of a million dollars against police agencies for sexual harassment.[115]

Sexual harassment is unwelcomed sexual advances; requests for sexual favors; and other verbal, visual, or physical conduct that results in sexual submission being expressed or implied as a condition of employment. It may also involve interfering with an individual's work performance or creating an intimidating, hostile, or offensive working environment. The unique aspect of sexual harassment is that, generally speaking, the *victim* defines it in terms of what is offensive. Touching is not required.

Since 1986, workers have had the right to sue for sexual harassment. Until 1998, however, the courts remained silent about the precise meaning of the term. During that year the U.S. Supreme Court clarified the issue with four historic decisions. The Court made it easier for a person who has been harassed to win a lawsuit, but it gave employers a greater measure of protection from lawsuits if they have a strong program in place to prevent and discipline harassment.[116] Following is an overview of the impact of each of these four decisions.

The old rule was that to prove harassment, a worker had to show that because sexual advances were resisted, the worker was punished in terms of salary, assignments, or promotions. The new rule is that an action can count as harassment even if an employee is otherwise treated well. In this case,[117] a supervisor kept making passes at a subordinate but never punished her; in fact, she was promoted once. The Supreme Court ruled that harassment is defined by the ugly behavior of the manager, not by what subsequently happened to the worker.

Another old rule was that if a manager was not informed that an employee was harassing other workers, the supervisor was not normally responsible for the harasser's actions. The new rule is that the administrator can be held responsible for a harasser's actions—unless the company has a strong system of dealing with such problems. This decision[118] involved a Florida lifeguard who for five years endured men requesting sexual favors, groping her person, attempting to break into her shower area, and directing vulgar epithets toward her. The Supreme

Court held that it is not enough to have a policy against sexual harassment; it must be disseminated and enforced effectively.

Third, the Court made clear that a worker who is being harassed has a duty to report it—beyond merely telling a friend or co-worker. The victim has to inform the person responsible under the sexual harassment policy.[119]

Finally, the Court unanimously held that sexual harassment at work can be illegal and violate federal antidiscrimination law even when the offender and victim are the same sex. In this case,[120] the harassment claim by a male victim stemmed from four months of work on a Gulf of Mexico oil rig, where he was sexually assaulted, battered, touched, and threatened with rape by his direct male supervisor and a second male supervisor. He quit because he feared the harassment would escalate to rape. The ruling allows victims of homosexual harassment to sue in federal court.[121]

The Americans With Disabilities Act (ADA)

Much has been written and many monographs and primers are available concerning the powerful Americans With Disabilities Act (ADA), which was signed into law in 1990. Therefore, we will cover the law only briefly here; however, persons in an administrative capacity are strongly urged to become familiar with the literature in order to avoid conflicts with ADA mandates. The law is implicated in background checks; psychological and medical exams; and agility, drug, and polygraph tests.

While certain agencies in the federal government, such as the Federal Bureau of Investigation, are exempt from the ADA, state and local governments and their agencies are covered by the law. It is critical for administrators to develop written policies and procedures consistent with the ADA and have them in place before a problem arises.[122]

Under the law, criminal justice agencies may not discriminate against qualified individuals with disabilities. A person has a disability under the law if he or she has a mental or physical impairment that substantially limits a major life activity, such as walking, talking, breathing, sitting, standing, or learning.[123] Title I of the ADA makes it illegal to discriminate against persons with disabilities. This mandate applies to the agency's recruitment, hiring, and promotion practices. The ADA is not an affirmative action law, so persons with disabilities are not entitled to preference in hiring. The law will cause police agencies throughout the United States to adjust and perhaps even completely overhaul their recruitment and selection procedures, however.

Employers are to provide reasonable accommodation to disabled persons. A reasonable accommodation—80 percent of which have been found to cost less than $100 to effect[124]—can include modifying existing facilities to make them accessible, job restructuring, part-time or modified work schedules, acquiring or modifying equipment, and changing policies. Hiring decisions must be made based on whether an applicant meets the established prerequisites of the position (for example, experience or education) and is able to perform the essential functions of the job. Under the law, blanket exclusions of individuals with a particular disability (such as diabetes) are, in most cases, impermissible.

Corrections agencies—jails, prisons, and detention facilities—are also covered by the ADA: Programs offered to inmates must be accessible. For example, if a hearing-impaired inmate wished to attend Alcoholics Anonymous meetings, the corrections facility would need to make reasonable accommodation to allow him or her to do so, through such means as providing a sign language interpreter or writing notes as needed.[125]

Summary

After providing an overview of related legislation, this chapter examined several areas of criminal justice employee rights, including the issues of drug testing, privacy, hiring and firing, sexual harassment, and disabilities. Criminal justice employers' responsibilities were also discussed.

Working in the field of justice administration has never been easy. The issues facing today's practitioners have probably never been more difficult, however.

This chapter demonstrated quite clearly that these are litigious times for the justice system: One act of negligence can mean financial disaster for an individual or a supervisor.

Questions for Review

1. What are criminal justice employees' rights in the workplace according to federal statutes?

2. What is the general employee-employer relationship in criminal justice regarding recruitment and hiring and affirmative action?

3. It has been stated that criminal justice employees have a "property interest" in their jobs as well as a right to a safe workplace. What does this mean?

4. What constitutional rights are implicated for criminal justice employees on the job? (In your response, address whether rights are held regarding freedom of speech, searches and seizures, self-incrimination, and religion.)

5. In what regard is a greater standard of conduct expected of criminal justice employees? (In your response, include discussions of sexual behavior, residency, moonlighting, use of firearms, and alcohol/drug abuse.)

Notes

1. Robert H. Chaires and Susan A. Lentz, "Criminal Justice Employee Rights: An Overview," *American Journal of Criminal Justice* 13 (April 1995): 259.
2. Ibid.
3. See *United Autoworkers v. Johnson Controls*, 111 S.Ct. 1196 (1991).

4. See for example, Kenneth J. Peak, *Policing America: Methods, Issues, Challenges* (3d ed.) (Upper Saddle River, N.J.: Prentice Hall, 2000), pp. 72–79.

5. Chaires and Lentz, "Criminal Justice Employee Rights," p. 260.

6. *U.S. v. Gregory,* 818 F.2d 114 (4th Cir. 1987).

7. *Harris v. Pan American,* 649 F.2d 670 (9th Cir. 1988).

8. Chaires and Lentz, "Criminal Justice Employee Rights," p. 267.

9. See Ken Peak, Douglas W. Farenholtz, and George Coxey, "Physical Abilities Testing for Police Officers: A Flexible, Job-Related Approach," *The Police Chief* 59 (January 1992): 52–56.

10. *Shaw v. Nebraska Department of Corrections,* 666 F.Supp. 1330 (N.D. Neb. 1987).

11. *Garrett v. Oskaloosa County,* 734 F.2d 621 (11th Cir. 1984).

12. Chaires and Lentz, "Criminal Justice Employee Rights," p. 268.

13. *EEOC v. State Department of Highway Safety,* 660 F.Supp. 1104 (N.D. Fla. 1986).

14. *Johnson v. Mayor and City Council of Baltimore* (105 S.Ct. 2717 (1985).

15. 460 U.S. 226, 103 S.Ct. 1054, 75 L.Ed.2d 18 (1983).

16. Chaires and Lentz, "Criminal Justice Employee Rights," p. 269.

17. Paul J. Spiegelman, "Court-Ordered Hiring Quotas After *Stotts*: A Narrative on the Role of the Moralities of the Web and the Ladder in Employment Discrimination Doctrine," 20 *Harvard Civil Rights Review* 339 (1985).

18. Chaires and Lentz, "Criminal Justice Employee Rights," p. 269.

19. *Regents of the University of California v. Bakke,* 98 S.Ct. 2733, 438 U.S. 265, 57 L.Ed.2d (1978).

20. See *Wygant v. Jackson Board of Education,* 106 S.Ct. 1842 (1986).

21. Chaires and Lentz, "Criminal Justice Employee Rights," p. 269.

22. *Ledoux v. District of Columbia,* 820 F.2d 1293 (D.C. Cir. 1987), at 1294.

23. Ibid.

24. Chaires and Lentz, "Criminal Justice Employee Rights," p. 270.

25. See *Parratt v. Taylor,* 451 U.S. 527, 536–37, 101 S.Ct. 1908, 1913–14, 68 L.Ed.2d 420 (1981).

26. *Board of Regents v. Roth,* 408 U.S. at 577, 92 S.Ct. at 2709.

27. *Cleveland Board of Education v. Loudermill,* 470 U.S. 532, 541 (1985).

28. *McGraw v. City of Huntington Beach,* 882 F.2d 384 (9th Cir. 1989).

29. *Loborn v. Michael,* 913 F.2d 327 (7th Cir. 1990).

30. *Palmer v. City of Monticello,* 731 F.Supp. 1503 (D. Utah 1990).

31. *Young v. Municipality of Bethel Park,* 646 F. Supp. 539 (W.D.Penn. 1986).

32. *McAdoo v. Lane,* 564 F.Supp. 1215 (D.C. Ill. 1983).

33. Ibid., at 1217.

34. Chaires and Lentz, "Criminal Justice Employee Rights," p. 273.

35. Lynn Lund, "The 'Ten Commandments' of Risk Management for Jail Administrators," *Detention Reporter* 4 (June 1991):4.

36. *National League of Cities v. Usery,* 426 U.S. 833 (1976).

37. 105 S.Ct. 1005 (1985).

38. Charles R. Swanson, Leonard Territo, and Robert W. Taylor, *Police Administration: Structures, Processes, and Behavior* (4th ed.) (Upper Saddle River, N.J.: Prentice Hall, 1998), p. 278.

39. *Jurich v. Mahoning County,* 31 Fair Emp. Prac. 1275 (BNA) (N.D. Ohio 1983).

40. *Eldridge v. Boulchard,* 620 F. Supp. 678 (D.C. Va.).

41. Chaires and Lentz, "Criminal Justice Employee Rights," p. 280.

42. Ibid.

43. *Collins v. City of Harker Heights,* 112 S.Ct. 1061 (1992).

44. See *Ruge v. City of Bellevue,* 892 F.2d 738 (1989).

45. *Galloway v. State of Louisiana,* 817 F.2d 1154 (5th Cir. 1987).

46. Chaires and Lentz, "Criminal Justice Employee Rights," p. 280-283.

47. *Pickering v. Board of Education,* 391 U.S. 563 (1968), p. 568.

48. *Keyishian v. Board of Regents,* 385 U.S. 589 (1967).

49. Swanson, Territo, and Taylor, *Police Administration,* p. 394.

50. *Muller v. Conlisk,* 429 F.2d 901 (7th Cir. 1970).

51. *Flynn v. Giarusso,* 321 F.Supp. 1295 (E.D. La. 1971), at p. 1299.

52. *Magri v. Giarusso,* 379 F.Supp. 353 (E.D. La. 1974).

53. Swanson, Territo, and Taylor, *Police Administration,* p. 395.

54. *Brukiewa v. Police Commissioner of Baltimore,* 263 A.2d 210 (Md. 1970).

55. *United Public Workers v. Mitchell,* 330 U.S. 75 (1947); *U.S. Civil Service Commission v. National Association of Letter Carriers,* 413 U.S. 548 (1973).

56. *Magill v. Lynch,* 400 F.Supp. 84 (R.I. 1975).

57. *Boston Police Patrolmen's Association, Inc. v. City of Boston,* 326 N.E.2d 314 (Mass. 1975).

58. *Phillips v. City of Flint,* 225 N.W.2d 780 (Mich. 1975).

59. *Elrod v. Burns,* 427 U.S. 347 (1976); see also, *Ramey v. Harber,* 431 F.Supp 657 (W.D. Va. 1977); and *Branti v. Finkel,* 445 U.S. 507 (1980).

60. *Connick v. Myers,* 461 U.S. 138 (1983); *Jones v. Dodson,* 727 F.2d 1329 (4th Cir. 1984).

61. Swanson, Territo, and Taylor, *Police Administration,* p. 397.

62. *Sponick v. City of Detroit Police Department,* 211 N.W.2d 674 (Mich 1973), p. 681; but see *Wilson v. Taylor,* 733 F.2d 1539 (11th Cir. 1984).

63. *Bruns v. Pomerleau,* 319 F.Supp. 58 (D. Md. 1970); see also *McMullen v. Carson,* 754 F.2d 936 (11th Cir. 1985), where it was held that a Ku Klux Klansman could not be fired from his position as a records clerk in the sheriff's department simply because he was a Klansman. The Court did uphold the dismissal because his active KKK participation threatened to negatively affect the agency's ability to perform its public duties.

64. *Civil Service Commission of Tucson v. Livingston,* 525 P.2d 949 (Ariz. 1974).

65. *Briggs v. North Muskegon Police Department,* 563 F. Supp. 585 (W. D. Mich. 1983), aff'd 746 F. 2d 1475 (6th Cir. 1984).

66. *Oliverson v. West Valley City,* 875 F. Supp. 1465 (D. Utah 1995).

67. *Henery v. City of Sherman,* 116 S.Ct.1098 (1997).

68. See *Hughes v. City of North Olmsted,* 93 F. 3d 238 (6th Cir., 1996).

69. Michael J. Bulzomi, "Constitutional Authority to Regulate Off-Duty Relationships: Recent Court Decisions." *FBI Law Enforcement Bulletin* (April 1999), pp. 26-32.

70. *425 U.S. 238* (1976).

71. *Katz v. United States,* 389 U.S. 347 (1967).

72. See *People v. Tidwell,* 266 N.E.2d 787 (Ill. 1971).

73. *McDonell v. Hunter,* 611 F.Supp. 1122 (S.D. Iowa, 1985), affd. as mod., 809 F.2d 1302 (8th Cir., 1987).

74. *Biehunik v. Felicetta,* 441 F.2d 228 (1971), p. 230.

75. 385 U.S. 483 (1967).

76. 392 U.S. 273 (1968).

77. See *Gabrilowitz v. Newman,* 582 F.2d 100 (1st Cir. 1978). Cases upholding the department's authority to order a polygraph examination for police officers include: *Eshelman v. Blubaum,* 560 P.2d 1283 (Ariz. 1977); *Dolan v. Kelly,* 348 N.Y.S.2d 478 (1973);

Richardson v. City of Pasadena, 500 S.W.2d 175 (Tex. 1973); *Seattle Police Officer's Guild v. City of Seattle,* 494 P.2d 485 (Wash. 1972); *Roux v. New Orleans Police Department,* 223 So.2d 905 (La. 1969); and *Farmer v. City of Fort Lauderdale,* 427 So.2d 187 (Fla. 1983), *cert. den.,* 104 S.Ct. 74 (1984).

78. 42 U.S.C. 200e(j).

79. *United States v. City of Albuquerque,* 12 EPD 11, 244 (10th Cir. 1976); see also *Trans World Airlines v. Hardison,* 97 S.Ct. 2264 (1977).

80. *United States v. Albuquerque,* 545 F.2d 110 (10th Cir. 1977).

81. *Potter v. Murray City,* 760 F.2d 1065 (10th Cir. 1985).

82. *Faust v. Police Civil Service Commission,* 347 A.2d 765 (Pa. 1975); *Stewart v. Leary,* 293 N.Y.S.2d 573 (1968); *Brewer v. City of Ashland,* 86 S.W.2d 669 (Ky. 1935); *Fabio v. Civil Service Commission of Philadelphia,* 373 A.2d 751 (Pa. 1977); *Major v. Hampton,* 413 F.Supp. 66 (1976).

83. *Major v. Hampton,* 413 F.Supp. 66 (1976).

84. *Briggs v. City of North Muskegon Police Department,* 563 F.Supp. 585 (6th Cir. 1984).

85. *National Gay Task Force v. Bd. of Ed. of Oklahoma City,* 729 F.2d 1270 (10th Cir. 1984).

86. *Board of Education v. National Gay Task Force,* 53 U.S.L.W. 4408, No. 83-2030 (1985).

87. *Rowland v. Mad River Sch. Dist.,* 730 F.2d 444 (6th Cir. 1984).

88. David J. Schall, "An Investigation Into the Relationship Between Municipal Police Residency Requirements, Professionalism, Economic Conditions, and Equal Employment Goals" (Unpublished dissertation, The University of Wisconsin-Milwaukee, 1996).

89. *Detroit Police Officers Association v. City of Detroit,* 190 N.W.2d 97 (1971), appeal denied, 405 U.S. 950 (1972).

90. *Miller v. Police Board of City of Chicago,* 349 N.E.2d 544 (Ill. 1976); *Williamson v. Village of Baskin,* 339 So.2d 474 (La. 1976); *Nigro v. Board of Trustees of Alden,* 395 N.Y.S.2d 544 (1977).

91. *State, County, and Municipal Employees Local 339 v. City of Highland Park,* 108 N.W.2d 898 (1961).

92. See, for example, *Cox v. McNamara,* 493 P.2d 54 (Ore. 1972); *Brenckle v. Township of Shaler,* 281 A.2d 920 (Pa. 1972); *Hopwood v. City of Paducah,* 424 S.W.2d 134 (Ky. 1968); *Flood v. Kennedy,* 239 N.Y.S.2d 665 (1963).

93. Richard N. Williams, *Legal Aspects of Discipline by Police Administrators,* Traffic Institute Publication 2705 (Evanston, Ill.: Northwestern University, 1975), p. 4.

94. *City of Crowley Firemen v. City of Crowley,* 264 So.2d 368 (La. 1972).

95. 471 U.S. 1, 105 S.Ct. 1694, 85 L.Ed.2d 1 (1985).

96. See *Lally v. Department of Police,* 306 So.2d 65 (La. 1974).

97. See, for example, *Peters v. Civil Service Commission of Tucson,* 539 P.2d 698 (Ariz. 1977); *Abeyta v. Town of Taos,* 499 F.2d 323 (10th Cir. 1974); *Baumgartner v. Leary,* 311 N.Y.S.2d 468 (1970); *City of Vancouver v. Jarvis,* 455 P.2d 591 (Wash. 1969).

98. Swanson, Territo, and Taylor, *Police Administration* (3d ed.), p. 433.

99. *Parker v. District of Columbia,* 850 F.2d 708 (1988), at 713, 714.

100. *Marusa v. District of Columbia,* 484 F.2d 828 (1973).

101. *Sager v. City of Woodlawn Park,* 543 F.Supp. 282 (D. Colo. 1982).

102. *Bonsignore v. City of New York,* 521 F.Supp. 394 (1981).

103. *Popow v. City of Margate,* 476 F.Supp. 1237 (1979).

104. Eloise Salholz and Frank Washington, "Detroit's Brutal Lessons," *Newsweek* (November 30, 1992):45.

105. Ibid.

106. See *Krolick v. Lowery,* 302 N.Y.S.2d 109 (1969), p. 115; *Hester v. Milledgeville,* 598 F.Supp. 1456, 1457 (M.D.Ga. 1984).

107. *McCracken v. Department of Police,* 337 So.2d 595 (La. 1976).

108. *Krolick v. Lowery,* op. cit.

109. 489 U.S. 602 (1989).

110. 489 U.S. 656 (1989).

111. Robert J. Aalberts and Harvey W. Rubin, "Court's Rulings on Testing Crack Down on Drug Abuse," *Risk Management* 38 (March 1991):36–41.

112. Ibid., p. 38.

113. Ibid., p. 40.

114. A. C. Germann, Frank D. Day, and Robert R. Gallatti, *Introduction to Law Enforcement and Criminal Justice* (Springfield, Ill.: Charles C. Thomas, 1976), p. 224.

115. See, for example, Ted Gest and Amy Saltzman, "Harassment: Men on Trial," *U.S. News and World Report* (October 21, 1991):39–40, concerning a $3.1 million award to two former Long Beach, California, female police officers.

116. Marianne Lavelle, "The New Sexual Harassment," *U.S. News and World Report* (July 6, 1998):30–31.

117. *Burlington Industries v. Ellerth,* 118 S.Ct. 2257, 141 L.Ed.2d 633 (1998).

118. *Faragher v. City of Boca Raton,* 118 S.Ct. 2275, 141 L.Ed.2d 662 (1998).

119. *Gebser v. Lago Vista Independent School District,* 118 S.Ct. 1989, 141 L.Ed. 2d 277 (1998).

120. *Oncale v. Sundowner Offshor Services, Inc.,* 523 U.S. 75, 118 S.Ct. 998 (1998).

121. "Court: Harassment Covers Same-Sex Torment." *Associated Press,* March 5, 1998.

122. Paula N. Rubin and Susan W. McCampbell, "The Americans With Disabilities Act and Criminal Justice: Providing Inmate Services," U.S. Department of Justice, National Institute of Justice Research in Action (July 1994), p. 2.

123. Paula N. Rubin, "The Americans With Disabilities Act and Criminal Justice: An Overview," U.S. Department of Justice, National Institute of Justice Research in Action (September 1993), p. 1.

124. U.S. Department of Justice, National Institute of Justice Journal, Research in Action, "Health and Criminal Justice: Strengthening the Relationship" (November 1994), p. 40.

125. Ibid., p. 41.

SPECIAL CHALLENGES: DISCIPLINE, LABOR RELATIONS, AND LIABILITY

Chapter

14

> *Responsibility is the price of greatness.*
>
> —Winston Churchill
>
> *Discipline must be maintained.*
>
> —Charles Dickens
>
> *No man is fit to command another that cannot command himself.*
> —William Penn

Introduction

Several previous chapters have either implied or overtly stated that while the major asset of any criminal justice agency is its personnel, so are personnel the major *challenge.* The ability of such agencies to accomplish their mission ultimately depends on the critically important element of human resources. The expanded labor movement and body of law concerning employees, the increased inclination of citizens to file suits against criminal justice personnel as well as criminal justice employees to sue their administrators—and the growing willingness of courts and juries to award large cash settlements in such cases—all point to the need for great effort and care to be directed to human resource management. Accordingly, this chapter examines three aspects of human resources/personnel administration that loom large in the administrator's coffer of challenges: *discipline, labor relations,* and *liability.*

Because of their power and authority, criminal justice employees—especially the police—are under greater public scrutiny than are most government employees. Therefore, this segment examines administrators' responsibilities to *discipline* their employees. Employee misconduct includes acts that harm the public, including corruption, harassment, brutality, and civil rights violations. Violations of agency policy, such as substance abuse and insubordination, or even minor violations of dress and tardiness, can also foster disciplinary action.

In the past 50 years, no force has had a greater impact on the administration of criminal justice agencies than *labor relations.* Labor unions represent a major force that must be reckoned with by criminal justice administrators. This chapter discusses how the unionization movement developed, as well as practices surrounding collective bargaining by labor and management groups.

Finally, the problem of *liability* is a matter that is closely related to employee discipline, because both can involve misbehavior and harm to others. This section discusses laws and legal concepts (such as negligence and torts) that serve to make criminal justice practitioners legally accountable, both civilly and criminally, for acts of misconduct and negligence.

Disciplinary Policies and Practices

Maintaining the Public's Trust

The public's trust and respect are precious commodities that can be quickly lost with improper behavior by criminal justice employees and with the improper handling of allegations of misconduct. Serving communities professionally and with integrity should be the goal of every agency and its employees in order to ensure that trust and respect are maintained. The public expects that criminal justice agencies will make every effort to identify and correct problems and respond to citizens' complaints in an equally judicious, consistent, fair, and equitable manner.

In this vein, the most important responsibilities held by criminal justice agencies are implementing sound disciplinary policies and practices and responding to employee misconduct or performance problems at an early stage. Employee misconduct and violations of departmental policy are the two principal areas where discipline is involved.[1]

Due Process Requirements

There are well-established minimum due process requirements for discharging public employees, who must

1. Be afforded a public hearing

2. Be present during the presentation of evidence against them and have an opportunity to cross-examine their superiors
3. Have an opportunity to present their own witnesses and other evidence concerning their side of the controversy
4. Be permitted to be represented by counsel
5. Have an impartial referee or hearing officer presiding
6. Have an eventual decision based on the weight of the evidence introduced during the hearing

Such protections apply to any disciplinary action that can significantly affect a criminal justice employee's reputation and/or future chances for special assignment or promotion. A disciplinary hearing that might result, say, in only a reprimand or short suspension may involve fewer procedural protections than one that could result in more severe sanctions.[2]

When a particular disciplinary action does not include termination or suspension, however, it may still be subject to due process considerations. An example is a Chicago case involving a police officer who was transferred from the neighborhood relations division to less desirable working conditions in the patrol division, with no loss in pay or benefits. The court found that the officer's First Amendment free speech rights were violated, as his de facto demotion was in retaliation for his political activities (inviting political opponents of the mayor to a civic function and in retaliation for a speech given there, criticizing the police department), and that he was thus entitled to civil damages. The court stated that "Certainly a demotion can be as detrimental to an employee as denial of a promotion."[3]

On the other hand, no due process protection may be required when the property interest (one's job) was fraudulently obtained. Thus, a deputy sheriff was not deprived of due process when he was summarily discharged for lying on his application about a juvenile felony charge, which would have barred him from employment in the first place.[4]

In sum, agency rules and policies should state what due process procedures will be utilized under certain disciplinary situations. The key questions regarding due process are whether or not the employer followed established agency guidelines, and, if not, whether the employer has a compelling reason not to follow them.

At times the administrator will determine that an employee must be disciplined or terminated. What are adequate grounds for discipline or discharge? Grounds for discipline or discharge can vary widely from agency to agency. Certainly, the agency's formal policies and procedures should specify and control what constitutes proper and improper behavior. Normally, agency practice and custom enter into these decisions. Sometimes administrators will "wink" at the formal policies and procedures, overlooking or only occasionally enforcing certain provisions contained in them. But the failure of the agency to enforce a rule or policy for a long period of time may provide "implied consent" by the employer that such behavior, although officially prohibited, is permissible. (In other words, do not allow an employee to violate the agency's tardiness policy for three months, and then decide one day to summarily fire him or her.) Attempts to fire employees for behavior that has been ignored or enforced only infrequently at best may give rise to a defense by the employee.

Hiring minority employees to meet state hiring goals and later attempting to terminate them as quickly and often as possible also violates employees' Title VII rights. Such a situation occurred in an Indiana case: It was alleged that black prison correctional officers were hired to fulfill an affirmative action program, only to be fired for disciplinary reasons for which white officers were not discharged.[5]

Generally, violations of an employee's rights occur in discharge and discipline when such actions are taken (1) in violation of a protected interest, (2) in retaliation for the exercise of protected conduct, (3) with a discriminatory motive, and (4) with malice.[6]

A Tradition of Problems in Policing

Throughout its history, policing has experienced problems involving misconduct and corruption. A number of events during the 1990s demonstrated that problems still exist and require the attention of police officials. Incidents such as the beating of Rodney King by officers in the presence of supervisors, the controversy surrounding the testimony of former Los Angeles police detective Mark Fuhrman during the O. J. Simpson trial, and major corruption scandals in several big-city police departments have led many people to believe that police misbehavior is at a higher level today than ever before.

Without question, police administrators need to pay close attention to signs of police misconduct and respond quickly and to enact policies to guide supervisors in the handling of disciplinary issues. Such policies should ensure that there is certainty, swiftness, fairness, and consistency of punishment when it is warranted.

Automated Records Systems

There have been many advances in the technological aspects of police discipline. For example, in 1991, the Fresno, California, Police Department automated its disciplinary process in an effort to establish a better system for tracking and sanctioning personnel for various offenses.[7] The principal objectives of this automated system were to assist the chief of police in administering the department in a more equitable fashion and to improve the department's ability to defend its personnel actions. Within minutes, the database provides supervisors with five years of history about standards of discipline for any category of violation. A variety of reports can be produced, showing patterns of incidents for the supervisor.

Determining the Level and Nature of Action

When an investigation against an employee is sustained, the sanctions and level of discipline must be decided. Management must be very careful when recommending and imposing discipline because of its impact on the overall morale of the agency's employees. If the recommended discipline is viewed by employees as too lenient, it may send the wrong message that the misconduct was insignificant. On the other hand, discipline that is viewed as too harsh may have a demoralizing effect on the officer(s) involved and other agency employees and result in allegations that the leadership is unfair. This alone can have a significant impact on the *esprit de corps* or morale of the agency.

In addition to having a disciplinary process that is viewed by employees as fair and consistent, it is also important that discipline is progressive and that more serious sanctions are invoked when repeated violations occur. For example, a third substantiated incident of rude behavior may result in a recommendation for a one-day suspension without pay, whereas a first offense may be resolved through documented oral counseling or a letter of reprimand. The following is a list of disciplinary actions commonly used by agencies in order of their severity:

Counseling: This is usually a conversation between the supervisor and employee about a specific aspect of the employee's performance or conduct. It is warranted when an employee has committed a relatively minor infraction or the nature of the offense is such that oral counseling is all that is necessary. For example, an officer who is usually punctual but arrives at briefing ten minutes late two days in a row may require nothing more than a reminder and warning to correct the problem.

Documented Oral Counseling: This is usually the first step in a progressive disciplinary process and is intended to address relatively minor infractions. It is provided when there are no previous reprimands or more severe disciplinary action of the same or similar nature.

Letters of Reprimand: These are formal written notices regarding significant misconduct, more serious performance violations, or repeated offenses. It is usually the second step in the disciplinary process and is intended to provide the employee and agency with a written record of the violation of behavior. It identifies what specific corrective action must be taken to avoid subsequent, more serious disciplinary action.

Suspension: This is a severe disciplinary action that results in an employee's being relieved of duty, often without pay. It is usually administered when an employee commits a serious violation of established rules or after a written reprimand has been given and no change in behavior or performance has resulted.

Demotion: In this situation, an employee is placed in a position of lower responsibility and pay. It is normally used when an otherwise good employee is unable to meet the standards required for the higher position, or when the employee has committed a serious act requiring that he or she be removed from a management or supervisory position.

Termination: This is the most severe disciplinary action that can be taken. It usually occurs when previous serious discipline has been imposed and inadequate or no improvement in behavior or performance has occurred. It may also be used when an employee commits an offense so serious that continued employment would be inappropriate.

Transfer: Many agencies use the disciplinary transfer to deal with problem officers. Officers can be transferred to a different location or assignment, and this action is often seen as an effective disciplinary tool.

Positive and Negative Discipline

When policies and procedures are violated, positive or negative disciplinary measures may be imposed. Although different in their philosophy, both positive and negative discipline seek to accomplish the same purpose: to correct negative behavior and promote the employee's voluntary compliance with departmental policies and procedures.

A positive discipline program (also known as positive counseling) attempts to change employee behavior without invoking punishment. An example of positive discipline or counseling is when an employee ("John") has been nonproductive and nonpunctual, causing interpersonal problems with co-workers, and/or is having other problems on the job. Until this point, John has been in control of the situation, on the offensive one might say, while the supervisor ("Jane") and his co-workers have been on the defensive. John is jeopardizing the morale and productivity of the workplace, but the preferred approach is to try to salvage him because of the agency's investment in time, funds, and training.

Finally, Jane calls John into her office. She might begin with a compliment (if indeed she can find one), and then she proceeds to outline all of his workplace shortcomings: This demonstrates to John that Jane is aware of his various problems. Jane explains to him why it is important that he improve (for reasons related to productivity, morale, and so on), and the benefits he might realize from improvement (promotions, pay raises, bonuses, or whatever). She also outlines what can happen if he does *not* show adequate improvement (demotion, transfer, termination, etc.). Now having gained John's attention, she gives him a certain time period (say, 30, 60, or 90 days) in which to improve. She emphasizes, however, that she will be constantly monitoring his progress. She might even ask John to sign a counseling statement form that sets forth all of the agreed upon terms, indicating that John has received counseling and understands the situation.

Note that Jane is now on the offensive, thereby putting John on the defensive and in control of his destiny. If he fails to perform, Jane would probably give him a warning, and if the situation continues, he will be terminated. If he sues or files a grievance, Jane has proof that every effort was made to allow John to salvage his position. This is a very effective means of giving subordinates incentive to improve their behavior, while at the same time being less vulnerable to successful lawsuits.

Negative discipline is punishment. It is generally used when positive efforts fail or the violation is so serious that punishment is required. Negative discipline may vary in its severity and involve simple documented oral counseling, a letter of reprimand, a demotion, days off without pay, or even termination.

Dealing with Complaints

Complaint Origin

A personnel complaint is an allegation of misconduct or illegal behavior against an employee by anyone inside or outside the organization. Internal complaints, those made from persons within the organization, may involve supervisors observing officer misconduct, officers complaining about supervisors, supervisors complaining about supervisors, civilian personnel complaining about officers, and so on. External complaints originate from sources outside the organization and usually involve the public.

Complaints may be received from primary, secondary, and anonymous sources. A primary source is one that is received directly from the victim. A secondary source is one that is made by another party on behalf of the victim, such as from an attorney, school counselor, parent of a juvenile, and so on. An anonymous source complaint derives from an unknown source and may be delivered to the organization via a telephone call or unsigned letter.

Every complaint, regardless of the source, must be accepted and investigated in accordance with established policies and procedures. Anonymous complaints are the most difficult to investigate because there is no opportunity to obtain further information or question the complainant about the allegation. Such complaints can have a negative impact on employee morale, as officers may view such complaints as unjust and frivolous.

Types and Causes

Complaints may be handled informally or formally, depending on the seriousness of the allegation and preference of the complainant. A formal complaint occurs when a written and signed and/or tape-recorded statement of the allegation is made and the complainant requests to be informed of the investigation's disposition. Figure 14.1 provides an example of a complaint form used to initiate a personnel investigation.

An informal complaint is an allegation of minor misconduct made for informational purposes that can usually be resolved without the need for more formal processes. When a citizen calls the watch commander to complain about the rude behavior of a dispatcher, but does not wish to make a formal complaint, the supervisor may simply discuss the incident with the dispatcher and resolve it through informal counseling as long as more serious problems are not discovered and the dispatcher does not have a history of similar complaints.

Few complaints involve acts of physical violence, excessive force, or corruption. Wagner and Decker[8] found that the majority of complaints against officers fall under the general categories of verbal abuse, discourtesy, harassment, improper attitude, and ethnic slurs.[9] Another study[10] found that 42 percent of complaints involved the "verbal conduct" of officers, and verbal conduct also accounted for 47 percent of all sustained complaints. The majority of repeated offenses also fell into this category. It is clear that the officers' verbal demeanor generates a significant number of complaints. Finally, minority citizens and those

```
*********************************************************************************
                                                          Control Number_____
Date & Time Reported    Location of Interview    Interview
_____        _____        _____Verbal  _____Written  _____Taped

Type of Complaint:      ____Force  ____Procedural  ____Conduct
                        ____Other (Specify)

Source of Complaint:    ____In Person  ____Mail  ____Telephone
                        ____Other (Specify)

Complaint originally    ____Supervisor    ____On Duty Watch Commander    ____Chief
Received by:            ____IAU           ____Other (Specify)

Notifications made:     _____Division Commander     _____Chief of Police
Received by:            _____On-Call Command Personnel
                        _____Watch Commander        _____Other (Specify)

Copy of formal personnel complaint given to complainant?    ____Yes ____No

*********************************************************************************
Complainant's name:                        Address:
_____          _____
                                           _____Zip_____
Residence Phone:                           Business Phone:
_____          _____
DOB:                 Race:                 Sex:              Occupation:
_____           _____            _____        _____

*********************************************************************************
Location of Occurrence:                    Date & Time of Occurrence:
_____          _____
Member(s) Involved:                        Member(s) Involved:
(1) _____          (2)_____
(3) _____          (4)_____
Witness(es) Involved:                      Witness(es) Involved:
(1) _____          (2)_____
(3) _____          (4)_____
*********************************************************************************
(1) _____  Complainant wishes to make a formal statement and has requested an investigation into the
           matter with a report back to him/her on the findings and actions.
(2) _____  Complainant wishes to advise the Police Department of a problem, understand that some type of
           action will be taken, but does not request a report back to him/her on the findings and actions.
*********************************************************************************
                              CITIZEN ADVISEMENTS
(1)   If you have not yet provided the department with a signed written statement or a tape-recorded
      statement, one may be required in order to pursue the investigation of this matter.
(2)   The complainant(s) and/or witness(es) may be required to take a polygraph examination in order to
      determine the credibility concerning the allegations made.
(3)   Should the allegations prove to be false, the complainant(s) and/or witness(es) may be liable for
      criminal and/or civil prosecution.
                              _____   _____
                                Signature of Complainant              Date & Time

_____
Signature of Member Receiving Complaint
```

Figure 14.1

Police department formal personnel complaint report.

with less power and fewer resources are more likely to file complaints of misconduct and to allege more serious forms of misconduct than persons with greater power and more resources.[11]

Receipt and Referral

Administrators should have in place a process for receiving complaints that is clearly delineated by departmental policy and procedures. Generally, a complaint will be made at a criminal justice facility and referred to a senior officer in charge to determine its seriousness and need for immediate intervention.

In most cases, the senior officer receiving the investigation will determine the nature of the complaint and the employees involved, then the matter will be referred to the employee's supervisor to conduct an initial investigation. The supervisor would complete the investigation, recommend any discipline, and send the matter to the internal affairs unit and the agency head for finalizing the disciplinary process. This method of review ensures that consistent and fair standards of discipline are applied.

The Investigative Process

Perez[12] indicated that all but a small percentage of the 17,000 police agencies in the United States have a process for investigating police misconduct. Generally, the employee's supervisor will conduct a preliminary inquiry into the complaint, commonly known as fact-finding. Once it is determined that further investigation is necessary, the supervisor may conduct additional questioning of employees and witnesses, obtain written statements from those persons immediately involved in the incident, and gather any evidence that may be necessary for the case, such as photographs. Care must be exercised that the accused employee's rights are not violated. The initial investigation would be sent to an appropriate division commander and forwarded to an IAU for review.

Making a Determination and Disposition

Once an investigation is completed, the supervisor or IAU officer must make a determination as to the culpability of the accused employee and report his or her findings to the administrator. Each allegation should receive a separate adjudication. Following are the categories of dispositions that are commonly used:

- *Unfounded:* The alleged act(s) did not occur.
- *Exonerated:* The act occurred, but it is lawful, proper, justified, and/or in accordance with departmental policies, procedures, rules, and regulations.
- *Not sustained:* There is insufficient evidence to prove or disprove the allegations made.
- *Misconduct not based on the complaint:* Sustainable misconduct was determined, but it is not a part of the original complaint. For example, a supervisor investigating an allegation of excessive force against an officer may find the force used was within departmental policy, but that the officer made an unlawful arrest.

- *Closed:* An investigation may be halted if the complainant fails to cooperate or if it is determined that the action does not fall within the administrative jurisdiction of the police agency.
- *Sustained:* The act did occur and it was a violation of departmental rules and procedures. Sustained allegations include misconduct that falls within the broad outlines of the original allegation(s).

Once a determination of culpability has been made, the complainant should be notified of the department's findings. Details of the investigation or recommended punishment will not be included in the correspondence. As shown in Figure 14.2, the complainant will normally receive only information concerning the outcome of the complaint, including a short explanation of the finding along with an invitation to call the agency if further information is needed.

Appeals and Grievances

Criminal justice personnel may complain and institute a grievance about contractual or other matters about which they are upset or concerned. Following is an overview of the grievance process.

Grievance procedures establish a fair and expeditious process for handling employee disputes that are not disciplinary in nature. Grievance procedures involve mostly collective bargaining issues, conditions of employment, or other terms and conditions of employment or employer-employee relations. More specifically, grievances may cover a broad range of issues, including salaries, overtime, leave, hours of work, allowances, retirement, opportunity for advancement, performance evaluations, workplace conditions, tenure, disciplinary actions, supervisory methods, and administrative practices. Grievance procedures are often established as a part of the collective bargaining process.

The preferred method for settling officers' grievances is through informal discussion, in which the employee explains his or her grievance to the immediate supervisor. Most complaints can be handled through informal discussion. Complaints that cannot be dealt with informally are usually handled through a more formal grievance process, as described in the following. A formal grievance begins with the employee submitting the grievance in writing to the immediate supervisor, as illustrated in Figure 14.3.

The process for formally handling grievances will vary among agencies and may involve as many as three to six different levels of action. Following is an example of how a grievance may proceed:

Level I: A grievance is submitted in writing to a supervisor. The supervisor will be given five days to respond to the employee's grievance. If the employee is dissatisfied, the grievance moves to the next level.

Level II: At this level, the grievance proceeds to the chief executive, who will be given a specified time (usually five days) to render a decision.

Level III: If the employee is not satisfied with the chief's decision, the grievance may proceed to the city or county manager, as is appropriate. The manager will usually meet with the employee and/or representatives from

Police Department
3300 Main Street
Downtown Plaza
Anywhere, USA. 99999
June 20, 2000

Mr. John Doe
2200 Main Avenue
Anywhere, USA.

Re: Internal affairs #000666-98
    Case Closure

Dear Mr. Doe:

Our investigation into your allegations against Officer Smith has been completed. It has been determined that your complaint is SUSTAINED and the appropriate disciplinary action has been taken.

Our department appreciates your bringing this matter to our attention. It is our position that when a problem is identified, it should be corrected as soon as possible. It is our goal to be responsive to the concerns expressed by citizens so as to provide more efficient and effective services.

Your information regarding this incident was helpful and of value in our efforts to attain that goal. Should you have any further questions about this matter, please contact Sergeant Jane Alexander, Internal Affairs, at 555-9999.

Sincerely,

I.M. Boss
Lieutenant
Internal Affairs Unit

Figure 14.2

Citizens' notification of discipline letter.

the bargaining association and attempt to resolve the matter. An additional 5 to 10 days is usually allowed for the manager to render a decision.

Level IV. If the grievance is still not resolved, either party may request that the matter be submitted to arbitration. Arbitration involves a neutral, outside person, often selected from a list of arbitrators from the Federal Mediation and Conciliation Service. An arbitrator will conduct a hearing, listening to both parties and usually concluding with a decision within 20 to 30 days. The decision of the arbitrator can be final and binding. This does not prohibit the employee from appealing the decision to a state court, however.

Failure to act on grievances quickly may result in serious morale problems within an agency.

Police Department
Formal Grievance Form

Grievance #_____

Employee Name: _____ Work Phone: _____
Department Assigned: _____
Date of Occurrence: _____
Location of Occurrence: _____

Name of: 1. Department Head:_____

2. Division Head:_____

3. Immediate Supervisor:_____

Statement of Grievance: _____
_____
_____
_____
_____

Witnesses:_____
_____
_____

What article(s) and or section(s) of the labor agreement of rules and regulations do
you believe have been violated? _____
_____
_____
_____

What remedy are you requesting?_____
_____
_____

_____   _____
Employee signature   Signature of labor representative

Figure 14.3

Employee grievance form.

Appealing Disciplinary Measures

Appeals processes—frequently outlined in civil service rules and regulations, labor agreements, and departmental policies and procedures—normally follow an officer's chain of command. For example, if an officer disagrees with a supervisor's recommendation for discipline, the first step of an appeal may involve a hearing before the division commander, usually of the rank of captain or deputy chief. The accused employee may be allowed labor representation or an attorney to assist in asking questions of the investigating supervisor, clarifying issues, and presenting new or mitigating evidence. The division commander would have five days to review the recommendation and respond in writing to the employee.

If the employee is still not satisfied, an appeal hearing before the chief executive is granted. This is usually the final step in appeals within the agency. The chief or sheriff communicates a decision to the employee in writing within five to 10 days. Depending on labor agreements and civil service rules and regulations, some agencies extend their appeals of discipline beyond the department. For example, employees may bring their issue before the civil service commission or city or county manager for a final review. Employees may also have the right to an independent arbitrator's review of discipline. The arbitrator's decision is usually binding.

The Early Warning System

Early identification of and intervention with employee misconduct or performance problems are vital to preventing ongoing and repeated incidents. An early warning system (EWS) allows police agencies to identify and intervene in employee problems at an early stage and before they become crises. These problems can eventually lead to misconduct or violations of departmental rules and regulations. EWS helps agencies to respond proactively to patterns of behavior that may lead to more serious problems. EWS views these patterns as precursors to more serious problems and may require that the officer's supervisor intervene with early prevention methods such as counseling or training.

In some cases, repeated incidents of violence may require that officers attend anger training or verbal judo to learn how to deescalate confrontational situations. Some preventive measure(s), such as counseling, remedial training, or temporary change of assignments, may also be used. A referral to an employee assistance program (EAP) to deal with more serious psychological or substance abuse problems may also be necessary.

Labor Relations

As indicated in the chapter introduction, labor relations—a term that includes the related concepts of unionization and collective bargaining—poses a major challenge to contemporary criminal justice administrators. This section discusses the unionization movement and current means and elements of collective bargaining that are employed by labor and management.

Unionization in Policing, Courts, and Corrections

Probably as a result of their difficult working conditions, as well as traditionally low salary and benefits packages, police and corrections groups have elected to band together within their disciplines to fight for improvement. It is probably also accurate to say that a major force in the development—and spread—of unionization of these two groups was the authoritarian, unilateral, and "do as I say, not as I do" management style that characterized many police and prison administrators of the past.

The Movement Begins: Policing

The first campaign to organize the police started shortly after World War I, when the American Federation of Labor (AFL) reversed a long-standing policy and issued charters to police unions in Boston, Washington, D.C., and about 30 other cities. August Vollmer and many other police chiefs promptly condemned this move, insisting that police officers had no more right to unionize than did military personnel. Many police officers were suffering from the rapid inflationary rate following the outbreak of the war, however, and believed that if their chiefs could not get them long-overdue pay raises, then perhaps unions could. Capitalizing on their sentiments, the fledgling unions signed about 60 percent of all officers in Washington, 75 percent in Boston, and similar proportions in other cities.[13]

The unions' success was short-lived, however. The Boston police commissioner refused to recognize the union, forbade officers to join it, and filed charges against several union officials. Shortly thereafter, on September 9, 1919, the Boston police initiated the famous three-day strike, causing major riots and a furor against the police all across the nation. Nine rioters were killed and 23 were seriously injured. During the strike, Massachusetts Governor Calvin Coolidge uttered his now-famous quote: "There is no right to strike against the public safety by anybody, anywhere, anytime."

During World War II, however, the effort was reignited. Unions issued charters to a few dozen locals all over the country and sent in organizers to help enlist the rank and file. Most police chiefs continued speaking out against unionization, but their subordinates were moved by the thousands to join, sensing the advantage in having unions press for higher wages and benefits.[14] But in a series of rulings, the courts upheld the right of police authorities to ban police unions.

The unions were survived in the early 1950s by many benevolent and fraternal organizations of police. Some were patrolmen's benevolent associations (PBAs), like those formed in New York, Chicago, and Washington, while others were fraternal orders of police (FOPs). During the late 1950s and early 1960s, a new group of rank-and-file association leaders came into power. They were more vocal in articulating their demands. Soon a majority of the rank and file vocally supported higher salaries and pensions, free legal aid, low-cost insurance, and other services. For the first time, rank-and-file organizations were legally able to insist that their administrators sit down at the bargaining table.[15]

Since the mid-1980s, the unionization of the police has continued to flourish. Today, the majority of all American police officers hold membership in unions.[16] The International Conference of Police Associations (ICPA) is the largest organization, with more than 100 local and state units representing more than 200,000 officers.[17] George Cole attributed this dramatic rise in union membership to several factors: job dissatisfaction, the belief that the public is hostile to police needs, and an influx of younger officers who hold less traditional views on relations between officers and the department hierarchy.[18]

With some justification, administrators fear that their control over the organization will be concomitantly reduced as union power increases and as traditional matters within their scope, such as promotion and transfer of personnel, become enmeshed in union negotiations. And, of course, there is always the specter of police job actions, including work slowdown, work stoppage (strikes or "blue flu"), work speedup, or votes of confidence. The threat of a police work stoppage is real, as a number of major strikes by police occurred during the mid-1970s. Several guidelines exist to prevent police strikes: Police and city administrators should work toward developing an atmosphere of trust and cooperation; an effective internal communications system must be developed in police agencies and between the police administrator, the city administration, and the union leaders; training must be provided to police management, city administration, and union leaders in the area of negotiation; and "eleventh-hour" bargaining and negotiation must be eliminated.[19]

Corrections Follows the Precedent

It is sometimes assumed that the movement to unionize correctional officers was a response to the increased power given inmates. While both occurred at about the same time, unionization grew out of a general impetus toward public employee organization (certainly fostered by the strong drive by the police in the 1950s and 1960s). Correctional officers (COs) were probably the last group of public workers to organize. Currently, more than half of the states have correctional unions. Like the police, most CO unions are prohibited by law from striking; only seven states legally recognize the right to strike.[20]

The results of correctional unionization are mixed. On the positive side, unions have helped improve working conditions. And as opposed to the conventional union concern of salary and benefits, COs are more concerned with secure and safe working conditions—keeping inmates in their place and neutralizing gains made in the individual rights of inmates. COs see unions as a way to return to the paternalistic model of authority, displacing the competitive model. In most institutions, CO unions seek to limit the power of inmates at every turn. But inmates also want safe and secure living conditions; thus inmates often privately support the demands of the unions.[21] CO unions also exert pressure on administration concerning prison policy. For example, the union in Walla Walla, Washington, put pressure on the warden to close the workshop run by the Bikers Club, because they were making weapons there as well as repairing their motorcycles.[22]

The biggest problem facing CO unions is their potential lawlessness. Since most such unions cannot legally strike, they are limited in their collective power against administrators. Most of the union's bargaining weapons are illegal. Unlawful strikes occur with some frequency, however. The most infamous strike action, on a plain with the Boston police strike of 1919, was in New York State in 1979, when 7,000 correctional workers simultaneously struck the state's 33 prisons.

The National Guard was called in to staff the prisons at a cost of $1 million per day. A court found the union in violation of the law, heavily fined the union for failing to return to work, and jailed union leaders for contempt of court.[23] The strike ended 17 days after it began. The guards gained very few concessions, and salary gains did not offset fines imposed on the strikers.[24]

Illegal strikes by COs have not been effective for several reasons. First, these workers are unlikely to obtain public sympathy. Furthermore, a strike does not actually close down the industry: The presence of the National Guard greatly strengthens the bargaining position of the state. COs will also lose face if overseers are appointed by the court in the aftermath of a strike to prevent CO retaliation against nonsupportive inmates. Further tension is created when prison administrators impose disciplinary actions against COs who struck.[25] And because not all COs belong to the union, there will probably be conflict between co-workers prior to and following the strike.

As corrections unions push to become a major instrument of institutional policy, the warden's troubles will increase. Wardens today must worry about both CO and inmate lawlessness. Many resign or seek early retirement as a result.[26]

Unionization in the Courts

The movement to exercise the right to bargain collectively, especially when compared with law enforcement and corrections, has been very rare in the courts, occurring on a random, localized basis. (There are unified court systems in which court personnel are organized statewide, however, as in Hawaii.) Many states adhere generally to model legislation on public employee relation commissions, which provides mediation and fact-finding services and makes determinations of unfair labor practices. On occasion, these commissions are asked to make decisions that greatly affect the management authority of the judiciary over its personnel.

When a collective bargaining unit exists in a court system, however, the process has all of the basic elements found in any such circumstance: (1) recognition (the employing court recognizes that henceforth employees will be represented by their chosen agent); (2) negotiation (there are established methods for arriving at a collective bargaining agreement, breaking deadlocks, ratifying contracts, etc); and (3) contract administration (the day-to-day management of a court is accomplished within the framework of the labor contract).[27]

Collective Bargaining: Types, Relationships, Negotiations, and Job Actions

Three Models

Each state is free to decide whether and which public-sector employees will have collective bargaining rights and under what terms. Therefore, there is considerable variation in collective bargaining arrangements across the nation. In states with comprehensive public-sector bargaining laws, the administration of the statute is the responsibility of a state agency, such as a Public Employee Relations

Board (PERB) or Public Employee Relations Commission (PERC). Three basic models are used in the states: *binding arbitration, meet and confer,* and *bargaining not required.*[28] Table 14.1 shows the use of these models in the various states.

The binding arbitration model is used in 25 states. There, public employees are given the right to bargain with their employers. If the bargaining reaches an impasse, the matter is submitted to a neutral arbitrator who decides what the terms and conditions of the new collective bargaining agreement will be.[29]

Only three states use the meet-and-confer model, which grants very few rights to public employees. As with the binding arbitration model, criminal justice employees in meet-and-confer states have the right to organize and to select their own bargaining representatives.[30] When an impasse is reached in meet-and-confer states, however, employees are at a distinct disadvantage. Their only legal choices are to accept the employer's best offer, try to influence the offer through political tactics (such as appeals for public support), or take some permissible job action.[31] The 22 states that follow the bargaining not required model either do not statutorily require or do not allow collective bargaining by public employees.[32] In the majority of these states, laws permitting public employees to engage in collective bargaining have not been passed.

States with collective bargaining must also address the issue of whether an individual employee must be a member of a union that represents his or her class of employees in a particular organization. In a "closed shop," employees must be dues-paying members or they will be terminated by the employer. "Open" shops, conversely, allow employees to choose whether or not to join, even though the union has an obligation to represent them.

The Bargaining Relationship

If collective bargaining is legally established, the process of establishing a bargaining relationship is straightforward, although opportunities still exist for disputes. In those states and agencies seeking to organize for collective bargaining, the process is as follows. First, a union will begin an organizational drive seeking to get a majority of the class(es) of employees it hopes to represent to sign authorization cards. At this point, agency administrators may attempt to convince employees that they are better off without the union. Questions may also arise, such as whether or not certain employees (for example, police or prison lieutenants) are part of management and therefore ineligible for union representation.

Once a majority ("50 percent plus one" of the eligible employees) has signed cards, the union notifies the criminal justice agency. If management believes that the union has obtained a majority legitimately, it will recognize the union as the bargaining agent of the employees it has sought to represent. Once recognized by the employer, the union will petition the PERB or other body responsible for administering the legislation for certification.

TABLE 14.1 State Collective Bargaining Laws Governing Law Enforcement Officers

STATE	BINDING ARBITRATION MODEL	MEET-AND-CONFER MODEL	BARGAINING-NOT-REQUIRED MODEL	STATE	BINDING ARBITRATION MODEL	MEET-AND-CONFER MODEL	BARGAINING-NOT-REQUIRED MODEL
Alabama	X			Montana	X		
Alaska	X			Nebraska			X
Arizona			X	Nevada	X		
Arkansas			X	New Hampshire	X		
California		X		New Jersey	X		
Colorado			X	New Mexico		X	
Connecticut	X			New York	X		
Delaware	X			North Carolina			X
District of Columbia	X			North Dakota			X
Florida		X		Ohio	X		
Georgia			X	Oklahoma	X		
Hawaii	X			Oregon	X		
Idaho			X	Pennsylvania	X		
Illinois	X			Rhode Island	X		
Indiana			X	South Carolina			X
Iowa	X			South Dakota			X
Kansas	X			Tennessee			X
Kentucky			X	Texas			X
Louisiana			X	Utah			X
Maine	X			Vermont	X		
Maryland			X	Virginia			X
Massachusetts	X			Washington	X		
Michigan	X			West Virginia			X
Minnesota	X			Wisconsin	X		
Mississippi			X	Wyoming			X
Missouri			X				

Source: Will Aitchison, *The Rights of Police Officers,* 3rd ed. (Portland, Oregon: Labor Relations Information System, 1996), p. 10. Used with permission.

Negotiations

Figure 14.4 depicts a typical configuration of the union and management bargaining teams. Positions shown in dashed boxes typically serve in a support role and may or may not actually partake in the bargaining. Management's labor relations manager (lead negotiator) is often an attorney assigned to the human resources department, reporting to the city manager or assistant city manager and representing the city in grievances and arbitration matters. The union's chief negotiator will normally not be a member of the bargaining unit; rather, he or she will be a specialist brought in to represent the union's position and provide greater experience, expertise, objectivity, and autonomy. The union's chief negotiator may be accompanied by some people who have conducted surveys on wages and benefits, trends in the consumer price index, and so on.[33]

Management's negotiating team chief negotiator may be the director of labor relations or human resource director for the unit of government involved or a professional labor relations specialist. The agency's chief executive should not appear at the table personally. It is extremely delicate for the chief to represent management one day and then return to work among the employees the next. Rather, management should be represented by a key member of the command staff having the executive's confidence.

The issues, and the way in which they are presented, will impact how the negotiations will proceed. The purpose of bargaining is to produce a bilateral

Figure 14.4

Union and management collective bargaining teams
(*Source:* Jerry Hoover, Chief of Police, Reno, Nevada.)

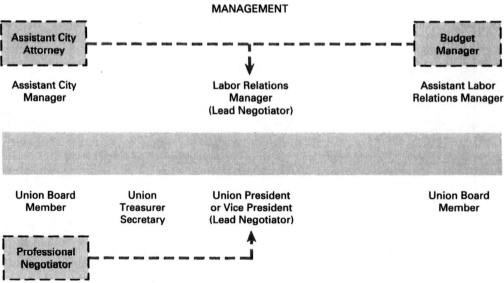

written agreement that both parties will bind themselves to during the lifetime of the agreement. Management normally prefers a narrow scope of negotiations because it means less shared power. Conversely, the union will opt for the widest possible scope. The number of negotiating sessions may run from one to several dozen, lasting from 30 minutes to 10 or more hours, depending on how close or far apart the union and management are when they begin to meet face to face.

In the initial session, the chief negotiator for each party will make an opening statement. Management's representative will often go first, touching on general themes such as the need for patience and the obligation to bargain in good faith. The union's negotiator will generally follow, outlining what the union seeks to achieve under the terms of the new contract. Ground rules for the bargaining may then be reviewed, modified, or developed. The attention then shifts to the terms of the contract that the union is proposing. Both sides need to understand what it is they are attempting to commit each other to. Ultimately, unless a total impasse is reached, agreement will be obtained on the terms of a new contract. The union's membership will vote on the contract as a whole. If approved by the membership, the contract then goes before the necessary government officials and bodies for approval.[34]

In the Event of an Impasse . . .

Even parties bargaining in good faith may not be able to resolve their differences by themselves, and an impasse may result. In such cases, a neutral third party may be used to facilitate, suggest, or compel an agreement. Three major forms of impasse resolution are *mediation, fact-finding,* and *arbitration.*

- *Mediation* occurs when a third party, called the mediator, comes in to help the adversaries with the negotiations.[35] This person may be a professional mediator or someone else in whom both parties have confidence. In most states, mediation may be requested by either labor or management. The mediator's task is to build agreement about the issues involved by reopening communications between the two sides. The mediator is without any means to compel an agreement, so an advantage of the process is that it preserves the nature of collective bargaining by maintaining the decision-making power in the hands of the involved parties.[36]

- *Fact-finding* primarily involves the interpretation of facts and the determination of what weight to attach to them. Appointed in the same way as mediators, fact-finders also do not have the means to impose a settlement of the dispute. Fact-finders may sit alone or as part of a panel—normally consisting of three people. The fact-finding hearing is quasi-judicial, although less strict rules of evidence are applied. Both labor and management may be represented by legal counsel, and verbatim transcripts are commonly made. In a majority of cases, the fact-finder's recommendations will be made public at some point.[37]

- *Arbitration* parallels fact-finding but differs in that the "end product of arbitration is a final and binding decision that sets the terms of the settlement and with which the parties are legally required to comply."[38] Arbitration may be compulsory or voluntary. It is compulsory when mandated by state law and is binding on the parties even if one of them is unwilling to comply. It is voluntary when the parties undertake of their own volition to use the procedure. Even when entered into voluntarily, arbitration is compulsory and binding on the parties who have agreed to it.

Grievances

The establishment of a working agreement between labor and management does not mean that the possibility for conflict no longer exists: The day-to-day administration of the agreement may also be the basis for strife. Questions can arise concerning the interpretation and application of the document and its various clauses, and grievances—complaints or expressions of dissatisfaction by an employee concerning some aspect of employment—may arise. The grievance procedure is a formal process that involves the seeking of redress of the complaints through progressively higher channels within the organization. The sequence of grievance steps are spelled out in the collective bargaining agreement and typically include the following five steps: (1) the employee presents the grievance to the immediate supervisor; and, if not receiving satisfaction, (2) a written grievance is presented to the division commander, then (3) to the chief executive officer, then (4) to the city or county manager, and, finally, (5) to an arbiter, selected according to the rules of the American Arbitration Association.[39]

The burden of proof is on the grieving party, except in disciplinary cases, where it is always on the employer. The parties may be represented by counsel at the hearing, and the format includes opening statements by each side, examination and cross-examination of any witnesses, and closing arguments in the reverse order of which opening arguments were made.[40]

Job Actions

A "job action" is an activity in which employees engage to express their dissatisfaction with a particular person, event, or condition or to attempt to influence the outcome of some matter pending before decision makers. Employees seek to create pressure that may shift the course of events to a position more favorable or acceptable to them.[41] Job actions are of four types: *vote of confidence, work slowdown, work speedup,* and *work stoppage.*

- *Vote of confidence:* This job action is used sparingly. A vote of no confidence signals employees' collective displeasure with the chief administrator of the agency. Although such votes have no legal standing, they may have high impact because of the resulting publicity.
- *Work slowdown:* Employees continue to work during a slowdown, but they do so at a leisurely pace, causing productivity to fall. As productivity declines, the unit of government is pressured to resume normal work production. For example, a police department may urge officers to issue more citations so revenues are not lost, or citizens may complain to politicians to "get this thing settled."[42]

- *Work speedup:* This action involves accelerated activity in the levels of services. For example, a police department may conduct a "ticket blizzard" to protest a low pay increase, pressure government leaders to make more concessions at the bargaining table, or abandon some policy change that affects their working conditions.

- *Work stoppage:* This action constitutes the most severe job action. The ultimate work stoppage is the strike, or withholding of all employees' services. This tactic is most often used by labor to force management back to the bargaining table when negotiations have reached an impasse. Criminal justice employee strikes are now rare, however. Short of a strike by all employees are briefer work stoppages, known in policing as "blue flu," that last only a few days.

Civil Liability

No group of workers (with the exception of physicians) is more susceptible to litigation and liability than police and corrections officers. Frequently cast into confrontational situations, and given the complex nature of their work and its requisite training needs, they will from time to time act in a manner that evokes public scrutiny and complaints. The price of failure among public servants can be quite high, in both human and financial terms. Coupled with that is the fact that some police and corrections officers are overzealous and even brutal in their work. They may intentionally or otherwise violate the rights of the citizens they are sworn to protect or the clients they are to detain or supervise. For these inappropriate actions, the public has become quick to file suit for damages for what are perceived to be egregious actions.

Another trend is for such litigants to cast a wide net in their lawsuits, suing not only the principal actors in the incident but supervisors and agency administrators as well. This breadth of suing occurs through the notion of "vicarious liability" or the doctrine of *respondeat superior,* an old legal maxim meaning "let the master answer." In sum, an employer can be found liable in certain instances for wrongful acts of an employee.[43] Such a case was that of *McClelland v. Facteau.*[44] McClelland was stopped by Officer Facteau for speeding and taken to the city jail. He was not allowed to make any phone calls, was questioned but not advised of his rights, and was beaten and injured by Facteau in the presence of two city police officers who were from different jurisdictions. McClelland sued, claiming that the two police chiefs were directly responsible for his treatment and injuries due to their failure to train and supervise their subordinates properly. Evidence was also produced of prior misbehavior by Facteau. The court ruled that the chiefs could be held liable if they knew of prior misbehavior yet did nothing about it.

Next we examine torts and negligent behaviors that can lead to civil liability and even incarceration for police and corrections personnel in the justice system. Following that is a discussion of two major legislative tools that are used to legally attack such activities: Title 42, U.S.C. Section 1983; and Title 18, U.S.C. Section 242.

Torts and Negligence

It is important to have a basic understanding of tort liability. A *tort* is the infliction of some injury on one person by another. Three categories of torts generally cover most of the lawsuits filed against criminal justice practitioners: negligence, intentional torts, and constitutional torts.

Negligence can arise when a criminal justice employee's conduct creates a danger to others. In other words, the employee did not conduct his or her affairs in a manner so as to avoid subjecting others to a risk of harm and may be held liable for the injuries caused to others.[45]

Intentional torts occur when an employee engages in a voluntary act that had a substantial likelihood of resulting in injury to another: Examples are assault and battery, false arrest and imprisonment, malicious prosecution, and abuse of process.

Constitutional torts involve employees' duty to recognize and uphold the constitutional rights, privileges, and immunities of others. Violations of these guarantees may subject employees to civil suits, most frequently brought in federal court under 42 U.S.C. Section 1983 (discussed later).[46]

Assault, battery, false imprisonment, false arrest, invasion of privacy, negligence, defamation, and malicious prosecution are examples of torts that are commonly brought against police officers.[47] False arrest is the arrest of a person without probable cause. False imprisonment is the intentional illegal detention of a person, not only in jail but in any confinement to a specified area. For example, the police may fail to release an arrested person after a proper bail or bond has been posted, they can delay the arraignment of an arrested person unreasonably, or authorities can fail to release a prisoner after they no longer have authority to hold him or her.[48]

A single act may also be a crime as well as a tort. For example, if Officer Smith, in an unprovoked attack, injures Jones, the state will attempt to punish Smith in a *criminal* action by sending him to prison, or fining him, or both. The state would have the burden of proof at criminal trial, having to prove Smith guilty "beyond a reasonable doubt." Furthermore, Jones may sue Smith for money damages in a *civil* action for the personal injury he suffered. In this civil suit, Jones would have the burden of proving Smith's acts were tortious by a "preponderance of the evidence"—a lower standard and thus easier to satisfy in civil court.

Development of Section 1983 Legislation: Use Against Police

Following the Civil War, Congress, in reaction to the activities of the Ku Klux Klan, enacted the Ku Klux Klan Act of 1871, later codified as Title 42, U.S.C. Section 1983. It states that

> Every person who, under color of any statute, ordinance, regulation, custom, or usage of any State or Territory, subjects, or causes to be subjected, any citizen of

the United States or any other person within the jurisdiction thereof to the deprivation of any rights, privileges, or immunities secured by the Constitution and laws, shall be liable to the party injured in an action at law, suit in equity, or other proper proceeding for redress.

This legislation was intended to provide civil rights protection to all "persons" protected under the act, when a defendant acted "under color of law" (misused power of office), and to provide an avenue to the federal courts for relief of alleged civil rights violations.

Section 1983 also allows for a finding of personal liability on the part of police supervisory personnel when improper training is shown or it is proven that supervisors knew, or should have known, of the misconduct of their officers yet failed to take corrective action and prevent future harm.

An example of such a case was *Brandon v. Allen*.[49] Two teenagers parked in a "lovers' lane" were approached by an off-duty police officer, Allen, who showed his police identification and demanded that the male exit from the car. Allen struck the male with his fist and stabbed him with a knife, then attempted to break into the car where the female was seated. The young male was able to reenter the car and managed to escape. As the two teenagers sped off, Allen fired a shot at them with his revolver, and the shattered windshield glass severely injured the youths to the point that they required plastic surgery. Allen was convicted of criminal charges, and the police chief was also sued under Section 1983. The plaintiffs charged that the chief and others knew of Allen's reputation. None of the other police officers wished to ride in a patrol car with him. At least two formal charges of misconduct had been filed previously, yet the chief failed to take any remedial action or even to review the disciplinary records of officers when he became chief. The court called this behavior "unjustified inaction," held the police department liable, and allowed the plaintiffs damages. The U.S. Supreme Court upheld this judgment.[50]

Police supervisors have also been found liable for injuries arising out of an official policy or custom of their department. Injuries resulting from a chief's verbal or written support of heavy-handed behavior resulting in excessive force by officers have resulted in such liability.[51]

Whereas Section 1983 is a civil action, Title 18, U.S.C. Section 242 makes it a *criminal* offense for any person acting under color of law to violate another's civil rights. Section 242 applies not only to police officers but also to the misconduct of public officials and prosecutions of judges, bail bond agents, public defenders, and even prosecutors.

Liability of Corrections Personnel

The liability of corrections workers often centers on their lack of due care for persons in their custody. This responsibility primarily concerns police officers and civilians responsible for inmates in local jails.

When an inmate commits suicide while in custody, police agencies are frequently—and often successfully—sued in state courts under negligence and wrongful death claims. The standard used by the courts is whether the agency's act or failure to act created an unusual risk to an inmate. A "special duty" of care exists for police officers to protect inmates suffering from mental disorders and those who are impaired by drugs or alcohol. Foreseeability—the reasonable anticipation that injury or damage may occur—may be found when inmates make statements of intent to commit suicide, have a history of mental illness, are in a poor emotional state, or are at a high level of intoxication or drug dependence.[52]

Suicides are not uncommon among jail inmates: Each year, between 150 and 300 jail inmates take their own lives.[53] As noted earlier, inmate suicide rates are higher in small jails and highest in small jails with lower population densities.[54] State courts generally recognize that police officials have a duty to care for persons in their custody.[55] Thus, jail administrators are ultimately responsible for taking reasonable precautions to ensure the health and safety of persons in their custody. They must protect inmates from harm, render medical assistance when necessary, and treat inmates humanely.[56]

Several court decisions have helped to establish the duties and guidelines of jail administrators for their employees concerning the care of their charges. An intoxicated inmate in possession of cigarettes and matches started a fire that resulted in his death. The court stated that "the prisoner may have been voluntarily drunk, but he was not in the cell voluntarily . . . [he] was helpless and the officer knew there was a means of harm on his person. . . ." The court concluded that the police administration owed a greater duty of care to such an arrestee.[57] Emotionally disturbed arrestees can also create a greater duty for jail personnel. In an Alaskan case, a woman had been arrested for intoxication in a hotel and had trouble talking, standing, and walking: Her blood-alcohol content was 0.26 percent. Two and a half hours after her incarceration, officers found her hanging by her sweater from mesh wiring in the cell. The Alaska Supreme Court said the officers knew she was depressed, and that in the past few months one of her sons had been burned to death, another son was stabbed to death, and her mother had died. Thus, the court felt officers should have anticipated her suicide.[58]

In New Mexico, a 17-year-old boy was arrested for armed robbery. Later he told his mother he would kill himself before he would go to prison, and he subsequently tried to cut his wrists with an aluminum can top. The assistant chief ordered the officers to keep watch over him, but he was found dead by hanging the following morning. The Supreme Court of New Mexico held that the knowledge officers possessed was an important factor to be considered in determining liability and negligence in such cases.[59] In a New Jersey case, a young man arrested for intoxication was put in a holding cell but officers failed to remove his leather belt, which he used to take his own life. The court found the officers' conduct could have been a "substantial" factor in his death.[60]

Courts have also found the design of detention facilities as a source of negligence. A Detroit holding cell did not permit officers to observe inmates' movements unless the inmates were standing directly in front of the door, and no electronic monitoring devices were in use. A suicide in this case led the court to hold that these conditions, and the absence of a detoxification cell, were proximate causes and constituted a building defect.[61] In another incident, an intoxicated college student was placed in a holding cell at the public safety building of the university. Forty minutes after being placed in the cell, officers found the man hanging from an overhead heating device by a noose fashioned from his socks and belt. The court found the university liable for operating a defective building and awarded the plaintiff $650,000.[62]

The behavior of jail personnel *after* a suicide or attempted suicide may also indicate a breach of duty. Officers are expected to give all possible aid to an inmate who is injured or has attempted suicide. Thus, when officers found an inmate slumped in a chair with his belt around his neck and left him in that position instead of trying to revive him or call for medical assistance, the court ruled that this behavior established a causal link between the officer's inaction and the inmate's death.[63]

It is clear that correctional administrators must ensure that their organizations are cognizant of their legal responsibilities and expanded custodial role with their detainees.

Summary

This chapter examined three aspects of administration that pose serious challenges: discipline, labor relations, and civil liability. It is clear from this triad of issues that administrators need to understand the current and developing laws that serve to make criminal justice practitioners legally accountable. This need cannot be overstated. It is far better to learn the proper means of discipline, areas of liability, and how to properly engage in collective bargaining through education and training—*in house*—than to learn about these issues as a defendant in a lawsuit—in the *courthouse*.

This requires criminal justice executives to be proactive and follow appropriate laws and guidelines as they recruit, hire, train, supervise, and negotiate with their subordinates in order to avoid legal difficulties. For administrators to avoid doing so could mean that they place themselves and their jurisdictions at serious financial, legal, and moral risk.

Questions for Review

1. What are the minimum due process requirements for discharging public employees?
2. Which forms of disciplinary actions are commonly used by police agencies?
3. How do positive and negative disciplinary measures operate, and how do they differ?
4. What is the preferred process for dealing with citizens' complaints against criminal justice personnel?

5. How does an employee's grievance proceed?

6. How did unionization begin among criminal justice employees?

7. What are the three basic models used for collective bargaining in the United States?

8. When parties bargaining in good faith reach an impasse, what three major forms of impasse resolution are available?

9. Who are some of the people participating in typical union and management bargaining teams?

10. Why was Title 42, U.S.C. Section 1983 enacted, and how is it used today?

11. How do the concepts of torts and negligence affect criminal justice employees?

12. For what reasons may corrections personnel be found liable?

Notes

1. V. McLaughlin and R. Bing, "Law Enforcement Personnel Selection." *Journal of Police Science and Administration* 15 (1987):271–276.

2. Ibid.

3. *McNamara v. City of Chicago,* 700 F.Supp. 917 (N.D. Ill. 1988), at 919.

4. *White v. Thomas,* 660 F.2d 680 (5th Cir. 1981).

5. *Yarber v. Indiana State Prison,* 713 F. Supp. 271 (N.D. Ind. 1988).

6. Robert H. Chaires and Susan A. Lentz, "Criminal Justice Employee Rights: An Overview," *American Journal of Criminal Justice,* 13 (April 1995): 273–274.

7. M. Guthrie, "Using Automation to Apply Discipline Fairly," *FBI Law Enforcement Bulletin* 5, 1996: 18–21.

8. A. E. Wagner and S. H. Decker, "Evaluating Citizen Complaints Against the Police," in R. G. Dunham and G. P. Alpert (eds.), *Critical Issues in Policing: Contemporary Readings* (Prospect Heights, Ill.: Waveland, 1997).

9. Ibid.

10. J. R. Dugan and D. R. Breda, "Complaints About Police Officers: A Comparison Among Types and Agencies, *Journal of Criminal Justice* 19 (1991): 165–171.

11. Kim Michelle Lersch, "Police Misconduct and Malpractice: A Critical Analysis of Citizens' Complaints," *Policing* 21 (1998): 80–96.

12. D. W. Perez, *Police Review Systems* (Washington, D.C.: Management Information Service, 1992).

13. W. Clinton Terry III, *Policing Society: An Occupational View* (New York: Wiley, 1985), p. 168.

14. Ibid., p. 168.

15. Ibid., pp. 170–171.

16. Samuel Walker, *The Police in America: An Introduction* (3rd ed.) (Boston: McGraw-Hill, 1999), p. 368.

17. George F. Cole and Christopher E. Smith, *The American System of Criminal Justice* (8th ed.) (Belmont, Calif.: West/Wadsworth, 1998), p. 240.

18. Ibid., p. 371.

19. Harry W. More Jr. (ed.), *Critical Issues in Law Enforcement* (4th ed.) (Cincinnati, Ohio: Anderson, 1985), pp. 155–161.

20. Scott Christianson, "How Unions Affect Prison Administration," *Criminal Law Bulletin* 15 (1979):238–247.

21. Richard Hawkins and Geoffrey P. Alpert, *American Prison Systems: Punishment and Justice* (Englewood Cliffs, N.J.: Prentice Hall, 1989), p. 354.

22. Ibid., p. 356.

23. James B. Jacobs, *New Perspectives on Prisons and Imprisonment* (Ithaca, N.Y.: Cornell University Press, 1983), p. 153.

24. Ibid., pp. 154–155.

25. Ibid., p. 156.

26. Hawkins and Alpert, *American Prison Systems,* p. 357.

27. U.S. Department of Justice, National Institute of Law Enforcement and Criminal Justice, Trial Court Management Series, *Personnel Management* (Washington, D.C.: U.S. Government Printing Office, 1979), pp. 42–47.

28. Will Aitchison, *The Rights of Police Officers* (3d ed.) (Portland, Ore.: Labor Relations Information System, 1996), p. 7.

29. Ibid.

30. Ibid.

31. Ibid., p. 8.

32. Ibid., p. 9.

33. Charles R. Swanson, Leonard Territo, and Robert W. Taylor, *Police Administration: Structures, Processes, and Behavior* (4th ed.) (Upper Saddle River, N.J.: Prentice Hall, 1998), p. 344.

34. Ibid., pp. 347–350.

35. Arnold Zack, *Understanding Fact-Finding and Arbitration in the Public Sector* (Washington, D.C.: Government Printing Office, 1974), p. 1.

36. Thomas P. Gilroy and Anthony V. Sinicropi, "Impasse Resolution in Public Employment," *Industrial and Labor Relations Review* 25 (July 1971–1972): 499.

37. Robert G. Howlett, "Fact Finding: Its Values and Limitations—Comment," Arbitration and the Expanded Role of Neutrals, Proceedings of the twenty-third annual meeting of the National Academy of Arbitrators (Washington, D.C.: Bureau of National Affairs, 1970), p. 156.

38. Zack, *Understanding Fact-Finding,* p. 1.

39. Charles W. Maddox, *Collective Bargaining in Law Enforcement* (Springfield, Ill.: Charles C. Thomas, 1975), p. 54.

40. Swanson, Territo, and Taylor, *Police Administration,* p. 355.

41. Ibid., p. 356.

42. Ibid.

43. *Monell v. Department of Social Services,* 436 U.S. 658 (1978).

44. 610 F.2d 693 (10th Cir., 1979).

45. H. E. Barrineau III, *Civil Liability in Criminal Justice* (Cincinnati, Ohio: Pilgramage, 1987), p. 58.

46. Ibid., p. 5.

47. Swanson, Territo, and Taylor, *Police Administration*, p. 374.

48. Ibid.

49. 516 F.Supp. 1355 (W.D. Tenn., 1981).

50. *Brandon v. Holt,* 469 U.S. 464, 105 S.Ct. 873 (1985).

51. See, for example, *Black v. Stephens,* 662 F.2d 181 (1991).

52. Victor E. Kappeler, *Critical Issues in Police Civil Liability* (2d ed.) (Prospect Heights, Ill.: Waveland, 1997), pp. 177–178.

53. U.S. Department of Justice, Bureau of Justice Statistics Special Report, *Population Density in Local Jails, 1988,* (Washington, D.C.: U.S. Government Printing Office, 1991), p. 9.

54. *Thomas v. Williams,* 124 S.E.2d 409 (Ga. App. 1962).

55. Victor E. Kappeler and Rolando V. delCarmen, "Avoiding Police Liability for Negligent Failure to Prevent Suicide," *The Police Chief* (August 1991):53–59.

56. Ibid., p. 53.

57. *Thomas v. Williams.*

58. *Kanayurak v. North Slope Borough,* 677 P.2d 892 (Alaska 1984).

59. *City of Belen v. Harrell,* 603 P.2d 711 (N.M. 1979).

60. *Hake v. Manchester Township,* 486 A.2d 836 (N.J. 1985).

61. *Davis v. City of Detroit,* 386 N.W.2d 169 (Mich. App. 1986).

62. *Hickey v. Zezulka,* 443 N.W.2d 180 (Mich. App. 1989).

63. *Hake v. Manchester Township,* op. cit.

FINANCIAL ADMINISTRATION

Chapter

How pleasant it is to have money, heigh ho! How pleasant it is to have money.

—Arthur Hugh Clough

Money is like muck, not good except it be spread.

—Francis Bacon

Introduction

The importance of financial administration to organizations for this country is unquestionable. Budgets are the key to financial administration: Their development involves planning, organizing, directing, and other administrative functions. If unlimited funds were available, planning would not be needed. As Frederick Mosher observed, "Not least among the qualifications of an administrator is [one's] ability as a tactician and gladiator in the budget process."[1]

Just as individuals need to be responsible with their personal finances to avoid legal and personal difficulties, so must governmental administrators be responsible stewards of the public's funds.

This chapter presents some of the fundamental elements of the control of fiscal resources through budgeting. It is not intended to prepare the reader to be an expert on fiscal management, but it provides an overview of some of the basic methods and issues surrounding financial administration.

Of the four component parts of financial administration—budgeting, auditing, accounting, and purchasing—budgeting is our primary focus. Specifically included are discussions of budget definitions and uses; the influence of politics and fiscal realities in budgeting, which often lead to constricted financial conditions for the organization; the several elements of a budget, including the budget cycle, formulation, approval, execution, and audit; budget formats; potential pitfalls in budgeting; and some strategies for augmenting criminal justice budgets in tight fiscal times.

The Budget

A Working Definition

The word *budget* is derived from the old French *bougette,* meaning a small leather bag or wallet. Initially, it referred to the leather bag in which the chancellor of the exchequer carried the documents to English Parliament stating the government's needs and resources.[2] Later, it came to mean the documents themselves. More recently, *budget* has been defined as a plan stated in financial terms, an estimate of future expenditures, an asking price, a policy statement, the translation of financial resources into human purposes, and a contract between those who appropriate the funds and those who spend them.[3] To some extent, all of these definitions are true.

In addition, the budget is a management tool, a process, and a political instrument. It is a "comprehensive plan, expressed in financial terms, by which a program is operated for a given period. It includes (1) the services, activities, and projects comprising the program; (2) the resultant expenditure requirements; and (3) the resources usable for their support."[4] It is "a plan or schedule adjusting expenses during a certain period to the estimated income for that period."[5] Lester Bittel added:

> A budget is, literally, a financial standard for a particular operation, activity, program, or department. Its data is presented in numerical form, mainly in dollars ... to be spent for a particular purpose—over a specified period of time. Budgets are derived from planning goals and forecasts.[6]

Although these descriptions are certainly apt, one writer warns that budgets contain an inherently irrational process: "Budgets are based on little more than the past and some guesses."[7]

Financial management of governmental agencies is clearly political. Anything the government does entails the expenditure of public funds.[8] Thus, the single most important political statement that any unit of government makes in a given year is its budget. Essentially, the budget causes administrators to follow the gambler's adage and "put your money where your mouth is."[9] When demands placed on government increase while funds are stable or decline, the competition for funds is keener than usual, forcing justice agencies to make the best case for their budgets. The heads of all departments, if they are doing their jobs well, are also vying for appropriations. Special interest groups, the media, politicians, and the public, with their own views and priorities, often engage in arm twisting during the budgeting process.

Elements of a Budget

The Budget Cycle

Administrators must think in terms of a budget cycle, which in government (and, therefore, in all public criminal justice agencies) is typically on a fiscal year basis. Some states have a biennial budget cycle: Their legislatures, such as those in Kentucky and Nevada, budget for a two-year period. Normally, however, the fiscal year is a 12-month period that may coincide with a calendar year or, more commonly, will run from July 1 through June 30 of the following year. The federal government's fiscal year, however, is October 1 through September 30. Obviously, the budget cycle is important because it drives the development of the budget and determines when new monies become available.

The budget cycle consists of four sequential steps, repeated every year at about the same point in time: (1) budget formulation, (2) budget approval, (3) budget execution, and (4) budget audit.

Budget Formulation

Depending on the size and complexity of the organization and the financial condition of the jurisdiction, budget formulation can be a relatively simple or exceedingly difficult task. It is by far the most complicated stage of the budgeting process. The administrator must anticipate all types of costs—overtime, gasoline, postage, maintenance contracts, and so on—and predict expenses related to major incidents or events that might arise. Certain assumptions based on the previous year's budget can be made while formulating the budget. Those assumptions are not necessarily accurate, however. One observer noted that "every expense you budget should be fully supported with the proper and most logical assumptions you can develop. Avoid simply estimating, which is the least supportable form of budgeting."[10] Another criminal justice administrator, discussing budget formulation, added that

> the most important ingredient for any budgeting process is planning. [Administrators] should approach the budget process from the planning standpoint of "How can I best reconcile the [criminal justice] needs of the community with the ability of my jurisdiction to finance them, and then relate those plans in a convincing manner to my governing body for proper financing and execution of pro-

grams?" After all, as budget review occurs, the document is taken apart and scrutinized piece by piece or line by line. This fragmentation approach contributes significantly to our inability to defend interrelated programs in an overall budget package.[11]

To illustrate, let us assume that a police department budget is being prepared in a city having a manager form of government. Long before a criminal justice agency (or any other unit of local government) begins to prepare its annual budget, the city manager and/or the staff of the city has made revenue forecasts, considered how much (if any) of the current operating budget will be carried over into the next fiscal year, analyzed how the population of the jurisdiction will grow or shift (affecting demands for public services), and examined other priorities for the coming year. The city manager may also appear before the governing board to obtain information about its fiscal priorities, spending levels, pay raises, new positions, programs, and so on. The city manager may then send all department heads a memorandum outlining the general fiscal guidelines to be followed in preparing their budgets.

Upon receipt of the city's guidelines for preparing its budget, the heads of functional areas, such as the chief of police, have a planning and research unit (assuming a city large enough to have this level of specialization) prepare an internal budget calendar and an internal fiscal policy memorandum. Table 15.1 shows an internal budget calendar for a large municipal police department. This memo may include input from unions and lower supervisory personnel. Each bureau is then given the responsibility for preparing its individual budget request.

In small police departments with little or no functional specialization, the chief may prepare the budget alone or with input from other officers or the city finance officer. In some small agencies, chiefs and sheriffs may not even see their budget or assist in its preparation. Because of tradition, politics, or even laziness, the administrator has abdicated control over the budget. This puts the agency in a precarious position indeed. It will have difficulty engaging in long-term planning and spending money productively for personnel and programs when the executive has to get prior approval from the governing body to buy items such as office supplies.

The planning and research unit then reviews the bureau's budget requests for compliance with the budgeting instructions and the chief's and city manager's priorities. Eventually, a consolidated budget is developed for the entire police department and submitted to the chief, who may meet with the planning and research unit and bureau commanders to discuss it. Personalities, politics, priorities, personal agendas, and other issues may need to be addressed. The chief may have to mediate disagreements concerning these matters, while sometimes rewarding the loyal and reducing allotments for the disloyal.[12] Requests for programs, equipment, travel expenses, personnel, or anything else in the draft budget may be deleted, reduced, or enhanced.

The budget is then presented to the city manager. At this point, the chief executive's reputation as a budget framer becomes a factor. If the chief is known to pad the budget heavily, the city manager is far more likely to cut their

TABLE 15.1   Budget Preparation Calendar for a Large
Police Department

WHAT SHOULD BE DONE	BY WHOM	ON THESE DATES
Issue budget instructions and applicable forms	City administrator	November 1
Prepare and issue budget message, with instructions and applicable forms, to unit commanders	Chief of police	November 15
Develop unit budgets with appropriate justification and forward recommended budgets to planning and research unit	Unit commanders	February 1
Review unit budget	Planning and research staff with unit commanders	March 1
Consolidate unit budgets for presentation to chief of police	Planning and research unit	March 15
Review consolidated recommended budget	Chief of police, planning and research staff, and unit commanders	March 30
Obtain department approval of budget	Chief of police	April 15
Forward recommended budget to city administrator	Chief of police	April 20
Review recommended budget by administration	City administrator and chief of police	April 30
Approve revised budget	City administrator	May 5
Forward budget document to city council	City administrator	May 10
Review budget	Budget officer of city council	May 20
Present to council	City administrator and chief of police	June 1
Report back to city administrator	City council	June 5
Review and resubmit to city council	City administrator and chief of police	June 10
Take final action on police budget	City council	June 20

(*Source:* National Advisory Commission on Criminal Justice Standards and Goals,
Police. Washington, D.C.: U.S. Government Printing Office, 1973, p. 137.)

STEPS IN BUDGET DEVELOPMENT

The following describes how the $885 million budget for the California Highway Patrol is typically developed. According to the Budget Section, it is an all-year and year-on-year process that begins at the level of the 120 area commands, where budget requests originate. The requests are dealt with in one of three ways: (1) funded within the department's base budget, (2) disapproved, or (3) carried forward for review by CHP personnel.

At the division level, managers review the area requests, make needed adjustments, and submit a consolidated request to the budget section at headquarters. This section passes input from the field to individual section management staff (e.g., personnel, training, communications, and so on) for review. Budget section staff meet with individual section management staff. Within two or three months, the budget section identifies proposals for new funding that have department-wide impact and passes them on to the executive level.

The commissioner and aides review the figures and agree on a budget to submit to the governor. The governor submits this budget to the legislature, which acts on it and returns it to the governor for signature.

Source: Budget Section, California Highway Patrol, Sacramento, California, personal communication.

---

department request than if the chief is known to be reasonable in the budget request, engage in innovative planning, and have a flexible approach to budget negotiations.

The city manager consolidates the police budget request with those from other municipal department heads and then meets with them individually to discuss their requests further. The city manager directs the city finance officer to make any necessary additions or cuts and then prepare a budget proposal for presentation to the governing body.

The courts have a similar budgetary process. In a large court, there may be five major procedures in the process: (1) developing an internal budgetary policy, (2) reviewing budget submissions, (3) developing a financial strategy, (4) presenting the budget, and (5) monitoring the budget. Figure 15.1 illustrates the relationships of the steps in the process.

Budget Approval

With the city manager's proposed budget requests in hand, the governing board begins its deliberations on the citywide budget. The city manager may appear before the board to answer questions concerning the budget, and individual department heads also may be asked to appear. Suggestions for getting monies approved and appropriated include the following:

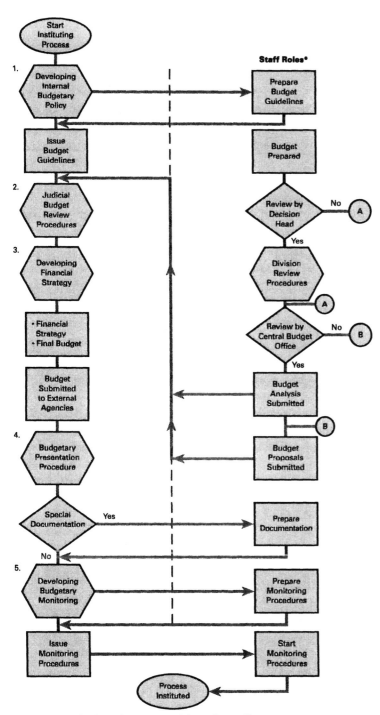

Staff Roles*

* Particularly applicable in a large court, much less so in a small court.

Figure 15.1

Steps in a judicial budgetary process.

1. Have a carefully justified budget.
2. Anticipate the environment of the budget hearing by reading news reports and understanding the priorities of the council members. Know what types of questions elected officials are likely to ask.
3. Determine which "public" will be at the police department's budget hearing and prepare accordingly. Public issues change from time to time. Citizens who were outraged over one issue one year may be incensed by another the next.
4. Make good use of graphics in the form of pie charts and histograms, but be selective and do not go overboard. Short case studies of successes are normal and add to graphics.
5. Rehearse and critique the presentation many times.
6. Be a political realist.[13]

After everyone scheduled has spoken, the city council gives directions to the city manager, such as make further cuts in the budget, or reinstate certain funds or programs cut earlier, and so on. The budget is then approved. It is fair to say that at this stage, budgeting is largely a legislative function that requires some legal action, as a special ordinance or resolution approving the budget is passed each year by the governing board.

The column headings in Table 15.2 (pp. 397–398) indicate (1) the budget amount requested by the chief of police, (2) the amount recommended by the city manager, and (3) the amount finally approved by the city council.

Budget Execution

The third stage of the budget process, execution, has several objectives: (1) to carry out the police department's budgeted objectives for the fiscal year in an orderly manner, (2) to ensure that the department undertakes no financial obligations or commitments other than those funded by the city council, and (3) to provide a periodic accounting of the administrator's stewardship over the department's funds.[14]

Supervision of the budget execution phase is an executive function that requires some type of fiscal control system, usually directed by the city or county manager. Periodic reports on accounts are an important element of budget control. They serve to reduce the likelihood of overspending by identifying areas in which deficits are likely to occur due to such things as gasoline prices, extensive overtime, natural disasters, and unplanned emergencies (such as riots). A periodic budget status report informs the administrator what percentage of the total budget has been expended to date (see Table 15.3, p. 399).

Prudent administrators normally attempt to manage the budget conservatively for the first eight or nine months of the budget year, holding the line on spending until most fiscal crises have been averted. Because unplanned incidents and natural disasters can wreak havoc with any budget, this conservatism is normally the best course. Then the administrator can plan how best to allocate funds if emergency funds have not been spent.

The Audit

The word *audit* means to verify something independently.[15] The basic rationale for the audit has been described by the Comptroller General of the United States as follows:

> Governments and agencies entrusted with public resources and the authority for applying them have a responsibility to render a full accounting of their activities. This accountability is inherent in the governmental process and is not always specifically identified by legislative provision. This governmental accountability should identify not only the object for which the public resources have been devoted but also the manner and effect of their application.[16]

After the close of each budget year, the year's expenditures are audited to ensure that the agency spent its funds properly. Audits are designed to investigate three broad areas of accountability: *financial* (focusing on proper fiscal operations and reports of the justice agency), *management* (determining whether funds were utilized efficiently and economically), and *program* (determining whether the city council's goals and objectives were accomplished.)[17]

Financial audits determine whether funds were spent legally, the budgeted amount was exceeded, and the financial process proceeded in a legal manner. For example, auditors investigate whether funds transferred between accounts were authorized, grant funds were used improperly, computations were made accurately, disbursements were documented, financial transactions followed established procedures, and established competitive bidding procedures were employed.[18]

Justice administrators should welcome auditors' help to identify weaknesses and deficiencies and correct them.

Budget Formats

The three types of budgets primarily in use today are the line-item (or object-of-expenditure) budget, the performance budget, and the program (or results or outcomes) budget. Two additional types, the planning-programming-budgeting system (PPBS) and the zero-based budget (ZBB), are discussed in the literature but are used to a lesser extent.

The Line-Item Budget

The line-item or object budget is the most commonly used budget format. It is the basic system on which all other systems rely because it affords control. It is so named because it breaks down the budget into the major categories commonly used in government (e.g., personnel, equipment, contractual services, commodities, and capital outlay items). Every amount of money requested, recommended, appropriated, and expended is associated with a particular item or class of items.[19] In addition, large budget categories will be broken down into smaller line-item budgets (in a police department, examples would include patrol, investigation, communications, or jail function). The line-item format fosters budgetary control because no item escapes scrutiny.[20] We show line-items for actual budgets in police (see Table 15.2), court (Table 15.4), probation and parole (Table 15.5), and state prison organizations (Table 15.6). Each demonstrates the range of activities and funding needs of each agency. Note in Tables 15.2, 15.5, and 15.6 how a recession affected budgets and requests from year to year in many categories, resulting in severe cuts and even total elimination of items previously funded. Also note some of the ways in which administrators are deviating from the norm in order to save money (e.g., the police budget shows the department finding it cheaper to lease its patrol vehicles rather than buying a huge fleet of its own).

The line-item budget has several strengths and weaknesses. Its strengths include ease of control development, comprehension (especially by elected and other executive branch officials), and administration. Weaknesses are its neglect of long-range planning and its limited ability to evaluate performance. Furthermore, the line-item budget tends to maintain the status quo. Ongoing programs are seldom challenged. Line-item budgets are based on history: This year's allocation is based on last year's history. Although that allows an inexperienced manager to prepare a budget more easily, it often precludes the reform chief's careful deliberation and planning for the future.

The line-item budget provides ease of control because it clearly indicates the amount budgeted for each item, the amount expended as of a specific date, and the amount still available at that date. See, for example, Table 15.3.

Virtually all criminal justice agencies are automated to some extent, whether the financial officer prepares his or her budget using a computerized spreadsheet or a clerk enters information onto a database that will be uploaded to a state's mainframe computer. Some justice agencies use an automated budgeting system (ABS) that can store budget figures, make all necessary calculations for generating a budget request, monitor expenditures from budgets (similar to that shown in Table 15.6), and even generate some reports.

The Performance Budget

The key characteristic of a performance budget is that it relates the types of volume of work to be done to the amount of money spent.[21] It is input-output oriented, and it increases the responsibility and accountability of the manager for output as opposed to input.[22] This format specifies an organization's activities, using a format similar to that of the line-item budget. It normally measures activities that are easily quantified, such as numbers of traffic citations issued, crimes solved, property recovered, cases heard in the courtroom, and caseloads of probation officers. These activities are then compared to those of the unit that performs the most. This ranking according to activity attempts to allocate funds fairly. Using a police department as an example, the commander of the traffic accident investigation unit requests an additional three investigators, which the chief

TABLE 15.2 Police Operating Budget in a Community of 150,000 Population

DESCRIPTION	FY 1998–99 EXPENSES	FY 1999–2000 EXPENSES	FY 2000–01 DEPT. REQ.	CITY MANAGER	CITY COUNCIL
Salaries/Wages					
Reg. salaries	$14,315,764	$14,392,639	$16,221,148	$16,221,148	$16,221,148
Overtime	988,165	782,421	951,875	951,875	711,875
Severence pay	36,194	226,465	82,000	–0–	–0–
Holiday pay	395,952	591,158	698,958	698,958	698,958
Call back pay	45,499	49,833	49,555	49,555	49,555
Subtotals	15,781,574	16,042,516	18,003,536	17,921,536	17,681,536
Employee benefits					
Retirement	3,345,566	3,485,888	4,069,521	4,069,521	4,069,521
Group ins.	1,256,663	1,467,406	1,752,718	1,752,718	1,752,718
Life ins.	43,797	53,164	117,590	117,396	117,396
Disability ins.	726,885	794,686	1,346,909	1,346,038	1,024,398
Uniform allowance	188,079	193,827	196,750	196,750	196,750
Medicare	77,730	80,868	100,058	99,739	99,739
Long-term dis.	11,583	21,974	48,517	48,517	48,517
Subtotals	5,650,303	6,097,813	7,583,546	7,630,679	7,309,039
Services and supplies					
Office supp.	62,357	49,292	51,485	51,485	51,485
Operating supp.	227,563	148,569	270,661	270,661	270,661
Repair/Maint.	248,922	195,941	233,118	233,118	233,118
Small tools	49,508	788	12,175	12,175	12,175
Prof. serv.	337,263	290,359	334,765	334,765	334,765
Communication	287,757	223,200	392,906	392,906	392,906

(table continues)

TABLE 15.2 (continued)

DESCRIPTION	FY 1998–99 EXPENSES	FY 1999–2000 EXPENSES	FY 2000–01 DEPT. REQ.	CITY MANAGER	CITY COUNCIL
Public utility	111,935	116,773	121,008	121,008	121,008
Rentals	81,840	96,294	113,071	113,071	113,071
Vehicle rental	834,416	1,193,926	1,363,278	1,363,278	1,169,278
Extradition	20,955	22,411	20,000	20,000	20,000
Other travel	4,649	5,123	23,500	23,500	23,500
Advertising	2,662	2,570	4,100	4,100	4,100
Insurance	328,360	595,257	942,921	942,921	942,921
Books/Manuals	16,285	12,813	12,404	12,404	12,404
Employee training	47,029	30,851	–0–	–0–	–0–
Aircraft exp.	–0–	–0–	15,000	15,000	15,000
Special inv.	11,527	13,465	15,000	15,000	15,000
Other serv. & supplies	1,386,201	1,039,651	1,386,201	1,386,201	1,386,201
Subtotals	4,059,229	4,037,283	5,311,593	5,311,593	5,117,593
Capital outlay					
Machinery and equipment	572,301	102,964	–0–	–0–	–0–
Totals	$26,063,407	$26,280,576	$30,898,675	$30,863,808	$30,108,168

TABLE 15.3 A Police Department's Budget Status Report

LINE ITEM	AMOUNT BUDGETED	EXPENSES TO DATE	AMOUNT ENCUMBERED	BALANCE TO DATE	PERCENTAGE USED
Salaries	$16,221,148	$8,427,062.00	–0–	$7,794,086.00	52.0
Professional services	334,765	187,219.61	$8,014.22	139,531.17	58.3
Office supplies	51,485	16,942.22	3,476.19	31,066.59	39.7
Repair/Maintenance	49,317	20,962.53	1,111.13	27,243.34	44.8
Communication	392,906	212,099.11	1,560.03	179,246.86	54.4
Utilities	121,008	50,006.15	10,952.42	60,049.43	51.4
Vehicle rental	1,169,278	492,616.22	103,066.19	573,595.59	51.9
Travel	23,500	6,119.22	2,044.63	15,336.15	34.7
Extraditions	20,000	12,042.19	262.22	7,695.59	61.5
Printing/Binding	36,765	15,114.14	2,662.67	18,988.19	48.4
Books/Manuals	12,404	5,444.11	614.11	6,345.78	48.8
Training/Education	35,695	19,661.54	119.14	15,914.32	55.4
Aircraft expense	15,000	8,112.15	579.22	6,308.63	57.9
Special investigation	15,000	6,115.75	960.50	7,922.75	47.2
Machinery	1,000	275.27	27.50	697.23	30.3
Advertising	4,100	1,119.17	142.50	2,838.33	30.8

TABLE 15.4 Operating Budget for a District Court in a County of 300,000 Population

CATEGORIES	AMOUNTS
Salaries and wages	
Regular salaries	$2,180,792
Part-time temporary	9,749
Incentive/Longevity	50,850
Subtotal	$2,241,391
Employee benefits	
Group insurance	170,100
Worker comp.	8,470
Unemployment comp.	3,220
Retirement	412,211
Social security	605
Medicare	13,503
Subtotal	$608,109
Services and supplies	
Computers and office equipment	22,865
Service contracts	2,000
Minor furniture/Equipment	1,000
Computer supplies	10,000
Continuous forms	4,000
Office supplies	36,066
Advertising	50
Copy machine expense	40,000
Dues and registration	4,000
Printing	24,000
Telephone	16,000
Training	2,000
Court reporter/Transcript	235,000
Court reporter per diem	265,000
Law books/Supplements	9,000
Jury trials	75,000
Medical examinations	80,000
Computerized legal research	20,000
Travel	1,500
Subtotal	$847,481
Child support	
Attorneys and other personnel	$66,480
Court-appointed attorneys	656,000
Grand juries	18,600
Family court services	762,841
Total	$5,200,902

TABLE 15.5 Probation and Parole Budget for a State Serving 3 Million Population

DESCRIPTION	FY 1999–2000 ACTUAL	FY 2000–01 AGENCY REQ.	FY 2000–01 GOV. RECOMM.	LEGIS. APPROVAL
Personnel	$13,741,104	$14,290,523	$13,620,991	$13,540,222
Travel	412,588	412,588	412,588	401,689
Operating expenses	1,307,020	1,395,484	1,307,020	1,256,787
Equipment	10,569	4,379	4,379	4,379
Loans to parolees	4,500	4,500	4,500	4,500
Training	9,073	9,073	9,073	9,073
Extraditions	200,000	200,000	200,000	185,000
Client drug tests	112,962	112,962	112,962	112,962
Home arrest fees	114,005	114,005	114,005	114,005
Community programs	50,000	50,000	50,000	47,500
Residential confinement	496,709	500,709	496,709	487,663
Utilities (paid by building lessors)				
Totals	$16,458,530	$17,094,223	$16,332,227	$16,163,780

TABLE 15.6 Operating Budget for a State Medium Security Prison with 1,000 Inmates

DESCRIPTION	FY 1999–2000 ACTUAL	FY 2000–01 AGENCY REQ.	FY 2000–01 GOV. RECOMM.	LEGISLATURE APPROVED
Personnel				
Salaries	$5,051,095	$5,370,979	$5,186,421	$5,105,533
Worker's comp.	184,362	143,462	201,198	198,016
Retirement	1,142,010	1,174,968	1,215,674	1,196,028
Recruit tests	49,447	51,528	45,692	44,972
Insurance	474,330	488,250	513,000	500,175
Retirement ins.	30,963	31,872	35,917	35,349
Unemployment comp.	6,003	6,383	6,162	6,065
Overtime	165,856	-0-	-0-	-0-
Holiday pay	150,519	158,500	154,643	151,936
Medicare	39,965	45,140	42,225	40,948
Shift differential	95,925	101,011	98,553	96,828
Standby pay	6,465	6,807	6,641	6,526
Longevity pay	18,095	18,095	18,095	18,095
Subtotals	$7,415,035	$7,596,995	$7,524,221	$7,400,471
Services and supplies				
Operating supplies	$180,672	$277,495	$180,647	$214,859
Communications/freight	4,877	5,314	5,023	5,023
Printing/copying	20,900	47,222	19,016	21,527
Equipment repair	14,385	13,542	14,817	14,817
Vehicle operation	20,405	21,601	21,016	21,016
Uniforms—custody	118,122	105,976	103,237	113,856

Inmate clothing	72,436	184,790	72,430	86,167
Equipment issued	20,403	13,236	15,451	17,086
Inmate wages	36,645	52,815	35,572	42,309
Food	895,897	1,299,838	895,759	1,065,403
Postage	7,738	8,793	7,036	7,738
Telephone	24,808	23,802	22,130	24,808
Subscriptions	382	401	725	401
Hand tools	110	286	113	113
Subtotals	$1,417,780	$2,055,111	$1,392,972	$1,635,123
Special equipment	$116,863	$34,088	$12,557	$13,661
Grounds maint.	150,098	209,003	138,560	185,843
Inmate law library	18,564	20,115	16,419	21,836
Special projects	53,237	8,887	8,887	8,887
Gas and power	554,478	586,604	505,823	604,335
Water	60,390	69,377	52,266	67,171
Garbage	80,035	101,240	82,436	82,436
Canine unit	13,936	2,521	4,260	2,543
Total	$9,880,416	$10,683,941	$9,738,401	$10,022,306

approves. Later the chief might compare the unit's output and costs of the unit to those before the three investigators were added to determine how this change affected productivity.[23] An example of a police performance budget is provided in Table 15.7.

The performance budget format could be used in other justice system components in addition to the police. For example, the courts could use such performance measures as filing cases, writing opinions, disposing of cases, and quality of presentence investigations.

Advantages of the performance budget include a consideration of outputs, the establishment of the costs of various justice agency efforts, improved evaluation of programs and managers, an emphasis on efficiency, increased availability of information for decision making, and the enhancement of budget justification and explanation.[24] The performance budget works best for an assembly line or other organization where work is easily quantifiable, such as paving streets. Its disadvantages include its expense to develop, implement, and operate because of the extensive use of cost accounting techniques and the need for additional staff (Figure 15.2 illustrates the elements used to determine the cost of providing a criminal justice service); the controversy surrounding attempts to determine appropriate workload and unit cost measures (in criminal justice, although many functions are quantifiable, such reduction of duties to numbers often translates to quotas, which is anathema to many people); its emphasis on efficiency rather than effectiveness; and the failure to lend itself to long-range planning.[25]

Determining which functions in criminal justice are more important (and should therefore receive more financial support) is difficult. Therefore, in terms of criminal justice agency budgets, the selection of meaningful work units is very difficult and irrational. How can a justice agency measure its successes? How can it count what does not happen?

The Program Budget

The best known budget for monitoring the activities of the organization is the *program budget,* developed by the RAND Corporation for the U.S. Department of Defense. This format examines cost units as units of activity rather than as units and subunits within the organization. This budget becomes a planning tool; it demands justification for expenditures for adding new programs and for deleting old ones that have not met their objectives.

A police agency probably has greater opportunities for creating new community-based programs than do the courts or corrections agencies. Some of these programs include crime prevention and investigation, drug abuse education, home security, selective enforcement (e.g., drunk driving) programs, and career development for personnel. Each of these endeavors require instructional materials or special equipment, all of which must be budgeted. For example, traffic accident investigation (TAI) may be a cost area. The program budget emphasizes output measures. Outputs for TAI, for example, include the numbers of accidents worked and enforcement measures taken (such as citations issued, DUI and other arrests made, public safety speeches given, and so on). If the budget for

TABLE 15.7   Example of a Police Performance Budget

TOTAL BUDGET		$
Units/Activities		
Administration (chief)	Subtotal	$
Strategic planning		$
Normative planning		$
Policies and procedures formulation		$
Etc.		
Patrol	Subtotal	$
Calls for service		$
Citizen contacts		$
Special details		$
Etc.		
Criminal investigation	Subtotal	$
Suspect apprehension		$
Recovery of stolen property		$
Transportation of fugitives		$
Etc.		
Traffic services	Subtotal	$
Accident investigation		$
Issuance of citations		$
Public safety speeches		$
Etc.		
Juvenile services	Subtotal	$
Locate runaways/missing juveniles		$
Arrest of offenders		$
Referrals and liaison		$
Etc.		
Research and development	Subtotal	$
Perform crime analysis		$
Prepare annual budget		$
Prepare annual reports		$
Etc.		

these programs were divided by the units of output, the administrator could determine the relative cost for each unit of output or productivity. The cost of TAI, however, entails more than just the TAI unit. Patrol and other support units also engage in this program.

Thus, the program budget is an extremely difficult form to execute and administer because it requires tracking time of all personnel by activity as well as figuring in the cost of all support services and supplies. For this reason, criminal

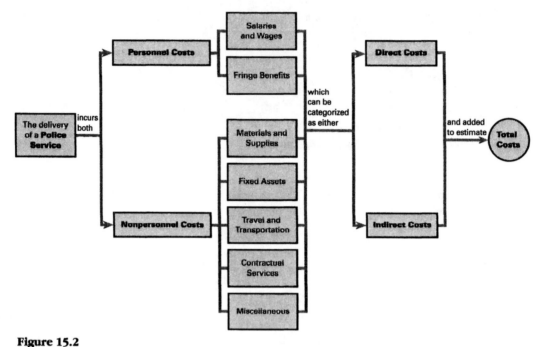

Figure 15.2

Elements of total costs for police services. (*Source:* U.S. Department of
Justice, National Institute of Justice, *Measuring the Costs of Police Services.*
Washington, D.C.: Author, 1982, p. 20.)

justice agencies rarely use the program budget.[26] Examples of police and court
program budgets are presented in Tables 15.8 and 15.9. Other disadvantages
include its cost in terms of time and money to develop, implement, and administer; development of objectives and performance measures is difficult; data collection may be costly; and agency managers may not have or want to develop the
skills necessary for directing large-scale, complex programs.[27]

Some advantages of the program budget include emphasis on the social utility of programs conducted by the agency, its clear relationship between policy
objectives and expenditures, its ability to provide justification and explanation of
the budget, its establishment of a high degree of accountability, and its format and
the wide involvement in formulating objectives, which lead employees at all levels of the organization to understand more thoroughly the importance of their
roles and actions.

PPBS and Zero-Based Budgeting Formats

General Motors used the planning-programming-budgeting system (PPBS) as
early as 1924,[28] and the RAND Corporation contributed to its development in a
series of studies dating from 1949.[29] By the mid-1950s, several states were using

TABLE 15.8 Example of a Police Program Budget

TOTAL BUDGET		$
Program Area		
Crime prevention	Subtotal	$
Salaries and benefits		$
Operating expenses		$
Capital outlay		$
Miscellaneous		$
Traffic accident investigation	Subtotal	$
Salaries and benefits		$
Operating expenses		$
Capital outlay		$
Miscellaneous		$
Traffic accident prevention	Subtotal	$
Salaries and benefits		$
Operating expenses		$
Capital outlay		$
Miscellaneous		$
Criminal investigation	Subtotal	$
Salaries and benefits		$
Operating expenses		$
Capital outlay		$
Miscellaneous		$
Juvenile delinquency prevention	Subtotal	$
Salaries and benefits		$
Operating expenses		$
Capital outlay		$
Miscellaneous		$
Special investigations	Subtotal	$
Salaries and benefits		$
Operating expenses		$
Capital outlay		$
Miscellaneous		$
Etc.		

it, and Secretary Robert McNamara introduced PPBS into the Defense Department in the mid-1960s.[30] By 1971, a survey revealed, however, that only 28 percent of the cities and 21 percent of the counties contacted had implemented PPBS or significant elements of it;[31] and in 1971, the federal government announced that it was discontinuing its use.

PPBS treated the three basic budget processes—planning, management, and control—as compatible: They were treated as co-equals. It was predicated on the

TABLE 15.9   Example of a Court's Program Budget

TOTAL BUDGET		$
Program Area		
Adjudicate criminal cases	Subtotal	$
Adjudicate felony cases	Total	$
Adjudicate misdemeanor appeals	Total	$
Adjudicate civil cases	Subtotal	$
Adjudicate major civil cases	Total	$
Adjudicate minor civil cases	Total	$
Adjudicate domestic relations cases	Total	$
Adjudicate juvenile cases	Subtotal	$
Adjudicate delinquency and dependent and neglect cases	Total	$
Adjudicate crimes against juveniles	Total	$
Provide alternatives to adjudication	Subtotal	$
Divert adult offenders	Total	$
Divert juvenile offenders	Total	$
Provide security	Subtotal	$
Handle prisoner transport	Total	$
Provide courtroom security	Total	$
Etc.		

(*Source:* U.S. Department of Justice, National Institute of Law Enforcement and Criminal Justice, *Financial Management.* Washington, D.C.: The American University, 1979, p. 41.1.)

primacy of planning.[32] This future orientation transformed budgeting from an annual ritual into "formulation of future goals and policies."[33] The PPBS budget featured a program structure, zero-based budgeting, the use of cost-budget analysis to distinguish between alternatives, and a budgetary horizon, often five years.[34]

Associated with PPBS, the zero-based planning and budgeting process requires managers to justify their entire budget request in detail rather than simply to refer to budget amounts established in previous years.[35] That is, each year all budgets begin at zero and must justify any funding. Following Peter Phyrr's use of zero-based budgeting at Texas Instruments, Governor Jimmy Carter adopted it in Georgia in the early 1970s, and then as president implemented it in the federal government for fiscal year 1979. An analysis of this experience at the Department of Agriculture indicates that although its use saved $200,000 in the department's budget, it cost at least 180,000 labor-hours of effort to develop it.[36]

It is important to note that few organizations have budgets that are purely one format or another. Therefore, it is not "bad" or unusual to find that because of time, tradition, and personal preferences, it is more likely that a combination of several is used.

Potential Pitfalls in Budgeting

The Need for Budgeting Flexibility

Ancient Greek mythology tells of a highwayman named Procrustes who had an iron bedstead. He measured all who fell into his hands on the bed. If they were too long, their legs were lopped off to fit it. If they were too short, they were stretched to fit the bed. Few criminal justice administrators have not seen their monies and programs laid out on the Procrustesean bed of a state or municipal budget officer and lopped off.

It therefore becomes imperative to build as much flexibility into the planned program and budget as possible. One technique utilized is to make up three budgets: an optimistic one, reflecting the ideal level of service to the jurisdiction and organization; an expected one, giving the most likely level of service that will be funded; and finally, an optimistic budget plan that will provide a minimum level of service.[37]

To maximize the benefits of using budgets, managers must be able to avoid major pitfalls, which, according to Samuel Certo,[38] include the following:

1. *Placing too much emphasis on relatively insignificant organizational expenses.* In preparing and implementing a budget, managers should allocate more time to deal with significant organizational expenses and less time for relatively insignificant organizational expenses. For example, the amount of time spent on developing and implementing a budget for labor costs typically should be more than the amount of time managers spend on developing and implementing a budget for office supplies.
2. *Increasing budgeted expenses year after year without adequate information.* Perhaps the best-known method developed to overcome this potential pitfall was zero-based budgeting, just discussed.[39]
3. *Ignoring the fact that budgets must be changed periodically.* Administrators must recognize that such factors as costs of materials, newly developed technology, and demand for services are constantly changing and that budgets should reflect that fact by being reviewed and modified periodically in response to those changes. A special type of budget, the performance budget (discussed earlier), is designed to assist in determining the amount of resources allocated for each organizational activity.

Common Cost and Waste Problems

To manage costs, administrators must be able to identify areas where waste and costs might be controlled. Louise Tagliaferri[40] identified 14 common cost factors that can be found in most organizations. Note that some costs are simply uncontrollable, but others are within the scope of the manager to reduce or at least maintain within a reasonable scope:

Absenteeism and turnover	Direct and indirect labor
Accident loss	Energy

Maintenance	Product quality
Materials and supplies	Productivity
Overtime	Tools and equipment
Paperwork	Transportation
Planning and scheduling	Waste

Tagliaferri also noted that "literally billions of dollars are lost to industry (and criminal justice!) each year through carelessness, inattention, waste, inefficiency, and other cost problems."[41]

Strategies for Augmenting Criminal Justice Budgets

In difficult fiscal times, criminal justice agencies welcome any means by which they can increase their operating budgets. Unfortunately, there are limited opportunities for doing so, especially for courts and corrections agencies. The police, however, have recently fared better in this regard, albeit some measures have been controversial. Prisons and jails have some income-producing inmate-labor programs (see Chapter 9), and the police can presently draw supplemental funds from several sources.

Federal and general foundation grants are available to police agencies. Police have used them for a variety of purposes, such as the purchase of vehicles and riot equipment, communications centers, regional crime laboratories, and programs for alcohol safety and accident prevention, rape victims, and the elderly. Potential grantors are located through such publications as the *Federal Directory of Domestic Aid Programs* and by preparing well-conceived grant proposals.

Criminal justice agencies also receive contributions. For example, the Erie County, New York, sheriff's office received $5,000 from a local bank to renovate an old van for use in a crime-prevention program. On a larger scale, the New York City Police Foundation has raised money since 1971 for endeavors such as scholarships, a police stress program, and a bomb squad. In one recent year, the foundation raised $1.3 million. Police departments have also raised funds to purchase bulletproof vests and canines and to renovate their facilities.[42]

Huge supplemental revenues for police agencies come from confiscated cash and property involved with narcotics and contraband goods trafficking, racketeering, gambling, and other offenses. States' forfeiture laws allow the police to initiate forfeiture proceedings on seized goods such as airplanes, cash, cars, boats, and guns. These laws can use criminals' assets against them by funding additional law enforcement initiatives.[43]

Extra income also comes from user fees, which some police departments have initiated. These fees for services formerly provided for free, such as unlocking vehicles and responding to false burglar alarms, are controversial. Less controversial have been fees for hooking up burglar alarms to the police alarm board or computer-assisted dispatch system.[44] In one year, Miami, Florida, collected $270,000 in alarm permit and false alarm fees.

Finally, Internal Revenue Service rewards have been paid to police agencies that capture racketeers who have not properly reported their income taxes. The program began in Atlanta, Georgia, where the police department approached the IRS about collecting the 10 percent informer's fee on unpaid taxes. Through a special city ordinance, the police department was awarded the informer's fee on behalf of the city. The IRS does not divulge the identities of agencies that have received such awards.[45]

Summary

This chapter focused on a singularly important area of financial administration, budgeting, and included its elements, formats, and potential pitfalls. Emphasis was placed on the need for administrators to develop skill in budget formulation and execution.

This chapter also discussed the budget process and different types of budgets. No single budgeting format is best, and based on tradition and personal preference, a hybrid format normally evolves in an organization. Nor should an administrator, under any normal circumstances, surrender control of the organization's budget to another individual or body: The budget is too integral to planning, organizing, and directing programs and operations. In seemingly endless times of fiscal shortages, the justice administrator should attempt to become knowledgeable about opportunities for enhancing the budget through grants, donations, user fees, forfeitures, rewards, and other such means of "fattening" the budget. Uncommon times call for uncommon methods.

Questions for Review

1. What is a budget? How is it used?
2. What is a budget cycle? What is its importance in budgeting?
3. What is involved in formulating a budget? Its approval and execution?
4. List four types of budget formats used in the past. Which type is used most frequently? What are its major advantages and component parts?
5. How are criminal justice agencies augmenting their budgets? Can additional means be used in this regard? Provide some examples.

Notes

1. Charles R. Swanson, Leonard Territo, and Robert W. Taylor, *Police Administration: Structures, Processes, and Behavior* (4th ed.) (Upper Saddle River, N.J.: Prentice Hall, 1998), p. 550.

2. See James C. Snyder, "Financial Management and Planning in Local Government," *Atlanta Economic Review* (November/December 1973):43–47.

3. Aaron Wildavsky, *The Politics of the Budgetary Process* (2d ed.) (Boston: Little, Brown, 1974), pp. 1–4.

4. Orin K. Cope, "Operation Analysis—The Basis for Performance Budgeting," in *Performance Budgeting and Unit Cost Accounting for Governmental Units* (Chicago: Municipal Finance Officers Association, 1954), p. 8.

5. Lester R. Bittel, *The McGraw-Hill 36-Hour Management Course* (New York: McGraw-Hill, 1989).

6. Ibid., p. 187.

7. Robert Townsend, *Further Up the Organization: How to Stop Management from Stifling People and Strangling Productivity* (New York: Alfred A. Knopf, 1984), p. 2.

8. Roland N. McKean, *Public Spending* (New York: McGraw-Hill, 1968), p. 1.

9. S. Kenneth Howard, *Changing State Budgeting* (Lexington, Ky.: Council of State Governments, 1973), p. 13.

10. Michael C. Thomsett, *The Little Black Book of Budgets and Forecasts* (New York: AMACOM, a division of the American Management Association, 1988), p. 38.

11. Quoted in V. A. Leonard and Harry W. More, *Police Organization and Management* (7th ed.) (Mineola, N.Y.: Foundation Press, 1987), p. 212.

12. Swanson, Territo, and Taylor, *Police Administration* (4th ed.), pp. 558–559.

13. Adapted, with some changes, from Aaron Wildavsky, *The Politics of the Budgetary Process* (2d ed.), pp. 63–123.

14. Lennox L. Moak and Kathryn W. Killian, *A Manual of Techniques for the Preparation, Consideration, Adoption, and Administration of Operating Budgets* (Chicago: Municipal Finance Officers Association, 1973), p. 5, with changes.

15. Lennis M. Knighton, "Four Keys to Audit Effectiveness," *Governmental Finance* 8 (September 1979):3.

16. The Comptroller General of the United States, *Standards for Audit of Governmental Organizations, Programs, Activities, and Functions* (Washington, D.C.: General Accounting Office, 1972), p. 1.

17. Ibid.

18. Peter F. Rousmaniere (ed.), *Local Government Auditing* (New York: Council on Municipal Performance, 1979), Tables 1 and 2, pp. 10, 14.

19. Swanson, Territo, and Taylor, *Police Administration* (4th ed.), p. 572.

20. Allen Schick, *Budget Innovation in the States* (Washington, D.C.: Brookings Institution, 1971), p. 14–15. Schick offered 10 ways in which the line-item budget fosters control.

21. Malchus L. Watlington and Susan G. Dankel, "New Approaches to Budgeting: Are They Worth the Cost?" *Popular Government* 43 (Spring 1978):1.

22. Jesse Burkhead, *Government Budgeting* (New York: Wiley, 1956), p. 11.

23. Larry K. Gaines, Mittie D. Southerland, and John E. Angell, *Police Administration* (New York: McGraw-Hill, 1991), p. 398. Swanson, Territo, and Taylor, *Police Administration* (3d ed.), p. 591.

24. Swanson, Territo, and Taylor, *Police Administration* (4th ed.), p. 574.

25. Ibid.

26. Gaines, Southerland, and Angell, *Police Administration*, pp. 396, 398.

27. Ibid., p. 600.

28. David Novick (ed.), *Program Budgeting* (New York: Holt, Rinehart, and Winston, 1969), p. xxvi.

29. Ibid., p. xxiv.

30. See Council of State Governments, *State Reports on Five-Five-Five* (Chicago: Council of State Governments, 1968).

31. International City Management Association, *Local Government Budgeting, Program Planning and Evaluation* (Urban Data Service Report, 1972):7.

32. Allen Schick, "The Road to PPBS: The Stages of Budget Reform," *Public Administration Review* 26 (December 1966):244.

33. Ibid.

34. Swanson, Territo, and Taylor, *Police Administration* (4th ed.), p. 576.

35. Peter A. Phyrr, "Zero-Base Budgeting," *Harvard Business Review* (November/December 1970):111–121; see also E. A. Kurbis, "The Case for Zero-Base Budgeting," *CA Magazine* (April 1986):104–105.

36. Joseph S. Wholey, *Zero-Base Budgeting and Program Evaluation* (Lexington, Mass.: Lexington Books, 1978), p. 8.

37. Donald F. Facteau and Joseph E. Gillespie, *Modern Police Administration* (Englewood Cliffs, N.J.: Prentice Hall, 1978), p. 204.

38. Samuel C. Certo, *Principles of Modern Management: Functions and Systems* (4th ed.) (Boston: Allyn and Bacon, 1989), pp. 484–485.

39. George S. Minmier, "Zero-Base Budgeting: A New Budgeting Technique for Discretionary Costs," *Mid-South Quarterly Business Review* 14 (October 1976):2–8.

40. Louise E. Tagliaferri, *Creative Cost Improvement for Managers* (New York: Wiley, 1981), p. 7.

41. Ibid., p. 8.

42. Swanson, Territo, and Taylor, *Police Administration* (4th ed.), p. 586.

43. Ibid., p. 586.

44. Ibid., p. 588.

45. Ibid., p. 590.

TECHNOLOGY REVIEW

Chapter

God hath made man upright; but they have sought out many
inventions.

—Ecclesiastes 7:29

Everything that can be invented has been invented.
—Charles H. Duell, Commissioner of Patents, 1899

*There is no reason for any individual to have a computer in their
home.*

—Kenneth Olsen, president and founder of Digital
Equipment Corp., 1977

Introduction

Criminal justice involves a wide range of professional participants. For decades,
even centuries, participants primarily have worked independently, sharing information by the printed page. As the world enters the fast lane of the Information
Age, criminal justice has fallen behind dramatically. As Judges George Nicholson
and Jeffrey Hogge pointed out,

It is not enough to shovel faster. Criminal justice must enter the Information Age by incorporating technology as a tool to make the system run efficiently and effectively. It doesn't take a brilliant futurist to know criminal justice will eventually be paperless. All documents will be created, filed, stored, and retrieved electronically, (at) lower costs, time savings, and improvements in storage, retrieval, portability, and access.[1]

The paperless era will probably not come soon, however. As Nicholson and Hogge noted, most of today's more experienced criminal justice participants learned to perform their basic functions the old way. Furthermore, these participants are reluctant to try new methods when past attempts have been disappointing and embarrassing because of partial or complete failure of the system to live up to its advance billing.[2] Another factor that militates against an infusion of technology is cost. Many smaller jurisdictions simply cannot afford to become high tech; and stacks of cardboard boxes full of files rise from the floor to the ceiling in many police departments, courthouses, and corrections facilities across the land. Still, one thing is clear: In order for the justice system to improve and become more coordinated, technology, planning, and cooperation are essential.

This chapter discusses the kinds of technological advances that are now used. Few involve getting the three justice system components working together, as Nicholson and Hogge advocate. The technologies described in this chapter demonstrate what each component is doing to help itself.

Technology in Policing

We begin with a discussion of several exciting developments involving computer technology in police work. It is not surprising that most of the technological developments today involve the police, given the nature of their work, tools, and crime problems. In this section, we discuss a wide variety of police technologies involving patrol officers, dispatchers, forensic scientists, crime analysts, and records personnel.

Use of Wireless Technology

The first digital data were transmitted from police headquarters to a police car in the mid-1980s. Until recently, this capability was limited only to those agencies that could afford private radio networks and mobile data terminals (MDTs). Today, however, even a small agency can afford a laptop and a modem to send encrypted data to officers in the field.[3]

A growing number of U.S. police departments, including small agencies, are using laptop computers with wireless connections to crime and motor vehicle databases. These systems are believed to pay for themselves in increased fines and officer safety. Officers can access court documents, in-house police department records, and a computer-aided dispatch (CAD) system, as well as enter license numbers into their laptop computers. Through a national network of motor vehicle and criminal history databases, the police can locate drivers with outstanding warrants, expired or suspended licenses, and criminal backgrounds. Furthermore, rather than using open radio communications, police officers use their computers to communicate with each other via e-mail.[4]

As the new millennium begins, police officers require computing tools with flexibility—a quality that MDTs lack. Advances in technology have pushed well beyond the ability to send and receive short bursts of alphanumeric data. Police administrators need to become more innovative. As one consultant put it,

> We see over and over the RFP [Request for Proposal] that says the agency wants to purchase the latest, greatest high-tech widget, but it has to be proven, have five previous installations, and have been in existence for four years. There's a phenomenal contradiction there.[5]

Technology Aids Community Policing

In Chapter 3, we discussed community oriented policing and problem solving (COPPS). This strategy entails identifying—through scanning and analysis—"hot spots" of neighborhood disorder that are in need of police attention. Certainly, technology can assist in these endeavors.

Some cities now employ a sophisticated system that uses an integrated CAD system, MDTs, and message switching and routing tools to collect, store, monitor, and retrieve information needed with COPPS. Officers can quickly perform license plate checks, produce slips if they tow a vehicle, check on stolen property, and write online incident and booking reports. The system also automatically captures shift activities to produce the daily shift-ending reports and helps officers sort data so they can present information to citizens in an easy to understand format at neighborhood meetings.[6]

Some cities are also developing a Geographic Information System (GIS), which enables officers to plot criminal activity on an electronic map. Layers of information can then be added to the map to create a picture of crime trends. One unique way officers can use community policing strategies is to develop a database of problems and solutions. When an officer answers a call for service or encounters a problem, he or she can enter it into the database, along with all information about the problem, the action taken, and a list of resources that were applied to the problem. The next time officers confront a similar problem, they can search the database and get a report on everything that has been done about that problem in the past.[7]

Electronics in Traffic Investigations and Enforcement

A multicar accident can turn a street or highway into a parking lot for many hours, sometimes days. The police must collect evidence relating to the accident and take measurements and make sketches of the scene and vehicle and body positions, skid marks, street or highway elevations, intersections, and curves.

These tasks typically involve a measuring wheel, steel tape, pad, and pencil. The cost of traffic delays—especially for commercial truck operators—is substantial for every hour traffic is stalled.

Some police agencies have begun using a version of a surveyor's total station that electronically measures and records distances, angles, elevations, and the names and features of objects. Data from the system can be downloaded onto a computer for display or printed out on a plotter. In vehicular homicide cases requiring reconstruction of the crime scene, some courts now prefer the precision, scope, and professional appearance of court exhibits collected and generated by the electronic system.

With this system, officers can spend an hour or so getting measurements at major traffic accidents, push a button, and have the system draw lines pertinent to the accident to scale. This process enables officers to get 40 percent more measurements in about 40 percent of the time, thus allowing the traffic flow to resume much more quickly. This system is also being used at major crime scenes. Its only drawback is that it cannot be used in heavy rain or snow.[8]

Technological development has also raised traffic enforcement to a higher level with the advent of traffic cameras, already nicknamed the *photocop,* and electro-optical traffic enforcement devices that include both radar and cameras. Traffic cameras, either mounted on a mobile tripod or permanently fixed on a pole, emit a narrow radar beam that triggers a flash camera when a targeted vehicle exceeds the speed limit by a certain amount, usually 10 miles per hour. The ticket is then mailed to the vehicle's registered owner. If the owner has a question about or defense to the citation (such as having loaned the vehicle to another person on the day of the violation), he or she may contact the police department or take the matter to court.

Several companies now manufacture and provide traffic cameras to the police: The devices cost nothing in taxes: The manufacturer receives a certain fee per paid ticket, so violators actually finance the program.

Expediting DUI Arrests

During a stop for driving under the influence (DUI), officers might spend a lengthy period of time questioning a driver and conducting a barrage of screening tests. Then, if an arrest is made, the officer necessarily devotes a good deal of time transporting and processing the arrestee at the jail, including administering a urine or blood test. This delay in formal testing can skew test results because it can allow the alcohol to metabolize.

Recently, the California Department of Justice and the California Highway Patrol began looking at another way to help automate the drunk-driver apprehension process. One tool used routinely during a drunk-driving stop is a small, portable machine that resembles a video-game cartridge for breath screening. The DUI suspect blows into it, and the officer takes the reading of the amount of alcohol in the suspect's system. Law enforcement officials hope that this device can be adapted so that the test can be used in court. If it can be, it could save time in transporting DUI suspects, testing them, and finding that their blood level was below the legal limit.

The revamped instrument would be attached to a notebook or laptop computer that an officer would use by running a mag-stripe driver's license through a reader on the computer to bring up pertinent information about the driver. The computer would then prompt the officer to start the test and would provide a readout of the results on the screen. The officer would transfer the test results over telecommunications lines to a central location to be recorded.

Another potential use of the system is the sharing of data, specifically a database of blood alcohol arrests and results,[9] with the division of motor vehicles and the courts.

Imaging and Sensing Technology

Another technological weapon in the war against crime is image processing, which can turn the most blurred video images into clear visions. Until recently, image processing usually meant enhancement by enlarging photographs, but they can be enlarged only to a certain extent before clarity is completely lost. The new image processing is based on technology created by NASA to clear up the blurred photos taken by the Hubble space telescope. The technique relies on linear mathematical equations that can manipulate a photo's shades of gray.[10] The U.S. Secret Service uses image enhancement to attempt to spot individuals under surveillance in large crowd photos.

Imaging technology has also been applied to fingerprints and mugshots. The Boston Police Department, like most departments in the country, was devoting tremendous resources to identifying prisoners with mugshots and fingerprints. Then the department, with what was the first system of its kind in North America, replaced all filmed mugshots and ink fingerprinting with a citywide integrated electronic imaging identification system. Its system also was the first to receive the FBI's certification for electronic fingerprint submission.

Instead of transporting prisoners to a central booking facility in downtown Boston—a task that took 40,000 hours of officers' time per year—officers at the 11 district police stations can electronically scan a prisoner's fingerprints, take digital photographs, and then route the images to a central server for easy storage and access. This network gives investigators timely access to information and mugshot lineups and saves the police department a million dollars in labor and transportation costs while freeing officers for duties other than transporting prisoners.[11]

Finally, a promising breakthrough in sensing technology may soon give the police the ability to detect previously undetectable items, such as drugs or explosives hidden in bags, suitcases, or clothing. The system is being heralded as one of the most important discoveries since the X-ray.

In the same way we use visible light to create a photograph or invisible radiation to reveal broken bones, terahertz radiation can likewise be used to *create* images. Many biological and organic compounds radiate distinct images in the terahertz band. This radiation passes through objects just as X-rays can, producing internal views that are difficult or impossible to see with existing detection systems. Ongoing research has been funded in part by a $100,000 federal government grant.[12]

Computerized Mapping for Crime Control

Police department crime analysts have long used paper pin maps to indicate criminal activity in a given area. The use of computers and mapping software has greatly extended the paper pin map and offers far greater flexibility and analytical capabilities. Although computers have been used to display and manipulate maps since the 1960s, widespread use of mapping software is a relatively new phenomenon resulting, in large part, from the availability of inexpensive yet sophisticated PC-based mapping software packages.[13] Computerized mapping is an effective tool to help police departments track criminal activity in neighborhoods known in community policing, as previously mentioned, as *hot spots*. Combined with a technique known as *geocoding* (which verifies addresses and links other geographic information with them), computer mapping software can combine data sets to provide a multidimensional view of crime and its potential contributing factors.[14]

Many large police agencies are using this technology, some in conjunction with their COPPS initiative. Computerized mapping is particularly useful for police departments with computer-aided dispatch and records management systems, which store and maintain calls for service and incident, arrest, and other data that are potentially mappable. Geographic information useful in planning includes the locations of crimes committed during the past month; the locations of abandoned houses, stripped cars, and other conditions indicating neighborhood decay; and the locations where persons who could benefit from crime prevention actually live. Perhaps the most important feature of mapping software is its ability to join or overlay disparate data sets. For example, one "layer" of a map display could represent the locations of crimes in the past month, and another layer could represent the unemployment rates of persons living on each city block, the locations of abandoned houses, or citizen reports of drug activity.[15]

Crime analysts use mapping software to prepare crime alert bulletins and other reports that police commanders use in planning operations. Patrol officers use this software to obtain quick visual overviews of current crime conditions in their patrol areas. Figure 16.1 shows a crime map of street gang homicide, other violence, and drug crime.

Three-Dimensional Crime Scene Drafting

For years, police have used tape and, when necessary, pieces of string to measure crime scenes and then used these measurements to painstakingly draw the scene to scale for later use in court. Today, three-dimensional computer-aided drafting (3-D CAD) software can be purchased for a few hundred dollars. By working in 3-D, CAD users can create scenes that can be viewed from any angle. Suddenly, very technical evidence can be visualized by nontechnical people. Juries can

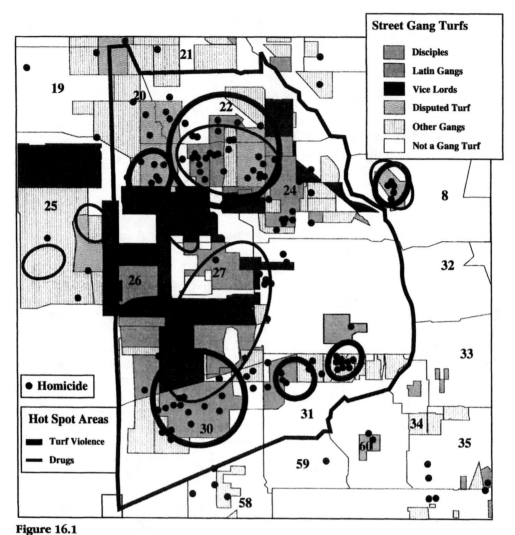

Figure 16.1

Street gang-motivated homicide, other violence, and drug crime,
1987–1990. (*Source:* Chicago Police Department.)

"view" crime scenes and see the locations of evidence: They can view just what the witness says he or she saw.

Police program the exact dimensions into the CAD system and receive a scaled drawing. What is also needed, however, is training to teach officers or detectives how to create such drawings. A five-day, 40-hour course is available for police investigators, traffic accident reconstructionists, and evidence technicians.[16]

Gunshot Locator Systems

In some cities, random gunshots have become such a problem that citizens are storming into city council meetings to demand action. During holidays such as New Year's Eve and the Fourth of July, people shooting guns in celebration create a potentially lethal problem.

A primary obstacle for the police in addressing this problem is determining the location of such gunshots. Technology that is similar to that used to determine the strength and epicenter of earthquakes is now available. Known as a *Gunshot Locator System,* it uses microphonelike sensors placed on rooftops and telephone poles to record and transmit the sound of gunshots by radio waves or telephone lines. A software program then alerts a dispatcher and pinpoints the origin of gunshots via a flashing icon on a computerized map. At minimum, the system, which bases location on how long it takes the sound to reach the sensors, has the potential to greatly reduce police response time to crime scenes, which can decrease the time needed to obtain aid for victims and can increase the likelihood of arrests.[17]

Firearms Technology

Training

Recruits and in-service officers alike use the Firearms Training System (FATS), which ranges in cost from $32,000 to a military model selling for $5 million and is said to be "as close to real life as you can get."[18] Users can be shown on a movie screen a wide variety of computer-generated scenarios led by an instructor at a console. Using laser-firing replicas of their actual weapons, users learn marksmanship as well as judgment—when to shoot and when not to shoot. The system, which consists of a container about the size of a large baby buggy with a computer, a laser disk player, a projector, and a hit detect camera, can be transported to various sites. At some sites, such as Miami-Dade County, Florida, FATS is combined with a driving simulator. Recruits drive to the scene of a bank robbery and then bail out of their cars into a FATS scenario.

Drugfire Network Connects Guns to Crimes

Drugfire is a federal networked system begun in 1992 that holds images of spent cartridges that can help link weapons to other shootings. It is essentially an imaging system with networked search capabilities. A dedicated microscope is attached to a computer, and an image of the cartridge case primer (the area where the firing pin hits the cartridge) is loaded into the system. The image is stored and accessible later by other crime laboratories checking for connections with evidence they hold. Forensic scientists compare fired bullets and used casings to determine whether a firearm in custody was used in other shootings. Since its inception in 1992, more than 1,000 matches have been made by labs around the country using Drugfire, and 68 firearms labs in 19 states and the District of Columbia were linked to Drugfire or are in the planning stages.[19]

"Smart Guns" That Save Lives

Historically, many police officers have been slain with their own guns. Furthermore, close to 500 children and adolescents are killed in firearms accidents each year, and some 1,400 youngsters commit suicide with guns.[20]

In the face of these facts, efforts are under way to create "smart" (or personalized) guns that can be fired only by their rightful owners along with a few other authorized users. Technological options are being explored in several areas. For example, radio signals that enable a weapon to recognize and respond to a transponder worn by the authorized user are being developed. The transponder's range is only a few inches, so the gun would not work for a stranger who steals it. A gun could be designed to recognize up to 50 transponders, so a number of officers could fire the weapon if necessary. Although such a system could increase the price of a standard service pistol from $600 to about $900, the development of this system is gaining momentum. States and localities are drafting laws that could require the use of personalized guns.[21]

Laser Aiming

In order to reduce the potential for use of deadly force, many police agencies have begun to authorize and issue laser sights as standard equipment. The high-tech laser system adapts to the officer's firearm by means of replacement grip panels. Packaged within the grips is a sophisticated laser aiming device that is pressure activated when the officer's gun is drawn. Police agencies have reported that the laser aiming device clearly adds an additional less-than-lethal force alternative. Often an officer's verbal commands to a suspect at gunpoint often go unheeded. The visual impact of the red laser dot on the suspect's chest, however, has assisted officers in gaining compliance and even surrender. In addition, lasers have been effective as an alternative sighting method around or over cover.[22]

The Search for the Consummate Less-Than-Lethal Weapon

For several decades, police administrators and inventors around the world have endeavored to find the "perfect" weapon for use against rioters and other offenders.

Until the 1960s, international policing witnessed only one major addition to the small array of less-than-lethal police tools: chemical weapons. Invented in 1869, CN gas was the first tear gas that produced a burning sensation in the throat, eyes, and nose. Chemical Mace was the most well-known variety.[23] Mace seemed to be manna from heaven and Mace-squirting nightsticks were developed. Wooden rounds, rubber bullets, the British riot police watercannons, and the Sound Curdler (consisting of amplified speakers that produce loud, shrieking noises at irregular intervals) were all developed.[24]

In 1970, another unique less-than-lethal weapon—a gun that shot beanbags rather than bullets—was introduced. The Photic Driver produced a strobe effect whose light caused giddiness, fainting, and nausea. Other inventions of this decade included an electrified water jet, a baton that carried a 6,000 volt shock, shotgun shells filled with plastic pellets, plastic bubbles that immobilized rioters, a chemical that created slippery street surfaces for combatting rioters, and an instant "cocoon" that, when sprayed over crowds, made people stick together.[25] The side-handle baton remains popular among police officers today. Two new types of projectiles were developed in the mid-1970s: the plastic bullet, and the TASER, which shot two tiny darts into its victim and delivered a 50,000-volt electrical shock that could knock down a person at a distance of 15 feet. Also introduced in the mid-1970s, the stun gun, shaped like an electric razor, delivered a 50,000 volt shock when its two electrodes were pressed directly against the body.

During the 1980s, flashlights that had stun capacity or contained chemical agents were marketed. The entanglement net and the action chain control device required four officers to operate, in what seems today much like a Keystone Cops scenario. An expandable baton (from 6 to 16 inches "with a flick of the wrist") and a six-inch steel whip that, when opened to its 13-inch length, projected three steel coils and was transformed into something resembling the Medieval "cat-o-nine-tails," were also available.

Pepper spray, or oleoresin capsicum (OC), introduced in the early 1990s, is now believed to hold much promise as a less-than-lethal police tool, reducing injuries and complaints about force. Although OC has been used in cases in which the suspects later died, a review by the International Association of Chiefs of Police found no evidence linking OC to such deaths.[26] The use of OC has spread across the country, even in many prisons, but a number of police agencies believe that it is not a panacea and have discontinued its use in the aftermath of these reported in-custody deaths.

Another possible solution to the ongoing search for a perfect less-than-lethal weapon, now being peddled to police agencies for use against criminals, uses two very strange types of foam. One is supersticky: Intruders would be drenched in a substance that, exposed to the air, turns into taffylike glue. The other creates an avalanche of very dense soap bubbles that leave offenders unable to see or move but able to breathe. Other chemical compounds, known as *slick'ems* and *stick'ems,* make pavements either too sticky or too slippery for vehicles to move.[27]

Gang Intelligence Systems

The escalating problem of street gangs prompted many police departments to search for a tool that could help them deal with the problem. Several agencies now use a system to collect information in a database, allowing officers to enter and access key pieces of data such as gang names, vehicles, weapons, suspect associates, and incident dates. Even if an officer has a very small piece of information to work with, such as a nickname or partial license plate number of a suspect's car, the system's cross referencing function connects that information to more information in the database about gang members, their activities, addresses, descriptions, and photos. Officers can even access the database in their patrol cars utilizing laptops. The system also allows photographs to be stored and linked with other information about suspects. A statewide gang intelligence system, California's CAL/GANG, is a relational database that holds and categorizes everything from nicknames to tattoos on suspected or known gang members. This system, which has been credited for solving a number of high-visibility gang crimes, is now being considered by other states, including Florida, which has a significant gang problem.[28]

Enhanced Dispatch Systems

Recently, when a call came in to the Edmonton, Alberta, dispatch center, its enhanced system displayed an icon indicating six prior calls to that address, four for family violence and two for a missing juvenile. The dispatcher called up the incident address in Canada's firearms registry and discovered that weapons were registered to the occupant; and in addition, a male occupant had threatened responding officers. This information was relayed to the two responding officers both verbally and via MDT in their patrol car. With this information, the officers acted with caution and did not stand in front of the occupant's front door. This information proved crucial, because the occupant shot through the door with a rifle, commencing a 16-hour standoff that ended with his suicide. Officers in Edmonton believe that dispatchers provide information that is as valuable as a bullet-proof vest.[29]

Many police departments have a similar system, but most are tied to only one database. The Edmonton police can access information from the national crime information center (on wants, warrants, and stolen vehicles); the Operational Support Communications and Records System, an incident database linked to other national, provincial, and municipal databases; and the Computer Aided Dispatch System (CAD), which handles call history. Officers also have direct links to databases of city utilities and the local telephone company.

NCIC 2000

The Federal Bureau of Investigation (FBI) began operating the National Crime Information Center (NCIC) in 1967. This system, now serving more than 80,000 agencies and making more than two million transactions daily,[30] is responsible for the recovery of billions of dollars of property, the capture of tens of thousands of criminals, and the location of thousands of missing persons.[31]

NCIC sorely needs replacing, however. In 1986, the FBI began a $46 million project to replace it with NCIC 2000. System enhancements will include new hardware and software; image capabilities for pictures of subjects, stolen property, and fingerprint matching; a choice of communications protocols; electronic validation of records submitted by state and local police agencies; electronic access to federal prison records as well as Canadian criminal justice records;

improved response times; the ability to multithread queries, which under NCIC were processed one at a time; improved system security; and live scan fingerprint capability.[32]

To take full advantage of NCIC 2000's enhancements, state and local police agencies must upgrade their hardware and software. At a minimum, they must each decide whether to replace their old terminals with personal computer work stations and laptop computers in patrol vehicles. Experts believe that because equipment costs are continually dropping, even the smallest police agencies can afford upgraded PCs or work stations.[33]

The Camcorder Era

Since the Rodney King incident in 1991, videotape technology has had an impact on all of the previously mentioned areas of policing and its administration. The use of videotaping by the general public after that incident and the benefits of utilizing camcorders as tools for police activities were recognized by police administrators, many of whom now equip their agency's patrol vehicles with videocameras.

A recent study found that one-third of all police and sheriff's departments serving populations of 50,000 or larger in the United States are also videotaping at least some interrogations. Furthermore, police videos have been particularly useful in drunk-driving arrests and at crime-scene and traffic accident investigations. Videocameras are also used to record eyewitness testimony and in-progress events, such as robberies and building checks. With little investment in money or personnel, police can make in-house tapes for police roll-call training, public relations, and programs such as drinking and driving.[34]

Other Police Technologies

The following are brief descriptions of other newly developed technologies for use by the police:

- *Voice recognition:* Police reports often require 45 minutes to an hour of writing. A software program uses a police knowledge base, which is a combination of filling in report form blanks and open writing (full form). Templates prompt questions on the screen and the officer responds verbally. This technology helps police officers input information without having to type it.[35]

- An air vehicle was recently produced that offers a variety of applications to police in counter-narcotics, search and rescue, surveillance, and other types of operations. The vehicle, with no driver aboard, is 6.5 feet in diameter and has a 50-horsepower engine enabling it to cruise at 80 knots at up to 8,000 feet. It has a remote video recorder that can assist SWAT teams and bomb disposal units in viewing dangerous situations without having to place officers in jeopardy.[36]

- A new video camera has been developed that is so small it can be hidden in a police badge, allowing officers to discreetly videotape every field interrogation, routine traffic stop, and domestic disturbance they encounter. The device, sure to stir a personal liberty debate, could also put a new twist on police brutality litigation.[37]
- Global positioning system (GPS) technology is being utilized by police around the world for finding drowning victims in deep oceans, rivers, and lakes with zero visibility.[38]
- More than 125 police agencies in the United States are using electric bicycles. These appear to be normal mountain bikes; however, the flip of a switch provides a turbo power boost of electric power of up to 20 miles per hour, allowing for faster acceleration for climbing hills.[39]

Issues and Trends: Cellular Phones and 911/311

Cellular phones are having a profound impact, both positive and negative, on policing. Sixty-five percent of all public safety agencies now use cellular phones, and 80 percent will use them by 2005. The positive side is that public safety agencies are being notified by citizens more quickly and more frequently about emergencies and other situations. The negative aspect is that many wireless callers cannot tell these agencies where they are, requiring that police spend an inordinate amount of time trying to locate them. New technology can pinpoint the location of any cell phone and its caller, posing for some a serious threat to privacy. It is generally accepted that people who dial 911 for assistance in an emergency waives their expectation of privacy in order to facilitate emergency responders.[40]

In a related vein, today's 911 telephone system drives police departments. With an estimated 268,000 911 calls per day—90 percent of which are for nonemergencies—911 has "broken the back" of many agencies. To relieve this burden, in August 1996, the federal Office of Community Oriented Policing Services (COPS) launched an experiment using 311 for nonemergency calls and a $350,000 grant in the Baltimore Police Department (BPD).[41] The 311 system has been declared a huge success, with 1,700 nonemergency calls per day, or more than 600,000 nonemergency calls per year diverted from 911 operators. The 311 program has now been replicated in other jurisdictions, including San Jose and Dallas.[42]

Court Technologies

"Courts *are* their records." This adage captures the essence of the important role played by the courts in serving as the primary repository for the records of the community's arrests, convictions, births, deaths, marriages, divorces, and so on. But in so doing, lawyers, judges, and society generally create a blizzard of paper documents daily, all of which require filing, sorting, and indexing for later retrieval. Most courthouses have file cabinets occupying every inch of wall space, as well as basements filled with boxes of decaying records.

The justice system is sagging under the weight of its paper at a time when few resources exist to deal with massive volumes of complaints, briefs, and motions. About 50 percent of the cost of running the courts is attributed to moving paper. The magnitude of the problem was demonstrated when one consulting firm estimated that if 80 percent of 19 million lawsuits in one year had been filed electronically, attorneys and their clients could have saved $646 million.[43]

In this section, we briefly examine two developments that exist toward greatly reducing this deluge of paperwork in the courts: electronic filing and document imaging. Then we look at videoconferencing, a system that greatly reduces staff time spent in transporting prisoners and security risks in courthouses. We also view a futuristic court that has been created to showcase technological products for the twenty-first century.

Electronic Filing

Electronic filing is an exciting advancement for courts that wish to streamline their expanding caseloads. The proliferation of computers, local area networks (LANS), and electronic mail technologies present a unique opportunity to cost effectively organize court procedures.

Various methods are available to file documents electronically. The first is the transfer of word-processing files from one computer to another through a file transfer program. This method has some drawbacks, however. Most file transfer programs require some technical knowledge, and the multiplicity of formats increases the chance that information will be lost or altered. The second method for filing documents electronically is the use of e-mail-enabled electronic forms with fields, or blank spaces, on which users place specific information that is stored in a database. Users send completed forms to the court via a modem, a mail service, or a diskette. Benefits of this system include the friendly graphical user interfaces of most software packages; the ability of users to send e-mail information simultaneously to multiple parties 24 hours a day; and the reduction of photocopy and postal charges, resulting in cost savings.[44]

In summary, using electronic forms offers many benefits for the courts. Automatic entry of information into case management systems reduces entry time and eliminates errors. The ability to control the information entered in a form is important. With an electronic form, one can prevent incorrect, inappropriate, or incomplete information from being entered and can place data in required formats automatically. This procedure saves the space that would be taken by paper forms and reduces time and costs of transferring information to appellate courts. The purchase and maintenance of equipment and software by which to complete electronic forms and the training for personnel are more costly than paper forms, however.[45]

Courts are realizing that computer filing and retrieval of documents can be faster and less expensive and more accurate and secure than the traditional method. Furthermore, computerized documents require far less space to store than paper.

Document Imaging

Another promising solution to the courts' record-keeping problem is document imaging, which can provide better control of document tracking and distribution as well as reduced costs and greater efficiency, because higher volumes of work can be handled more rapidly and accurately, requiring less paper and office space. Imaging offers significant, exponentially growing advantages for high-volume, paper-intensive, service-oriented operations such as courts. Next is a list of advantages of document imaging for the courts.

Courts enter information into case-processing systems from numerous sources. Some documents submitted directly to the administrator's or clerk's office could be scanned into the imaging system locally. Other documents come from such external sources as attorneys, police and probation agencies, and community services. These documents could be scanned into the system remotely or faxed directly into the system.[46]

As with any system, imaging has its disadvantages, including its initial cost; difficulty of system implementation (for integration with other systems) and of reading lengthy imaged documents on a computer screen; the impossibility of modifying, manipulating, or copying text in imaged documents; the potential need for additional staff; and the potential for the entire operation to be immobilized by system failures.[47] Figure 16.2 shows a sample page of document imaging.

Videoconferencing

Videoconferencing has evolved using relatively simple technology because of the security risks and costs of transporting prisoners between jail and court buildings. For these reasons, videoconferencing is becoming one of the most demanded systems in today's court systems. First used with videophone bail hearings in 1972, the primary components of a simple videoconferencing system are television cameras, monitors, microphones, speakers, and a communications network. The latter can be as simple as a pair of coaxial cables running between the court and the jail or as complicated as a satellite transmission and reception facilities.[48]

Although each state has different statutes that govern the use of technology, courts in at least 30 states use video arraignment for first appearance felonies and misdemeanors,[49] which represent about three-fourths of 12 million new criminal cases each year. Approximately 200 video arraignment sites exist in state court systems today. Thus, it is evident that this technology is becoming established as an accepted criminal justice practice. As video technology becomes even more affordable, interest in video arraignment should increase.

Video arraignment provides several benefits, including reduced security risks associated with transporting and handling inmates, reduced overcrowding of courthouse holding facilities, improved custody conditions for defendants while

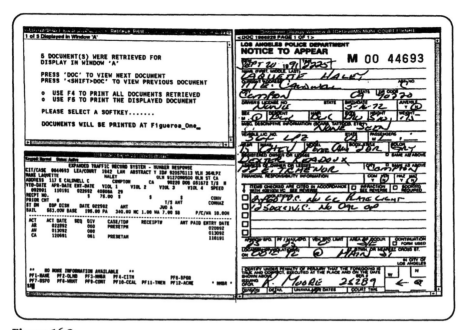

Figure 16.2

Document imaging screen. (*Source:* National Center for State Courts, *Court Technology Reports.* Vol. 4. Williamsburg, Va.: Author, p. 15. Copyright 1992. Used with permission.)

they await arraignment, improvements in the overall efficiency of court proceedings, reduced tension levels among guards and prisoners, minimized delays, and the commingling of first-time offenders with hardened offenders.[50] Criticisms of video arraignments commonly come from defense attorneys, who believe that such technology interferes with the defendant's right to adequate defense representation. In addition, some judges believe that this procedure does not afford them the same control over the courtroom environment or guarantee confidential communication between defendant and counsel.[51]

In addition to arraignments, videoconferencing can eliminate travel and waiting time when attorneys can meet with judges from their own offices. Videoconferencing can also be used for bond hearings, probation revocation hearings, and child support hearings.[52] In addition, court reporters can transcribe these hearings.

Courtroom 21

Recently, the College of William and Mary and the National Center for State Courts unveiled Courtroom 21, the most technologically advanced courtroom in the United States. All of its technology should be available soon after the arrival of the twenty-first century. This project demonstrates how technology can enrich the legal process by assisting judges, court administrators, counsel, jurors, court reporters, and other staff. Courtroom 21 includes the following integrated capabilities:[53]

- *Automatic video recording of proceedings using ceiling-mounted cameras with voice activation.* Courtroom 21 has five ceiling television cameras in the courtroom. When someone in the courtroom speaks, the microphone and camera closest to that person are activated. With cameras properly aimed, the entire courtroom is visible via small video windows, while the person speaking is visible through a large video window. (Such a video record is viewed as superior to a written transcript because appellate judges can observe the demeanor of witnesses and their voice inflections, facial expressions, and gestures.)
- *Recorded televised evidence display with analog optical disk storage.* Evidence can be prerecorded on small analog disks for later use at trial. Counsel may present documentary or real evidence to judge and jury via television display. Trial evidence and events may also be preserved on disk for later trial use or for appeals.
- *Remote two-way television arraignment.* Video arraignment (i.e., teleconferencing, described earlier) is possible between the bench and some remote site. Audio and video signals are received by the control center and then are sent to the several courtroom computer monitors.
- *Jury box computers.* Courtroom 21's jury box contains computers for information display. Each monitor can display documents, real evidence, live or recorded video, transcription, and the usual graphics (charts, diagrams, pictures).
- *LEXIS legal research.* Judges and counsel are provided immediate access to legal resources through the LEXIS online legal database. If an unanticipated legal question arises during trial, judges and counsel can use the computers to consult the database.
- *Video deposition playback facilities.* Because more depositions are being video recorded by attorneys in preparation for trial, Courtroom 21 has video deposition playback. To impeach a witness or present expert witness testimony, video depositions can be played on court monitors.

Court Reporters Work with Technology

It is not uncommon for a court reporter who spends three or four days working on one case, sits in court in one place, and works without breaks to develop a variety of physical ailments because of the intense nature of the work.

Now a system that can afford relief to reporters is available: a digital audio transcription system. This system captures the spoken word on ultrasensitive condenser microphones located at specific points in the courtroom, including the witness stand, judge's bench, and counsel tables. Audio is transmitted to a central control room, where it is digitized by system audio servers and stored on a hard disk and tape.[54]

Instead of sitting in the courtroom, court reporters monitor proceedings from the control room. For every four courtrooms, one reporter is required to sit and monitor all of the activities; thus, the system allows one reporter to do the work of four. The initial investment for the system is about $15,000, versus paying about $50,000 per year for each reporter. Therefore, the court realizes a heavy return on its investment. Accuracy is enhanced by taking the human factor out of the recording process.

Other Court Technologies

Other court technologies have been developed around the country, such as the following:

- Court dates often pose problems for police officers who report to court unnecessarily on their days off (also resulting in millions of dollars of overtime expenses nationally). A number of agencies now use an automated system that reconciles planned court appearances with officers' work schedules. A screen accesses both the officer's and the court's schedules and determines the best dates for scheduling proceedings.[55]

- A Florida circuit court has developed an Automated Telephone Calendaring System that diverts hundreds of calls a month from judicial assistants. Attorneys interact directly with the scheduling computer by telephone to schedule civil hearings. Figure 16.3 shows the concise one-page instruction sheet that serves as a reference for attorneys using the system.

- New York's Automated Budget System (ABS) has databases and spreadsheets that have replaced a paper-driven budgetary process, resulting in significant savings for budget preparers and reviewers. Figure 16.4 shows a sample screen for "worksheet navigation" through this system.

- Oregon's Financial Information and Accounting System tracks all financial transactions of a case, integrating financial and case management. Figure 16.5 shows a sample case financial history screen.

- Arkansas's Supreme Court has a CD-ROM legal research database that saves time and increases the effectiveness of legal research in state appellate courts.[56] Figure 16.6 shows a sample computer screen for a case search.

Technology in Corrections Facilities

In Chapter 11, we discussed two types of electronic monitoring devices that have been used since the mid-1980s as part of intensive supervision programs in corrections. Indeed, computers have been used extensively in the corrections field

```
┌──────────────────────────────────────────────────────────────┐
│                                                                │
│  ┌──────────────────────────────────────────────────────────┐ │
│  │         AUTOMATED COURT SCHEDULING REFERENCE SHEET        │ │
│  │                                                          │ │
│  │    Attorney Name: _____   Bar No: _____ │ │
│  └──────────────────────────────────────────────────────────┘ │
└──────────────────────────────────────────────────────────────┘
```

Caller Supplied Information:			System Generated Responses:		
CASE	LENGTH	TYPE (Request Code)	DAY-DATE	TIME	CONFIRM #

DIVISION A: 951-5742
DIVISION D: 364-4685

TO ACCESS THE SYSTEM:

1) Dial the phone number given above.
When you hear the greeting, press
the appropriate response on your phone.

2) After you have choosen to use the
automated scheduler, the system will
ask for the Attorney Bar no.
Enter the 7-digit Bar no.

(All Bar #'s are 7 digits long!
If necessary, add leading 0's
until the Bar no. is 7 digits long.)

TO SCHEDULE A HEARING TIME:

3) Press 7 - (S)chedule if the court
appearance will be in person;
Press 8 - (T)elephone Appearance if
the appearance will be by telephone.
4) Enter the 6-digit numeric portion of
the case no. when asked to do so.
5) Enter the 2-digit Request Code using
the table to the right as a guideline.
6) A list of time choices will be played;
press a no. (1-4) which represents
the amount of time you are requesting.
7) If the date and time are OK, press 9
(Y)es; otherwise, press 6 for (N)o.
8) Once you have accepted a hearing time,
it will be repeated; write it down.
9) The system will give you a special
confirmation #. You should write it
down! This number provides a secure
and convenient way for you to cancel
the hearing if it is necessary.

TO CANCEL A HEARING TIME:

3) Press 2 - (C)ancel when prompted.
4) Enter the 4-digit special confirmation #
when you asked to do so.
5) System will inform you if the hearing
was successfully cancelled.

Hearing Request Codes:

01 - DISMISS
02 - STRIKE
03 - COMPEL
04 - CONTINUE
05 - QUASH
06 - SUMMARY JUDGEMENT
07 - FINAL DEFAULT JUDGEMENT
08 - VACATE
09 - INTERVENE
10 - TAX FEES/COSTS
11 - ABATE
12 - AMEND
13 - DEFAULT
14 - SEVER
15 - CONSOLIDATE
16 - LIMINE
17 - PROTECTIVE ORDER
18 - CONTEMPT
19 - WITHDRAW
20 - STAY
21 - SANCTIONS
22 - SET ASIDE
23 - DEFICIENCY JUDGEMENT
24 - EXTEND TIME
25 - FINAL HEARING
26 - QUIET TITLE
27 - OBJECTION TO INTERROG.
28 - ORDER TO SHOW CAUSE
29 - OBJECTION TO REQUEST FOR
          PRODUCTION
30 - ANY OTHER SINGLE MOTION
31 - ALL PENDING MOTIONS OR
          MULTIPLE MOTIONS
32 - NEW TRIAL
33 - TEMPORARY INJUNCTION

TO LIST ALL OF YOUR HEARINGS:

3) Press 5 - (L)ist to play
a list of the hearings
you have auto-scheduled.

TO DISCONTINUE A CALL:

3) Press 4 - (H)angup

Figure 16.3

Automated court scheduling reference sheet. (*Source:* National Center for
State Courts, *Court Technology Reports,* Vol. 4. Williamsburg, Va.: Author,
p. 62. Copyright 1992. Used with permission.)

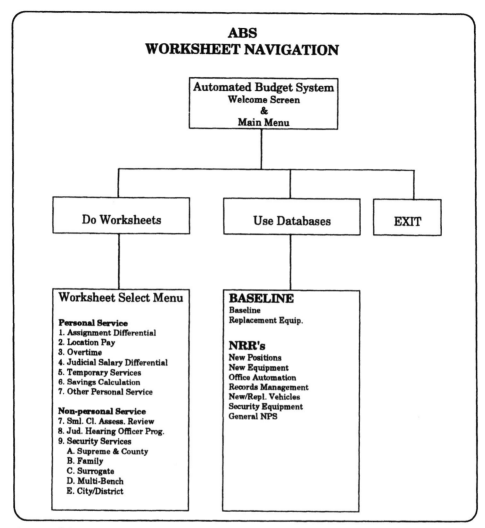

Figure 16.4

Automated budget system worksheet navigation. (*Source:* National Center for State Courts, *Court Technology Reports,* Vol. 4. Williamsburg, Va.: Author, p. 46. Copyright 1992. Used with permission.)

for many years. In state-of-the-art prisons, automated systems control access gates and doors, individual cell doors, and the climate in cells and other areas of the prison. Corrections agencies have also used computers to manage inmate records, conduct presentence investigations, supervise offenders in the community, provide instruction to inmates, and train correctional personnel. With computer assistance, jail administrators receive daily reports on court schedules, inmate rosters, time served, statistical reports, maintenance costs, and other data.

```
                                                            AEH  5/14/92 10:09 AM
    Financial History.... Clackamas County Circuit Court     Status Open      VBL
    Case#......    UNAS16 Oregon State Of/Doe John
                        __Offense_Misdemeanor_-_Comm_Weight/Measure_Viola_-_U/MIS_
    Trust                        Received        Disbursed         Balance
      A/R Payment                1,300.00        -1,300.00            0.00
      Restitution                  500.00          -500.00            0.00
    Trust Balance                                                     0.00
    -----------------------------------------------------------------------------
    Accounts Receivable          Deferred         Applied          Balance
      A/R Payment                    0.00             0.00            0.00
      Fine                       1,000.00          -725.00          275.00
      Restitution                  500.00          -500.00            0.00
      Unitary Assessment            75.00           -75.00            0.00
    Accounts Rcv Balance         1,575.00        -1,300.00          275.00
    -----------------------------------------------------------------------------
        4/30/92 VBL  100786 Due:  4/30/92 Distribution: S REST        500.00
                IMP   1 CRD Mr Measure It
                SNT   1
    ------------------------------------------------------------------------- +


    CF05-DSPPMT     CF07-DSPTRSLGR   CF08-DSPVBLLGR   CF10-BROWSE FWD CF11-BROWSE BCK
```

Figure 16.5

Computer-assisted case financial history. (*Source:* National Center for State Courts. *Court Technology Reports,* Vol. 4. Williamsburg, Va.: Author, p. 95. Copyright 1992. Used with permission.)

Technological advancement in the corrections field has been adapted to much greater advantage than by courts. Next we discuss some of these other uses of technology in prisons, jails, and probation and parole agencies.

Tracking Prison Inmates

The California Department of Corrections (CDC) is one of the largest criminal justice agencies in the world. It tracks more than 130,000 inmates in 27 state institutions and 38 camps during and after incarceration. This Herculean task includes monitoring inmates movements, medical histories, visitors, restitution fines, and job assignments.[57]

The foundation of the CDC's inmate tracking program is an integrated information sharing system with at least one computer located at each institution. Pertinent data are entered by custody staff each day and are transmitted via a wide area network to the central office in Sacramento. When entering a prison, a new inmate is assigned a unique CDC number. This number helps the staff track the inmates' movements and status at all times. A complex data file that consists of information ranging from medical problems and cell assignment to previous escape history is maintained on each inmate. CDC also accounts for the money an inmate may have arrived with, any money sent to him or her through the mail, and amounts deducted to pay court-ordered restitution fines.[58]

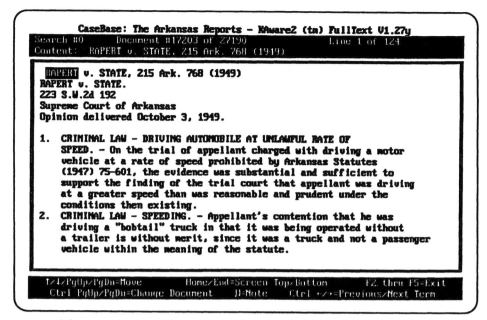

Figure 16.6

Computer-assisted legal research system. (*Source:* National Center for State Courts, *Court Technology Reports*, Vol. 4. Williamsburg, Va.: Author, p. 122. Copyright 1992. Used with permission.)

Automated Direct Supervision in Jails

Direct supervision jails are springing up across the country, eschewing typical jail cells with steel bars. Some of these facilities—including those in Knox County, Tennessee; Forsythe County, North Carolina; and Pima County, Arizona—are replacing the bars with bar-coded wristbands and state-of-the-art computerized information management systems. As one data communications engineer stated, "Everything from the toilets to the telephones is fully computerized" in these facilities.[59]

The information technology package used in these kinds of facilities includes live-scan fingerprinting, an automated fingerprint identification system, digitized mug shots, and computerized inmate and records management. Each inmate's wristband is keyed into the central computer system, which contains his or her name, physical description, picture, and prisoner number. It is used to track each inmate's location, visitations, library use, medical treatment, and court appointments. The system is expected to reduce costs, provide an unheard of level of records integrity, and increase the safety of both officers and inmates by allowing the administrators to develop a completely cashless inmate society. Without cash and with limits set on how much an inmate can spend each week, correctional officers hope to curtail contraband problems. This cashless system virtually eliminates the illicit transactions that once were common, because the administration can regulate and monitor the flow of cash.[60]

Kiosk Check-In for Probationers

Several problems plague probation agencies in America. Probation caseloads continue to rise, and many probation practitioners feel that something has to be done to alleviate their overworked and understaffed condition. Many are turning to automated means of doing so.

A new computer system allows probationers who pose little or no public risk and need very little personal supervision to check in from a remote location rather than making a trip to the probation officer's office. The probationers simply push a few buttons at an electronic kiosk to show they have not left town and perhaps breathe into a breathalyzer if abstention from alcohol is a condition of probation. The system is user-friendly, very accessible, and works without invading privacy.[61]

The kiosks are strategically located and linked to a network of personal computers in the probation department. During the initial meeting with a probation officer, a probationer's biometric keys (fingerprints, voice, retina scan, signature, hand structure) and digital photo of the face are captured electronically. They are entered, along with case-specific information, into the database. The system's server can be programmed to expect check-ins from several times a day to weekly, monthly, or longer intervals. Specific questions can be written for each client. A probationer may check in at any kiosk, where a biometric sample is taken via scanner and compared to the one collected during enrollment. Once identification is established, the probationer may check in. The kiosk operates every day, serving a maximum of 180 people per day.

Evaluations of the system by academics give it high marks for its efficiency in computerized record keeping and for giving probation officers more time to deal with their more serious offenders.[62]

An excellent resource for both criminal justice practitioners and students wishing to travel the information superhighway is *Internet Investigations in Criminal Justice* by Cynthia B. Leshin.[63] This book includes discussion and hands-on practice in using the Internet, finding information and resources, using criminal justice web sites, and employing cyberspace to find a job. Furthermore, persons wishing to access new developments in technology may find the following World Wide Web address useful: http://www.govtech.net. This resource provides information about new products, solutions to problems, jobs, training resources, and conferences. For Internet access to the National Criminal Justice Reference Service Online, use Telnet to access ncjrsbbs.aspensys.com or Gopher to access ncjrs.aspensys.com 71. UNOJUST, the United Nations Online Justice Information System, may be reached at http://ncjrs.org/unojust. Many more relevant web sites are provided in Appendix I.

Summary

This chapter reviewed several exciting technological nuances that are in use by or available to police, courts, and correctional organizations. Readers, especially present and future administrators, managers, and supervisors, are encouraged to stay tuned in this area, because the age of computer technology makes almost anything possible. Computer-assisted systems can also be very economical.

Questions for Review

1. What can technology do to help the police answer calls? Investigate traffic accidents?

2. Which technologies described in this chapter have the primary benefit of making the environment safer for employees and clients? Which are primarily advantageous in their cost savings?

3. What are some of the major technological capabilities now in use in the nation's courts? What are some of the futuristic technological items or methods found in a twenty-first century courtroom?

4. What technologies are available to help all criminal justice agencies to become paperless?

5. Try to conceive of areas in which computer hardware and software could provide greater assistance in criminal justice. What cost issues come into play with these technologies?

Notes

1. George Nicholson and Jeffrey Hogge, "Retooling Criminal Justice: Interbranch Cooperation Needed," *Government Technology* 9 (February 1996): 32.

2. Ibid.

3. Tod Newcombe, "Bandwidth Blues," *Government Technology* 9 (August 1996): 1, 52.

4. Kaveh Ghaemian, "Small-Town Cops Wield Big-City Data," *Government Technology* 9 (September 1996): 38.

5. Meghan Cotter, "Will Integrated Public Safety and Criminal Justice Become a Reality?" *Government Technology* 8 (December 1995): 52.

6. Justine Kavanaugh, "Community Oriented Policing and Technology," *Government Technology* 9 (March 1996): 14.

7. Ibid.

8. Bill McGarigle, "Electronic Mapping Speeds Crime and Traffic Investigations," *Government Technology* 9 (February 1996): 20–21.

9. Justine Kavanaugh, "Drunk Drivers Get a Shot of Technology," *Government Technology* 9 (March 1996): 26.

10. Tod Newcombe, "Image Processing Sharpens Crime Video," *Government Technology* 9 (March 1996): 22.

11. Tod Newcombe, "Imaged Prints Go Online, Cops Return to Streets," *Government Technology* 9 (April 1996): 1, 31.

12. J. Douglas Page, "Terahertz Sensing Technology," *Law Enforcement Technology* (August 1997): 42.

13. U.S. Department of Justice, National Institute of Justice Research in Action, "The Use of Computerized Mapping in Crime Control and Prevention Programs" (July 1995): 1.

14. U.S. Department of Justice, National Institute of Justice Program Focus, "The Chicago Police Department's Information Collection for Automated Mapping (ICAM) Program" (July 1996): 2.

15. U.S. Department of Justice, National Institute of Justice Research in Action, "The Use of Computerized Mapping in Crime Control and Prevention Programs," p. 2.

16. Tod Newcombe, "Adding a New Dimension to Crime Reconstruction," *Government Technology* 9 (August 1996): 32.

17. Justine Kavanaugh, "Locator System Targets Shooters," *Government Technology* 9 (June 1996): 14-15.

18. Patrick Joyce, "Firearms Training: As Close to Real as it Gets," *Government Technology* 8 (July 1995): 14-15.

19. Brian Miller, "Spent Cartridges Nail Shooters," *Government Technology* 9 (October 1996): 15.

20. Ted Gest, "Can 'Smart' Guns Save Many Lives?" *U.S. News and World Report* (December 2, 1996) 37.

21. Ibid., p. 38.

22. Adam Wollander, "Tactical Technology for the Next Millennium," *Law Enforcement Technology* (April 1998): 80.

23. Ken Peak, "The Quest for Alternatives to Lethal Force: A Heuristic View," *Journal of Contemporary Criminal Justice* 6(1) (1990): 8-22.

24. Ibid.

25. Sarah Manwaring-White, *The Policing Revolution: Police Technology, Democracy, and Liberty in Britain* (Brighton, Sussex: The Harvester Press, 1983).

26. "IACP 'Acquits' OC Spray in 22 In-Custody Deaths," *Law Enforcement News* (April 30, 1994): 1.

27. John Barry and Tom Morganthau, "Soon, 'Phasers on Stun,' " *Newsweek* (February 7, 1994): 24-25.

28. Raymond Dussault, "CAL/GANG Brings Dividends," *Government Technology* 11 (December 1998): 124.

29. Raymond Dussault, "Dispatchers Provide Information Age Kevlar," *Government Technology* 9 (January 1996): 14-15.

30. Christina Fusilero and Tod Newcombe, quoting Tom Tolman in "The Grid," *Government Technology* 11 (August 1998): 23.

31. Milford H. Sprecher, "States Gearing Up for NCIC 2000," *Government Technology* 8 (January 1995): 12.

32. Ibid.

33. Ibid., quoting Jack Keating, p. 23.

34. U.S. Department of Justice, National Institute of Justice Research in Brief, *Videotaping Interrogations and Confessions.* (Washington, D.C.: Author, March 1993), p. 2.

35. Keith W. Strandberg, "Law Enforcement Computers and Software," *Law Enforcement Technology* (May 1998): 40.

36. Richard Morrison, "Eye in the Sky," *Law Enforcement Technology* (June 1998): 66.

37. Douglas Page, "Picture This: Oak Ridge National Laboratory (ORNL) Has Developed a Police Shield That Doubles as a Video Camera," *Law Enforcement Technology* (June 1998): 70.

38. "The Vanishing," *Government Technology* 11 (July 1998): 50.

39. "Utah Offers First Electric Bike School," *Law Enforcement Technology* (December 1998): 36.

40. Ibid., quoting Bill Munn, p. 22.

41. U.S. Department of Justice, Office of Community Oriented Policing Services, "COPS Facts: 3-1-1 National Non-Emergency Number," October/November 1996, p. 1.

42. Jennifer Nislow, "Who Ya Gonna Call?" *Law Enforcement News* (December 15/31, 1998): 1, 14.

43. James Evans, "JusticeLINK: Maryland's Electronic Court Test," *Government Technology* (July 1995): 34.

44. David J. Egar, "Electronic Filing," paper presented at the Fourth National Court Technology Conference, National Center for State Courts, Nashville, Tennessee, October 1994, p. 3.

45. Ibid., pp. 3–4.

46. Carter C. Cowles, National Center for State Courts, "Document Imaging," *Court Technology Reports* 5 (1992): 26–27.

47. Carter C. Cowles, "Document Imaging," *Court Technology Bulletin* 7(5) (September/October 1995): 5.

48. National Center for State Courts Court Technology Briefing Paper, "Videoconferencing," 1995, p. 1.

49. Ibid.

50. Ibid., pp. 24–25.

51. Ibid., p. 25.

52. Ibid.

53. Fredric I. Lederer, "Courtroom 21: A Model Courtroom of the 21st Century," *Court Technology Bulletin* 6(1) (January/February 1994): 1, 5.

54. Michelle Gamble-Risley, "A Smart Tool for Modern Courtrooms," *Government Technology* 9 (October 1996): 32.

55. Alison Sonntag, "Court System Saves More Than Time," *Government Technology* 10 (April 1997): 1, 61.

56. National Center for State Courts, *Court Technology Reports* 4 (1991): iii.

57. Dona Snow, "Stretching Corrections Resources With Project Management," *Government Technology* 8 (January 1995): 78.

58. Ibid.

59. Raymond Dussault, "Direct Supervision and Records Automation," *Government Technology* 8 (August 1995): 36.

60. Ibid., p. 37.

61. James Evans, "Kiosk Check In for Probationers," *Government Technology* 8 (May 1995): 42.

62. Ibid., pp. 42, 44.

63. Cynthia B. Leshin, *Internet Investigations in Criminal Justice* (Upper Saddle River, N.J.: Prentice Hall, 1997).

PEEKING OVER THE RIM: WHAT LIES AHEAD?

Chapter

I like the dreams of the future better than the history of the past.
—Patrick Henry

The trouble with our times is that the future is not what it used to be.
—Paul Valery

Introduction

We all have probably wished at some time that we could gaze into a crystal ball and have what former President George Bush termed "the vision thing." Criminal justice students—our administrators of tomorrow—must listen to what the prognosticators tell us about the future and understand their methods. Like current justice administrators, these future administrators must take the time today to peek over the rim to anticipate and plan for the future.

This final chapter examines some of the things that futurists believe that the future holds. We also look at what appears to be imminent with respect to demographics and crime in the United States. We consider what the experts predict in terms of police methods for coping with crime as well as forecasted changes in courts and corrections. We also examine the methods of police, courts, and corrections in the future. Some areas for which reforms are needed are identified.

We close the chapter with a general discussion of the necessary steps administrators need to take to reinvent their agencies, specifically whether they can bring about changes in governance in order to become more customer oriented and streamline and enhance many of their operations by joining the information technology revolution.

How to Predict the Future

Many variables can affect justice agencies: One of the most important is money. In the future, the economy will be the driving force for major changes.

Contemporary futures research involves environmental scanning and scenario writing. Environmental scanning is an effort to put a social problem under a microscope and to predict its future. We may consult experts, such as demographers, social scientists, technologists, and economists. A Delphi process may be used to assist in gathering data from experts, looking at all possible factors, and getting an idea of what will happen in the future. Thus, environmental scanning permits us to identify, track, and assess changes in the environment.[1]

Through scanning, we can examine the factors that seem likely to "drive" the environment. *Drivers* are factors or variables—economic conditions, demographic shifts, governmental policies, social attitudes, technological advances, and so on—that will have a bearing on future conditions. Three categories of drivers will serve to identify possible trends and impacts on the American criminal justice system beyond the year 2000: (1) social conditions (e.g., size and age of the population, immigration patterns, nature of employment, and lifestyle characteristics); (2) shifts in the amounts and types of crimes (including the potential for new types of criminality and for technological advances that might be used for illegal behavior); and (3) possible developments in the criminal justice system itself (e.g., changes in the way the police, courts, and corrections subsystems operate and important innovations).[2]

Scenario writing is simply the application of drivers to primary situations or elements. In the context of our discussion, three scenarios are public tolerance of crime, amount of crime, and the capacity of the criminal justice system to deal with crime. An important consideration is whether each will occur in high or low degrees. For example, drivers may be analyzed in a scenario of *low* public tolerance of crime, a *high* amount of crime, and a *high* capacity of the criminal justice system to deal with crime. Conversely, a scenario may include a view of the future where there is a *high* tolerance of crime, a *low* amount of crime, and a *low* capacity for the system to cope with crime, and so on.

The Changing Face of America

In 1996, the first wave of "baby boomers" turned 50. By 2010, one in every four Americans will be 55 or older. By the year 2000, an estimated 34.9 million elderly people constituted 13 percent of the population. The minority population is increasing rapidly. By the year 2000, an estimated 34 percent of American children were Hispanic, African American, or Asian. As of 1990, more than 25 million women headed their own households, 28 percent of the nation's 91 million households. Two-thirds of African American and Hispanic households are headed by women.[3]

In our postindustrial society, the number of blue-collar jobs has decreased and the number of white-collar jobs has increased. Jobs that are declining in number are those that could be filled by those with fewer skills. The fastest-growing jobs are those requiring more language, math, and reasoning skills. For the first decade of the twenty-first century, 90 percent of all new jobs will be in the service sector—fields that often require high levels of education and skill. In the mid-1980s, about three-fourths of all jobs required some type of generating, processing, retrieving, or distributing information. By the year 2000, heavily computerized information processing is involved in 95 percent of all jobs. Statistics indicate that America is becoming a bifurcated society, with more wealth, poverty, and a shrinking middle class. The gap between the "haves" and "have nots" is widening. An underclass of people who are chronically poor and live outside of society's rules is growing. Between 1970 and 1980, the underclass tripled.[4]

The influence of immigration on America and the growth of minority group populations in general cannot be overstated. The United States accepts nearly a million newcomers per year, which equates to about 10 million new residents each decade, excluding their offspring, even if immigration rates do not rise. Shortly after the turn of the twenty-first century, Asians are expected to reach 10 million. In less than 100 years, we can expect white dominance of the United States to end, as the growing number of African Americans, Hispanics, and Asians together become the new majority.

History has shown that where newcomers cluster together in poor neighborhoods with high crime rates, the criminal justice system is soon involved. When these various minority groups are forced to compete for increasingly scarce low-paying service jobs, intergroup relations are strained and can become combative, as has occurred recently in major cities.[5]

The Changing Nature of Crime

Three important drivers have contributed to the changing nature of crime in the West: (1) the advent of high technology, (2) the distribution and use of narcotics, and (3) a declining population in the 15 to 24 age bracket.[6]

The nature of crime is rapidly changing. The new crimes of data manipulation, software piracy, bank card counterfeiting, and embezzlement by computer are here to stay. The traditionally illegal means of obtaining funds—robbery and burglary—will be used less frequently. These new crimes will require the development of new investigative techniques, specialized training for police investigators, and the employment of people with specialized, highly technological backgrounds.

The abuse of narcotics is increasing throughout various social classes and continues to demand an ever-increasing amount of police time and resources. The true solution to the drug problem is for people to stop demanding a supply. This is probably an impossible goal, however.

The decline in the size of the 15 to 24 age cohort, the crime-prone youth of our society, has significantly affected crime rates. With the exception of violent crime, we have witnessed a decline in several types of crime involving youth. This demographic benefit is about to change, however. As a consequence of the "baby boomerang" (the offspring of the baby boomers), there are now 39 million children in this country who are under the age of 10, millions of them living in poverty and without parental supervision. Thus, we likely face a future wave of youth violence that will be even worse than that of the past 10 years.[7]

The nation's shift in demographic makeup also has implications for future criminal justice recruiting efforts. A change toward older workers; fewer entry-level workers; and more women, minorities, and immigrants in the population will force criminal justice and private industry to become more flexible to compete for qualified applicants. With the aging of the United States, justice agencies that recruit only recent high school graduates will probably face a shortage of qualified workers. Agencies must devise new strategies to attract 21- to 35-year-olds, an age group that will be at a premium over the next 10 years, a trend that will continue well into the middle of the twenty-first century. Criminal justice will also need to offer better wage and benefits packages (such as day care, flexible hours, and paid maternity leave) in order to compete with private businesses.[8]

Policing Methods of the Future

The technological revolution discussed in Chapter 16 will result in new weapons for both criminals and the police. Some futurists believe that traditional methods and equipment for doing police work will be replaced. Electric and methane-fueled scooters and bubble-topped tricycles will be used in densely populated areas; police in rural and suburban areas will employ steamwagons and diesel superchargers; and methane-filled helium dirigibles, equipped with infrared night goggles and sophisticated communications and lighting devices will assist in setting traps for high-speed drivers and in performing search and rescue operations.[9]

Patrol officers in this scenario will type in the facts of a crime and receive a list of suspects. With a bit more analysis and data, the computer will give a probability that various suspects committed the particular crime at that particular place. All homes and businesses will be linked to a central dispatch system in a police-approved, computer-based remote linkage system that will combine burglar and fire alarms. Community policing teams will be assigned by zone, the officers wearing blazers instead of paramilitary uniforms. Basic police training will last a minimum of 10 months and will be geared so that the lower one-third of the class will not succeed.[10]

Others see the future of policing differently. The twenty-first century police officer may patrol by means of jet backpack flight equipment, and officers will be able to tie in to "language banks" of translators via their wrist radios. Holographic, or three-dimensional, photography may be used for mug photos, and satellite photography will probably be used to assist in criminal investigations. Police vehicles will have all electronic equipment built in, and private vehicles will have a factory-installed "kill switch" that can be activated by pressing a button in a nearby patrol vehicle, thus preventing high-speed pursuits.[11]

Obviously, police administrators need to assign some of their best thinkers to the task of probing the future. What should the agency's budget be? How should police personnel be trained? What skills will be needed? What new technologies will the police face? How should forces be deployed?

An area of concern among futurists is policing's organization structure. Increasing numbers of police executives are beginning to question whether the pyramid-shaped police bureaucracy will be effective in the future. Indeed, the spread of community policing and problem solving (discussed in Chapter 3) has allowed many police executives to flatten their organizations. And, as we discussed in Chapter 2, communication within the pyramid structure is often stymied by many barriers and frustrated by the levels of bureaucracy. Perhaps the organization structure, the argument goes, could be changed to a more horizontal design to facilitate the flow of information and ideas.

Personnel and labor/management problems will continue to loom large in the future. Because opportunities for police graft and corruption will not decline, so police administrators must be sure to develop personnel policies that will protect the integrity of the profession. Such matters as age discrimination, employment misconduct, sexism, new employee attitudes, and poor work habits will not be resolved in the near future.

Future Changes in the Courts

Shifts in Philosophy and Practices

Futurists have also been considering the future of the courts as their caseloads expand, society demands greater assistance from the courts in addressing its social ills, and technology continues to advance. Looking at current trends, futurist Clement Bezold offered some interesting court-related speculations for the early twenty-first century:

1. Private businesses offering adjudication, arbitration, and mediation will increasingly compete with public courts to resolve disputes more quickly and fairly.

2. The adversary system, which is slow, costly, and fraught with unfairness, will die.

3. The vast majority of judicial decision making (in such areas as small claims, traffic courts, and status offenses) will be by nonlawyer, citizen pro-tempore judges.

4. Courts will be depoliticized. Appointed professional managers will become the norm, and the merit selection of judges will become more commonplace.

5. Courts will increasingly be called on to resolve social problems involving drugs, poverty, and domestic violence, but with little success.

6. Court programs will become increasingly decentralized and closer to client groups.

7. Court organization structures will become more informal, with less reliance on hierarchical bureaucratic structures, and shared leadership.[12]

Certainly not to be overlooked in the courts' future is the impact of high technology on their internal operations. Next we examine the technological advances that are now developing.

Help on the Horizon with Technology

On a Tuesday evening, in the suburbs of a large, traffic-choked city, Smith is in court to contest a speeding ticket. Instead of getting into his car and driving into the city for night court, Smith strolls a few blocks to a public library and enters a small enclosed booth and stares at a computer screen that displays a menu of functions and colorful icons. He touches the symbol of a courthouse and then the one indicating traffic court. A pleasant voice instructs him to insert his driver's license into a slot on the monitor. Seconds later he sees a description of the date, time, and nature of the charged offense. Smith is told that his case will be called in two minutes. Soon the monitor shows a black-robed figure who addresses the man and asks how he pleads ("not guilty"). The testimony of Smith and the arresting officer, who appears on another monitor, are then given to the judge, who also calls up and views Smith's DMV record on the monitor. After the case is resolved, Smith pays any assessed fine and removes his driver's license from the monitor and exits the booth to go home.[13]

Many problems must be solved before this scenario can become a reality. Virtually none of the problems are technological ones, however. In Chapter 16 we discussed document imaging, electronic filing, and other high-technology developments that are either already here or are on the horizon. With the assimilation of these developments, the courts have the fundamental tools to create this scenario. The tough issues are those involving the way we view the judicial process. Artificial intelligence, or "AI" (where computers are programmed to exhibit characteristics of human intelligence), expert systems (AI programs that capture the knowledge of experts for use with new situations), virtual reality (AI that combines computers and sensory apparatus to create simulated, controlled environments and experiences), robotics (using computers to accomplish a useful action), speech recognition (the interface between people and computers), and high-technology access systems for court security are some of the tools that can be implemented in the courts to ease their burden, provided that the public will accept their use.

Corrections and the Future

Continuing the Boom Industry

Probably the most difficult area in the justice system to make future projections is corrections. The most ominous problems for corrections will continue to be those we have concentrated on already and those that are the most difficult to predict, crowding and its related costs.

Many attempts have been made in the past to estimate future state prison populations. Mathematical models were used to extrapolate crime, incarceration, and demographic patterns.[14] Reality has a way of outstripping forecasts and mathematical models, however, especially in corrections. Forecasters cannot anticipate changes in sentencing policy or capture adequately the subtle and possibly changing interactions among age, race, crime, and criminal justice processing. For example, the baby boom never really stopped in the black and Hispanic communities, and these groups will constitute an increasingly large proportion of the young male cohort in the coming decades—a cohort that has higher arrest and incarceration rates.

Even more ominous are predictions that the U.S. prison population might double again in the next 10 years: The current rates of growth are pointing in that direction. If the prison population doubles, governments will rapidly have to construct as many cells as exist now to handle the demand, in addition to replacing currently substandard facilities. The cost of this construction, which is based on a cost that is upwards of $100,000 per bed, will be astronomical.[15]

The situation will be more severe in those states having high incarceration rates, few plans for alternatives to incarceration, and higher levels of poverty (with, by extension, weaker tax bases). Most states in the South are so characterized. Local governments maintaining jails will fare even worse than state governments because their revenue bases are narrower.[16]

Future Needs of Correctional Managers

With all of the issues and problems affecting corrections (discussed in this chapter and in more depth in Chapter 12), it is clear that more than ever the effective correctional administrator is one who, in the words of Alvin Cohn, "not only recognizes the inevitability of change, but tries to harness and direct the change process."[17] Cohn suggested that the pedestrian correctional manager reacts to crises, fails to plan, views his or her position as one of a sinecurist (requiring little or no work), and otherwise fails to lead the organization. Conversely, the progressive correctional manager is proactive, views the organization as a system, and plans for and attempts to control its future.[18]

Three significant developments in the fields of business and industry can be transferred to correctional practice. First is *technology.* At the beginning of the twenty-first century, more information is recorded and processed in ways that are faster and more complete and accurate than ever before. The second major development is *total quality management,* which is a philosophy that practices participative management and moves attention to customers. The third development is *reinventing government,* or finding ways to reduce both the size and complexity of government operations. Each of these developments has a critical impact on government but is not always employed by correctional administrators to affect current and projected programs and services.[19]

Cohn believes that the traditional role of correctional managers—much of which revolves around information gathering and case reviewing—may be unnecessary with today's technology. If middle managers and supervisors can be recycled to demonstrate a willingness to change from traditional ways of doing business and incorporate these developments into their work, restructuring today's correctional agencies will be an easier process.[20]

Prisons: To Reform or Not to Reform

Given the extent of corrections' responsibilities and problems throughout its history, it is not surprising that many people have called for its reform. The story of penal reform in the United States is an old and discouraging one. From the development of the penitentiary in the late eighteenth and early nineteenth centuries to the determinate sentencing movement of the last two decades, penal "reforms" in this country have led to few real improvements in the practice of punishment. Even if the reforms alleviated problems, in so doing they often created new ones, requiring new reforms, which led to further problems, and so on.[21] Now that we are ending the current reform cycle, that of determinate sentencing, however, it is timely and perhaps even necessary to consider why reforms fail and whether anything will work. According to Samuel Pillsbury,

> Reform begins with the proposal of a scheme for penal improvement. In most instances it is suggested by an idealist who links the proposed penal reform to a view of the ideal society prominent at the time. The idealist promotes a penal ideology which emphasizes the rightness or goodness of the proposed change in terms of society's relation to the offender.[22]

George Bernard Shaw warned against penal reform more than 70 years ago. He urged persons interested in pursuing penal reform for benevolent purposes:

> to put it down and go about some other business. It is just such reformers who have in the past made the neglect, oppression, corruption, and physical torture of the old common gaol the pretext for transforming it into that diabolical den of torment, mischief, and damnation, the modern model prison.[23]

Many have sought, both within and without the system, to make prisons better places. Internally initiated reform has from time to time been sought by inmates through rioting. Although this method is not the most effective tool for the expression of inmate grievances, it has focused attention on prison problems and helped pave the way for inmate councils, grievance procedures, conflict resolution, and the position of ombudsmen.

Another means of attempting internal reform is changing the internal administration. Normally, internally initiated reform by the staff is short-lived: Either the familiar routine returns or the reforms settle into a new but equally sterile routine. Unless real reform occurs at all levels, little incentive for initiating new programs exists. The most lasting reforms appear to be those that have been initiated by external sources or with the knowledge and support of the outside community and public leaders.[24]

At the state level, externally induced reform is usually brought by legislative or executive action. A state's criminal code may be revised to allow such benefits as educational and home furloughs. The executive branch of government can enact executive orders. At the federal level, the most active reformer has been the Supreme Court. As noted previously, a number of major court decisions have affected prisoners' rights and the ability to file writs of habeas corpus in death penalty cases. External pressure is also brought to bear by private organizations, such as The John Howard Association, the American Correctional Association, and the National Council on Crime and Delinquency. All seek reform through prison certification visits and suggestions to correctional administrators. Organizations of former offenders who work with prisoners, such as the Seventh Step Foundation, Man-to-Man, and the Fortune Society, also seek correctional reform.[25] An official of the California school system provided some food for thought for simple prison reform, saying

> You want to know where prison reform starts? I'll tell you. It's the third grade. We know the high risk groups who will drop out of school. We know individuals from these groups make up a disproportionate share of prison inmates. Give me part of the $20,000 a year we now spend on these kids as adults [in prison], give it to me now, and we can make sure they won't wind up in prison, costing the state money not only to lock them up, but for the crimes they've committed, and for the welfare payments if they have a family.[26]

According to prison expert John DiIulio Jr., prison officials could take three steps to help create better prisons in the short and long terms:

1. Provide continuity in the commissioner's office (and, it should be added, in the warden's office; both have an average tenure that is often less than five years). The current situation of high turnover for the past 20 years fosters a power vacuum at many levels of management.

2. Adopt the practice of unit management (the concept described earlier in this chapter) as a means of reducing prison violence. In addition to its potential for calming the institution and its residents, there are fewer staff rotations, allowing management to measure performance better. Officers are given more authority, act more as professionals, and morale is boosted.

3. Allow products manufactured by inmates in state prisons to be sold to the federal government. This would eliminate endless hours of idleness for inmates. The federal system has a large and ready market for its products.[27]

Building More Prisons: Large, Small, or None at All?

No issue has brought criminal justice more to the forefront of public policy—and into the living rooms of America—than that of corrections costs. In fact, state spending for corrections throughout the nation grew by more than 50 percent during the 1980s—the greatest increase of any state-funded service.[28] Furthermore, from 1975 to 1985, the cost of operating corrections in the country rose by nearly 240 percent.[29] Americans now spend more than $16 billion annually to confine adult offenders.[30]

As discussed earlier, legal reforms have expanded the use of determinate and mandatory sentences and thus enlarged the correctional population. With the annual cost of incarceration running in some states now more than $50,000 per inmate, concern over the cost of incarcerating such large numbers of offenders and crowding in general is increasing. As a result, a variety of proposals have surfaced to cope with the problem of population and save money. As presented previously, one purported cost-saving mechanism is privatization, by which correctional institutions are run by for-profit enterprises. Others include marginally credible ideas ranging from that of a New York City politician, who suggested using old tugboats to hold prisoners,[31] to politically volatile solutions such as early-release programs,[32] to electronic surveillance home-detention programs.

Although it is clear that the concern among legislators, correctional administrators, and the public over the cost of corrections is justified, the public is sending mixed messages. For example, legislative changes to penal codes in the late 1980s, in the form of mandatory prison terms for drunk drivers and for those who commit gun crimes and calls for the abolition of parole boards, seemed to indicate a popular sentiment for more prison space. More recently, however, the public seems to be gradually reversing itself, balking at the prospect of spending more than $50 to $100 million every few years to construct a new prison for housing offenders (especially when schools, highways, health care, and social services are suffering). Thus, we now see a movement toward early release and other types of programs designed to reduce the overload and divert offenders away from incarceration.

Douglas McDonald determined that larger prisons were less expensive on a per prisoner basis than smaller ones. In addition, the average per capita cost of operating maximum security prisons was lower than the cost of minimum security camps, which in turn were less expensive than medium security facilities. These cost differences resulted largely from variations in the way each type of facility was staffed. Maximum security prisons were larger, on average, and had fewer staff persons per inmate than other facilities. "As the staff/inmate ratio increased, so did cost." [33]

All is not gloom and doom in the area of corrections costs, however. Construction and financing costs can make building prisons seem overwhelmingly expensive. According to the National Institute of Justice (NIJ), however, when these charges are amortized over the useful life of a facility, they become quite modest. The NIJ also noted that other unintended costs of imprisonment for a community exist. Imprisoning breadwinners may force their families into welfare dependency. If an inmate were unemployed at the time of imprisonment, however, the state would actually gain by paying less unemployment compensation. [34]

In addition to being sensitive to the high cost of imprisonment and the political sensitivity of this issue, correctional administrators must be adept at determining the best approach to keeping abreast with the structural needs of their criminal population. Timing can be a hidden yet important variable, as the public is not always amenable to new, normally expensive construction proposals. Legislative enactments (such as those concerning mandatory sentencing or early-release proposals) also weigh into the prison construction decision. Alternatives to imprisonment (such as those discussed in Chapter 11) must also be considered.

Can Administrators "Reinvent" Criminal Justice?

Casting Off Old Ways

Reinventing Government, the book that swept the country and was on the bookshelves of many governors, city managers, and criminal justice administrators, provides ideas about how government can and should work as efficiently and productively as the best-run private businesses. It uses myriad examples of government agencies that have slashed red tape, begun focusing on the "customer," cut costs tremendously, revamped the budget-expenditure process to provide incentives for saving money, abandoned archaic civil service systems, decentralized authority, and empowered their employees. The book shows how these agencies can become more entrepreneurial and "steer" rather than "row," be driven by missions rather than by rules, encourage competition over monopoly, and invest in prevention rather than cure. The reason for the book's widespread popularity is that it demonstrates what can be accomplished when government leaders decide to "break the mold" and try new methods.

The authors of *Reinventing Government,* David Osborne and Ted Gaebler, went beyond the five principles of total quality management, espoused by W. Edwards Deming in 1950, which focused on results, customers, decentralization, prevention, and a market (or systems) approach. Osborne and Gaebler found that most entrepreneurial governments focus on promoting *competition* between service providers; they *empower* citizens by pushing control out of the bureaucracy and into the community; and they measure the performance of their agencies, focusing not on inputs but on *outcomes*. They are driven by their goals—their *missions*—rather than by rules and regulations. They redefine their clients as *customers* and offer them choices between levels of involvement, training programs, and so on. They *prevent* problems before they emerge rather than simply offering services afterward. They *decentralize* authority, embracing participatory management. They prefer *market* mechanisms to bureaucratic mechanisms. They focus not simply on providing public services, but on *catalyzing* all sectors—public, private, and voluntary—into action to solve their community's problems.[35]

A Shift in Governance

Unfortunately, the great majority of our federal, state, and local government agencies do not operate as entrepreneurs. Instead, they reward failure and enhance bureaucracies rather than create incentives to save money or serve customers. When the crime rate increases, justice agencies are given more money; if they continue to fail, they are given even more. As police departments entered the professional era in the 1930s, they began focusing on chasing criminals, not on solving community problems. This approach encourages agencies to ignore the root causes of crime and not to consider possible solutions to problems.

What Osborne and Gaebler call for is nothing less than a shift in the basic model of governance used in the United States—a shift that is already under way, doubtless largely because of demands on government agencies to "do more with less." It is now essential that justice administrators engage in strategic planning, looking beyond tomorrow and anticipating the future. Some police administrators have begun coping with revenue shortfalls in some new and unique—if not always popular—ways: as noted earlier, charging fees for traditionally free public services, such as unlocking vehicles and responding to false alarms.

It will become increasingly important for justice administrators to think of such revenue-enhancing possibilities and ways to save money. They must also listen more to one of their greatest resources—the rank and file—although a revamped or "inverted" pyramidal organization structure may be necessary for accomplishing this goal. Increased collaboration with the public is also needed. The police must insist that private citizens, institutions, and organizations within their communities shoulder greater responsibility for assisting in crime control. Some examples of excellent collaborative efforts are DARE, MADD, Neighborhood Watch, and Court Watch.

In sum, justice administrators and members of society must rethink their approach to crime. They must play a catalytic role rather than merely reducing services or, as in the past, throwing money and personnel at ongoing problems. They must steer rather than row, with a clear map in hand. In short, they need a new vision of government.

Computer Applications

Although we discussed the uses of technology in criminal justice in Chapter 16, this subject should be discussed again here in brief because computers are a major component of our future perspective.

Advances in computer technology have revolutionized many organizational and operational aspects of administration. We are clearly witnessing an "information technology revolution."[36] When a police officer investigates a crime, a probation officer prepares a presentence report, a court schedules a case for trial, a victim calls the district attorney's office to learn the status of his or her case, or a parole board tracks an inmate's parole eligibility date, information is collected, analyzed, and stored for future use. Computers also allow justice administrators to engage in *planning* at a level never before possible. As we saw earlier in this chapter, strategic planning and forecasting are essential for developing and implementing policy within the limitations of present knowledge and decision making within political and economic realities.[37]

Mainframe computer systems are designed to store, retrieve, manipulate, and analyze massive amounts of information. Three well-known mainframe databases in criminal justice are (1) the National Criminal Justice Information Center (NCIC), which contains detailed arrest and intelligence information on known and wanted offenders; (2) the *Uniform Crime Reports* (UCR), published annually by the FBI, which compiles and summarizes reported national crime data on a quarterly and annual basis; and (3) the *Sourcebook of Criminal Justice Statistics*, published by the federal Bureau of Justice Statistics, which includes a comprehensive summary of justice activities across the country. Mainframe data-based management systems are also used extensively in criminal justice at all levels of government in functions ranging from psychological profiles of terrorists and kidnappers to automobile registration and descriptions and sketches of criminal subjects. Computers are also used as investigative tools in crime laboratories across the country.[38]

Our ability to use computer technology for additional purposes is limited only by our imaginations and available funds. Clearly, today's criminal justice students and practitioners must become knowledgeable about computer applications, particularly word-processing, the Internet, and use of modems. The future holds far greater growth and development in our information-processing society. The future is high-technology. Criminal justice cannot drive into the future looking into the rear-view mirror as far as technology is concerned.

Summary

This chapter discussed how the future may be predicted, the changing face of America and its crime problem, and future changes that are anticipated in police, courts, and corrections organizations. Emphasis was also placed on shifts in governance and computer applications.

For criminal justice organizations to implement innovation successfully, administrators and their staffs must have an abiding commitment to change and must motivate personnel to support innovations. Criminal justice agencies must become proactive.

Questions for Review

1. What are the primary methods that justice administrators use for predicting the future? Discuss each.
2. What are some of the country's major demographic changes on the horizon? Which of them is/are most significant for criminal justice?
3. What does the future hold concerning crime? What criminal justice technology will be developed? How must justice agencies adapt to change?
4. What are some of the issues involved in the construction of correctional institutions?
5. What are some specific means by which government—and justice administrators in particular—can "reinvent" their operations? Why do so many people feel they must do so?
6. How has computer technology changed criminal justice? In what ways will it continue to change justice administration in the future?

Notes

1. Kenneth J. Peak, *Policing America: Methods, Issues, Challenges* (3d ed.) (Upper Saddle River, N.J.: Prentice Hall, 2000), p. 360.
2. Ibid., p. 361.
3. Ibid.
4. Ibid., p. 362.
5. Ibid., p. 361.
6. Ibid., pp. 362–363.
7. James Alan Fox, *Trends in Juvenile Violence* (Washington, D.C.: U.S. Department of Justice, Bureau of Justice Statistics, 1996), p. i.
8. Rob McCord and Elaine Wicker, "Tomorrow's America: Law Enforcement's Coming Challenge," *FBI Law Enforcement Bulletin* 59 (January 1990):31.
9. Edward A. Thibault, "Proactive Police Futures," in Gene Stephens (ed.), *The Future of Criminal Justice* (Cincinnati, Ohio: Anderson, 1982), pp. 67–85.
10. Ibid., p. 73–77.
11. Clyde L. Cronkhite, "21st Century Cop," *The National Centurion* (April 1984):26–29, 47–48.
12. Adapted from Clement Bezold, "On Futures Thinking and the Courts," *The Court Manager* 6 (Summer 1991): 4–11.

13. Adapted from Lawrence P. Webster, James E. McMillan, J. Douglas Walker, and Barbara C. Kelly, "What's New in Court Technology: An Overview," *Judges' Journal* 32(3) (Summer 1993): 11, 73.

14. See, for example, Thomas F. Rich and Arnold I. Barnett, "Model-Based U.S. Prison Population Projections," *Public Administration Review* 45 (November 1985): 780–789.

15. Douglas C. McDonald, "The Cost of Corrections: In Search of the Bottom Line," in Joan Petersilia (ed.), *Research in Corrections* (U.S. Department of Justice, National Institute of Corrections) 2 (February 1989): 23.

16. Ibid., pp. 23-24.

17. Alvin W. Cohn, "The Failure of Correctional Management: Recycling the Middle Manager," *Federal Probation* 59(2) (June 1995): 10.

18. Ibid.

19. Ibid.

20. Ibid., p. 15.

21. Samuel H. Pillsbury, "Understanding Penal Reform: The Dynamic of Change," *The Journal of Criminal Law and Criminology* 80 (1989): 726–780.

22. Ibid., pp. 726-727.

23. George Bernard Shaw, *Imprisonment* (New York: Brentanos, 1924), p. 1.

24. For an excellent discussion of corrections reform through legislation, executive order, and judicial decree, see Harry E. Allen and Clifford E. Simonsen, *Corrections in America: An Introduction* (8th ed.) (Upper Saddle River, N.J.: Prentice Hall, 1998).

25. Ibid., p. 71.

26. Quoted in Jim Bencivenga, "State Prisons: Crucibles for Justice," *The Christian Science Monitor* (July 28, 1988): 14–15.

27. Quoted in Ibid.

28. National Institute of Corrections, *Research in Corrections* 2 (February 1989): Editor's Note.

29. Ibid., p. 1.

30. Kathleen Maguire and Ann L. Pastore, *Sourcebook of Criminal Justice Statistics—1997* (Washington, D.C.: U.S. Department of Justice, Bureau of Justice Statistics, 1998), p. 11.

31. *New York Times* (October 14, 1986).

32. *Gainesville Sun* (June 16, 1987): 3B; (April 21, 1988): 3B

33. McDonald, "The Cost of Corrections," p. 19.

34. U.S. Department of Justice, National Institute of Justice Research in Brief, *Making Confinement Decisions* (Washington, D.C.: Author, 1987), pp. 2–3.

35. David Osborne and Ted Gaebler, *Reinventing Government: How the Entrepreneurial Spirit Is Transforming the Public Sector* (Reading, Mass.: Addison-Wesley, 1992), pp. 19–20.

36. William G. Archambeault and Betty J. Archambeault, *Computers in Criminal Justice Administration and Management: Introduction to Emerging Issues and Applications* (2d ed.) (Cincinnati, Ohio: Anderson, 1989), pp. 1, 3.

37. William G. Archambeault and Betty J. Archambeault, *Correctional Supervisory Management: Principles of Organization, Policy, and Law* (Englewood Cliffs, N.J.: Prentice Hall, 1982), p. 10.

38. Archambeault and Archambeault, *Computers in Criminal Justice Administration and Management* (2d ed.), p. 63.

APPENDIX I

Related Web Sites

World Wide Web (WWW) Sites

American Bar Association
http://www.abanet.org/
Publications, journals, LawMart, and Continuing Legal Education.

American Correctional Association: The Corrections Connection
http://www.corrections.com/
This site lists corrections links to federal, state, and local agencies, in addition to international associations.

Asian and Diversity Crime Page
http://www.halcyon.com/arthurhu/index/acrime.htm
Provides crime statistics broken down by race and other demographics.

Association of Certified Fraud Examiners
http://www.acfe.org/
Provides occupational fraud and abuse statistics, such as costs, methods, perpetrators, and victims.

Bomb Data Center (FBI)
http://www.fbi.gov/lab/bomsum/eubdc.htm
Provides data on the number of bombs, individuals killed and injured, and monetary damages.

Bureau of Alcohol, Tobacco and Firearms (BATF)
http://www.atf.treas.gov/
Information on firearms manufacturing and licensing, frequently asked questions and answers about the Brady law, and a listing of states subject to comply with the Brady law.

Bureau of Justice Statistics
http://www.ojp.usdoj.gov/bjs
This agency is the United States' primary source for criminal justice statistics. BJS collects, analyzes, publishes, and disseminates information on crime, offenders, crime victims, and the operation of justice systems. Numerous publications are available.

Centers for Disease Control and Prevention (CDC)
http://www.cdc.gov
Statistics on firearm-related injuries and deaths, death investigation, and health-related data.

College and University Crime Statistics
http://www.soconline.org./STATS/index.html
Provides crimes statistics for colleges and universities across the United States.

Computer Security Institute
http://www.gocsi.com
Provides statistics on computer crime, financial losses due to computer fraud and abuse, in addition to usage data on current technology and products by security professionals.

The Consumer Law Page
http://consumerlawpage.com/
Information and data from both the national Fraud Information Center and the Federal Trade Commission on fraudulent insurance schemes, specifically fraud involving automobiles, banks, funerals, credit cards, health/medical, timeshares, investments, products and services, and loans and mortgages.

Courts.net
http://www.courts.net
Provides links to federal and state courts.

Crime Statistics Site
http://www.crime.org/links.html
Provides crime statistics for colleges, universities, counties, cities, states, and aggregate data for the United States and countries worldwide.

Crime Stoppers International, Inc.
http://www.c-s-i.org/stats.htm
Crime Stopper statistics based upon results submitted from crime stopper programs around the world. These include cases cleared, rewards paid, property recovered, narcotics recovered, total dollars recovered, total prosecutions, etc.

Court TV Library: Death Penalty
http://www.courttv.com
Provides current information on high profile, civil right, Supreme Court, and death penalty cases.

Database of U.S. Supreme Court Opinions
http://www.usscplus.com/
Citation search, party search, docket, case name search, and view current term cases.

Death Penalty Information Center (DPIC)
http://essential.org/dpic/
Analysis and information on issues surrounding the death penalty including publications on costs, racial disparities, and trends in capital punishment.

Drug Enforcement Administration (DEA)
http://www.usdoj.gov/dea/
Data on the supply of illicit drugs to the United States, including manufacturing, trafficking, and eradication efforts by drug type.

Federal Bureau of Investigation (FBI)
http://www.fbi.gov
Crime data from the annual Uniform Crime Report (UCR); status of FBI investigations, including the Unabomber case and computer crimes; and a list of the 10 most wanted fugitives.

Federal Bureau of Prisons (FBOP)
http://www.bop.gov
Provides statistics on federal inmate demographics, sentence, offense, and facility populations.

Federal Judicial Center
http://www.fjc.gov
Information on judicial administration and reports from the Administrative Office of the U.S. Courts and the U.S. Sentencing Commission on mandatory minimum prison terms, gender disparity in sentencing, and the rates of federal civil appeals.

Federal Justice Statistics Resource Center (FJSRC)
http://fjsrc.urban.org/
The Federal Justice Statistics Resource Center (FJSRC) maintains the Bureau of Justice Statistics (BJS) Federal Justice Statistics Program (FJSP) database, which contains information about suspects and defendants processed in the federal criminal justice system. Using data obtained from federal agencies, the FJSP compiles comprehensive information describing defendants from each stage of federal criminal case processing.

FEDSTATS
http://www.fedstats.gov
Provides powerful link and search utilities to find statistical information generated by any federal statistics agency without knowing in advance what agency produces or publishes the data.

Financial Crimes Enforcement Network
http://www.ustreas.gov/fincen/

Fraud Information Center
http://www.echotech.com/
Collection and dissemination of fraud-related information, specifically prevention, detection, and prosecution of fraud.

The International Association of Chiefs of Police
http:www.theiacp.org/
Established in 1893, the IACP is the world's oldest and largest organization of police executives (with 16,000 members). It launches programs, conducts research and training, and promulgates standards. Publishes *The Police Chief* monthly.

Justice Research and Statistics Association (JRSA)
http://www.jrsainfo.org
Provides information on the collection, analysis, dissemination, and use of data concerning crime and criminal justice at the state level.

National Archive of Criminal Justice Data (NACJD)
http://www.icpsr.umich.edu/NACJD/home.html
This web site provides browsing and downloading access to over 500 data collections relating to criminal justice.

National Association for Justice Information Systems (NAJIS)
http://www.statesattorney.org/nhome.htm
Promotes exchange of ideas among individuals and organizations at the federal, state, and local levels who are responsible for the acquisition, operation, and management of criminal justice information systems.

National Center for State Courts (NCSC)
http://www.ncsc.dni.us
Findings from the Court Statistics Project, including caseload highlights from state courts on caseload trends, tort filings, DWI caseloads, and arrests. Information on court management, court technology, and administrative data from different divisions of NCSC.

National Center for Statistics and Analysis, National Highway Traffic Safety Administration
http://www.nhtsa.dot.gov/people/ncsa
Provides state data on traffic fatalities, alcohol use, driver demographics, and speeding.

National Criminal Justice Association (NCJA)
http://www.acsp.uic.edu/ncja/nasbo.htm
Access to the National Association of State Budget Officers' report on state juvenile justice expenditures and innovations.

National Criminal Justice Commission (NCJC)
http://www.ncianet.org/ncia/
State rankings on public safety issues and crime, a summary of the latest release "The Real War on Crime," and a copy of the citizen crime questionnaire.

National Institute of Justice
http://www.ojp.usdoj.gov/nij
A component of the Office of Justice Programs, NIJ is the research agency of the Department of Justice. NIJ supports research, evaluation, and demonstration programs as well as the development of technology. Programs and publications are numerous.

National Institute for Standards and Technology (NIST)
Computer Security Resource Clearinghouse
http://www.first.org
Computer security information on a variety of subjects, including computer-related threats, vulnerabilities, general risks, privacy, and legal issues.

National Judicial College (NJC)
http://www.judges.org
A not-for-profit educational corporation located on the campus of the University of Nevada, Reno, the NJC offers many different short courses for trial court and administrative law judges and court personnel and cosponsors a Master's of Judicial Studies degree program.

National Law Enforcement and Corrections Technology Center
http://www.nlectc.org
This site publishes and distributes a large collection of free publications concerning computers and software, equipment of all types, weapons and ammunition, and communications.

National Sheriff's Association
http://www.sheriffs.org
Established in 1940 and serving over 20,000 sheriffs, deputies, jail administrators, corrections officials, court security officers, chiefs of police, and federal law enforcement agents. Provides training, information, and other services. Publishes *Sheriff* magazine monthly and other bulletins.

The National Transportation and Safety Board
http://www.ntsb.gov
Provides statistics on aviation accidents, fatalities, and accident rates, in addition to highway, marine, pipeline/hazardous material, and railroad accident reports.

National White Collar Crime Center (NWCCC)
http://www.iir.com/nwccc/nwccc.htm
Provides a description of the center and its services.

Office of Community Oriented Policing Services (COPS)
http://www.usdoj.gov/cops
Established by Congress with passage of the 1994 Violent Crime Control and Law Enforcement Act, it was authorized $8.8 billion over six years for grants to add community policing officers to the streets and to advance community policing. Publishes newsletters and conducts various programs and activities.

The Prison Privatization Research Site
http://www.ucc.uconn.edu/~logan/
Provides data on the number of adult correctional facilities under private contract or construction in the U.S., U.K., and Australia, including trend charts, tables and figures, privatization surveys, capacities, and performance measures.

Rand Corporation
http://www.rand.org/areas/CRIM/Toc.html
Research and analysis of pressing policy problems to inform the revision of public policy. Reports on topics such as child abuse, decriminalization, economic aspects of imprisonment, juvenile delinquency, and mandatory sentences and costs.

Rominger Legal
http://www.romingerlegal.com/supreme.htm
U.S. Supreme Court Links-decisions, history, information about the Justices, and U.S. Constitution.

Roper Center for Public Opinion Research
http://www.ropercenter.uconn.edu/
Public Opinion Location Library (POLL) that provides online access to an enormous database that includes many of the public opinion poll questions asked nationally in the United States from 1936 to the present. Also, the International Survey Library Association (ISLA) is linked to this site.

SEARCH
The National Consortium for Justice Information and Statistics
http://www.search.org

National clearinghouse for criminal justice information systems, including an automated index and an online forum for discussion of criminal justice software and application needs and benefits.

The Sentencing Project
http://www.sproject.com
Provides national and international incarceration statistics, and facts about sentencing disparity.

Social Science Data Archive
http://www.uib.no/nsd/diverse/utenland_no.htm

Social Sciences Data Collection
http://odwin.ucsd.edu/jj/idata/
406 sites that have numeric data ready to download, 87 searchable catalogs of data and lists of data from data libraries, archives, and vendors.

The Social Statistics Briefing Room
http://www.whitehouse.gov/fsbr/ssbr.html
Provides current data on the United States including demographic, education, health, and crime statistics. In addition, the site provides links to information produced by a number of federal agencies.

Sourcebook of Criminal Justice Statistics
http://www.albany.edu/sourcebook
The *Sourcebook* presents a broad spectrum of criminal justice data from the more than 100 sources in six section.

State Justice Institute (SJI)
http://www.statejustice.org/
Fact sheet, grant programs, court links, and publications.

Supreme Court Collection: LII-Legal Information Institute
http://supct.law.cornell.edu/supct
Current month's decisions and historic decisions.

U.S. Bureau of the Census
http://www.census.gov
Statistical abstracts of the United States that contain frequently requested statistical tables on expenditures, employment, salary, births, deaths, and other census-based general data on the U.S. population, state rankings, and state and county profile statistics.

U.S. Department of Justice (DOJ)
http://www.usdoj.gov
Press releases, crime bill information, and statistics from DOJ agencies including the Bureau of Justice Statistics, Federal Bureau of Investigation, and the Federal Bureau of Prisons.

U.S. Sentencing Commission
http://www.ussc.gov
Provides Federal sentencing statistics

State World Wide Web (WWW) Sites

The Council of State Governments (CSG)
http://www.csg.org/
Listing of state government web sites and state information center reference services with online data bases and newsletters for use in responding to information requests on state issues.

Justice Research and Statistics Association (JRSA)
http://www.jrsainfo.org
Provides information on the collection, analysis, dissemination, and use of data concerning crime and criminal justice at the state level.

National Association of State Information Resource Executives (NASIRE)
http://www.nasire.org
Topical clearinghouse to state government information on the Internet. State listings of criminal justice and judicial links, including law enforcement agencies, departments of corrections, attorney general's offices, administrative offices of the courts, and public defenders.

National Network of State Polls
http://www.unc.edu/depts/nnsp/archives.htm
Contains over 350 state-level studies (consisting of over 31,000 questions) from 22 survey organizations in 19 states. Archived data are included in the IRSS Public Opinion Poll Question Database.

Parole Watch
http://www.parolewatch.org
Posts information about violent felons in the United States who are set for parole hearings by state and by offense.

State and Local Government on the Net
http://www.piperinfo.com/state/states.html
Listing of all state and local government web sites accessible online, including all statistics divisions for state and local criminal justice agencies.

APPENDIX II

Analects of Confucius and Machiavelli

The writings of two major figures have stood the test of time. The analects (or brief passages) of Confucius (551–479 B.C.) and the work of Machiavelli (A.D. 1469-1527) are still quite popular today. Many graduate and undergraduate students in a variety of academic disciplines have been compelled to analyze the writings of both, especially Machiavelli's *The Prince*. Both men tend to agree on many points regarding the means of governance, as the following will demonstrate. After reading some excerpts of each philosopher, we will consider their application to justice administration.

Confucius often emphasized the moralism of leaders, saying:

> He who rules by moral force is like the pole-star, which remains in its place while all the lesser stars do homage to it. Govern the people by regulations, keep order among them by chastisements, and they will flee from you, and lose all self-respect. Govern them by moral force, keep order among them . . . , and they will . . . come to you of their own accord. If the ruler is upright, all will go well even though he does not give orders. But if he himself is not upright, even though he gives orders, they will not be obeyed.[1]

Confucius also believed that those whom the leader promotes are of no small importance: "Promote those who are worthy, train those who are incompetent; that is the best form of encouragement."[2] He also believed that leaders should learn from and emulate good administrators:

In the presence of a good man, think all the time how you may learn to equal him. In the presence of a bad man, turn your gaze within! Even when I am walking in a party of no more than three I can always be certain of learning from those I am with. There will be good qualities that I can select for imitation and bad ones that will teach me what requires correction in myself.[3]

Unlike Confucius, Machiavelli is often maligned for being cruel; the "ends justifies the means" philosophy imputed to him even today has cast a pall over his writings. Nevertheless, although often as biting as the "point of a stiletto"[4] and seemingly ruthless at times ("Men ought either to be caressed or destroyed, since they will seek revenge for minor hurts but will not be able to revenge major ones"[5] "If you have to make a choice, to be feared is much safer than to be loved"[6]), he, like Confucius, often spoke of the leader's need to possess character and compassion. For all of his blunt, management-oriented notions of administration, Machiavelli was prudent and pragmatic.

Like Confucius, Machiavelli believed that administrators would do well to follow examples set by other great leaders:

Men almost always prefer to walk in paths marked out by others and pattern their actions through imitation. A prudent man should always follow the footsteps of the great and imitate those who have been supreme. A prince should read history and reflect on the actions of great men.[7]

Machiavelli's counsel also agreed with that of Confucius in the sense that leaders should surround themselves with persons both knowledgeable and devoted: "The first notion one gets of a prince's intelligence comes from the men around him."[8]

But, again, like Confucius, Machiavelli believed that administrators should be careful of their subordinates' ambition and greed:

A new prince must always harm those over whom he assumes authority. You cannot stay friends with those who put you in power, because you can never satisfy them as they expected. The man who makes another powerful ruins himself. The reason is that he gets power either by shrewdness or by strength, and both qualities are suspect to the man who has been given the power.[9]

On the need for developing and maintaining good relations with subordinates, Machiavelli wrote:

If ... a prince ... puts his trust in the people, knows how to command, is a man of courage and doesn't lose his head in adversity, and can rouse his people to action by his own example and orders, he will never find himself betrayed, and his foundations will prove to have been well laid. The best fortress of all consists in not being hated by your people. Every prince should prefer to be considered merciful rather than cruel. The prince must have people well disposed toward him; otherwise in times of adversity there's no hope.[10]

In this current era of collective bargaining and a rapidly changing workforce, contemporary criminal justice administrators might do well to heed the writings of Confucius and Machiavelli.

Perhaps a leader, in the purest sense, also influences others by example. This characteristic of leadership was recognized in the sixth century B.C. by Lao-Tzu, who wrote:

> The superior leader gets things done
> With very little motion.
> He imparts instruction not through many words
> But through a few deeds.
> He keeps informed about everything
> But interferes hardly at all.
> He is a catalyst.
> And although things wouldn't get done as well
> If he weren't there.
> When they succeed he takes no credit.
> And because he takes no credit
> Credit never leaves him.[11]

Notes

1. Arthur Waley (trans.), *The Analects of Confucius* (London: George Allen and Unwin, 1938), pp. 88, 173.
2. Ibid., p. 92.
3. Ibid., pp. 105, 127.
4. Robert M. Adams (trans.), *The Prince* (New York: W.W. Norton, 1992), p. xvii.
5. Ibid., p. 7.
6. Ibid., p. 46.
7. Ibid., pp. 15, 41.
8. Ibid., p. 63.
9. Ibid., pp. 5, 11.
10. Ibid., pp. 29, 60.
11. Quoted in Wayne W. Bennett and Karen M. Hess, *Management and Supervision in Law Enforcement,* (2d ed.) (Minneapolis/St. Paul, Minn.: West, 1996), p. 61.

INDEX

466